Finance capital

Finance capital

A study of the latest phase of capitalist development

Rudolf Hilferding

Edited with an Introduction by
Tom Bottomore

From Translations by
Morris Watnick and Sam Gordon

Routledge & Kegan Paul
London, Boston, Melbourne and Henley

First published in Vienna as Das Finanzkapital: Eine Studie über die jüngste
Entwicklung des Kapitalismus

*This translation
first published in 1981
First published as a
paperback in 1985
by Routledge & Kegan Paul plc
14 Leicester Square, London WC2H 7PH, England
9 Park Street, Boston, Mass. 02108, USA
464 St Kilda Road, Melbourne,
Victoria 3004, Australia and
Broadway House, Newtown Road,
Henley-on-Thames, Oxon RG9 1EN, England
Set in Monophoto Times 11 on 13 pt
and printed in Great Britain by
Thomson Litho Ltd*

British Library Cataloguing in Publication Data

Hilferding, Rudolf

*Finance capital.
1. Capitalism
I. Title
II. Bottomore, Thomas Burton
III. Watnick, Morris
IV. Gordon, Sam
330.12'2   HB501   80-41226*

ISBN 0 7100 0618 7 (c)

ISBN 0 7102 0532 5 (p)

Contents

Acknowledgments

The publishers and the editor are grateful to the late Professor David Spitz (who was the literary executor of Professor Morris Watnick) and to Mr Sam Gordon and the Monthly Review Press for permission to make use of the translations which were in their possession, and to Rudolf Hilferding's son, Dr Peter Milford, for his permission to publish this English edition.

I am also grateful to Dr Milford for his advice on some matters concerning the translation, and especially for the additional information and extensive comments which he provided in connection with my Introduction. He is not, of course, in any way responsible for the interpretation of Hilferding's theories and political views which I have presented.

After the death of Professor David Spitz in April 1979, his widow, Professor Elaine Spitz, was kind enough to send me the manuscript material on Hilferding which formed part of Morris Watnick's literary estate, and I have acknowledged my use of this material more fully in the Introduction.

The English version of a passage from Aristophanes' *The Frogs*, translated by David Barrett, is reprinted on pp. 381–2 by permission of the publishers, Penguin Books Ltd.

Finally, I should like to express here my very great appreciation of the work of my secretary, Eileen Plume, and of Pat Bennett, who between them produced, with great accuracy and dispatch, an excellent typescript from a much revised and untidy original.

Tom Bottomore

Note on the translation

This English edition of Rudolf Hilferding's *Finance Capital*, which appears seventy years after the original publication of the work in German, is based upon two existing English translations, by the late Professor Morris Watnick, and by Mr Sam Gordon. I have worked mainly from Professor Watnick's translation, although I have drawn upon that by Mr Gordon at many points; but I have also revised the translation extensively, with the aim of providing an English version of this classic work which is as accurate, clear and readable as possible.

There are occasional difficulties in finding appropriate English equivalents of German technical terms, and where necessary I have added explanatory notes. One more general matter should be mentioned here: in Chapter 18 particularly, but also in many other places, Hilferding refers to 'England' when it would be more usual, and correct, to say 'Britain'. This was, and to some extent still is, a fairly common practice in continental Europe, and rather than changing Hilferding's text I have thought it best simply to call the reader's attention to this usage.

At various points in the book Hilferding quotes extensively from *Capital*, and I have referred the reader to page numbers in the Kerr edition, which I have used here with some modifications.

Dr Milford drew my attention to two printing errors in the original German text, which were reproduced in subsequent editions, and Professor Watnick had noted one or two further errors which he corrected. In going carefully through the translation I have also found a few other minor mistakes. All these errors have been corrected in the present edition, and the more important corrections are indicated in footnotes.

Finally, in providing annotations to the text where it seemed necessary for the benefit of the present-day English reader I have drawn, in some cases, upon annotations which Professor Watnick had included in his translation.

Tom Bottomore

Introduction to the translation*

I

When Rudolf Hilferding's *Finance Capital* first appeared in 1910 it was at once recognized as a major original contribution to Marxist economic theory. Otto Bauer, in a review published in *Der Kampf*,[1] observed that the book could almost be regarded as a further volume of *Capital*, in which Marx's bold anticipations of the concentration of capital and of the next stage in the development of the capitalist economy were shown to correspond with the real course of events in the period since his death. Similarly Karl Kautsky, in a long essay in *Die Neue Zeit*,[2] described the work as a continuation of *Capital*; a brilliant demonstration of the fruitfulness of the Marxist method, applied particularly in a study of those phenomena which Marx himself, in the unfinished second and third volumes of *Capital*, had not succeeded in investigating or analysing fully.

Somewhat later Lenin based his study of imperialism [3] upon Hilferding's 'very valuable theoretical analysis', and distinguished the principal features of imperialism – monopolies, finance capital, export of capital, formation of international cartels, territorial division of the world – in terms which were obviously derived from Hilferding's work. Nikolai Bukharin, who was the most talented of the Bolshevik social theorists, particularly in the economic field, showed his indebtedness to Hilferding's work in a number of his own writings.[4] In *Imperialism and World Economy*, which was completed some months before Lenin's study (and was used by Lenin), Bukharin's 'starting point and essential inspiration'[5] was *Finance Capital*; but he presented Hilferding's theory in a more intransigent way, by insisting that 'finance capital cannot pursue any policy other than an imperialist one', leading inevitably to war, and also extended it by arguing that the structural changes in capitalism had resulted in a system of 'state capitalism', in which an interventionist state acquired immense new

---

*Details of the works, other than minor articles and reviews, referred to in this Introduction and in Hilferding's text are given in the Bibliography at the end of the volume.

powers, regulating and 'militarizing' the whole economy. This conception of modern capitalism underlay much of Bukharin's subsequent work, including his well-known book *The Economics of the Transformation Period* (1920), and as will be seen later it had some affinities with Hilferding's notion of 'organized capitalism', although its political significance was conceived in a different way.

It was Hilferding's theory of imperialism, set out in the final part of his book, which had the greatest immediate influence, as may be seen not only from the response of Marxist thinkers, but also from the attention which a critic such as Joseph Schumpeter gave to it in his references to the Austro-Marxist school.[6] *Finance Capital*, however, contained many other new conceptions, dealing with the nature of modern capitalism, the class structure, the state, and working-class politics, which Hilferding continued to develop and revise in his later writings; and before embarking upon a closer examination of its principal themes it will be useful to set the book in the context of Hilferding's life and work as a whole.

II

Rudolf Hilferding was born on 10 August 1877 in Vienna, the only son of Emil Hilferding, who was chief cashier of the 'Allianz' (an old-established insurance company) and of Anna Hilferding (neé Liss). After attending the Staatsgymnasium in District 2 of Vienna (Leopoldstadt) he entered the University of Vienna to study medicine, obtaining his doctorate in 1901. After graduating he practised as a doctor at least until 1906 (and again during his military service in the First World War) but he also devoted much of his time to economic studies, in which he had been interested since joining the Association of Socialist Students at the age of fifteen. He began to write on economic and social questions while still at university, and some of his earliest articles appeared in *Le Mouvement Socialiste* (Paris) in 1899–1900. From 1902 he was a frequent contributor on economic subjects to *Die Neue Zeit* (the leading Marxist theoretical journal of that period, edited by Karl Kautsky), and he became more widely known when he published, in 1904, his rejoinder to Böhm-Bawerk's criticism of Marx's economic theory.[7]

At this time Hilferding was also engaged in establishing, with Max Adler, the *Marx-Studien* (published irregularly from 1904 to 1923) which were intended to provide a means of expression for Austrian socialism and for the newly emerging Austrian version of Marxist theory. Shortly afterwards, in 1906, he was invited to become a lecturer in economics at the

Social Democratic Party school in Berlin, but had to give up this position when the appointment of aliens as lecturers was prohibited, and then became the foreign editor of *Vorwärts*. From 1907 he contributed frequently (sometimes under the pseudonym 'Karl Emil') to *Der Kampf*, the newly established monthly journal of the Austrian Social Democratic Party, and he was also engaged during this period in completing his major work, *Finance Capital*. In 1904 Hilferding married Margarethe Hönigsberg, also a doctor, whom he had first met in the socialist student movement, and had two sons, Karl Emil (1905–42) and Peter (b. 1908), but later divorced and remarried.

On the outbreak of the First World War Hilferding associated himself with the minority in the German party who opposed the voting of war credits. He was mobilized as a doctor in the Austrian army in 1915, and spent the rest of the war on the Italian front. Immediately after the war he was invited back to Berlin by the leaders of the Independent Social Democratic Party of Germany[8] as editor of its journal *Freiheit*. He opposed affiliation of the party with the Third International, took part in the discussions which led to the creation of the 'Second-and-a-half' International,[9] and eventually rejoined the majority German Social Democratic Party after its reunification in 1922. Having acquired Prussian citizenship in 1920 Hilferding was appointed to the Reich Economic Council, became Minister of Finance, from August to October 1923, in the coalition government of Gustav Stresemann, and was again Minister of Finance, from June 1928 until December 1929, in the government of Hermann Müller. He was elected to the Reichstag in 1924, and remained a member until 1933. During this time he also edited the journal *Die Gesellschaft*, to which he contributed many articles, and he took a prominent part in the activities of the Social Democratic Party.

After Hitler's accession to power Hilferding went into exile, initially in Denmark, then in Zürich. He participated actively in the work of the Social Democratic Party while it was in exile in Czechoslovakia, and contributed frequently to the socialist press.[10] In 1938 he went to Paris, where he joined his friend Rudolf Breitscheid, and after the collapse of France in 1940 they moved to the unoccupied zone, living at the Hotel Forum in Arles. Here Hilferding began to write his last work – a reassessment of the materialist conception of history – entitled *Das historische Problem*. But on 11 February 1941 the Pétain government, yielding finally to repeated demands from the German authorities, handed Breitscheid and Hilferding over to the SS liaison officer, Hugo Geissler, in Vichy. They were then taken to Paris, where Hilferding either committed suicide, or more probably was murdered, after being tortured by the Gestapo.[11]

III

As I have indicated, Hilferding published articles on economic questions in *Die Neue Zeit* from 1902 onwards, but his first major contribution to Marxist economic theory was his defence of that theory against the criticisms of Böhm-Bawerk.[12] The context in which this work should be seen is the general aim of the Austro-Marxist school of thinkers[13] to engage in critical debate with the representatives of new currents of thought in philosophy and the social sciences,[14] and more specifically, to counter the influence of the 'revisionists' in the socialist movement.[15]

Hilferding's principal thesis is that Marx's theory of value rests upon a conception of 'society' and 'social relations', whereas the marginalist theory begins from individuals. In the first chapter of the book, after noting that 'the analysis of the commodity constitutes the starting point of the Marxist system', he goes on to say that 'the term commodity . . . is the expression of social relationships between mutually independent producers in so far as these relationships are effected through the instrumentality of goods'. Hence 'the object of political economy is the social aspect of the commodity, of the good, in so far as it is a symbol of social interconnection'. On the other hand, 'every theory of value which starts from use value, that is to say from the natural qualities of the thing, whether from its finished form as a useful thing, or from its function, the satisfaction of a want, starts from the individual relationship between a thing and a human being instead of from the social relationships of human beings with each other. This involves the error of attempting to derive an objective social measure from the subjective individual relationship. . .'

In the second chapter, on value and average profit, Hilferding replies to Böhm-Bawerk's specific criticisms of Marx s argument in the third volume of *Capital*.[16] According to Böhm-Bawerk, the theory of the average rate of profit and of the prices of production cannot be reconciled with the theory of value; there is a fundamental contradiction in Marx's system. I shall not attempt here to summarize Hilferding's counter-criticisms, but only state his general argument; which is that value is 'the necessary theoretical starting point from which we can elucidate the peculiar phenomenon of prices resulting from capitalist competition', and that the 'law of value' does govern the transformation of value into price of production in a long historical process.

Finally, in the third chapter, Hilferding sums up his argument and formulates his own criticism of the marginalist school: 'the law of value becomes a law of motion for a definite type of social organization based upon the production of commodities; for in the last resort all change in social structure can be referred to changes in the relationships of production, that is to say to changes in the evolution of productive power and in the organization of (productive) labour' On the other hand, 'the representative of the psychological school of political economy [Böhm-Bawerk] fails to see this social nexus, and he therefore necessarily misunderstands a theory which specifically aims to disclose the social determinism of economic phenomena, a theory whose starting point therefore is society and not the individual'.

The publication of *Böhm-Bawerks Marx-Kritik* – which is probably still, as Paul Sweezy once claimed, 'the best criticism of subjective value theory from the Marxist standpoint'[17] – was a first step in Hilferding's elaboration of a Marxist theory of the development of modern capitalism. In the years following 1904 he published numerous articles and reviews on economic questions in *Die Neue Zeit*, and at the same time worked on *Finance Capital*, the main structure of which, as he claims in his preface, was substantially completed by 1906.

In *Finance Capital* Hilferding analyses more thoroughly, in the light of recent changes in the capitalist economy, a number of problems which had been treated very briefly, or only referred to, by Marx in the second and third volumes of *Capital*. The work is conceived and presented, therefore, as a development of Marx's theory, in which several new conceptions are formulated.[18] Hilferding begins with a discussion of money and credit, then examines the growth of joint stock companies and cartels, analyses the phenomena of economic crises, and finally outlines a theory of imperialism.

Perhaps the least successful part of the book is that which deals with the theory of money. Few later writers have paid much attention to it, and Schumpeter dismissed it laconically, and somewhat cryptically, as offering a 'rather old-fashioned monetary theory'.[19] Nevertheless, this part of Hilferding's study has at least two important features. In the first place, it is one of the very few attempts to develop further a Marxist theory of money, in the course of which Hilferding also makes a brief comment on the role of money in a socialist economy.[20] Second, the analysis of 'credit money' is an essential preliminary to Hilferding's account of the dominant position of the banks in the recent development of capitalism.[21]

Only after this analysis of money and credit does Hilferding embark upon the main themes of his study, which are the increasing concentration and centralization of capital in large corporations,[22] the formation of cartels and trusts, the role of banks, and, finally, the economic and political consequences of these changes in the structure of the capitalist economy. The most important economic aspect of the growth of corporations is 'the liberation of the industrial capitalist from the function of industrial entrepreneur'.[23] This transformation has several consequences. One is the emergence of 'promoter's profit' (*Gründergewinn*), which arises from the possibility of selling shares in a newly formed joint stock company for considerably more than the capital already invested in the enterprise, if the yield on that capital is higher than the current rate of interest on investments.[24] Promoter's profit is not only an incentive to the formation of joint stock companies but also a source of considerable wealth which becomes available for further investment. In both ways it stimulates the centralization of capital, the growth of giant corporations and eventually of cartels and trusts controlling whole industries.[25]

Hilferding could rightly claim that his analysis of the tendencies in modern capitalism went considerably beyond Marx's own brief comments on joint stock companies, by treating dividends and promoter's profit as distinct economic categories, and by working out more fully the significance of the separation between the ownership and the control of production, which allows a small number of people to acquire control over a large number of companies, and to establish personal connections which then facilitate the formation of cartels and trusts.[26] What has been most criticized in Hilferding's analysis is his attribution of a dominant role in this process to bank capital, a notion which is summed up in his remark that 'taking possession of six large Berlin banks would mean taking possession of the most important spheres of large scale industry'.[27] This thesis was contested very soon after his book first appeared,[28] and an equally critical view was taken subsequently by Eduard Heimann[29] and Paul Sweezy[30] among others. Hilferding himself seems to have introduced some qualification of his thesis later on, by characterizing finance capital not as the 'final stage of capitalism', but as a condition preceding the emergence of 'organized capitalism'.[31] It has sometimes been claimed that Hilferding's analysis was based too exclusively upon the experience of Germany[32] and Austria[33] and took too little account of the different relationship between the banks and industry in other capitalist countries; but Eduard März, in his introduction to the new German edition of *Finance Capital* (1968) argues that while critics of Hilferding's thesis may have been right on particular points, the substance of his thesis remains unaffected, for the banks did play an important part in the development of industry from the mid nineteenth century onwards, especially in the relatively backward countries of Central Europe, and there did in fact grow up the close personal and organizational links between industrial and bank capital which Hilferding described as 'finance capital'.[34] Another recent writer has argued that in the case of American capitalism too (which Sweezy, for example, contrasted with European capitalism), for many years 'the outstanding feature ... was undoubtedly the "empires of high finance" [and] in these empires, the bankers undoubtedly played a dominant and organizing role'.[35]

It is only quite recently, perhaps, that the situation described by Hilferding at the beginning of this century has begun to change significantly. Eduard März suggests that a decline in the power of finance capital in Western Europe since 1945 can be attributed to the nationalization of many banks in the European countries, and to the greatly enlarged role of the state in promoting and financing industrial development.[36] On the other hand, Michael Barratt Brown observes that 'the banker's role is now more a partnership with the finance directors of the giant companies and the bankers themselves have become most important as intermediaries between the companies and the state. What the finance groups did before to coordinate movements of private capital in an otherwise anarchic market, the bankers do now to coordinate the otherwise unplanned allocation of state funds and unplanned international trade and investment.'[37] On this interpretation, the interventionist state, however greatly its own power has grown, still has to deal with other powers – especially the multi-national corporations and the international bankers, themselves closely associated – and the influence of finance capital remains far from negligible.

The conclusions which Hilferding, in the later chapters of his book, drew from his analysis of finance capital, and of the general tendency towards an ever greater centralization of capital, were brought together under two heads: the theory of economic crises and the theory of imperialism. In his discussion of the causes of crises,[38] Hilferding makes clear that he regards the general condition responsible for crises as being the restricted consumption which lies at the base of capitalist production, but he goes on to remark that 'such expressions as "overproduction of commodities" and "underconsumption" tell us very little',[39] and he therefore proceeds to examine the more specific causes suggested by Marx in the second volume of *Capital*; in particular, the disproportionality which arises between the capital goods and consumer goods industries. After presenting this 'disproportionality' theory,[40] Hilferding considers the changes in the character of crises which are brought about by the growth of cartels.[41] In his view, cartels cannot prevent the emergence of disproportional relations, but they can shift the main burden of a crisis onto non-cartelized industries, and in a more general way they introduce a measure of planning and overall control into the capitalist economy. One can see in this discussion the germs of Hilferding's later conception of 'organized capitalism', which I shall examine in the next section.

The theory of imperialism[42] initially attracted more attention than any other part of Hilferding's work, and it was also the most significant in providing a general view of his political ideas. Its main argument is easily presented. The development of monopolies and cartels leads to a new form of protectionism designed to restrict or eliminate foreign competition in the domestic market. Monopoly prices, however, tend to reduce domestic sales, and in order to maintain and extend large-scale production exports become increasingly important. At the same time a new kind of expansionism emerges with the export of capital, which extends the economic region and the scale of production, and by developing production in areas where labour is very cheap helps to maintain a high rate of profit. Such expansion requires the support and active intervention of the state, in acquiring and maintaining control over the new economic areas (often by colonial conquest), and it leads eventually to national expansionist policies and an intensification of conflict among the major capitalist states. Nationalism itself, Hilferding argues, is transformed from a doctrine of national independence, cultural autonomy, and self-determination into the idea of world domination; it becomes the ideology of imperialism.

Schumpeter, in his early essay on imperialism,[43] attributes considerable value to the Austro-Marxist theory,[44] and he concludes his exposition by saying:

> Thus we have here, within a social group [the entrepreneurs] that carries great political weight, a strong, undeniable, economic interest in such things as protective tariffs, cartels, monopoly prices, forced exports (dumping), an aggressive economic policy, an aggressive foreign policy generally, and war, including wars of expansion with a typically imperialist character.

But he also argues that there are countervailing tendencies, and that imperialism is not a 'necessary stage of capitalism'. Hilferding, clearly, did conceive it as a necessary stage – indeed as the 'final stage' of capitalism – but his interpretation of its significance differed considerably from that of some other Marxists. Unlike Bukharin, he did not regard war as an inevitable outcome of imperialist rivalries, but pointed to the various forces opposed to militarism and war, prominent among them the socialist movement itself;[45] and his general view of the transition to socialism diverged widely from the sequence outlined in Bukharin's *Imperialism and World Economy*: monopoly capitalism → imperialism → war → proletarian revolution.[46] His conception was also very different from that of Rosa Luxemburg, who presented in *The Accumulation of Capital* an account of imperialism which was intended to provide an explanation of capitalist economic expansion and to reveal the point at which this expansion would cease and capitalism would inevitably collapse.

In Hilferding's view 'the collapse of capitalism will be political and social, not economic'; and in the final part of *Finance Capital*, as well as in his subsequent writings, he devotes his attention to the diverse social and political tendencies connected with the economic changes which can be discerned in modern capitalism. He argues, first, that the monopolies and cartels have introduced some degree of regulation and planning into the economy, and this 'socialization effected by finance capital has made it enormously easier to overcome capitalism'. The socialization of the economy has been reinforced by the greatly enhanced role of the state. There has been, he says, 'a complete change in the relationship of the bourgeoisie to the state', and a growing desire to strengthen the state. With this development of the interventionist state there must come, Hilferding argues, a change in the attitude of the socialist movement toward the state; it is no longer a question of 'smashing' the bourgeois state as a purely repressive apparatus, but of taking it over and extending its role in planning and controlling socialized production.[47]

Hilferding may have exaggerated somewhat when he said that 'taking possession of six large Berlin banks . . . would mean taking possession of the most important spheres of large scale industry';[48] but it is in fact the case that the development of the capitalist welfare states since the Second World War has depended very largely upon gaining control of the 'commanding heights'[49] of the economy in this sense, and that any further advance toward democratic socialism in the Western societies can only follow the same course.

Hilferding also explores the conditions of working class political struggle in relation to the changes in the class structure, and to imperialism. He notes that the small producers have become increasingly hostile to the working class, but that the salaried employees, although they are still firmly allied with the bourgeoisie, may change their political allegiance in the future as they begin to suffer economically from monopoly prices and from the high taxes necessary to finance national expansion; and he discusses more generally the possibility of finding allies for the working class movement in the middle class, in terms which have a very modern ring.[50] At the same time, however, he observes that the growth of salaried employment has created a new hierarchical system which helps to sustain the bourgeois social order:

> The interest in a career, the drive for advancement which develops in
> every hierarchy, is thus kindled in each individual employee and
> triumphs over his feelings of solidarity. Everyone hopes to rise above
> the others and to work his way out of his semi-proletarian condition
> to the heights of capitalist income.[51]

The protectionist and expansionist policies of finance capital, Hilferding shows, are fundamentally detrimental to the working class – increasing the power of employers' organizations, raising the cost of living, imposing a heavy burden of taxation, weakening democracy, strengthening an ideology which glorifies force, and tending to produce an armed conflict between capitalist states in which workers would be the principal sufferers – even though, from another aspect, finance capital creates economic precon-

ditions for a socialist society. Hence, working class politics should express
an implacable hostility to militarism and to belligerent foreign policies.
There is no suggestion in Hilferding's analysis that imperialist war is to be
considered the most favourable occasion for the overthrow of capitalism;
on the contrary, it is in a successful struggle against expansionist policies
and preparations for war that the working class has the best chance of
attaining a socialist society.

Since the first decade and a half of this century when Hilferding,
Luxemburg, Bukharin and Lenin wrote their studies of imperialism no
major revision of the Marxist theory has been undertaken, although the
characteristics of imperialism have changed considerably. It may be
doubted indeed whether a new theory of imperialism which followed
closely the mainstream of Marxist thought on the subject could any longer
comprehend adequately these characteristics. For although there is still
capitalist imperialism – or what is sometimes called 'neo-imperialism', after
the dissolution of the colonial empires – the competition among capitalist
states has been very highly, and largely successfully, regulated since the end
of the Second World War; and the threat of armed conflict among
capitalist states is one of the least of the dangers which humanity now faces.
On the other side, it is evident that expansionist policies are being pursued
by states which are not capitalist; and some of the most acute conflicts of
the present time arise between states which claim to be socialist and to be
guided by Marxist doctrine. The situation in the late twentieth century thus
lends some credibility both to Schumpeter's view that imperialism is not a
necessary feature of capitalism, and to the later Austro-Marxist conception, formulated particularly by Karl Renner, of 'social imperialism', or
the imperialism of a whole people, which is an outgrowth of extreme
nationalism.[52]

IV

From the very beginning of his career Hilferding, like the other Austro-
Marxists, was deeply involved in party politics; first in Austria, and
subsequently, for the greater part of his adult life, in Germany.[53] After
participating in the student socialist movement and the Social Democratic
party, and helping to found the *Marx-Studien*, in Vienna, he became, in
1906, the foreign editor of *Vorwärts* in Berlin and was active in the
leadership of the German Social Democratic Party. In the period up to
1914 three main groups could be distinguished in the SPD – 'revisionists',
'left radicals' and 'centrists' – and Hilferding associated himself with the
'centrists', being particularly closely linked with Karl Kautsky.[54] Thus, in

the debates about the mass strike which took place from 1904 on, Hilferding supported the position of the 'centrists'; arguing that the political mass strike was a weapon of last resort, either as a defence of the working-class movement against bourgeois violence, or as a means to be used in the final stage of the struggle for socialism, and at the same time emphasizing the importance of electoral politics and parliamentary action.[55]

After his war service as a doctor in the Austrian army Hilferding returned to Germany, and as I noted earlier, he then became editor of *Freiheit*, the newspaper of the Independent Social Democratic Party (USPD). He took an active part in the debate about the workers' councils[56] and about the 'socialization' programme,[57] and was one of the eleven members of the Commission on the Socialization of Industry established by the Social Democratic government in November 1918, as well as being a member of the Commission which dealt particularly with the socialization of the coal mining industry.[58] At the same time he was engaged in a fierce political controversy inside the USPD, in an attempt to maintain the unity of the party, and to prepare the way for a reunification of the whole working class political movement, in opposition to the efforts to create a new Communist Party affiliated to the Third International.[59] In 1921 he also took part in the founding of the 'Second-and-a-half' International, which was a further attempt to reunite the labour movement, strongly supported by many of the Austro-Marxists.[60]

The most active period of Hilferding's political career extends from 1920, when he became a member of the Reich Economic Council, to 1933, during which time he was a member of the Reichstag (from 1924) and finance minister in two German governments. It is difficult, in the present state of knowledge, to assess Hilferding's policies or achievements as finance minister.[61] On the first occasion, in the government of Gustav Stresemann, he was in office only for seven weeks, from the middle of August to the beginning of October 1923, and had no opportunity to implement his policies. During September, however, he did work out a plan for currency reform involving the introduction of a *Rentenmark* backed by gold, and he insisted that the successful introduction of a new currency to halt inflation also depended upon ending the reckless financing of the passive resistance to the French and Belgian occupation of the Ruhr.[62]

On the second occasion Hilferding was finance minister in the government of Herman Müller from June 1928 to December 1929. By this time the financial difficulties of the German state had increased enormously, largely through the incompetence of previous governments; and as Schumpeter wrote 'we now have a socialist minister who faces the exceptionally difficult task of curing or improving a situation bequeathed by non-socialist financial policies'.[63] Hilferding was criticized by some commentators for not undertaking a major reform of public finance, but he considered this impossible until the problem of reparations had been solved. On the other hand, he saw clearly that in the immediate situation an increase in taxes was necessary, but his proposals encountered strong opposition, even within his own party, and were not approved. Finally, in December 1929, while the Ministry of Finance was engaged in negotiations for a loan with an American banking group, the president of the Reichsbank, Hjalmar Schacht, published a memorandum in which he criticized vehemently the government's policies and demanded emergency measures, whereupon Hilferding resigned.

During these years, and in the following period up to 1933, Hilferding and the other SPD leaders had also to confront extremely difficult and dangerous political problems arising from the economic depression and the rapidly increasing strength of the National Socialist party. In 1928, as Julius Braunthal writes, 'German Social Democracy was at the height of its powers', having won more than nine million votes in the Reichstag elections of May 1928, and emerging as by far the strongest party; but 'only two years later it was locked in a life-and-death struggle with the National Socialists',[64] who had vastly increased their vote in the September 1930 elections and had now become the second largest party in the Reichstag. Much criticism has since been directed against the policy of the SPD leadership after 1930, which involved 'accepting the lesser evil'; that is to say, supporting Brüning's presidential government, which ruled by emergency decrees, as the only alternative to a government which would be either directly or indirectly under Hitler's control, and would destroy all democratic rights.[65] What has been most sharply criticized, however, is the policy which the SPD leadership pursued after the events of June/July 1932 – in which Hindenburg dismissed Brüning, dissolved the Reichstag, removed the ban on the Nazi paramilitary formations (SA and SS), and declared a state of emergency in Berlin and Brandenburg – when they continued to uphold this idea of 'legal opposition', and to rest their hopes in a decline of National Socialist support by the time of the next Reichstag elections.

But what was the alternative? The Social Democratic leaders, Braunthal writes, 'shrank in deadly fear from the prospect of the carnage of civil war'; they were 'profoundly convinced that democracy and the Weimar Republic would be destroyed in a civil war and the advance of the working classes would be held up for decades'. There is no doubt that Hilferding fully shared these convictions, which were in any case those of the Austro-Marxists generally.[66] Nevertheless, both the German and Austrian Social Democratic parties accepted the idea of 'defensive violence' – a mass strike and armed resistance – in certain circumstances, and it may be argued, as Braunthal and others have done, that such tactics would have been more effective in halting the advance of Fascism.[67] Some critics of the SPD's failure to oppose National Socialism more vigorously have attributed it to a loss of dynamism, resulting in part at least from the reluctance of an ageing leadership to give any responsibility to younger elements in the party, and its inability to attract the enthusiastic support of German youth.[68] While this may have had some importance, along with other influences which are discussed by Bracher,[69] I think the major factor – certainly in the case of Hilferding – was a profound commitment to democratic socialism, and a conviction that preparations for a violent struggle could only hasten the final destruction of the Weimar democracy. This outlook gave rise to an excessive confidence that a legal regime could in fact be maintained, and to Hilferding's interpretation of the substantial fall in the National Socialist vote in the November 1932 election, and the dismissal of the Chancellor, von Papen, as the first step toward the restoration of a democratic system in which the SPD would once again be able to take its place in the government. Hilferding seems to have clung to these hopes (though perhaps with growing despair), until finally, in early February 1933, he was obliged to go precipitately into hiding to escape the Gestapo, and then to flee the country.

However, it is also clear, I think, that National Socialism could have been much more effectively opposed at an earlier time, without the risk of civil war, had it not been for the division in the German working class movement between the SPD and the Communist Party (KPD) and the policies of the KPD itself. Since 1928 the KPD, by that time completely subservient to the Comintern (that is, to the USSR), had obediently followed Stalin's directive to intensify the struggle against Social Democracy, which was now referred to as 'social fascism'. The phenomenal increase in the National Socialist vote in September 1930 did not alarm the KPD leaders, who argued that there was no essential difference between bourgeois democracy and Fascist dictatorship; and even as late as April 1932, in the presidential election campaign, Ernst Thälmann declared that the struggle of the KPD was 'directed in the first place against the most important counter-revolutionary mass parties, the Social Democratic party and the Nazi Party [and that] even in this struggle the main blow must be directed against the Social Democratic party. . .'[70] It is scarcely surprising, in these circumstances, that Hilferding who, like the other Austro-Marxists, had long been a vigorous critic of the Soviet dictatorship, should reply[71] to its representatives in Germany with the argument that the Social Democrats' own struggle against the leadership of the KPD was an essential counterpart of its struggle to restore democracy in Germany by ending the regime of 'presidential rule'. Hilferding had opposed the withdrawal of the SPD ministers from the coalition government of 1928–30 and he regarded the outcome of the November 1932 election as opening the way for their renewed participation in government.

Gottschalch suggests[72] that Hilferding misinterpreted the social and political situation in Germany during the crisis years, and was led into political errors, as a result of his theory of 'organized capitalism', which overestimated the capacity of the working class movement to limit and control the economic and political power of the great cartels and corporations through the machinery of the existing state, and in this way advance gradually and peacefully toward socialism. Hilferding had little opportunity, in the years between the First World War and the National Socialist seizure of power, to devote himself to any major theoretical study, but in addition to his articles on current economic and political problems, he wrote several important essays in which he developed further some of the ideas adumbrated in *Finance Capital*, and in particular his notion of 'organized capitalism'.[73] This conception involved three main elements; first, that modern capitalism at the national level had succeeded – as a result of the economic dominance of the large corporations and the banks and the changed relation of the bourgeoisie to the state, which had led to extensive state intervention in the economy – in introducing a degree of planning into economic life; second, that such planning had spread, to some extent, into the international economy, with the consequence that the postwar relations between capitalist nation states had come to be characterized, in Hilferding's view, by a 'realistic pacifism';[74] and third, that these developments had necessarily altered the relation of the working class to the state. On this last question Hilferding argued that, in the new democratic system of the Weimar Republic, the task of the working class was to extend democracy by reforming the educational system and the administration of justice, reducing the powers of the president of the Reich, and providing real opportunities for the mass of the people to participate in political life; and at the same time to use its political power to transform an economy organized and planned by the great corporations into one which was planned and controlled by the democratic state. He rejected entirely the idea that the Weimar republic was a mere 'bourgeois democracy', as well as the facile antithesis between 'real' and 'formal' democracy, arguing that socialism had always constituted the core of the democratic movement and was inseparable from democracy.[75] In the essay which I quoted earlier,[76] he had noted, in terms which have become very familiar again in recent political analyses, that two options faced the working class in 'organized capitalism'; either to become assimilated into a more effectively planned, but still hierarchical, capitalist society, capable of assuring high material levels of living, or to advance toward a democratic socialist society – and he returned to this theme again later.[77]

It is no doubt possible to interpret Hilferding's conception of 'organized capitalism', in the manner of Gottschalch, as reflecting a purely temporary stabilization of capitalism in the period 1924–9,[78] and then attribute the political failures of the SPD in the following years of crisis to this erroneous theoretical analysis. But if we take a longer view, and consider the whole period from the 1920s to the 1970s, it seems to me that Hilferding's general theory should be regarded as substantially correct. Even in the economic crisis of the 1930s most capitalist states did not experience that degree of instability which would have allowed a significant revolutionary movement to develop, and the principal result of the crisis was to promote a further growth of state intervention which, as in the case of Roosevelt's New Deal, helped to 'save capitalism', to create the conditions in which it was able to resume its rapid growth after 1945, and to make possible the development of 'welfare states' and 'mixed economies'. In so far as Hilferding did make serious political misjudgments – and this would have to be demonstrated by a more thorough and detailed study of his career – these should be attributed, in my view, to the complexity, and from another aspect the hopelessness, of the German situation, in a highly unfavourable international context, rather than to fundamental weaknesses in his theoretical analysis. The crucial features of German society were its profound authoritarianism and nationalism, which the revolutionary movement of 1918 (as Hilferding recognized) had failed to eradicate, or even seriously diminish, because the right-wing SPD leaders did not attempt to destroy the power of the old landowning and military groups; and the total absence of an established and vigorous democratic tradition.[79] It was these social and cultural conditions which provided such a favourable environment for the growth of the fascist movement,[80] and on the other hand made it a matter of vital importance for the Social Democrats to uphold, so far as they could, the frail and weakly democracy of the Weimar Republic.

V

By the mid 1930s, as the National Socialists consolidated their rule in Germany and fascism was victorious in Austria, Hilferding, like other Austro-Marxists and other SPD leaders, recognized the need for a more revolutionary kind of politics, and the use of force, in order to oppose fascism effectively.[81] These preoccupations are clearly to be seen in his last, unfinished work, *Das historische Problem*,[82] a theoretical summation of three decades of political thought and experience which encompassed two world wars, the economic crisis of the 1930s, the triumph of fascism in Germany and Austria, and the establishment of the Stalinist dictatorship in the USSR. Hilferding now undertook a systematic revision of his conception of the state, which he – along with other Austro-Marxists[83] – had long regarded as an increasingly independent element in the industrial and democratic societies of the West. He now recognized that this independent power, rather than being used within a democratic system, might be transformed into an instrument of total oppression.

Hilferding's new analysis of the state is presented briefly in an article, 'State Capitalism or Totalitarian State Economy' (1940), which discusses the nature of Soviet society,[84] and is developed more fully in *Das historische Problem*. In the latter text he argues that 'the political superstructure of society is a power in its own right, with its own agencies, its own tendencies and its own interests. The development of *state power* accompanies the development of the modern economy.' And he continues:

> The political problem of the postwar period consists in the change in the relation of the state to society, brought about by the *subordination of the economy* to the coercive power of the state. The state becomes a totalitarian state to the extent that this process of subordination takes place . . .[85]

Later he observes that:

> The subordination of all historically significant social processes to the consciousness of the state, to the conscious will of the state, means the suppression of those areas of social life which previously were free from state influence and were regulated by autonomous laws.[86]

Hilferding then turns to a critical exposition of the 'Marxian interpretation of history', devoting particular attention to Marx's conception of the state, which did not 'attribute to it any independent power',[87] and to the 'most difficult problem' of 'the relation between *class interests* and *class consciousness*'. Here he discusses the long and complex historical process in which particular interests undergo a transformation in consciousness, and are 'sublimated into general interests, with the result that the economic and social demands of the group are transformed into a claim to rule society as a whole'.[88] The manuscript ends at the point where Hilferding embarks upon an analysis of the problems of working class consciousness, and notes in the first place that 'nowhere has *socialist* consciousness taken hold of the entire working class'.[89] This was clearly the prelude to a discussion of the reasons for the failure of the working class movement to oppose effectively the rise of fascism and the establishment, in diverse forms, of an unlimited, despotic state power.

Finance Capital is one of the classical works of Marxist theory, and, as I have tried to show in this introduction, it possesses far more than a purely historical interest for the present generation. The ideas which Hilferding formulated here, and in some cases developed further in his later writings – about the role of cartels and trusts, both nationally and internationally, the influence of the banks, 'organized capitalism' as a stage in the movement toward a socialized economy, the growth of the 'interventionist state' with its inherent potentiality for becoming a system of total power, and the politics of imperialism – are all highly relevant in the analysis of recent and current economic and political trends, and they are more widely debated than at any time since the 1920s. Above all, Hilferding's book stands as a model for any renewed attempt to 'attain a scientific understanding . . . of the latest phase of capitalist development' in the vastly changed circumstances of today, after a further seventy years of tempestuous growth.

Finance capital

Preface

In the following pages an attempt will be made to arrive at a scientific understanding of the economic characteristics of the latest phase of capitalist development. In other words, the object is to bring these characteristics within the theoretical system of classical political economy which begins with William Petty and finds its supreme expression in Marx. The most characteristic features of 'modern' capitalism are those processes of concentration which, on the one hand, 'eliminate free competition' through the formation of cartels and trusts, and on the other, bring bank and industrial capital into an ever more intimate relationship. Through this relationship – as will be demonstrated later – capital assumes the form of finance capital, its supreme and most abstract expression.

The mystery which always surrounds the position of capital becomes more inscrutable than ever in this case. The distinctive movement of finance capital, which seems to be independent, though in reality it is a reflection; the diverse forms which this movement assumes; the dissociation and relative independence of this movement from that of industrial and commercial capital – these are all processes which it becomes more urgent to analyse the more rapidly finance capital grows, and the greater the influence which it exercises on the current phase of capitalism. No understanding of present-day economic tendencies, and hence no kind of scientific economics or politics, is possible without a knowledge of the laws and functioning of finance capital.

The theoretical analysis of these processes must therefore deal with the interconnection of all these phenomena, and thus leads to an analysis of bank capital and its relation to other forms of capital. Our inquiry must seek to discover whether the legal forms in which industrial enterprises are established have a specific economic significance; and this is a problem to the solution of which the economic theory of the joint stock company may perhaps contribute. But in the relation of bank to industrial capital we only observe in their most mature form the same relationships that can be discerned in the more elementary forms of money and productive capital. Thus there emerges the problem of the nature and function of credit, which in turn can be dealt with only after the role of money has been clarified. This task was all the more important because, since the formulation of the Marxian theory of money, many important problems have emerged, particularly in the monetary systems of Holland, Austria and India, which monetary theory up to now has apparently been incapable of resolving. It was this situation which led Knapp, acute though he was in his appreciation of the problems raised by modern monetary experience, to attempt to set aside any kind of economic explanation, and replace it by a terminology drawn from jurisprudence which can indeed provide no explanation, and hence no scientific understanding, but may at least offer the possibility of a neutral and unprejudiced description.* A more thorough treatment of the problem of money was all the more necessary because only in this way can we provide an empirical test of the validity of a theory of value, which is fundamental to any system of economics. Furthermore, only a valid analysis of money enables us to understand the role of credit and thereby the basic forms of the relations between bank and industrial capital.

The plan of this study thus took shape of its own accord. The analysis of money is followed by an inquiry into credit, and connected with these is the theory of the joint stock company and the analysis of bank capital in its relation to industrial capital. This leads in turn to an examination of the stock exchange in its role as a 'capital market'. The commodity market, however, embracing as it does the activities of both money capital and commercial capital, requires separate treatment. The progress of industrial concentration has been accompanied by an increasing coalescence between bank and industrial capital. This makes it imperative to undertake a study of the processes of concentration and the direction of their development, and particularly their culmination in cartels and trusts. The hopes for the 'regulation of production', and hence for the continuance of the capitalist system, to which the growth of monopolies has given rise, and to which some people attribute great significance in connection with the problem of the trade cycle, require an analysis of crises and their causes. With this, the theoretical part of the work is completed. But the developments studied at this theoretical level also exert a powerful influence on the class structure of society, and it seems desirable, therefore, in a concluding section of our study, to trace their principal influences on the policies of the major classes of bourgeois society.

Marxism has often been reproached with failing to advance economic theory, and there is some objective justification for this reproof. Nevertheless, it must be insisted that the failure is very easily explicable. Economic theory, by virtue of the infinite complexity of its subject matter, is among the most difficult of scientific enterprises. But the Marxist finds

---

* The reference is to G.F. Knapp, *The State Theory of Money*. [Ed.]

himself in a peculiar situation; excluded from the universities, which afford the time required for scientific research, he is obliged to defer his scientific work to those leisure hours which his political struggles may spare him. To demand of active participants in a struggle that their labours on the mansion of science should progress as rapidly as those of more peaceful builders would be quite unjust if it did not indicate at the same time a healthy respect for their creative capacity.

In view of the numerous methodological controversies of recent times, my treatment of economic policy merits perhaps a brief word of explanation, if not of justification. It has been claimed that the study of policy is normative, and determined in the final analysis by valuations; and that, in as much as such value judgments do not belong to the realm of science, the study of policy questions lies outside the domain of scientific investigation. Naturally, it is impossible here to enter fully into the epistemological controversies about the relation of the normative disciplines to the explanatory sciences, of teleology to causality, and I omit such a discussion all the more readily since Max Adler has thoroughly investigated the problem of causality in the social sciences in the first volume of the *Marx-Studien*.* Here it is enough to say that so far as Marxism is concerned the sole aim of any inquiry – even into matters of policy – is the discovery of causal relationships. To know the laws of commodity-producing society is to be able, at the same time, to disclose the causal factors which determine the willed decisions of the various classes of this society. According to the Marxist conception, the explanation of how such class decisions are determined is the task of a scientific, that is to say a causal, analysis of policy. The practice of Marxism, as well as its theory, is free from value judgments.

It is therefore false to suppose, as is widely done *intra et extra muros*, that Marxism is simply identical with socialism. In logical terms Marxism, considered only as a scientific system, and disregarding its historical effects, is only a theory of the laws of motion of society. The Marxist conception of history formulates these laws in general terms, and Marxist economics then applies them to the period of commodity production. The socialist outcome is a result of tendencies which operate in the commodity producing society. But acceptance of the validity of Marxism, including a recognition of the necessity of socialism, is no more a matter of value judgment than it is a guide to practical action. For it is one thing to acknowledge a necessity, and quite another thing to work for that necessity. It is quite possible for someone who is convinced that socialism will triumph in the end to join in the fight against it. The insight into the

* The reference is to Max Adler, *Kausalität und Teleologie im Streite um die Wissenschaft* (1904). [Ed.]

laws of motion which Marxism gives, however, assures a continuing advantage to those who accept it, and among the opponents of socialism the most dangerous are certainly those who partake most of the fruits of its knowledge.

On the other hand, the identification of Marxism with socialism is easy to understand. The maintenance of class rule depends upon the condition that its victims believe in its necessity. Awareness of its transitory character itself becomes a cause of its overthrow. Hence the steadfast refusal of the ruling class to acknowledge the contribution of Marxism. Furthermore, the complexity of the Marxist system requires a difficult course of study which will be undertaken only by those who are not convinced in advance that it will prove either barren or pernicious. Thus Marxism, although it is logically an objective, value-free science, has necessarily become, in its historical context, the property of the spokesmen of that class to which its scientific conclusions promise victory. Only in this sense is it the science of the proletariat, in contradistinction to bourgeois economics, while at the same time it adheres faithfully to the requirements of every science in its insistence upon the objective and universal validity of its findings.

The present work was ready in its main outlines four years ago, but extraneous circumstances have repeatedly delayed its completion. However, I must permit myself the comment that the chapters dealing with monetary problems were finished before the appearance of Knapp's work, which led me to make only minor changes and to add some critical remarks. These chapters are also the most likely to present difficulties, for in monetary matters, unfortunately, not only pleasure but also theoretical understanding is soon exhausted, as Fullarton was well aware when he lamented:

> The truth is that this is a subject on which there can never be any efficient or immediate appeal to the public at large. It is a subject on which the progress of opinion has been and always must be exceeding slow.*

Matters have certainly not improved since then. I hasten to assure the impatient reader, therefore, that once the preliminary discussion has been mastered, the rest of the study should not give rise to any complaints about difficulties of comprehension.

Berlin-Friedenau, Christmas 1909   Rudolf Hilferding

---

* J. Fullarton, *On the Regulation of Currencies* (1845), p. 5–[Ed.]

Part I

Money and credit

1

The necessity of money

In principle the human productive community may be constituted in either of two ways. First, it may be consciously regulated. Whether its scale is that of a self-sufficient patriarchal family, a communistic tribe, or a socialist society, it creates the organs which, acting as the agents of social consciousness, fix the extent and methods of production and distribute the social product thus obtained among the members. Given the material and man-made conditions of production, all decisions as to method, place, quantity and available tools involved in the production of new goods are made by the *pater familias*, or by the local regional or national commissars of the socialist society. The personal experience of the former gives him a knowledge of the needs and productive resources of his family; the latter can acquire a like knowledge of the requirements of their society by means of comprehensively organized statistics of production and consumption. They can thus shape, with conscious foresight, the whole economic life of the communities of which they are the appointed representatives and leaders in accordance with the needs of the members. The individual members of such a community consciously regulate their productive activity as members of a productive community. Their labour process and the distribution of their products are subject to central control. Their relations of production are directly manifest as social relations, and the economic relations between individuals can be seen as being determined by the social order, by social arrangements rather than by private inclination. Relations of production are accepted as those which are established and desired by the whole community.

Matters are different in a society which lacks this conscious organization. Such a society is dissolved into a large number of mutually independent individuals for whom production is a private matter rather than a social concern. In other words, its members are individual proprietors who are compelled by the development of the division of labour to do business with one another. The act by which this is accomplished is the exchange of commodities. It is only this act which establishes connections in a society otherwise dismembered into disparate units by private property and the division of labour. Exchange is the subject matter of theoretical economics only because, and to the extent that, it performs this mediating function in the social structure. It is of course true that exchange may also take place in a socialist society, but that would be a type of exchange occurring only after the product had already been distributed according to a socially desired norm. It would therefore be merely an individual adaptation of the distributive norm of society, a personal transaction influenced by subjective moods and considerations. It would not be an object for economic analysis. It would have no more importance for theoretical analysis than does the exchange of toys between two children in the nursery, an exchange which is fundamentally different in character from the purchases made by their fathers at the toy shop. For the latter is only one element in the sum of exchanges by which society realizes itself as the productive community which it really is. A productive community must express itself in such acts of exchange because only in this way can the unity of society, dissolved by private property and the division of labour, be restored.

Just as Marx said that a coat is worth more within the exchange relationship than outside it, so we may say that exchange has far greater significance in one social context than in another.[1] It becomes a distinctive social force when it supplies the integrating factor in a society in which private property and the division of labour have dissociated individuals and yet made them interdependent. Only in a society of this type does it acquire the function of assuring the social life process. The outcome of completing all possible acts of exchange in such a society is what would have been accomplished in a communist, consciously planned, society by the central authorities; namely, what is produced, how much, where, and by whom. In short, exchange must allocate among the producers of commodities what would be allocated to the members of a socialist society by the authorities who consciously regulate production, plan the labour process, and so on. The task of theoretical economics is to discover the law which governs this type of exchange and regulates the course of production in a commodity producing society, just as the laws, decrees and directives of the authorities regulate production in a socialist society. The difference between the two systems is that in a commodity producing society economic law is not directly imposed on production by the deliberations of human intelligence, but operates in the manner of a natural law, having the force of a 'natural social necessity'.[2]

In addition, exchange must also provide the answer to another question: whether production is to be undertaken by the independent artisan or by the capitalist entrepreneur? The answer to this question is to be found in the change in the exchange relationship with the development from simple commodity production to capitalist production. The act of exchange itself differs qualitatively only as between different social systems; for instance, between the socialist and the commodity producing society. In a commodity producing society the act of exchange is qualitatively uniform, however much the quantitative ratios at which goods exchange may vary. In such a society, an objective social factor constitutes the basis of exchange relations: the socially necessary labour time embodied in the things exchanged. In communist society, on the other hand, the only basis of exchange is a subjective equalization, an equal desire. Under such conditions, exchange is purely accidental and is not therefore a possible object of investigation for theoretical economics. Not being susceptible to theoretical analysis, it can be grasped only in psychological terms. But since exchange always appears as a quantitative ratio between two things, people do not notice the difference.[3]

The act of exchange becomes the necessary mediator in the circulation of social goods because their circulation is itself a social necessity. A single or isolated exchange may be purely fortuitous, but exchange becomes a general and established practice if it makes possible the social circulation of goods and ensures the productive and reproductive processes of society. Social production is thus a condition of exchange among individuals, and only in this way are they integrated into society and enabled to share in the aggregate social product which has to be distributed among them. This situation removes an act of exchange from the sphere of the accidental, the arbitrary and the subjective, and raises it to the level of the uniform, the necessary and the objective. And as a condition of the social circulation of goods, it is also a vital necessity to every individual. A society based upon private property and the division of labour is only possible by virtue of this exchange relationship among its members; it becomes a society through exchange, which is the only social process it recognizes from an economic standpoint. Only in this society does the exchange act become the object of a specific analysis, which asks how the exchange act, as a means of circulating social goods, arises.

Exchange converts a good into a commodity, an object no longer intended for the satisfaction of an individual need or brought into existence and vanishing with that need. On the contrary, it is intended for society, and its fate, now dependent on the laws which govern the social circulation of goods, can be far more capricious than that of Odysseus; for what is one-eyed Polyphemus compared with the argus-eyed customs officials of Newport, or the fair Circe compared with the German meat inspectors? It has become a commodity because its producers participate in a specific social relationship in which they have to confront each other as independent producers. Originally a natural, quite unproblematic thing, a good comes to express a social relation, acquires a social aspect. It is a product of labour, no longer merely a natural quality but a social phenomenon. We must therefore discover the law which governs this society as a producing and working community. Individual labour now appears in a new aspect, as part of the total labour force over which society disposes, and only from this point of view does it appear as value-creating labour.

Exchange is thus accessible to analysis because it not only satisfies individual needs, but is also a social necessity which makes individual need its instrument while at the same time limiting its satisfaction. For a need can be satisfied only to the extent that social necessity will permit. It is of course a presupposition, for human society is inconceivable without the satisfaction of individual needs. This does not mean, however, that exchange is simply a function of individual need, as indeed it would be in a collectivist economy, but that individual needs are satisfied only to the extent that exchange allows them to participate in the product of society. It is this participation which determines exchange. The latter appears to be simply a quantitative ratio between two things,[4] which is determined when this quantity is determined. The quantity which is turned over in exchange, however, counts only as a part of social production, which itself is quantitatively determined by the labour time that society assigns to it. Society is here conceived as an entity which employs its collective labour power to produce the total output, while the individual and his labour power count only as organs of that society. In that role, the individual shares in the product to the extent that his own labour power participates, on average, in the total labour power (assuming the intensity and productivity of labour to be fixed). If he works too slowly or if his work produces something useless (an otherwise useful article would be considered useless if it constituted an excess of goods in circulation), his labour power is scaled down to average labour time, i.e. socially necessary labour time. The aggregate labour time for the total product, once given, must therefore find expression in exchange. In its simplest form, this happens when the quantitative ratios between goods exchanged correspond to the quantitative ratios of the socially necessary labour time expended in their production. Commodities would in that case exchange at their values.

In fact, this can happen only when the conditions for commodity production and exchange are equal for all members of society; that is to say, when they are all independent owners of their means of production who use these means to fabricate the product and exchange it on the market. This is the most elementary relationship, and constitutes the starting point for a theoretical analysis. Only on this basis can later modifications be understood; but they must always satisfy the condition that, whatever the nature of an individual exchange may be, the sum of exchange acts must clear the market of the total product. Any modification can be induced only by a change in the position of the members of society within production. In fact, the modification must take place in this manner because production and the producers can only be integrated as a social unit through the operation of the exchange process. Thus the expropriation of one section of society and the monopolization of the means of production by another modify the exchange process, because only there can the fact of social inequality appear. However, since the exchange relationship is one of equality, social inequality must assume the form of a parity of prices of production rather than an equality of value. In other words, the inequality in the expenditure of labour (which is a matter of indifference to capitalists since it is the labour expenditure of others) is concealed behind an equalization of the rate of profit. This kind of equality simply underlines the fact that capital is the decisive factor in a capitalist society. The individual act of exchange no longer has to satisfy the requirement that units of labour in exchange shall be equal, and instead the principle now prevails that equal profits shall accrue to equal capitals. The equalization of labour is replaced by the equalization of profit, and products are sold not at their values, but at their prices of production.

If the exchange act may thus be regarded as a creation of society, it is no less true to say that both society and the individual become aware of this only after exchanges have been completed. The work of an individual is, first and foremost, his own individual endeavour, motivated by his own self-interest. It is his personal labour, not the labour of society. But whether or not it conforms with the requirements of the total circulation of goods, of which his labour is necessarily a component part, can be determined only when all the component elements have been compared and the aggregate requirements of that circulation have been completely satisfied.

Commodities are the embodiment of socially necessary labour time. But labour time as such is not expressed directly, as it is in the society envisaged by Rodbertus, in which the central authority establishes the unit of labour time which it will accept as valid for each commodity. Labour time is expressed only in the exchange commensurability of two articles. Thus the value of an article, i.e., its average time of production, is not expressed directly as eight, ten or twelve hours, but as a specific quantity of another article. In other words, a natural object with all its material attributes expresses the equivalent value of another thing. For example, in the equation, one coat equals twenty metres of linen, the twenty metres of linen are the equivalent of one coat simply because both are embodiments of socially necessary labour time. It is in this sense that all commodities are commensurable.

The value of an article is a social relationship and is always represented in terms of another article regardless of the differences in their respective use values. Such a definition of value is implicit in, and inseparable from, the nature of commodity production. A use value belonging to one person becomes a commodity and then a use value to another person, thereby giving rise to the social relationship peculiar to members of a commodity producing society in which all are under the same compulsion to exchange their goods. The producer does not learn whether his commodity really satisfies a social need or whether he has made the correct use of his labour time until after the completion of the exchange. The confirmation that he is a fully-fledged member of a commodity producing society does not come to him from some person authorized to speak in its name, and able to criticize, approve or reject his work, as the merchant might do with his weavers. The only proof he has of his usefulness as a member of society is another article which he obtains in exchange for his own. Society entrusts its destiny to things, rather than to people and its own collective consciousness; and notwithstanding Stirner's views to the contrary this is the root of its anarchy. The thing which can give the producer this assurance must therefore have the necessary authorization to speak in the name of society. It obtains this authorization in precisely the same way as other agents receive their authorization, by the common action of those who confer it. Just as people meet and authorize someone from among their own number to take specific action on their behalf, so commodities must meet to authorize a single commodity to confer full or partial citizenship in the world of commodities. The act of exchange is the occasion for such a meeting of commodities. The social activity of commodities on the market is to capitalist society what collective intelligence is to a socialist society. The consciousness of the bourgeois world is concentrated in the market report. It is only after the successful completion of the exchange that the individual can have any insight into the process as a whole, or any guarantee that his product has satisfied a social need, as well as the incentive to begin his production anew. The object which is thus authorized by the common action of commodities to express the value of all other commodities is – money. The authority of this particular commodity develops along with the development of the exchange of commodities.

A and B, as owners of commodities, may begin a social relationship merely by exchanging their products, say a coat for twenty metres of linen. As the production of commodities becomes the general rule, the tailor must perforce satisfy all his needs by exchange. Instead of limiting this relationship to the maker of linen, he now develops similar arrangements with many other people. One coat may be worth twenty metres of linen; but it is also worth five pounds of sugar, ten pounds of bread etc. As all commodity producers engage in transactions of this type, there emerges a pattern of numerous exchange equations by which commodities are paired off and their value measured against one another. In the development of this process, commodities gradually come to measure their respective values, with increasing frequency, by a single commodity, thus making that commodity a general standard of value.

A simple expression of value, e.g., one coat equals twenty metres of linen, already expresses a social relationship, but one which may be quite accidental or isolated. In order to be a genuine expression of a social reality, it must first lose its isolated character. When the production of commodities becomes the universal form of production, the social circulation of goods, and hence the social interdependence among workers asserts itself in innumerable acts of exchange and value equations. The concerted action of commodities in exchange transforms private, individual and concrete labour time into the general, socially necessary and abstract labour time which is the essence of value. As the value of commodities comes to be measured in multifarious exchanges, so it comes to be measured increasingly in terms of a single commodity, and this needs only to become established as the standard of value in order to become money.

The exchange of values is essential to production and reproduction in a commodity producing society. Only in this way is private labour socially recognized, and a relationship between things turned into a relationship between producers. However exchange takes place, whether directly or through the medium of money, it is necessarily an exchange of equivalent values. As a value, therefore, money is like any other commodity, and the necessity for it to have value arises directly out of the nature of the commodity producing society.[5]

Money is a commodity like all other commodities and thus embodies value, but it is differentiated from all other commodities by being the equivalent of all of them and thus expressing their value. It acquires that status as a result of the whole process of exchange.[6] It becomes the legitimate standard of value. The money commodity, a substance with all its natural characteristics, is now the direct expression of value, of this quality which only arises from the social relations of commodity production and their embodiment in objects. It can now be seen how the necessity for a common measure of value – in which the value of every other commodity is directly expressed, and with which every commodity can consequently be directly exchanged – arises from the process of exchange, from the need continually to equate commodities with each other. Money is, therefore, on the one hand a commodity, but on the other hand it is always forced into the unique position of acting as a general equivalent for all the others. This has happened through the action of all other commodities, which have legitimated it as their sole and universal equivalent.

The exchange value of all commodities is thus expressed in a socially valid form, in the money commodity, in a definite quantity of its use value. Through the reciprocal action of all other commodities, which are measured by it, the money commodity appears as the direct embodiment of socially necessary labour time. Money is thus 'the exchange value of commodities as a particular, exclusive commodity'.[7] All commodities thus acquire a standardized social position through their transformation into money.

Just as, according to Ernst Mach, the ego is merely a focal point for an infinite variety of sensations, from the interplay of which it forms a picture of the world, so money is a knot in the skein of social relationships in a commodity producing society, a skein woven from the innumerable threads of individual exchanges. In money, the social relationships among human beings have been reduced to a thing, a mysterious, glittering thing the dazzling radiance of which has blinded the vision of so many economists when they have not taken the precaution of shielding their eyes against it.

In so far as commodities come into relation with each other in the exchange process they are reduced to products of socially necessary labour time and, as such, are equal. The bond which ties a commodity, as a use value, to some particular individual need is severed while it is in circulation, where it counts only as an exchange value. It resumes its role as a use value and re-establishes its relevance to another individual need only after the process of exchange has been completed. As an exchange value, however, a commodity finds its immediate expression in money, the use value of which is nothing but the embodiment of socially necessary labour time, that is, exchange value. Money, therefore, makes the exchange value of a commodity independent of its use value. Only the transformation of money into a good realizes the use value of the good. As a use value it then leaves the sphere of circulation and enters that of consumption.

Money can serve as a general equivalent for all commodities only because it is itself a commodity, that is, exchange value. But as an exchange value, any commodity can serve as a standard of value for all other commodities. Hence, it is only when commodities, by common action, align themselves with one special commodity that it can become an adequate expression of exchange value, or universal equivalent. The fact that all commodities are exchange values means that the producers in this society atomized by the division of labour and private property – which nevertheless forms a production community despite the fact that it does not possess a common consciousness – have a relationship to each other only through the medium of their material products. This becomes evident in the fact that the products of their labour, as exchange values, merely represent different fractions of the same object – money. General labour time, the economic expression of the productive community, and indeed its essential feature, thus appears as a unique object, a commodity alongside, and yet distinct from, all other commodities.

A commodity enters the process of exchange as a use value, having proved that it can satisfy a need to the extent required by society. It then becomes an exchange value for all other commodities which fulfil the same condition. This symbolizes its conversion into money, as the expression of exchange value in general. In becoming money, it has become the exchange value for all other commodities. The commodity must therefore become money, because only then can it be expressed socially, as both use value and exchange value; as the unity of both which it really is. However, since all commodities transform themselves into money by divesting themselves of their use values, money becomes the transformed existence of all other commodities. Only as a result of this transformation of all other commodities into money does money become the objectification of general labour time, that is, the product of the universal alienation and suppression (*Aufhebung*) of individual labours.

The necessity of money thus arises from the nature of commodity producing society, which derives its law from the exchange of commodities as products of socially necessary labour time. It arises from the fact that the social relationship of the producers is expressed as the price of their products, which prescribes their share in the production and distribution of the product. The law of price is the regulative principle of this society, the distinctive feature of which is that it requires a commodity as a means of exchanging commodities, since only a commodity embodies socially necessary labour time. The need for the means of exchange to have value follows directly from the character of a society in which goods have become commodities and must be exchanged as such. 'The very same process which makes commodities out of goods, turns the commodity into money.' Social association is thus brought about unconsciously through the exchange of commodities, and the confirmation that this has taken place in an appropriate way is provided by the same process of exchange. But the confirmation comes only after the process of production, which had already established this social association, is finished and unalterable. The anarchy of the capitalist mode of production consists in the fact that there is no conscious organization of production in advance to accomplish its goal. For the individual members, conscious only of themselves and not of society as a whole, social association appears to be a natural law, functioning independently of the will of the participants, although it exists only because of their own unconscious social action. Their action indeed is never conscious and purposive with respect to social association, but only with respect to the satisfaction of individual needs. In this sense it may be said therefore that the necessity to mediate exchange through money, that is, through a substance which is valuable in itself, arises from the anarchy of commodity producing society.

While money is thus, on the one hand, a necessary product of commodity exchange, it is, on the other hand, the condition for generalizing the exchange of products as commodities. It renders commodities directly commensurable by becoming their standard of value. This is because, as value, it is the same as the commodities, and within the value form their opposite; an equivalent which has the form of a use value in which [exchange] value is expressed.

Money thus originates spontaneously in the exchange process and requires no other precondition. The exchange process makes that commodity into money which is best qualified for the role by its natural attributes. The use value of this commodity, of gold for example, makes it money *material*. Gold is not money by nature (but only due to a definite structure of society); but money is by nature gold. Neither the state nor the legal system determines arbitrarily what the nature or medium of money shall be. Their primary function is to coin money. The state changes nothing except the units into which gold is divided. While at first these were distinguished or measured according to weight, they are now classified according to another arbitrary standard, necessarily based upon conscious agreement. Since the supreme conscious organization in a commodity producing society is the state, it falls to the state to sanction this agreement, so that it shall be generally accepted throughout society. Its procedure in this instance is the same as in establishing any other standard, for example, a measure of length. Only in this case, since it is a standard of value that is involved, and value always inheres in a particular thing, and in every such thing according to the time devoted to its production, the state must also declare what the thing, the money substance, shall be. The standard is valid only within the area covered by the agreement, for example, within the boundaries of the state, outside of which it becomes unacceptable. On the world market gold and silver are accepted as money, but they are measured in terms of their weight.[8]

In the absence of state intervention an agreement with respect to a specific money can also be worked out by private persons – for example, by the merchants of a city – in which case, of course, it is valid only within the jurisdiction of the group.[9]

Gold is therefore divided up in some way by the state, and every piece is stamped with the government seal. All prices are then expressed in terms of this standard. The state, then, has established the unit of price. As a standard of value, the value of gold, because it is a commodity and hence value, embodying socially necessary labour time, varies with any alteration in its time of production. As a measure of price, however, it is divided into pieces of equal weight, and this division is by definition invariable. The state coinage is simply a guarantee that a piece of coined money contains a specified weight of the money material; for example, gold. It is also an important technical simplification, since money need no longer be weighed, but only counted. Any quantity of value required in exchange can then be conveniently supplied.

Money in the circulation process

The circulation process takes the form: Commodity – Money – Commodity, or C–M–C. In this process the social exchange of goods is completed. A sells a commodity which does not have use value for him, and then buys another which does. In this process, money simply furnishes the evidence that the individual conditions of production for any single commodity coincide with the general conditions of social production. The essential purpose of the process, however, is the satisfaction of individual wants through general exchange of commodities. A commodity is exchanged for another of equal value. The latter is then consumed and disappears from circulation.

While commodities are continuously disappearing from circulation, money continues to circulate without interruption. The place formerly occupied by a commodity is merely taken by a unit of money of equal value. The circulation of money, therefore, really consists of a rotation of commodities. The question then arises as to the quantity of money required in circulation. This involves asking what is the real relation between money and commodities. The quantity of circulating media is determined primarily by the aggregate price of commodities. Given the quantity of commodities, changes in the quantity of money in circulation follow the fluctuations of commodity prices, regardless of whether such price changes arise from real changes in value or only from fluctuations of market prices.[1] Such is the rule when sales and purchases take place in the same locale. If, on the other hand, they constitute a sequential series, the following equation holds good: the sum of commodity prices, divided by the velocity of circulation of a unit of money, equals the total quantity of money serving as a medium of exchange. The law that the quantity of the medium of exchange is determined by the sum of the prices of commodities in circulation and the average velocity of circulation of money can also be expressed by saying that 'given the sum of the values of commodities and the average rapidity of their metamorphosis, the quantity of precious metal current as money depends on the value of that precious metal'.[2]

We have seen that money is a social relationship expressed in the form of an object. This object serves as a direct expression of value. In the sequence

C–M–C, however, the value of a commodity is always exchanged for the value of another commodity, and money is a transitory form or a mere technical aid, the use of which causes expense which should be avoided as far as possible. Simultaneously with money itself arises the effort to dispense with money.[3] Money provides circulation with a value-crystal into which a commodity can be converted, only to be subsequently dissolved into the equivalent value of another commodity.[4]

Money can be dispensed with as an expression of equivalence. But it is indispensable as a symbol of value because it is a necessary means of giving society's sanction to the value of a commodity. Thanks to money, it is possible for value to be reconverted from its monetary form into any other commodity. However, since the monetary expression of value is ephemeral, and unimportant in itself (except when the process C–M–C is interrupted and the money itself has to be stored for a longer or shorter time in order to make possible the completion of the M–C sequence at a later date), what is important for our purpose is the social aspect of money – its quality of being the value equivalent of a commodity. This social aspect of money finds its palpable expression in the substance used as money: for example, gold. But it can also be expressed directly through conscious social regulation or, since the state is the conscious organ of commodity producing society, by state regulation. Hence the state can designate any token – for example, a piece of paper appropriately labelled – as a representative of money, a money token.

It is clear that tokens of this type can only function as a medium of circulation between two commodities; they are useless for other purposes. Their entire work is done in circulation where money, as a form of value, is always a temporary transition stage to the value of a commodity. The volume of circulation is extremely variable because, given the velocity of circulation of money, it depends, as we know, upon the sum total of prices. This sum changes constantly, and is affected particularly by the periodic fluctuations within the annual cycle (as when farm products enter the market at harvest time, increasing the sum of prices), and by the cyclical fluctuations of prosperity and depression. Hence, the volume of paper money must always be kept down to the minimum amount of money required for circulation.[5] This minimum can, however, be replaced by paper, and since this amount of money is always necessary for circulation there is no need for gold to appear in its place. The state can therefore make paper money legal tender. In other words, within the limits set by the minimum required for circulation, a consciously regulated social relationship can take the place of a relationship which is expressed through an object. All this is possible because metallic money, although concealed in a material garb, is itself a social relation. Unless this is understood, we cannot hope to understand the nature of paper money.[6] We have already seen how the anarchy of the commodity producing society generates the need for money. The anarchy is more or less eliminated with respect to the minimum required for circulation. A certain minimum of commodities with a given value must be bought and sold whatever the circumstances. The exclusion of the effects of anarchic production manifests itself in the possibility of replacing gold by mere value tokens.

Nevertheless, the minimum of circulation places a definite limit on this kind of conscious control. The money token can serve as a full-fledged substitute for money, and paper can serve as a token for gold, only within the limits thus set. Since the volume of circulation fluctuates constantly, the use of paper money must be accompanied by a perpetual ebb and flow of gold in circulation. Where this is not possible a discrepancy arises between the nominal value of paper money and its actual value, or in other words, depreciation of the paper money.

In order to understand this process let us first envisage a system of pure paper currency (as legal tender). Let us assume that, at a given time, circulation requires 5,000,000 marks for which 36.56 pounds of gold would be needed. We should then have a total circulation as follows; 5,000,000 marks in C −5,000,000 marks in M −5,000,000 marks in C. If paper tokens were substituted for gold, their sum would have to represent the total value of commodities (5,000,000 marks in this case) whatever their nominal value. In other words, if 5,000 notes of equal value were printed, each note would be worth 1,000 marks; if 100,000 notes were printed, each would be worth 50 marks. If the velocity of circulation remained constant and the sum of prices were to double without any corresponding change in the quantity of paper money, the value of the paper would rise to 10,000,000 marks; *per contra*, if the sum of prices were to decline by one half, the value of the paper would fall to 2,500,000 marks. In other words, under a system of pure legal-tender paper currency, given a constant velocity of circulation, the value of paper money is determined by the total price of all the commodities in circulation. The value of paper money in such circumstances is completely independent of the value of gold and reflects directly the value of commodities, in accordance with the law that its total amount represents value equal to the sum of commodity prices divided by the number of monetary units of equal denomination in circulation. It is obvious that paper money can appreciate as well as depreciate in relation to its original value.

Naturally, not only paper but a more valuable material, say silver, can also function as a money token. If a depreciation of silver results from a fall in its cost of production, the silver price of commodities will rise, but their price in terms of gold, other things being equal, will remain unchanged. The depreciation of silver would be reflected in its exchange rate with gold, and the degree of depreciation could be measured by the exchange rate obtaining between a silver currency country and a gold currency country. Under a system of free coinage, the depreciation of the legal-tender silver would be equal to the depreciation of the uncoined bullion. But this would not be the case if free coinage were suspended.[7] If, in the latter circumstances, there were an increase in the aggregate price of commodities in circulation, say from 5,000,000 marks to 6,000,000 marks, and if the silver used in circulation had a value of only 5,500,000 marks, the value of silver coins in circulation would appreciate until their sum was equal to 6,000,000 marks. In other words, their value as currency would exceed their bullion value. If we accept the foregoing explanation, phenomena which seemed inexplicable to such eminent monetary theorists as Lexis and Lotz – namely, the appreciation of the Dutch and Austrian silver guilder, and later of the Indian rupee, above their bullion value – cease to be a mystery.[8]

The proof that value is a purely social category is thus supplied by the fact that the value of paper money is determined by the value of the total quantity of commodities in circulation. A mere slip of paper, worthless in itself, but discharging the social task of circulating commodities, thereby acquires a value which is out of all proportion to its negligible value as paper. Just as the moon, long since extinguished, is able to shine only because it receives light from the blazing sun, so paper has a value only because commodities are impregnated with value by social labour. It is therefore a reflection of labour value which converts paper into money just as it is reflected sunlight which enables the moon to shine. The lustre of commodity value is to paper currency what the rays of the sun are to moonlight.

Austria had an inconvertible paper currency from 1859. Silver guilders were at a premium in relation to paper. More paper was issued than was required in circulation. A condition was thus brought about similar to the one described above. The purchasing power of a guilder no longer depended on the value of silver, but on the value of commodities in circulation. If the value of the quantity of commodities in circulation equalled 500,000,000 guilders but 600,000,000 paper guilders were printed, the paper guilders would then purchase the same volume of commodities as were formerly purchased by 5/6ths of that quantity of paper money. As a result silver guilders became, in effect, commodities. Paper guilders were used for most purchases while silver guilders were sold abroad; the latter fetched 6/5ths of a paper guilder and with the proceeds one could then repay debts previously contracted in silver. As a result silver disappeared from circulation.

A change in the ratio of silver to paper guilders may take place in two ways. If the value of silver guilders remains fixed, the ratio could change if the turnover of commodities were to increase as a result of the development of commodity circulation. If there were no new issue of paper money to meet the increased demand, the paper guilder could regain its former value as soon as the volume of commodities in circulation required 600,000,000 guilders for its disposal. The paper guilder could also appreciate above its former value if there were a continued increase in the volume of commodities. Thus, if they required 700,000,000 guilders and only 600,000,000 paper guilders were available in circulation, the paper guilder would appreciate to 7/6ths of the value of the silver guilder. If free coinage were in force, people would continue to coin silver until a quantity of silver guilders would enter circulation which, together with the paper guilders, would amount to 700,000,000. If that happened, there would be a restoration of parity as between paper and silver guilders, and with a continuation of free coinage, paper guilders would no longer be governed by the value of commodities, but by the value of silver. In a word, they would resume their function as silver tokens.

The same result, however, can come about in another way. Let us assume that the circulation of commodities does not change. In that case, the paper guilder would be rated at 5/6ths of the silver guilder. Now let us imagine that there is a decline in the value of silver, say by 1/6th. Silver guilders would then have the same purchasing power as paper guilders. The silver premium having disappeared, the silver would now remain in circulation. If silver continued to decline, say by 2/6ths of its former value, it would be profitable to purchase silver and coin it in Austria. This would continue until the sum of both paper and silver had grown large enough for the requirements of circulation, in spite of the 2/6ths reduction in the purchasing power of silver. We assumed an original value of 500,000,000 guilders in commodities, and 600,000,000 paper guilders in circulation. The latter therefore had 5/6ths of the value of the original guilders. Silver guilders, rated at 4/6ths of their former purchasing power, then enter the process. To circulate commodities, we therefore need 6/4 times 500,000,000 guilders or 750,000,000 guilders. This would consist of 600,000,000 paper guilders and 150,000,000 newly minted silver guilders. If the state wishes to prevent any further depreciation of its currency it need only suspend the free coinage of silver. Guilders would then become independent of the price of silver. Their value would be pegged at the previous level, 5/6ths of the value of the original guilder. The decline in the value of silver would not be expressed in the silver currency.

This analysis contradicts the traditional theory according to which a silver guilder is only a piece of silver, weighing 1/45th of a pound, which must therefore have the same value under all circumstances. But this is easily explained by bearing in mind that, when coinage is suspended, the value of money simply reflects the total value of commodities in circulation. According to our assumption, silver declined by 2/6ths, but the Austrian guilder fell by only 1/6th as assumed at the beginning of our inquiry. Hence, the Austrian silver guilder still in circulation will stand 1/6th higher than the price of an equal quantity of silver bullion. In other words, it will be over-valued. Such a state of affairs actually occurred in Austria in the middle of 1878. It was caused, on the one hand, by the fact that the value of paper guilders was forced up by the expansion of circulation without any corresponding increase in the quantity of paper money: and, on the other hand, by the decline in the value of silver, evidenced in the fall of the price of silver in London.

Schematic though this analysis may be, it does full justice to the realities of the problem. Free coinage of silver was introduced in the Netherlands in May 1873. The coined silver money increased appreciably in value at the same time as silver bullion depreciated in relation to gold.

Whilst at the beginning in 1875 the price of silver in London fell to about 57½ pence, the rate of exchange for Dutch money stood at only 11.6 guilder for one pound sterling instead of 12 guilder as heretofore. This showed that the value of the Dutch guilder had risen by about 10 per cent above the value of the silver it contained.[9]

The 10-guilder coin was first introduced as legal tender in 1875.

Already in 1879, the value of the silver in the guilder was only 95.85 kreuzer, and this figure fell further in 1886 to 91.95 kreuzer, and to 84.69 kreuzer in 1891.[10]

The development of the Austrian currency system is briefly described in the following passage:

The currency of the Monarchy was established by the patents of 19 September 1857 and 27 September 1858. From 1 November 1858 there existed legally, and at first also in practice, a silver currency based on a standard unit of 45 guilders per metric pound of fine silver (90 guilders or florins per kilogram). Conversion into silver through the bank of issue persisted only for a short while, until the end of 1858. Moreover, in consequence of the prolonged critical political and financial situation [Which had as a consequence an over-issue of notes–R. H.] prevailing until 1878, silver was at a premium against paper money, and silver coins were progressively driven out of circulation. In 1871, this silver premium exceeded 20 per cent but it diminished during the 1870s as a consequence of the extraordinary slump in silver prices on the world market. After 1875 the price of silver was so low that it frequently approached its legal price (45 florins per pound) and actually reached it in 1878. At times, in view of the

London exchange rate on the Vienna exchange, it became quite profitable to deliver silver to the mints of Vienna and Kremnitz for coinage into Austrian currency. Indeed, the influx of silver into the Austro-Hungarian Customs Union reached extraordinary heights in 1878, and the coinage that year as well as in the ensuing one attained a volume never previously reached (on the basis of reports available up to this point).[11]

In order to prevent depreciation of the currency, free coinage of silver was suspended at the beginning of 1879. This suspension of silver coinage

had the effect of relieving the purchasing power of the Austrian guilder from the almost mechanical pressure of silver prices, and allowing it to develop almost entirely independently of the value of the quantity of silver contained in the Austrian silver guilder. On the basis of the prices of silver in London, and of London exchange quotations, the average value of pure silver contained in 100 silver guilders was as follows:

1883	97 fl.	64 kr.
1887	91 fl.	— kr.
1888	86 fl.	68 kr.
1889	82 fl.	12 kr.
1891	84 fl.	70 kr.

On these assumptions the value of 100 florins of Austrian currency in gold guilders should have been as follows:[12]

1883	82 fl.	38 kr.
1887	72 fl.	42 kr.
1888	69 fl.	34 kr.
1889	69 fl.	38 kr.
1891	73 fl.	15 kr.

But the actual quoted value of 100 such florins in terms of gold guilders for the respective years was, on the average, 84.08, 79.85, 81.39, 84.33, 86.33.[13]

In other words, Austrian silver guilders were overvalued in those years; that is to say, their purchasing power exceeded that of the silver they contained. The difference for every 100 florins of Austrian money was:

1883	1 fl.	70 kr.	
1887	7 fl.	43 kr.	
1888	12 fl.	05 kr.	(in gold guilders)
1889	14 fl.	90 kr.	
1891	13 fl.	18 kr.	

It will be seen from this table that the price of silver guilders was not only *nearly* (as Spitzmüller suggests) but *completely* independent of the silver price in its fluctuations.

Spitzmüller calls this currency 'credit currency', but he is unable to account for the manner in which its price is determined. He says:

> The purchasing and exchange power of the Austrian silver guilder, as well as the paper guilder, in the period 1879–1891, therefore, were not primarily determined by the value of bullion. Indeed, to go further, the Austrian guilder of the period, as Karl Menger has so cogently demonstrated (in the *Neue Freie Presse*, 12 December 1889) showed that the exchange value was not determined by the intrinsic value of any coin in circulation.
>
> Actually, the Austrian currency was no longer a silver currency. Realistically considered, it could not even be called an emasculated silver currency. It could more aptly be called a credit currency, the international value of which depended on the Austro-Hungarian balance of payments, and the domestic value of which, in addition to this, was determined by other price-determining factors [sic!] within the Customs Union.[14]

His uncertainty is clearly shown in the following passage:

> In spite of everything, it would be misleading to assume that the credit character of the Austrian currency was completely [!] independent of the price structure of the silver market. On the contrary, during the transition period from 1879 to 1891, the high valuation of silver was ascribable, in part, to the suspension of coinage of silver for private persons by an administrative decree which could be abrogated at any time, while coinage for government purposes continued. The aforementioned factors were thus responsible for the completely uncertain future of our currency. In particular, it was certainly no accident that the recent fall of silver prices, 1885 to 1888, paralleled the sharp rise in foreign exchange rates.[15]

It would be interesting indeed if it could be shown how purely conjectural opinions concerning the future of a currency could at any time be translated into a mathematically exact rise or fall in exchange rates. As a matter of fact, however, these subjective influences were of no importance, and the decisive factor was the objective configuration of the social requirements of circulation.

Helfferich comes much closer to the correct explanation when he says:

The premium on coin in currencies with restricted coinage is created by the fact that . . . only coined, and not the uncoined metal, can function as money; and that the state refuses to convert metal into coins on demand.

In the case of inconvertible paper money also, value attaches to the currency exclusively by reason of the state having declared it legal tender for the payment of all debts and taxes. The state thus, in fact, confers upon it the privilege of fulfilling all the economically indispensable functions of money.

Both these types of currency, therefore, derive their value not from that of their substance, nor again from any implied promise to pay, but solely from their acquired character as a statutory medium of payment.[16]

The suspension of free coinage in a silver currency system is a condition of, and an explanation for, the emancipation of coined silver from the value of bullion, as Helfferich correctly indicates. But this does not tell us anything about the crucial issue; namely, the amount of value that the coin retains. That value is determined, of course, by the quantity of circulating media required by society which, in turn, is determined in the final analysis by the value of the sum of commodities. Helfferich's subjective theory of value prevents him from recognizing this fact.

On the other hand, he is entirely correct in his criticism of Spitzmüller's credit hypothesis:

In free currencies, with suspended coinage of the standard metal, in which the intrinsic value of all types of money is less than the actual value as money, the higher value cannot be ascribed to 'credit', if only because no standard coins exist into which the other coins are exchangeable and from which they derive their value by way of cre- dit. In the Dutch monetary system between 1873 and 1875, in the Austrian between 1879 and 1892, and in the Indian from 1893 to 1899, there actually existed no money of full standard value. The money value of Dutch and Austrian silver guilden, and of the Indian rupee, a value which was in excess of the intrinsic value of these coins, was an absolutely independent thing, not based upon any other object of value. It was not even based on any rating in terms of standard money, and certainly not upon any claim to standard money, but sprang solely from the legal-tender power assigned to these coins and from the restriction of coinage.

How little, up to that time, monetary theory managed to free itself from the erroneous conception that overrated money must be credit money and must at least derive its value from that of some standard money is shown by the confused views widely held concerning the position of the Austrian currency from the year 1879 onwards. The phenomenon of the rise in the value of the coined Austrian silver guilden, after the suspension of the free coinage of silver, above the value of its silver content, puzzled people mainly because it was not apparent from which type of money of higher intrinsic value, the silver guilden derived a value exceeding that of its silver content. Recourse was had, therefore, to the extraordinary explanation that the value of the silver guilden had been raised above its metallic value only because of its connection with paper guilden; but it was not explained by what kind of connection the paper guilden should have been kept at a higher value than its paper value.[17]

Similar phenomena were observable in India. In 1893 the free coinage of silver was discontinued. The object was to raise the rupee exchange to 16 pence. Under free coinage this rate corresponded to a silver price of about 43.05 pence. In other words, at that price, the silver content of the rupee, if melted down and sold, would have fetched a price of 16 pence on the London (world) market. The suspension of free coinage had the following effect: the price of the rupee rose to 16 pence after having previously stood at 14.87 pence. But a few days later the price of silver fell from 38 pence before the closing of the silver mints to 30 pence on 1 July. After that date the price of the rupee declined while the price of silver rose to 34.75 pence and remained around that price until the suspension of American silver purchases on 1 November 1893 (the monthly amount was 4,500,000 ounces fine). The price of silver then fell and reached the low point of 23.75 pence on 26 August 1897. On the other hand, the value of the Indian currency reached the desired level of 16 pence at the beginning of September 1897, when the bullion in the rupee was quoted at about 8.87 pence.

From the very beginning it was possible to observe the gratifying result that once the Indian mints were closed to private coinage, the price of the rupee always remained higher than the value of its metal content by an amount far in excess of the costs of coinage. From the middle of 1896 onward, there was also a severance of the last link between the price of silver and the price of the rupee. Any parallelism in their movements, however weak it may have been recently, has now completely disappeared.[18]

Monetary theorists are still plagued by the question: What constitutes the standard of value when coinage is suspended?[19] Obviously it is not silver (nor gold, when gold coinage is suspended).[20] The value of money and the price of bullion follow completely divergent courses. Further, ever since Tooke's demonstration, the quantity theory of money has been rightly regarded as untenable. Finally, it is impossible to establish a relation between a mass of bullion on one side and a mass of commodities on the other. What relation is supposed to exist between 7 kilograms of gold or silver, or even paper, and A million boots, B million cases of shoe polish, C bushels of wheat, D hectolitres of beer, etc? A reciprocal relation between money and commodities presupposes that they have something in common; in other words, it presupposes the value relation, which is precisely what has to be explained.

It is equally useless to invoke the power of the state as an answer to the question. In the first place, it remains a complete mystery how the state can possibly confer a purchasing power on a piece of paper or a gram of silver which wine, boots, shoe polish, etc., do not have. Furthermore, such attempts by the state have always come to grief. The mere desire of the Indian government to raise the price of the rupee to 16 pence did not avail it to the slightest degree. The rupee showed no regard for the government's desire in this matter, and the closest the government ever came to success in its undertaking was the complete unpredictability of the price of the rupee after it ceased to bear any relation to the price of silver. Again, the appreciation of silver guilders relative to their metallic content came as a complete surprise to the Austrian government. It came without warning, almost overnight as it were, without any previously prepared plan of intervention on the part of the government. What confounds the theorists is the circumstance that money has apparently retained its quality of being a standard of value.[21] Naturally, commodities are still expressed in money terms or 'measured' in money, as they were before the suspension of coinage. And as before, money continues to serve as a 'measure of value'. But the magnitude of its value is no longer determined by the value of the constituent commodity, gold, or silver, or paper. Instead, its 'value' is really determined by the total value of commodities in circulation, assuming the velocity of circulation to be constant. The real measure of value is not money. On the contrary, the 'value' of money is determined by what I would call the *socially necessary value in circulation*. If we also take account of the fact that money is a medium of circulation, which I have so far ignored for the sake of simplicity, and shall deal with more thoroughly below, this socially necessary value in circulation can be expressed in the formula:

$$\frac{\text{total value of commodities}}{\text{velocity of circulation of money}} \quad \text{plus the sum of}$$

payments falling due minus the payments which cancel each other out, minus finally the number of turnovers in which the same piece of money functions alternately as a means of circulation and as a means of payment. This is, of course, a standard the magnitude of which cannot be calculated in advance. Society itself is the only mathematician capable of solving the problem. It is a fluctuating magnitude and the value of the currency rises and falls in consonance with its movements. The changes in the value of the Indian rupee from 1893 to 1897, and the fluctuations of the Austrian currency, offer clear evidence in favour of this proposition. These fluctuations are eliminated as soon as a commodity of full-fledged value (gold, silver) resumes the role of money. As we have already seen, it is not at all necessary for this purpose that paper money or depreciated money disappear from circulation; all that is required is that it be reduced to the minimum of circulation and that any fluctuations over and above that minimum be eliminated by the introduction of money of full value.

The remarkable history of currencies based on suspended coinage – the 'silver currencies with golden borders' or the 'gold margin system', as the Indian and similar currencies have been called – loses its mystery when it is examined in the light of the Marxist theory of money, while in terms of the 'metallistic' theory, it remains completely unintelligible. Knapp, although he exposed many of the latter's inadequacies with great acuteness (he takes no account of the Marxist theory and apparently confuses it with the 'metallistic' theory) offers no economic explanation of his own for these phenomena and contents himself with a highly ingenious system of classification of the types of money, which neglects both their origin and their development. It is a specifically juridical analysis, characterized by an excessive attention to terminology, while the fundamental economic problem of the value and purchasing power of money is completely excluded from consideration. Knapp is, as it were, the Linnaeus of monetary theory, while Marx is its Darwin; but in this case Linnaeus comes long after Darwin!

Knapp is the most consistent follower of the theory which, because it cannot explain the phenomenon of a paper currency, and especially the obvious phenomenon of the influence of the quantity of paper issued in the case of legal tender paper money, treats it as an aspect of metallic money and of general circulation (including bullion, bank notes and government paper money). The theory takes account only of quantitative ratios and overlooks the factor which determines the value of both money and commodities. Its error originates in the experience with paper money economies, especially that of England following the suspension of specie payments in 1797.

The historical background for the controversy was furnished by the

history of paper money during the eighteenth century: the fiasco of
Law's bank; the depreciation of the provincial bank notes of the
English colonies in North America from the beginning till the middle
of the eighteenth century which went hand in hand with the increase
of the number of tokens of value; further, the Continental bills issued as legal tender by the American government during the War of
Independence; and finally, the experiment with the French assignats,
carried out on a still larger scale.[22]

Even the penetrating mind of Ricardo could not escape this erroneous
conclusion, and this furnishes an interesting example of the powerful
psychological effect which empirical impressions can exert on abstract
thought. For it is precisely Ricardo who, in other cases, always abstracts
from the quantitative ratios which influence prices (supply and demand) in
an attempt to discover the fundamental factors which underlie and
dominate these quantitative ratios, namely value. Yet when he comes to a
consideration of the money problem, he puts aside the very value concept
he had previously formulated. He says:

> If a mine of gold were discovered in either of these countries, the
> currency of that country would be lowered in value in consequence
> of the increased quantity of the precious metals brought into circu-
> lation and would, therefore, no longer be of the same value as that
> of other countries.[23]

Here it is quantity alone that reduces the value of gold, and gold is regarded
exclusively as a medium of circulation, from which it follows quite
naturally that the entire quantity of gold immediately enters into circulation. And since quantity is the only factor considered, gold can without
further ado be equated with bank notes. It is true that Ricardo says
expressly at the very outset that he is presupposing convertible bank notes,
but later he gives the impression that convertible bank notes are similar to
legal tender paper money under the conditions of the English currency
system at that time. He can therefore say:

> If instead of a mine being discovered in any country, a bank were
> established, such as the Bank of England, with the power of issuing
> its notes as circulating medium; after a large amount had been is-
> sued, ... thereby adding considerably to the sum of currency the
> same effect would follow as in the case of the mine.[24]

The influence of the Bank of England is thus placed on a par with that of the
discovery of a gold mine; both increase the medium of circulation.

This identification prevented any proper understanding of the laws of metallic money and bank note circulation alike. Knapp, for his part, was greatly impressed by the more recent developments described above: the stable 'paper currencies' and the divergence of silver money from its bullion value. The divergence is, of course, characteristic of silver money (or any metallic money) as well as of paper money. But the value of paper money nevertheless appears to be determined by the state which issues it; and since, in this sense, silver seems to approximate the position of paper money when free coinage is suspended, the illusion is created that paper money, like metallic money and money in general, is a creature of the state. A state theory of money, having nothing to do with economic theory, is then formulated. Marx criticized the illusion on which it is based as follows:

> The interference of the state which issues paper money as legal tender . . . seems to do away with the economic law. The state which in its mint price gave a certain name to a piece of gold of a certain weight, and in the act of coinage only impressed its stamp on gold, seems now to turn paper into gold by the magic of its stamp. Since paper bills are legal tender, no one can prevent the state from forcing as large a quantity of them as it desires into circulation and from impressing upon it any coin denominations such as £1, £5, £20. The bills having once entered circulation, cannot be removed since, on the one hand, their course is hemmed in by the frontier posts of the country, and on the other hand, they lose all value, use value as well as exchange value, outside of circulation. Take away from them their function and they become worthless rags of paper. Yet this power of the state is a mere fiction. It may throw into circulation any desired quantity of paper bills of whatever denomination, but with this mechanical act its control ceases. [And therefore Knapp's theory ceases to be useful precisely at the point where the economic problem begins – R.H.] Once in the grip of circulation, and the token of value or paper money becomes subject to its intrinsic law.[25]

The difficulty in understanding the matter comes from confusing the different functions of money with the different types of money (government paper money and credit, of which more later). It was a defect of the quantity theory, from which not even Ricardo was free, that it confounded the laws of government paper money with those of circulation in general and the circulation of bank notes in particular. Today the opposite error is just as common. The quantity theory being rightly regarded as refuted, there is a reluctance to give due recognition to the influence of quantity on the value of money even where it really is the determining factor, as in the case of paper money and depreciated currency. All sorts of explanations are resorted to, and because no account is taken of the causal role of the social factor subjective explanations seek to ascribe the value of government paper to this or that credit evaluation. Since on the other hand, however, the intrinsic value of metallic money has to be vindicated, one cannot follow Knapp, because his theory would involve a general abandonment of all economic explanation. The result is that no satisfactory explanation has been advanced for overvalued money. Ricardo explained all changes in the value of money as a consequence of a change in its quantity. According to his theory such changes in the value of money occur very frequently, the value rising or falling inversely with the increase or decrease in its quantity. Every currency is therefore subject to depreciation or overvaluation; and overvaluation, as such, is not a problem for him. He says:

> Though it [paper money] has no intrinsic value, yet by limiting its quantity, its value in exchange is as great as an equal denomination of coin, or of bullion in that coin. On the same principle, too, namely, by a limitation of its quantity, a debased coin would circulate at the value it should bear if it were of the legal weight and fineness, and not at the value of the quantity of metal which it actually contained. In the history of British coinage, we find, accordingly, that the currency was never depreciated in the same proportion that it was debased; the reason of which was that it never was increased in quantity in proportion to its diminished intrinsic value.[26]

Ricardo's mistake consists in applying without modification the laws which regulate currency in a system of suspended coinage to a currency based on a system of free coinage. The majority of German monetary theorists are also guilty of confounding the two types of currency, but in an opposite sense; hence they have a bad conscience with regard to the quantity theory and continually fall back upon the old notions of the quantity theory whenever they deal with the circulation of bank notes, while rejecting any quantitative explanation when they deal with problems arising in a system of suspended coinage.

In contrast, Fullarton offers an interesting and essentially correct formulation of the problem in a system of restricted coinage. He presupposes:

> the case of a nation having no commercial intercourse with its neighbors, maintaining no mint establishment for the renewal of its coin, but transacting its interior exchanges by means of an old and debased metallic circulation, which preserves a high rate of exchangeable value merely by limitation of its amount – of a nation making use, nevertheless, of the precious metals on a large scale for the pur-

poses of ornament and luxury, and exporting yearly the products of its industry, to the value, say, of half a million sterling, to some distant mining country, for the purchase of an equivalent in gold and silver, to replace the annual tear and wear of its stock, and to meet an increasing demand for consumption. Under these circumstances, let it be imagined, that by some extraordinary improvement in the method of working the mines, or by the discovery of some new and richer veins of ore, the cost of procuring the gold and silver in the mining country were reduced to one half of what it had been before; that, in consequence of this discovery, the annual production were doubled, and the price of the metals on the spot lowered in a corresponding proportion, and that, in consequence of this change in circumstances, the merchants of the country first mentioned were, in return for the same quantity of exported goods which had hitherto been merely sufficient for the purchase of gold and silver to the amount of the required half-million, enabled to procure and bring home a million of those metals – what would be the effect? I certainly am not aware that any effect would be produced, under such circumstances, differing materially from the effect of an oversupply of any other equally durable commodity. The previous annual consumption of gold and silver in the country, for plate, gilding, and trinkets having been fully supplied by an importation to the value of half a million, there would be no purchase for more until a new demand should be created by a reduction of price; the prices, accordingly, of the newly imported stock of metals, as estimated in the base currency, would decline with more or less rapidity, as the merchants might be more or less eager to realize their returns . . . . But, all this time, the price of every other commodity but gold and silver, as measured in the local currency of the country, would remain unmoved; and, unless some of the surplus stock of the metals thus acquired could be turned to account in commercial exchange with some third country less favorably circumstanced for procuring its supplies of gold and silver direct from the mines, the importing country would derive no advantage from these periodical accessions of metallic wealth, beyond such gratification as can be derived from the more generally diffused application of gold and silver to domestic uses.[27]

This, in theoretical form, is the case of overvaluation as found in the Austrian silver guilder. But Fullarton fails to show that the quantitative ratios are determined by the social minimum of circulation.

He then proceeds to investigate the fundamentally different conditions which would prevail under what we today would call a system of free coinage:

> But let us next picture to ourselves the effect which a similar succession of incidents would produce in a country more advanced in its commercial relations, and with its monetary system on a more improved footing, possessing already a full metallic circulation of standard weight and fineness, an unrestrained traffic in metals, and a mint open for coinage of all the standard bullion which might be brought to it. Under such circumstances, the effect of a sudden duplication of the annual supply from the mines would be very different. There would, in that case, be no rise of the market price of bullion, for the price of gold, measured in coin of the same metal, of equal fineness, can never vary; they may both rise or fall together, as compared with commodities, but there can be no divergence. Neither would there be any unusual pressure on the bullion market in consequence of the increased importation, nor, at least in the first instance, any inducement to a larger consumption of the imported metals in the arts. The market would take off at par nearly such proportion of the importation as had hitherto sufficed for the purposes of consumption, and the rest would all be sent to the mint for coinage, yielding an enormous accession of wealth to importers, who, to the extent of the means thus placed in their hands, would immediately become competitors for every description of productive investment in the market as well as for all material objects which contribute to human enjoyment. But as the supply of such objects is always limited, and would in no way be augmented by this great inundation of circulating coin, the inevitable results would be first, a decline of the market rate of interest; next, a rise in the value of land and of all interest-bearing securities; and lastly, a progressive increase in the prices of commodities generally, until such prices should have attained a level corresponding with the reduced cost of procuring the coin, when the action on interest would cease, the new stock of coin would be absorbed in the old, and the visions of sudden riches and prosperity would pass away, leaving no trace behind them but in the greater number and weight of coin to be counted over on every occasion of purchase and sale.[28]

Still another characteristic type of overvaluation of money remains to be mentioned: characteristic because it occurs automatically, without any state intervention. During the last credit crisis in the United States, in the autumn of 1907, there suddenly appeared a premium on money; not merely on gold money, but on all types of legal tender (gold and silver coins, government paper greenbacks, and bank notes). Initially the premium amounted to more than 5 per cent. The facts are set forth in the following dispatch from New York to the *Frankfurter Zeitung*, 21 November 1907.

> In a good many American commercial centres, cash payments have ceased completely and private money certificates are used there instead. In a few instances, payments are made partly in cash and partly in these certificates. In many places cash circulates only as small change. In 77 American cities, emergency money has been issued; either in the form of clearing house certificates or bank cheques specially issued for the occasion, mostly however, the former type. Before the crisis, perhaps only a dozen American cities had clearing house institutions, but they have now been established in some hundred places. As soon as the crisis broke out in New York, the money institutions in these places combined for common protection against the impending danger. Departing from the practice of New York, where clearing house certificates were issued only for large sums, these clearing institutions created emergency money intended for general use, in denominations of 1,2,5 and 10 dollars, suitable for use in small transactions. These money tokens circulate unhindered in the vicinity of the clearing houses. Workers accept them as wages, merchants in payment for goods, and so forth. They pass from hand to hand and usually there is only a small discount on them as compared with cash. How great the dearth of cash was even in New York, is shown, for example, by the fact that even the powerful Standard Oil Company has had to pay its workers in certified cheques. Only in transactions with government agencies is emergency money not used. Public agencies insist on legal tender payments, so that cash money has to be obtained. This is the main reason for the premium on cash money. During the last few days, when the American Sugar Refining company could not muster sufficient cash to clear a shipment of sugar through the customs, it had to close down several establishments for a day or two.

What is unique in this occurrence is that the quantity of means of circulation available became inadequate for the needs of commerce. The credit crisis provoked a strong demand for cash payments because there was a disturbance in the settlement of balances by credit money (bank drafts, etc.), and a passion for cash money ensued. At the very moment when circulation required more cash, it disappeared from circulation, to be hoarded as a reserve.[29] In place of the vanished money, an effort was made to create new money in the form of clearing house certificates which were actually notes issued under a common guarantee by the banks belonging to the clearing house. The legal restriction on the issue of notes was simply ignored *contra*, or at least *praeter legem*, just as, in a similar case in England, the Peel Act [The Cash Payments Act of 1819.Ed.] was suspended. But this credit money was not legal tender, and cash money was insufficient. Hence, the latter was soon overvalued and remained overvalued (it commanded a premium) until gold imports from Europe, the re-establishment of normal credit conditions, and the enormous contraction of circulation immediately after the crisis, eliminated the 'money famine' and transformed it into a condition of great cash liquidity. The amount of the premium varied, depending upon the social value in circulation. It is characteristic that the premium was the same both for paper and metal; the best evidence that it had nothing to do with an increase in the value of gold.

The issue of legal tender paper money is a well-known and frequently used means for the state to meet its debts when no other means are available. Above all, paper money drove full value metallic money out of circulation,[30] the latter being sent abroad to meet, for example, war expenditures. Continued issues of paper money then led to its depreciation. The quantity theory, then, holds good for a currency with suspended coinage. After all, the theory was formulated as a generalization of the experience with unsettled currencies at the end of the eighteenth century in America, France and England. In such cases, one may also speak of inflation, of a circulation glut, and (in specific cases) of a shortage of the means of circulation. In contrast to this, under a system of free coinage inflation is impossible even when the minimum of circulation is amply covered by legal tender paper money. Convertible credit money, when present in surplus amounts, reverts back to the point of issue; and the same happens to gold itself, which is accumulated in the coffers of the banks as a gold reserve. As a universal equivalent, gold is both a universally valid and always coveted form of value and wealth accumulation. It would be senseless to accumulate legal tender paper money, since it appears as value only in the domestic circulation of a country. Gold, on the other hand, is an international money and constitutes a reserve for all expenditures. Hence its accumulation is always a rational act. Gold is an independent bearer of value even when it is not in circulation. Paper money, on the other hand, acquires a 'rate of exchange' only in circulation.

An overissue of paper money is indicated whenever there is a diminution of its value in terms of the metal it represents. At any given moment, however, the volume of paper money is neither larger nor smaller than is required in circulation. Let us assume that circulation requires 1,000,000 guilders but that state expenditures have put 2,000,000 guilders into circulation. This would cause a 100 per cent rise in nominal prices which would absorb the 2,000,000 guilders. They would, of course, constitute a depreciated paper currency because they have been issued in excess quantities; but once issued they are absorbed into circulation. Hence, they cannot automatically drop out of circulation. Given a constant volume of commodities, the quantity of such paper money can be reduced only if the state destroys part of it, thus increasing the relative value of the balance which continues to circulate. For the state this would naturally mean a loss, just as the previous issue of paper had yielded a profit. The essential thing to bear in mind in this case, is that under a system of suspended coinage and a depreciated or worthless medium of circulation, the entire sum of money must remain in circulation because, regardless of the volume issued, it derives its value from the commodities in circulation. The case is entirely different with free coinage. Money, in this case, enters or leaves circulation according to the prevailing demand for it, and if an excess occurs it is accumulated in the banks as a store of value. The assumption of the quantity theory that changes in value are caused by either an excess or deficiency of money in circulation must therefore be ruled out at once.

Under a system of pure paper currency, then, given a constant velocity of circulation, the sum of prices denoted by the paper money varies directly with the sum of commodity prices and inversely with the quantity of paper money issued. The same is true in a system of suspended coinage when the metal in circulation is depreciated. In the latter case, however, the proviso should be added that the price of the metal on the world market constitutes the lowest limit to its depreciation, so that even if there were an increased issue of the coin, its value would not fall below that limit. Furthermore, even under a system of gold currency in which free coinage (that is, the right of individuals to have their gold coined at any time) has been discontinued, the value of coin can increase in terms of uncoined bullion.[31] In all such cases, the media of circulation are value tokens, rather than money or gold certificates. They do not acquire their value from a single commodity, as is the case in a system of mixed currency where paper is simply a gold certificate which acquires its value from gold, but instead the total quantity of paper money has the same value as the sum of commodities in circulation, given a constant velocity of circulation of money. Its value simply reflects the whole social process of circulation. At any given moment, all the commodities intended for exchange function as a single sum of value, as an entity to which the social process of exchange counterposes the entire sum of paper money as an equivalent entity.

From what has been said thus far, it also follows that a pure paper currency of this kind cannot meet the demands imposed on a medium of circulation for any extended period of time. Since its value is determined by the value of the circulating commodities, constantly subject to fluctuations, the value of money would also fluctuate constantly, Money would not be a measure of the value of commodities; on the contrary, its own value would be measured by the current requirements of circulation, that is to say, by the value of commodities, assuming a constant velocity of circulation. A pure paper currency is, therefore, impossible as a permanent institution, because it would subject circulation to constant disturbances.

A system of pure paper currency might be envisaged in the abstract along the following lines. Imagine a closed trading nation which issues legal tender state paper money in a quantity sufficient for the average requirements of circulation, and further, that this quantity cannot be increased. The needs of circulation would be met, aside from this paper money, by bank notes etc., exactly as in the case of a metallic currency. By analogy with most modern legislation governing banks of issue, the paper money would serve as cover for these bank notes, which would also be covered by the resources of the banks. The impossibility of increasing the supply of paper money would protect it against depreciation. Under such circumstances, paper money would behave as gold does today; it would flow into the banks or be hoarded by individuals when circulation contracts, and would return to circulation when that expands. The minimum of circulating media required at any time would remain in circulation, while the fluctuations in circulation would be covered by an expansion or contraction of bank notes. The value of the state paper money would therefore remain stable. Only in the event of a collapse of the credit structure, and a monetary crisis, would there be any likelihood of an insufficiency in the amount of paper money. It would then command a premium, as was the case with gold and greenbacks during the recent monetary crisis in the United States.

In reality, however, such a system of paper currency is impossible. In the first place, this paper money would be valid only within the boundaries of a single state. For the settlement of international balances, metallic money with an intrinsic value would be required; and if this requirement is to be satisfied, the value of the money in domestic circulation must be kept on a par with the medium of international payments to avoid the disruption of commercial relations. This condition, incidentally, was fulfilled by the Austrian currency system and policy; and we may note that it is not necessary for this purpose to put metal into domestic circulation. Marx virtually foresaw this recent experience with currencies when he wrote:

All history of modern industry shows that metal would indeed be required only for the balancing of international commerce, whenever its equilibrium is disturbed momentarily, if only national production were properly organized. That the inland market does not need any metal even now is shown by the suspension of cash payments of the so-called national banks that resort to this expedient whenever extreme cases require it as a sole relief.[32]

But this type of currency can never succeed in practice for the simple reason that there is no possible guarantee that the state will not increase the issue of paper money. Finally, money with an intrinsic value – such as gold – is always needed as a means of storing wealth in a form in which it is always available for use.[33]

For this reason money and precious bullion, such as gold, can never be replaced completely by mere money tokens without introducing disturbances into the process of circulation. Hence, in practice, even under a system of exclusive paper currency, full value money is always available in circulation, if only for the purpose of making payments abroad. The paper currency can replace only the minimum quantity below which experience has shown that circulation does not fall. This is proof afresh, however, that the value of both money and commodities, far from being imaginary, is an objective magnitude. The impossibility of an absolute paper currency is a rigorous experimental confirmation of the objective theory of value, and only this theory can explain the peculiar features of pure paper currencies, and more particularly, of currencies with suspended coinage.

On the other hand, it is perfectly rational to substitute relatively worthless tokens for money of full value (gold) so long as it is done within the limits set by the minimum of circulation. For in the process C – M – C money is superfluous from the standpoint of its essential content, the social exchange of goods, and is only an unnecessary expense.[34]

If paper money circulates in this volume, it does not represent the value of commodities but the value of gold, it is not a commodity token but a gold token. Within these limits, Marx's conclusions remain valid:

In the process C – M – C, in so far as it represents the dynamic unity or direct alternations of the two metamorphoses – and that is the aspect it assumes in the sphere of circulation in which the token of value discharges its function – the exchange value of commodities acquires in price only an ideal expression and in money only an imaginary symbolic existence. Exchange value thus acquires only an imaginary though material expression, but it has no real existence except in the commodities themselves, in so far as a certain quantity of labor time is embodied in them. It appears, therefore, that the token of value represents directly the value of commodities, by figuring not as a token of gold, but as a token of the value which exists in the commodity alone and is only expressed in its price. But it is a false appearance. The token of value is directly only a token of price, i.e., a token of gold, and only indirectly a token of value of a commodity. Unlike Peter Schlemihl, gold has not sold its shadow but buys with its shadow. The token of value operates only in so far as it represents the price of one commodity as against that of another within the sphere of circulation, or in so far as it represents gold to every owner of commodities. A certain comparatively worthless object such as leather, a slip of paper, etc., becomes by force of custom, a token of money material, but maintains its existence in that capacity only so long as its character as a symbol of money is guaranteed by the general acquiescence of the owners of commodities, i.e. so long as it enjoys a legally established conventional and compulsory circulation. Paper money issued by the state and circulating as legal tender is the perfected form of the token of value, and the only form of paper money which has its immediate origin in metallic circulation, or even in the simple circulation of commodities.[35]

Thus our hypothesis of a pure paper currency which exists without a gold complement has merely demonstrated once again that it is impossible for commodities to act as direct expressions of each other's value. On the contrary, it serves to demonstrate the need for advancing to a universal equivalent which itself is a commodity and therefore a value.

Obviously, if concerted action by producers is required to guarantee the validity of coined money, this is all the more true of paper money. The natural agency for this purpose is the state, for it is the only conscious organization known to capitalist society, which possesses coercive power. The social character of money then appears directly in the regulation of society by the state. At the same time, the limits of circulation for coins and paper money are set by the frontiers of the state. As international money, gold and silver function in terms of their weight.

Money as a means of payment. Credit money

Up to this point we have considered money only as a medium of circulation. We have shown that it is necessary for it to have objective value, that this necessity has limits, and that it can be replaced by money tokens. In the process of circulation, C – M – C, value appears in a double guise: as money and as a commodity. Now a commodity can be sold and paid for later. It can be transferred to another owner before its value is converted into money. The seller thereby becomes a creditor, and the buyer a debtor. As a result of this hiatus between sale and payment money acquires still another function; it becomes a means of payment. When this happens commodity and money do not necessarily have to appear simultaneously as the two parties to a sales transaction. In fact, the means of payment first begins to circulate when the commodity itself drops out of circulation. Money ceases to be an intermediary in the process but concludes it independently. If the debtor (buyer) has no money he must sell commodities to pay his debt, and if he cannot do this his property can be compulsorily sold. The value form of the commodity, money, thus becomes the essential purpose of the sale, through a necessity which itself arises from the relations of the circulation process. When money is used as a medium of circulation it facilitates the dealings between buyer and seller, and mediates their interdependence as members of society. But when it is used as a means of payment it expresses a social relationship which arose before it began to be used. The commodity is handed over and perhaps even consumed long before its value is realized in the form of money. The contraction of a debt and its repayment are separated by a period of time. This means that the money which is turned over in payment can no longer be regarded as a mere link in the chain of commodity exchanges or as a transitory economic form for which something else may be substituted. On the contrary, when money is used as a means of payment it is an essential part of the process. Thus, when M becomes a debt in the process C – M – C the seller of the first commodity can proceed with the second part of the cycle M – C only after debt M has been repaid. What was previously a simple transaction is now divided into two component parts, separated in time.

Needless to say, the seller has an alternative course. He can proceed with the purchase M – C by contracting, in turn, a debt for the M in anticipation of repayment for the original sale of his commodity. Should this payment fail to materialize, however, he may be forced into bankruptcy and drive his creditors into bankruptcy too. When money is used as a means of payment, therefore, it must continue to flow back to prevent the cancellation of the entire series of exchanges which has already been completed. The creditor has parted with a commodity even if the debtor does not pay the money. The social relationship, once brought into being by this transaction, cannot be undone. Nevertheless, it is rendered null and void for the individual owner of the commodity. He does not recover the value which he previously advanced, and in consequence he cannot acquire any new values, nor pay for those already acquired.

The function of money as a means of payment, therefore, presupposes a mutual agreement between buyer and seller to defer payment. The economic relation arises in this case from a private act. Purchase and sale have their counterpart in a second relationship between creditor and debtor, an obligation between two private individuals.

From another aspect, money used as a means of payment represents only a completed purchase and sale. In that case money functions only nominally as a measure of value, and payment is made later. When purchases and sales take place among the same people they can be cancelled out, and only the balance need be paid in money. When this happens money is only a symbol of value and can be replaced. But as a medium of circulation money simply mediated the exchange of commodities; the value of one was replaced by the value of the other. With this, the whole process was completed. This was a social process, an act by which the social exchange of objects is completed, and therefore unconditionally necessary in a particular context. Since gold money only mediated in this process it could be replaced by tokens which have the sanction of society (the state). When money functions as a means of payment, the direct substitution of one value for another is abolished. The seller has parted with his commodity without acquiring the socially valid equivalent, money, or another commodity of equal value which would have made the use of money in this act of exchange superfluous. All he has received is a promise to pay from the buyer, which is not backed by a social guarantee but only by the private guarantee of the purchaser.[1] That he delivers a commodity against a promise is a private matter. What such a promise is really worth can only be determined when it falls due and must be translated into cash. In the meantime, however, he has parted with a commodity in return for a promise of payment, that is a 'promissory note'. If others, in turn, are sure that the note will be redeemed, they may accept it in exchange for commodities. The note therefore serves as a medium of circulation, or means of payment, within the circle of those who accept such promises of payment at their face value, and who are bound together only by their personal, though for the most part well-founded, judgments. In short it functions as money, credit money. All these acts of exchange are finally and definitively concluded, in this circle, only when credit money is converted into real money.

In contrast to legal tender paper money which emerges from circulation as a social product, credit money is a private affair, not guaranteed by society; consequently, it must always be convertible into money. If its convertibility becomes doubtful it loses all its value as a substitute for the means of payment. Money, as a means of payment, can be replaced only by promises to pay, and these have to be redeemed to the extent that they do not balance out.

This accounts for the difference between the circulation of promissory notes and that of legal tender paper money. The latter is based upon the minimum social requirements of circulation. All requirements over and above this minimum are served by the circulation of notes which, since they depend on the sale of commodities at definite prices, are simply personal instruments of indebtedness, either cancelled against other notes or redeemed in money. The note is a private obligation which becomes transformed into a socially recognized valid equivalent. It has arisen from the use of money as a means of payment, replaces money by credit, by a private relation between contracting parties based upon a mutual confidence in each other's social standing and ability to pay. Such business transactions among individuals are not a prerequisite for state paper money. In fact, the opposite is true: where paper money is in use, an exchange is possible only with its help. When notes do not cancel each other out, the balance must be paid in cash if the exchange is to be socially valid, but there is no such requirement when an exchange is made with the use of state paper money. It is completely misleading to characterize paper money as a state debt, or as credit money, because it is not based upon a credit relationship.

If notes and state paper money are not subject to the same type of depreciation, it is because notes rest upon private obligation while paper money rests upon a social obligation. The sum total of state paper is an entity in which each element is, as it were, equally and uniformly responsible for the other. It can depreciate or appreciate only as a whole, with the same effect on all members of sociey The endorsement of society stands behind the entire sum and is therefore uniform for all its component parts. Society, acting through its conscious organ, the state, establishes money as a medium of circulation. Credit money, on the other hand, is created by individuals in their business transactions, and functions as money only so long as it is convertible into money at all times. It is therefore possible for a single note to depreciate (notes do not appreciate) when such private transactions are not concluded in a socially valid manner and the note is not redeemed on the due date. Indeed, in that event, it may become entirely worthless, but only the individual note becomes worthless, and the depreciation affects only one other person, whose own obligations, moreover, remain unaffected.

Inconvertible paper money cannot be issued in excess of the minimum of circulation. The quantity of credit money depends only on the aggregate price of those commodities for which money functions as a means of payment. At given prices, its magnitude depends upon the volume of credit transactions, which is extremely variable. Since it must always be convertible, however, it can never depreciate in or through its relations with commodities. Convertible credit money (unlike inconvertible paper money) can never be depreciated merely because a large volume of it has been put into circulation, but only when it cannot be redeemed in money. The crucial test, therefore, is its convertibility. When that test comes, the owners of commodities, who had forgotten all about gold amidst their delightful 'pieces of paper' now, as one man, make a mad rush for gold. *'On revient toujours à ses premiers amours!'*

The number of promissory notes due for payment at any given time represents the total price of the commodities for which they were issued. The quantity of money necessary to pay this sum depends upon the velocity of circulation of the means of payment, and this is affected by two factors: (a) the chain of obligations between creditors and debtors, in which a payment to A from B will enable him to pay C and so on; and (b) the length of time between the dates when the various notes fall due. The closer together these dates are, the more often can the same piece of gold be used to make the various payments.

If the process C – M – C takes place in such a way that sales occur simultaneously and in the same place, the effect is to curtail the rate of turnover of the means of circulation, and thus to limit the possibility of substituting velocity for quantity. On the other hand, when payments are made simultaneously and in the same place they can offset one another, so that the quantity of money required as a means of payment is reduced. When these payments are concentrated in one place, specialized institutions and methods for settling them come into existence spontaneously. The *virements* of medieval Lyons were one example of this. All that is required is that the various claims to payment be collated, in order to cancel each other out, up to a certain point, leaving only a residue to be settled in cash. The larger the volume of payments which are thus concentrated the smaller, relatively speaking, is the balance which must be paid in cash and the smaller too, therefore, is the required quantity of means of payment in circulation.

We have found that the volume of money in circulation, in the process C – M – C (including the gold which covers the minimum of circulation and which can be replaced by gold certificates), is equal to the sum of commodity prices divided by the average number of turnovers of a unit of money. Similarly, the volume of means of payment is equal to the sum of obligations incurred (which in turn is equal to the aggregate price of all the commodities from the sale of which the promissory notes arose) divided by the average number of turnovers of a unit of money used as a means of payment, minus the sum of payments which are offset against each other. Assuming the velocity of circulation at a certain time to be given, say 1, then the quantity of money to be used for all purposes is equal to the aggregate price of commodities entering into circulation, plus the sum of payments falling due, minus the payments which cancel out, and finally, minus the units of money which functioned first as a means of payment and then as a medium of circulation. If the volume of commodities turned over amounts to 1,000 million marks altogether, and payments due are the same; if 200 million marks serve first for payments and then for circulation; and if 500 million marks cancel out, then 1,300 million marks represent the necessary money which is required at that particular time. This is the amount which I call the socially necessary value in circulation.

The greater part of all purchases and sales takes place through this private credit money, through debit notes and promises to pay which cancel each other out.[2] The reason why means of payment outweigh in importance the media of circulation is that the development of capitalist production has vastly complicated the circulation process, separated purchases and sales, and generally dissolved the old connection which used to tie purchases closely to sales.

Credit money originates in circulation, that is, in purchases and sales by capitalists. Its importance consists in making the circulation of commodities independent of the amount of gold available. In other words, credit money makes gold unnecessary as a medium of circulation for commodities which has to be physically present, and limits its function to that of settling the final balances. These balances are immense in comparison with the amount of gold, and their final settlement is a function of special institutions. But as we have already noted, circulation is both a precondition and an outcome of capitalist production, which can be undertaken only after the capitalist has acquired the elements of production through an act of circulation. To the extent that circulation is independent of real money, it is also independent of the quantity of gold. Finally, since this gold costs labour and represents a large item of *faux frais*, it follows that the replacement of money constitutes a direct saving of unnecessary costs in the circulation process.

Because of its origin, the quantity of credit money is limited by the level of production and circulation. Its purpose is to turn over commodities, and in the final analysis, it is covered by the value of the commodities the purchase and sale of which it has made possible. But unlike state paper money, credit money has no inflexible minimum which cannot be increased. On the contrary, it grows along with the quantity of commodities and their prices. But credit money is nothing but a promise to pay. When a commodity is sold for gold, the payment of gold is the end of the transaction, value is exchanged against value, and further disturbances are excluded; but in the case of credit money, the settlement is only a promise to pay. Whether promises of this kind can be honoured depends on whether or not debtors who have purchased commodities can resell them or sell other commodities of equal value. If an exchange act does not correspond to social conditions, or if these conditions have undergone a change in the interim, the debtor cannot meet his obligation and the promise to pay becomes worthless. Real money must now take its place.

It follows, therefore, that during a crisis the decline in commodity prices is always accompanied by a contraction in the volume of credit money. Since credit money consists of obligations assumed during a period of higher prices, this contraction is tantamount to a depreciation of credit money. As prices fall sales become increasingly difficult, and the obligations fall due at a time when the commodities remain unsold. Their payment becomes doubtful. The decline in prices and the stagnation of the market mean a reduction in the value of the credit money drawn against these commodities. This depreciation of credit instruments is always the essential element of the credit crisis which accompanies every business crisis.

The function of money as the means of payment implies a contradiction without a *terminus medius*. In so far as the payments balance one another, money functions only ideally as money of account, as a measure of value. In so far as actual payments have to be made, money does not serve as a circulating medium, as a mere transient agent in the interchange of products, but as the individual incarnation of social labour, as the independent form of existence of exchange value, as the universal commodity. This contradiction comes to a head in those phases of industrial and commercial crises which are known as monetary crises. Such a crisis occurs only where the ever-lengthening chain of payments, and an artificial system of settling them, has been fully developed. Whenever there is a general and extensive disturbance of this mechanism, no matter what its cause, money becomes suddenly and immediately transformed from its merely ideal shape of money of account into hard cash.[3]

Legal tender paper money registers its greatest success when this devaluation of credit money has run its full course. Like gold coin, it is a legally established means of payment. The failure of credit money creates a gap in circulation, and the *horror vacui* requires that it be filled at all costs. When this happens it is a perfectly rational policy to expand the circulation of state paper money or the bank notes of the central bank, the credit of which has not been impaired. As we shall see in due course, these bank notes, thanks to legal regulation, enjoy an intermediate position between state paper money and credit money. In the event that such a policy is not followed, money (bullion or paper money) acquires a premium, as gold and greenbacks did in the recent American crisis.

In order to perform its task properly credit money requires special institutions where obligations can be cancelled out and the residual balances settled; and as such institutions develop so is a greater economy achieved in the use of cash. This work becomes one of the important functions of any developed banking system.[4]

In the course of capitalist development there has been a rapid increase in the total volume of commodities in circulation, and consequently of the socially necessary value in circulation. Along with this, the importance of the place occupied by legal tender state paper money has increased. Further, the expansion of production, the conversion of all obligations into monetary obligations, and especially the growth of fictitious capital, have been accompanied by an increase in the extent to which transactions are concluded with credit money. State paper money and credit money together bring about a great reduction in the use of metallic money in relation to the volume of circulation and payments.

Money in the circulation of industrial capital

We turn now to the role which money plays in the circulation of industrial capital. Our path does not lead to the capitalist factory, with its marvels of technology, but to the monotony of the recurrent market process, in which money changes into commodity and commodity into money, in the same endlessly repeated way. Only the hope that by this means we can discover the secret of how the processes of circulation themselves endow capitalist credit with the power eventually to dominate the whole social process, can give the reader courage to traverse patiently the 'stations of the cross' in the present chapter.

Money would be superfluous in circulation if aggregate prices were always constant; that is to say, if the volume and prices of commodities never changed and all commodities exchanged at their respective values. But this is an unattainable condition in an unregulated, anarchic method of production. On the other hand, consciously directed social production would make impossible the appearance of value as exchange value, as a social relationship between two things, and the use of money. Claims to the social product issued by society are no more money than is a theatre ticket which is a claim to a reserved seat. It is the nature of commodity production which makes money necessary as a measure of value and a medium of circulation.[1]

Once money is used as a means of payment a complete mutual cancellation of payments at any given time must be seen as a sheer accident, which will never occur in reality. Money concludes independently the process of moving commodities from place to place. It is entirely arbitrary when the money received in payment for a commodity is itself transformed into a commodity, and the value of the first commodity is replaced by another. The link in the sequence $C - M - C$ is broken. Money must necessarily intervene in the process in order to satisfy the requirements of the seller who does not necessarily intend to buy another commodity.

This disruption of the circulation process, which would seem to us arbitrary and accidental in a system of simple commodity circulation, becomes absolutely necessary in the sphere of capitalist commodity circulation. An analysis of the circulation of capital will demonstrate this.

Value becomes capital when it is used to produce surplus value. This is
what takes place in the process of capitalist production based on the
monopolization of the means of production by the capitalists and the
existence of a free wage-earning class. The wage-labourers sell to the
capitalist their labour power whose value equals the value of the means
necessary for the subsistence and reproduction of the working class. Their
labour creates new value, one part of which replaces the capital advanced
by the capitalist for the purchase of labour power (Marx calls it variable
capital) and the other accrues to the capitalist in the form of surplus value.
Since the value of the means of production (constant capital) is simply
transferred to the product in the course of the labour process, the value
which the capitalist advanced for production has increased, has become
value-breeding value, has confirmed itself as capital.

All industrial capital goes through a circular flow, but the only thing
which is of interest to us in the present context is the change in form which it
undergoes. The creation of surplus value, the valorization of capital, is of
course the rationale of the process. This is accomplished in the process of
production, which has a double function in capitalist society: (1) as in every
form of society, it is a labour process which produces use values; (2) but at
the same time it is a value-creating process, characteristic of capitalist
society, in which the means of production are employed as capital to
produce surplus value. Marx has given us an exhaustive analysis of this
process in the first volume of *Capital*. Our present inquiry, however, need
concern itself only with the transformation of the form of value rather than
with its origin. This transformation does not affect the magnitude of value,
the increase of which occurs in production, but concerns the sphere of
circulation. There are only two forms which value can assume in a
commodity-producing society: the commodity form and the money form.

If we examine the cycle of the capitalist process we find that every capital
makes its debut as money capital. Money intended for use as capital is
converted into commodities of various kinds (C), comprising means of
production (Mp) and labour power (L). These are then put to use in
production (P) which, as such, does not involve any transformation in the
form of value. The value remains a commodity. But in the production
process, first, the use value of the commodity is changed (which does not
affect value at all), and second, the value is increased by the expenditure of
labour. The original value of the commodity is increased by the addition of
surplus value, and it is in this expanded form (C_1) that it emerges from the
place of production to experience its second and last change of form, when
it is converted into money (M_1).

The cycle of capital, then, consists of two phases of circulation, M–C and
C_1–M_1, and one phase of production. In circulation, it appears as money
capital and commodity capital; in production, as productive capital. The
capital which passes through all these metamorphoses is industrial capital

Money capital, commodity capital, and productive capital are not distinct types of capital, but merely particular functional forms of industrial capital. Thus we get the following schema: $M-C-P \ldots C_1-M_1$.

The original form of every new capital is money capital. Money does not bear a label announcing it as capital. What makes it capital is the fact that it is intended for conversion into the elements of productive capital.[2] Otherwise it is only money and can only fulfil money functions, as a means of circulation or payment.

We have already seen that the function of money as a means of payment may also include credit relationships. M–C, the first stage of the circulation process of capital is divided into two parts: M–Mp and M–L. Since the wage-labourer lives only by the sale of his labour power, the maintenance of which requires daily consumption, he must be paid at relatively short intervals, so that he can make the purchases necessary for his sustenance. Consequently, in dealing with him the capitalist must be in the position of a money capitalist and his capital must consist of money.[3] Credit plays no role here.

The same is not true, however, of the process M–Mp; in this case, credit can play a greater part. Means of production are purchased in order to realize value. The money spent for them has only been advanced by the capitalist. It is intended to return to him at the end of the period of circulation, and in the normal course of events it will return increased in amount. Since money, therefore, is only advanced by the capitalist, and returns to him, it can also be advanced to him, i.e. lent. This, in general, is the basis of production credit: money is loaned only on condition that it is used by the borrower in such a way that in normal circumstances it will return to him. The security for the loan consists of the commodities for the purchase of which the money has been advanced.

We are concerned at this point only with credit which arises from commodity circulation itself, from the change in the function of money, and its transformation into a means of payment after being a medium of circulation. For the present, therefore, I shall not consider the type of credit which arises from the division of the functions of the capitalist between the pure money owner and the entrepreneur. When money is advanced by the money capitalist to the entrepreneur, the advance is only a transfer; there is no change in its amount. Such a change may well take place, however, in the case which concerns us at the moment. The seller of the means of production credits the customer with commodities, and in return receives a promise to pay in the form of a note. When the note falls due, the capitalist may perhaps be able to repay the capital advanced to him from the proceeds of its circulation. Under these circumstances, his total capital can be smaller than it would have to be if credit were not available. Credit, then, has increased the power of his own capital.

But the existence of credit in no way changes the fact that capital must have the form of money in order to be able to buy commodities. It merely reduces the quantity of metallic money that would otherwise be required for exchange, in so far as payments cancel each other out. But this quantity does not depend at all upon the fact that money is being used as capital in this transaction; it is determined by the laws of commodity circulation. Other things being equal, the quantity of money advanced is determined by the aggregate price of the commodities which have to be bought. Thus, an increase in the quantity of capital advanced simply denotes an increase in the purchase of commodities intended for use as productive capital (Mp + L); that is, an increased volume of media of circulation and payment.

Two opposed tendencies are at work in the case of an increase of this kind. During a period of prosperity, a rapid accumulation of capital is accompanied by an increased demand for certain commodities and consequently by an increase in their prices, which makes necessary an increase in the quantity of money. On the other hand, credit also grows in such a period, since regular returns seem to assure the valorization of capital, and there is a greater readiness and opportunity to make credit available. The expansion of credit makes possible a rapid growth of circulation beyond what would be possible on the basis of metallic money.

This is true, naturally, only of the process M–Mp; not of the process M–L. With the growth of variable capital there is a corresponding increase in the amount of extra money which serves consumers' purchases and flows into circulation. It is evident that as capitalist production develops there constantly takes place an absolute, and even more a relative, increase in the use of credit. The latter is accounted for by the progress toward a higher organic composition of capital, in which the growth of M–Mp outpaces the growth of M–L, with the resulting more rapid increase in the use of credit as compared with the use of cash.

Thus far, in our examination of the cycle, we have not observed credit performing any new function. This changes, however, when we consider the influence of the rate of turnover upon the magnitude of money capital. For we shall soon see that sums of money are periodically set free during the cycle. Since idle money can yield no profit, the attempt is constantly being made to prevent such idleness; and this task can be accomplished only by credit, which thereby acquires a new function. It is to this new function of credit that we must now direct our inquiry.

The periodic release and idleness of money capital

The movement of capital through the sphere of production and the two phases of circulation takes place in a sequence of time. The duration of its sojourn in the sphere of production constitutes its production time, that of its stay in the sphere of circulation its time of circulation. The entire time of rotation is therefore equal to the time of production plus time of circulation.[4]

The rotation of capital, considered as a periodical process, not as an individual event, constitutes its turnover. The duration of this turnover is determined by the sum of its time of production plus its time of circulation. This sum constitutes its time of turnover.[5]

In our schema, the time necessary to complete the process M–M, therefore, constitutes the turnover time, which is equal to the time required by the transactions M–L and M–Mp plus the time required by C_1–M_1; while production time proper is equal to the time in which capital as productive capital (P) engages in the process of generating value.

Let us assume that the turnover time of a given capital is nine weeks, of which production takes six weeks, and circulation three weeks, and that 1,000 marks are required for production each week. If production is not to be interrupted for three weeks (the period of circulation) at the end of the period of production, the capitalist must advance a new capital of 3,000 marks (capital II), for during the three weeks in which the capital is in circulation it does not exist at all so far as production is concerned.[6]

The period of circulation therefore calls for additional capital, and this additional capital stands in the same ratio to the total capital as the circulation time stands to the turnover time; in our example, a ratio of 3:9. The additional capital would therefore amount to one-third of the total capital.

The capitalist, then, must have at his disposal 9,000 marks, rather than 6,000, in order to avoid the suspension of production for three weeks. But the additional 3,000 marks first begins to function at the beginning of the circulation time, in the seventh week, and hence must lie idle for the first six weeks. This periodic release and idleness of 3,000 marks goes on unceasingly. The 6,000 marks which were transformed into commodity capital in the first working period are sold at the end of the ninth week. The capitalist now has 6,000 marks in hand. By this time, however, the second working period, which began in the seventh week, is half completed. During this time the additional capital of 3,000 marks has gone to work, and to complete this second period, only 3,000 marks are required, and this sum is provided by releasing again half of the original 6,000 marks. The process now repeats itself again and again.

Additional capital, money capital used to purchase means of production and labour power, has become necessary in order to maintain the continuity of production, and to prevent its interruption by the circulation of capital. The additional capital itself does not generate surplus value

continuously and to that extent does not really function as capital. The
mechanism of rotation has simply set it free for a time so that it can
function during the rest of the time.

Looking at it from the point of view of the aggregate social capital,
there will always be a more or less considerable part of this additional capital for a prolonged time in the form of money capital.[7]

And this released capital is equal to that portion of capital which has
to fill out the excess of the circulating period over the working period or over a multiple of working periods.[8]

The advent of the additional capital [3,000 marks] required for the
transformation of the circulation time of capital I [6,000 marks] into
a time of production increases not only the magnitude of the advanced capital and the length of time for which the aggregate capital
must necessarily be advanced, but it also increases specifically that
portion of the advanced capital which exists in the form of a money
supply, which persists in the condition of money capital, and has the
form of potential capital.[9]

These 3000 marks are not necessarily the entire amount of money capital
lying idle at any given moment.[10] Assume that our capitalist divides the
6,000 marks required at the beginning of the period of production into
3,000 marks for the purchase of means of production and 3,000 marks for
wages. He pays his workers weekly, which means that once a week, until the
end of the sixth week, the sum is reduced by 500 marks, the balance
remaining idle during the interim. Similarly, it is possible that he will not
purchase some of the means of production (say, coal) in bulk at the
beginning of the period of production, but will buy it in successive
instalments during production. Conversely, it may happen that market
conditions or delivery practices dictate purchases in excess of the requirements of a single period of production, in which case it would be necessary
to convert a larger part of money capital into commodity capital.

In so far as process $M{<}^{L}_{Mp}$ does not require that money be immediately
transformed into labour power and means of production, idle money
capital comes into existence, quite apart from the additional capital II. One
part of this money concludes that act M–C, while another part remains in
monetary form in order to be used for simultaneous or successive acts of
M–C when conditions require it. This second part is only temporarily
withdrawn from circulation, in order to become active at an appropriate

time. This hoarding is, therefore, a state in which money continues to exercise one of its functions as money capital. Although it is temporarily inactive it still forms part of the money capital (M) which is equal to the value of the productive capital from which the cycle began. On the other hand, all the money which has been withdrawn from circulation exists in the form of a hoard.

In the form of a hoard, money is thus likewise a function of money capital, just as the function of money in M–C as a medium of purchase or payment becomes a function of money capital. For capital value here exists in the form of money, and the money form is a condition of industrial capital in one of its stages, prescribed by the interrelations of processes within the cycle. At the same time, it is here once more obvious that money capital performs no other functions than those of money within the cycle of industrial capital, and that these functions assume the significance of capital functions only by virtue of their interrelations with the other stages of this cycle.[11]

A third very important reason for money capital lying idle arises from the manner in which capital flows back from the process of realization. Here two principal causes should be distinguished. Looked at from the point of view of its turnover, industrial capital may be divided into two parts. One is completely consumed during a single turnover period and its value is transferred in toto to the product. In a spinning mill, for example, in which 10,000 pounds of yarn are produced monthly and sold at the end of the month, a corresponding value of cotton, lubricants, lighting gas, coal, and labour power is consumed during the month and their value returns to the capitalist when the yarn is sold. This portion of capital which is replaced during a single turnover period is circulating capital. On the other hand, installations, machinery, etc., are also needed for production, and these continue their productive service over many periods of turnover. Hence, only a part of their value, equal to the average depreciation for a single turnover period, is transferred to the product. If their value is, say, 100,000 marks, and their functional life 100 months, then 1,000 marks will be taken from the sale of the yarn for replacement of installations and machinery. The part of the total capital which thus functions over a series of turnover periods is fixed capital.

The owner of the spinning mill therefore, receives a steady flow of money from circulation which he uses for the replacement of his fixed capital. He must hold it in the form of money until 100 months have elapsed, at which time it will amount to the 100,000 marks required for the purchase of new machinery, etc. The process, therefore, constitutes still another occasion for the formation of a hoard, which is itself

a factor in the capitalist process of reproduction; it is the reproduction and storage, in the form of money, of the value of its fixed
capital, or its individual elements, until such time as the fixed capital,
shall be worn out, until it shall have transferred its entire value
to the commodities produced, and must be reproduced
in its natural form.[12]

Obviously, then, some capitalists are always withdrawing money from
circulation as replacement for the consumed value of the fixed capital. The
essential thing here is the money form. The value of the fixed capital can be
replaced in money form only because the fixed capital itself can continue to
function in production without having to be replaced in kind. It is thus the
particular form of the reproduction of fixed capital which makes money
necessary in this connection.[13] In the absence of money, it would not be
possible to separate the circulation of the value of fixed capital from its
technical continuity in production. The manner in which fixed capital is
renewed thus requires periodic hoarding, and hence also the periodic
idleness of money capital.

The capitalist mode of accumulation supplies the final cause of the
release of money capital which is of interest to us here. Surplus value must
attain a certain volume, depending upon the prevailing technical and
economic conditions of an enterprise, before it can begin to function as
capital, either in the expansion of existing enterprises or the formation of
new ones. Every cycle ends with surplus value in money form. As a rule, a
whole series of cycles is required before the realized surplus value is large
enough to be converted into productive capital. The result is idle money
capital which originates in production and must remain in money form
until such time as it can be put to productive use.

Hoarding can occur even in simple commodity circulation. All that is
required is that in the sequence C – M – C, the second part, M – C, should
fail to take place; that the seller of the commodity refrains from buying
other commodities and hoards his money instead. But this kind of action
seems quite accidental and arbitrary, whereas in the circulation of capital
such hoarding is essential and ensues from the nature of the process itself.
Another difference between the two types of circulation is that in the
circulation of capital not only are means of circulation set free and
hoarded, but also money capital which was a stage in the valorization
process and a potential starting point for a new cycle of production. In this
way pressure is exerted on the money market.

Thus there arises from the very mechanism of capital circulation the
necessity for a larger or smaller amount of money capital to remain idle for
longer or shorter periods. During these periods of inactivity, of course, it
can earn no profit – a mortal sin from the standpoint of capitalists. As in

most cases of sinning, however, the extent to which capital commits this sin depends upon objective factors, which we must now consider.

The changing volume of idle capital and its causes

As we already know, additional money capital which periodically lies idle is required in order to continue production during the turnover period. In our first example, if the period of turnover were reduced from three to two weeks, 1,000 marks would become superfluous and would therefore be withdrawn in the form of money capital. It would then enter the money market as an addition to the capital already there. Prior to its release, only part of the 1,000 marks was in money form, namely the 500 marks which served to purchase labour power. The balance of 500 marks had been used to purchase means of production and therefore existed in commodity form. The entire sum, in the form of money, is now disengaged from this cycle.

> The 1,000 marks thus withdrawn in money now form a new money capital seeking investment, a new constituent part of the money market. True, they were previously periodically in the form of released money capital, and of additional productive capital, but these latent forms were the conditions for the promotion and continuity of the process of production. Now they are no longer needed for this purpose, and for this reason they form a new money capital and a constituent part of the money market, although they are neither an additional element of the existing social money supply (for they existed at the beginning of the business and were thrown by it into circulation) nor a newly accumulated hoard.[14]

This shows how, given a constant money reserve, any increase in the supply of money capital must be the result of an abbreviation of the turnover period. Money, having once served as capital, is fated to return to that role.

Conversely, if the turnover period were prolonged, say for another two weeks, an additional capital of 2,000 marks would be required. This sum would have to be obtained from the money market in order to re-enter the cycle of productive capital (including its circulation). Of this sum, half would be gradually converted into labour power, and the other half, perhaps all at once, would be invested in means of production. Any prolongation of the turnover period therefore produces an increased demand in the money market.

The most important factors which affect the turnover period itself are the following:

To the extent that the greater or smaller length of the period of turn-over depends on the working period, strictly so called, that is to say, on the period which is required to get the product ready for the market, it rests on the existing material conditions of production of the various investments of capital. In agriculture, they partake more of the character of natural conditions of production; in manufacture and in the greater part of extractive industry they vary with the social development of the process of production itself.[15]

Two tendencies are at work here. The development of technology shortens the working period and makes it possible to finish a product and bring it to the market with greater speed. In the case of particular products, the scale of production is enlarged and a larger capital is turned over more rapidly. Technological progress thus shortens the working period and accelerates the turnover of circulating capital and of surplus value. At the same time, however, this progress also means an increase of fixed capital, which has a longer turnover period, spanning many turnover periods of circulating capital. Since fixed capital tends to increase more rapidly than circulating capital, the result is that a growing proportion of the total capital has a slower rate of turnover. Leaving aside credit, this slowing down of the rate of turnover provides another reason – in addition to the expansion of the scale of production itself – for an increased advance of money capital, of which a larger proportion, however, would remain unoccupied and available.

To the extent that the length of the working period is conditioned on the size of the orders (the quantitative volume in which the product is generally thrown upon the market), this point depends on con-ventions. But convention itself depends for its material basis on the scale of production, and it is accidental only when considered individually.[16]

In this connection, too, the quantity produced generally increases and with it the requirements for money capital. Nevertheless, it should be observed that technological progress makes it possible to produce a larger volume of commodities at lower prices, and this may reduce the capital outlay required.

Finally, so far as the length of the period of turnover depends on that of the period of circulation, the latter is indeed conditioned on the incessant change of market conditions, the greater or lesser ease of selling, and the resulting necessity to throw a part of the product on to more or less remote markets. Apart from the volume of general demand, the movement of prices plays here a principal role, since sales are deliberately restricted when prices are falling, while production continues; and conversely, production and sales keep in step when prices are rising, or sales may even be made in advance. But we must consider the actual distance of the place of production from the market as the real material basis.[17]

Since profit originates in production and is only realized in circulation, there is a never-ending search for ways and means of converting the greatest possible amount of capital into production capital. This accounts for the tendency to reduce the costs of circulation to a minimum, first by substituting credit money for metallic money, and second by reducing the circulation time itself, by improving commercial methods and selling products as quickly as possible. There is also a counter-tendency resulting from the expansion of markets and the development of the international division of labour, but the effect of these factors is moderated in turn by the development of transport facilities.

Finally, it should be emphasized that the length of the period of capital turnover is the decisive factor which determines the rapidity with which surplus value is reconverted into capital and accumulated. The shorter the turnover period the more rapidly can surplus value be realized in the form of money and converted into capital.

The factors mentioned above – the organic composition of capital (especially the ratio of fixed to circulating capital), the development of commercial methods which reduce the turnover time, the improvement of means of transportation which achieves the same result (though it also has the opposite effect when it opens up distant markets), periodic business fluctuations which change the rate at which money flows back, and finally, changes in the speed of productive accumulation – all play some part in determining the quantity of idle capital and the period of its inactivity.

Still another important factor is the influence exerted by changes in commodity prices. If the price of raw materials falls, the capitalist (in our example) need not advance the weekly sum of 1,000 marks, but only, say, 900 marks, in order to continue production on the same scale. His capital for the whole turnover period would then be 8,100 marks rather than 9,000 marks, leaving 900 marks free.

This eliminated, and now unemployed, capital which seeks investment in the money market, is nothing but a portion of the originally advanced capital [of 9,000 marks]. This portion has become superfluous by the fall in the price of the materials of production so long as the business is carried along on the same scale and not expanded. If this fall in prices is not due to accidental circumstances such as a

rich harvest, oversupply, etc., but to an increase of productive power
in the line which supplies the raw materials, then this money capital
is an absolute addition to the money market, or in general to the
capital available in the form of money capital because it no longer
constitutes an integral portion of the capital already invested.[18]

Conversely, a rise in the price of raw materials would necessitate additional
money capital and would increase the demand on the money market.

It is evident that the factors we have just considered are of great
importance for the development of the money market during the periodic
fluctuations caused by the business cycle. At the beginning of a period of
prosperity, prices are low, the turnover of capital is very rapid and the time
of circulation is short. As the upswing approaches its peak, prices rise and
the circulation time is extended. There is a stronger demand for credit in
circulation, while at the same time the demand for capital credit has
increased as a result of the expansion of production. The extended
circulation time and the rise in prices make additional capital necessary,
and this must be obtained from the money market, thus reducing the
amount of loan capital available.

Along with its progress toward a higher organic composition, the general
turnover time of the capital generally increases. Both the quantity of capital
and the period of time during which it is engaged in production increase. A
longer time elapses before the capital which has been advanced returns to
its starting point again. For example, if the turnover time is ten weeks, the
capitalist must advance 10,000 marks. If he introduces a new method of
production which requires an advance of 60,000 marks and has a turnover
time of thirty weeks, he would need to draw 60,000 marks from the money
market. The capital, increased sixfold, would have to be advanced for
thrice the length of time.

The longer the turnover time of the capital the longer it takes for the
equivalent value of the commodities (means of production and means of
subsistence for the workers) withdrawn from the market, to return to the
market in the form of commodities. Thus commodities are withdrawn from
the market and money takes their place. Money is now not an ephemeral
but an enduring value form for the commodities withdrawn from the
market. Its value has become independent of the commodity. The
commodity value must now be replaced absolutely by money, since its
replacement by another commodity can only follow at an entirely different
point of time.

If we assume that society were not capitalist but communist, then
money capital would be entirely eliminated, and with it, the disguises
which it carries into the transactions. The question is then simply
reduced to the problem that society must calculate beforehand how

much labour, means of production, and means of subsistence it can utilize without injury for such lines of activity as, for instance, the building of railways, which do not furnish any means of production or subsistence, or any useful thing, for a long time, a year or more, while they require labour and means of production or subsistence out of the annual social production. But in capitalist society, where social intelligence does not act until after the fact, great disturbances will and must occur under these circumstances. On the one hand there is pressure on the money market, while on the other an easy money market creates just such enterprises in mass that bring about the very circumstances by which a pressure is subsequently exerted on the market. A pressure is exerted on the money market, since an advance of money for long terms is always required on a large scale. And this is so quite apart from the fact that industrialists and merchants invest the money capital needed for carrying on their business in railway speculation, etc., and reimburse themselves by borrowing on the money market. On the other hand, there is a pressure on the available productive capital of society. Since elements of productive capital are continually withdrawn from the market and only an equivalent in money is thrown on the market in their place, the demand of cash payers for products increases without providing any elements of supply. Hence a rise in prices of means of production and of subsistence. To make matters worse, swindling operations are always carried on at this time, involving the transfer of large sums of capital . . . . [19]

In such circumstances, variations in the rate of turnover constitute a disturbing factor in the proportionality of reproduction, and thereby, as will be shown later, an element in crises.

Our investigation so far has therefore yielded the following conclusions: (i) a portion of the total social capital devoted to production is always lying idle in the form of money capital; (2) the magnitude of this idle money capital is subject to great variations which exert an immediate influence on the demand for and supply of money capital in the money market. But the existence of idle money is in contradiction with the very function of capital, which is to produce profit. Hence every effort is made to reduce this idleness to a minimum, and this task constitutes yet another function of credit.

The transformation of idle money into active money capital by means of credit

It is easy to see how credit can perform this function. We have seen already that money capital is periodically released in the cycle of capital. Once released from the cycle of any one individual capital, it can function as money in the cycle of another capital if it is made available to other capitalists in the form of credit. In other words, this periodic release of capital is an important basis for the development of the credit system. All the factors, therefore, which have led to the idleness of capital now become so many causes for the emergence of credit relations, and all the factors which affect the quantity of idle capital also determine the expansion and contraction of credit.

If, for example, there are interruptions in the cycle of any capital which cause it to remain in the form of money capital, a potential supply of money capital comes into existence and can be made available to other capitalists through the medium of credit. Such is the case in discontinuous processes of production, like those which prevail in the seasonal industries, whether as a result of natural causes (in agriculture, the herring catch, sugar production, etc.) or of conventional arrangements (where there is, for example, so-called seasonal work). Every release of money capital involves the possibility of applying this capital, by means of credit, to other productive purposes beyond those of the individual capital which released it.[20]

If, on the contrary, the interruption occurs at a point in the cycle where no money capital is released, then the reverse holds true. The continuity of the process can only be maintained if recourse can be had to liquid reserves, or, where a developed credit system exists, to credit.

On the one hand, the nature of the cycle creates the possibility of granting loans for use as capital. But since money is always needed to defray the cost of circulation, and capitalist production has a tendency to expand more rapidly than the supply of money capital, the resort to credit becomes a necessity. On the other hand, every disturbance in the process of circulation, every prolongation of the process C–M or M–C, makes an additional reserve capital essential to maintain the continuity of the production process.

I have already noted that the quantity of money depends, *ceteris paribus*, on the aggregate price of commodities in circulation. Any changes in value which occur while capital is going through its cycle will therefore affect the quantity of money capital. If prices rise, the additional money capital is tied up; if they fall, money capital is released.

But to the extent that these disturbances increase in volume, the industrial capitalist must have at his disposal a greater money capital in order to tide himself over the period of compensation; and as the scale of each individual process of production, and thus the minimum size of the capital to be advanced, increase in the process of capitalist production, we have here another circumstance in addition to those others which transform the functions of the industrial capi-

falls more and more into a monopoly of great money capitalists, who may be individuals or associations.[21]

Credit which is thus based upon the release of money capital is radically different from the commercial credit which originates only from the changed function of money in simple commodity circulation. This subject requires a closer examination.

The banks and industrial credit

Credit first appears as a consequence of the changed function of money as a means of payment. When payment is made some time after the sale has taken place, the money due is credited for the intervening period. Naturally, this form of credit presupposes commodity owners and, in a developed capitalist society, productive capitalists. Assuming that we are dealing with a single isolated example of this practice this simply means that capitalist A has enough reserve capital to wait for payment from B who did not have the necessary cash at the time of the purchase. In this kind of unilateral advance of credit, A must have available the sum of money which B will have to pay when the debt falls due. Money is not economized thereby; it is merely transferred. Things are different if the promissory note itself functions as a means of payment. To take an example; if A not only advances credit to B, but also receives credit from C by giving him B's note, C can use that note to make any payments he owes to B. Sales and purchases between A and B, A and C, C and B have taken place without the intervention of money. Money is therefore saved, and since this money must have been in the possession of productive capitalists as money capital for the circulation of their commodity capital, it follows that for them money capital has been saved, The promissory note, in other words, has replaced money by performing the work of money, by functioning as credit money. A large part of the circulation processes, including the largest and most concentrated operations, take place among the productive capitalists, and all these transactions can, in principle, be accomplished by promissory notes or bills of exchange.* The majority of such bills cancel out and hence only a small amount of cash is required to settle the balances. In this case productive capitalists are mutually providing each other with credit. What the capitalists lend each other is commodities, which constitute for them commodity capital. At the same time, however, these

---

* Throughout his study Hilferding uses the term Wechsel to denote a variety of credit instruments which are usually given distinct names in the English-speaking world. I have therefore translated the term in different ways according to the context. [Ed.]

commodities are looked upon as mere bearers of a given amount of value, which is assumed to have been realized in its socially valid form at the time of sale. In other words, they are regarded as the bearers of a specific sum of money represented by the bill. The circulation of bills, therefore, is based upon the circulation of commodities, but of commodities which have been sold and converted into money, even if the conversion is one which society has not yet accepted as valid, but which only exists as a private act in the buyers' promises to pay.[1]

This type of credit, advanced by productive capitalists to one another, I shall call circulation credit. I have already noted that it is used as a substitute for money and that, by facilitating the transfer of commodities without the use of money, it helps to conserve precious bullion. The expansion of this type of credit is based on the increased use of this method of transferring commodities, and since commodity capital is involved here – transactions between productive capitalists – it depends also upon the expansion of the reproduction process. Whenever the scale of reproduction increases, there is also an increased demand for productive capital (machinery, raw materials, labour power).

An increase in production means a simultaneous increase in circulation; and the enlarged circulation process is made possible through an increase in the quantity of credit money. The circulation of bills expands, and can expand, because the quantity of commodities entering circulation is larger. This growth of circulation can proceed without any rise in the demand for gold money. Equally, the relation between the supply of and demand for money capital need not change, because the greater need for means of payment can be met simultaneously, and in the same proportion, by a larger supply of credit money based upon the increased volume of commodities.

What increases in this case is the circulation of bills of exchange.[2] This increased credit need not in any way affect the relation between the demand for and supply of the elements of real productive capital. Rather, both are likely to increase at the same rate. The process of production is expanded, and commodities are thus produced which are required to carry on production on an enlarged scale. We therefore have an increase in credit as well as an increase in productive capital, both of which are reflected in an increased circulation of commercial bills. But this does not entail any variation in the relation of the supply to the demand for capital in money form. Yet it is only *this* demand which affects the rate of interest. It is therefore possible for the supply of credit to increase without any change in the rate of interest, provided that the additional credit consists exclusively of circulation credit.

The circulation of bills is limited only by the number of business transactions actually concluded. An overissue of state paper money will depress the value of each individual money unit without changing the value of the total supply of paper money, but commercial bills can in principle only be issued when a business transaction has been concluded, and for this reason bills cannot be overissued. If a particular transaction is fraudulent, the bill of course will become worthless. But the worthlessness of one bill has no effect on all the others.

The impossibility of an overissue of bills does not, however, preclude the possibility that capitalists may assume excessive monetary obligations in the form of credit instruments of this type. During a crisis, for instance, the prices of commodities fall and obligations cannot be redeemed in full. Market stagnation makes the conversion of commodities into money impossible. The manufacturer of machines who issued bills in payment for coal and iron, hoping to redeem them through the sale of his product, now finds himself unable to liquidate his obligation or to satisfy his creditor by giving him a bill drawn on a purchaser of his own machines. If he has no reserves his bills become worthless, notwithstanding the fact that they represented commodity capital at the date of issue (coal and iron converted into machines).[3]

In providing credit for the period of circulation bills are a substitute for the additional capital that would otherwise have been required to bridge over that period. These bills are normally issued by productive capitalists to one another. But if returns fail to materialize the money has to be obtained from a third party, the banks. The banks are also involved whenever the normal conditions of bill circulation are disturbed; for instance, when commodities become temporarily unsaleable or are withheld for speculative or other purposes. In this case the banks merely extend and supplement the credit provided by bills.

Circulation credit thus extends the scale of production far beyond the capacity of the money capital in the hands of the capitalists. Their own capital simply serves as the basis for a credit superstructure and provides a fund for the settlement of balances, as well as a reserve against losses when bills depreciate.

The saving in cash money tends to increase to the extent that bills cancel each other out. Special institutions are required for this purpose. The collection and clearance of credit instruments is a task performed by the banks. At the same time, more money can be saved the more frequently a single bill can be used as a means of payment. Bills will circulate in this more extensive way only if there is certainty that they will be redeemed; that is, if their security as a medium of circulation and means of payment is publicly recognized. This, too, is one of the tasks of the banks. Banks perform both functions by buying bills. In so doing, the banker becomes a guarantor of credit and substitutes his own bank credit for commercial credit in so far as he issues a bank note in place of industrial and commercial bills. The bank note is simply a draft on the banker which is more readily acceptable than the notes of the industrialist or merchant. Thus the bank note rests upon the circulation of bills. The state note is backed by the socially necessary minimum of commodity transactions, and the bill of exchange by the completed commodity transaction as a private act of the capitalist. The bank note, on the other hand, is secured by the bill, or promissory note, which is backed by the total assets of all the drawers who were parties to the exchange. At the same time, the issue of bank notes is limited by the volume of discounted bills and hence by the number of completed acts of exchange.

Originally, therefore, the bank note was simply a bank draft which replaced bills issued by productive capitalists.[4] Prior to the use of bank notes bills often circulated with a hundred or more signatures before they fell due. On the other hand, the first bank notes resembled ordinary commercial bills in being issued for the most varied amounts rather than in round sums. Nor were they always payable on demand.

In past times, it was not uncommon for banks to issue notes, payable on demand, or at a distant day from that of presentation, at the option of the issuer, but in such case, the notes bearing interest till the day of payment.[5]

A change (which, however, does not affect the economic laws involved) was first introduced when the state intervened. The purpose of its legislation was to guarantee the convertibility of the bank note by limiting, directly or indirectly, the quantity that might be issued, and by making the issue of bank notes a monopoly of a bank operating under state control. In countries where there is no state paper money, or where its volume is far below the socially required minimum, the bank note takes its place. Where such notes are made legal tender during certain periods of crisis they become in effect state paper money.[6]

The artificial regulation of the issue of bank notes fails as soon as circumstances require an increased issue. For instance, when the credit structure collapses during a crisis, the credit money (bills) of many individual capitalists is impaired, and the place it occupied in circulation has to be filled by additional means of circulation. The law becomes impotent and is either disregarded (as recently occurred in the United States) or suspended (as in the case of the Peel Act in England). People will accept bank notes while they reject many other bills simply because the credit of the bank has not been impaired. If it were impaired the notes would have to be made legal tender, or state paper money would have to be issued. If this were not done, purely private means of circulation would be contrived, as they were in the recent American crisis. But this is a much less effective method of combating a money crisis, especially when such a crisis is aggravated by unsound legislation with respect to the issue of bank notes.[7]

Like the bill of exchange the convertible note cannot be issued in excess quantities. (The inconvertible note is really identical with legal tender state paper money.)[8] A bank note which is not required in circulation is returned to the bank. Since it can be used in lieu of the bill of exchange, the issue of notes is subject to the same laws as is the circulation of bills, and expands along with the latter so long as credit remains undisturbed. The credit behind a bank note can hold its own even during a crisis and consequently, when the circulation of bills contracts during a crisis, bank notes and cash are used in their place.

With the development of the banking system, as unemployed money flows into the banks, bank credit is substituted for commercial credit, so that increasingly all bills serve as means of payment not in the original form in which they circulate among productive capitalists, but in their converted form as bank notes. Banks become the institutions for clearing and settling balances, a technical improvement which extends the range of possible mutual cancellation and reduces the amount of cash required for settling balances. The money which productive capitalists had previously been obliged to keep on hand for settling the bills they had drawn now becomes superfluous, and flows as deposits to the banks who can use it to settle the balances.

Since the banker substitutes his own credit for the commercial bills, he requires credit, but only a relatively small money capital of his own, in order to guarantee his ability to pay. What the banks do is to replace unknown credit by their own better known credit, thus enhancing the capacity of credit money to circulate. In this way they make possible the extension of local balances of payment to a far wider region, and also spread them over a longer time period as a consequence, thus developing the credit superstructure to a much higher degree than was attainable through the circulation of bills limited to the productive capitalists.

Nevertheless, we should be on guard against the error of double counting with regard to the capital which banks supply to producers by discounting their bills. The greater part of bank deposits belong to the productive capitalists who, as the banking system evolves, keep the whole of their liquid money capital in the banks. This money capital, as we have seen, is the basis for the circulation of bills. But it is that class's own capital, and the class does not receive any new capital through the discounting of bills. All that has happened is that capital in one money form (as a private promise to pay) has been replaced by capital in another money form (as a promise to pay by the bank, ultimately in cash). Money capital is involved only to the extent that it replaces the realized commodity capital. In other words, money is regarded here from a generic point of view. In a functional sense, however, money is always involved, either as a means of payment or of purchase.

The substitution of bank credit for the credit of the productive capitalist can, of course, take place in other forms than the issue of bank notes. For instance, in countries where the note issue is a monopoly, private banks may supply bank credit to producers by 'accepting' their bills; that is by endorsing them, and thus guaranteeing their redemption. By this means, the bill benefits from the credit of the bank, and its ability to circulate is increased as if it had been replaced by a note of that particular bank. It is well known that a large part of international commercial transactions, in particular, are carried on by means of such bills. In principle, there is no difference between such 'acceptances' and the notes of private banks.[9]

Circulation credit, in the sense in which I have used the term, simply consists in the creation of credit money. Thanks to the service it performs, production is not limited by the volume of available cash which is part of the socially necessary minimum of circulation (full value metallic money, standard currency, gold and silver coins, plus legal tender state paper money and small change).

But circulation credit as such does not transfer money capital from one productive capitalist to another; nor does it transfer money from other (unproductive) classes to the capitalist class, for transformation into capital by the latter. If circulation credit is merely a substitute for cash, that credit which converts idle money of whatever kind (whether cash or credit money) into active money capital is called capital (or investment) credit, because it is always a transfer of money to those who use it, through the purchase of the various elements of productive capital, as money capital.

We saw in the last chapter how hoards of idle money accumulate in the course of capitalist production which can be used as money capital. It is these sums, which are sometimes involved in the circulation process and are sometimes idle, which are hoarded either for the replacement of fixed capital or as saved-up surplus value until they are large enough for accumulation. Three aspects need to be distinguished here: (1) the individual sums must be collected until, through centralization, they are sufficiently large to be used in production; (2) they must be made available to the right people; and (3) they must be available for use at the right time.

We have seen earlier how credit money originates in circulation. We are now dealing with money which lies idle. But money can only perform the functions of money, and can do so only in circulation. Credit, therefore, can do no more than put non-circulating money into circulation. As capitalist credit, however, it puts money into circulation only in order to withdraw more money. It puts money into circulation as money capital in order to convert it into productive capital. Thus it expands the scale of production, and this expansion presupposes the expansion of circulation. The scale of circulation is enlarged not by the injection of new money, but simply by the utilization of old, previously idle money for the purposes of circulation.

There is thus a need for an economic function which consists of collecting idle money capital and then distributing it. But credit assumes here an entirely different character from ordinary circulation credit. Circulation credit merely makes it possible for money to serve as a means of payment. Payment for a commodity which has been sold is credited, and the money which would otherwise have had to enter circulation is saved because it is replaced by credit money. Actual money which might otherwise be required thus becomes superfluous. On the other hand, no new capital is made available to the capitalist. Circulation credit merely gives his commodity capital the form of money capital.

Capital (investment) credit, however, involves the transfer of a sum of money from the owner, who cannot employ it as capital, to another person who intends to use it for that purpose. This is the purpose of the money. For if it were not employed as capital, its value would not be maintained or recovered. From the standpoint of society as a whole, however, the borrower must always repay his debt if lending is to take place with any degree of security. In this case, therefore, there is a transfer of money which already exists, and no money is economized. Investment credit thus transfers money and converts it from idle into active money capital.[10] Unlike ordinary commercial credit, it does not reduce the costs of circulation. Its primary purpose is to enable production to expand on the basis of a given supply of money. The possibility of investment credit arises from the conditions of circulation of money capital, from the fact that in the cycle of capital money periodically falls idle. Some capitalists are always paying such funds into the banks which, in turn, make them available to others.

If, therefore, we view the matter from the standpoint of the capitalist class as a whole, the money is not idle. No sooner is it hoarded at any point in circulation, than it is immediately converted by the use of credit into an active money capital in another process of circulation. The class as a whole can economize in its advances of money capital, because the transferability of money available during intervals of circulation obviates the formation of idle money hoards. The relatively small part of the money supply which the capitalist class needs to lay by as a hoard, is required only to cope with irregularities and interruptions in circulation.

Previously we were dealing with productive capitalists (producers and merchants) who conducted their business (for instance, the purchase of means of production) by means of credit money. Now the productive capitalist has become a money capitalist or a loan capitalist. This new guise, however, is temporary, lasting only for the period during which his money capital lies idle, anxious to be turned into productive capital. And just as he is a lender at one moment, so he is a borrower from some other productive capitalist at another. The character of loan capitalist is at first only transitory, but with the development of the banking system it becomes the specialized function of the banks.

Credit causes the available supply of money capital to do a larger volume of work than would be possible in the absence of credit. It reduces idle capital to the minimum which is necessary to avoid interruptions and unforeseen changes in the capitalist cycle. It thus tries to eliminate, for the benefit of the whole social capital, the idleness of money capital which an individual capital experiences for a certain period of time in the course of the cycle.

It follows that deposits and withdrawals by productive capitalists take place in accordance with definite laws, which can be inferred from the nature of the circulation process of productive capital and the length of its cycle. Experience has familiarized the banks with these regularities, which indicate the minimum amount of deposits under normal conditions, and hence the amount which they can make available to productive capitalists.

The cheque is a direct order upon a deposit, while the commercial bill draws upon it only indirectly. The cheque draws upon an individual deposit, while the bill is based upon the aggregate deposit of the whole class. For it is essentially their own deposits which are made available to the capitalist class for discounting bills, and when the bills which fall due are paid the money, which has accrued in fact from the sale of commodities, returns to the banks as deposits. Should this reflux of money diminish, and the repayment of these bills be reduced, capitalists would have to secure additional capital. They would then draw upon their deposits, and thus reduce the fund which is available for discounting their bills. The bank now has to intervene and discount bills with its own credit, but since the deposits which provide the basis for the circulation of bills have been reduced, and the bank's liquidity has declined, it is dangerous for the bank to expand its own credit. The retarded reflux of money, in this case, has increased the demand for bank credit and thus – since credit cannot be expanded – for bank (i.e. loan) capital. This is expressed by a rise in the rate of interest. The functioning of the bill as credit money has declined in importance, and actual money obtained from the bank has had to take its place, as is revealed by the increased demand for money capital. Thus we see a reduction of deposits, while the circulation of commercial bills remains constant or even increases, and the interest rate rises.

It is obvious that the total volume of deposits is many times greater than the available supply of cash. Metallic money circulates rapidly and is also the basis for the circulation of credit money. Any transfer of either metallic money or credit money may result in a deposit with the banker, and the fact that the volume of deposits can thus greatly exceed the stock of cash is shown by the rate of circulation (including credit money).

A deposits 1,000 marks in a bank. The bank lends these 1000 marks to B who, in turn, uses them to pay his debt to C. C then again deposits the 1,000 marks in the bank. The bank lends them out again and receives them once again as a deposit, and so on.

> The deposits . . . play a double role. On the one hand . . . they are loaned out as interest-bearing capital, and are not found in the cash boxes of the banks, but figure merely in their books as credits of the depositors. On the other hand, they figure as such book entries to the extent that the mutual credits of the depositors in the shape of cheques on their deposits are balanced against one another and so recorded. In this procedure, it is immaterial whether these deposits are entrusted to the same banker who can thus balance the various credits against each other, or whether this is done in different banks, which mutually exchange cheques and pay only the balances to one another.[11]

In terms of the preceding account the bank has performed two functions: (1) it has facilitated the process of making payments, and by concentrating them and eliminating regional disparities, it has enlarged the scale of this process; (2) it has taken charge of the conversion of idle capital into active money capital by assembling, concentrating and distributing it, and in this way has reduced to a minimum the amount of idle capital which is required at any given time in order to rotate the social capital. The bank assumes a third function when it collects the money income of all other classes and makes it available to the capitalist class as money capital. Capitalists thus receive not only their own money capital, which is managed by the banks, but also the idle money of all other classes, for use in production.

In order to perform this function the banks must be able to assemble, concentrate, and lend out as much of the available idle money as possible. Their principal means of doing so are the payment of interest on deposits and the establishment of branch banks where such deposits can be made. This 'decentralization' – a misnomer perhaps, because the decentralization is purely geographical rather than economic – is essential to the bank's job of transferring idle money to productive capitalists.

The money capital which is thus supplied by the banks to industrial capitalists can be used to expand production in two different ways: by increasing either fixed capital or circulating capital. The distinction is a very important one because it determines the way in which the money capital flows back. Money capital which is advanced for the purchase of circulating capital flows back in the same manner; that is, its value is fully reproduced during a single turnover period and reconverted to the money form. This is not the case, however, when the advance is made for investment in fixed capital. Invested in this way, the money returns in piecemeal fashion, in the course of a long series of turnovers, during which time it remains tied up. This difference in the reflux of money is responsible for a difference in the way in which the bank invests its money. When it invests its capital in a capitalist enterprise the bank becomes a participant in the fortunes of the enterprise; and this participation is all the more intimate the more the bank capital is used as fixed capital. The bank enjoys far more freedom of action in its dealings with a merchant than with an industrial entrepreneur. In the case of merchant capital, only credit for payments is involved, and as we shall see, this explains why bank capital stands in an altogether different relationship to merchant capital than it does to industrial capital.

Bank capital (including other funds, as mentioned above) is supplied to industrial capitalists in a number of ways; by allowing them to overdraw their own deposit accounts, by establishing open credit accounts, or by current account operations. There is no difference in principle between these three methods. What really counts is the purpose for which the funds are applied, that is, whether they are used as fixed or circulating capital.[12]

To the extent that banks tie up their funds, they are obliged to keep a comparatively large capital of their own, as a reserve fund, and as security for the uninterrupted convertibility of deposits. Thus banks which are engaged in supplying long-term credit, in contrast to pure deposit banks, must have at their disposal a substantial capital. In England the ratio of paid-up share capital to liabilities is extraordinarily small: 'In the excellently managed London and County Bank, the ratio in 1900 was 4.38 to 100.'[13] On the other hand, this ratio also explains why the dividends of the English deposit banks are so high.

Originally, the principal credit instrument was the bill of exchange used as payment credit by productive capitalists – industrial and commercial – in their dealings with one another; its outcome is credit money. When credit is concentrated in the hands of the banks, investment credit becomes increasingly important in comparison with payment credit. At the same time the credit which industrialists extend to one another may change its form. Since all their money capital is held in liquid form in the banks, it becomes a matter of indifference to them whether they extend credit to one another by means of commercial bills or by claims upon their bank credit. Bank credit can therefore be substituted for bills, and the

circulation of the latter begins to diminish. Industrial and commercial bills
are replaced by bank drafts, which are based upon an obligation of the
industrialist to the bank.[14]

The transition from commercial to investment credit is also apparent in
international markets. In the early stages of development England (and
Dutch policy was similar in the early period of capitalism) extended
commercial credit to countries which bought English products, while
paying for a larger proportion of her own imports in cash. The situation is
different today: credit is not provided exclusively or mainly in the form of
commercial credit, but for capital investment, the object of which is to gain
control of foreign production. The principal international bankers today
are not so much the industrial countries like the United States and
Germany; it is primarily France, and then Holland and Belgium, which
were already financing English capitalism in the seventeenth and eighteenth
centuries, which are the main providers of investment credit. England, in
this regard, occupies an intermediate position. This accounts for the
differences in the gold movements in and out of the central banks of these
countries. For a long time London has been the only genuinely free market
for gold and hence the centre of the trade in gold, so that the movement of
gold through the Bank of England has served as an index of international
credit relations. The free movement of gold has been impeded in France by
the gold premium policy, and in Germany by various policies of the
Reichsbank management. Since the credit extended by England to this very
day is still largely commercial credit, the fluctuations of England's gold
reserve depend, in the main, on the state of industry and trade, and the
balance of payments. The Bank of France, on the other hand, enjoys a far
greater degree of freedom in making its dispositions, thanks to its
enormous gold reserve and relatively small commercial obligations.
Whenever there is any disturbance in the market for commercial credit, it is
the Bank of France which comes to the assistance of the Bank of England.

The important thing about this relative independence of bank credit
from ordinary commercial credit is that it gives the banker certain
advantages. Every merchant and industrialist has commitments which must
be honoured on a specified date, but his ability to meet these obligations
now depends upon the decisions of his banker, who can make it impossible
for him to meet them by restricting credit. This was not the case when the
bulk of credit was commercial credit and banks were only dealers in bills. In
such circumstances, the banker himself was dependent upon the state of
business and the payment of bills, and had to avoid so far as possible any
restrictions of the credit required by business, since otherwise he might
destroy the whole commercial credit structure. Hence the expansion of his
own credit to the full, even to the point of overextending himself and
inviting bankruptcy. Today, when commercial credit is far less important

than investment credit, the bank is able to dominate and control the situation much more effectively.

Once the credit system has attained a certain degree of development, the utilization of credit by the capitalist enterprise becomes a necessity, imposed upon it by the competitive struggle. The use of credit by an individual capitalist means an increase in his rate of profit. If the average rate of profit is 30 per cent and the rate of interest 5 per cent, a capital of 1,000,000 marks will produce a profit of 300,000 marks. (This will appear in the accounts of the capitalist as 250,000 marks entrepreneurial profit and 50,000 marks interest on capital.) If the capitalist succeeds in obtaining a loan of another 1,000,000 marks, he will make a profit of 600,000 marks, less 50,000 marks interest on his loan, leaving him a net profit of 550,000 marks. If this is calculated on his own capital of 1,000,000 marks it amounts to an entrepreneurial rate of profit of 50 per cent as compared with the original 25 per cent. And if the larger capital also makes it possible for him to increase his output, and so produce more cheaply, his profit might well be even larger. If other capitalists do not have access to credit on the same scale, or on equal terms, the favoured capitalist can make an extra profit.

Under unfavourable market conditions the use of credit has other advantages. A capitalist who uses borrowed capital under these circumstances can reduce his prices, for that proportion of his output produced with borrowed capital, below production prices (cost price plus average profit) to the point where they equal cost price plus interest, and can therefore sell his whole output below the production price without diminishing the profit on his own capital. All that he sacrifices is the entrepreneurial profit on the borrowed capital, not the profit on his own capital. In periods of economic depression, therefore, the use of credit bestows an advantage in price competition, which is all the greater the larger the amount of credit. For productive capitalists, therefore, their own productive capital becomes only the basis of an enterprise which is expanded far beyond the limits of the original capital with the aid of borrowed capital.[15]

The increase of entrepreneurial profit through the use of credit accrues to the individual capitalist and to his own capital. It leaves unchanged, at first, the average social rate of profit, but it does, of course, increase the total sum of profit and accelerate the pace of accumulation. Those capitalists who use credit before others do so, or more extensively, are able to enlarge their scale of production, increase the productivity of labour, and thus gain initially an extra profit; but as this process continues the rate of profit tends to fall, because the expansion of production is usually associated with a tendency toward a higher organic composition of capital. The increase in the entrepreneurial profit of individual capitalists stimulates their demand for further credit, and the supply of such credit is made possible by the increasing concentration of money capital from all sources in the banks. This tendency arising in industry is bound to react upon the banks' methods of providing credit.

One of the first results of this intensified demand is that credit is sought for use as circulating capital. An increasing proportion of the entrepreneur's own capital is transformed into fixed capital while the bulk of circulating capital comes from the borrowed funds. But as the scale of production expands, and fixed capital becomes much more important, so this limitation of credit to circulating capital is felt to be too restrictive. If credit is then required for fixed capital, however, the terms on which credit is made available undergo a fundamental change. Circulating capital is reconverted into money at the end of a period of turnover, whereas fixed capital is converted into money very gradually, over a long period of time, as it is slowly used up. Consequently, money capital which is turned into fixed capital must be advanced on a long-term basis because it will remain tied up in production for a long time. The loan capital available to the bank, however, is usually repayable at short notice to its owners. For this reason the bank can only lend for fixed capital investment that amount which remains in its own possession for a sufficiently long time. This does not apply, of course, to any particular unit of loan capital; but there always remains in the hands of the bank a large proportion of the total loan capital, the composition of which will naturally change, while a certain minimum amount will always be available, and can therefore be lent for fixed capital investment. While individual capital is not suitable for fixed investment in the form of loan capital – for it ceases then to be loan capital and becomes industrial capital, and the loan capitalist is turned into an industrial capitalist – the minimum which the banks always have available is appropriate for fixed investment. The larger the aggregate capital at the disposal of the bank, the larger and more constant will be the portion which it can lend in this way. Hence a bank cannot lend funds for investment in fixed capital until it has attained a certain size; and it must expand as rapidly, or more rapidly, than industrial enterprises themselves. Moreover, a bank cannot limit its participation to a single enterprise, but must distribute the risks by participating in many different enterprises. This policy will in any case be adopted to ensure a regular flow of repayments on its loans.

This way of providing credit has changed the relation of the banks to industry. So long as the banks merely serve as intermediaries in payment transactions, their only interest is the condition of an enterprise, its solvency, at a particular time. They accept bills in which they have confidence, advance money on commodities, and accept as collateral shares which can be sold in the market at prevailing prices. Their particular sphere of action is not that of industrial capital, but rather that of commercial capital, and additionally that of meeting the needs of the stock exchange. Their relation to industry too is concerned less with the production process than with the sales made by industrialists to wholesalers. This changes when the bank begins to provide the industrialist with capital for production. When it does this, it can no longer limit its interest to the condition of the enterprise and the market at a specific time, but must necessarily concern itself with the long-range prospects of the enterprise and the future state of the market. What had once been a momentary interest becomes an enduring one; and the larger the amount of credit supplied and, above all, the larger the proportion of the loan capital turned into fixed capital, the stronger and more abiding will that interest be.

At the same time the bank's influence over the enterprise increases. So long as credit was granted only for a short time, and only as circulating capital, it was relatively easy to terminate the relationship. The enterprise could repay the loan at the end of the turnover period, and then look for another source of credit. This ceases to be the case when a part of the fixed capital is also obtained through a loan. The obligation can now only be liquidated over a long period of time, and in consequence the enterprise becomes tied to the bank. In this relationship the bank is the more powerful party. The bank always disposes over capital in its liquid, readily available, form: money capital. The enterprise, on the other hand, has to depend upon reconverting commodities into money. Should the circulation process come to a halt, or prices fall, the enterprise will require additional capital which can only be obtained in the form of credit. Under a developed credit system, an enterprise maintains its own capital at a minimum; any sudden need for additional liquid funds involves obtaining credit, and failure to do so may lead to bankruptcy. It is the bank's control of money capital which gives it a dominant position in its dealings with enterprises whose capital is tied up in production or in commodities. The bank enjoys an additional advantage by virtue of the fact that its capital is relatively independent of the outcome of any single transaction, whereas the fate of the entire enterprise may depend entirely upon a single transaction. There may, of course, be cases in which a bank is so deeply committed to one particular enterprise that its own success or failure is synonymous with that of the enterprise, and it must then meet all the latter's requirements. In general, however, it is always the superiority of capital resources, and particularly disposal over freely available money capital, which determines economic dependency within a credit relationship.

The changed relationship of the banks to industry intensifies all the tendencies toward concentration which are already implicit in the technical conditions of the banking system. A consideration of these tendencies must again distinguish the three main functions of the banks: the supply of commercial credit (circulation of bills), the supply of capital credit, and, anticipating somewhat, investment banking.

As regards commercial credit, the paramount factor is the development of international connections, which requires an elaborate network of relations. Foreign bills take longer to circulate and therefore immobilize a larger volume of resources. Furthermore, the balancing of payments through the mutual cancellation of bills is seldom so complete. Dealings in foreign exchange thus require a large and efficient organization.

> The important thing is that the banks tend to concentrate because of certain technical banking operations which are extremely important to growing industries. Foreign and domestic bills which industrial producers use to pay for raw materials and finished goods require an organization of the banking system sufficiently ramified to enable it to handle all transactions – especially foreign exchange operations – on a large scale, and also to guarantee their collateral. It requires, in other words, large banks with numerous foreign and domestic branches. It is true, of course, that industries use bills as a means of payment or to secure commercial credit. Institutions which furnish the credit do not thereby get a chance to intervene deliberately in the affairs of their debtor enterprises. In such a relationship between the bank and the enterprise, the bank's jurisdiction is limited to the reliability of the borrower and the discount return.[16]

In order to be profitable foreign exchange transactions must be closely linked with arbitrage operations. This requires extensive connections, and a large volume of liquid resources, because arbitrage must be carried out quickly and on a large scale to be profitable at all. Arbitrage transactions in bills are based on the fact that whenever, say, the London demand for Paris bills exceeds their supply and their price rises accordingly, firms which have deposits or credits in Paris will take advantage of the situation by drawing bills on Paris. The Paris firm, on the other hand, on which the bills have been drawn, waits for a similar favourable opportunity in that market to transfer the sums again to England.[17]

The fostering of capital credit can best be seen in the growing importance of current account operations.[18]

> These transactions play a significant part in the relationship of the banks to industry for three reasons: (1) Since they are so indispensable to the smooth expansion of an enterprise, they make it dependent on the creditor. (2) The technical complexities of bank credit for industry have a far greater influence on the organization of the

banking system than any of the credit operations we have discussed previously. They create a tendency toward concentration in banking. . . . The unique relation (of the banks) to industry . . . requires new principles and an entirely new knowledge of industry on the part of bankers. (3) Finally, current account transactions for industry are the keystone for all other banking activities in industry, such as promotion and the flotation of shares, direct participation in industrial enterprises, participation in management through membership of the board of directors. In a large number of cases such activities are related to bank credit as effect to cause. [At the same time current account work] is an excellent means of judging the soundness of an industrial enterprise and of obtaining control over it; regularity of turnover means that the business is going well.[19]

The exact knowledge which a bank obtains as a result of this continuous relationship can also serve it in good stead in many other ways; for example, in its business on the stock exchange. On the other hand, the danger of over-extending credit makes it necessary for the bank to exercise a high degree of control over the industrial enterprise, and this presupposes that the enterprise works in association with a single bank.

If the concentration of bank capital tends to increase along with the expansion of industry when the banks simply provide credit, it reaches its zenith when they take over the job of floating shares. The large bank enjoys an unmistakable superiority in this activity because it can undertake the most profitable operations. Its transactions are more numerous, on a larger scale, and more efficient. Its flotations are more secure, and it can sell a large part of the issue to its own customers. On the other hand, the large bank must be able to provide the even greater sums of capital which may be required; and for this purpose, it needs a large capital of its own and a great deal of influence on the market.

The large bank is able to choose the appropriate time for issuing shares, to prepare the stock market, thanks to the large capital at its command, and to control the price of shares after they have been issued, thus protecting the credit position of the enterprise. As industry develops, it makes increasing demands on the flotation services of the banks. Once the mobilization of capital is assured, only one condition governs the expansion of industry; namely, the technical possibilities. The expansion of enterprises also ceases to depend upon their own surpluses resulting from production, and indeed during periods of prosperity an industry may grow rapidly, often by leaps and bounds. The sudden increase in the demand for capital which such expansion involves can only be satisfied by the large, concentrated funds of the banks. The banks alone can

Money and credit

obtain the capital without disrupting the money market. This operation can be carried out only if the capital which the bank provides is recovered quickly, or if the issue is performed as a simple book-keeping transaction, which will more probably be the case if the bank sells the issue to its own customers and receives the proceeds of the sale by deducting them from deposits, thus reducing its liabilities.

The technique of banking itself generates tendencies which affect the concentration of the banks and of industry alike, but the concentration of industry is the ultimate cause of concentration in the banking system.

6

The rate of interest

In the capitalist system of production, every sum of money is able to function as capital, that is, to produce a profit, so long as it is made available to productive capitalists.

> Take it that the average rate of profit is 20 per cent. In that case, a machine valued at £100, employed as capital under the prevailing average conditions and with an average exertion of intelligence and adequate activity, would yield a profit of £20. In other words, a man having £100 at his disposal holds in his hands a power by which £100 may be turned into £120. . . . He holds in his hands a potential capital of £100. If this man relinquishes these £100 for one year to another man who uses this sum actually as capital, he gives him the power to produce a profit of 20 per cent, a surplus value which costs this other nothing, for which he pays no equivalent. If this man should pay, say £5, at the close of the year to the owner of the £100, out of the produced profit, he would be paying for the use value of £100, the use value of its function as capital. . . . That part of the profit which he pays to the owner is called interest. It is merely another name, a special term for a certain part of the profit which capital in the process of its function has to give up to the owner, instead of keeping it in its own pocket.
>   It is evident that the possession of £100 gives to their owner the power to absorb the interest, a certain portion of the profit produced by his capital. If he did not give the £100 to the other man, then this other could not produce any profit, and could not act in the capacity of capitalist at all with reference to these £100.[1]

From the standpoint of the owner of money, the money he lends is capital because it returns to him after a time in an increased amount. Capital, however, can acquire an added value only in production, through the exploitation of labour-power, and the appropriation of unpaid labour. Consequently, the money capital of the lenders cannot yield a profit unless it becomes the money capital of producers and is used in production. The

profit which results is now divided, one part returning to the loan capitalist
as interest, the other remaining with the productive capitalist. Under
normal conditions, therefore, profit constitutes the upper limit of interest
because the interest is a fraction of profit. This is the only possible
relationship between interest and profit. On the other hand, interest is not
some definite fixed part of profit. The level of interest depends upon the
demand for and supply of loan capital. It is possible to conceive, and to
formulate the bases of, capitalist society on the assumption that money
owners and productive capitalists are identical, or in other words, that all
productive capitalists have at their disposal the necessary money capital. In
that case, there would be no such thing as interest. But capitalist
production without the production of profit is inconceivable; the two mean
the same thing. The production of profit is both the condition and the
purpose of capitalist production. Its production of surplus value (embodied in the surplus product) is determined by objective factors. Profit
arises directly from the economic relationship, from the capital relationship, from the separation of the means of production from labour,
and from the opposition of capital and wage labour. Its size depends upon
the new value which the working class produces with the available means of
production, and upon the division of this new value between the capitalist
class and the working class, which, in turn, is determined by the value of
labour power. We are dealing here with factors which are determined in a
completely objective manner.

Interest, however, is another matter. It does not arise from an essential
feature of capitalism – the separation of the means of production from
labour – but from the fortuitous circumstance that it is not only productive
capitalists who dispose over money. In consequence, the whole money
capital need not enter the cycle of the individual capital at all times, but may
lie idle occasionally. What part of the profit the loan capitalists can
appropriate depends upon the changing level of producers' demand for
money capital.[2]

If interest is determined by supply and demand, we have to ask how
supply and demand themselves are determined. On one side there is a sum
of money temporarily lying idle but seeking investment; and on the other,
the demand of the capitalists for money which can be converted into capital
for use in production. Capital credit makes this allocation, and the state of
the capital market determines the rate of interest. At any given moment, a
definite sum of money, which represents the supply, is available to capitalist
society, and on the other side, there is at the same time a demand for money
capital arising from the expansion of production and circulation. In other
words, the 'loan price of money', or rate of interest, at any given time is
determined by the confrontation on the market between supply and

demand as two determinate magnitudes. This determination of the rate of interest presents no further problem, and difficulties only arise when we begin to analyse fluctuations in the rate of interest.

This much, at least, is clear; that an increase in production and thus in circulation means an increased demand for money capital which, if it were not matched by an increased supply, would induce a rise in the rate of interest. The problem is that the supply of money would also change along with, and precisely because of, the change in demand. The quantity of money which constitutes the supply comprises two elements: the available cash, and credit money. In our analysis of commercial credit, we found it to be a variable quantity which increases when production increases. This involves an increased demand for money capital, but the increased demand is accompanied by an increased supply in the form of credit money generated by the expansion of production. Hence the interest rate will change only if the demand for money capital changes more than the supply; it will rise, for instance, if the demand for money capital increases more rapidly than the supply of credit money. Under what conditions is this likely to occur?

In the first place, any increase in the quantity of credit money requires an increase in the cash reserves which are needed to ensure that credit money can always be converted. Further, an increase in the circulation of credit money is accompanied by an increase in that part of the total cash supply which is needed to settle uncleared balances. An increased circulation, moreover, is accompanied by an increase in the number of transactions in which credit money plays only a minor part: wage payments to workers and payments for increased retail purchases, for instance, are usually made in cash. Thus the sums available for lending tend to be reduced because part of the cash is needed for these other purposes. Finally, it should be noted that the increase in credit money will lag behind the requirements of increasing production and circulation when the marketing of goods ceases or slows down at the end of a period of prosperity. For this means that the bills drawn against commodities will no longer cancel out, and that at the very least their period of circulation will increase. But if the bills that fall due do not cancel each other out they must be settled in cash. The various forms of credit money (bills, and bank notes issued on the basis of such bills) can no longer perform their money functions, the circulation of commodities, on the same scale as formerly. There is an increased demand for cash to redeem commercial paper, and at the same time to make up the reduced supply of credit money in actual use. It is this demand for cash which brings about the rise in the rate of interest.

If the absolute level of the interest rate thus depends upon the state of the capital market, fluctuations in the rate of interest depend primarily upon the state of commercial credit. A closer analysis of these fluctuations belongs more properly to a .discussion of the trade cycle, and will be presented in that connection.

I am not in complete agreement with Marx's view that variations in the rate of interest depend upon the supply of capital which is loaned in the form of money, cash and notes. He states:

> The variations of the rate of interest (aside from those occurring over long periods or from differences of the rate of interest in different countries; the first-named are conditioned by the variations of the general rate of profit, the last named by differences in the rates of profit and in the development of credit) depend upon the supply of loan capital, all other circumstances, state of confidence etc., being equal; that is, of the capital loaned in the form of money, hard cash and notes; this is distinguished from industrial capital which, in the shape of commodities, is loaned out by means of commercial credit among the agents of reproduction themselves.[3]

This leaves open the question of how large the volume of bank notes can be. For England, whose situation Marx evidently has in mind, the answer is, of course, given by the legal provisions of the Peel Act, according to which the total volume of cash and notes is constituted by the cash in circulation, the gold reserve of the Bank of England, and £14,000,000 in notes, being the volume of unsecured notes in circulation. In fact, these notes assume the function of state paper money to the extent that they represent – or at least represented in Peel's day – the minimum of circulation replaceable by money tokens. Thus the law provided once and for all that the quantity of bank notes should remain at a prescribed figure. But if we put the question in a more general form, variations in the rate of interest depend upon the supply of loanable money. All money, however, can be loaned which is not in circulation. There is in circulation, first the money tokens, covering the minimum requirements of circulation, and second, a certain quantity of gold. The remainder of the gold is in the coffers of the bank or banks, serving partly as a reserve for domestic circulation, and partly as a reserve for international circulation (since gold must perform the function of international money). Only experience can show the minimum quantity of gold required for these two purposes. The remainder can be loaned out, and in the final analysis constitutes the supply whose use determines the rate of interest. But the extent to which it is employed depends upon the state of the commercial credit advanced by producers to one another. As long as this commercial credit can increase fast enough to satisfy the increased demand, the rate of interest will not change. We should not forget, however, that the greater part of the demand is satisfied by a supply which increases together with the demand. The bulk of credit is commercial credit, or as I prefer to call it, 'circulation credit', and both the demand for and the supply (or if you wish, means of satisfaction) of such commercial credit increase together, and *pari passu* with the expansion of production. The expansion of credit is possible without any effect on the rate of interest, and indeed occurs at the beginning of a period of prosperity without such effects. The interest rate first begins to rise when the gold holdings of the banks are reduced and the reserves approach the minimum requirements, forcing the banks to raise their discount rate. This happens at the peak of the trade cycle because circulation then requires more gold (with the growth of variable capital, of turnover generally, and of the amount needed to settle balances). The demand for loan capital becomes greatest precisely when the stock of gold is at its lowest point owing to the absorption of gold by the requirements of circulation. The depletion of the gold stock available for loans becomes the immediate occasion for an increase in the bank discount rate, which in such periods becomes the regulator of the rate of interest. The purpose of raising the discount rate is precisely to bring about an influx of gold. The various restrictions imposed by misconceived banking legislation only have the effect of bringing about the higher discount rate sooner than purely economic conditions require. The mistake of all such restrictions is that in one way or another (indirectly in Germany, directly in England) they underestimate the minimum required in circulation and thereby limit the supply of loan capital.

It follows, then, that the rate of interest would show a downward tendency only if it could be assumed that the relation of the existing gold stock to the demand for loan capital is always becoming more favourable, that is to say, that the gold stock increases more rapidly than the demand for loan capital. But if we consider only developed capitalist systems, such a tendency for interest rates to decline steadily cannot be established.[4] Nor can it be postulated theoretically, because simultaneously with the increase in the gold reserve and in the minimum of circulation there is an increase in the amount of gold entering circulation in a period of prosperity.

A fall in the rate of profit would involve a decline in the rate of interest only if interest were a fixed part of profit; but this is not the case. At most, a decline in the rate of profit means that there has been a reduction in the theoretical maximum level of interest, namely the total profit. But this is of no significance, because interest does not generally reach this ceiling in the long term.[5]

But there is another important factor which should not be overlooked. In a developed capitalist system, the rate of interest is fairly stable, while the rate of profit declines, and in consequence the share of interest in the total profit increases to some extent at the expense of entrepreneurial profit. In other words, the share of rentiers grows at the expense of productive capitalists, a phenomenon which does indeed contradict the dogma of the falling interest rate, but nevertheless accords with the facts. It is also a cause of the growing influence and importance of interest-bearing capital, that is to say, of the banks, and one of the main levers for effecting the transformation of capital into finance capital.

Part II

The mobilization of capital. Fictitious capital

The joint-stock company

1 Dividends and promoter's profit

Up to the present, economics has sought to distinguish between the individually owned enterprise and the joint-stock company (or corporation) only in terms of differences in their organizational forms and of the consequences which flow directly from them. It has indicated the 'good' and the 'bad' features of the two forms of enterprise, emphasizing partly subjective factors such as the greater or lesser degree of interest and responsibility of their managers, and the relative ease or difficulty of exercising a general supervision over the enterprise, and partly objective factors such as the ease of access to capital, and their relative capacity for accumulation. But it has neglected to investigate the fundamental economic differences between the two forms of enterprise, even though these differences are crucial to any understanding of modern capitalist development, which can only be comprehended in terms of the ascendancy of the corporation and its causes.[1]

The industrial corporation, our first object of inquiry, involves above all a change in the function of the industrial capitalist. For it converts what had been an occasional, accidental occurrence in the individual enterprise into a fundamental principle; namely, the liberation of the industrial capitalist from his function as industrial entrepreneur. As a result of this change the capital invested in a corporation becomes pure money capital so far as the capitalist is concerned. The money capitalist as creditor has nothing to do with the use which is made of his capital in production, despite the fact that this utilization is a necessary condition of the loan relationship. His only function is to lend his capital and, after a period of time, to get it back with interest; a function which is accomplished in a legal transaction. So also the shareholder functions simply as a money capitalist. He advances money in order to get a return (to use a very general expression at this stage). Like any money capitalist who risks only such sums of money as he sees fit, the shareholder makes the decision as to how much money he will advance and be held liable for. Nevertheless, a distinction already emerges here. The rate of interest paid on money capital which is provided in the form of shares is not fixed in advance; it is only a claim on the yield (profit) of an enterprise. A second difference as against loan capital is that the return of capital to the money capitalists is not guaranteed. Neither the contract which defines their relationship to the enterprise, nor the relationship itself, gives them any such assurance.

Let us consider the first point. To begin with, it should be realized that the return on money capital offered in the form of shares is by no means completely indeterminate. A capitalist enterprise is founded in order to make a profit, and its creation is undertaken on the assumption that it will achieve a profit; in normal circumstances, the prevailing average rate of profit. In any case, the shareholder is in a situation similar to that of the money capitalist, who counts on the realization of his capital in production so long as the debtor remains solvent. Generally speaking, the somewhat greater insecurity of the shareholder by comparison with the money capitalist will bring him a certain risk premium. But one should not suppose that this premium is somehow fixed and known in advance to the shareholder as a definite measurable claim. The risk premium is simply a result of the fact that the supply of free money capital, which the founders of companies are seeking, which is available for investment in shares, will normally be smaller, other things being equal, than that for particularly safe, fixed interest investments. It is just this difference in supply which explains the variations in interest rates and in the market quotations of interest-bearing securities. Greater security or insecurity is the reason for a larger or smaller supply, and from the variations in this relation between supply and demand results the diversity of interest yields. The probable profit yield on a share is therefore determined by industrial profit and this profit, other things being equal, is determined by the average rate of profit.

The shareholder, however, is not an industrial entrepreneur (capitalist). He is primarily a money capitalist, and one of the essential characteristics which differentiates the loan capitalist from the industrial capitalist is that he holds his capital – money capital – in an entirely different way, available for use just as he pleases. The industrial capitalist invests his entire capital in a particular enterprise. Unlike the shareholder, who need have only a negligible amount of capital available, the industrial capitalist must command a capital which is large enough to function independently in the given branch of industry. The industrial entrepreneur has tied up his capital in his enterprise, he works productively only in that enterprise, and his interests are bound up with it over a long period. He cannot withdraw his capital unless he sells the enterprise, and this means only that the person of the capitalist changes, that one industrialist is replaced by another. He is not a money capitalist but an industrial (productive, functioning) capitalist, who draws a return from his enterprise in the form of industrial profit. The shareholder, on the other hand, if we consider him only as a money capitalist will make his capital available to anyone so long as he gets interest on it.

For the shareholder to become a money capitalist, however, he must be able to regain possession of his capital as money capital at all times. But his capital, like that of an individual capitalist, seems to be tied up in the enterprise, as indeed it is. His money has gone to buy machines and raw materials, to pay workers etc.; in short it has been converted from money capital into productive capital $(M\underset{L}{\overset{M_P}{<}})$ and enters into the cycle of industrial capital. Once the shareholder has parted with this capital, he cannot recover it. He has no claim upon it, but only a claim to a pro-rata share of its yield. In capitalist society, however, every sum of money has the capacity to bear interest; and conversely every regularly recurring income which is transferable (as is usually the case, so far as it is not tied to a purely personal, and therefore transitory and indeterminate condition, such as wages, etc.) is regarded as interest on capital and has a price which is equal to the yield capitalized at the current rate of interest.[2] This is easily explained by the fact that large sums of money are always available for realization and find such realization in a claim upon the profit. Consequently, the shareholder is in a position to recover his capital at any time by selling his shares or claims to profit, and to that extent he is in the same position as the money capitalist. This possibility of selling is created by a special market, the stock exchange. The establishment of this market endows share capital, which the individual can now always realize, completely with the character of money capital. Conversely, the money capitalist retains his character even when he invests in shares. Liquid money capital competes, as interest-bearing capital, for investment in shares, in the same way as it competes in its real function as loan capital for investment in fixed interest loans. The competition for these various investment opportunities brings the price of shares closer to the price of investments with a fixed interest, and reduces the shareholders' yield from the level of industrial profit to that of interest.

This reduction of the share yield to the level of the rate of interest is a historical process which accompanies the development of stocks and the stock exchange. When the joint-stock company is not the dominant form, and the negotiability of shares is not fully developed, dividends will include an element of entrepreneurial profit as well as interest.

To the extent that the corporation is prevalent, industry is now operated with money capital which, when converted into industrial capital, need not yield the average rate of profit, but only the average rate of interest. This appears to be a patent contradiction. The money capital which is provided in the form of share capital is transformed into industrial capital. The fact that in the minds of its owners it functions in exactly the same way as does loan capital, certainly cannot affect the yield of the industrial enterprise. Just as before, the enterprise will yield, under normal conditions, an average profit. We cannot possibly assume that the corporation will sell its commodities at below the average profit, and voluntarily sacrifice a part of the profit, simply in order to distribute among its shareholders a return no higher than the rate of interest. After all, every capitalist enterprise seeks to maximize its profit, which it can succeed in doing if it sells its output at prices of production (cost price plus average profit). Apparently, then, the factors previously mentioned which make money capital, invested in shares appear subjectively as simple loan capital yielding interest, are not adequate to explain the reduction of the yield from shares to the level of interest. What they would leave unexplained is where the other part of the profit (average profit minus interest), in other words the actual entrepreneurial profit, had gone. Let us examine the matter more closely.

With the transformation of an individually owned enterprise into a corporation a doubling of the capital seems to have occurred. The original capital advanced by the shareholders has been definitively converted into industrial capital, and actually exists only in that form. The money was used to purchase means of production, and thus disappeared definitively from the circulation process of money capital. When these means of production are converted into commodities in production, and the commodities are then sold, money – quite different money – can flow back from circulation. Thus the money which is acquired from subsequent sales of shares is not the same money which was originally supplied by the shareholders and then used in production. It is not a constituent part of the corporation's capital, but rather an additional quantity of money required for the circulation of the capitalized claims to income. Similarly, the price of a share is not determined as if it were part of the capital of the enterprise, but rather as a capitalized claim to a share in the yield of the enterprise. In other words, the price of a share is not determined as an aliquot part of the total capital invested in the enterprise and therefore a relatively fixed sum, but only by the yield capitalized at the current rate of interest. Since the share is not a claim to a part of the capital in active use in the enterprise, its price does not depend upon the value, or price, of the industrial capital which is actually being used. It is a claim to a part of the profit, and therefore its price depends, first, on the volume of profit (which makes it far more variable than it would be if it were part of the price of the elements of production of the industrial capital itself), and second, on the prevailing rate of interest.[3]

The share, then, may be defined as a title to income, a creditor's claim upon future production, or claim upon profit. Since the profit is capitalized, and the capitalized sum constitutes the price of the share, the price of the share seems to contain a second capital. But this is an illusion. What really exists is the industrial capital and its profit. But this does not prevent the fictitious 'capital' from existing in an accounting sense and from being treated as 'share capital'. In reality it is not capital, but only the price of a revenue; a price which is possible only because in capitalist society every sum of money yields an income and therefore every income appears to be the product of a sum of money. If this deception is assisted in the case of industrial shares by the existence of genuinely functioning industrial capital, the fictitious and purely accounting nature of this paper capital becomes unmistakable in the case of other claims to revenue. State bonds need not in any way represent existing capital. The money lent by the state's creditors could long ago have gone up in smoke. State bonds are nothing but the price of a share in the annual tax yield, which is the product of a quite different capital than that which was, in its time, expended unproductively.

The turnover of shares is not a turnover of capital, but a sale and purchase of titles to income. The fluctuations in their price leave the actually functioning industrial capital, whose yield, not value, they represent, quite unaffected. Aside from the yield their price depends upon the rate of interest at which they are capitalized. The movements of the rate of interest, however, are quite independent of the fate of any particular industrial capital. These considerations make it obvious that it is misleading to regard the price of a share as an aliquot part of industrial capital.

If this is so, then the total sum of 'share capital', that is, the aggregate price of capitalized claims to profit, need not coincide with the total money capital, which was originally converted into industrial capital. The question then arises how this discrepancy comes about and how large it is. Let us take, for example, an industrial enterprise with a capital of 1,000,000 marks, and assume that the average profit is 15 per cent and the prevailing rate of interest 5 per cent. The enterprise makes a profit of 150,000 marks. The sum of 150,000 marks capitalized as annual income at 5 per cent, will have a price of 3,000,000 marks. Usually, at a rate of 5 per cent money capital would seek out only absolutely secure paper at a fixed rate of interest. But if we add a high risk premium, say of 2 per cent, and take into account various costs of administration, directors' fees, etc., which would have to be deducted from the profit of the corporation (and which an individually owned enterprise would be spared), and assume that this results in the available profit being reduced by 20,000 marks, then 130,000 marks can be distributed giving shareholders a return of 7 per cent. The price of the shares would then be 1,857,143 marks, or in round figures, 1,900,000 marks. But only 1,000,000 marks are needed to produce a profit of 150,000 marks, and 900,000 marks are left free. This balance of 900,000 marks arises from the conversion of profit-bearing capital into interest- (or dividend-) bearing capital. If we disregard the higher administrative costs of a corporation, which reduce the total profit, the 900,000 marks represent the difference between the yield capitalized at 15 per cent and the same yield capitalized at 7 per cent; or in other words, the difference between capital which earns the average rate of profit and capital which earns the average rate of interest. This is the difference which appears as 'promoter's profit', a source of gain which arises only from the conversion of profit-bearing into interest-bearing capital.

The prevalent view, which emphasizes so strongly the higher administrative costs of the corporation as compared with an individually owned enterprise, has neither recognized nor explained the remarkable problem of how a profit arises with the change from a cheaper to a more expensive form of productive enterprise, but has been content with mere phrases about costs and risks. But promoter's profit is neither a swindle, nor some kind of indemnity or wage. It is an economic category *sui generis*.

In so far as they make any distinction at all between interest and entrepreneurial profit, economists conceive dividends simply as interest plus entrepreneurial profit, or in other words, the equivalent of profit for an individual entrepreneur. It is evident that such a view overlooks the distinctive features of the corporation. Rodbertus, for example, says:

> For the sake of agreement on terminology, I wish at this point merely to remark that while the dividend on a stock contains not only interest but also an entrepreneurial profit, the interest on a loan is without any trace of entrepreneurial profit.[4]

This of course, makes it impossible to explain promoter's profit.

> The technical form[5] of the corporate enterprise makes it possible for the owner of capital (who would receive only the current rate of interest had he loaned it to an individual entrepreneur) to receive entrepreneurial profit as well, with the same ease as he would get the interest. This is why the corporate form of enterprise is so attractive to our capitalists, and may be expected increasingly to dominate the industrial field. The so-called swindle of company promotion is merely foam, or rather dross, on the surface of genuine business.[6]

Beyond the moral judgment, there is no attempt to explain promoter's profit, which is not itself a swindle, although it certainly makes swindles possible. Rodbertus's view is one-sided and thus misleading:

> In short, what was once ordinary loan capital ceases to be loan capital when it is converted into shares, and becomes in the hands of

its owners something which creates its own value, and indeed in a form which allows them, in their godlike existence as loan capitalists, to pocket almost the entire capital income.[7] [By income from capital, Rodbertus means entrepreneurial profit plus interest – R.H.]

Rodbertus sees only the content of the process; the transformation of money capital into industrial capital. He fails to notice that what is essential is the form in which it is done, which enables the money capital to become fictitious capital and at the same time to retain for its owners the form of money capital.[8]

Turning now to the peculiar form which the circulation of fictitious capital takes, we find the following: The shares (S) are issued; that is, sold for money (M). One part of this money (m_1) constitutes the promoter's profit, accrues to the promoter (say, the issuing bank) and drops out of circulation in this cycle. The other part (M_1) is converted into productive capital and enters the cycle of industrial capital which is already familiar to us. The shares have been sold; if they are to circulate again then additional money (M_2) is needed as a medium of circulation. This circulation ($S-M_2-S$) takes place in its own specific market, the stock exchange. Hence, the scheme of circulation in Figure 1.

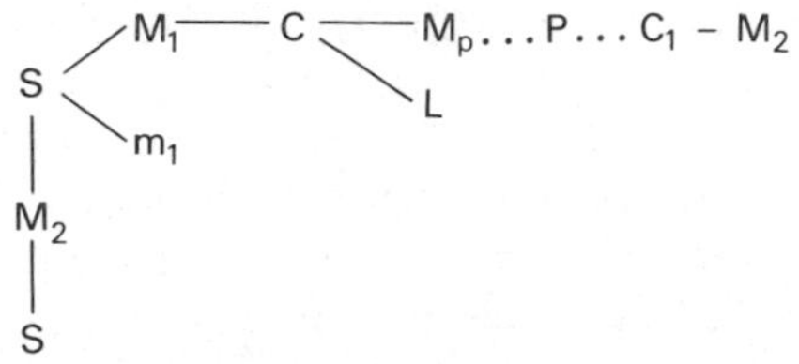

Figure 1

Once a share has been issued it has nothing more to do with the real cycle of the industrial capital which it represents. None of the developments or misfortunes which it may encounter in its circulation have any direct effect on the cycle of the productive capital.

The commerce in shares, and in all certificates of fictitious capital, requires new money, both cash and credit money (for instance, bills of exchange). But whereas bills were previously covered by the value of commodities, they are now covered by the 'capital value' of the shares, which in turn depends upon the yield. Since the yield depends upon the realization of the commodities which the corporation produces, that is upon the sale of the commodities at their values or prices of production, so this credit money is only indirectly covered by the value of commodities. Furthermore, while the volume of payments in trade is determined by the value of commodities, in the commerce in shares it is determined by the capitalized amount of the net yield. But the amount of money needed in this case is greatly reduced by the negotiability of these papers.

If we remember that capital is equal to one hundred times the interest, divided by the rate of interest, the formula for promoter's profit is:

$$P = \frac{100 \, Y}{d} - \frac{100 \, Y}{p}$$

where P is the promoter's profit, p the average profit, d the dividend, and Y the yield of the enterprise. If the gross yield of the enterprise is considered to be reduced by the costs of administration, $Y - e$ may be substituted for the first Y in the formula. It is evident that the separation of the entrepreneurial function, which economics has so far dealt with only in a descriptive manner, involves at the same time a transformation of the industrial capitalist into a shareholder, into a particular kind of money capitalist, so that there emerges a tendency for shareholders to become increasingly pure money capitalists. This tendency is reinforced by the fact that shares are always readily saleable on the stock exchange.

My analysis of the economics of the corporation goes considerably beyond that provided by Marx. In his brilliant sketch of the role of credit in capitalist production, which he was unfortunately denied the opportunity to elaborate, Marx conceives the corporation as a consequence of the credit system, and describes its effects as follows:

1   An enormous expansion of the scale of production and enter-
     prises which were impossible for individual capitals. At the
     same time, such enterprises as were formerly carried on by
     governments are socialized.
2   Capital, which rests on a socialized mode of production, and
     presupposes a social concentration of means of production and
     labour-power is here directly endowed with the form of social
     capital (a capital of directly associated individuals) as disting-
     uished from private capital, and its enterprises assume the form
     of social enterprises as distinguished from individual enterprises.
     It is the abolition of capital as private property within the boun-
     daries of capitalist production itself.
3   Transformation of the actually functioning capitalist into a mere
     manager, an administrator of other people's capital, and of the
     owners of capital into mere owners, mere money capitalists. Even
     if the dividends which they receive include the interest and profits
     of the enterprise, that is, the total profit (for the salary of the
     manager is, or is supposed to be, a mere wage of a certain kind
     of skilled labour, the price of which is regulated in the labour

market like that of any other labour), this total profit is henceforth received only in the form of interest, that is, in the form of a
mere compensation of the ownership of capital, which is now
separated from its function in the actual process of reproduction,
in the same way in which this function, in the person of the manager, is separated from the ownership of capital. The profit now
presents itself (and not merely that portion of it which derives its
justification as interest from the profit of the borrower) as a mere
appropriation of the surplus labour of others, arising from the
transformation of means of production into capital, that is, from
its alienation from its actual producer, from its antagonism as
another's property opposed to the individuals actually at work in
production, from the manager down to the last day labourer.

In the joint stock companies, the function is separated from the
ownership of capital, and labour, of course, is entirely separated
from ownership of the means of production and of surplus labour. This result of the highest development of capitalist production is a necessary transition to the reconversion of capital
into the property of the producers, no longer as the private property of individual producers, but as the common property of
associates, as social property outright. On the other hand, it is a
transition to the conversion of all functions in the process of
reproduction, which still remain connected with capitalist private
property, into mere functions of the associated producers, into
social functions.

Before we proceed any further, we call attention to the following fact which is economically important; since profit here assumes purely the form of interest, enterprises of this sort may still
be successful, if they yield only interest, and this is one of the
causes which stem the fall of the rate of profit since these enterprises, in which the constant capital is so enormous, compared
to the variable, do not necessarily come under the regulation of
the average rate of profit.[9]

What Marx considers here are primarily the economic and political
effects of the corporations. He does not yet conceive dividends as a distinct
economic category and hence fails to analyse promoter's profit. As regards
the concluding remarks concerning the influence upon the formation of the
average rate of profit, and the tendency of the rate of profit to fall, it is clear
that with the spread of the corporation its profit, just like that of an
individually owned enterprise, must contribute to the equalization of the
general rate of profit. We have seen already that the output of the
corporation, under normal conditions, is subject to exactly the same price

laws as is that of the individually owned enterprise. Marx was thinking of
the railway corporations of his day, and in this connection his comments
were perhaps partly justified. I say 'partly' because even then promoter's
profit had already absorbed some part of the profit, and this was bound to
be reflected in railway prices.

2   The financing of corporations. Corporations and banks

When a corporation is founded its share capital is calculated so that the
profit of the enterprise will be adequate to distribute a dividend on the
capital which will provide each individual shareholder with interest on his
investment.[10] Should an economic boom, or other favourable circumstances, make it possible later on to distribute a larger dividend, the price
of the shares will rise. If we assume that the shares of a corporation yielding
a dividend of 6 per cent stand at 100, then they will rise to 150 if the
dividend is raised to 9 per cent. These variations in dividends reflect the
varying fortunes of individual enterprises. Such variations, however, are
overridden, in the case of new purchasers of shares, by the rise or fall of the
general level of share prices.[11]

The difference between the value of the capital in actual use and the
(fictitious) share capital can increase during the lifetime of a corporation. If
the enterprise yields dividends much higher than the average, and if the
necessity, or opportunity, of increasing its capital then arises, this higher
yield becomes the basis of the new capitalization, and the nominal share
capital is increased far beyond the extent of the capital in actual use.
Conversely, it is also possible to increase the functioning capital without
any increase in the nominal share capital. This is the case, for example,
when the net profit is ploughed back into the operations of the enterprise
rather than being distributed as dividends to the shareholders. But as such a
use of profit encourages the expectation of an increased future yield, there is
a simultaneous rise in the market quotation of the shares.

Share prices will fluctuate not only as a result of changes in the yield, or
of increases and decreases in the amount of capital in active use, but also
because of changes in the general rate of interest. A low rate of interest over
a long period will make it possible, *ceteris paribus*, for share prices to rise,
while a high rate of interest will have the opposite effect.

From the nature of dividends it is obvious that there are no average
dividends in the sense in which there is an average rate of interest or an
average rate of profit. A dividend is originally equal to interest plus a risk
premium, but it may either increase or decrease, and then remain at this
level, in the course of time, because in this case competition does not

equalize the yield, as it does with the interest rate or the rate of profit, but only the price of shares.

The market price of share capital is therefore always higher, under normal conditions, than the value of productive capital; that is, of capital which yields an average profit. On the other hand, given the yield of the enterprise and the rate of interest, the market price of the share capital depends upon the number of shares issued. Thus, if the interest rate is 5 per cent the shares of an enterprise which has a productive capital of 1,000,000 marks and yields a profit of 200,000 marks will have a market price of 4,000,000 marks. If 1,000,000 marks of shares are issued, a share with a nominal value of 1,000 marks will sell for 4,000 marks; if 2,000,000 marks of shares are issued, it will sell for 2,000 marks; if 4,000,000 marks of shares are issued, it will sell for 1,000 marks., etc.

The issue of shares in such a quantity as to depress the price below the nominal value, below par, is referred to as 'stock watering'. It is clear that this is purely a matter of accounting. The yield is given, and this determines the price of the shares as a whole. Naturally, the larger the number of shares, the lower the price of each individual share. The practice of 'watering' stock has nothing to do with promoter's profit, which arises whenever a corporation is formed, through the transformation of productive, profit-yielding capital into fictitious, interest-yielding capital. In fact the watering of stock is not at all essential, and unlike promoter's profit it can as a rule be prevented by law. The provision in the German law relating to shares which requires that any premium on shares must be credited to the reserves has simply had the effect that shares are turned over at par, or at a small premium, to a bank consortium which then sells them to the public at a profit (promoter's profit).

Under certain conditions, however, stock watering is a convenient financial device for increasing the share of the founders of a corporation beyond the normal promoter's profit. In the United States, for example, two distinct kinds of shares are usually issued when large corporations are formed; preferred and ordinary shares. Preferred shares have a limited rate of interest, usually between 5 per cent and 7 per cent. They are also frequently cumulative, in the sense that if in any year the whole dividend to which they are entitled has not been paid they have a right to have it made up from the yield of subsequent years. Only after the claims of the preferred shares have been met can dividends be paid on the ordinary shares. The volume of preferred shares is usually calculated when the corporation is founded, so that it exceeds the capital actually required for the conduct of the business. The greater part of the promoter's profit is embodied in the preferred shares. The ordinary shares are usually issued for a similar amount. In most cases, the price of ordinary shares is at first very low, but preferred and ordinary shares together stand somewhat above par. A large part of the ordinary shares is usually retained by the promoters, and this makes it easier for them to ensure their majority control.[12] Moreover, in the more important flotations the preferred shares earn the equivalent of a fixed interest rate, whereas ordinary shares do not have a fixed dividend. Their yield depends upon general business conditions; and since the yield is subject to extremely sharp fluctuations, ordinary shares are a favourite with speculators. Well-informed large shareholders, who paid nothing for the shares anyway, can use them for lucrative speculation.

Furthermore, this method of financing guarantees to the founders, who own the ordinary shares, the extra profit which accrues from the foundation of the corporation and the return from all future progress and favourable market conditions. The public, on the other hand, which owns the preferred shares, must content itself with a fixed rate of return which is little higher than the current rate of interest. To some extent, finally, the real situation of the enterprise can be concealed,[13] and this concealment makes possible various fraudulent activities. Nevertheless, overcapitalization has no effect whatsoever on prices. It is a curious notion that the inflation of the nominal value of fictitious capital can alter in any way the laws of price. Of course, it is self-evident that holders of large blocks of share capital will desire high prices so that they can be assured of a return. But even if the capital were written down to zero, no capitalist will sell more cheaply than he has to, whether he directs an individually owned enterprise, a joint-stock company, or a trust.

The corporation is an association of capitalists. It is formed by each capitalist contributing his share of capital, and the extent of his participation, his voting rights, and the degree of his influence, are determined by the amount of capital he contributes. The capitalist is a capitalist only in so far as he owns capital, and he is differentiated from other capitalists only in a quantitative way. Hence the control of the enterprise as a whole is in the hands of those who own a majority of the shares. This also means that a corporation can be controlled by those who own half the capital, whereas in an individually owned enterprise it is necessary to own the whole capital. This doubles the power of the large capitalists. Disregarding here the role of credit, a capitalist who decides to turn his enterprise into a joint-stock company needs only half his capital in order to retain complete control. The other half becomes disposable and can be withdrawn from the enterprise. It is true, of course, that he would then lose the dividends on this half. Nevertheless, the control of outside capital is extremely important, and his domination of the enterprise is, aside from everything else, a crucial means of influencing the sale and purchase of shares on the stock exchange.

In practice, the amount of capital necessary to ensure control of a corporation is usually less than this, amounting to a third or a quarter, or even less. Whoever controls the corporation also has control over the outside capital as if it were his own. But this kind of control is by no means synonymous with control over outside capital in general. With the development of the credit system in an advanced capitalist society every unit of owned capital is at the same time the exponent [in the mathematical sense – Ed.] of outside loan capital; and other things being equal, the amount of credit depends upon the size of one's own capital, although the former increases more rapidly than the latter. The capital of the large shareholder is such an exponent in two senses. His own capital controls that of the other shareholders, and in turn the total capital of the enterprise serves to attract outside capital in the shape of loan capital which is made available to the enterprise.

The large capital dominating a corporation has an even greater impact when it is no longer a question of a single corporation, but of a system of interdependent companies. Suppose that capitalist X controls, with 5,000,000 shares, corporation A whose share capital is 9,000,000. This corporation now establishes a subsidiary company, B, with a share capital of 30,000,000, and retains 16,000,000 of these shares in its own portfolio. In order to pay for these 16,000,000 shares, A issues 16,000,000 fixed-interest debentures without voting rights. With his 5,000,000 capitalist X now controls both corporations, or a total capital of 39,000,000. Following the same procedure, A and B can now create other new companies, so that X, with a relatively small capital, acquires control over an exceptionally large amount of outside capital. With the development of the joint-stock system there emerges a distinctive financial technique, the aim of which is to ensure control over the largest possible amount of outside capital with the smallest possible amount of one's own capital. This technique has reached its peak of perfection in the financing of the American railway system.[14]

Along with the development of the corporations on one side, and the increasing concentration of property on the other, the number of large capitalists who have distributed their capital among diverse corporations also increases. Substantial ownership of shares gives access to the management of the company. As a member of the board of directors, the large shareholder first of all receives a share of the profit in the form of bonuses;[15] then he also has the opportunity to influence the conduct of the enterprise, and to use his inside knowledge of its affairs for speculation in shares, or for other business transactions. A circle of people emerges who, thanks to their own capital resources or to the concentrated power of outside capital which they represent (in the case of bank directors), become members of the boards of directors of numerous corporations. There develops in this way a kind of personal union,[16] on one side among the various corporations themselves, and on the other, between the corporations and the bank; and the common ownership interest which is thus formed among the various companies must necessarily exert a powerful influence upon their policies.

In order to achieve the concentration of capital in an enterprise the corporation assembles its capital from individual particles of capital, each of which is too small, taken separately, to function as industrial capital, either generally or in the branch of industry where the corporation is located. It should be borne in mind that initially the corporations assembled their capital by direct appeals to individual capitalists, but this changed at a later stage, when the individual sums of capital were already accumulated and concentrated in the banks. In these conditions, the appeal to the money market is mediated by the banks.

No bank can think of raising the capital for an individually owned enterprise. The most it can do as a rule is to provide it with commercial credit. With the corporation it is an entirely different matter. To provide the capital in this case, the bank need only advance it, divide the sum into parts, and then sell these parts in order to recover the capital, thus performing a purely monetary transaction (M–M1). It is the transferability and nego-tiability of these capital certificates, constituting the very essence of the joint-stock company, which makes it possible for the bank to 'promote', and finally gain control of, the corporation. Similarly, a corporation can obtain bank loans far more readily than the individually owned enterprise. The latter, generally speaking, must be able to cover such loans out of its earnings, and their extent is consequently restricted. But precisely for this reason, because the debts are small, they leave the private entrepreneur relatively independent. The corporation, on the other hand, is able to repay these bank loans not only out of its current earnings, but also by increasing its capital through the issue of shares and bonds, by issuing which the bank also gains an additional promoter's profit. The bank can therefore provide more credit, with much greater security, to a corporation than to an individually owned enterprise, and above all a different type of credit; not only credit as a means of payment, commercial credit, but also credit for the expansion of the enterprise's productive capital, that is, capital credit. For if it seems necessary, the bank can always curtail this credit and insist that the enterprise should obtain fresh capital by a new issue of shares or bonds.[17]

The bank can not only extend more credit to a corporation than to an individual entrepreneur, but can also invest a part of its money capital in shares for a longer or shorter period. In any event, the bank acquires a permanent interest in the corporation, which must now be closely watched to ensure that credit is used for the appropriate purpose, and so far as possible controlled by the bank in order to make the latter's profitable financial transaction secure.

The interests of the banks in the corporations give rise to a desire to establish a permanent supervision of the companies' affairs, which is best done by securing representation on the board of directors. This ensures, first, that the corporation will conduct all its other financial transactions, associated with the issue of shares, through the bank. Second, in order to spread its risks and to widen its business connections, the bank tries to work with as many companies as possible, and at the same time, to be represented on their boards of directors. Ownership of shares enables the bank to impose its representatives even upon corporations which initially resisted. In this way there arises a tendency for the banks to accumulate such directorships.[18]

Industrialists who serve on the boards of directors of other corporations have a different role, namely to establish business relations between the companies involved. Thus, the representative of an iron firm who sits on the board of directors of a colliery aims to ensure that his firm obtains its coal from this colliery. This type of personal union, which also involves an accumulation of positions on boards of directors in the hands of a small group of big capitalists, becomes important when it is the precursor or promoter of closer organizational links between corporations which had previously been independent of one another.[19]

3 The corporation and the individually owned enterprise

At its foundation the corporation does not have recourse to the relatively small stratum of working capitalists who must combine ownership with the entrepreneurial function. From the beginning, and throughout its life, the corporation is quite independent of these personal qualities. Death, inheritance, etc., among its owners, have absolutely no effect upon it. But this is not the decisive difference between the corporation and the individually owned enterprise, since the latter can also replace the personal qualities of its owners, at a certain stage of development, by those of paid employees. Equally unimportant in practice is another distinction made in the literature on the subject: namely, that on one side there is the individual entrepreneur, who is an independent and responsible agent with a stake in his enterprise, and on the other side a crowd of uninformed, powerless entrepreneurs (shareholders) who have only a minor interest in their enterprise, and understand nothing about its management. In fact the corporations – especially the most important, profitable and pioneering ones – are governed by an oligarchy, or by a single big capitalist (or a bank) who are, in reality, vitally interested in their operations and quite independent of the mass of small shareholders. Furthermore, the managers who are at the top of the industrial bureaucracy have a stake in the enterprise, not only because of the bonuses they earn, but, still more important, because of their generally substantial shareholdings.

The objective difference between the two kinds of enterprise is much more important. Recourse to the money market is a recourse to all those who have money (including the credit at their disposal). The corporation is independent of the size of individual amounts of capital, which must first be brought together in a single hand if they are to function as the industrial capital of a privately owned enterprise. Not only does it broaden the circle of people involved (anyone who has money can be a money capitalist), but every sum of money above a certain minimum (which need only amount to a few schillings) is capable of being combined with other sums in a joint-stock company and used as industrial capital. It is therefore much easier to establish, or to expand, a corporation than a privately owned enterprise.

In their capacity to assemble capital the corporations have a similar function to that of the banks. The difference is that the banks retain the accumulated capital in its original form as money capital, and make it available as credit for production after it has been assembled, whereas the corporations combine the atomized money capital in the form of fictitious capital. But this should not lead us to identify the combination of small capitals into a large capital with the participation of small capitalists. These small amounts of capital may belong to very big capitalists. The small sums of the petty capitalists are more likely to be assembled by the banks than by the corporations.

The corporations can accumulate capital just as easily as they acquire it in the first place. The privately owned enterprise has to accumulate capital out of its profits. Assuming that it has reached a certain size, that part of its profit which is not consumed is brought together as potential money capital until it becomes large enough for new investment and expansion. The corporation, on the other hand, usually distributes dividends to its shareholders, but in this case, too, a part of the profit can be accumulated, especially during periods when the dividends are well above the average rate of interest. The main point, however, is that the expansion of the corporation does not depend upon its own accumulation out of earnings, but can take place directly through an increase of its capital. The limitation which the amount of profit produced by the enterprise places upon the growth of the privately owned firm is thus removed, giving the corporation a much greater capacity for growth. The corporation can draw upon the whole supply of free money capital, both at the time of its creation and for its later expansion. It does not grow simply by the accumulation of its own profits. The entire fund of accumulated capital which is seeking to realize value provides grist for its mill. The obstacles which arise from the fragmentation of capital among a host of indifferent and casual owners are removed. The corporation can draw directly upon the combined capital of the capitalist class.

The size of an enterprise which does not have to depend upon individual capital is independent of the amount of wealth already accumulated by an individual, and it can expand without regard to the degree of concentration of property. Hence it is through the joint-stock company that enterprises first become possible, or possible on a scale which, because of the magnitude of their capital requirements, could never have been achieved by an individual entrepreneur, and were, therefore, either not undertaken at all, or else had to be undertaken by the state, in which case they were removed from the direct control of capital. The outstanding example is evidently the railways, which provided such a powerful stimulus to the growth of corporations. The significance of the corporation in breaking through the personal limits of property, and thus being constrained not by the extent of personal capital, but only by the aggregate social capital,[20] was greatest in the early stages.

The expansion of the capitalist enterprise which has been converted into a corporation, freed from the bonds of individual property, can now conform simply with the demands of technology. The introduction of new machinery, the assimilation of related branches of production, the exploitation of patents, now takes place only from the standpoint of their technical and economic suitability. The preoccupation with raising the necessary capital, which plays a major role in the privately owned enterprise, limiting its power of expansion and diminishing its readiness for battle, now recedes into the background. Business opportunities can be exploited more effectively, more thoroughly, and more quickly, and this is an important consideration when periods of prosperity become shorter.[21]

All these factors play an important part in the competitive struggle. As we have seen, a corporation can procure capital more easily than can a privately owned enterprise, and is able, therefore, to organize its plant according to purely technical considerations, whereas the individual entrepreneur is always restricted by the size of his own capital. This applies even when he uses credit, since the amount of credit is limited by the size of his own capital. No such limitation of personal property hampers the corporation, either when it is founded or when it later expands and makes new investments. It can, therefore, acquire the best and most modern equipment and is free to install it whenever it chooses, unlike the private entrepreneur who must wait until his profit has reached a level sufficient for accumulation. The corporation can thus be equipped in a technically superior fashion, and what is just as important, can maintain this technical superiority. This also means that the corporation can install new technology and labour-saving processes before they come into general use, and hence produce on a larger scale, and with improved, modern techniques, thus gaining an extra profit, as compared with the individually owned enterprise.

In addition, the corporation has a great superiority in the use of credit, which deserves attention at this point. The private entrepreneur, as a rule, can obtain loans only up to the amount of his circulating capital. Anything beyond this would turn the borrowed capital into fixed industrial capital, and would *de facto* deprive it of its character as loan capital so far as the loan capitalist is concerned. The loan capitalist would, in effect, be transformed into an industrial capitalist. Consequently, credit can only be extended to private entrepreneurs by people who are thoroughly familiar with all their circumstances and ways of running their business. This being so, credit for the private entrepreneur is provided by small local banks, or private bankers, who have a detailed knowledge of the business affairs of their customers.

The corporation can obtain credit more easily, because its structure greatly facilitates supervision. One of the bank's employees can be delegated for this purpose, and the private banker is thus replaced by a bank official. The bank will also provide large amounts of credit more readily to a corporation, because the corporation itself can easily raise capital. There is no danger that the credit which has been provided will be immobilized. Even if the corporation were to use the credit for the creation of fixed capital, it could, under favourable conditions, mobilize capital by issuing shares, and repay its bank debts, without having to wait for the fixed capital to return from circulation. In fact, this is a daily occurrence. Both these factors – easier supervision, and the possibility of using credit for purposes other than circulation – enable the corporation to obtain more credit and so enhance its competitive advantage.

Thus, from the economic advantages attributable to the greater accessibility of credit when the corporation is formed, and its greater capacity to expand, there also results a technical superiority. Thanks to its structure the corporation also has an advantage in price competition. As we have seen, the shareholder is, in a sense, a money capitalist who does not expect more than interest on his invested capital. In favourable circumstances, however, the earnings of a corporation may well exceed considerably the rate of interest, in spite of deductions from total profit in the form of promoter's profit, high administrative costs, bonuses, etc.

But as we have already noted, the increasing yield does not always benefit the shareholders. A part of it may be used to strengthen the enterprise, or to build up reserves, which enable the corporation to face a period of crisis more successfully than an individually owned enterprise. These large reserves also make possible a more stable dividend policy and thus raise the market price of the shares. Alternatively, the corporation can accumulate a part of its profit, and so increase its productive, profit-yielding capital, without increasing its nominal capital. This also increases, even more than does the growth of reserves, the real value of the shares. This rise in value, which perhaps only becomes manifest at a later stage, benefits the large, permanent shareholders, while the small, temporary owners of shares contribute by being deprived of a part of their profit.

If business conditions deteriorate, and competition becomes keener, a corporation which has followed the dividend policy just outlined, thereby reducing or eliminating the original difference between its share capital and its actually functioning capital, can reduce its prices below the price of production $c + p$ (cost price plus average profit) to a price equal to $c + i$ (cost price plus interest), and will still be able to distribute a dividend equal to, or a little below, the average interest.

The power of resistance of the corporation is thus much greater. The individual entrepreneur strives to realize the average profit, and if he realizes less, he must consider withdrawing his capital. This motive, however, is not present with the same degree of urgency in the corporation, certainly not among its directors and probably not among its shareholders. The private entrepreneur must make his living from the yield of his business, and if his profit falls below a certain level, his working capital will dwindle, since he has to use part of it for his own sustenance. Eventually he goes bankrupt. The corporation does not face this problem, because it seeks only to earn interest on its shares. It can generally continue in business so long as it does not operate at an actual loss. There is no pressure upon it to operate at a net profit,[22] the kind of pressure which threatens the individual capitalist with immediate disaster if he eats into his capital. Such pressure might perhaps affect the shareholder and oblige him to sell his shares, but this would have no effect on the functioning capital. If the net profit has not been eliminated, but only reduced, the corporation can continue in business indefinitely. If the net profit has fallen below the average rate of dividend, the share prices will fall, and new buyers as well as the existing owners will now calculate their yield on a lower capital value. In spite of the lower share price, and even though an industrial capitalist would pronounce the enterprise unprofitable because it no longer produces the average rate of profit, it remains quite profitable for the new purchasers of shares, and even the existing shareholders would lose more by disposing of all their shares. Even when it is operating at a loss the corporation still has greater powers of resistance. The individual entrepreneur, in such a case, is usually lost, and bankruptcy is inevitable, but the corporation can be 'reorganized' with comparative ease. The facility with which it can raise capital makes it possible to assemble the amounts of money which are necessary in order to maintain and reorganize production. As a general rule, the shareholders must give their approval, because the price of their shares expresses the condition of the enterprise and reflects, if only nominally, the real losses it has sustained.

The usual procedure is to deflate share values so that the total profit can be calculated on a smaller capital. If there is no profit at all, new capital is obtained which, together with the existing deflated capital, will then produce an adequate profit. In passing, it is worth mentioning that these reorganizations are important in two ways for the banks; first as profitable business, and second as an opportunity to bring the companies concerned under bank control.

The separation of capital ownership from its function also affects the management of the enterprise. The interest which its owners have in obtaining the largest possible profit as quickly as possible, their lust for booty, which slumbers in every capitalist soul, can be subordinated to a certain extent, by the managers of the corporation, to the purely technical requirements of production. More energetically than the private entrepreneur they will develop the firm's plant, modernize obsolete installations, and engage in competition to open up new markets, even if the attainment of these goals entails sacrifices for the shareholders. Those who manage capital drawn from outside pursue a more vigorous, bold, and rational policy, less influenced by personal considerations, especially when this policy meets with the approval of the large, influential shareholders, who can very easily sustain temporary reductions in their profits, since in the long run they are rewarded by higher share prices and larger profits, resulting from the sacrifices made by small shareholders who have long since had to dispose of their property. The corporation, then, is superior to the individually owned enterprise because it gives priority to purely economic conditions and requirements, even in opposition to the conditions of individual property, which in some circumstances may come into conflict with technological-economic needs.

The concentration of capital is always accompanied by the detachment of units of capital which then function as new and independent capitals:

> the division of property within capitalist families plays a great part
> . . . . Accumulation and concentration accompanying it are, there-
> fore, not only scattered over many points, but the increase of each
> functioning capital is thwarted by the formation of new and the sub-
> division of the old capitals. Accumulation, therefore, presents itself,
> on the one hand, as an increasing concentration of the means of
> production, and of the command over labour; on the other, as re-
> pulsion of many individual capitals one from another.[23]

The growth of the corporate form of enterprise has made the course of economic development independent of contingent events in the movement of property, the latter being now reflected in the fate of shares on the market, not in the fate of the corporation itself. Consequently the concentration of enterprises can take place more rapidly than the centralization of property. Each of these processes follows its own laws, although the tendency towards concentration is common to both; it seems, however, to be more fortuitous and less powerful in the movement of property, and in practice is frequently interrupted by accidental factors. It is this surface appearance which leads some people to speak of a democratization of property through shareholding. The separation of the tendency towards industrial concentration from the movement of property is important because it allows enterprises to be guided only by technological and economic laws, regardless of the limits set by individual property. This type of concentration, which is not simultaneously a concentration of property, must be distinguished from the concentration and centralization[24] which ensue from, and accompany, the movement of property.

As a result of the transformation of property into share ownership the rights of the property owner are curtailed. The individual, as a shareholder, is dependent upon the decision made by all other shareholders; he is only a member of a larger body, and not always an active one. With the extension of the corporate form of enterprise, capitalist property becomes increasingly a limited form of property which simply gives the capitalist a claim to surplus value, without allowing him to exercise any important influence on the process of production. At the same time, this limitation of property gives the majority shareholders unlimited powers over the minority, and in this way, the property rights and unrestricted control over production of most of the small capitalists are set aside, and the group of those who control production becomes ever smaller. The capitalists form an association in the direction of which most of them have no say. The real control of productive capital rests with people who have actually contributed only a part of it. The owners of the means of production no longer exist as individuals, but form an association in which the individual has only a claim to his proportionate share of the total return.

4   The flotation of shares

As intermediaries in the circulation of bills and notes, the banks substitute their own bank credit for commercial credit, and as intermediaries in the conversion of idle funds into money capital, they furnish new capital to producers. They also perform a third function in supplying productive capital, not by lending it, but by converting money capital into industrial capital and fictitious capital, and taking charge of this process themselves. On the one side, this development causes all funds to flow into the banks, so that only through their mediation can they be transformed into money capital. On the other side, when bank capital is converted into industrial capital it ceases to exist in the form of money and hence ceases to be part of bank capital. This contradiction is resolved by the mobilization of capital, by its conversion into fictitious capital or capitalized claims to profit. Since this conversion process is accompanied by the growth of a market for such claims, in which they become convertible into money at any time, they can again become components of bank capital. In all this the bank does not enter into a credit relationship, nor does it receive any interest. It merely supplies the market with a certain amount of money capital in the form of fictitious capital which can then be transformed into industrial capital. The fictitious capital is sold on the market and the bank realizes the promoter's profit which arises from the conversion of the industrial capital into fictitious capital. The expression 'flotation credit', therefore, does not describe a credit relationship, but simply indicates the more or less well founded confidence of the public that it will not be defrauded by the bank.

This function of the bank, to carry out the mobilization of capital, arises from its disposal over the whole money stock of society, although at the same time it requires that the bank should have a substantial capital of its own. Fictitious capital, a certificate of indebtedness, is a commodity *sui generis* which can only be reconverted into money by being sold. But a certain period of circulation is required before this can happen, during which the bank's capital is tied up in this commodity. Furthermore, the commodity cannot always be sold at a particular time, whereas the bank must always be prepared to meet its obligations in money. Hence it must always have capital of its own, not committed elsewhere, available for such transactions. Moreover, the bank is compelled to increase its own capital to meet the increasing demands which the growth of industry makes upon it.[25]

The more powerful the banks become, the more successful they are in reducing dividends to the level of interest and in appropriating the promoter's profit. Conversely, powerful and well-established enterprises may also succeed in acquiring part of the promoter's profit for themselves when they increase their capital. Thus there emerges a kind of competitive struggle between banks and corporations over the division of the promoter's profit, and hence a further motive for the bank to ensure its domination over the enterprise.

It is self-evident that promoter's profit is not only produced by founding corporations in the strict sense, whether this involves the creation of completely new enterprises or the transformation of existing privately owned enterprises into joint-stock companies. Promoter's profit, in the economic sense, can be obtained just as readily by increasing the capital of existing corporations, provided its yield exceeds the average interest.

To some extent what appears as a decline in the rate of interest is only a consequence of the progressive reduction of dividends to the level of interest, while an over increasing share of the total profits of the enterprise is incorporated, in a capitalized form, in the promoter's profit. This process has as its premise a relatively high level of development of the banks, and of their connections with industry, and a correspondingly developed market for fictitious capital, the stock exchange. In the 1870s, for example, the interest on railway bonds in the United States stood at 7 per cent, as against 3.5 per cent today[26] and this reduction is due to the fact that the part of the 7 per cent which once constituted the entrepreneurial profit has been capitalized by the founders. The importance of these figures lies in the fact that promoter's profit is on the increase because the yield on stocks and bonds is being continuously depressed to the level of simple interest. This upward trend in promoter's profit runs counter to the falling rate of profit, but it may be assumed that this fall, which is frequently interrupted or even checked by counter tendencies, will not in the long run put an end to the rising trend of promoter's profit. The latter has shown a continuous increase in recent times, especially in those countries where there has been a very rapid development of banks and stock exchanges, and where the influence of the banks on industry has been most marked.

While the money capitalist receives interest on the money he lends, the bank which issues shares lends nothing and therefore does not receive interest. Instead, the interest goes to the shareholders in the form of dividends. The bank receives a flow of entrepreneurial profit, not in the form of an annual revenue, but as capitalized promoter's profit. Entrepreneurial profit is a continuous stream of income, but it is paid to the bank as a lump sum in the form of promoter's profit. The bank assumes that the capitalist distribution of property is eternal and unchangeable, and it discounts this eternity in the promoter's profit. The bank is thus compensated once and for all, and it has no claim to further compensation if this distribution of property is abolished. It already has its reward.

8

The stock exchange

1 Securities and speculation

The stock exchange is the market for securities. By 'securities' I mean here every kind of scrip which represents sums of money. They fall into two main groups: (1) certificates of indebtedness, or credit certificates, which bear a statement of the amount of money for which they are issued, the principal example being the bill of exchange; (2) certificates which do not represent a sum of money but its yield. The latter may be further subdivided into two groups: (a) fixed-interest paper, such as debentures and government bonds; and (b) dividend certificates (shares). As we know, in a capitalist society, every regular (annual) return is regarded as the revenue on a capital, the amount of which is equal to the capitalized yield at the current rate of interest. Thus these securities also represent sums of money, but they differ from those in the first group in the following way. The prime consideration in the case of credit certificates is the amount of money they represent; money, or value of equal magnitude, has actually been lent and now bears interest. The certificates circulate for a specified period of time and are withdrawn when the capital is repaid. The bill has fallen due. Bills are always falling due and the capital which has been lent then flows back to the lender. The latter now has the money in his hands once more and can proceed to lend it again. The cycle in which bills fall due and the capital flows back continually to its owner, is a condition for the constant renewal of the process.

The situation is different with the second group of securities, since here the money is definitively surrendered. In the case of government bonds it may have been withdrawn from productive uses for a long time, and thus ceased to exist; or if it was put into industrial shares, it has been used to buy constant and variable capital, has served as a means of purchase, and its value is now incorporated in the elements of productive capital. The money is in the hands of the sellers of this productive capital and will never return to its starting point. It follows, therefore, that shares cannot represent this money, because it has now passed to the sellers of commodities (of the elements of productive capital) and has become their property. But neither do they in any way represent the productive capital itself. In the first place, the shareholders have no claim to any part of the productive capital, but only to the yield; and second, the share, unlike vouchers or bills of lading, does not represent any specific use value, as it would have to do if it were really a share in the capital actually used in production, but is only a claim to a certain amount of money. It is this which constitutes the 'mobilization' of industrial capital. This money is, however, nothing more than the yield capitalized at the current rate of interest. Hence the yield, or annual income, is the basis on which the certificates are valued, and only after the yield is known is the amount of money calculated.

Fixed-interest certificates have some resemblance to those in the first group, in the sense that a fixed return at a given point of time always represents a definite sum of money. Nevertheless, they really fall into the second category, because the money which they originally represented has been definitively given up and does not have to return to its starting point. The capital which they represent is fictitious, and its magnitude is calculated on the basis of its yield. The difference between fixed-interest certificates and other titles to income seems to be (if we disregard fortuitous influences) that the price of the former depends only upon the rate of interest, while the price of the latter depends upon both the rate of interest and the current yield on capital. The former group, therefore, is subject to only comparatively minor fluctuations in price; and when such fluctuations occur, they are gradual and follow the more easily predictable fluctuations in the rate of interest. By contrast, the rate of return in the second group is indeterminate, and subject to countless changes which cannot always be foreseen; and this produces considerable fluctuations in the price of these certificates. As a result, they are a favoured target of speculation.

It follows from what has been said that the customary description of the stock exchange as the 'capital market' misses the essential nature of that institution. The certificates in the first group are certificates of indebtedness. The vast majority of them originate in circulation, in the transfer of commodities without the intervention of money except as a means of final settlement. They are a form of credit money which replaces cash. When they are traded on the stock exchange, a grant of credit is simply transferred from one person to another. The circulation of credit money, as we have seen, requires as its premise and complement the circulation of real money. Since credit money is used in foreign as well as domestic payments, the stock exchange must be able to supply both domestic credit money and foreign credit money as well as metallic money. Hence, in order to complement the traffic in credit money the stock exchange also becomes the centre of dealings in foreign exchange, both credit and cash. Into the stock exchange streams the ever available money capital seeking investment, which it finds in the various types of credit certificates. In this activity the stock exchange competes with the credit institutions proper, the banks. Nevertheless, there is a quantitative as well as a qualitative difference between the two institutions. From a quantitative standpoint, the stock exchange differs in its activities from the banks because it is not mainly concerned with collecting small savings, but attracts large amounts of already accumulated capital which are seeking investment. The concentration of funds, which is such an important function of the banks, is here an accomplished fact. The qualitative difference between the two institutions turns on the fact that the stock exchange is not concerned with the diverse ways of making credit available. It simply provides the money which is necessary to sustain the circulation of credit money. The money is supplied in large amounts, in the form of first-class bills. Both demand and supply involve large, concentrated sums of money, and it is on the stock exchange that the market price of loan capital (the rate of interest) is established. It is pure interest, devoid of any risk premium, for these are the best certificates that can be had in this wicked capitalist world, and their excellence is even less open to doubt than is the goodness of the Almighty. The interest which is paid on these finest of all bills (finest, of course, not in terms of their lowly use value, for even first-class bills are not written on handmade paper) seems to stem directly from the mere possession of money capital. It is as though the money had not been given away at all, since it can always be recovered simply by transferring the bill again. In any case, the money is only temporarily invested and is always available for some other use. The absolute security and short term of repayment make for a low rate of interest on such investments, which are suitable only for very large, temporarily available, capital sums. The interest rate on such investments is the basis for calculating the interest rate on other types of investment, and it also determines the movement of available floating money capital from one exchange to another. These funds, in ever-varying amount, flow in and out of the circulation of world money.

The stock exchange constitutes the market for the traffic in money among the banks and the big capitalists. Bills usually bear the signature of one or other of the leading banks. Both domestic and foreign banks, or other big capitalists, put their funds in these bills, which bear interest and are absolutely secure. On the other side, the large credit institutions can sell such bills on the exchange to obtain whatever funds they may need to meet obligations in excess of their freely available capital.[1]

Although the sums of money required for such operations vary from time to time, a certain minimum amount is always available, which is used to purchase the bills and then returns to its starting point when they fall due. This continual reflux of money, and its function as a mere intermediary in the credit process, at once distinguishes the circulation of money which belongs to the first category of stock exchange securities from the circulation of money in the second category; for example, that which is invested in shares. In the latter case the money is definitively relinquished, converted into productive capital, and comes into the hands of those who sell commodities. It does not return to the stock exchange. In place of money there are now capitalized claims to interest. Money is here actually withdrawn from the money market.

The stock exchange and the banks are competitors in the bill market, and the development of the latter has actually cut into this business of the stock exchange. The banks have even taken over the major part of the business of supplying payment credit to industrial capitalists, which was initially the principal function of the stock exchange, and all that is left to the latter is the function of an intermediary between the banks themselves and the foreign exchange market, where foreign payments are dealt with and foreign exchange rates are determined. Even here a considerable part of the business is handled directly by the banks, which maintain foreign branches for this purpose. The development of the banks has reduced this part of the business of the stock exchange in two ways: first directly, inasmuch as the banks invest their ever growing funds in bills, to an increasing extent without involving the stock exchange; and second, by substituting, in part, other forms of credit for bills.

The bill of exchange represents a credit given by one productive capitalist (understood as any capitalist who produces profit, thus including the merchant) to another in lieu of cash payment. The capitalist who receives it discounts it at the bank, which now becomes the creditor. If, however, both the capitalists have deposits or open credits at the bank, they can make their payments by cheque or by a transfer on the books of the bank. The bill has become superfluous. Its place has been taken by a book-keeping transaction in the bank, and this, in contrast to the bill which can be circulated, is a private affair. The increasing involvement of the banks in making payments for their clients has brought about a contraction of the traffic in bills, which has further affected that part of stock exchange business. Furthermore, in those countries where the note issue is a monopoly, the note-issuing bank has a dominant position on the foreign exchange market, and if that position is weakened the change benefits the large banks rather than the stock exchange. There is, therefore, no specific and exclusive stock exchange activity in the sphere of credit money circulation, except speculation in foreign exchange. The stock exchange is only a concentrated market for the sums of money which are made available for credit transactions.

The true sphere of stock exchange activity is as a market for titles to interest, or fictitious capital. Here the investment of capital as money capital, which is to be converted into productive capital, takes place. The money is committed definitively in the purchase of these titles, and does not return. Only the interest yield flows back annually to the stock exchange, whereas in the case of money invested in credit instruments the capital itself is also returned. Hence, new money, serving stock exchange circulation itself, is required for the sale and purchase of titles to interest. The amount of new money is small in relation to the aggregate sums turned over. Since the interest titles represent claims to money, they can be cancelled out against one another, and there is never more than a small balance to be settled. The balances are calculated by specialized institutions which ensure that cash is used only for settling these. Nevertheless, the absolute amount of means of circulation required on the stock exchange is quite consider- able, especially during periods of heavy speculation, when speculative activity is usually oriented in one direction, and the balance for cash settlement tends to grow appreciably.

The question now arises whether the activities and functions of the stock exchange have any distinctive features. We have already seen that its activity in the bill market overlaps with that of the banks. Equally, the purchase of securities for investment is not a specific function of the stock exchange, for they can be bought just as easily from the banks, and indeed it is increasingly common for them to be bought there. The specific activity of the stock exchange is really *speculation*.

At first sight, speculation looks like any other purchase and sale. What is purchased, however, is not commodities but titles to interest. A productive capitalist must convert his commodity capital into money – that is, sell it – before he can realize a profit. If another capitalist assumes the task of selling, the industrialist must assign him part of the profit.

The entire profit contained in the commodity is definitively realized only when it is sold to the consumer. The commodity is thus transferred from the producer to the consumer, but it would be absurd to regard this as a change in location (just think of the sale of a house) and to confuse trade with transport. Buying and selling do not consist in changes of location, but in economic events, transfers of property; although in all processes which are not purely intensional a change of position in space is also involved. But who would conceive the essential element in visiting the theatre as being to find the theatre building itself?

The commodity is finally consumed and disappears from the market. The title to interest, however, is by its very nature eternal. It never disappears from circulation in the way a commodity does. Even when it is temporarily withdrawn from the market for investment purposes, it can return at any time, and in fact such titles do return sooner or later, in larger or smaller quantities. But the withdrawal of interest titles from the market is neither the aim nor the consequence of speculation. Speculative stock is constantly circulating on the stock exchange. Its movement is always back and forth, or circular, not straight ahead.

The purchase and sale of commodities is a socially necessary process, through which the essential conditions of social life in a capitalist economy are met. It is the *conditio sine qua non* of this society. Speculation, on the other hand, is nothing of the sort. It does not affect the capitalist enterprise; neither the plant nor the product. An established enterprise is not affected by a change of ownership or by the constant circulation of shares. Production and its yield is not affected by the fact that claims to the yield change hands; nor is the value of the yield changed in any way by changes in share prices. On the contrary, it is the value of the yield, other things being equal, which determines these changes in share prices. The purchase and sale of these claims to interest is a purely economic phenomenon, a mere fluctuation in the distribution of private property, without any influence upon production or upon the realization of profit (by the sale of commodities). Speculative gains or losses arise only from variations in the current valuations of claims to interest. They are neither profit, nor parts of surplus value, but originate in fluctuations in the valuations of that part of surplus value which the corporation assigns to the shareholders; fluctuations which, as we shall see, do not necessarily arise from changes in the volume of profit actually realized. They are pure marginal gains.[2] Whereas the capitalist class as a whole appropriates a part of the labour of the proletariat without giving anything in return, speculators gain only from each other. One's loss is the other's gain. '*Les affaires, c'est l'argent des autres.*'

Speculation consists in taking advantage of price changes, though not of changes in commodity prices. Unlike the productive capitalist the speculator does not care whether commodity prices rise or fall; all that concerns him is the price of his titles to interest. These prices depend upon the amount of profit, which can rise or fall, whether prices rise, fall, or remain stationary. The decisive factor affecting profit is not the absolute level of prices, but the relationship between costs and prices. But it is also unimportant to the speculator whether profits rise or fall; he is only concerned with being able to foresee these fluctuations. His interests, therefore, are entirely different from those of the productive capitalist or the money capitalist who desire the maximum stability of profit, and whenever possible, a constantly increasing profit. Increases in commodity prices only have an influence upon speculation in so far as they are an indication of increased profit. Speculation is affected only by such changes in profits as are either bound to occur, or can be expected. But the profit which an enterprise produces is distributed to the owners of productive capital or to holders of shares without regard to speculation. The speculator as such does not derive his gain from the increase in profit. He can gain just as easily from a fall in profit. In general, therefore, he does not think in terms of a rise in profit but in terms of changes in the price of securities induced by a rise or fall in profit. He does not hold securities in the hope of sharing in the higher profit – as an investor does – but seeks to gain by buying and selling his securities. His gain does not arise from a share in the profit, for he gains also from declining profits, but from price changes, which means that at a particular time he can buy securities more cheaply than he sold them, or sell them more dearly than he bought them. If all speculators played the same side of the market, that is, if they all simultaneously placed the same higher or lower value on securities,[3] there would not be any speculative gains at all. These arise only because contradictory valuations are made, only one of which can turn out to be correct. The different valuations made by buyers and sellers, at a particular time, result in losses for some speculators and gains for others. The profit of one is the other's loss; and this is in sharp contrast with the profit of the productive capitalist; for the profit of the capitalist class is not a loss for the working class, which cannot expect, under normal capitalist conditions, to receive more than the value of its labour power.

What are the factors which speculators must reckon with in their operations? The principal objects of speculation are securities which do not bear a fixed rate of interest. Their price fluctuations depend essentially upon two factors: the level of profit and the rate of interest. Theoretically, the level of profit is given by the average rate of profit. But the latter is simply the expression of innumerable individual profit, which may diverge widely from the average. An outsider, however, is not in a position to know the level of any individual profit, for this is determined not only by general factors, such as the amount of surplus value and the quantity of invested capital, but also by all the fortuitous variations in market prices and by the entrepreneur's skill in taking advantage of business opportunities. The external observer can see only the market price of the commodity; he cannot have any knowledge of the really decisive factor, which is the relation between market price and cost price. Even the entrepreneur frequently does not know what this relation is until he has made an exact calculation at the end of a period of turnover. Moreover, aside from the actual amount of profit, a whole series of more or less arbitrary factors affect the sum which is actually paid out on the securities; among them the level of depreciation, bonuses, allocations to reserves, etc. These factors give the directors of an enterprise the power, within limits, to fix in an arbitrary fashion the amount of profit available for distribution and so influence stock market prices. At all events, the majority of speculators are completely in the dark about the crucial factor which determines the price of shares. A general, more or less superficial knowledge of an enterprise will avail them little should they wish to take advantage of the slight price differences which sometimes occur, or of those movements in the price of its securities which result from the capitalization of changed profits. Conversely, the intimate knowledge of an enterprise which an insider enjoys gives him the confidence and ability to use this knowledge for speculative gain with scarcely any risk.

It is a different matter with respect to the second factor which determines share prices: the rate of interest. As we have seen, the activities of speculators depend upon differences of opinion about the probable movement of share prices; such differences, for instance, as those which arise from uncertainty about future profits. The rate of interest, on the other hand, is like the market price of commodities; at any given time it has a definite magnitude, which is known to all speculators.

Furthermore, changes in the rate of interest – or at least their direction – can be predicted with a high degree of probability, except when there are sudden and more or less powerful disturbances, caused by extraordinary events such as wars, revolutions, or natural disasters, which react directly upon the demand for money. Besides, the influence of fluctuations in the rate of interest upon share prices tends to diminish; thus during a depression, a low rate of interest usually prevails, speculative activity is sluggish, confidence is impaired, and share prices are low, in spite of the low rate of interest. Conversely, during a period of prosperity and unlimited speculation, the effect of a high rate of interest is lost in the general anticipation of increased stock market gains. Hence, although the level of the rate of interest is a more certain factor than any estimate of future profits, it is still essentially the latter which determines the direction and intensity of speculation. It is, therefore, precisely the uncertain, incalculable factor which speculators are obliged to take into consideration. In short, no certain foresight is possible in speculative activity, which is essentially a groping in the dark. Stock market speculation is like a game of chance or a wager, but for insiders it is a wager *à coup sûr*.

As in the case of all prices, we can distinguish the real causal factors which determine stock market prices from the incidental influences expressed in changes in the relation between supply and demand. This distinction is, of course, of no concern to the speculator, who is interested only in the price changes themselves, not in their causes. Nevertheless, it is speculation itself, and the ever changing moods and expectations of speculators, arising largely from their uncertainties, which produces the ceaseless fluctuations in supply and demand and hence the changes in the price of shares. Every price change, in turn, provides the impetus for a fresh wave of speculation, new commitments and changes of position, and further changes in supply and demand. In this way, speculation creates an ever ready market for the securities which it controls itself, and thus gives other capitalist groups the opportunity to convert their fictitious capital into real capital, to change from one investment in fictitious capital to another, and to convert fictitious capital back into money capital at any time.

But the uncertainty which characterizes speculation has still another consequence; it creates the possibility of influencing the direction of speculative activity, through the large speculators drawing in the small ones. Since the speculator is not 'in the know' (frequently even with regard to general conditions, and invariably when it is a matter of particular cases)[4] he tends to be influenced by superficial indications, by the mood and the general trend of the market. This mood, however, can be manufactured, and is actually manufactured, by the big speculators, who can be regarded more or less correctly as 'insiders'. The petty speculators follow their lead. The big speculators stiffen the market by making large purchases, thus driving up the price of shares, and once the trend is under way demand increases further as a result of the purchases by all those people who think they are following the example of the big speculators, so that prices continue to rise although the latter have already withdrawn. They can now either take their profit, or maintain the higher price level for a longer or shorter time, depending upon their aims. In this case, disposal over a larger sum of capital gives rise directly to a superior position on the market because market trends themselves are determined by the way in which this capital is used. In the sphere of production, a large capital enjoys an advantage because it can produce more cheaply and so reduce prices, but in the stock market, capital acts upon prices directly. The large dealers in securities, the banks, can take advantage of this situation to push speculation in a particular direction. They need only drop a hint to their numerous customers to buy or sell certain securities, in order to bring about, in most cases, a change in the relation between supply and demand, which is thus known to them in advance, and like all foreknowledge in the field of speculation produces a profit for them. We can now also appreciate the importance of the hangers-on, the outsiders, and the public at large. Gains and losses among professional speculators may balance out, but the great public which simply follows the lead of the big speculators, and continues in the same course after the latter have already pulled out with the gains they have made – these naive people who believe the moment has now come for them to share in the fruits of prosperity – are the ones who have to bear the losses, and to pay the balances arising with every turn in the business cycle or in the mood of the stock exchange, which are pocketed by the speculators as the reward for their 'productive activity'.

Nevertheless, the fact that speculation is unproductive, that it is a form of gambling and betting (and is rightly regarded as such by public opinion) does not run counter to its necessity in a capitalist society, at least during a certain period of capitalist development. Obviously, it is nothing but an apologetic artifice to regard everything which is necessary in capitalist society as being productive. The truth is rather that the anarchy of capitalist production, the antagonism between those who own and those who use the means of production, and the capitalist mode of distribution, all generate a large volume of expenses and payments which contribute nothing to the increase of wealth, which would be eliminated in an organized society, and in this sense are unproductive.[5] The fact that they are necessary in capitalist society does not show that they are productive but simply testifies against the way in which this society is organized. Speculation is essential, however, if the stock exchange is to carry out its various functions, which we shall now examine more closely.

2 The functions of the stock exchange

The function of the stock exchange changes in the course of economic development. Originally it provided for the circulation of currency and bills; for which purpose it was only necessary to accumulate free money capital which could be invested in such bills. Later, it became a market for fictitious capital, which first emerged with the development of state credit. It became the market for state loans. But it was radically transformed when industrial capital began to assume the form of fictitious capital, and the corporate form of enterprise began to spread throughout industry. The resources at the disposal of the stock exchange now increase rapidly and without limit, and on the other hand the existence of the stock exchange as a market which is always available is a prerequisite for the conversion of industrial capital into fictitious capital and for the reduction of dividends to interest.

The development of a market for fictitious capital makes speculation possible. In turn, speculation is necessary to keep this market open for business at all times, and so give money capital as such the possibility of transforming itself into fictitious capital, and from fictitious capital back into money capital, whenever it chooses. For the fact that marginal gains can be made by buying and selling is a constant stimulus to engage in these activities and to ensure the permanent existence of an active market. The essential function of the stock exchange is to provide such a market for the investment of money capital. Only in this way is the investment of capital as money capital made possible on a large scale. For if capital is to function as money capital it must in the first place yield a steady income (interest), and second, the principal itself must flow back, or if it does not actually flow back it must always be recoverable through the sale of titles to interest. The

stock exchange first made possible the mobilization of capital. From a legal
standpoint this mobilization involves a transformation, and at the same
time a duplication, of property rights.[6] Ownership of the actual means of
production is transferred from individuals to a legal entity, which consists,
to be sure, of the totality of these individuals, but in which the individual as
such no longer has ownership rights in the property. The individual has
only a claim upon the yield; his property, which once meant real,
unrestricted control over the means of production, and hence over the
management of production itself, has been transformed into a mere claim
to income and has been deprived of   control over production.

From an economic standpoint, however, the mobilization of capital
consists in the possibility for the capitalist to withdraw his invested capital
in the form of money at any time, and to transfer it to other branches of
production. The higher the organic composition of capital becomes, the
less possible is it to make this change by altering the real structure of the
material components of productive capital. The tendency to equalize the
rate of profit encounters increasing obstacles in the growing difficulty of
withdrawing productive capital, which consists in the main of fixed capital,
from a particular branch of production. The process of equalization which
actually takes place is very slow, gradual, and imperfect, occurring mainly
as a result of the investment of newly accumulated surplus value in those
spheres with a higher rate of profit, and the withholding of new investment
from those with a lower rate of profit. The rate of interest, in contrast to the
rate of profit, is equal and uniform throughout the system at any given
time. The equivalence of all capital – which, for the individual capitalist,
consists not in the fact that they are equal in value, but that equal values
produce equal yields – finds a satisfactory expression, first of all, in the
uniformity and equality of the rate of interest. The capitalist is indifferent to
the use value of his capital, to the specific field in which it is invested at any
time; for him it is only a sum of value which breeds surplus value, is only
regarded from this quantitative aspect, as an entitlement to profit.

Hence the actual differences in yield (profit) lead to differences in the
valuation of capitals of equal size. If there are two capitals which have a
value of 100, one of which produces a profit of 10, while the other produces
a profit of 5, the first will be valued at twice the amount of the second. These
disparities in profit as between different units of capital lead on one side,
through the striving of each individual capitalist to maximize his profit, to
competition among the various capitals for spheres of investment, and thus
to the tendency towards an equalization of rates of profit (and the prior
equalization of rates of surplus value), and the establishment of a general
average rate of profit. On the other side, since inequalities in rates of profit
constantly re-emerge, and constantly provoke movements of capital, the
individual capitalist can only surmount them by valuing his capital in terms

of its income, capitalized at the current rate of interest. If this valuation is to be achieved in practice, if capitalists are really to be equal, if the equality of everything which yields profit is finally to be accomplished, the capital must always be realizable in accordance with this standard of valuation, and realizable in the socially valid form, as money. Only then is the equality of the rate of profit achieved for every individual capitalist. But this realization is an inversion of the real relationship. Capital no longer appears as a definite magnitude which determines the amount of profit. On the contrary, it is profit which seems to be a fixed magnitude determining the magnitude of the capital. This way of determining the magnitude of capital emerges in practice whenever a corporation is formed, makes possible promoter's profit, and determines its level. The real relationships seem to have been stood on their head. No wonder that those economists who observe economic affairs through the eyes of stock exchange operators regard any presentation of the real conditions as being itself perverse and absurd!

The equality of all capital is thus realized by its being valued according to its yield. But it is only realized, like all capital which is given a value in this way, on the stock exchange, the market for capitalized titles to interest (fictitious capital). If the inherent tendency of capitalism, its need to place all the available social wealth at the disposal of the capitalist class, in the form of capital, and to ensure the same yield for each unit of capital, obliges it to mobilize capital, and thus to make a valuation of it as mere interest-bearing capital, then it is the function of the stock exchange to facilitate this mobilization, by providing the machinery for the transfer of capital.

The mobilization of capital transforms an increasing proportion of capitalist property into titles to income, and in so doing it makes capitalist production increasingly independent of the movement of capitalist property. The trading in income titles which goes on in the stock exchange involves only the transfer of property, which can take place quite independently of the course of production, and without any effect upon it. The movement of property has now acquired independence, and is no longer determined by the processes of production. In the past, a transfer of property also involved a transfer of the capitalist entrepreneurial function, and vice versa, but this is no longer the case. And whereas, in earlier times, the principal cause of changes in the distribution of property was the variability of achievements in production, and industrial competition was thus a crucial determinant of the distribution of property, this cause, still operative today, is now supplemented by others which stem from the circulation of income titles and may produce movements of property which neither originate in any change in production relations nor exert any influence on production.

In the circulation of commodities the transfer of goods and the transfer of ownership go hand in hand. In simple commodity production the transfer of goods seems to be the essential thing, the incentive for transferring property; and the latter is only the means for accomplishing the former. The determining motive for production is still the creation of use value, the satisfaction of needs. But in capitalist commodity circulation the circulation of goods also involves the realization of the profit which arose in production, and this profit is the mainspring of economic activity. In capitalist society the transfer of labour power, as a commodity, to capitalists augments their property through the production of surplus value. The circulation of securities, on the other hand, involves only a transfer of property, the circulation of mere paper titles to property, without any corresponding transfer of goods. In this case, the movement of property is not accompanied by the movement of goods, and capitalist property has lost any direct connection with use value. The market for this circulation of property in itself is the stock exchange.

Mobilization, the creation of fictitious capital, is in itself an important cause of the emergence of capitalist property outside the process of production. Capitalist property used to arise essentially from the accumulation of profit, but the creation of fictitious capital now opens up the possibility of promoter's profit. By this means, a large part of the profit is channelled into the hands of the great money powers, who alone are in a position to give industrial capital the form of fictitious capital. This profit does not flow to them in the way dividends are paid to shareholders, in the form of fragmented annual payments, but is capitalized as promoter's profit, and received in the form of money, both relatively and absolutely considerable in amount, which can immediately function as new capital. Thus every new enterprise pays, from the very outset, a tribute to its promoters, who have done nothing for it and need never have any dealings with it. It is a process which is always concentrating large new sums of money in the hands of the big money powers.

A process of concentration of property takes place in the stock exchange, quite independently of concentration in industry. The big capitalists, who are thoroughly familiar with the activities of the corporations, and have a comprehensive view of business conditions, are thus able to foresee the future trend of share prices. The strength of their capital enables them, through appropriate buying and selling, to influence stock exchange prices themselves, and to collect the resulting profit. This power also makes it possible for them to intervene in the market, amid universal acclaim, in order to buy up securities during a crisis or panic, and later sell them at a profit when conditions have returned to normal.[7] In short, they are in the know, and 'all fluctuations of business are advantageous to those in the know' as that crafty banker Samuel Gurney assured a committee of the House of Lords.[8]

An essential element in the functioning of the stock exchange as a means of endowing industrial capital, through its transformation into fictitious capital, with the character of money capital for the individual capitalist, is the size of the market, because its character as money depends upon the real possibility of selling shares and bonds at any time without substantial losses. That is why there is a tendency to concentrate all transactions to the greatest possible extent in a single market; hence all bank and stock exchange business is increasingly concentrated in the main centre of economic life, in the capital city, while the provincial stock exchanges are becoming progressively less important. In Germany the Berlin stock exchange surpasses all others in importance. Outside Berlin only the stock exchanges in Hamburg and Frankfurt are of some account, but their importance is declining.

According to petty bourgeois theory the development of shareholding should bring about the 'democratization of capital'; but petty bourgeois practice, which is always more sensible, tries to limit share ownership to the capitalists. The representatives of big business practice subscribe whole-heartedly to such warnings as the following, in the comfortable knowledge that they will have little effect: 'Anyone who needs a fixed income', the authoritative Arnhold maintains, 'should not buy shares.'[9] He goes on to say that the fluctuating return on shares will only be a source of capital losses for anyone who has to live on the interest he receives, because high dividends will probably encourage him to increase his expenditure. Such a person will not sell his holdings when prices are high, but as a rule decides to sell when he becomes uneasy about the small dividends and low share prices (as he always does, because he has no insight into the real condition of the business, and must therefore rely upon the market quotations and the 'verdict' of the stock exchange), or for some other reason.

3　Stock exchange operations

Transactions on the stock exchange involve a kind of buying and selling which differs radically from other kinds, not by virtue of its procedure, but because of the commodity which is dealt in. The crucial factor from an economic standpoint is not the technique employed in such operations, but their substance; and an account of these technical details would be more appropriate in a manual for practical dealers than in a theoretical treatise. Nevertheless, these technical aspects of the subject acquire a more general interest and importance to the extent that the manner of conducting the transactions facilitates certain results which stem from the nature of these operations.

The distinctive regulations which govern the conduct of stock exchange transactions – the practices of the stock exchange – are primarily designed to promote the maximum utilization of credit, the curtailment of risk, and the greatest possible rapidity of turnover. The maximum utilization of credit is already made possible by the nature of the 'commodities' involved. Primarily these 'commodities' are claims to money, either in the direct form of bills or in the indirect form of claims to capitalist profit. As such claims to money, stock exchange values are all equivalent and interchangeable, differing from each other only quantitatively. Even the so-called qualitative differences which exist between the different types of stock exchange paper, as for example those between fixed interest certificates and shares, as well as differences in their reliability, are always converted into quantitative differences by stock exchange transactions, and cannot be expressed otherwise than as differences in valuation. These differences, however, unlike differences in the price of different brands of the same commodity, which are primarily the result of differences in their costs of production, arise exclusively from differences in the supply–demand ratios. When, for example, a sugar share and a railway share give the same return, the railway share may still be quoted at a higher price because more people want to buy the railway share in the belief that it promises more stable earnings. Qualitative differences in the security of the yield are given quantitative expression in share quotations. This interchangeability of stock exchange values thus makes it possible for most purchase and sale transactions to cancel each other out, leaving only a small proportion of the difference to be settled by payment in cash.

The granting of credit is associated with such transactions, since money functions merely as account money and only a small amount is needed for cash payments. In order to reduce these payments to a minimum, there are special institutions to settle the claims which result from purchase and sale operations.[10] For this purpose, however, it is essential that the prices at which transactions on the stock market are concluded should be known; hence, stock exchange quotations are public. At the same time the publication of share prices achieves the main purpose of the stock exchange; namely, to be the market where securities can be traded at any time, and at a known price. Since the price which can be obtained at any time is fixed it becomes much easier to provide the other form of credit – loans – than it was previously in the case of payment credit, because the creditor now knows exactly the price of the object on which he is lending money. The speculator deposits as security with his creditor the papers which he has paid for with the borrowed money. At the same time there emerges a new and surer way of using money capital to earn interest, by using stock exchange securities as collateral.

The provision of credit enables the speculator to take advantage even of minor price fluctuations, in so far as he can extend his operations far beyond the limits of his own resources, and thereby make a good profit, through the scale of his transactions, despite the small extent of the fluctuations. On the other side, credit has not only permitted speculation to increase, and to take advantage of market conditions at any time, but has also had the effect, since speculative operations are always accompanied by counter-operations, of moderating price fluctuations. The use of credit also gives a further advantage to the large speculator. The weight of his resources is multiplied by the use of credit, which grows much more rapidly than his own wealth.

Another distinctive feature of stock exchange transactions is the speed with which they are concluded, which results from a certain informality of procedure. This rapidity is due essentially to the need to take advantage of slight, short-term price fluctuations. The rapid changes in supply and demand, and the speed with which market quotations vary, make it extremely important to conclude transactions as fast as possible. Every new turnover gives speculators a new possibility to make a profit. Hence any time-consuming formality is abhorrent, and in this sphere the expression 'time is money' is literally true. Hence, also, the hostility to any legal specification of settlement times, and to legislative intervention in general, which would always involve a loss of time.

Futures trading, which defers the completion of all transactions to the same date, is the best way to take advantage of credit. Since such transactions are mainly the work of speculators, buying and selling are synchronized in such a way that most of the transactions offset each other, leaving only the balances to be settled in money (and most of these payments, for that matter, are also settled by credit or by book transfers in the banks). Money may also be needed in cases where there is only a sale or a purchase, but such transactions are few compared with those which cancel each other out. Here, too, the effect of credit is to expand the market. Futures trading allows a great extension of operations: securities which are dealt in for future delivery always find a market, and it is always possible, therefore, to bring a speculative operation to an end by buying or selling, to realize the profit or minimize the loss, unless the market is disrupted by a panic. Furthermore, since actual possession of the securities is not involved when speculating in futures, but the aim is simply to make a marginal profit, and the securities can be sold at any time, the extent of the commitment is determined not by the price of the securities, but only by the amount of the marginal differences which may arise from the speculation. At the same time, the securities actually available on the market are required only to the extent that the speculative operations of buying and selling do not cancel out. The volume of dealings entered into is therefore likewise independent of the total sum of prices for the securities actually available on the market and can be many times that amount. Furthermore, the typical conditions under which deals are concluded give the most complete assurance that such transactions will be completed very speedily.

The greater simplicity of the futures market, the increased possibility of cancelling out purchases and sales, reduces the amount of capital which is needed in order to take part in speculation. Accordingly, the circle of people who can participate in speculation has been extended, and the scale of individual transactions has increased. The futures market is expanded as against the market for cash operations. At the same time it absorbs fewer resources in order to maintain and develop speculative operations, and so affects less strongly the rate of interest on the capital which is made available for speculation. However, since a great deal of speculation is always carried on with borrowed capital, and the rate of interest on this capital has a strong influence upon the continuation of speculation, there is always a general tendency for the futures market to continue to promote speculation. This greater continuity of operations results in smaller variations in the relation between supply and demand, and more moderate fluctuations in share prices. At the same time, given the large scale of the transactions, much smaller fluctuations are sufficient to induce speculators to engage in their activities. A similar consequence follows from the fact that futures operations also make it possible to *sell* securities for speculative purposes, so that it is easier here to counteract a one-sided increase in the supply than it is on the cash market.[11]

Trading in futures makes it possible to invest capital, which will only become due at a later date, at predetermined prices, or to obtain capital on favourable terms for use at a later date. In addition, there is the expansion of the market, already mentioned, which futures trading assures through the ease of obtaining credit and of business procedures generally. The absorbent capacity of the futures market is greater than that of the cash market, and this facilitates the issue of securities by making it possible for the issue houses to place their offerings gradually without depressing the price of securities.[12] Trading in futures is also the standard method of carrying out arbitrage operations and equalizing price differences between the various stock exchanges.

Speculation requires that a certain quantity of securities should be made available for its own purposes. A security which is in 'safe' hands, and has been withdrawn from the market as an investment for a long period of time, cannot serve the purposes of speculation. The same is true of securities which have a very small aggregate value. In such a case, small purchases and sales can exert a strong influence on the price level and give a few capitalists the opportunity, by buying up all the available 'material', to dictate monopoly prices to their competitors. Speculation presupposes a large market which cannot be too easily dominated; monopoly is the death of speculation.

As we have seen, credit transactions always go hand in hand with speculative operations. What is involved in speculation is not the total sum of quoted security prices, but the size of the possible variations in price. In accepting securities as collateral, the supplier of credit cannot extend himself beyond the sum which is guaranteed against changes in price. Thus, for example, if the price of a security subject to relatively small fluctuations is 110, a speculator can pledge it as collateral at any time and obtain 90 for it, and need then only advance 20 out of his own funds. This is the most common method by which stockbrokers, bankers and banks extend credit to enable their clients to participate in stock exchange transactions. The withdrawal of such credit, or making it more difficult to obtain, is a favourite means of putting these clients 'out of commission', making it impossible for them to go on speculating, forcing them to unload their securities at any price, and by this sudden increase in supply, depressing prices and enabling creditors to pick up these securities very cheaply. In this case too the provision of credit is a means of expropriating small debtors.

The provision of credit for the really large speculators is arranged in an entirely different manner. In this case the speculators obtain the necessary funds on a contango basis. In a formal sense, such contango operations consist of buying and selling. If a bullish speculator wants to hold on to his securities beyond settlement day until the next due date, because he hopes for a further rise in their price in the interim, he simply sells them to a money capitalist and buys them back for the next term. The interest which the lender receives on his money is contained in the difference between purchase and sale price. But this is only a matter of form. In reality, the lender has simply taken over the securities for the specified period of time, and has assumed the place of the speculator. Yet there is a difference between him and the speculator in that he assumes no risk and does not seek any speculative profit, but has merely invested his money for that period of time and received interest on it. It is the specific form in which the advance is made that is important here. For since the credit transaction here takes the form of a purchasing transaction, ownership of the securities is transferred during the interim period to the supplier of credit. This enables him to make such use as he pleases of the securities during that time, and this may be important where industrial shares are concerned. It may be a matter, for example, of a bank securing a decisive voice in the decisions taken by a general shareholders' meeting, thanks to its large shareholdings. Through contango business the bank is enabled to acquire temporary ownership of the shares and thus to obtain control of the corporation. By reducing charges, and thus making contango arrangements more attractive, a bank may find it easier to obtain these securities from speculators. Quite frequently the banks co-operate with each other in this field, in order to eliminate competition in contango business for certain securities during a given period of time.[13] In this way shares acquire a dual function. They serve, on the one hand, as objects of speculation and as the source of marginal profits. At the same time they also serve the banks in their effort to gain a controlling influence in the corporations and to impose their will on the shareholders' meetings without being obliged to make long-term investments of their funds in the shares concerned.[14]

Other things being equal, the extent of stock exchange speculation depends essentially upon the volume of money which is available to speculators. For the frequency of turnover of the securities – and every turnover brings a marginal profit – is obviously independent of the number of existing securities. This accounts for the influence which banks have upon stock exchange speculation, for by granting or withholding credit they affect very strongly the scale of speculation. The greatest demand for credit arises from contango operations. Very considerable sums, of floating capital, for the most part, are invested in these operations,[15] and such investments have an influence in establishing the rates for call money. During periods when money is less mobile, they also have an influence on the discount rate and thus on the movement of gold. By restricting the supply of credit, therefore, the banks can directly influence the rate of interest, because in this case the supply of credit is to an exceptional degree at the discretion of the banks. These are purely financial transactions which have no crucial effect, one way or the other, on the course of the economy. It is a different matter when credit is being supplied to traders and industrialists, for in this case a sudden and excessive restriction of credit would be bound to lead to a collapse and an acute crisis.

The development of the banking system has been accompanied by a change in the organization of trading in securities. At first the banker is simply a broker who handles a business affair for his client. But the more the capital resources of the bank and its interest in the share market increase, the more actively does it go into business on its own account. A great many of the transactions no longer take place on the stock exchange, but instead the bank simply cancels out the orders of its clients against one another, and only the outstanding balance is settled on the stock exchange or covered by the bank's own funds. Up to a certain point, then, the sums which will be provided for buying and selling on the stock exchange are at the discretion of the bank, and this gives it a means of influencing the movement of security prices. The bank thus ceases to be simply a middleman in securities trading and becomes a dealer itself. 'In fact, banking today is no longer a brokerage business, but has become a business which trades on its own account.'[16]

At the same time the large bank also takes over part of the function of the

stock exchange, and itself becomes a securities market; all that remains for
the stock exchange is the balance which cannot be cleared in the banks.[17]
'A large bank represents in itself a volume of supply and demand such as
was previously represented only by one of the larger stock exchanges.'[18]

With the increasing concentration of the banking system the power of
the big banks over the stock exchange has grown enormously, especially
during those periods when the participation of the general public in stock
exchange speculation declines.

> Considering the way in which affairs have developed on the stock
> exchange, one should speak today of the trend in banking rather
> than the trend of the stock exchange, because the big banks are in-
> creasingly turning the latter into a subservient instrument and direct-
> ing its movements as they see fit. Just as last spring there was much
> talk of how an unfavourable forecast of business conditions by one
> of the big banks gave the external impetus to the sudden collapse of
> security prices, which had, of course, more profound inherent causes,
> so the contrary attempts by the *haute banque* this week to reassure
> and stimulate have brought about a change of mood on the stock
> exchange, which is now alert to auspicious signs instead of paying
> attention only to the unfavourable aspects.[19]

In addition to this powerful influence on the trend of the stock market,
the banks, as a result of their increasingly close relations with industry, now
have an intimate knowledge of the situation of particular enterprises, can
anticipate their earnings, and under certain conditions influence the level of
earnings as they wish. All these factors enable the banks to carry on all their
speculations with considerable security. The declining importance of the
stock exchanges is obviously connected with this development of the large
banks.[20]

On the stock exchange capitalist property appears in its pure form, as a
title to the yield, and the relation of exploitation, the appropriation of
surplus labour, upon which it rests, becomes conceptually lost. Property
ceases to express any specific relation of production and becomes a claim to
the yield, apparently unconnected with any particular activity. Property is
divorced from any connection with production, with use value. The value
of any property seems to be determined by its yield, a purely quantitative
relationship. Number is everything; the thing itself is nothing! The number
alone is real, and since what is real is not a number, the relationship is more
mystical than the doctrine of the Pythagoreans. All property is
capital – and not simply property. Debts are also capital, as every state
loan demonstrates. All capital is equal, and is embodied in those printed
certificates which rise and fall in value on the stock exchange. The actual

formation of value is a process which remains entirely outside the sphere of property owners but determines their property in a completely mysterious way.

The magnitude of property seems to have nothing to do with labour; the direct connection between labour and the yield on capital is already partially obscured in the rate of profit, and completely so in the rate of interest. The apparent transformation of all capital into interest-bearing capital, which the fictitious capital form involves, makes any insight into this relationship impossible. It seems absurd to connect interest, which is always fluctuating and can change regardless of what is happening in the sphere of production, with labour. Interest seems to be a consequence of the ownership of capital as such, a *Tóros*, the fruit of capital which is endowed with productive powers. It is fluctuating and indeterminate, and the 'value of property', a category, fluctuates along with it. This 'value' seems just as mysterious and indefinite as the future itself. The mere passage of time seems to produce interest, and Böhm-Bawerk has founded his theory of the interest on capital upon this illusion.

The commodity exchange

The stock exchange is the birthplace of the trade in securities. As it develops, so also do the investment banks, which compete with it, and at the same time use it as an intermediary. The futures business, while it facilitates the trade in securities, is not essential to it, and has no decisive influence upon prices. The situation is different in the case of commodity trading which follows stock exchange procedures.[1]

The turnover of securities on the stock exchange has the function of mobilizing capital. By the sale of shares the fictitious capital of individual capitalists (which had previously been converted into industrial capital) is reconverted into money capital. Such turnovers are unique, having nothing in common with the trade in commodities except the formal character of purchase and sale, which is the universal economic form in which values and property are transferred. Trade in commodities is entirely different; for it is in the circulation of commodities that the metabolism of society takes place. From the outset, the commodity exchange and the stock exchange are differentiated from each other just as commodities are from securities. Putting them in the same category as 'exchanges' is bound to create confusion if this fundamental distinction is disregarded, and especially if speculation is identified with trade. The concept of trade in commodities according to stock exchange procedures – that is, the specific characteristics of the commodity exchange which distinguish it from other types of trade – therefore requires closer examination.

We generally say that trade is exchange trading if it takes place on an exchange; that is, at a place in which numerous merchants gather. But it is obvious that whether merchants do business over their own counters or in another place, on the exchange, is a purely technical distinction, not an economic one. On the exchange, deals may be concluded more quickly, and traders may have a better view of the market as a whole, but these are still technical, not economic, differences.

The difference remains merely technical even if one important function of the individual merchant, namely the testing and confirmation of the quality of goods, becomes redundant when only commodities of a standard quality can be supplied to the market. Whether these conditions of delivery are met or not is decided, in disputed cases, by expert bodies of the exchange itself. The elimination of this function, for the individual merchant, is a precondition for commodity exchange trading, which also requires, however, other economic circumstances.

Only commodities of a standard quality are traded on the commodity exchange. For this purpose, each commodity has to be a fixed use value, a standard commodity, any unit of which can be replaced by any other. It is as a quantum of equal use value that the commodity has become an exchangeable good. The mass of commodities is distinguishable only quantitatively on the commodity exchange. According to the nature of the commodity, and the exchange regulations, a given quantity – so many kilograms, so many sacks – is taken as the unit in concluding a deal. Hence only those commodities are suited to commodity exchange trading which are by their nature readily interchangeable, or can be made so by relatively simple and inexpensive regulations.

The interchangeability of commodities is a natural attribute of their use value, which some commodities have and others lack. But more than this is required for commodity exchange trading. In an ordinary commercial transaction the manufacturer sells his commodity to the merchant at its price of production, and the latter then sells it to the consumer with his trading profit added. Such a transaction becomes feasible as a commodity exchange operation only if a marginal profit in the form of a speculative gain can be added to the commercial profit. The precondition for speculation, however, is frequent variations of price; and the commodities most suitable for trading on the exchange are those which undergo considerable price fluctuations over relatively short periods of time. These are primarily agricultural products (wheat, cotton), and those semi-finished or finished goods, the prices of which are strongly influenced by sharp fluctuations in the price of the raw materials from which they are produced, e.g. sugar.

According to Robinow, futures trading in England developed first in metals, talc, etc.[2] With the introduction of the telegraph and steamship lines it was extended to overseas products which are only produced seasonally, and are then thrown on to the market all at once, while consumption is spread over the whole year. The reason for futures trading is therefore the short period of production as against the long circulation time resulting from continuous consumption. The introduction of futures operations in the securities business was stimulated by the interchangeability of the objects dealt in, which themselves, as capitalized claims to income and thus representatives of money, are interchangeable. In commodity trading, however, the introduction of futures operations resulted from specific circumstances in the turnover of commodities, such as the difference between their time of production and their period of circulation. Only the requirements of futures trading lead to the creation, often by artificial means, of fully interchangeable commodities; that is to say, commodities of which every unit has the same use value as every other.[3] When price fluctuations cease, as a result of the formation of cartels, as for example in oil, then commodity exchange transactions in such products also cease, or become purely nominal.

A third important factor, directly related to those already noted, is that it is seldom possible to control price fluctuations by adjusting supply to demand. This is particularly difficult in the case of agricultural products. The supply of such products is more or less fixed, once the crops are harvested, and it can only be adjusted to the demand for them over a long period of time. And finally, it should be noted that the supply of such commodities as are traded on the commodity exchange must be large enough to preclude the danger of a 'ring' being formed, or the market 'cornered'; for the establishment of a monopoly price would eliminate price fluctuations and hence speculation.

The distinctive feature of commodity exchange trading is that by standardizing the use value of a commodity it makes the commodity, for everyone, a pure embodiment of exchange value, a mere bearer of price. Any money capital is now in a position to be converted into such a commodity, with the result that people outside the circle of professional, expert merchants hitherto engaged in the trade can be drawn into buying and selling these commodities. The commodities are equivalent to money; the buyer is spared the trouble of investigating their use value, and they are subject only to slight fluctuations in price.[4] Their marketability and hence their convertibility into money at any time is assured because they have a world market; all that need be considered is whether the price differences will result in a profit or a loss. Thus they have become just as suitable objects of speculation as any other claims to money; for instance, securities. In futures trading, therefore, the commodity is simply an exchange value. It becomes a mere representative of money, whereas money is usually a representative of the value of a commodity. The essential meaning of trade – the circulation of commodities – is lost, and along with it the characteristics of, and the contrast between, commodity and money. This contrast reappears only when speculation ceases, because the market has been cornered, and suddenly money has to take the place of the profane commodity which is no longer available. Just as money plays an evanescent role in the circulation process, so does the commodity in commodity speculation, Similarly, speculation turns over much larger quantities of commodities than really exist, just as more money is turned over on paper than is actually available.[5]

Eventually, of course, all futures trading in commodities must be followed by a real transfer of commodities from producers to consumers;

there must be real trading operations rather than speculation, and indeed these operations are a precondition for speculation. A series of futures operations has to begin with a producer (or his agent, the merchant), and terminate with a consumer (for example, the miller). We can regard the matter in the following way: some part of the stock of commodities always remains at the disposal of the speculators, serving merely as a reserve stock whose composition naturally varies, which would otherwise be stored elsewhere and would be at the disposal of other capitalist agents, not the speculators but producers and merchants, and would eventually reach the consumers. This stockpile must always be of a certain minimum size, to avert the danger of the market being cornered and rings being formed.

When speculators get their hands on these commodities, a whole new wave of buying and selling begins. This sequence of purchase and sale transactions is purely speculative; its object is to reap a marginal profit. These are not commercial operations, but speculative dealings. The categories of purchase and sale do not have the function, in this case, of circulating commodities, or moving them from producers to consumers, but have taken on an imaginary character. Their object is the acquisition of a marginal profit. The price of a commodity which a merchant sells on the exchange already includes the normal trading profit. If the manufacturer had sold it directly, he would simply have acted as his own dealer and pocketed the trading profit himself. The exchange, however, buys and sells in a purely speculative fashion, and speculators make a marginal gain, not a profit. If one gains, another loses. Nevertheless, this continuous chain of transactions ensures that it is always possible to convert a commodity on the exchange into money, and thus permits, to a certain extent, the investment of money in the commodity, and its reconversion into money at any time. Hence, a commodity which is dealt in on the exchange becomes suitable as a security for money which is temporarily idle. The banks, therefore, can use their capital in a new way by underwriting such commodities, or carrying them on a time basis, up to a certain proportion of their price. But when bank capital is used to participate in trading operations, it is used in the appropriate form, as interest-bearing capital. The commodities into which it has converted its money can be reconverted at any time into money. A well-managed bank will never tie up more money in these commodities than it can reconvert even under the most unfavourable conditions. The bank can be sure of recovering its money because there exists a commodity exchange in which a continuous round of buying and selling, which constitutes speculation, goes on. Consequently, the bank's money is not tied up, but remains money capital which has been invested in accordance with banking practice only in interest-bearing investments. Nevertheless, the entry of bank capital into this field provides both speculators and merchants with opportunities for expanding their operations. They can now purchase commodities without paying the full price in cash. Instead, they only need that amount of money which will cover any possible marginal differences, the balance being supplied by the bank. For speculators, this is tantamount to an expansion of their operations. Speculation is thus encouraged even if the price differentials are slight, provided the volume of trading grows; and so indeed the number of transactions steadily increases, while price differentials diminish.

An entirely different, and much more interesting, question concerns the effect which bank capital has on trade. Traders too can now have commodities underwritten, and need only pay interest on the borrowed capital. But profit is not produced in trading. Trade only realizes the average profit corresponding to the size of the capital employed. Since the trader now has access to a larger volume of credit, he need only use a small capital of his own to turn over the same volume of commodities as before. The trading profit on his own capital is consequently spread over a larger quantity of commodities, thus reducing the commercial mark-up on the price of these commodities. Since trading profit is only a deduction from industrial profit, the latter will increase proportionately, while the price of the commodity for the consumer remains the same. The incursion of bank capital thus has three consequences: (1) it increases industrial profit; (2) it reduces commercial profit, both in the aggregate and per unit of commodity; and (3) it converts a part of the commercial profit into interest. This last is a necessary consequence of the substitution of bank capital for a part of commercial capital, which has been made possible by commodity exchange trading.

It should be noted here that, with the exception of consumer credit, interest is always a portion of profit or ground rent. Nevertheless, it is also important to observe that borrowed capital which is employed in production serves as industrial capital, and therefore produces a profit. Since it only receives interest, it increases the industrial capitalist's profit by the difference between the average profit and the interest paid on the borrowed capital. In trade, where no profit is produced, but commercial capital has to be paid the average rate of profit out of the general fund of profit, bank capital works in a different way. It receives interest, but produces no profit for the merchant, who receives the average profit on his capital, excluding the capital borrowed from the bank, plus the interest on the latter, which he then pays over to the bank. Trade now requires less commercial capital and consequently a smaller amount of profit. The profit thus saved remains with its producer, industrial capital. Bank capital functions here like any other progressive measure which reduces commercial costs. The different effect is due simply to the fact that industrial capital produces surplus value while commercial capital does not.

This tendency is reinforced by another circumstance. Futures operations on the exchange create a stable market for those commodities in which they deal. The producer or importer can always sell his commodities, and so the circulation time of his capital is reduced. As we know already, however, every such contraction of circulation time releases capital. Hence, in this way too, the futures trade reduces the amount of capital required to carry out purely commercial operations, the circulation of commodities, which served only to realize profit, not to produce it.

The futures trade is the most satisfactory form for all speculation, since every kind of speculation is a way of taking advantage of price differences which occur over periods of time. Speculation is not production, and since time represents a sheer loss to a speculator unless he is engaged in buying or selling, he must be able to exploit immediately all price differences, including those which will occur in the future. He must therefore be able to buy or sell at any moment, for any future moment of time, and this is precisely the essential characteristic of futures trading. In this way speculation creates a price for every instant of the year. It thus gives manufacturers and merchants the possibility of avoiding the unforeseen consequences of price movements, of protecting themselves against price fluctuations, and of passing on the risks of price changes to the speculators. The manufacturer of unrefined sugar is willing to pay 100,000 marks for beets today, when he can sell the unrefined sugar on the exchange for 130,000,000 marks, for delivery on a stipulated future date. If he sells unrefined sugar at this price today, he will not be affected by any ensuing price fluctuations and will have secured his own profit. Futures trading is thus a means by which industrialists and merchants can confine themselves to their proper function. A part of the reserve capital which would otherwise be needed as an insurance against such price fluctuations, and thus tied up in industry or commerce, is thereby set free. Part of it is now used for speculation on the exchange, but since such capital is more concentrated on the exchange, it may be smaller in total than the capital which was dispersed in small units among individual industrialists and merchants.

Capitalist profit originates in production and is realized in circulation. It is natural that both producers and merchants should try to insure their profits against fortuitous price fluctuations occurring during circulation, when production has long since ended, and the amount of profit for the producer, and for the merchant who has already bought the commodity, is settled. At a certain stage of development, and for those commodities which are liable to particularly large and unpredictable price fluctuations because the output of them is governed by natural (for example, climatic) conditions, futures trading serves this aim. It smoothes out, so far as possible, the price fluctuations resulting from speculation, but can only do so by creating smaller and more frequent oscillations. This speculation, which is completely senseless from the standpoint of society, appears necessary because it brings about the required volume of participation by buyers and sellers, so that the necessary quantity of commodities is always being traded. This insurance against price fluctuations brings the market price increasingly close to the price of production. A specific class of capitalists, the speculators, is formed, who assume the burden of these price fluctuations. The question is: how does their capital realize its value?

In dealing with speculation in securities, we saw that this capital produces a marginal gain. The profit of one speculator is the loss of another. As a rule it is the large speculators, who can afford to wait, and can themselves influence the trend of prices, and the knowledgeable insiders, who profit at the expense of small speculators and outsiders.[6] The only problem which remains is whether speculators also get a risk premium. The risk premium is frequently alluded to, but very little studied. The first thing to establish is that the risk premium is not the source of profit and cannot explain it. Profit originates in production and is equivalent to the surplus value incorporated in the surplus product of the worker, which has cost the capitalist class nothing. Varying degrees of risk, or to put it another way, varying degrees of certainty that the profit which originates in production will actually be realized in circulation, can only bring about variations in the distribution of profit. Those branches of industry which have a higher risk, which must express itself in greater losses, seek higher prices so that in the end the rate of profit on their capital will be equal to the average rate of profit. It is clear that in so far as the special circumstances prevailing in any branch of production tend to reduce its yield, these circumstances must be offset by a level of prices high enough to assure the equality of the rate of profit. Thus, the price of optical lenses must include the cost of the glass which is spoilt during the pouring process. They form part of the cost of production. Similarly the average amount of damage and wastage which occurs while commodities are in transit to the market must be included in their price. The position is entirely different in the case of risk arising from fortuitous events in the course of circulation, which alter the costs of production themselves. For example, if there is a product still on the market, which was manufactured with old machines, while new ones allow it to be produced in half the time, there is no compensation for such a 'risk'. The sellers of this product will have to bear the loss.

The same conditions apply in the case of products which are most frequently dealt in on the futures market. The uncertainty may arise, for example, from the fact that the price of German grain is determined not only by the outcome of the German harvest, that is, by the German costs of production which would be directly expressed in the price, but also by American, Indian, Russian, etc. costs of production. For these price factors, there is no adjustment in the price of German grain.[7]

In so far as large, unforeseen fluctuations occur in circulation, the capitalists in such a branch of production must maintain reserves which will enable them to cover losses arising from price fluctuations, and to continue their production without interruption. This reserve fund is a part of the necessary circulation capital, and an average rate of profit is calculated for it. The profit imputed to it may therefore be regarded as the risk premium. Productive capitalists may still need such a reserve fund even when the futures trade has developed, for the latter cannot eliminate in any way those price fluctuations which result from a change in the conditions of production. The impact of the world market upon domestic prices must be borne by the producer.

The commodity market can insure only against those fluctuations which arise in the course of circulation. The miller insures the price at which he sells flour on a given day by buying grain on the same day. The grain dealer insures his profit by selling the grain which he has bought today, on the commodity exchange, for delivery on an agreed future date. The insurance consists in the fact that he ensures a definite current price for a later date when he will actually have to meet his obligation. In other words, purchase and sale have taken place concurrently, rather than independently and unilaterally, for the merchant or producer. This presupposes, however, that there is a large and constantly receptive market such as the futures trade creates, and along with that, agents who do not seek insurance for themselves, but anticipate the later state of the market; in short, speculators who take over the risk from the merchant who has insured himself. Their profit, therefore, is not a risk premium, but a marginal profit, which must be compensated by a corresponding loss. This characteristic of speculative gains has as its consequence that professional speculators only thrive when large numbers of outsiders participate in speculation and bear the losses. Speculation cannot flourish without the participation of the 'public'.[8]

Increasing concentration gradually makes this kind of insurance unnecessary. For a commercial enterprise which has become sufficiently large the favourable and unfavourable circumstances tend to balance out. The large commercial firm provides its own 'insurance' and does without the futures market. Furthermore, the small speculators are gradually forced out because they have to foot the bill more and more frequently.[9] The development of shares, and of speculation in securities, draws them away from the commodity exchange. Finally, the syndicates and trusts bring to an abrupt end speculation in those commodities which they control.

If we ask which business circles find the futures market necessary the answer is that the medium-size merchant has the most pressing need of it. It also has a certain utility for the producer to the extent that he would otherwise be obliged to undertake these important commercial functions himself. This will be the case if the processing of goods is already done by large capitalist enterprises, while the production of raw materials remains fragmented. In these circumstances the commodity exchange provides the necessary concentration of the products. A good example is to be found in the period when modern commercial milling was developing. The commodity exchange brings about this kind of concentration more quickly and more thoroughly than would be the case if a wholesale trade had first to be developed. The futures market is particularly desirable for commerce in those products which have a long circulation time, are produced by widely scattered plants which are difficult to supervise, with a variable yield which is difficult to anticipate, and hence are characterized by considerable, irregular price fluctuations during circulation.

Once futures trading is well established, participation becomes increasingly necessary for both merchants and producers, because the futures market is a major factor in price formation. On the other hand, if the futures trade were limited to the professional traders, it would be deprived of its most important function; namely the possibility of insuring oneself by unloading the losses due to price fluctuations upon the speculators.

Since speculators have no desire to hold on to speculative objects for any length of time, it is evident that every speculator is always a seller as well as a buyer. The bearish speculator, selling a commodity, will become a buyer of it in order to cover himself. But he buys and sells at different times and takes advantage of price fluctuations within this period of time, whereas the security of real trading consists precisely in avoiding such fluctuations, thus allowing sale and purchase to take place at the prices which prevail at a given time.

The speculator takes advantage of price fluctuations which are produced, not by him, but by the actual trade in goods. Such fluctuations may arise either from a fortuitous relation between supply and demand, or from more profound changes in the cost of production of a commodity. Supply and demand by the speculators then change the price level further, and produce fluctuations which must in the end cancel each other out just because every speculator is a buyer as well as seller. Naturally, this does not prevent one speculative trend – for example, a 'bullish' trend – from becoming dominant for a time, and so long as this trend persists the price will be higher than the actual trading in goods would dictate. Thus speculation causes more frequent, and therefore, in many cases, smaller price fluctuations, which cancel each other out in the long run.

The futures trade concentrates all business in one place, and gives the wholesale merchants in the vicinity of the exchange a preponderance over the provincial merchants, who are gradually disappearing.[10] But it also makes possible, on the commodity exchange itself, the entry of previous outsiders, who now compete with the old established houses. That is why the introduction of the futures trade frequently meets with opposition from the old professional merchants. The futures traders, by and large, are less qualified than the traditional professional merchants, and the participation of bank capital enables people who have little capital of their own to become involved. Yet even here concentration occurs, on a new basis, and in general one has the impression that the participation of mere speculators, and of outsiders, in the futures markets is declining.[11] Conversely, the abolition of the futures trade would strengthen the position of the large merchants who can do without this insurance.

One of the dangers of futures trading lies in the possibility of 'cornering'. If the seller does not deliver the commodity on the specified date, the buyer has the right to buy it on the market itself, on the seller's account. If the available supply of the commodity does not meet the demand, because the buyer has previously had the available stock bought up, very high fictitious prices will result, determined entirely by the decisions of buyers, and the sellers are then at their mercy. Cornering is all the easier the smaller the available stocks of the commodity. This situation can also be contrived artificially if the terms of delivery in futures trading specify a very high standard of quality for the commodity. Conversely, if the standard is lowered cornering is made more difficult. Cornering is usually possible only in special circumstances and for brief periods; for example, when grain stocks are low just before the harvest, and most of the old supply has already been sold. But unusually high prices generally cause supplies to appear on the market which were thought to have been long since consumed. If these new supplies exceed the demand from the buyers, the 'corner' collapses. In general, even successful 'corners' only involve the expropriation of groups of speculators who are outsiders, and they have only a slight effect on the actual commerce and the real prices.

As is well known, the German Stock Exchange law of 22 June 1896 has partly abolished the futures trade, and partly made it more difficult. The grain trade has greatly declined, especially since court decisions jeopardized delivery contracts regulated by commercial law. Hence 'the circle of people taking part in the delivery business has grown even smaller until it scarcely suffices to carry on the trade'. This has also increased the difficulties of the insurance business. What have the consequences been?

Already there are some large firms which believe that, because of the difficulties involved, they can get along better without insurance on the futures market, and these firms, helped by several years of stable and even rising prices, have achieved quite satisfactory profits. But, generally speaking, the more reliable firms regard such procedures as dangerous speculation and prefer to content themselves with a smaller but more certain profit. . . . In the present situation it is quite evident that the two or three large firms referred to are capturing an increasing share of the whole business. In this case, as in the case of banking, legislation has favoured concentration. But it is very doubtful whether the trend in this direction will, in the long run, really satisfy those who praise the success of this legislation so highly today. Widespread competition would provide far better guarantees of more favourable prices to farmers than do prices dictated by giant firms.[12]

The provincial merchants are all the more interested in the delivery business because the sale of futures enables them to offer their goods as collateral on more favourable terms. Since these commodities have already been sold at a firm price, they cannot lose in value, should prices fall. The merchant can thus once again obtain capital and is in a position to buy new lots of grain from the producers at good prices.[13]

By reducing the circulation time for productive capitalists, and assuming the risks, speculators can have an effect upon production itself. Before trading in futures was introduced it was mainly the partial producer who had to bear the risk. When this is no longer necessary, and there is no further need to hold stocks of the commodity, which are now concentrated at the location of the commodity exchange, this restricted productive function ceases to be enough. By combining his business with another one the partial producer becomes a full-fledged entrepreneur. He can do this all the more easily because a part of his circulation and reserve capital has been set free. It is in this way that independent wool carders have become superfluous, because the risk which they had to carry previously has now been transferred to the futures trade. They now become spinners themselves; or conversely, spinners merge with wool-carding firms.[14]

Futures trading saves the producers circulation capital, first by reducing the circulation time, and second by reducing their self-insurance (reserve fund) against price fluctuations. This strengthens the capital resources of the large enterprises, which are the principal beneficiaries of the futures market. The capital which is thus set free becomes productive capital.

The division of labour within enterprises is not determined solely by technological considerations, but also by commercial factors. Many partial processes, especially the conversion of raw materials into semi-manufactured goods, remain independent simply because the partial producers also perform important commercial functions. They take over the raw materials from the producers or importers, with whom they share the risks involved in price fluctuations. This independence becomes superfluous if the manufacturer can protect himself against risk without their help by resorting to the futures market. He then processes the raw material in his own plant. The elimination of the commercial function renders the technological independence superfluous. There is also a tendency here to eliminate the middleman. It is true that commodity markets give the appearance of multiplying trading operations, but as we have seen, such purchases and sales are forms of speculation, not trading operations.

We have seen that the futures trade is a means of enabling bank capital to participate in commodity trading by the provision of credit, either against collateral, or through contango operations. But the bank can also use its great capital resources and its general overview of the market to engage in speculation on its own account with comparative safety. Its numerous connections, extending over a wide range of futures markets, and its knowledge of the market, give it the opportunity to engage in safe arbitrage dealings, which bring considerable profits because of the large scale on which they are conducted. The bank can carry on such speculative dealings all the more safely the larger the quantity of the commodity that it controls and the greater its influence over the supply. That is why the bank tries to extend its control over the commodities which are dealt in on the futures market. The bank tries to obtain the commodity directly from the producer and to exclude other dealers. It either buys the commodity outright, or operates on a commission basis; and in the latter case it can afford to accept a much smaller profit, in competition with other dealers, because it is also able to gain speculative profits, and to employ a far larger volume of credit. The bank uses the influence it possesses through its other business connections with industry, in order to take the place of the merchant in relation to the industrialist. Once the bank has control of the marketing, the mutual relations between the bank and industry become closer. The bank's interest in the price of the commodity is no longer exclusively that of a speculator; it desires a high price in the interest of the enterprise with which it has all kinds of credit connections. At the same time, since the bank wants to acquire the greatest possible control over the commodity, it seeks connections with as many enterprises as possible, and so acquires an interest in an entire branch of industry. The bank's interest, therefore, is to protect this branch of industry as much as possible against the impact of a depression, and so it will use its influence to accelerate the process of cartelization, which will, to be sure, make the bank's speculative activity on the domestic market (though not on the world market) superfluous, but will amply compensate it by participation, in various ways, in the cartel's profits. This is a development which has occurred whenever historical factors have prevented the emergence of a strong and effective wholesale trade, either generally or in a specific branch of production. In Austria, for example, the banks penetrated the sugar industry, and with somewhat less success, the oil industry, through commerce, and became the animators of the trend towards cartelization in these industries, which are now heavily dependent upon them. Thus the futures trade encourages a development, which is in any case a general trend, that culminates in the elimination of the futures trade itself.

Monopolistic combines are completely eliminating the commodity exchanges. This is self-evident, because they establish long-term prices and thus make it impossible to take advantage of price fluctuations. The 'division over time', of course, continues as before, which would only surprise someone like Professor Ehrenberg! The German coal syndicate and the steel combine have made exchange quotations at Essen and Düsseldorf purely nominal.

> Thus the Essen coal exchange is nothing more than a folder containing a list of coal quotations which is carried regularly from the coal syndicate building to the hall of the exchange, while the whole so-called Düsseldorf commodity exchange consists of an epistle which an industrialist conveys at regular intervals to the governing body of the exchange.[15]

The same is true of the futures trade in alcohol:

> It has been noted quite correctly that a part of the trade through the central office (for the regulation of alcohol sales) had become insignificant, and that a part of the wholesale trade no longer found a place in the syndicate. This is the part which is mainly concerned with commodity exchange business. The commission and brokerage business, and all the merchants who had no direct dealings with producers, have become superfluous with the creation of the syndicate and have been eliminated.[16]

The actual traders have been transformed into agents of the syndicate, working on a fixed commission (30 to 40 pfennigs), and it seems that their number has been kept more or less constant. In 1906 there were 202 such agents, selling about 40 per cent of the output.

To the extent that the profits of the commodity exchange derive from commercial profit, they accrue to producers if the exchange is eliminated. This is also the case with those profits which arise from differences between the time of production (the 'working season') and the time of consumption. For example, the price of alcohol is higher in summer than in winter. At the end of the working season, the output is turned over to dealers. Summer prices are higher because they must cover storage costs, loss of interest, etc. But the distillers must sell as soon as possible after the end of the season, and the supply becomes excessive. Conversely, there is no production during the summer, the supply cannot be increased, and the dealers have enough capital not to be obliged to release the commodity at an unfavourable time. The difference between the capital resources of the dealers (who also have at their disposal bank capital against collateral or on a contango basis) and the capital resources of the often small-scale producers plays a role in determining the price; not, of course, the price which consumers pay but that which is paid by the dealer to the producer. These conditions can be changed by a cartel of producers in their own favour and to the detriment of merchants. Mr Stern, the managing director of the *Zentrale für Spiritusverwertung*, expresses this concisely when he says: 'The syndicate allows the price to rise after the end of the distilling season to the advantage of the distillers; the free market, to the advantage of speculators.'

Cartelization is particularly advantageous in agricultural production – and the agricultural producers' 'co-operatives' are often nothing but embryonic or small-scale cartels – for it is precisely here that capitalist regulation by the price mechanism is least appropriate, and the anarchy of capitalist society is least compatible with the natural and technical conditions of agricultural production. By contrast with its success in industry, capitalism cannot realize the ideal of a rational system of production in agriculture. This contradiction between capitalist price formation and the natural and technical conditions of agricultural production is brought to a head by the existence of a futures market, which makes price fluctuations continuous. Hence there is a tendency to blame the futures trade, with its frequently dramatic changes in the movement of prices – brought about, or at least exaggerated, by speculation – for a situation which is the fault of the whole capitalist mode of production. If this is demagogically exploited it can easily lead to a vigorous movement against the futures trade among agricultural producers.[17]

In so far as a cartel is able to diminish economic anarchy it is particularly effective in the domain of agriculture. Agriculture is inherently subject to extreme variations of output from year to year, in accordance with natural conditions, and the volume of products directly affects prices. An abundant yield exerts a strong deflationary pressure on prices, and increases consumption for that year. The depressed prices will result in production being restricted in the following year. If there is, in addition, a poor harvest, shortages will occur, driving up prices sharply and reducing consumption drastically. Small-scale, fragmented production is more or less helpless in the face of such phenomena. A cartel, on the other hand, has a much greater influence upon price formation, because it is able to stockpile in good time, and this, together with the regulation of production, enables it to prevent excessive price fluctuations. It is true, of course, that the capitalist cartel uses this power in order to maintain high prices over the long term by reducing output, but none the less it creates more stable conditions for agricultural producers.

Mr Stern, the managing director mentioned earlier, observes:

The syndicate can store a very considerable, though not unlimited, surplus. In a free market, an excessive surplus causes a fall in prices, which only stops when they have fallen below the cost of production. The syndicate can separate the export price from the domestic price. If the available surplus is directed abroad, the price level for the entire output on the free market depends upon the income from exports. For example: in 1893–4 there was a surplus of 20,000,000 litres [of alcohol], by no means a dangerous surplus, but enough to depress the average price for that year to 31 marks. Had the syndicate exported an extra 10,000,000 litres that year, sustaining a loss of 5 to 8 marks per 100 litres, or a total of 500,000 to 800,000 marks, on these exports, then the whole distillery trade would have been spared a very considerable loss, for if I assume that the price would have been 5 marks higher for the output as a whole, then taking into account the loss of 500,000 to 800,000 marks on exports, the value of the entire output of some 300,000,000 litres would have been increased by some 15,000,000 marks.

The exchange did not allow stocks to increase substantially, and very quickly offset any surplus by a decline in production. The surplus stocks of alcohol at the end of the season (30 September) during the period when a free market prevailed was regularly about 30 million litres. In several years the stocks were smaller, falling on one occasion by 9 million litres, but only once, in 1893–4, were they larger, by some 15 million litres. These fluctuations of 10 million litres or so, up or down, amount to only 3 to 5 per cent of total output, but they are enough to put an intense pressure on prices. Even small surpluses make the speculator nervous, and he gets rid of them when he anticipates a good harvest. The apparent equilibrium of the exchange was fundamentally nothing but a state of anxiety and nervousness.

He continues by explaining why he does not like equalization through the exchange: 'The exchange achieves equilibrium at low prices' – whereas his employers, the cartelized distillers and alcohol producers only desire equilibrium at high prices.

Many advocates of the futures trade also argue that it is an instrument for the more precise determination of prices. The futures market embraces a larger number of expert participants and the outcome of so many expert opinions must generally be more accurate than those of a smaller number. But the quality of being a good grain dealer does not endow a person with the mystical ability to foresee the size of the coming harvest. Such an ability is possessed neither by a single grain dealer, nor by any number of them, however great. Perhaps the saying 'Understanding has always been confined to the few' does not apply to the gentry of the commodity exchange, but whatever other Old Testament qualities they may possess, they are certainly not endowed with the gift of prophecy. In reality, futures prices are purely speculative. Even a syndicate like the alcohol syndicate, which undoubtedly has a direct influence upon domestic price formation, and would therefore be in a position to make tenders for futures, does so with extreme reluctance. The managing director of the alcohol syndicate, Untucht, declares:

> We have always had certain difficulties with futures tenders. If it had
> been up to us we would have been more cautious about them. . . .
> When someone offers a product, he must know in advance how
> much of it he will have in order to fix a price. Naturally, we can
> determine this only after several months of the season have passed.
> Even then, we cannot be sure of avoiding mistakes, for it is the out-
> put of the spring months which determines whether the output for
> the entire season will be large or small; and this is especially the case
> when the overall situation is not too clear. One must concede, how-
> ever, that the head office of the syndicate, which has an overall view
> of production, and controls about 80 per cent of the output, has
> more reliable information than is available to the commodity ex-
> change operators.

The reason for wishing to know futures prices is that the processing industry must know the price of its raw materials when it has to make tenders. If the raw materials season does not coincide with the time when the processing industry orders materials, it will need to know futures prices, especially in the case of commodities subject to sharp price fluctuations. In this way the processor transfers the risk to the supplier of his raw materials. But syndicates also use their power to free themselves of this risk, either by maintaining stable prices, or by setting futures prices so high that in that way too they avoid all risk. Herr Untucht is quite frank about it: 'Since we face uncertain conditions, we have been very prudent [sic!] and set our prices too high rather than too low.' And in a memorandum by the syndicate, it is noted:

> In the first four years of the syndicate's existence, futures tenders
> were issued promptly at the beginning of each business year, but since

1904-5 we have adopted the practice of not quoting general supply prices until we have formed some idea of how production is developing.

In the German stock exchange inquiry, those members of the commission who were not businessmen themselves (like Privy Counsellor Wiener, and the Independent Conservative deputy, von Gamp) took the view that the securities business was legitimate, but market transactions based on marginal price differences were not, whereas the businessmen consistently rejected this distinction. The former simply could not understand that in all capitalist transactions the use value of a commodity is a matter of complete indifference, and at most a regrettable necessity (a *conditio sine qua non*). The pure margin business is actually the most complete expression of the fact that for the capitalist only exchange value is essential. The margin business is indeed the most legitimate offspring of the basic capitalist spirit. It is business-in-itself, from which the profane phenomenal form of value – the use value – has been abstracted. It is only natural that this economic thing-in-itself should appear as something transcendental to non-capitalist epistemologists who, in their anger, describe it as a swindle.[18] They do not see that behind the empirical reality of every capitalist transaction there stands the transcendental business-in-itself, which alone explains the empirical reality. The remarkable thing is that the protagonists of use value themselves forget the concept of use value as soon as they come into contact with the exchange. All transactions are then regarded as equally real, whether they concern titles to income or commodities, provided the titles or commodities are actually delivered. They ignore completely the fact that the circulation of securities is quite immaterial to the metabolism of society, whereas the circulation of commodities is its lifeblood.

An example will show the idiocies which result from this indifference to use value. In order to be exchangeable a commodity must conform to certain fixed and definite standards; a specific weight for a given volume, a particular colour, aroma, etc. Only then does it constitute the 'type' or brand suitable for delivery. The 'type' used in the coffee futures trade in Hamburg was of inferior quality. Accordingly, all superior brands of coffee were adulterated by adding black beans, kernels, etc. In Berlin the type was superior, so that the additives incorporated in Hamburg had to be carefully removed in order to make the coffee fit for delivery. A most remarkable instance of unproductive capitalist costs![19] But there is still better to come. In Hamburg, the market was cornered, and supplies of coffee became scarce. The only coffee available was that mixed with kernels, etc. Superior brands, because they did not conform to the quality required, had to pay a premium. In other words, a fine had to be paid for supplying the better grades of coffee! But this is a consistent application of capitalist logic; for the buyer, the member of the combine, is not at all concerned with use value, but exclusively with exchange value. Exchange value determines the whole of economic action, the aim of which is not the production or supply of use values, but the achievement of profit.[20]

The apologists of the capitalist mode of production attempt to demonstrate the necessity of all its particular features by identifying the specific economic, and therefore historical, form which results from capitalist production with its technological content, which is always necessary and permanent, whereas the form is transitory; and on the basis of this erroneous identification they then infer the necessity of the form. Thus they insist strongly that every social labour process must be managed and supervised from above, in order to demonstrate the necessity of capitalist management, which arises from private ownership of the means of production, and hence the necessity of this private ownership itself. They regard commerce not as a specific act of circulation but as a way of distributing goods among consumers. Ehrenberg, for example, explains trade as distribution through space and speculation as distribution through time.[21] And since distribution, naturally, is always necessary at a certain level of technological development, so trade and speculation are always necessary, their elimination an impossibility, a Utopia. If 'necessary' is then identified with 'productive', one arrives with Ehrenberg at the grotesque conclusion that speculation is just as much a branch of production as agriculture. And why not, when land and shares alike yield money? Commerce is simply confused with transportation, packing, sorting, etc., and speculation is identified with storage; operations which are, of course, essential in any technologically developed mode of production. Even a sagacious person like Professor Lexis, who certainly deserves to be taken more seriously than Ehrenberg, becomes confused in his testimony concerning the futures trade[22] because he too fails to see that, unlike real trade in commodities, market trading in commodity futures is a specific form of economic activity. He ignores the role of speculation, and tries to demonstrate that the futures trade is a necessity, by attempting to depict it as genuine trade.

His opponent, Gamp, then has no difficulty in showing that the futures trade creates an enormous number of commodity turnovers which contribute nothing whatsoever to the distribution of commodities from the producer to the consumer. Lexis points out that futures trading makes it easier to find buyers. That is correct; only this 'buyer' is not usually the consumer, but another 'seller', namely a speculator. It is quite mistaken to attempt to derive trade, especially the futures 'trade' and speculation in futures, from some absolute requirement of distribution. Trade only meets distribution needs in a capitalist society, and even within capitalist society it is only a transitory necessity, as its elimination by syndicates and trusts demonstrates. Anyone who regards trade as 'productive', that is, as not merely realizing profit but producing it, faces an insoluble dilemma; he lauds the saving in trading costs as one of the advantages of cartelization, but then implicity admits that this is only an advantage if commercial operations produce a deficit, or in other words, are unproductive.

In fact, the futures trade is only a necessity in so far as: (1) it allows the productive capitalists (industrialists and merchants) to reduce their circulation time to zero, and thereby to protect themselves against price fluctuations during the period of circulation by transferring the burden to the speculators whose specific function it is to cope with them; (2) it permits money (bank) capital to replace commercial capital in carrying out a part of the commercial functions, the return on this part of the operating being interest, rather than average profit, with the difference between them going to increase industrial (entrepreneurial) profit; and (3) futures trading allows money capital – and this is closely related to the second point – to be converted into commercial capital while retaining its character as money capital, which opens the way for bank capital to extend its domination over trade and industry, and to impose upon an ever larger part of productive capital the character of money capital which is under the control of the bank.

Bank capital and bank profit

The mobilization of capital opens up a new sphere of activity for the banks: share flotation and speculation. From a theoretical standpoint, it makes no difference whether these activities are combined with the payment and credit functions of a bank, or are handled by separate banking institutions. What is important is the economic significance of this differentiation of functions. In any case, the modern trend is increasingly to combine these functions, either in a single enterprise, or else in several different institutions whose activities complement each other, and which are controlled by a single capitalist or group of capitalists. In the final analysis, the factor which leads to the combination of these activities is that capital emerges in all of them as money capital in the strict sense, as loan capital which can be withdrawn at any time, in the form of money, from its current commitment. Even where this combination does not take place in a single enterprise, it is still to some extent the same money capital which performs all the various functions inasmuch as one enterprise makes it available to others. Only after an analysis of these various functions is it possible to investigate the sources from which bank capital draws its profit, and the structure of the relationship, in this sphere, between profit and capital (both the bank's own capital and the other capital which it has at its disposal).

We know that profit originates in production and is realized in circulation; and we also know that additional capital is required for the operations of circulation, the purchase and sale of commodities. A part of these operations is taken over by merchants from the industrialists, and becomes an independent function of one section of social capital, commercial capital. The capital used by merchants yields an average profit, which is simply part of the profit generated by industrialists in the process of production, that is, a *pro tanto* (proportional) deduction from the profit which would otherwise accrue to industrialists.[1] Circulation also requires a series of financial transactions (the maintenance of reserve funds, preparation and despatch of payments, collection and payment of accounts, etc.). These accounting operations can be concentrated in order to economize labour, representing costs of circulation, and to reduce the amount of capital needed for such work.

The purely technical movements performed by money in the circulation process of industrial capital, and, as we may now add, of commercial capital, which assumes a part of the circulation movement of industrial capital as its own peculiar movement – these movements, if individualized into an independent function of some particular capital that performs nothing but just this service, convert a capital into financial capital. In that case, one portion of the industrial capital and of commercial capital persists not only in the form of money, of money capital in general, but as money capital which performs only these technical functions. A definite part of the total social capital separates from the rest and individualizes itself in the form of money capital, whose capitalist function consists exclusively in performing the financial operations for the entire class of industrial and commercial capitalists. As in the case of the commercial capital, so in that of financial capital, a portion of the industrial capital in process of function in circulation separates from the rest and performs these operations of the process of reproduction for all the other capital. These movements of such money capital, then, are once more merely movements of an individualized part of industrial capital in the process of reproduction.[2]

The money trade in its pure form, which we considered here, that is the money trade not complicated by the credit system, is concerned only with the technique of a certain phase of the circulation of commodities . . . namely with the circulation of money, and the different functions of money . . . following from its circulation. . . . It is evident that the mass of money capital with which the money dealers have to operate is the money capital of the merchants and industrial capitalists in the process of circulation, and that the operations of the money dealers are merely those originally performed by the merchants and industrial capitalists. It is equally evident that the profit of the money dealers is nothing but a deduction from the surplus value, since they are operating merely with the already realized values (even when they have been realized in the form of creditors' claims).[3]

In the course of development the banks have taken over the business of keeping accounts. The amount of capital required for this work is determined by the technical nature and the scale of the operations. On this capital the banks realize average profit just as merchants do on their commercial capital and industrialists on their productive capital.[4] This is the only part of bank capital, however, on which the profit can be described as average profit in the strict sense. The profit on the rest of bank capital is fundamentally different.

As a provider of credit, the bank works with all the capital at its disposal; its own and that of others. Its gross profit consists of interest paid on the capital which it has lent. Its net profit – after deduction of expenses – is the difference between the interest paid to it and the interest which it pays on deposits. This profit is not, therefore, profit in the strict sense, and its level is not determined by the average rate of profit. Like that of any other money capitalist it arises from interest. The position of middleman that the bank occupies in credit circulation enables it to profit not only from its own capital, like any other money capitalist, but also from that of its creditors to whom it pays a lower interest than it demands from its debtors. This interest is only part of, or a deduction from, the average social profit prevalent at the moment. But unlike the profit of the merchant or the money-dealing capitalist it has no influence whatsoever in determining the average rate of profit.

The level of interest depends upon supply and demand of loan capital in general, of which bank capital is only a part. This level of interest determines the gross profit. In order to attract the greatest possible amount of money for their use, the banks in turn pay interest on their deposits; and the amount of such capital at the disposal of any bank depends, *ceteris paribus*, upon the level of interest which it pays on deposits. Competition for deposits compels the banks to pay the highest possible rate of interest. The difference between the interest which the banks receive as creditors and the interest which they pay as debtors constitutes their net profit.

The process can be summarized as follows: the rate of interest is governed in the first place by supply and demand of loan capital as a whole, and this determines the gross profit of the banks, which they make by lending the money – their own and that which is deposited with them – at their disposal. The ratio between the bank's own assets and its customers' deposits is quite immaterial for the interest rate or the amount of gross profit. Of course, only part of the deposited money is actually at the disposal of the bank, while another part must be kept as a reserve fund, but this reserve, which earns no interest, is very small compared with the total sum. Competition among the banks determines the rate of interest which they have to pay to depositors, and on this rate, given the gross profit and expenses, depends the net profit. It is evident that what is important is not the banks' own capital, since their profits do not depend upon this, but the total loan capital at their disposal. The basic datum is the level of profit, and the amount of their own capital must be adjusted in accordance with it. The banks can convert into their own capital only as much of the total loan capital as their profits allow. For capital, however, banking is a sphere of investment like any other, and it will only flow into this sphere if it can find the same opportunities for realizing profit as in industry or commerce; otherwise it will be withdrawn. The bank's own capital must be reckoned in such a way that the profit on it is equal to the average profit. Let us assume that a bank has at its disposal a loan capital of 100,000,000 marks, and makes a gross profit of 6,000,000 marks and a net profit of 2,000,000 marks. If the prevailing rate of profit is 20 per cent, the bank's own capital can be reckoned at 10,000,000 marks, while the other 90,000,000 marks are available as deposits of its customers. This also explains why, when joint-stock banks are founded, or increase their capital, there is an opportunity to make promoter's profit, even though bank capital does not produce entrepreneurial gains (industrial profit), but only realizes interest. Since the bank's profit is equal to the average rate of profit, while the shareholders need only be paid interest, the possibility of promoter's profit follows, and if the bank has a dominant position on the money market it can take the whole, or part, of the promoter's profit, to strengthen its reserves. The reserves are, of course, the bank's own capital, except that from an accounting standpoint, the profit is attributed to the smaller, nominal capital. In turn, the reserves allow the bank to invest a larger part of its capital in industry.

The fact that the distinction between the bank's own capital and the capital deposited with it is immaterial so far as profit is concerned, and that the ratio of one to the other is not fixed, creates the impression that the amount of the bank's own capital is arbitrary, and allows it to be reckoned in such a way that the profit, although not really average profit itself, none the less becomes equal to it. If the banking system is already highly developed, so that the available loan capital is at the disposal of the existing banks, it becomes very difficult to found new banks, because there would be insufficient outside capital available to them, or it could be attracted only after a fierce competitive struggle with all the other banks, the outcome of which would be very doubtful.

Bank capital is not only entirely different from industrial capital, but also from commercial and money-dealing capital. In the latter branches of activity the amount of capital is technically determined by the objective conditions of the processes of production and circulation. The magnitude of industrial capital depends upon the general development of the process of production, the extent of the means of production available, including natural resources and the ability to exploit them, and the available working population. The manner in which this capital is used, and the degree of exploitation of the working population, determine the amount of profit which is distributed in similar fashion to industrial, commercial, and money-dealing capital. In the latter two spheres, the amount of capital required is also determined by the technical conditions of the circulation process. Since circulation does not produce a profit, and simply represents costs, there is a tendency to reduce the capital applied in this sphere to a minimum. Bank capital, on the other hand, including both the bank's own capital and deposited capital, is nothing but loan capital and as such it is, in reality, only the money form of productive capital. The important feature is that the greater part of it has a merely formal existence, as a pure unit of account.

The same relation that exists between bank profit and the amount of the bank's own capital, is also to be found in the case of the profit which arises from issuing shares and from speculative activities. Promoter's profit, or the profit from issuing shares, is neither a profit, in the strict sense, nor interest, but capitalized entrepreneurial revenue. It presupposes the conversion of industrial into fictitious capital. The level of gains from issuing shares is determined, first, by the average rate of profit, and second, by the rate of interest. Average profit minus interest determines the entrepreneurial gain which, capitalized at the current rate of interest, constitutes the promoter's profit. The latter does not depend in any way upon the amount of the bank's own capital. The convertibility of industrial into fictitious capital depends solely upon the quantity of loan capital available which, while retaining the form of interest-bearing capital, is ready to be converted into productive capital. There must be enough money available for investment in shares. But a distinction must be made here: the conversion of existing industrial capital into share capital ties up only as much money as is necessary for the circulation of the shares on the stock exchange, and this in turn depends upon the extent to which these shares remain in 'safe hands' as long-term investments, or experience a very rapid turnover as speculative stocks. Alternatively, the issue of share capital may represent the founding of a new enterprise or the expansion of an existing one. In that case enough money capital is needed, first, to complete the turnover $M-\begin{smallmatrix} L \\ < \\ M_P \end{smallmatrix}-P \ldots C^1-M^1$, and second, in order to issue the shares themselves. The amount of loan capital available determines both the rate of interest, which is the crucial factor in capitalization, and hence the size of the profit gained by issuing shares, which is therefore independent of the amount of the bank's own capital. In the long term, nevertheless, the gain from issuing shares must equal the average rate of profit on that capital. On the other hand, the bank will tend to increase its own capital in order to enhance its credit standing and its security. The case of speculative profits is analogous. The participation of the banks in speculation does not depend upon the distinction between their own capital and that of their depositors, but upon the size of the total sum.

As we already know, however, both the provision of credit, and financing and speculation, give rise to a tendency towards concentration, and at the same time, to the endeavour to hold as much of the capital as possible as the bank's own capital. For unlike the borrowed capital, the bank's own capital is not subject to sudden demands for repayment, and it can, therefore, be invested much more safely in industrial enterprises. In particular, the founding of companies involves tying up money capital in industry for a longer or shorter period until such time as it flows back to the bank through the sale of shares. This means that by increasing its own capital the bank is able to participate more fully, and on a more enduring basis, in industrial enterprises, eventually establishing control over them; and can exert a stronger influence upon speculation in commodities and securities. Consequently, when its gains from interest and share issues permit, the bank will tend constantly to enlarge its own capital.

But aside from the fact that the bank must be able to realize the value corresponding to its increased capital, it cannot convert deposited capital into its own capital at will. The bank tries to enlarge its own capital in order to invest it in industry, to make gains by issuing shares, and to acquire control over industry. If the sole function of the bank were to provide payment credit, an increase of its own capital beyond a certain limit would be unnecessary, since in this case disposal over deposited money is the crucial factor, and the bank cannot gain anything but interest on capital which must be immediately available as a means of payment. It is not the case that the bank, once it holds a larger part of the total available loan capital as its own capital, can then invest a larger amount of capital in industry on its own account. Quite the contrary. Since only part of the available loan capital is required as means of payment (circulation credit) the remainder is available for industrial investment (capital credit). This division of the total available loan capital between the purposes of circulation credit and capital credit has its own objectively conditioned grounds, which result from the prevailing state of the production and circulation processes; and even though these limits are flexible, the banks cannot ignore them if bank capital is to retain its money form, and the ability of the bank to meet its payments is not to be endangered. On the other hand, this division of the available loan capital does not depend upon how much of the capital at the bank's disposal is its own and how much belongs to its depositors..

The bank wants to increase its own capital in order to invest it in industry; and the limits to the amount of outside capital which a bank can convert into its own capital are set by that part of the total available capital which can be used for capital investment. Within these limits, the trend of development is for the banks to convert an ever increasing proportion of loan capital into their own capital. Thus the magnitude of the bank's own capital does not depend solely upon its own wishes, nor upon investment opportunities for the increased capital.

The increase of bank capital is a purely juridical transaction, not a change in its economic function. The bank can only increase its capital, which must have the form of money capital, by converting deposited money capital into its own. Since in any developed monetary system all the available money is assembled by the banks, an increase in bank capital simply means that a part of the deposits held by the bank has now been converted into bank capital by an issue of shares. This conversion of deposited capital into the bank's own capital, of course, leaves the supply and demand of money capital entirely unaffected, and consequently has no influence upon the rate of interest.[5]

Other things being equal, an increase in industrial capital will result in an increase in the amount of profit because industrial capital generates surplus value in the process of production. An increase in bank capital obviously leaves the total amount of interest received by the banks quite unchanged; for given a constant demand this depends upon the supply of loan capital which is not altered in any way by a change in the distribution of loan capital as between banks and private individuals, by a mere change in ownership. What changes is only the calculation of the net profit of the banks, which is smaller in percentage terms as the bank's own capital has increased.

Industrial, commercial, and money-dealing capital are distinct parts of social capital, which at any given moment must have a definite relation to each other. Abstractly considered, all social capital could also be bank capital. For bank capital, after all, is only capital which is at the disposal of the banks, and there is no inherent reason why all capital should not pass through the banks. Of course, most of this bank capital is fictitious, being merely a monetary expression for genuinely productive, functioning capital, or simply capitalized claims to surplus value. An increase in bank capital, therefore, unlike an increase in industrial capital, is not a precondition for increased profit. On the contrary, for the bank it is the profit which is the given factor. If the profit rises, then the bank will increase its own capital, because the increased capital enables it to convert more of its bank capital into industrial capital without assuming any greater risk. The fact that it is essentially the supply of credit to industry, and participation in industrial enterprises through the issue and ownership of shares, which induce the banks to increase their own capital is demonstrated by the example of the exclusively deposit banks in England, which are not increasing their capital, despite their vastly increased turnover, but are distributing very high dividends.

It should not be supposed therefore that the influx or outflow of bank capital would affect the profits of the banks in such a way as to change the rate of interest. Only the distribution of the profit changes, in so far as it has to be allotted to either a larger or a smaller amount of the bank's own capital.

There is also a certain significance in the fact that the increase of bank capital takes the form of share capital, that is to say, fictitious capital. We have already seen that the conversion of money into fictitious capital leaves the character of the individual capitalist as a money capitalist, or loan capitalist, quite unchanged. The money which is converted into fictitious capital remains bank capital, and so, in the economic sense, money capital. A part of this bank capital is converted into industrial capital, in one of two ways: either by providing credit to an industrial enterprise (that is, simply lending capital to the enterprise), or by acquiring shares in the enterprise which the bank then owns permanently if the size of its capital permits. In the latter case, the increase of bank capital has taken place by first converting money capital into bank capital, and then converting this in turn into industrial capital. Instead of private money capitalists investing their money directly in industrial shares, they invest it in bank shares, and it is the bank which converts it into industrial capital by buying industrial shares. The difference is that the bank is now not only an intermediary in the operation, but as the owner of bank capital has become co-owner of the industrial enterprise. Furthermore, this property right of the bank has altogether different consequences from that of individual shareholders. A tendency emerges to convert the greatest possible amount of the disposable money capital of individuals into bank capital, and only then to convert the latter into industrial capital. In the process fictitious capital has been doubled. Money capital assumes a fictitious form as shares in bank capital, and thereby becomes in reality the property of the bank; and this bank capital then assumes the fictitious form of industrial shares, and is converted in reality into the elements of productive capital, means of production and labour power.

The dividend policy of the banks, which operate with large amounts of outside capital (deposits), must be more stable than that of industrial enterprises. This is particularly so if the deposits come from sources which can only judge whether the management of the bank is good or bad on the basis of external criteria such as the stability of dividends, and withdraw their deposits when these fluctuate. It is a matter here of deposits from non-capitalist sources. An industrial enterprise can be more independent in its dividend policy; first, because its creditors are generally well informed about its ability to pay, and second, because the payments credit to which it has regular recourse must be covered by the commodities which it produces, while other credit is not required continuously, as in the case of the banks, but only at longer intervals. This greater independence enables it to influence share prices, and gives 'insiders' the opportunity to make speculative gains on the stock exchange. It also facilitates adaptation to market fluctuations and to the needs of accumulation, both of which are more important for the industrial enterprise than for the banks.

On the other hand, the banks can adapt a stable dividend policy more easily than can industrial enterprises, because business fluctuations do not affect bank revenues so strongly or one-sidedly as they affect industrial profit. In the first place, a large part of bank profit depends less upon the absolute level of the interest rate than it does upon the difference between the interest on the capital which they lend and that on the capital which they borrow. This margin, however, is much more stable than the fluctuations in the absolute level of interest, particularly if the concentration of banking is already well advanced. In the course of the business cycle there are favourable and unfavourable moments which, in part, cancel each other out. The most favourable one is a period of increasing prosperity characterized by a gradual rise in the rate of interest, strong demand for capital in industry, and consequently brisk activity in share issues and larger promoter's profits. At the same time the banks make larger profits from the management of accounts, advances of commercial credit, and stock exchange speculation. At the peak of the boom both the absolute rate of interest and the difference between interest received and interest paid out increase; but, on the other hand, share issues and promoter's profit begin to decline. Bank credit replaces the issue of shares and debentures as a means of meeting the capital requirements of industry, while speculation in securities is usually curbed some time before the onset of the crisis by the high interest rate. The first stage of the depression, when the rate of interest has reached its lowest point, is the most favourable time for issuing fixed-interest obligations. Bank gains from the acquisition of government and municipal bonds, and from the sale of fixed-interest securities in their own possession at the current inflated prices, grow appreciably. A part of the bank debt previously incurred by industry is converted into share and debenture issues, since the money market is fluid, and yields new gains on capital issues. All these factors compensate, to a greater or lesser extent, for the smaller revenue derived from interest on the supply of credit.

The competition among the banks is not conducted only with their own capital but with the entire capital at their disposal. Competition on the money market, however, is essentially different from that on the commodity market. The most important difference is that on the money market capital has the form of money, whereas on the commodity market it must first be converted from commodity capital into money capital, and this implies that the conversion may miscarry, that the commodity capital may decline in value, resulting in a loss rather than a profit. In commodity competition it is a matter of realizing capital, not only of realizing value. In the competition of money capital the capital itself is secure and it is only a matter of the level of value it attains, the level of interest. But interest is determined in such a way as to leave the individual competitors very little room for manoeuvre. It is primarily the discount policy of the central financial institutions which determines the situation for everyone else and sets rather narrow limits to their freedom of action. This is particularly important in the strictly credit operations of the banks (either lending or borrowing) where there is little competition. The less room for manoeuvre there is, however, the more important is the purely quantitative volume of business. Only if this is very large can the bank reduce its commission charges and increase the interest it pays on deposits. These conditions, however, are more or less the same for all enterprises of the same size. Furthermore, there is no extra profit in credit operations for large enterprises as against small ones, except perhaps in respect of economy of operation, and the greater ease with which losses can be avoided and risks distributed. On the other hand, the extra profit arising from patented technical improvements in industry, which plays such an important part in the competitive struggle, has no counterpart in this sphere.

Competition is more important in the financing of enterprises through share issues than in the provision of credit. Here the size of the promoter's profit leaves scope for competitive underbidding, though even in this case the limits are still rather narrow, and it is the extent to which industry is in a condition of dependence as a result of previous loans, rather than the terms offered by the banks, which is the crucial factor.

In industry, it is necessary to distinguish between the technical and the economic aspects of competition, but in the case of the banks, technical differences play a minor part and banks of the same type use the same technical methods. (Banks of different types do not compete directly with each other at all.) Here there is only an economic, purely quantitative, difference which involves simply the size of their competing capitals. It is this quite distinctive type of competition which makes it possible for the banks alternately to compete and to co-operate with one another in such varied and changing ways. An analogous situation can sometimes be observed among equally large enterprises in industry, which may occasionally enter into agreements about particular business matters; for example, in the case of tenders. In industry, however, such an agreement is frequently the precursor of a cartel, that is, of an enduring co-operation which excludes competition.

If the general rate of interest is the barrier to competition in the provision of credit, so the average rate of profit constitutes a limit in the field of payment transactions. Here the volume of business is crucial in determining the amount of commission charged, and it gives a great advantage to the large banks.

The professional banking principle of maximum security makes the banks inherently averse to competition, and predisposed in favour of the elimination of competition in industry through cartels, and its replacement by a 'steady profit'.

Bank revenue is not profit. Nevertheless, the total revenue, calculated on the basis of the bank's own capital, must equal the average rate of profit. If it is lower, capital will be withdrawn from the banking business, while if it is higher new banks will be established. Since bank capital is in the form of money, or to a great extent can easily be converted into money at any time, the equalization of profit can be achieved very quickly. For that reason there is also no 'overproduction' of bank capital. An excessive increase in the bank's own capital leads to a withdrawal of capital, and its investment elsewhere, rather than to a general crash, accompanied by depreciation, etc., as may be seen in industry. A bank crash results only from industrial overproduction or excessive speculation, and manifests itself as a scarcity of bank capital in money form, due to the fact that bank capital is tied up in a form which cannot be immediately realized as money.

With the development of banking, and the increasingly dense network of relations between the banks and industry, there is a growing tendency to eliminate competition among the banks themselves, and on the other side, to concentrate all capital in the form of money capital, and to make it available to producers only through the banks. If this trend were to continue, it would finally result in a single bank or a group of banks establishing control over the entire money capital. Such a 'central bank' would then exercise control over social production as a whole.[6]

In credit transactions the material, business relationship is always accompanied by a personal relationship, which appears as a direct relationship between members of society in contrast to the material social relations which characterize other economic categories such as money; namely, what is commonly called 'trust'. In this sense a fully developed credit system is the antithesis of capitalism, and represents organization and control as opposed to anarchy. It has its source in socialism, but has been adapted to capitalist society; it is a fraudulent kind of socialism, modified to suit the needs of capitalism. It socializes other people's money for use by the few. At the outset it suddenly opens up for the knights of credit prodigious vistas: the barriers to capitalist production – private property – seem to have fallen, and the entire productive power of society appears to be placed at the disposal of the individual. The prospect intoxicates him, and in turn he intoxicates and swindles others.

The original pioneers of credit were the romanticists of capitalism like Law and Pereire; it was some time before the sober capitalist gained the upper hand, and Gunderman vanquished Saccard.*

*The reference is to the two principal characters in Zola's novel, *L'Argent*. [Ed.]

Part III

Finance capital and the restriction of free competition

11

Surmounting the obstacles to the equalization of rates of profit

The aim of capitalist production is profit. The achievement of the largest possible profit is the motive of every individual capitalist, and becomes the guiding principle of his economic action as a necessary consequence of the capitalist competitive struggle. For the individual capitalist can only survive if he strives continually not simply to keep pace with his competitors, but to outstrip them; and he can do this only if he succeeds in raising his profit above the average, thus achieving an extra profit.[1]

The subjective desire for maximum profit, which animates all individual capitalists, nevertheless results objectively in the tendency to establish a uniform average rate of profit for all capital.[2]

This result is assured by the competition of capitals for spheres of investment, by the constant influx of capital into those spheres with above average rates of profit, and by its withdrawal from those spheres where the rate of profit is below average. This perpetual ebb and flow of capital, however, encounters obstacles which become more formidable as capitalism continues to develop.

The increasing productivity of labour, the progress of technology, can be seen in the fact that the same amount of living labour sets in motion an ever growing quantity of means of production. This process is reflected, in economic terms, in the higher organic composition of capital, in the increasing proportion of constant capital to variable capital in the total capital.[3] This change in the ratio C:V expresses the changing image of manufacturing industry, from handicraft production and the early capitalist factory, with its cramped working space and the workers crowded around a few small machines, to the modern factory in which the few diminutive human figures, visible here and there behind the gigantic frames of automatic machines, seem to be continually disappearing.

Technological development also brings about a change in the component elements of constant capital. Fixed capital increases more rapidly than does circulating capital. The following account illustrates this point:

Technical advances in the smelting process have led to an increase in the size of firms and to an ever greater concentration of capital. Ac-

cording to Lürmann, *Die Fortschritte im Hochofenbetrieb seit 50
Jahren*, the cubic capacity of furnaces has increased since 1852 by a
ratio of 1:4.8, the productivity per furnace by 1:33.3, and the productivity per ton of output by 1:7.

In 1750, 14 Silesian charcoal fired blast furnaces together produced
25,000 cwts of pig-iron, and in 1799 the two Königshütten coke fired
furnaces projected an annual output of 40,000 cwts. Oechelhäuser in
1852 boasted a daily output of 50,000 to 60,000 Prussian pounds.
The most recent records per day and per furnace are: Gewerkschaft
Deutscher Kaiser (Thyssen), 518 tons; Ohio Steel Co. No.3, 806
tons. In other words, the American furnace is producing in about 30
hours what a Silesian furnace previously produced in a year, and, in
36 hours, the same amount that 14 Silesian furnaces produced annually 150 years ago.

Accordingly the investment costs of a furnace have risen enormously. The Königshütten furnaces mentioned above were valued at
40,000 thalers, or about 20,000 marks, investment per ton of daily
output. In 1887, according to Wedding, this figure was down to between 5,400 to 6,000 marks per ton of daily output, with an investment of almost 1 million marks per furnace. Recently, however, the
costs per ton of daily output have risen again to about 10,000 marks
as a result of the introduction of many new devices and the almost
complete elimination of manual labour. This means that an average
250-ton furnace in the Ruhr today costs 2,500,000 marks, while the
giant American furnaces have devoured as much as 6,000,000 marks.

Except in Siegerland [Alsace-Lorraine – Ed.] and Upper Silesia
there are scarcely any furnaces in Germany today with a daily output capacity of less than 100 tons. The minimum annual output of a
newly constructed furnace must be set at least at 30,000 to 40,000
tons, but there are considerable advantages in operating several furnaces, hence the endeavour to increase the number of furnaces belonging to a single enterprise. In this way, general overhead costs
(administration, laboratories, maintenance engineers) as well as expenditure on necessary reserve machines (blast engines, air heaters)
can be spread over a larger output. Only by owning several furnaces
can an enterprise also use one of them year in, year out, exclusively
for the production of one type of pig-iron. By this means the
troublesome problem of converting a furnace from the production of
one type of pig-iron to another disappears, making it possible to
construct furnaces which are specially designed to produce a particular kind of pig-iron. Finally, it becomes economically feasible to
utilize modern inventions (controlled feeding of raw materials, cast-

ing machines, mixers, furnace generators) when production figures are high and several furnaces are available.[4]

It is interesting to compare, with this branch of industry in which there is an extremely high organic composition of capital, another branch which also makes extensive use of machinery, but in which, owing to different technical conditions, there is a considerably lower organic composition of capital.

The amount of capital required for the manufacture of shoes can be illustrated by taking the example of a factory which has a daily output of 600–800 pairs of shoes, half of which are sewn and half nailed:

Buildings	100,000 marks
Site	50,000
Steam engine (50 h.p.)	21,000
Electrical installations	20,000
Manufacturing machinery and other equipment	80,000
Lasts	25,000
Fixed capital	296,000 marks

If we assume that the circulating (working) capital is turned over twice a year we get the following:

Raw materials for 6 months	350,000 marks
Wages for 6 months	100,000
Other costs for 6 months	90,000
Circulating capital	540,000 marks

We may say, therefore, that in addition to a fixed capital of about 300,000 marks, a circulating capital of about 500,000 marks is required; and this factory employing 180 to 200 workers will need a total capital of 800,000 marks.[5]

In sharp contrast to this:

The total cost of building a new large combined Thomas plant with a capacity of 300,000/400,000 tons, in western Germany today, and purchasing its mineral fields site, would be at least:

1,000 hectares of iron ore fields	10,000,000 marks
6 coal fields in the Ruhr	3,000,000
Colliery with 1 million tons capacity, including coke installations	12,000,000
Blast furnace installations	10,000,000
Steel and rolling mills	15,000,000
Site, branch railway, workers' dwellings etc.	5,000,000

Total   55,000,000 marks

Such an enterprise would need 10,000 workers. In America an investment of 20 to 30 million dollars is indicated as necessary for a steel works with double this capacity (2,500 tons per day). By contrast, the capital invested in the whole Nassau iron industry in 1852 was 1,235,000 florins.[6]

This enormous inflation of fixed capital means, however, that once capital has been invested, its transfer from one sphere to another becomes increasingly difficult. Circulating capital is reconverted into money at the expiration of each turnover period, and can then be invested in any other branch of production; but fixed capital is tied up in the production process through a whole series of turnover periods. Its value is only gradually transferred to the product, and hence only gradually reconverted into money. The turnover time of the total capital is therefore prolonged. The larger the fixed capital, the greater its weight in the balance of investments, and the larger its proportion in relation to the total capital, the more difficult it becomes to realize the value embodied in it without very considerable losses, and to transfer it to a more advantageous sphere. This circumstance modifies the competition between capitals for investment outlets. In place of the old legal restrictions imposed by medieval tutelage, new economic restrictions have emerged which limit the mobility of capital, although admittedly they only affect the capital which has already been transformed into means of production, not the capital which still awaits investment. A second limitation consists in the fact that technical progress expands the scale of production, and that the increasing volume of constant capital, especially fixed capital, requires an ever greater absolute sum of capital in order to expand production itself on a corresponding scale or to establish new enterprises. The sums which are gradually accumulated from surplus value are far from adequate to be transformed into independent capitals. It is conceivable, therefore, that the influx of new capital is insufficient or arrives too late. The free movement of capital, however, is a necessary condition for the establishment of an equal rate of profit. This equality is violated whenever the ebb and flow of capital is impeded in any way. Since the tendency towards equality of profit is identical with the striving of the individual capitalist to maximize his profit, the removal of this limitation must also begin with the individual. This occurs through the mobilization of capital.

In order to centralize capital it suffices to create a capital association. But the mobilization of capital simultaneously broadens the extent of the capital which can be associated, for it makes the continuous reconversion of industrial capital (including fixed capital) into money capital as independent as possible from the actual reflux of capital at the end of the turnover period during which the fixed capital has to function. This reconversion is not possible, of course, on a society-wide scale, but is only available to a certain number of continually changing individual capitalists. Nevertheless, this constant reconvertibility into money endows capital with the fluidity of loan capital, that is, of money capital which is advanced for a certain period and then returns as a sum of money enhanced by interest. Thus it makes sums of money suitable for industrial investment which would otherwise not have functioned as industrial capital.

Such sums of money must either lie idle for a longer or shorter time in the hands of their owners, or be invested temporarily as pure loan capital. These sums change constantly in their composition, contract and expand, but a certain amount of such idle money is always available to be converted into industrial capital, and thus tied up. The continual changes in this sum of money are expressed in the continual changes in the ownership of shares. Its conversion into industrial capital, of course, occurs only once, and once for all. Idle capital is converted definitively into money capital, and this, in turn, into productive capital. The fresh sums of money which flow out of this fund of idle capital function as means for purchasing shares, and then as means of circulation for the turnover of shares. For the owners of the money which was initially converted into industrial capital they make possible the return of their money, which can now be applied to other purposes, after having served them in the meantime as capital. It should be noted, by the way, that when share prices rise, more money will be required, *ceteris paribus*, for the turnover of shares, and more money can then enter into circulation than was originally converted into industrial capital. Here we should observe that, as a rule, the share prices are higher than the value of the industrial capital into which the money was converted. The mobilization of capital, of course, has no effect upon the process of production. It affects only property, only creates the form for the transfer of property which functions in a capitalist way, the transfer of capital as capital, as a sum of money which breeds profit. Since it leaves production unaffected this transfer is in effect a transfer of property titles to profit. The capitalist is concerned only with profit, and is quite indifferent to its source.

He does not make a commodity, but what is in a commodity, namely profit.

One share is, therefore, just as good as another if, other things being equal, it brings the same profit. Every share is thus valued according to the profit it brings. The capitalist who buys shares, buys just the same stake in the profit as does any other capitalist who pays the same amount of money. Hence, at the individual level, the mobilization of capital ensures that the equalization of the rate of profit is realized for every capitalist. But this happens only in the case of the individual, since for him the inequalities which really exist are effaced when he buys shares. In reality, these inequalities persist, as does the tendency to balance them out.

The mobilization of capital does not affect the real tendency of capital to equalize the rate of profit. The constant effort of individual capitalists to maximize their profits remains, and now shows itself in the form of larger dividends and higher share prices, which indicate the proper direction for new capital investment. The level of profit achieved, once the business secret of the individual enterprise, is now more or less adequately expressed in the level of dividends, and facilitates the decision as to where to invest new capital. For example, if a capital of 1,000 million marks in the iron industry makes a profit of 200 million marks, whereas the same capital in another industry makes only 100 million marks, then assuming a capitalization of 5 per cent, the market price of the iron shares will be 4,000 million marks, and that of the other shares 2,000 million marks. In this way, the difference is obliterated for the individual owners. But this will not deter new capital from seeking investment in the iron industry, where it can make above-average profits. It is the share system, in fact, which facilitates the flow of capital into such areas, not only because, as has already been pointed out, it removes the difficulty presented by the large amounts of capital required, but also because the capitalization of the extra profit in this sphere holds out the promise of large promoter's profits, and encourages the banks to participate in this branch of production. The disparities in the rates of profit take the form, in this case, of differences in the amount of promoter's profit, but they are then evened out by the flow of newly accumulated quantities of surplus value into those spheres which have the highest promoter's profit.

Similarly the mobilization of capital does not affect the difficulties which obstruct the equalization of the rate of profit. On the other hand, however, the combination of capitals which always accompanies their mobilization removes the limitations which arise from the magnitude of the capitals required for new investment. With the increasing wealth of capitalist society, and the ability to combine many individual sums of money, the size of an enterprise is no longer an obstacle to its establishment. The result is that the equalization of the rate of profit is possible, increasingly, only through the influx of new capital into those spheres in which the rate of profit is above the average, whereas the withdrawal of capital from those branches of production which have a large amount of fixed capital is extremely difficult. In the latter case the capital can only be reduced by a process of gradual obsolescence of old installations, or by the destruction of the capital in the event of bankruptcy.

At the same time the extension of the scale of production gives rise to a further difficulty. A new business in a highly developed sphere of capitalist production must be established from the outset on a very large scale, and its establishment will at once increase enormously the output of that branch of industry. Technological imperatives do not allow the careful and discriminating increase of production which might be indicated by the capacity of the market. The rapid spurt in production may have an over-compensating effect on the rate of profit, which from having been above the average, may now fall below the average.

Thus obstacles to the tendency to equalize rates of profit emerge, and they increase as capitalism develops. The strength of these obstacles varies, of course, in different spheres in accordance with the composition of capital, and in particular with the relative proportion of fixed to total capital. The difficulties are greatest in the most advanced branches of capitalist production, in the heavy industries, where fixed capital is by far the most important factor, and where it is most difficult to withdraw capital once it has been invested.

What effect does this have on the rate of profit in these spheres? One might conceivably argue that since these industries require a very large initial capital, such as few people possess, there will be less competition and a higher profit. This argument, however, is only valid for the period when capital still functioned in an individual capacity. The possibility of combining capitals easily overcomes this limitation. The fact that a very large amount of capital is required presents no impediment to obtaining it. On the other hand, in such branches of industry, it is wellnigh impossible to equalize the rate of profit by withdrawing capital, and extremely difficult to write off the capital. These highly developed industries are precisely the ones in which competition eliminated the small firms most rapidly, or in which there were no small firms to begin with (as in many branches of the electrical industry). Not only does the large firm predominate, but these large, capital-intensive concerns tend to become more equally matched, as the technical and economic differences which would give some of them a competitive advantage are steadily reduced. The competitive struggle is not one between the strong and the weak, in which the latter are destroyed and the excess capital in that sphere is eliminated, but a struggle between equals, which can remain indecisive for a long time, imposing equal sacrifices on all the contending parties. The enterprises involved must all find ways of continuing the struggle, if the whole immense capital invested in each of them is not to depreciate in value. Consequently, it has become extremely difficult, in this sphere, to ease the situation by writing off capital; and at the same time the establishment of any new enterprise, because of the high production capacity which it must possess from the outset, has a powerful influence upon supply. A situation may easily develop, in these areas, in which the rate of profit remains below the average over a long period, and this situation is all the more dangerous, the lower the average rate of profit. The decline in the rate of profit which is associated with the development of capitalist production continually narrows the range within which production is still profitable. If the rate of profit is only 20 per cent, as compared with a previous rate of 40 per cent, a much smaller decline in price is enough to eliminate the profit entirely and defeat the very purpose of capitalist production. It is just these industries, with their large amounts of fixed capital, which are particularly vulnerable to competition and to the resulting decline in the rate of profit, while at the same time they find it increasingly difficult to change the established distribution of capital resources. Assuming free competition, the rate of profit which emerges in such industries may well be below the average, and it can be equalized only very gradually, if the influx of new capital comes to an end and consumption slowly increases as a result of the growth of population. The tendency toward a lower rate of profit may be reinforced by the fact that new capital (share capital) can only expect to receive, from the outset, a rate of profit below the average.

On the other side, a lower-than-average rate of profit will be the rule in those spheres in which individual capital is still dominant and the capital required is relatively small. These spheres attract capital sums which cannot compete in the advanced sectors of industry, and which are too small to allow their owners to invest them as interest or dividend-bearing capital. They are the spheres of retail trade and petty capitalist production, characterized by a bitter competitive struggle and the continual destruction of old capital which is at once replaced by new capital; spheres populated by those elements in society who always have one foot in the proletariat, are always threatened by bankruptcy, and of whom only a few gradually develop into big capitalists. These are the sectors of production which, in very diverse ways, are increasingly forced into a position of indirect dependence upon big business.

Aside from the fact that these sectors of production are overcrowded, there is another reason for the reduction of their rate of profit. There is savage competition for trade, which involves large expenditures to accelerate the turnover of goods and increase sales. Large advertising campaigns are undertaken and hordes of salesman are sent out. Ten salesmen battle for every customer. All this requires money, which swells the capital in these sectors, but since it is not used productively and does not increase profit, the rate of profit, which must now be calculated on this larger capital, declines.

Thus we see how, for entirely different reasons, the rate of profit tends to be depressed below the average at both poles of capitalist development. Where capital is sufficiently powerful a counter tendency emerges in order to overcome this trend. The final outcome is the abolition of free competition, and a trend towards the maintenance of a lasting inequality of rates of profit, until eventually this inequality itself is eliminated by the removal of the division between different sectors of production.[7]

The tendency which thus arises within industrial capital, and more particularly in its most developed sectors, is given a further impetus by the interests of bank capital. We have seen that concentration in industry also promotes a concentration of the banks, which is reinforced by the specific conditions of development of the banking business. We have also noted how bank capital can expand industrial credit by the issue of shares, and encouraged by the prospect of promoter's profit acquires an ever increasing interest in the financing of enterprises. Other things being equal, promoter's profit depends upon the overall level of profit. Hence bank capital becomes directly interested in industrial profits. As concentration proceeds in banking, so the range of industrial enterprises in which the bank participates as a supplier of credit, and as a financing agency, grows.

An industrial enterprise which enjoys technical and economic superiority can count upon dominating the market after a successful competitive struggle, can increase its sales, and after eliminating its competitors, rake in extra profits over a long period, which more than compensate it for the losses sustained in the competitive struggle; but the bank has other considerations in mind. The triumph of one enterprise means defeat for the others, in which the bank is equally interested. These enterprises had drawn heavily upon bank credit and the borrowed capital is now endangered. The competitive struggle itself involved all the enterprises in losses. The bank had to curtail its credit and forego profitable financial transactions, for which the victory of one of the enterprises provides no compensation. A powerful enterprise of this kind is an adversary from which the bank cannot earn very much. In general, it can only stand to lose from competition among enterprises which are its customers. Hence the bank has an overriding interest in eliminating competition among the firms in which it participates. Furthermore, every bank is interested in maximum profit, and other things being equal, this will be achieved by the complete elimination of competition in a particular branch of industry. That is why the banks strive to establish monopolies. In this way the tendency of both bank capital and industrial capital to eliminate competition coincides. At the same time, the increasing power of bank capital enables it to attain this goal even if it is opposed by some enterprises which, on the basis of particularly favourable technical conditions, would perhaps still prefer competition. Industrial capital has bank capital to thank for eliminating competition at a stage of economic development in which, without intervention, free competition would still prevail.[8]

These general tendencies to restrict competition are supplemented by other tendencies which arise from certain phases of the industrial cycle. It should be noted, first, that during a period of depression the drive to increase profits asserts itself with particular strength. In times of prosperity demand exceeds supply, as is shown by the fact that output is sold long before it has been produced.[9] But it should also be noted that during such a period demand frequently has a speculative character. People buy in the expectation that prices will continue to rise, and while the rise in prices restricts consumer demand it stimulates that of speculators. If demand exceeds supply the market price is determined by the least efficient enterprises, and those which have more favourable conditions of production realize an extra profit. Entrepreneurs are a tightly knit group, even without any formal agreement.

The contrary is true in a depression, when there is a scramble to save whatever can be saved, and everyone acts without regard to others.

That side of competition which is momentarily the weaker is also that in which the individual acts independently of the mass of his competitors and often works against them, whereby the dependence of one upon the other is impressed upon them, while the stronger side always acts more or less unitedly against its antagonist. If the demand for this particular commodity is larger than the supply, then one buyer outbids another within certain limits, and thereby raises the price of the commodity for all of them above the market price, while on the other hand the sellers unite in trying to sell at a high price. If, vice versa, the supply exceeds the demand, someone begins to dispose of his goods at a cheaper rate and the others must follow, while the buyers unite in their efforts to depress the market price as much as possible below the market value. The common interest is appreciated only so long as each gains more by it than without it. And common action ceases as soon as this or that side becomes the weaker, when each one tries to get out of it by his own devices with as little loss as possible. Again, if someone produces more cheaply and can sell more goods, thus assuming more room on the market by selling below the current market price, or market value, he does it, and thereby he begins an action which gradually compels the others to introduce the cheaper mode of production and reduces the socially necessary labour to a new and lower level. If one side has the advantage, everyone belonging to it gains. It is as though they had exerted their common monopoly. If one side is the weaker, then anyone may try on his own to be the stronger (for instance, anyone working with lower costs of production) or at least to get off as easily as possible, and, in that case, he does not care in the least for his neighbour, although his actions affect not only himself, but also all his fellow strugglers.[10]

Thus a contradiction arises: the restriction of competition can be accomplished most easily when it is least necessary, namely in a period of prosperity, because the agreement among producers then only sanctions an accomplished fact. Conversely, during a depression, when the restriction of competition is most essential, it becomes extremely difficult to conclude any agreement. This accounts for the fact that cartels are most easily organized in periods of prosperity, or at least after the end of a depression, but frequently collapse during a depression, unless they are very strictly organized.[11] It is also clear that monopolistic combines will control the market much more effectively in good years than in times of depression.[12]

Besides the tendencies which give rise to a protracted decline in the rate of profit and in its average level, which can only be overcome by eliminating their cause – competition – there is also the phenomenon of a fall in the rate of profit in one industry resulting from an increase of profit in another. Whereas the first kind of decline is due to long-term causes, the second arises from the conditions of the industrial cycle; and while the first will eventually occur in all branches of advanced capitalist production, the second will only affect particular branches of production. Finally, while the former results from competition within an industry, the latter originates in the relation between different branches of industry in which one supplies the raw materials of the other.

In times of prosperity production expands. This expansion occurs most rapidly where the amounts of capital involved are relatively small and production can be increased quickly at many points. To a certain extent this rapid expansion of production checks the rise in prices, notably in a large part of the finished goods industry. On the other hand, production cannot be expanded so rapidly in the extractive industries, where sinking a new shaft, or installing new blast furnaces, requires a comparatively long period of time.[13] During the initial phase of prosperity the increasing demand is met by a more intensive use of the existing productive capacity. But at the height of the boom demand from the manufactured goods industries increases more rapidly than the output of the extractive industries. Raw material prices therefore rise more rapidly than those of manufactured goods. The rate of profit in extractive industries thus increases at the expense of the processing industries, and the latter may be still further impeded by the shortage of raw materials in their efforts to take advantage of the boom.

In a depression the situation is reversed. The drain of money and the curtailment of production are more marked and produce greater losses in the industries which supply raw materials than in the manufacture of finished goods. The rate of profit in the former industries therefore remains below the average for a longer period of time, and this is a factor which contributes to restoring the rate of profit in the processing industries to its normal level, whereas in the production of raw materials the depression is more profound and prolonged. The crisis in the iron and steel industry of the United States between 1874 and 1878 shows how acute and prolonged such depressed conditions may be under a regime of free competition. Pig-iron prices in Philadelphia fell from $42.75 in 1873 to a low of $17.63 in 1878.[14] The violent price fluctuations in the course of an industrial cycle are also illustrated by the following figures, bearing in mind that costs of production of pig-iron generally declined during this period: Base ore No. 1 Bessemer-Hematite fell continuously from $6.00 in 1890 until it reached a low of $2.90 in 1895. Messabi-Bessemer sold at $2.25 in 1894; non-Bessemer at $1.85. This was followed by a brief upswing in the steel industry, and immediately the price of these ores rose to $4.00, $3.25 and $2.40 respectively.[15] Bessemer pig-iron in Pittsburgh was priced at $2.37 in 1884, $10.13 in 1897, $20.67 in 1902, $13.76 in 1904. The best English pig-iron sold at $10.86 in 1888, $11.30 in 1895, $20.13 in 1900, $13.02 in 1903.[16] Levy provides the following instructive table to show the price relationship between raw materials and manufactured pig-iron during the downswing:

	Price of 2240 lbs Bessemer pig-iron	Price of 2240 lbs Lake Superior ore	Price of 2000 lbs coke	Price of 4122 lbs ore plus 2423 lbs coke	Difference in price between pig-iron and ore plus coke
Year	$	$	$	$	$
1890	18.8725	6.00	2.0833	13.56	5.31
1891	15.9500	4.75	1.8750	11.01	4.94
1892	14.3667	4.50	1.8083	10.47	3.99
1893	12.8963	4.00	1.4792	9.15	3.72
1894	11.3775	2.75	1.0583	6.34	5.04
1895	12.7167	2.90	1.3250	6.94	5.78
1896	12.1400	4.00	1.8750	9.63	2.51
1897	10.1258	2.65	1.6167	6.84	3.29

We can see from these figures the kind of situation which these firms, wholly dependent on the flow of coal and ore, found themselves in after 1890. The price of raw materials did indeed fall appreciably, but the difference between their costs and the price of the finished product declined even more, so that the situation of the consumers of raw materials deteriorated greatly. The old tendency was at work again whereby the price of pig-iron declined more rapidly and steeply than that of the raw materials, and this tendency, as I indicated, led to the combination of enterprises.[17]

This discrepancy in rates of profit has to be overcome, and can only be overcome by a union of the extractive industries with the processing industries; that is, by the formation of combines. The impetus to combination will vary, of course, according to the phase of the business cycle. In times of prosperity it will come from the processing firms, which in that way overcome the problem of high raw material prices or shortages. In a depression, the producers of raw materials will attach processing plants to their own enterprise in order to avoid having to sell their raw material below the price of production. They will process it themselves, and realize a larger profit in the finished product. Stated in general terms, there is a tendency for that branch of business which is less profitable at any given time to attach itself to that which is more profitable.[18]

The various types of combination may be distinguished in terms of the way in which they are formed. Downward integration, for example, is illustrated by a rolling mill which acquires blast furnaces and coal mines; upward integration by a coal mine which buys blast furnaces and rolling mills. Or there may occur a 'mixed' type of combination in which a steel plant acquires coal mines on one side and rolling mills on the other.

It is, therefore, the differences in rates of profit which lead to combinations. An integrated firm can eliminate fluctuations in the rate of profit, whereas one that is not integrated sees its profit reduced to the advantage of some other firm.

Another advantage of combination is that it makes possible the elimination of commercial profit, and an increase in industrial profit by the amount that is thus saved. The elimination of commercial profit becomes possible when industrial concentration is well advanced. The function of commerce – that of integrating the activities which are fragmented among individual capitalist firms, thus enabling the demand of other industrial capitalists to be satisfied in the required quantities – becomes superfluous. A weaver prefers to obtain his different kinds and qualities of yarn from one yarn dealer rather than to deal with a host of individual spinners. Equally, the spinner prefers to sell his whole output to one dealer, rather than to a number of weavers. In this way circulation time and circulation costs are saved and the reserve capital reduced.

It is a somewhat different matter in the case of large integrated firms which produce standardized goods (mass consumption goods) and where the production of one branch of the enterprise meets the demand of another branch. Commerce then becomes entirely superfluous. The merchant and his profit can be eliminated, and he is eliminated by such combinations of enterprises. The elimination of commercial profit is peculiar to a combine as distinct from an association of businesses of the same kind, between which no commercial relations have developed in the natural course of events. Commercial profit, however, is simply a part of the total profit, and its disappearance increases the industrial profit proportionately. As long as the integrated concerns compete with those which remain independent, this increased profit gives them a competitive advantage.

If the rates of profit were the same for both types of concern, and equal to the average rate of profit, the combine would not enjoy any initial advantage, since it could only realize the average rate of profit. But combination smoothes out the fluctuations of the business cycle and so assures a more stable rate of profit for the integrated firm. Second, it eliminates the middleman's trade. Third, by the opportunity it offers for the introduction of technical improvements, it achieves an extra profit as compared with the non-integrated concerns. Fourth, it strengthens the competitive position of the integrated concerns as compared with others during a severe depression, when raw material prices fall less rapidly than the prices of finished goods.

Combination, which involves a contraction of the social division of labour, at the same time as it gives an impetus to the division of labour within the new integrated concern, extending increasingly to management functions as well, has been a feature of the capitalist mode of production from the beginning.

Finally, just as manufacture arises in part from the combination of various handicrafts, so too it develops into a combination of various manufactures. The large English glass manufacturers, for instance, make their own earthenware melting pots, because on the quality of these depends, to a great extent, the success or failure of the process. The manufacture of one of the means of production is here united with that of the product. On the other hand, the manufacture of the product may be united with other manufactures, of which that product is the raw material, or with the products of which it is itself subsequently mixed. Thus we find the manufacture of flint glass combined with that of glass cutting and brass founding; the latter for the metal settings of various articles of glass. The various manufactures so combined form more or less separate departments of a larger

manufacture, but are at the same time independent processes, each
with its own division of labour. In spite of the many advantages
offered by this combination of manufactures, it never grows into a
complete technical system on its own foundation. That happens only
on its transformation into an industry carried on by machinery.[19]

The enormous strides made by combination during the most recent
phase of capitalist development are attributable to powerful economic
forces, and particularly to the formation of cartels. However, once a
combination has come into existence as a result of economic forces it will
very soon present opportunities for the introduction of technical improvements in the process of production. One need only consider, for example,
the linking of blast furnaces with processing plants, which first made
possible an efficient utilization of blast furnace gases as a motive power.
These technical advantages, once achieved, in turn become a powerful
motive for forming combinations where purely economic factors would not
have brought them about.

By combination, therefore, we mean an association of capitalist
enterprises in which one supplies the raw materials for another; and we
distinguish this kind of association, which arises from variations in the rate
of profit in different sectors of industry, from the association of enterprises
within the same branch of industry. The latter is formed with the object of
raising the rate of profit in that branch of industry above its sub-average
level by suppressing competition. In the first case the rates of profit in the
different branches of industry to which the enterprises belonged before they
were combined do not undergo any change. The different rates of profit
remain, except for the integrated enterprise itself. In the second case a rise
in profits is expected in this branch of industry as a result of decreasing
competition. Theoretically, this can happen even when only two enterprises unite, either because they put an end to the competition between
themselves, or because the combination of the two enterprises is large
enough to dominate the market and by this means to raise prices, thus
limiting competition also for the other enterprises. Of course, a situation
may also arise in which the unified enterprises use their more powerful
position chiefly in order to beat down their rivals in competition, and only
after this goal has been achieved does the rate of profit begin to rise.

The unification of enterprises can take two forms. The enterprises may
retain a formal independence, and affirm their association only by
agreements, in which case we are faced with a 'consortium' (*Interessenge-
meinschaft*). If, however, the enterprises are dissolved in a new enterprise,
this is called a 'merger' (*Fusion*). Both a consortium and a merger may be
either partial, in which case free competition continues to prevail in the
branch of industry concerned, or monopolistic.[20]

A consortium comprising as many enterprises as possible, which is intended to raise prices, and hence profits, by excluding competition as completely as possible, is a cartel. Or, in other words, a cartel is a monopolistic consortium. A merger which is designed to attain the same end, by the same means, is a trust. A trust, then, is a monopolistic merger.[21]

Furthermore, a consortium and a merger may both be either horizontally integrated, i.e. encompass enterprises in the same branch of production, or vertically integrated, i.e. link enterprises which operate at successive stages of production.* We therefore refer to horizontal or vertical mergers and consortia, or to horizontal or vertical cartels and trusts. It should also be noted that consortia are quite frequently formed today, not by formal contracts, but through personal connections which express relations of interdependence among capitalist firms. Mergers and consortia are possible in commerce and banking as well as in industry. Such associations occur in the same sphere of activity, and I therefore refer to them as 'homospheric'. But combinations can also be formed which link, for example, a commercial enterprise with a bank, as happens when a bank establishes a commodities department, or a department store opens a deposit bank. Similarly, an industrial enterprise may establish a commercial firm; thus, for example, shoe manufacturers in large cities often establish retail shops to sell directly to the final consumers. In this case, I refer to the combinations as 'heterospheric'.

It should be noted here that the various branches of industry are no more immutable than are the species of the natural world. Combination, carried to its logical conclusion, only constructs a comprehensive branch of industry out of previously separated branches. It is easily conceivable that the iron industry will come to constitute a single branch of industry comprising everything from the mining of coal and ore to the production of rails and wire, since every single iron works will encompass all these kinds of production and the specialized enterprise will have disappeared. In such a branch of industry all the means of limiting competition become possible, from the consortium to the trust.

Vertical integration, whether in the form of a consortium or a merger, does not restrict competition, but only strengthens the combined firm in its competition with those which remain independent. On the other hand, horizontal integration, even if it is partial, always reduces competition, and if it is complete, eliminates it altogether. Aside from their economic advantages, the combine, the merger, and the trust also enjoy the technical advantages which characterize large firms as against smaller ones. These vary according to the nature of the enterprise and the industry. Such technical advantages themselves may be enough to lead to the formation of

---

*Hilferding uses the terms *homogen* and *kombiniert* for what is referred to in English as horizontal and vertical integration. [Ed.]

combinations and mergers, but consortia and cartels, on the other hand, only arise from purely economic advantages.

As a rule all these unifications of industrial enterprises are facilitated by the common interests which link the enterprises with a bank. For example, a bank which has a strong interest in a coal mine will use its influence with an iron works to persuade the latter to purchase its coal from that mine. This is an embryonic form of combination. Or the bank's interest in two similar enterprises which are engaged in fierce competition in various markets, may lead it to attempt some agreement between them, and this prepares the way for a horizontal integration in the form of a consortium or a merger.

This kind of intervention by the banks expedites and facilitates a process which is implicit in the trend toward industrial concentration. But the banks employ different means to achieve this end. The outcome of the competitive struggle is anticipated; hence, unnecessary waste and destruction of productive forces is avoided, but on the other hand there is no immediate concentration of ownership such as usually results from competition. The owner of the other factory is not expropriated. There is simply a concentration of production and enterprises without concentration of ownership. Just as on the stock exchange there is concentration of ownership without any concentration of production, so there now takes place in industry a concentration of production without any concentration of ownership; a striking expression of the fact that the function of ownership has become increasingly separated from the function of production.

On the other hand the bank's involvement in these processes means, first, greater security for the capital it has lent as credit, and second, the opportunity for profitable business in buying and selling shares, floating new share issues, and the like. For the unification of these enterprises means larger profits for all of them. A part of this increased profit is capitalized and appropriated by the bank. The bank is interested in the process of unification not only as a credit institution, but also and primarily as a financial institution.

The growing concentration also creates obstacles to its own further progress. The larger, stronger, and more similar the enterprises, the less chance there is that any one of them will be able to expand its production by eliminating one of the others through competition. Furthermore, the low rate of profit and the fear that prices, which are low anyway, will be further depressed by an increase in production, prevents expansion, which might otherwise be desirable on technical grounds. But the advantages of large-scale production cannot be dispensed with in depressed market conditions, and a way out is offered by the unification of previously separate enterprises into a larger concern by means of a merger.

How large a share of the total production must a monopolistic combination have in order to dictate the market price? There is no general answer to this question valid for all branches of production. Yet there is a basis for an answer if we recall what was previously said about the differences in the behaviour of competitors in periods of prosperity and depression. When business is good, and demand exceeds supply, the price of the product will be as high as possible, and at such times outsiders sell above rather than below the cartel price. It is different during a depression when supply exceeds demand. This is the time when it must be made clear whether or not the combination does really control the market. This will be so only if its output is absolutely indispensable to meet the requirements of the market. It will only sell if its price is met, and this price must be met simply because the market cannot dispense with the output of the cartel. The latter can then sell the quantity lacking in the market, at its own chosen price. But it must restrict production sufficiently not to flood the market, whereas outsiders are able to dispose of their entire output. This kind of price policy is most likely to be followed first in those branches of production in which restriction of output does not involve too great a sacrifice, that is to say, particularly where human labour constitutes one of the main elements and the depreciation of constant capital does not play a very important part. Both these conditions prevail in the extractive industries. Ore and coal do not depreciate and human labour is the main factor in their production. Second, this price policy can be followed in the case of products, the consumption of which contracts only slightly during a depression. When both the above-mentioned features are absent, however, the cartel is obliged to make price concessions to meet the competition of outsiders if it is to maintain its sales. This is the point at which a cartel which does not dominate the total production loses its control over the market and free competition is re-established.

The necessity of curtailing production makes for higher production costs on a diminished output and a lower rate of profit; and so runs counter to the tendency to maintain prices even during a depression, which reflects the cartel's domination of the market. The cartel can avoid this restriction of production, however, if it meets only the average demand of the market, and leaves the satisfaction of cyclical demand to the outsiders. But this is possible only if the outsiders cannot produce more than is required by the additional demand in a period of prosperity (for otherwise there is a danger that the sales of the cartel itself would be restricted), and second, the outsiders' costs of production are higher than those of the cartel. Only under these conditions would price levels that are still profitable for the cartel drive its competitors out of the market and guarantee its own sales. In other words, it is essentially the outsiders upon whom the entire burden of business fluctuations is imposed. The cartel makes large additional profits during periods of prosperity, and normal profits during a depression, when its competitors are eliminated. Under such conditions it is undoubtedly in the interest of the monopolistic combination not to prevent the activities of outsiders altogether, as it would have the power to do in many cases, thanks to its dominant position.

In what circumstances can production by outsiders be expected to operate at such a disadvantage? This may be the case when the size and technical equipment of the monopolistic combination ensure its superiority, but such advantages are often transient or not sufficiently great. It is a different matter when the cartels concerned have at their disposal more favourable natural conditions of production, and can therefore connect a natural monopoly with an economic one. Such, for example, are the cartels which have acquired particularly high-grade coal or ore mines, or advantageous water-power sites, leaving the outsiders at a disadvantage. The latter will then be unable to increase their production sufficiently to endanger the cartel's sales, and they will only be able to produce at all when the high prices during a period of prosperity cover their high costs of production.

The steel trust provides an excellent example of this kind of policy. The corporation could easily increase its output, but it does not do so, simply in order to avoid the burden of overproduction during a depression.

The large combined enterprises in the pig-iron industry consider it desirable to have a basic output which will always find a market. In order to achieve this, they allow the outsiders who do not belong to the combine, and whose costs of production are high, to expand steadily during times of lively demand and even give them more work by passing on orders to them. With rising prices the backward firms become profitable again, a speculative fever leads to the establishment of new independent concerns, and in short, production increases at a higher level of costs compared with the previous very low costs. This trend continues until the increasing demand is satisfied and prices begin to fall again. Now the blast furnaces which were brought into operation during the boom disappear from the market if their costs of production are too high, since they cannot show a profit. Only the firms with the lowest costs of production survive, because they are still able to produce profitably; and these are above all the steel trust, the large combines, and here and there a particularly well favoured, independent blast furnace concern.

This is how the large enterprises, and above all this corporation, establish a pattern of production which, in the main, can operate at a profit and find a market for its output in bad times as well as good. During good times, the corporation is not hurt by the increased competition of outsiders, for if it undertook to meet the increased demand itself it would suffer more keenly from the effects of overproduction in the subsequent recession, whereas the outsiders now have to bear the brunt of it.[22]

A somewhat different situation prevails, to take one example, in the case of the Rhenish-Westphalian Coal Syndicate. Here outsiders are not very important. In 1900 the syndicate mines accounted for 87 per cent of total production in the Dortmund Oberberg district, those outside the syndicate for only 13 per cent. The syndicate therefore controlled the market and prices. That is why it preferred to maintain the prosperity prices of 1900 even during the crisis of 1901, and to restrict production. As a result, the outsiders could increase their output somewhat in 1901 and 1902, whereas the output of the syndicate, which attached more importance to maintaining prices, declined.[23]

On the other hand, a monopolistic combination is obliged to follow a different policy in cases where the expansion of production is not restricted by any natural monopolies, and where it can be increased far beyond the amount of the additional demand in a period of prosperity, while costs remain the same or even lower. Control of the market will then depend essentially upon whether the combine controls an overwhelming part of the total output; otherwise a depression would make the cartel valueless to its participants, and perhaps destroy it.

The presence or absence of a natural monopoly has a crucial influence upon price formation and costs of production, and hence also upon the stability and durability of a monopolistic combination and the extent of its power to control the market. It is a crucial determinant of the proportion of total production which the combine must have in its own hands in order to be able to dominate the market.

The degree of assurance that control of the market is being maintained may vary greatly. It will be greatest when an economic monopoly can be effectively reinforced by a natural monopoly. At the same time, an established monopolistic combine has a great advantage because its large capital funds allow it to keep massive resources tied up over long periods of time. The strength of the syndicates which produce raw materials is largely due to their monopolization of the natural conditions of production, which is also greatly facilitated, in most cases, by mining legislation.

An economic monopoly is bolstered by a legal monopoly through the possession of patent rights by the monopolistic combinations. In this case too, because of their larger capital resources, they are in a better position than their individual competitors to acquire new patents and so to strengthen their monopolistic position.[24]

An intermediate stage between a natural and legal monopoly, and a purely economic monopoly, is that which encompasses means of transport.

Hence the effort of the trusts to acquire control over both land and water transport. Nationalization of the means of transport reduces monopolistic power and, to a certain extent, slows down the concentration of enterprises and property. Economic monopoly as such becomes all the stronger the larger the amount of capital necessary in order to establish a new enterprise, and the closer the connection between the banks and the monopolistic combination becomes; for without the help of a bank, and certainly if the banks oppose it, a large industrial enterprise can scarcely remain viable today.

Cartels and trusts

The ways in which combinations of capitalist enterprises are formed have been considered from three aspects. The distinction between horizontal and vertical combinations is one of a purely technical kind, and we have observed how the formation of such combinations depends upon diverse technical and economic causes.

The distinction between partial and monopolistic combinations rests upon the difference in their position on the market; whether they determine prices, or on the contrary have to conform to market prices. In this connection it should be noted that the ability to control prices does not depend upon *all* enterprises of the same type being brought into a combination. It is enough if the combination controls that part of the output which is indispensable for meeting market demand during all phases of the business cycle, and can keep its costs of production lower than those of the outsiders. Only then will the restriction of production which is necessary in a depression fall upon the outsiders, while prices need only be reduced to the level where they cover the cartel's costs of production.

Finally, the distinction between a consortium and a merger is simply one of formal organization. The consortium is based upon an agreement between two or more previously independent enterprises, while a merger is the unification of two or more enterprises in a new enterprise. This contrast is only one of organizational form, and tells us nothing about the substance of the difference, which depends upon the content of the agreement upon which the consortium is based. At all events, an agreement limits in certain respects the independence of the participating enterprises, while in a merger their independence is abolished altogether. But there is no sharp line of distinction between limited independence and complete loss of independence. The more an agreement limits the independence of the enterprises taking part in a consortium, the more its economic consequences lead them towards a merger. Furthermore, the restrictions upon the independence of an enterprise may proceed in a number of different ways. First, the organization of an enterprise can be established contractually in such a way that its management is obliged to submit to supervision by a common, central body which restricts certain kinds of competition in the sphere of circulation by establishing uniform terms and conditions of payment, etc.; that is to say, by standardizing the 'conditions' on which trade is transacted. Subsequently, restrictions may be imposed which affect economic and business practices.

The terms of an agreement establishing a monopolistic consortium are defined by its purpose, which is to increase profit by raising prices. The simplest way of doing this is to enter into a price agreement. But prices are not arbitrary; they depend upon supply and demand. A mere price agreement will only be effective in periods of prosperity when prices tend to rise, and even then only to a limited extent. Higher prices encourage an expansion of production, the supply increases, and in the end the price agreement cannot be maintained, so that this type of cartel usually collapses, at the very latest when a depression arrives.[1]

If the cartel is to endure the agreement must go further and bring about a relationship between supply and demand such that the agreed market price can be maintained. It must therefore regulate the supply and set production quotas. The pursuit of such a policy is certainly in the interest of the cartel as a whole, but not always in that of the individual members, who could lower their production costs by expanding production, and are constantly tempted to circumvent the cartel regulations. The best protection against such evasions is to remove the function of selling the product from the members, and to assign it to a central sales agency of the cartel.

The greater certainty of control, however, is not the only consequence of such measures. They also suspend any direct dealings between the individual enterprises and their customers while the cartel is in existence, and so eliminate the commercial independence of these enterprises. The cartel thus binds its members together not only by the terms of the agreement, which can easily be broken or circumvented at any time, but by common economic arrangements. A member enterprise which leaves the cartel has to renew relations with its customers, re-establish its sales outlets; and such attempts may well fail, or succeed only at considerable cost. In this way the cartel acquires greater stability and permanence. A cartel which is transformed from a simple agreement among its member enterprises into a commercial unit through the elimination of their commercial independence is called a syndicate. The syndicate form of combination is possible, however, only if it is a matter of indifference to customers which of the cartelized enterprises they patronize, and this, in turn, presupposes a certain standardization of production, which is a prerequisite for the establishment of a more tightly knit, durable and disciplined organization such as a syndicate. Incidentally, this explains why it is much more difficult to cartelize enterprises which produce speciality articles, since they derive an extra profit from the use of trade marks, patents, and the like, and the elimination of competition is therefore less important for them. They are only forced to enter into a cartel or combination themselves in cases where the industries which supply them with raw materials have been cartelized. In general, cartelization brings about a greater simplification of production.[2]

In a rather simplified and schematic form the development of the substance of agreements in monopolistic consortia may be depicted as follows, though of course it should be borne in mind that one or other stage in the process may be missed out. The first, weakest form, which is in fact a preparatory stage, is that which Grunzel calls a 'cartel of conditions' [see footnote 2 – Ed.]. Next comes the joint regulation of prices, but in order to maintain the level of prices the appropriate supply must also be determined. Price regulation, if it is not to be simply spasmodic and transitory, therefore requires that production should be regulated. In order to prevent circumventions of the agreement, it has been found desirable to transfer responsibility for marketing from the individual enterprise to a collective body of all the enterprises, in the form of a sales office. Thus each enterprise loses its commercial independence and its direct contact with customers. The agreement is also maintained more effectively if the profits do not go to the enterprise which actually produced them, but are distributed among all the participants according to some predetermined formula. Similarly, the purchase of raw materials may also be undertaken on a collective basis. Finally, there may eventually be interference with the technical autonomy of the individual firms. Poorly equipped factories may be closed down, while others may be made to specialize in certain products for which they are especially suited by reason of their technical equipment or their proximity to appropriate markets.[3] All these developments can occur in consortia, through the conclusion of agreements. But this type of consortium differs from a merger only in the sense that its organization is more top-heavy. It is therefore misleading to regard a cartel and a trust as mutually exclusive alternatives. The cartel form of organization can limit the independence of the participating enterprises to such a degree that it becomes practically indistinguishable from a trust. The real question is rather what advantages are offered in return for the restriction of independence. If there are such advantages the trust has them from the very outset, whereas in the case of a cartel they depend upon the nature and consequences of the agreement on which it is based.[4]

The monopolistic association is an organization for economic domination, and there is therefore a close analogy with the organizations of state domination. The relation between cartel, syndicate, and trust thus resembles that between a confederation, a federal state and a unitary state. The manner of speaking which lauds the cartel as 'democratic' by contrast with the trust appears in all its absurdity if one thinks of applying the same notion to the late German confederation.

The trust has an advantage over the cartel in fixing prices. The cartel is obliged to base its fixed price on the price of production of the most expensive producer among its member firms, whereas for the trust there is only one uniform price of production in which the costs of the more efficient and less efficient concerns are averaged out. The trust can set a price which allows it to maximize its output and make up for its small profit per unit by the volume of its turnover. Furthermore, the trust can close down the less profitable concerns much more easily than can the cartel. When production has to be cut down, the trust can effect this exclusively in the high-cost enterprises, and thus reduce average costs of production; and conversely, when there is an expansion of production it can concentrate the increase in the technically more efficient firms. As a rule, the cartel has to distribute the increased production evenly among its member enterprises. In this way, the technically superior enterprises gain, from the prices fixed by the cartel, extra profits which are not averaged out through competition, since the cartel excludes this, and seem to assume the character of a differential rent. The difference from ground rent consists in the fact that the least efficient enterprise, unlike the worst agricultural land, is not needed in order to meet market demand. The marginal enterprise can be closed down if its production can be transferred to more efficient concerns. Since the cartel price is meanwhile maintained, however, increased production means extra profit for the low-cost producers, and it becomes profitable to discontinue production in the high-cost plants. But in that case the 'differential rent' disappears and only the high cartel profit remains.

Differences in cost of production are especially important in cartels which produce raw materials, because the amount of ground rent (or mine rent) is a crucial item in their production prices. In such cases, therefore, we find, on the one hand, a very marked tendency to close down the less profitable enterprises (specifically those which yield a smaller ground rent), and on the other, a tendency to maintain high prices, which in turn entails a relatively severe limitation of output. A natural monopoly also helps to make such a policy effective. High raw material prices then have an effect upon prices, and also upon the volume of production in the processing industries.

The capitalist monopolies and commerce

Capitalist combinations in industry have repercussions upon circulation and its mediation through commerce. I refer here to commerce as a specific economic category, and treat it as distinct from such technical functions as weighing, measuring, and transporting. Commodity production necessarily entails a multilateral change of position of commodities which is accomplished through purchase and sale. If these become independent functions of a unit of capital, then this capital is trading or commercial capital. Clearly, when these activities (which otherwise would have to be carried out by the producers themselves) become autonomous they do not thereby become value-creating operations, and merchants do not become producers. Nevertheless, the autonomy of commerce does effect a concentration of buying and selling, savings on storage and maintenance costs, etc. Commerce, in short, reduces the necessary circulation costs and so eliminates some of the unproductive expenses of production. But in order to engage in trade a sum of money is necessary which must then be converted into commodities. In capitalist society every sum of money takes on the character of capital, and if commercial functions are to become independent the money invested in commerce must become capital, that is, yield a profit. It is clear, however, that this profit does not arise from commerce, from the mere activity of buying in order to sell again, but is only appropriated there. The magnitude of the profit is determined by the amount of capital, for in an advanced capitalist society capitals of equal size bring equal profits. Nevertheless, this profit itself is derived from the profit created in production. The industrialists must hand over a part of the profit which was originally theirs to the merchants, and it must be large enough to attract the necessary capital into commerce.

Commerce, which antedates the generalization of commodity production, and hence the development of capitalism, is – like usury and loan capital – older than industrial capital, and provides the starting point of capitalist development, by bringing together the bulk of the monetary wealth of society. Through credit, which has always been an important means of establishing capitalist relations of dependence – frequently in the form of commodity credit – it made the old handicraft system of production dependent on it and thus launched capitalist domestic industries as well as the first manufacturing industries. The later development of industrial capital put an end to the dependence of industry upon commerce and separated the two activities.

The development of commerce itself is determined by two factors. On one side it is determined by the technical conditions of trade. Commerce assembles products from the various centres of production and eventually sells them to the final consumers. The more dispersed the population is, the more retail sales have to be divided up not only quantitatively, but also seasonally and geographically. The character of retail trade depends upon the income structure and the geographical concentration of the final consumers, and both these factors vary with the social development and social structure of a given country. It is precisely in respect of commercial techniques that the superiority of a large firm over a small one becomes evident. The costs of buying and selling, book-keeping, etc., do not increase by any means proportionately to the turnover. Hence, there is a trend toward concentration. On the other hand, it is the nature of commerce that as it comes closer to the final consumer sales become more fragmented in terms of place and time. The size of a commercial firm is thus limited by its proximity to the final consumer; and these limits, which are always elastic, tend to expand as a country develops, but have an influence, in all cases, upon the size of businesses. At every stage the trend toward larger firms asserts itself, but it varies in its strength and tempo. The need to decentralize commerce geographically is met by establishing branches of the same large firm. On the other hand, the concentration of population in cities allows retail trade to be concentrated in large department stores. But this is only the beginning of concentration. The technical requirements of trade link department stores themselves with large purchasing houses, which combine large numbers of department stores and come to control them financially to a greater or lesser extent. On the other hand, the enormous financial needs of the large department stores force them into a close relationship with the banks.[1]

Alongside this process of concentration, there is also a trend in retail trade to eliminate the independent trader in so far as the producers in the consumer goods industries themselves take over the sale of their products. This process is most advanced where a trust has completely eliminated the independent retail trade, as the American Tobacco Trust has done.[2]

On the other hand, there are obstacles which tend to retard the process of concentration. It is comparatively easy to open a small retail business – all the easier, the smaller it is – because credit is available (all that is needed being commodity credit) particularly when it is sought from producers, for whom it is a means of competition for markets. In these small retail businesses a low rate of profit prevails and this makes the tradesman into a mere agent of the capitalist, whose products he sells. Consequently, there is no strong economic motive for eliminating him.

Aside from these technical factors which play a role in the case of products destined for the final consumers, that is to say, in retail trade, the repercussions of the relationships within industry are of major importance, where it is a matter of the turnover of commodities among industrial capitalists themselves or between them and the wholesalers. Here concentration in industry reacts upon the development of commerce, which is obliged to adapt to it. The more concentrated industrial enterprises are, and the greater their output, the larger the capital required by the dealers who dispose of this output. Furthermore, as concentration reduces the number of industrial concerns, the more superfluous do dealers become, and the simpler does it appear for the large concentrated industrial concerns to enter directly into contact with each other without any independent merchant as an intermediary. Concentration in industry not only brings about concentration in commerce, but also makes it superfluous. There are fewer turnovers, because each individual turnover is larger, and increasingly the services of an independent merchant capitalist can be dispensed with. In this way, however, a part of the capital available in commerce becomes superfluous and can be withdrawn from circulation.

The capital invested in commerce is equal to the value of the annual social product, divided by the number of turnovers of commercial capital, and multiplied by the number of intermediate stages through which it passes before it reaches the final consumer. But this is only the amount of commercial capital in book-keeping terms. The greater part of commercial capital consists of credit. Commercial capital is used only to circulate commodities, but as we have seen, this circulation can be carried on, for the most part, without the use of actual money. Productive capitalists simply extend credit to each other, and the loans are later cancelled out. The actual merchant capital is very much smaller, and it is only from this capital that the merchant derives a profit. The industrialist's profit depends upon his entire capital, regardless of whether it is his own capital or borrowed capital, because it is productive capital. The merchant's profit depends only upon the capital which is actually used, for this is not productive capital, but functions simply as money or commodity capital. The use of credit in this case does not entail merely a partition of property and hence a division of the profit, but an absolute contraction of the capital and along with it a reduction of the profit which accrues to the commercial class and is paid to it by the industrial capitalists. Here, credit reduces directly the costs of circulation just as paper money does.

Commercial profit, however, is part of the total surplus value generated by production. Other things being equal, the larger the share which falls to commercial capital, the smaller will be the share of industrial capital. Thus there exists a conflict of interest between industrial and commercial capital. These conflicting interests lead to a struggle which ends with the victory of one of the parties and the subordination of the other in a relation of dependence. In any such struggle between capitalist interests, the deciding factor is the relative strength of the capitals involved, but this should not be conceived in purely quantitative terms. The whole preceding discussion shows that the form of the capital is also important. Other things being equal, control over money capital assures superiority, because both industrialists and merchants become increasingly dependent upon money capital as the credit system develops. Thus, in a variety of ways, the dependency of both industry and commerce is accomplished.

As long as free competition prevailed, commerce could exploit the competitive struggle among industrialists to its own advantage. This was especially true in those branches of industry in which production was still relatively widely dispersed among many firms, while commerce had reached a more advanced stage of concentration. Credit relations worked in the same direction. As long as credit was largely payment credit which the banks extended mainly to commercial capitalists, the merchants enjoyed a financial superiority, which they used in order to obtain advantageous prices, as well as favourable delivery and payment terms, from the producers. By this means the merchants were able to skim the cream from a period of prosperity, and to impose some of the losses during a depression on the producers. This was a time when there were constant complaints from industrialists about the dictatorship of the merchants. Later on, the behaviour of the merchants served the industrialists as a justification for the establishment of cartels. This situation changed fundamentally, however, with the change in the relations between the banks and industry, and with the rise of capitalist combinations in industry.

Partial industrial combinations reduce the amount of trade. Vertical combinations do this directly by making trading operations entirely superfluous. Horizontal combinations have the same effect as does concentration in general. Monopolistic combinations, on the other hand, tend to eliminate independent trading altogether. We have seen that real control of the market first becomes possible when commodities are sold through a central agency. But in order to regulate production in its branch of industry the central agency must be able constantly to estimate the likely volume of sales. Since consumption always depends on the level of prices, the monopolistic combine must be able to fix prices at every stage up to the final consumer, without any interference by independent elements. But these independent elements are precisely the merchants. If commercial operations, including the determination of prices, were left to the merchants, they would be in a position to exploit the market situation, which is the principal advantage of the cartel. They could hoard stocks for speculative purposes, and particularly during periods of prosperity sell them at higher prices. This would result, on the one hand, in a contraction of production, without any compensating benefits to the cartel in the form of a higher profit, and on the other hand, in the directors of the cartel misjudging the market if they planned their production solely on the basis of this speculative and perhaps misleading demand from the merchants. The monopolistic combination will therefore strive to eliminate all forms of independent commerce, since only then will it be able to bring its full influence to bear upon the level of prices.

As we have seen, however, cartelization itself already involves an intimate connection between industry and bank capital; hence the cartel is usually stronger and can dictate its own terms to commerce. Its aim in doing so will be to deprive commerce of its independence and to remove its power to fix prices. Thus cartelization will eliminate commerce as a sphere of capital investment. It restricts commercial operations, eliminating some of them entirely, and performing the others through its own salaried employees, the sales personnel of the cartel. Some former merchants, indeed, may well become agents for the cartel, which then prescribes exactly what their buying and selling prices should be, the difference between them constituting the commission for these 'merchants'. The level of this commission is no longer determined, however, by the average rate of profit, but is simply a wage fixed by the cartel.

But if the balance of power between the two forms of capital is different, the relationship between commerce and cartels may also be somewhat different. It is possible that conditions could be more favourable to concentration in commerce rather than in industry. In this case a small number of merchants would confront many industrial enterprises with comparatively small capitals who are dependent on the merchants for the sale of their products. The merchants are then able to make use of their greater resources to convert a part of their capital into industrial capital by participating financially in these enterprises. They can then take advantage of the dependent position of industry to compel the enterprises to sell to them at lower prices, and so increase their commercial profit at the expense of industrial profit. In recent years such relations of dependence have been developing quite rapidly in some consumer goods industries which sell their products to large capitalist department stores.

These relations of dependence reproduce, at a higher stage of capitalist development, the process which led to the emergence of capitalist domestic industry, in which the merchant displaced the artisan. But similar relations may also be found in industries which are ripe for cartelization. Here commercial capital, which is perhaps involved in a whole series of enterprises, can play the role which would otherwise be assumed by bank capital.

In these cases merchants participate directly in the cartel, but they do so because, in fact, they were already involved in industrial production through their financial participation.[3] In reality, nothing has changed. For here too commerce is deprived of its power to fix prices, and ceases to serve as a market for the industrialists, who now enter into direct relations with the consumers.

The monopolistic combination thus eliminates independent trade by making some commercial operations entirely unnecessary and by reducing the cost of the others. The reduction of those circulation costs which arise from the attempt to win over consumers to the products of a particular enterprise, at the expense of the sales of other enterprises, has the same effect. What is involved here is the outlay on sales representatives (in so far as their number is determined by the fragmentation of production among individual enterprises) and on advertising. Such outlays are unproductive costs of circulation. They produce profit for the individual entrepreneur to the extent that he succeeds in increasing his turnover. For the branch of production as a whole these outlays constitute a deduction from the profit which would otherwise accrue to it. Cartelization reduces these costs enormously, by limiting advertising to what is necessary for product recognition, and reducing the number of sales representatives to the minimum required for the performance of these diminished, simplified and accelerated trading operations.

Austria has experienced a unique development. For historical reasons a genuine capitalist wholesale trade has not developed fully here. In the mass consumer goods industries, particularly where speculation plays a role, as in the sugar trade, the bank has assumed the functions of the wholesale dealer. Bank capital could do this all the more easily since it involved tying up only very small amounts of capital. As a result bank capital acquires an interest in cartelization both as a dealer and as a supplier of credit. Austria, therefore, provides the clearest example of the direct and deliberate influence of bank capital upon cartelization. The bank then retains its function as a sales agent for the cartel and receives a fixed commission for these services. A similar trend has emerged recently in Germany. Thus, for example, the Schaaffhausen Bank has established its own commodities department for the sale of cartelized products.[4]

The outcome of the whole process is a reduction of the amount of commercial capital. But if the capital is reduced, so also is the amount of profit accruing to it, which derives, as we know, from industrial profit. This reduction of commercial capital is also a diminution of unproductive costs. What effect does this have on prices? The price of a product is determined by its cost price plus the gross profit. The division of this profit between entrepreneurial profit, interest, commercial profit, and rent, has no effect on the price. The fact that a cartel has taken the place of the merchant, and that some trading operations have been eliminated, means only that the industrialist no longer has to surrender any part of his profit to the merchant. So far as the consumer is concerned the price of the product remains unchanged.[5] The costs of circulation constitute a deduction from profit, and the diminution of these costs means that industrial profit, entrepreneurial gain, increases by the same amount. It is only the superstition that profit arises from trade, the belief that the merchant makes a profit simply by adding a mark-up to his cost price, which leads some writers to entertain the hope that a reduction of commercial costs could somehow bring down the price of products for the consumer.[6]

The diminution of commercial operations also has the effect of releasing capital previously employed in commerce, which now seeks new investment opportunities. In certain circumstances this may increase the pressure to export capital.

It is in the interest of the cartels to retain the external forms of commerce. On this point Kirdorf, the overlord of the coal syndicate, observes:

> To reach the ultimate source of consumption, the individual con-
> sumer, requires an enormous apparatus, and the increased adminis-
> trative cost would definitely exceed the advantages derived from
> higher prices for direct delivery. The business would become into-
> lerably costly and the bureaucracy would become too large to super-
> vise and control. Hence, within certain limits, a strong middleman's
> trade remains an absolute necessity which can never be entirely
> eliminated.[7]

In fact, of course, it is no longer a question of dealers and merchants, but of agents of the syndicates whose independence is as fictitious as that of the artisan in domestic industry who passes for a master craftsman. The only difference is that while technical changes in production make domestic industry unprofitable beyond a certain point, this is less so in commerce. There is no real economic difference between a commercial representative on a fixed salary and an 'independent' merchant who, in reality, receives a commission; for by determining the extent of sales areas, and fixing prices for the various areas, the syndicate moderates divergences to the point where, in effect, the income of the employee and the income of the merchant are about the same. The fiction of independence created by a different type of remuneration – and in this case it is a matter of a wage, the income of the 'merchant' consisting of the profit on his capital plus the wage which the syndicate would have to pay to an agent – saves the costs of supervision and control, just as piecework wages do as against time rate wages. Furthermore, the system greatly reduces the amount of capital required: the merchant's own capital can be very small since the stability of cartel prices and the territorial monopoly diminish the risks. Hence, most of his turnover can be carried on by means of credit, and he can usually obtain a loan for any payments he has to make, paying only interest on this part of his capital. The syndicate is only concerned with reducing the number of dealers, since its own marketing is thereby simplified, and with lowering the rate of commission for dealers' services (which are regarded as highly skilled) to the level of workers' wages. How far this fiction of independence is maintained is a matter of indifference from an economic point of view. Kirdorf himself says that the extent to which trading by middlemen has been eliminated at the present time is not something definitive, but 'has to be seen in relation to the historical development of the coal industry', and he also emphasizes that it is evident that 'the coal trade carried on by large numbers of dealers, as it developed when the mining industry was fragmented among many independent producers, is no longer necessary today'.[8]

Even the large coal dealers, in spite of their obvious reticence, have given a similar account of the situation. A few quotations will suffice here. Vowinkel (Düsseldorf) declares:

When I say that we are no longer real merchants, I base this view upon the following considerations. The coal syndicate prescribes for us the types of coal we are to buy, the prices at which to buy, where to sell the coal, and the sale price. Obviously, very little remains of commercial freedom. But I do not believe the coal syndicate can do anything else under the circumstances. In future, we wholesale dealers must be clear that things cannot proceed differently, and that our numbers will diminish. This is so obvious that today it is impossible to start a wholesale business of any size because the necessary supplies are not available. Even an existing business is restricted in the sense that it cannot possibly expand.[9]

These 'merchants' are deprived of every vestige of independence. For as the coal dealer Bellwinkel (Dortmund) says: 'the syndicate has a representative with voting rights on the board of directors of every marketing association', and 'is moreover authorized to examine the books at any time'. He concludes quite rightly: 'In the final analysis our freedom of action has been taken away, and we have become more like sales representatives.'

The outlook for the future is even worse. Mr Vowinkel describes it thus:

The syndicate has created a marvellous organization, from which, I am led to think, the wholesale trade, excepting an unimportant part, will be eliminated. What justification is there then for any wholesale trade? All that will remain for the wholesaler in the end will be to supply the small consumers and those who need credit, and to accumulate large stocks of coal during periods when sales are sluggish, in order to moderate fluctuations. These are the only activities which will justify his existence in the future, and in all probability the coal trade, which has already declined by 45 per cent, as we heard this morning, will fall by at least another 20 per cent.[10]

This is an accurate description of how the specific function of commerce, the circulation process C-M-C, is becoming superfluous. All that remains is the task of distributing, conserving and storing the product, which is necessary to meet the needs of consumption in any social system based upon mass production. Mercantile trade as such has ceased, and as Mr Vowinkel laments, has become a completely automatic process.[11]

Vowinkel also shows in detail how the wholesale merchant is gradually replaced by the agent of the syndicate, and quite rightly characterizes his participation in a marketing association as a 'sinecure' which is held only at the pleasure of the syndicate. On the death of the current participant his share reverts to the syndicate, which 'becomes the participant. It is then perfectly obvious that this sub-syndicate [meaning the dealers' association] will eventually be taken over by the main syndicate.'[12]

The monopoly of the large dealers, or of the marketing associations, gives them the power to bring the smaller merchants into a condition of dependence, and to dictate their selling prices; in short, to turn them into their agents. Thus, for instance, the wholesale coal dealer Heidmann (Hamburg) says: 'When I discovered from my books that the debts of these people [the small dealers who obtained their coal from him] were steadily mounting, I told them: you will receive coal only when you agree to charge such and such a price.'[13]

City Councillor (Stadtrat) Dr Rive says of the wholesale merchants of Upper Silesia:

> The wholesalers with whom we are concerned here, that is, the first-class dealers (the firms of César Wollheim and Friedlander) have, of course, a whole series of second rank wholesalers in tow who, to be perfectly frank, are completely dependent upon them; and the wholesalers of the second rank are backed up by dealers of the first, second and nth rank. They are all interdependent, and the front rank wholesalers act voluntarily in accord with the agreement [meaning the Upper Silesian coal agreement] even if they are not bound by a contract.

It should be noted briefly here that the independent position of these two coal firms in Upper Silesia is due to the fact that they had gained control of the coal trade long before the conclusion of the agreement. The mines were mostly privately owned, and both firms had some degree of financial interest in them. Not only did they control the marketing organization, but they also had a share in the mine property, either directly or as creditors.

In Rhineland-Westphalia the joint-stock system has made the mines quite independent of commerce. In the west trade was also less concentrated, perhaps because the available market was larger there, and as a result competition was less intense; and even more important may have been the fact that the western mines are more recent than the old privately owned mines of Upper Silesia. That is why, in Upper Silesia, the two most powerful merchant firms have at least managed to maintain their position, even if commerce as such was not able to hold its own. They have become in effect the trading organization of the cartel (in reality, that is, not in a formal manner, because the cartel does not concern itself formally with trade, but leaves marketing to the mines themselves). They hold this position, not as 'merchants', but because of their capital resources; whereas the western merchants, who are less important because commerce is less concentrated, are losing ground and even the wholesale merchant is becoming 'more or less an agent', as a principal mine inspector, Dr Wachler, tells us.[14]

The subordination of commerce to the syndicate also makes it easier for the latter to check foreign competition, which is more dependent on the services of commerce than is domestic manufacture. Thus, the merchant Klöckner (Duisburg) says: 'the commercial firms which sell cast iron have to subscribe to the conditions of the pig-iron syndicate which forbid them to deal in foreign iron or to import it into Germany.'[15]

The dependence of small manufacturers in industries which are not ready for cartelization upon large capitalist dealers provides a sharp contrast to the overweening power of cartelized industry. Such dependence becomes particularly onerous when it is reinforced by the provision of credit:

> Many small manufacturers are, from a business point of view, completely at the mercy of the dealers. In our industry, which produces finished goods, there are unfortunately very many manufacturers who have insufficient capital and cannot really stand on their own feet, so that in order to stay in business they are obliged to sell their goods at any price they can obtain. The goods are taken by a dealer, or they may be turned over to him as collateral for a loan, and he then has the small manufacturer in the palm of his hand for the foreseeable future; he can dictate to him the conduct of his whole business.[16]

Mr Gerstein, Secretary of the Hagen Chamber of Commerce, is referring here to the small-scale iron industry, and he sees the resistance of the dealers as an important obstacle to the formation of cartels.

On the other hand, cartelization cannot by itself give the finished goods industries any significant advantage with respect to prices:

> If the manufacturers of finished goods combine and fix prices which would give them a modest return, we have unfortunately often had the experience that large-scale industry throws a spanner in the works by finishing the articles which it needs itself in its own plants, incurring of course quite different costs from those of the manufacturers, who have to buy their raw materials at prices determined by the cartels of large-scale industry. As we have already heard, this manufacture of required articles in one's own plant is already widely developed. Director Fuchs told me only yesterday that large concerns such as Bochum, Dortmunder Verein, Königshütte and Laurahütte are now entering into competition with factories which only produce railway waggons – which cannot, of course, be classified as products of the small-scale iron and steel working industries, but are nevertheless finished products. In reply, I told him that this will hurt not only the waggon manufacturers, but also small iron and steel working concerns which manufacture the fittings for waggons; for the large steel firms do not only produce for themselves the finished cars, but all the related fittings – buffers, crossings, couplings – in short, every item. The Königshütte and Laurahütte make everything they need for their waggons, from the wheels to the very last part, with the possible exception of springs, screws and rivets. The Dortmunder Union also turns out almost all the parts for its waggons, as well as other small iron and steel products, such as bolts for rail couplings.[17]

But if commerce, through its influence upon the smaller capitalists, impedes the formation of cartels, it nevertheless tries to strengthen this influence by forming rings of its own. Gerstein also provides some examples of this practice. The large ironmongery dealers of Berlin, for instance, have formed an association which exerts a strong influence on the level of prices. The dealers in Danzig bought a firm collectively, and then formed an ironmongers' association as a limited liability company. The Federation of German Ironmongers, with its headquarters in Mainz, has drawn up regulations concerning the purchase of its goods. Members of the Federation are required to obtain a written guarantee from their suppliers that 'they will not sell their products at fairs'. Members of the Federation also undertake not to buy from manufacturers who sell directly to consumers, and in some places this has gone so far that the big state railways were regarded as consumers and the attempt was made to prevent manufacturers from supplying various articles directly to the state railways.[18]

The following is a good example of how easily larger capital resources create relations of dependency, sometimes in the form of a wholesale merchant increasing his commercial profit at the expense of the industrialist and passing on the very risks which his own speculation has created.

On the other hand, speculation in newsprint interferes with the effort of the syndicate to stabilize prices and to adjust supply to demand. Paper generally, and newsprint in particular, is not an article of speculation, and according to the accounts of what happens in almost all German paper mills it is always those wholesalers who sell short when paper prices are falling, without regard to costs of production, who put pressure on the paper manufacturers with regard to prices, in the most reprehensible manner, when they make purchases from the latter when they are in need of orders. This has gone so far that such dealers spread false rumours to impel the paper manufacturers, located in the mountains and remote from the paper market, to sell far below the market price.

Conversely, when prices are rising on the paper market the same wholesalers use all their wiles and arts of persuasion to press the paper manufacturers into large contracts with them, or to sell them large quantities of paper, even though they themselves have not yet made any sales to their own customers. The principal victims in this case are the printers, who are obliged to pay through the nose for the dealer's speculative *coup*, but the paper manufacturers regularly form a second group of victims, since in periods of ephemeral prosperity the dealer concerned will put pressure on the price as soon as market prices begin to fall, or if he cannot take the paper himself will leave the manufacturer sitting on his goods. Only in rare instances does a manufacturer decide to bring any kind of legal action against the dealer, because he is afraid of losing the dealer's custom in the future.[19]

The formation of a syndicate immediately changes the situation. The individual dealers now confront a unified industry, and the power of capital is on the side of the industrialists. But this is not all. The dealer now appears as he really is, as a mere auxiliary, by contrast with the indispensable process of production. The natural necessity of production now asserts its predominance over the capitalist necessity of distribution by means of commerce. The syndicate restricts commerce within its 'legitimate bounds'. 'Commerce is regarded as legitimate when the dealer resells the paper on the basis of a stable purchase price plus an adequate profit, and observes the conditions which the paper manufacturers consider acceptable and which are traditional in the paper trade.' Thus the paper dealer becomes an agent of the syndicate working on a fixed commission. Deprived of his freedom, he complains vociferously about his shabby treatment and recalls nostalgically the good old days of *le doux commerce*. Of all the conditions now imposed on him, he finds most onerous the fact that he is now compelled to buy exclusively from the syndicate. He is prevented from taking advantage of competition among producers, and he himself becomes an instrument for consolidating the syndicate and perpetuating the monopoly which holds him in its grip. He must abandon all hope, for above the door of the syndicate's sales office are inscribed words which inspire in him a fear as great as that of the sinner beholding the words above the portal of Dante's Inferno: 'Buy only from the syndicate and sell only at the prices fixed by the syndicate.' This is indeed the nemesis of the capitalist merchant.[20]

One means of eliminating speculation from commerce is the conclusion of long-term contracts. The coal syndicate, for example, fixes its prices for a term of one year, during which time they may not be changed. No conceivable circumstances would persuade it to depart from this 'fundamental rule'.[21]

Tempora mutantur! At the time of the stock exchange inquiry of 1893 speculation was the alpha and omega of capitalism. Everything is speculation: manufacturing, commerce, hedging operations. Every capitalist is a speculator, and even the proletarian who considers where he can best sell his labour power is a speculator. But in the cartel inquiry, the sanctity of speculation is forgotten. It is now the unmitigated evil from which crises, overproduction, and, in short, all the defects of capitalist society flow. Eliminate speculation is now the slogan. In place of the ideal of speculation we now have speculation about an ideal condition of 'stable prices' and of the demise of speculation. The stock exchange and commerce are now speculative, reprehensible activities, which must be cast aside in favour of industrial monopoly. Industrial profit incorporates commercial profit, is itself capitalized as promoter's profit, and becomes the booty of the trinity which has attained the highest form of capital as finance capital. For industrial capital is God the Father, who sent forth commercial and bank capital as God the Son, and money capital is the Holy Ghost. They are three persons united in one, in finance capital.

The contrast between the certainty of cartel profit and the uncertainty of speculative gains is reflected in the psychological differences between those who engage in the two activities, and in the degree of confidence with which they appear before the public. The cartel magnate regards himself as the master of production; his function is evident. He attributes his success to the effective organization of production and the elimination of unproductive costs. He regards himself as the representative of social necessity as against individualist anarchy, and considers his profit a well deserved remuneration for his activity as an organizer. His capitalist way of thinking takes it for granted that he is entitled to the fruits of an organization even if he is not its sole creator. He is the representative of a new age. 'The day of the individual', Havemeyer hectors the defenders of the old order, 'has passed; if the mass of the people profit at the expense of the individual, the individual should and must go.'[22] The meaning of what he says is socialism, but drunk with victory he does not notice that one fine day he and his like may well be among those who will have to go. The cartel magnate has no scruples, and while Havemeyer declares, with delightful candour, that he doesn't care two cents for other people's ethics,[23] Kirdorf insists no less proudly upon the right of the master in his own house.

In their own ethical code the most heinous crime is a breach of solidarity, free competition, secession from the brotherhood of monopoly profit; for which social ostracism and economic destruction are the appropriate punishment.[24] Lists were distributed in which the names of those distillers who would not join the syndicate were printed in bold type.[25]

The public image of the speculator is quite different. He makes his appearance in an unassuming, guilty fashion. His own gain is simply others' loss. Even if he is necessary, the need for him is simply an indication of the imperfections of capitalist society. The source of his gain remains obscure, for he is clearly not a producer who creates values. If his gains are exceptionally large, admiration of his achievement is mingled with suspicion. He is never quite at ease in face of public opinion, and is for ever fearful of new stock exchange legislation. He is apologetic and implores people not to judge him too harshly. 'This is the fate of all human institutions, which are without exception imperfect and liable to err.'[26]

He is content when he finds trusting individuals such as Professor van der Borght, who consoles him by saying: 'It is in the nature of human beings to be seized with a gambling fever from time to time', and can then deflect the criticisms of his detractors by assuring them that 'all these adverse effects are due, in the final analysis, to the ineradicable weaknesses and passions of human nature'.[27]

But of course we must not be too hard on any capitalist. One of them had just admitted that 'Money has a demoralizing power, and a person's character changes very rapidly with an increase of income',[28] and then he became furious. He had been concerned throughout by Professor Cohn's lack of understanding, quite inconsistent with his religious faith, of his sensitive soul. He had endured very patiently the worthy professor's exhaustive, if not particularly enlightening, account of the working of the stock exchange, and had listened with placid good humour to his interesting observations on the functions of the Prussian universities. But things should not be carried to extremes. He certainly had no objection to the professor's pronouncement that the purpose of the university is to be a mediator between the stock exchange and Social Democracy, defending and justifying the stock exchange from an ethical standpoint. But when the learned gentleman goes on to say that 'if the universities were not there these contradictions would explode', he finds these delusions of grandeur simply laughable. He cannot take the professor seriously in this respect, and so he would reply: 'I agree that the stock exchanges pursue ethical aims [be it noted that he remains a speculator], but that is not why they were founded; it was for reasons of self-interest. Is the merchant to found stock exchanges in order to turn them into charitable institutions?'[29]

The ethical school of political economy has no answer to this question, and Professor Cohn resembles in this instance a poodle with its tail between its legs, but one in which no Mephistopheles lies concealed.

The capitalist monopolies and the banks. The transformation of capital into finance capital

The development of capitalist industry produces concentration of banking, and this concentrated banking system is itself an important force in attaining the highest stage of capitalist concentration in cartels and trusts. How do the latter then react upon the banking system? The cartel or trust is an enterprise of very great financial capacity. In the relations of mutual dependence between capitalist enterprises it is the amount of capital that principally decides which enterprise shall become dependent upon the other. From the outset the effect of advanced cartelization is that the banks also amalgamate and expand in order not to become dependent upon the cartel or trust. In this way cartelization itself requires the amalgamation of the banks, and, conversely, amalgamation of the banks requires cartelization. For example, a number of banks have an interest in the amalgamation of steel concerns, and they work together to bring about this amalgamation even against the will of individual manufacturers.

Conversely, a consortium established in the first place by manufacturers can have the consequence that two previously competing banks develop common interests and proceed to act in concert in a particular sphere. In a similar fashion, industrial combinations may influence the expansion of the industrial activities of a bank, which was perhaps previously concerned only with the raw materials sector of an industry, and is now obliged to extend its activities to the processing sector as well.

The cartel itself presupposes a large bank which is in a position to provide, on a regular basis, the vast credits needed for current payments and productive investment in a whole industrial sector. But the cartel also brings about a still closer relationship between banking and industry. When competition in an industry is eliminated there is, first of all, an increase in the rate of profit, which plays an important role. When the elimination of competition is achieved by a merger, a new undertaking is created which can count upon higher profits, and these profits can be capitalized and constitute promoter's profit.[1] With the development of trusts this process becomes important in two respects. First, its realization constitutes a very important motive for the banks to encourage monopolization; and second, a part of the promoter's profits can be used to induce reluctant but significant producers to sell their factories, by offering a higher purchase price, thus facilitating the establishment of the cartel. This can perhaps be expressed in the following way: the cartel exerts a demand on the enterprises in a particular branch of industry; this demand increases to a certain degree the price of the enterprises[2] and this higher price is then paid in part out of the promoter's profit.

Cartelization also means greater security and uniformity in the earnings of the cartelized enterprises. The dangers of competition, which often threatened the existence of the individual enterprise, are eliminated and this leads to an increase in the share prices of these enterprises, which involves further promoter's profit when new shares are issued. Furthermore, the security of the capital invested in these enterprises is significantly increased. This permits a further expansion of industrial credit by the banks, which can then acquire a larger share in industrial profits. As a result of cartelization, therefore, the relations between the banks and industry become still closer, and at the same time the banks acquire an increasing control over the capital invested in industry.

We have seen that in the early stages of capitalist production, the money available to the banks is derived from two sources: on one side, from the resources of the non-productive classes, and on the other side, from the capital reserves of industrial and commercial capitalists. We have also seen how credit develops in such a way as to place at the disposal of industry not only the whole capital reserves of the capitalist class but also the major part of the funds of the non-productive classes. In other words, present-day industry is carried on with an amount of capital far exceeding that which is owned by the industrial capitalists. With the development of capitalism there is also a continual increase in the amount of money which the non-productive classes place at the disposal of the banks, who in turn convey it to the industrialists. The control of these funds which are indispensable to industry rests with the banks, and consequently, with the development of capitalism and of the machinery of credit, the dependence of industry upon the banks increases. On the other side, the banks can only attract the funds of the non-productive classes, and retain their continually growing capital over the long term, by paying interest on them. They could do this in the past, so long as the volume of money was not too great, by employing it in the form of credit for speculation and circulation. With the increase in the available funds on one side, and the diminishing importance of speculation and trade on the other, they were bound to be transformed more and more into industrial capital. Without the continuous expansion of credit for production, the availability of funds for deposit would have declined long ago, as would the rate of interest on bank deposits. In fact, this is to some extent the case in England, where the deposit banks only furnish credit for commerce, and consequently the rate of interest on deposits is minimal.

Hence deposits are continually withdrawn for investment in industry by the purchase of shares, and in this case the public does directly what is done by the bank where industrial and deposit banks are closely linked. For the public the result is the same, because in neither case does it receive any of the promoter's profits from the merger, but so far as industry is concerned it involves less dependence on bank capital in England as compared with Germany.

The dependence of industry on the banks is therefore a consequence of property relationships. An ever-increasing part of the capital of industry does not belong to the industrialists who use it. They are able to dispose over capital only through the banks, which represent the owners. On the other side, the banks have to invest an ever-increasing part of their capital in industry, and in this way they become to a greater and greater extent industrial capitalists. I call bank capital, that is, capital in money form which is actually transformed in this way into industrial capital, finance capital. So far as its owners are concerned, it always retains the money form; it is invested by them in the form of money capital, interest-bearing capital, and can always be withdrawn by them as money capital. But in reality the greater part of the capital so invested with the banks is transformed into industrial, productive capital (means of production and labour power) and is invested in the productive process. An ever-increasing proportion of the capital used in industry is finance capital, capital at the disposition of the banks which is used by the industrialists.

Finance capital develops with the development of the joint-stock company and reaches its peak with the monopolization of industry. Industrial earnings acquire a more secure and regular character, and so the possibilities for investing bank capital in industry are extended. But the bank disposes of bank capital, and the owners of the majority of the shares in the bank dominate the bank. It is clear that with the increasing concentration of property, the owners of the fictitious capital which gives power over the banks, and the owners of the capital which gives power over industry, become increasingly the same people. As we have seen, this is all the more so as the large banks increasingly acquire the power to dipose over fictitious capital.

We have seen how industry becomes increasingly dependent upon bank capital, but this does not mean that the magnates of industry also become dependent on banking magnates. As capital itself at the highest stage of its development becomes finance capital, so the magnate of capital, the finance capitalist, increasingly concentrates his control over the whole national capital by means of his domination of bank capital. Personal connections also play an important role here.

With cartelization and trustification finance capital attains its greatest power while merchant capital experiences its deepest degradation. A cycle in the development of capitalism is completed. At the outset of capitalist production money capital, in the form of usurers' and merchants' capital, plays a significant role in the accumulation of capital as well as in the transformation of handicraft production into capitalism. But there then arises a resistance of 'productive' capital, i.e. of the profit-earning capitalists – that is, of commerce and industry – against the interest-earning capitalists.[3] Usurer's capital becomes subordinated to industrial capital. As money-dealing capital it performs the functions of money which industry and commerce would otherwise have had to carry out themselves in the process of transformation of their commodities. As bank capital it arranges credit operations among the productive capitalists. The mobilization of capital and the continual expansion of credit gradually brings about a complete change in the position of the money capitalists. The power of the banks increases and they become founders and eventually rulers of industry, whose profits they seize for themselves as finance capital, just as formerly the old usurer seized, in the form of 'interest', the produce of the peasants and the ground rent of the lord of the manor. The Hegelians spoke of the negation of the negation: bank capital was the negation of usurer's capital and is itself negated by finance capital. The latter is the synthesis of usurer's and bank capital, and it appropriates to itself the fruits of social production at an infinitely higher stage of economic development.

The development of commercial capital, however, is quite different. The development of industry gradually excluded it from the ruling position over production which it had occupied during the period of manufacture. This decline is definitive, and the development of finance capital reduces the significance of trade both absolutely and relatively, transforming the once proud merchant into a mere agent of industry which is monopolized by finance capital.

Price determination by the capitalist monopolies and the historical tendency of finance capital

Partial combinations represent a further stage of concentration. They differ from the earlier form of concentration, which involved the destruction of the weaker enterprises, by the fact that in this case the combination of plants and enterprises is not necessarily accompanied by a unification of ownership; but they do not imply any fundamental change in the conditions of competition. In so far as their costs are lower than those of other enterprises, or of their own enterprises before they were combined, they are more effective in the competitive struggle; and if the combinations are sufficiently numerous and large, so that they produce the greater part of the total output, then their costs of production will have a decisive influence upon prices. Hence the combinations tend to depress prices. This does not prevent the advantages of combination from bringing an extra profit to the combined enterprises, and indeed this is taken for granted.

It is a different matter in the case of monopolistic combinations, the cartels and trusts. Their purpose is to raise the rate of profit, which they can achieve primarily by raising prices once they are in a position to eliminate competition. The question then arises: how are cartel prices determined? This problem is usually confounded with that of monopoly price in general, and there has been much controversy about whether a monopolistic combination is really a monopoly, or whether its monopolistic character is limited in some way, and if so, whether the prices fixed by such combinations must be equal to or lower than monopoly prices. The latter would themselves be determined, however, by the reciprocal relationship between costs of production and volume of output on the one hand, and prices and the volume of sales on the other. The monopoly price would be that price which makes possible a volume of sales such that the scale of production does not increase the costs of production so greatly as to reduce the profit per unit significantly. A higher price would reduce sales, and hence the scale of production, thus raising costs and reducing the profit per unit of output; a lower price would reduce profit so greatly that even the greater volume of sales would not compensate for it.

The indeterminate and incalculable factor, where monopoly prices prevail, is demand. It is impossible to say how demand will respond to an increase in price. Monopoly price can indeed be fixed empirically, but its proper level cannot be apprehended in an objective theoretical manner, only grasped psychologically and subjectively. For this reason the classical school of economics, in which I also count Marx, excluded monopoly price, that is, the price of goods the supply of which cannot be expanded at will, from their reasoning. The favourite pursuit of the psychological school, on the contrary, is to 'explain' monopoly prices, which it chooses to do by regarding all prices as monopoly prices, on the ground that all goods are limited in supply.

Classical economics conceives price as the expression of the anarchic character of social production, and the price level as depending upon the social productivity of labour. But the objective law of price can operate only through competition. If monopolistic combinations abolish competition, they eliminate at the same time the only means through which an objective law of price can actually prevail. Price ceases to be an objectively determined magnitude and becomes an accounting exercise for those who decide what it shall be by fiat, a presupposition instead of a result, subjective rather than objective, something arbitrary and accidental rather than a necessity which is independent of the will and consciousness of the parties concerned. It seems that the monopolistic combine, while it confirms Marx's theory of concentration, at the same time tends to undermine his theory of value.

Let us examine this more closely. Cartelization is a historical process which affects the various branches of capitalist production in sequence, as the conditions become favourable. We have already seen how the development of capitalism tends to create such conditions in all branches of production. Other things being equal – that is, assuming that the banks have attained the same degree of influence in all industries, in the same phase of the industrial cycle, and that the organic composition of capital is the same for all industries – a particular branch of industry will be more ripe for cartelization the larger the capital and the smaller the number of the individual enterprises which constitute it.

Let us assume that these conditions are first attained in the extraction of iron ore; that iron ore mines are cartelized and raise their prices. The immediate result is an increase in the rate of profit for the mining enterprises. The higher sale price of iron ore, however, means a higher cost price for the pig-iron producers. But this has no immediate effect on the sale price of pig-iron, the market for which has not been changed by the cartelization of the iron ore mines. The ratio of supply and demand, and hence prices, remain the same. The rise in the cartel's rate of profit thus has as its consequence a fall in the rate of profit of the pig-iron producers. But what does this mean?

Theoretically, the following consequences might ensue. Capital flows out of the sphere with the lower rate of profit into the sphere with the higher rate of profit. Capital which was previously invested in pig-iron production would now be used in iron ore mining. Competition would then emerge in iron ore mining and would be all the sharper because of the contraction of pig-iron production. The price of ore would fall while that of pig-iron rose, and after a period of fluctuations during which the cartel would probably have disintegrated, the previous conditions would be restored. But we already know that it is precisely in such branches of production as these that the inflow and outflow of capital will encounter almost insurmountable obstacles, and so this route toward equalizing the rate of profit cannot be followed.

The cartel prices are important only to those pig-iron producers who have to buy their ore on the market, and in order to avoid the effects of cartelization the pig-iron enterprises need only take over iron ore mines themselves. In this way they become independent of the cartel and their rate of profit returns to its normal level. Those enterprises which first become vertically integrated undertakings will also make an extra profit as compared with the others, who are obliged to pay higher raw material prices as well as the trading profit of the ore merchants. The same is true, however, of iron ore mines which have extended their activities to pig-iron production, for as vertically integrated enterprises, they too have an advantage in competition with non-integrated firms. The cartel thus proves to be a very powerful stimulus to combination, and hence to the further concentration of capital. The stimulus makes itself felt most strongly in those branches of industry which buy and process the products of the cartel.

The preceding account shows how the trend toward combination is brought about or intensified by certain features of the business cycle. This trend is reinforced and at the same time modified by cartelization. A monopolistic combination can maintain high prices even during a crisis, whereas that would be impossible for its non-cartelized customers. In the case of the latter the effects of the crisis are aggravated by the impossibility of reducing their production costs by buying raw materials more cheaply. In such periods the pressure upon non-cartelized firms to obtain cheap raw materials from mines which they own themselves becomes particularly strong, but if they do not succeed a whole row of otherwise viable, technically well-equipped concerns will be unable to survive. They must either go bankrupt or sell out cheaply to an iron ore mining enterprise, for which the acquisition of the plant at a low price guarantees future profitability.

But there is also another way open to the pig-iron industrialists. They confronted the combined power of the mine owners as isolated individual producers, who for this reason were powerless in face of the rising cost of raw materials. They were equally powerless when it came to incorporating the increased cost of raw materials into the price of pig-iron. All this changes as soon as they themselves form a cartel. They are then in a position to face the mining cartel as a united body and to assert their power as customers. On the other side, they can themselves now fix the selling price of their products and raise their rate of profit above the norm. In practice, both the above-mentioned roads are being followed, vertical integration as well as cartelization, and the outcome of this process is likely to be a vertically integrated monopolistic combine of iron ore and pig-iron producers.

It is evident that this process is bound to spread to the subsequent buyers of pig-iron, and will penetrate one branch of capitalist production after another. The influence of the example set by cartels is widely diffused. The immediate effect of cartelization is a change in the rate of profit for the cartels at the expense of other capitalist industries. These different rates of profit cannot be equalized by the transfer of capital, because cartelization means that the competition of capitals for spheres of investment is restricted. The limitation of the free movement of capital by various economic factors or property relations (such as a monopoly of raw materials) is indeed a precondition for the abolition of market competition among sellers. Equalization of the rate of profit can only take place by participation in the higher rate of profit through self-cartelization, or through the elimination of cartels by vertical integration. Both methods involve a growth of concentration and thus facilitate further cartelization.

If, however, further cartelization is impossible for any reason, what effect does the cartel price then have, and what can we say about its level. We have seen that the increase in the rate of profit resulting from the higher cartel price can only be achieved by the reduction of the rate of profit in other branches of industry. The cartel profit is, in the first place, nothing but a participation in, or appropriation of, the profit of other branches of industry. There is a tendency, as we know, for the rate of profit to fall below the social average in branches of industry in which small capitals are employed and where there is considerable fragmentation of production. Cartelization reinforces this tendency, and depresses still further the rate of profit in these branches. Just how far it can be depressed depends on the nature of the industry. If there is an excessive reduction in the rate of profit capital responds by withdrawing from these spheres, as it can do without too much difficulty in view of the technical form of the capital in such industries.

The real difficulty begins with the problem of where this capital shall go, since the other branches of production in which small amounts of capital might be invested are similarly exploited by the cartelized industries.[1] The eventual outcome is that the profit of the capitalists in these industries, who still appear to be independent, becomes nothing more than a supervisor's salary, and these capitalists become, in fact, employees of the cartel, intermediary capitalists or entrepreneurs analogous to the intermediary masters of the handicraft period.

In fact, the cartel price depends upon demand, but this is itself capitalist demand. Theoretically, therefore, the cartel price must in the end be equal to the price of production plus the average rate of profit. But this average rate has undergone a change. There is one rate for the large cartelized industries and another for the spheres of small-scale industry which have become dependent upon them; and the capitalists in the cartelized industries rob the latter of a part of their surplus value, so reducing their income to a mere salary.

Nevertheless, this kind of price fixing, like the single or partial cartel itself, is only provisional. Cartelization involves a change in the average rate of profit. The rate of profit rises in the cartelized industries and falls in the non-cartelized ones, and this discrepancy leads to new combinations and further cartelization. For those industries which remain non-cartelized the rate of profit continues to fall. The cartel price will rise by the same amount above the price of production as it has fallen below the price of production in the non-cartelized industries. In so far as there are joint-stock companies in the non-cartelized industries, their prices cannot fall below c + i (cost price plus interest), because otherwise the investment of capital would be impossible. Thus the increase in the cartel price is limited by the extent to which it is possible to reduce the rate of profit in the non-cartelized industries. Among the latter the rate of profit is equalized at a low level through the competition of capital for spheres of investment.

The rise in the cartel price does not leave the price of non-cartelized products unaffected. The change arises from the equalization of the rate of profit among the non-cartelized industries. If non-cartelized industry were to form a combination of its own the price of non-cartelized products would not change. The same price would then produce a lower rate of profit than before, because the price of raw materials (that is, the cost price) had risen. If, previously, the price of the product was 100 and the rate of profit 20 per cent, the latter would now fall to 10 per cent because the cost price which was 80 will have risen to 90 as a result of cartelization. But since the cost price increases in different proportions in various non-cartelized industries in accordance with the organic composition of their capital, an equalization must occur. Those industries which use large quantities of raw materials, the price of which has been increased by cartelization, have to raise the price of their products, while those which use less will be able to reduce prices. In other words, the price of production will rise in industries in which the organic composition of capital is above the average,[2] fall in industries in which it is below the average, and remain unchanged in industries which have an average organic composition of capital. Attention is usually focussed only upon the rise in price, and it is assumed that any increase (in production costs) can be passed on without further ado to the consumers. But a rise in costs of production may lead, under certain circumstances, to a fall in price.

There are also some other peculiarities of price formation. Let us assume that the capital of the cartelized* industries amounts to 50 billions. If the rate of profit is 20 per cent, the price of production will be 60 billions, of which, let us say, 50 billions would be bought by non-cartelized industries. Their production price, at the same rate of profit, would also amount to 60 billions, and the value of the total product would therefore be 120 billions. But the cartelized industries have raised their rate of profit, and hence reduced that of the non-cartelized industries, say to 10 per cent. Their profit is reduced because they must now pay 55 billions instead of 50 billions for raw materials. (I leave out of account here the variable capital which has no bearing on this example.) But if the cartel now gets 55 billions instead of 50 billions, it must likewise get 66 billions instead of 60 billions. Prices must be the same not only for capitalist consumers but for all consumers. In accordance with our assumptions, therefore, the final 10 billions which go directly to consumers will be sold for 11 instead of 10 billions. Thus the consumers pay the old prices for the non-cartelized products and higher prices for the cartelized products. A part of the cartel profit comes therefore from the consumers, that is to say, from all the non-capitalist groups which derive their income from other sources. But the higher prices may lead consumers to reduce their consumption. Here we encounter the second limitation upon cartel prices. A price rise must, in the first place, allow the non-cartelized industries a rate of profit sufficient for them to continue production. Second, it must not reduce consumption too severely. This second limitation depends in turn upon the amount of income at the disposal of the classes which are not directly productive. But since productive consumption is far more important than unproductive consumption for cartelized industry as a whole, the first limitation is the decisive one.

The reduction of profit in the non-monopolized industries is bound to retard their development. The fall in the rate of profit means that new capital will flow very slowly into these branches of production. At the same time, however, this fall involves a much more intense struggle for markets, which is all the more dangerous since the small margin of profit can be wiped out by a comparatively slight reduction in price. There is also a further consequence: where the superior power of the cartelized industries

* The original text has 'non-cartelized', but this is clearly an error. [Ed.]

enables them to reduce profit to a mere managerial salary there is no longer any scope for organizing joint-stock companies, since both promoter's profit and dividends can only be paid out of the balance remaining after the managerial salary has been paid. Thus cartelization tends to retard the development of the non-cartelized industries, but at the same time it intensifies competition and hence the tendency toward concentration in these industries, until a point is finally reached when they are also ripe for cartelization, or for incorporation into an already cartelized industry.

Free competition promotes a constant expansion of production as a result of the introduction of improved techniques. For the cartels, such technical improvements also involve a rise in profit. They are obliged to introduce these improvements, for otherwise there is a danger that some outsider will get hold of them and will use them in a renewed competitive struggle against the cartel. Whether such a danger materializes depends upon the type of monopoly the cartel has established. A cartel enjoys a high degree of protection against fresh competition if it has a monopoly of the natural conditions of production (for example, in the case of a mining syndicate) or if its production requires a very high organic composition of capital, so that a new enterprise would need enormous capital resources which could be provided only by the banks, who would not want to act against the interests of the cartel. In this case technical improvements mean an extra profit, which is not eliminated by competition, and the prices of products do not fall. The introduction of improved techniques does not benefit consumers, but only the tightly organized cartels and trusts. Technical improvements might, of course, lead to increased output, the disposal of which would required a reduction in price in order to expand consumption, but this is not necessarily the case. It would be quite possible for the steel trust, for example, to apply the new techniques in some of its plants, so that their production would then suffice to meet the entire demand at existing prices, and to close down other plants. Prices would remain the same, production costs would fall and profits would increase, but there would be no expansion of production, and the technical improvements would simply lay off workers who would have no prospect of finding other employment. The same thing can happen in a cartel type of organization. The largest concerns introduce the improvements and expand their production; in order to do so, and still remain in the cartel, they buy up the quotas of the smaller concerns and then close them down. The technical improvement has been put into effect, and at the same time has brought about further concentration, without any expansion of production.

Cartelization brings exceptionally large extra profits,[3] and we have seen how these extra profits are capitalized and then flow into the banks as concentrated sums of capital. But at the same time cartels tend to slow down capital investment; both in the cartelized industries, because the first concern of a cartel is to restrict production, and in the non-cartelized industries because the decline in the rate of profit discourages further capital investment. Consequently, while the volume of capital intended for accumulation increases rapidly, investment opportunities contract. This contradiction demands a solution, which it finds in the export of capital, though this is not in itself a consequence of cartelization. It is a phenomenon that is inseparable from capitalist development. But cartelization suddenly intensifies the contradiction and makes the export of capital an urgent matter.

If we now pose the question as to the real limits of cartelization, the answer must be that there are no absolute limits. On the contrary there is a constant tendency for cartelization to be extended. As we have seen, the independent industries become increasingly dependent upon the cartelized industries until they are finally annexed by them. The ultimate outcome of this process would be the formation of a general cartel. The whole of capitalist production would then be consciously regulated by a single body which would determine the volume of production in all branches of industry. Price determination would become a purely nominal matter, involving only the distribution of the total product between the cartel magnates on one side and all the other members of society on the other. Price would then cease to be the outcome of factual relationships into which people have entered, and would become a mere accounting device by which things were allocated among people. Money would have no role. In fact, it could well disappear completely, since the task to be accomplished would be the allocation of things, not the distribution of values. The illusion of the objective value of the commodity would disappear along with the anarchy of production, and money itself would cease to exist. The cartel would distribute the product. The material elements of production would be reproduced and used in new production. A part of the output would be distributed to the working class and the intellectuals, while the rest would be retained by the cartel to use as it saw fit. This would be a consciously regulated society, but in an antagonistic form. This antagonism, however, would concern distribution, which itself would be consciously regulated and hence able to dispense with money. In its perfected form finance capital is thus uprooted from the soil which nourished its beginnings. The circulation of money has become unnecessary, the ceaseless turnover of money has attained its goal in the regulated society, and the *perpetuum mobile* of circulation finds its ultimate resting place.

The tendencies towards the establishment of a general cartel and towards the formation of a central bank are converging, and from their combination emerges the enormous concentrated power of finance capital, in which all the partial forms of capital are brought together into a totality. Finance capital has the appearance of money capital, and its form of development is indeed that of money which yields money (M – M') – the most general and inscrutable form of the movement of capital. As money capital it is made available to producers in two forms, as loan capital or as fictitious capital. The intermediaries in this process are the banks, which endeavour at the same time to convert an ever increasing part of this capital into their own capital, thus endowing finance capital with the form of bank capital. This bank capital becomes increasingly the mere form – the money form – of actually functioning capital, that is, industrial capital. At the same time as finance capital eliminates the division between bank capital and productive capital, commercial capital also increasingly loses its independence, and within industrial capital itself the progress of combination among previously separate and independent branches of production breaks down the barriers between different spheres. The social division of labour – the division into diverse spheres of production which were only integrated as parts of the whole social organism through exchange – is constantly diminished, while on the other hand the technical division of labour within the combined enterprises continues to advance.

Thus the specific character of capital is obliterated in finance capital. Capital now appears as a unitary power which exercises sovereign sway over the life process of society; a power which arises directly from ownership of the means of production, of natural resources, and of the whole accumulated labour of the past, and from command over living labour as a direct consequence of property relations. At the same time property, concentrated and centralized in the hands of a few giant capitalist groups, manifests itself in direct opposition to the mass of those who possess no capital. The problem of property relations thus attains its clearest, most unequivocal and sharpest expression at the same time as the development of finance capital itself is resolving more successfully the problem of the organization of the social economy.

Part IV

Finance capital and crises

The general conditions of crises

It is an empirical law that capitalist production passes through a cycle of prosperity and depression. The transition from one phase of the cycle to another is marked by a crisis. At a certain point during a period of prosperity sales begin to decline in a number of branches of production, and prices consequently fall; the sluggish market conditions and falling prices become more widespread and production is curtailed. This phase of the cycle, marked by low prices and profits, may be more or less prolonged, but then production gradually begins to expand again, prices and profits rise, and the volume of production becomes greater than ever, until a new turning point is reached. The periodic recurrence of this phenomenon raises a question as to its causes, which can only be discovered by an analysis of the mechanism of capitalist production.

The general possibility of a crisis arises from the dual existence of the commodity, as commodity and as money. This involves the possibility of an interruption in the process of commodity circulation if money is hoarded instead of being used to circulate commodities. The process $C_1 - M - C_2$ comes to a halt because M, which had previously realized the value of C_1, does not go on to realize the value of C_2. C_2 cannot be sold and so a glut develops.

But as long as money functions only as a means of circulation, as long as commodities exchange directly for money and money directly for commodities, the hoarding of a sum of money need only be a single isolated occurrence which would make it impossible to sell some particular commodity, but would not involve a general slump in sales. This situation changes, however, when the function of money as a means of payment, and commercial credit, develop. A slump in sales now makes it impossible to meet previously contracted debts. As we have seen, however, such promises to pay have been used as means of circulation or payment in many other transactions. If one person cannot meet his obligations, then others also become unable to pay. The chain of debtors resulting from the use of money as a means of payment is broken, and a slump at one point is transmitted to all the others, so becoming general. Payment credit thus makes the various branches of production interdependent and creates the conditions in which a partial slump may be transformed into a general one.

But the general possibility of a crisis is only a condition of its occurrence. Without the circulation of money, and the development of its function as a means of payment, a crisis would be impossible. But possibility is a long way from being actuality. Under simple commodity production – or more precisely, pre-capitalist commodity production – there are no crises. The breakdowns in the economy are not crises which conform with some economic law, but catastrophes arising from particular natural or historical circumstances such as poor harvests, drought, pestilence and war. What they have in common is a deficiency in reproduction, not any kind of overproduction. This is indeed self-evident if we reflect that this kind of production is still essentially production for the satisfaction of personal needs, that production is related to consumption as means to end, and that the circulation of commodities is relatively unimportant. Only capitalist production generalizes commodity production, allows all possible products to assume the commodity form, and finally – this is the crucial point – makes the sale of the commodity a precondition for the resumption of reproduction.[1]

This transformation of products into commodities makes the producers dependent on the market, and turns the inherent irregularity of production, which already existed in simple commodity production because the private economic households were independent units, into that anarchy of capitalist production which, as commodity production is generalized and local isolated markets are expanded into an all-inclusive world market, becomes the second general condition of crises.

Capitalism establishes a third general condition of crises by separating production from consumption. In the first place, it separates the producer from his product and leaves him only that part of the value produced which is equivalent to the value of his labour power. Thus it creates out of its wage labourers a class whose consumption has no direct relation to total production, but only to that part of it which equals wage capital. The output which these wage labourers produce does not, however, belong to them, hence it does not serve their consumption needs. On the contrary, their consumption, and its extent, depends upon production over which they have no influence. The production of the capitalists does not serve needs, but profits. The inherent purpose of capitalist production is the realization and increase of profit.

In other words, it is not consumption and its growth, but the realization of profit, which is the decisive factor in determining the direction that production takes, its volume, and its expansion or contraction. Goods are produced in order to obtain a specific profit and to achieve a specific degree of valorization of capital. Production, therefore, does not depend upon consumption, but upon capital's need for valorization, and there will be a contraction of production whenever the opportunities for the valorization of capital deteriorate.

Even in the capitalist mode of production there is, of course, a general connection between production and consumption. This is a natural condition which is common to all social formations. But whereas, in an economy based upon the satisfaction of needs, consumption determines the expansion of production, the limits of which are set in this case only by the level of technological development, in a capitalist economy, on the contrary, it is the scale of production which determines consumption. Production is restricted by the current opportunities for valorization, by the level at which capital can be valorized, and by the necessity for existing capital, as well as any additions to it, to achieve a certain rate of profit. The expansion of production here encounters a purely social barrier, which originates in, and is specific to, this social structure. The possibility of crises is implicit in unregulated production, that is to say, in commodity production generally, but it only becomes a real possibility in a system of unregulated production which eliminates the direct relationship between production and consumption characterizing other social formations, and interposes between production and consumption the requirement that capital shall be valorized at a particular rate.

Such expressions as 'overproduction of commodities' and 'underconsumption' tell us very little. Strictly speaking, one can use the term underconsumption only in a physiological sense; it has no sense in economics except to indicate that society is consuming less than it has produced. It is impossible, however, to conceive how that can happen if production is carried on in the right proportions. The total product is equal to constant capital, plus variable capital, plus surplus value $(C + V + S)$. Since V and S are consumed, and the elements of the constant capital which have been consumed must be replaced, production can be expanded indefinitely without leading to the overproduction of commodities. In other words, it cannot lead to a condition in which more commodities, that is to say goods (in this context, and for the purpose of this analysis, commodities are regarded as use values), are produced than can be consumed.[2]

One thing is clear; namely, that since the periodic recurrence of crises is a product of capitalist society, the causes must lie in the nature of capital. It must be a matter of a disturbance arising from the specific character of society. The narrow basis provided by the consumption relations of capitalist production constitutes, from that point of view, the general condition of crises, since the impossibility of enlarging this basis is the precondition for the stagnation of the market. If consumption could be readily expanded, overproduction would not be possible. But under capitalist conditions expansion of consumption means a reduction in the rate of profit. For an increase in consumption by the broad masses of the population depends upon a rise in wages, which would reduce the rate of surplus value and hence the rate of profit. Consequently, if the demand for labour, as a result of the accumulation of capital, increases so greatly that the rate of profit is reduced, to a point (at the extreme) where an increased quantity of capital would not produce a larger profit than did the original capital, then accumulation must come to an end, since its essential purpose – the increase of profit – would not be achieved. This is the point at which one necessary precondition of accumulation, the expansion of consumption, enters into contradiction with another precondition, namely the realization of profit. The conditions of realization   cannot   be reconciled with the expansion of consumption, and since the former are decisive, the contradiction develops into a crisis. That is why the narrow basis of consumption is only a general condition of crises, which cannot be explained simply by 'underconsumption'. Least of all can the periodic character of crises be explained in this way, since no periodic phenomenon can be explained by constant conditions. There is therefore no contradiction between Marx's argument in the following passage and the passage cited previously:

> The entire mass of commodities, the total product, which contains a
> portion which is to reproduce the constant and variable capital, as
> well as a portion representing the surplus value, must be sold. If this
> is not done, or only partly accomplished, or only at prices which are
> below the prices of production, the labourer has been none the less
> exploited, but his exploitation does not realize as much for the capi-
> talist. It may yield no surplus value at all for him, or only realize a
> portion of the produced surplus value, or it may mean a partial or
> complete loss of his capital. The conditions of direct exploitation and
> those of the realization of surplus value are not identical. They are
> separated logically as well as by time and space. The first are only
> limited by the productive power of society, and the last by the pro-
> portional relations of the various lines of production and by the
> consuming power of society. This last named power is not deter-
> mined either by the absolute productive power or by the absolute
> consuming power, but by the consuming power based on antagonis-
> tic conditions of distribution which reduce the consumption of the
> great mass of the population to a variable minimum within more or
> less narrow limits. The consuming power is furthermore restricted by
> the tendency to accumulate, the greed for an expansion of capital and
> a production of surplus value on an enlarged scale. This is a law of

capitalist production imposed by incessant revolutions in the methods of production themselves, the resulting depreciation of existing
capital, the general competitive struggle and the necessity of improving the product and expanding the scale of production, for the sake
of self-preservation and on penalty of failure. The market must
therefore be continually extended, so that its interrelations and the
conditions regulating them assume more and more the form of a
natural law independent of the producers and become ever more
uncontrollable. This internal contradiction seeks to balance itself by
an expansion of the outlying fields of production. But to the extent
that the productive power develops, it finds itself at variance with the
narrow basis on which the conditions of consumption rest. On this
self-contradictory basis, it is no contradiction at all that there should
be an excess of capital simultaneously with an excess of population.
For while a combination of these two would indeed increase the
mass of the produced surplus value, it would at the same time intensify the contradiction between the conditions under which this
surplus value is produced and those under which it is realized.[3]

Periodic crises are a distinctive feature of capitalism and can only be
deduced from its specific characteristics.[4]

In general, a crisis is a disturbance of circulation. It manifests itself as a
massive unsaleability of commodities, as the impossibility of realizing the
value of commodities (their price of production) in money. It can only be
explained, therefore, in terms of the specific capitalist conditions of
commodity circulation, not in terms of simple commodity circulation. The
specifically capitalist feature in the circulation of commodities is that
commodities are produced by capital, as commodity capital, and must be
realized as such. Their realization of based upon conditions peculiar to
capital; namely the conditions for the realization of value.

The analysis of these conditions from the standpoint of both individual
and (what is more important here) social capital, was provided by Marx in
the second volume of *Capital*, thus continuing an undertaking which only
Quesnay had previously attempted. Marx described Quesnay's *tableau
économique* as the most brilliant conception that political economy had so
far produced, and we can say that his own analysis of the social process of
production is undoubtedly the most outstanding elaboration of that
brilliant notion. Indeed, the largely ignored analyses in the second volume of
Capital are, from the standpoint of pure economic reasoning, the most
brilliant in that whole remarkable work. Above all, an understanding of the
causes of crises is quite impossible without taking into account the results
of Marx's analysis.[5]

Equilibrium conditions in the process of social reproduction

Let me recapitulate briefly the most important results of Marx's analysis. First, it is assumed in this study that capitalist production remains at the same level of development, and only simple reproduction takes place, while changes in value or price are disregarded.

The total product, that is the total production of society, falls into two major divisions: (1) means of production, being commodities of such a kind that they must, or at least can, enter into productive consumption; and (2) means of consumption, consisting of those commodities which enter into the individual consumption of the capitalist class and the working class.

The capital in each of these departments is again divided into two parts: variable (V) and constant (C) capital. The latter, in turn, is sub-divided into fixed and circulating capital.

The portion of value (C) which represents the constant capital consumed in production is not identical with the value of the constant capital invested in production, because the fixed capital has transferred only a part of its value to the product. In the following example the fixed capital will initially be disregarded.

The total production of commodities is represented in the following schema:

$$\text{I} \quad 4,000 \text{ C} + 1,000 \text{ V} + 1,000 \text{ S} = 6,000 \text{ means of production}$$
$$\text{II} \quad 2,000 \text{ C} + 500 \text{ V} + 500 \text{ S} = 3,000 \text{ means of consumption}$$

The total value is 9,000, excluding the fixed capital (disregarded here) which continues to function in its natural form.

If we now examine the necessary exchanges on the basis of simple reproduction, in which the entire surplus value is consumed unproductively, and leave out of account for the time being the circulation of money through which these exchanges are accomplished, then we obtain at once three main points of reference:

1 The 500 V, wages of workers, and the 500 S, surplus value of the capitalists, in department II must be spent for means of consumption. But their value exists in the means of consumption to the value of 1,000, in the hands of the capitalists of department II, which replace the 500 V advanced and represent the 500 S. The wages and surplus value of department II therefore are exchanged within department II against the products of this department. In this way there disappears from the total product the sum of (500 V + 500 S)II, which equals 1,000 means of consumption.

2 The 1,000 V and 1,000 S of department I must likewise be spent on means of consumption, that is, on the product of department II. Hence

they must be exchanged against what remains of this product, namely against the amount of the constant capital, 2,000 C. In return, department II receives an equal amount of means of production, the product of department I, in which the value of 1,000 V and 1,000 S of this department is embodied. In this way there now disappears from the calculation 2,000 C from II and (1,000 V + 1,000 S) from I.

3 There now remains the 4,000 C of department I. This comprises means of production which can only be used up in department I. It serves for the replacement of the consumed constant capital, and is disposed of by mutual exchanges among the individual capitalists of department I, just as the (500 V + 500 S) in department II is disposed of by exchanges between workers and capitalists or among individual capitalists in that department.

The replacement of the fixed capital plays a special role. Part of the value of constant capital is transferred from the instruments of labour to the product of labour. These instruments of labour continue to function as elements of productive capital in their original natural form; it is the wear and tear, the loss of value which they suffer as a result of continuous use over a period of time, which reappears as an element of value in the commodities which they produce.

Money, on the other hand, in so far as it embodies this part of the value of commodities which represents the depreciation of fixed capital, is not reconverted into a component part of the productive capital whose loss of value it replaces. It settles down alongside the productive capital and retains its money form. This precipitation of money is repeated during a period of reproduction, which may be longer or shorter, while the fixed element of constant capital continues to perform its function in the process of production in its old natural form. When the elements of fixed capital – buildings, machinery, etc. – are worn out and can no longer function in the process of production, their value already exists alongside them, fully transformed into money; namely in the sum of money, the values, which were gradually transferred from the fixed capital to the commodities in the production of which it assisted, and through the sale of these commodities converted into the money form. This money then serves to replace the fixed capital (or elements of it, since its various elements have different life spans) in kind, and thus effectively to renew this component of productive capital. It is the money form of a part of the value of constant capital, its fixed part.

The formation of this hoard is therefore itself a factor in the capitalist process of reproduction. It is the reproduction and storage, in the form of money, of the value of fixed capital or its individual elements, until such time as the fixed capital is worn out and has transferred its entire value to the commodities produced, and needs to be replaced in kind. This money, however, only loses its form as a hoard and actively re-enters the reproduction process of capital, mediated through circulation, when it is reconverted into new elements of fixed capital which will replace the worn out elements. But if there is to be no interruption of this process of simple reproduction, that part of the fixed capital which is depreciated annually must equal that which has to be renewed.

Let us consider, for instance, an exchange of (1,000 V + 1,000 S) of I against 2,000 C of II. In this 2,000 C, 200 in fixed capital has to be replaced. The 1,800 C which is to be converted into circulating constant capital is exchanged for 1,800 (V + S) of I. Department II must also obtain the 200 which remains in I in the natural form of fixed capital, but this can only be done if the capitalists of II have 200 on hand in money with which to buy the 200 of their fixed capital and retain it in its money form. In other words, the capitalists who in previous years had hoarded the depreciation of their fixed capital in money reserves will this year renew their fixed capital in kind, by using 200 in money to purchase the balance of 200 (V + S) from I. Department I, in turn, will use another 200 in money to buy the remainder of the means of consumption from the other capitalists of II, who hoard this money as a reserve against the depreciation of their own fixed capital. Thus those capitalists in department II who renew their fixed capital in kind during this year provide the money with which the other capitalists of II create a reserve against depreciation which they retain in money form. We must assume therefore a constant proportion between fixed capital which is depreciating and fixed capital which has to be renewed; and further, that there is a constant proportion between the depreciating fixed capital (which has to be replaced) and the fixed capital which continues to function in its original natural form. For if the depreciating fixed capital increased to 300, then the circulating capital would have declined, and II C, having less circulating capital, would not be able to continue production on the same scale. Moreover, if the fixed capital increased to 300, and II had only 200 in money to spend for the replacement of its capital in kind, 100 of the fixed capital in I would be unsaleable.

Hence, even when the amount of fixed capital is simply maintained, a disproportion in the production of fixed and circulating capital may still occur if – as is indeed always actually the case – the ratio of the annual depreciation of fixed capital to the fixed capital which continues to function in production varies. We have also seen that definite proportional relations must exist if simple reproduction is to be possible. I (V + S) must be equal to II C. The anarchy of capitalist society, however, always interferes with the realization of this proportional relation. In order to ensure continuity of production a certain amount of overproduction is always necessary as a safeguard against unpredictable consumer wants and constant fluctuations in demand. There are always disruptions and irregularities in the reflux of the value of capital which is being turned over. In order to overcome these irregularities, and to cope with the disruptions capitalists must always have at their disposal a reserve supply both of commodities and of money, and this requires additional money, a reserve of money capital, which must necessarily be in liquid form because it is precisely the turnover of commodity capital which may be disrupted, and in that case the capitalist must be able to obtain other commodities as quickly as possible. Only in the form of money is value a universal equivalent, always readily convertible into any other desired commodity. In this case, too, the necessity of money arises from the anarchy of the capitalist mode of production.

Once the capitalist form of reproduction is abolished, the problem resolves itself into the simple proposition that the magnitude of the expiring portion of the fixed capital, which must be reproduced in its natural form every year (which served in our illustration for the pro- duction of articles of consumption) varies in successive years. If it is very large in a certain year (in excess of the average mortality, the same as among men), then it is so much smaller in the next year. The quantity of raw materials, half-wrought materials and auxiliary materials required for the annual production of the articles of consumption – other circumstances remaining the same – does not decrease in consequence. Hence, the aggregate production of means of production would have to increase in the one case and decrease in the other. This can be remedied only by a continuous relative over- production. There must be, on the one hand, a certain quantity of fixed capital in excess of that which is immediately required; on the other hand, there must be above all a supply of raw materials etc. in excess of actual requirements of annual production (this applies par- ticularly to articles of consumption). This sort of reproduction may take place when society controls the material requirements of its own reproduction. But in capitalist society, it is an element of anarchy.[6]

Within certain limits this relative overproduction must also occur constantly in capitalist society, and is represented by the ever present reserve stock of commodities which serves to cushion disturbances, as well as by the reserve of money capital at the disposal of the industrial capitalists which enables them, in case of any disruption, to draw upon the commodity reserve for those items which are necessary in order to carry on their production. But this reserve of money capital which must be available to capitalists as a protection against temporary disruptions even in normal times, should not be confused with the reserve of money capital which is necessary when trade is slack. In times of prosperity production expands rapidly, and on the other hand, the money capital previously kept as a reserve is converted into productive capital. The reserve thus diminishes and this means that one factor which helps to smooth out disturbances is removed. This is, therefore, one of the causes of crises.

On the other hand, it should be emphasized that the necessity of this relative overproduction is grounded not upon capitalist society itself but upon the nature of the reproduction process once those elements of production, which appear as fixed capital in capitalist society, have attained a much greater importance. This 'overproduction', which is made necessary by technical and natural circumstances, is really only a building up of stocks, and as such would also be required by a regulated economy directed to the satisfaction of needs. It should not be confused with the general overproduction which occurs during a crisis. Nevertheless, in a capitalist society, this kind of overproduction may also be a factor which helps to intensify the crisis.

Equilibrium conditions in the capitalist process of accumulation

Simple reproduction – which does not actually occur in a capitalist society, in which the accumulation of capital is a matter of life and death, though of course this does not exclude the possibility of stagnant or even diminished reproduction in any particular year of the business cycle – already requires certain complicated relations of proportionality; and these become still more complicated if the process of accumulation is to proceed without disruption. Marx gives the following schema:

> I   Production of the means of production:
> $$4,000\,C + 1,000\,V + 1,000\,S = 6,000$$
> II Production of the means of consumption:
> $$1,500\,C + 750\,V + 750\,S = 3,000$$
> Total value of the social product $= 9,000$

Assume that I accumulates half its surplus value ($= 500$) and consumes the other half as income. We would then have the following turnovers: ($1,000\,V + 500\,S$) of I, which are spent as income, are turned over by I against $1,500\,C$ of II. In this way II replaces its constant capital and supplies I with the required means of consumption, a turnover which is exactly analogous to that which we encountered in the case of simple reproduction. Of the 500 S which remains in I and should be converted into capital, 400 will become constant capital and 100 variable capital if the organic composition remains unchanged. The 500 S exists as means of production, and

400 of these must exist in a form appropriate to the expansion of constant capital in department I, which thus adds this amount to its constant capital. The balance of 100 S must be converted into variable capital, that is to say, into means of subsistence which must be purchased from II. Since the 100 S are actually means of production, II would have to use them to enlarge its own constant capital. For I, then, we have a capital of 4,400 C + 1,100 V = 5,500.

Department II now has 1,600 C as constant capital, and in order to put it to work needs an additional 50 V in money for the purchase of new labour power, so that its variable capital grows from 750 to 800. This expansion of the constant and variable capital of II by a total of 150 is provided out of its surplus value, so that only 600 of the 750 S in II remain for the consumption of the capitalists of this department, whose annual product is now distributed as follows:

II   1,600 C + 800 V + 600 S (consumption fund) = 3,000

Thus we now have the following schema:
  I   4,400 C + 1,100 V + 500 (consumption fund) = 6,000
  II   1,600 C + 800 V + 600 (consumption fund) = 3,000

Total =   9,000 as above

Of these amounts, the following are capital:

$$\left.\begin{array}{l} \text{I} \quad 4,400\,\text{C} + 1,100\,\text{V (money)} = 5,500 \\[4pt] \text{II} \quad 1,600\,\text{C} + 800\,\text{V (money)} \quad = 2,400 \end{array}\right\} = 7,900$$

whereas production began with:

$$\left.\begin{array}{l} \text{I} \quad 4,000\,\text{C} + 1,000\,\text{V} = 5,000 \\[4pt] \text{II} \quad 1,500\,\text{C} + 750\,\text{V} \quad = 2,250 \end{array}\right\} = 7,250$$

We can see here a series of new complications. For one thing, the 500 S in I, which are to be accumulated, must be produced as means of production in such a way that 4/5ths of them are suitable as constant capital for I, and 1/5th as constant capital for II. Hence the scale of accumulation in II depends upon the accumulation in I. In I half the surplus value is accumulated, but in II this is impossible; from the surplus value of 750 only 150, 1/5th, can be accumulated while 4/5ths must be consumed.

Let us now consider the further development of accumulation. If production is actually undertaken with the enlarged capital, we shall have at the end of the following year:

$$\left.\begin{array}{l} \text{I} \quad 4{,}400\,\text{C} + 1{,}100\,\text{V} + 1{,}100\,\text{S} = 6{,}600 \\[6pt] \text{II} \quad 1{,}600\,\text{C} + \phantom{1{,}}800\,\text{V} + \phantom{1{,}}800\,\text{S} = 3{,}200 \end{array}\right\} = 9{,}800$$

If accumulation continues in the same way we shall obtain in the next year:

$$\left.\begin{array}{l} \text{I} \quad 4{,}840\,\text{C} + 1{,}210\,\text{V} + 1{,}210\,\text{S} = 7{,}260 \\[6pt] \text{II} \quad 1{,}760\,\text{C} + \phantom{1{,}}880\,\text{V} + \phantom{1{,}}880\,\text{S} = 3{,}520 \end{array}\right\} = 10{,}780$$

In this example we have assumed that half the surplus value in I is accumulated, and that I $(V + \frac{1}{2}S) = $ II C. If accumulation is to take place, I $(V + S)$ must always be greater than II C because a part of I S cannot in fact be converted into II C, but must function as means of production. On the other hand, I $(V + \frac{1}{2}S)$ may be greater or smaller than II C. For present purposes it is unnecessary to examine the matter in greater detail.[7]

Increased production requires a larger quantity of gold for its turnover. Given a constant velocity of circulation, and disregarding credit, this increased amount of gold must be provided by gold production. Capitalist production here encounters a natural barrier, and although the credit system pushes back this limit very considerably it cannot do away with it altogether.

Let us now consider for a moment the necessary preconditions under which the processes of circulation required by accumulation can take place. In our example, we have assumed that 500 S in I is accumulated and that of this amount 400 is converted into constant capital. What circulation processes make this possible, and with what money does I purchase the 400?

Let us look first at accumulation by a single capitalist. He cannot convert the surplus value into capital until it has reached a certain magnitude. The surplus value which is converted into money at the end of each year must therefore be hoarded in the form of money over a number of years. The capitals of the various branches of industry, as well as the individual capitals within each industry, are at different stages in the process of converting surplus value into capital. Hence, while some capitalists are always converting their potential money capital into productive capital, when it has grown large enough for that purpose, others are still engaged in amassing their potential money capital. The capitalists in these two categories therefore face each other, one group as buyers and the other as sellers, each performing one of these roles exclusively.

Suppose, for example, that A sells 600 (400 C + 100 V + 100 S) to B (who may represent more than one buyer). He has sold 600 in commodities for 600 in money, of which 100 represents surplus value which he withdraws from circulation and hoards as money. But this 100 in money is only the money form of the surplus product in which a value of 100 is incorporated. The formation of a hoard is in no way a part of production, or an increment of production. The action of the capitalist consists merely in withdrawing from circulation 100 obtained by the sale of his surplus product, and holding on to it, hoarding it. This operation is carried on not only by A, but at numerous points on the periphery of circulation by other capitalists – A^1, A^2, A^3 – all of whom are just as busily engaged in this sort of hoarding. These numerous points at which money is withdrawn from circulation and accumulated in many individual hoards of potential money capital appear as so many obstacles to circulation, because they stop the movement of money and deprive it of its capacity to circulate for a longer or shorter time.

A can accumulate such a hoard, however, only in so far as he is a seller of his surplus product, not as a buyer. His continuous production of surplus product, embodying his surplus value which is to be converted into money, is a precondition for the formation of his hoard. Hence, although A withdraws money from circulation and hoards it, from another side he throws commodities into circulation, without withdrawing other commodities in return, so that B^1, B^2, B^3 etc., for their part, are enabled to throw money into circulation and only withdraw commodities in return.

Once more we find here, as we did in the case of simple reproduction, that the disposal of the various elements of annual reproduction, that is to say, their circulation which must comprise the reproduction of the capital to the point of replacing its various elements such as constant, variable, fixed, circulating, money, and commodity capital, is not based upon the mere purchase of commodities followed by a corresponding sale, or a mere sale followed by a corresponding purchase, so that there would actually be a bare exchange of commodity for commodity [in which money would be only a means of circulation and therefore relatively superfluous – R.H.] as the political economists assume, especially the free trade school from the time of the physiocrats and Adam Smith [led astray by their own polemical interests in the struggle against the bullionist and mercantilist systems – R.H.]. We know that the fixed capital, once its investment is made, is not replaced during the entire period of its function, but serves in its old form until its value is gradually precipitated in the form of money.[8]

What money here makes possible for the first time is this separation and emancipation of the circulation of value from the constancy of the technical function in the process of production. For society as a whole this separation is not possible, and new fixed capital must be provided whenever the old capital wears out, but in the case of an individual that part of value which is retained for depreciation can be held for years in money form.

Now we have seen that the periodical renewal of the fixed capital of II C – the entire value of the capital of II C being converted into elements of I valued at $(V + S)$ – presupposes on the one hand the mere purchase of the fixed portion of II C, which is reconverted from the form of money into its material form, and to which corresponds the mere sale of I S; and presupposes on the other hand a mere sale on the part of II C, the sale of its fixed (depreciating) value, which is precipitated in money and to which corresponds the mere purchase of I S. In order that the transaction may take place normally in this case it must be assumed that the mere purchase on the part of II C is equal in value to mere sale on the part of II C. . . otherwise simple reproduction is interrupted. The mere sale on one side must be offset by a mere purchase on the other. It must likewise be assumed that the mere sale of that portion of I S which forms the hoards of A^1, A^2, A^3, is balanced by the mere purchase of that portion of I S which converts the hoards of B^1, B^2, B^3, into elements of additional productive capital.

So far as the balance is restored by the fact that the buyer acts later on as a seller to the same amount, and vice versa, the money returns to the side that has advanced it in the first place, which sold first before it bought again. But the actual balance, so far as the exchange of commodities itself is concerned, that is to say, the disposal of the various portions of the annual product, is conditioned on the equal value of the commodities exchanged for one another.

But to the extent that only one-sided purchases are made, a number of mere purchases on the one hand, a number of mere sales on the other – and we have seen that the normal disposal of the annual product on the basis of capitalist production requires such one-sided metamorphoses – the balance can be maintained only on the assumption that the value of the one-sided purchases and one-sided sales is the same.

In all these one-sided transactions money does not function merely as a mediator in the exchange of commodities, but as the initiator or concluder of a process in which there is only the commodity on one side and the value of the commodity in its independent form – money – on the other; so that money is essential to enable these one-sided processes to continue.

The fact that the production of commodities is the general form of capitalist production implies the role which money is playing, not only as a medium of circulation, but also as money capital, and creates conditions peculiar to the normal transaction of exchange under this mode of production, and therefore peculiar to the normal course of reproduction, whether it be on a simple or expanded scale. These conditions become so many causes of abnormal movements, implying the possibility of crisis, since a balance is an accident under the crude conditions of this production.[9]

Through the sale of their surplus product, capitalists A^1, A^2, A^3, form a hoard of additional potential money capital. In the present case, this surplus product consists of means of production which B^1, B^2, B^3 use in the production of means of production. Only in their hands does this surplus product serve as additional constant capital, although it is virtually such while it is in the hands of the accumulators of hoards, A^1, A^2, A^3 in department I, even before it is sold. If we consider simply the volume of values of reproduction on the part of I, then we are still moving within the limits of simple reproduction. The only difference is that other use values have been produced. Within the same sum of value more means of production for means of production, instead of for means of consumption, have been produced.

A part of I S which was previously exchanged for II C under simple reproduction, and had therefore to consist of means of production exchanged for means of consumption, now comprises means of production exchanged for means of production, which can be incorporated as such in the constant capital of I. Considering the matter only from the point of view of the volume of value, it follows that the material basis of expanded reproduction is being produced within simple reproduction, by the surplus labour of the working class in department I, expended directly in the production of means of production, the creation of virtual additional capital for I.

The formation of virtual additional money capital by A^1, A^2, A^3, through the successive sales of their surplus product, which was formed without any capitalist expenditure of money, is in this case the mere money form of the additional means of production produced by I.

The production of virtual additional money capital on a large scale, at numerous points on the periphery of circulation, is therefore only a result and expression of a multifarious production of virtual additional productive capital whose rise does not itself require any additional expenditure of money on the part of industrial capitalists.[10]

The successive transformation of this virtual additional productive capital into virtual money capital (hoard) on the part of A^1, A^2, A^3, etc. (I), conditioned on the successive sale of their surplus product, which is a repeated one-sided sale without a compensating purchase, is accomplished by a repeated withdrawal of money from circulation and a corresponding formation of a hoard. This hoarding, except where the buyer is a gold producer, does not in any way imply additional wealth in precious metals, but only a change of function on the part of money previously circulating. A while ago, it served as a medium of circulation, now it serves as a hoard, as a virtual additional money capital in process of formation. In other words, the formation of additional money capital and the quantity of precious metals existing in a country are not causally related.

Hence it follows further that the greater the productive capital already functioning in a particular country (including the labour power incorporated in it as the producer of the surplus product), the more developed the productive power of labour and at the same time the technical means for the rapid extension of the production of means of production, and the greater therefore the quantity of the surplus product both as to its value and to the quantity of use values in which it is expressed, so much greater is:

1 The virtual additional productive capital in the form of a surplus product in the hands of A^1, A^2, A^3, etc., and
2 The mass of this surplus product transformed into money, in other words, the virtual additional money capital in the hands of A^1, A^2, A^3.

The fact that Fullarton, for instance, will have nothing to do with any overproduction in the ordinary meaning of the term, but only with the overproduction of capital, meaning money capital, shows how pitifully little even the best bourgeois economists understand about the mechanism of their own system.[11]

While the surplus product, directly produced and appropriated by the capitalists, A^1, A^2, A^3 (I), is the real basis of the accumulation of capital, that is to say, of expanded reproduction, although it does not actually serve in this capacity until it reaches the hands of the capitalists, B^1, B^2, B^3, etc. (I), it is on the contrary quite unproductive in its chrysalis stage of money, as a hoard representing virtual money capital in process of formation. It runs parallel with the process of production, but moves outside it. It is a dead weight of capitalist production. The desire to utilize this surplus value, which is accumulating as virtual money capital, for the purpose of deriving profit or revenue from it, finds its consummation in the credit system and paper securities. Money capital thereby gains in another form an enormous influence on the course and the stupendous development of the capitalist system of production.

The surplus product converted into virtual money capital will grow so much more in volume, the greater the aggregate amount of capital already functioning which brought it into existence. With the absolute increase in the volume of the annually reproduced virtual money capital, its segmentation also becomes easier, so that it is more rapidly invested in a particular business, either in the hands of the same capitalist or in those of others (for instance, members of the family in the case of division of inheritances, etc.). By segmentation of money capital is meant here that it is wholly detached from the parent capital in order to be invested as new money capital in a new and independent business.[12]

While the sellers of the surplus product, A, A^1, A^2 (I), have obtained it as a direct outcome of the process of production, B, B^1, B^2, can only obtain it through an act of circulation. Having first accumulated the money for this, just as A, A^1, A^2 are now doing by the sale of their respective surplus products, they have now attained their goal. Their virtual money capital, accumulated as a hoard, now functions effectively as additional money capital.

The money which is necessary for these exchanges of surplus products must be available in the hands of the capitalist class. In simple reproduction money which served only as revenue for expenditure on means of consumption, returned to the capitalists in the same amount as they advanced it in order to turn over their respective commodities; but in this case, although the same money reappears it has a changed function. The As and Bs (I) supply each other alternately with the money for converting their surplus product into additional virtual capital, and alternately throw the newly formed money capital back into circulation as a means of purchase.

All that is presupposed here is that the volume of money existing in the country (assuming a constant velocity of circulation, etc.) is also adequate for the active circulation; the same presupposition which, as we saw, had to be made in the case of simple commodity circulation. Only the function of the hoard is different here.

This schematic presentation is, of course, greatly simplified. Clearly, the proportional relations between the capital goods and the consumer goods industries as a whole must also prevail in each separate branch of production. These schemas also show, however, that in capitalist production, both simple reproduction and expanded reproduction can proceed without interruption as long as these proportions are maintained. Conversely, a crisis can occur even in the case of simple reproduction if the proportions are violated; for example, that between depreciated capital and capital ready for new investment. It does not follow at all, therefore, that a crisis in capitalist production is caused by the underconsumption of the masses which is inherent in it. A crisis could just as well be brought about by a too rapid expansion of consumption, or by a static or declining production of capital goods. Nor does it follow from these schemas themselves that a general overproduction of commodities is possible; but rather that any expansion of production allowed by the available productive forces appears possible.

17

The causes of crises

If one considers the complicated relations of proportionality which must exist in production, despite its anarchic character, one is led to pose the question as to where the responsibility for maintaining these relations lies. Clearly, it is the price mechanism which performs this function, since prices regulate capitalist production, and changes in price determine the expansion or contraction of production, the initiation of a new line of production, etc. This also explains the necessity of an objective law of value as the only possible regulator of the capitalist economy. The disruption of these proportional relations must be explained in terms of a disruption in the specific regulatory mechanism of production, or in other words, in terms of a distortion of the price structure which prevents prices from giving a proper indication of the needs of production. Since such disruptions occur periodically, the distortions of the price structure must also be shown to be periodic.

The capitalist is not primarily concerned with the absolute price level of his product, but with the relation between the market price and the cost price, or in other words, with the level of profit. It is this which determines the branches of production in which he invests his capital. If there is a marked decline in profit, new investment is abandoned, particularly when it is a matter of large-scale investment in fixed capital, because such capital is tied up for a long time and the price of fixed capital is crucial in calculating the rate of profit.

As we already know, the organic composition of capital changes. For technological reasons, constant capital increases more rapidly than does variable capital, fixed capital than circulating capital. The relative reduction of the variable component of capital results in a fall in the rate of profit. A crisis involves a slump in sales. In capitalist society this presupposes a cessation of new capital investment, which in turn presupposes a fall in the rate of profit. This decline in the rate of profit is entailed by the change in the organic composition of capital, which has taken place as a result of the investment of new capital. A crisis is simply the point at which the rate of profit begins to fall. But the crisis is preceded by a long period of prosperity, in which prices and profits are high. How does this turn of fortune in the capitalist world occur, this transition from the blessed state of feverishly intense activity, high profits, and accelerated accumulation, to the hopelessness and despair of a slump in sales, dwindling profits and widespread idleness of capital?

Every industrial cycle begins with an expansion of production, the causes of which vary according to particular historical circumstances but which in general can be attributed to the opening of new markets, the establishment of new branches of production, the introduction of new technology, and the expansion of needs resulting from population growth. As demand increases prices and profits rise in particular branches of production, and they expand their output, which in turn increases the demand for products from those sectors of industry which supply their means of production. New investments of fixed capital, and the replacement of old and technically outmoded equipment, are undertaken on a large scale. The process becomes general as the expansion of each branch of industry creates a demand for the output of other industries. The various sectors of production feed upon each other and industry becomes its own best customer.

Thus the cycle begins with the renewal and growth of fixed capital, which is the main source of the incipient prosperity, and as the expansion continues this new investment is accompanied by the most intensive possible utilization of all the available forces of production.

To the same extent, therefore, that the magnitude of the value and the duration of the fixed capital develop with the evolution of the capitalist mode of production, so does the life of industry and of industrial capital develop in each particular investment into one of many years, say of ten years on average. If the development of fixed capital extends the length of this life on one side, it is on the other side shortened by the continuous revolution of the instruments of production, which likewise increases incessantly with the development of capitalist production. This implies a change in the instruments of production and the necessity of continuous replacement on account of their virtual depreciation long before they are worn out physically. One may assume that this life-cycle, in the essential branches of large-scale industry, now averages ten years. However, it is not a question here of the precise figure. So much at least is evident, that this cycle, extending over several years, through which capital is compelled to pass by its fixed part, furnishes a material basis for the periodical commercial crises in which business goes through successive periods of lassitude, average activity, frantic acceleration, and crisis. It is true that the periods in which capital is invested are different in time and place. But a crisis is always a starting point for a large amount of new investment Therefore it also constitutes, from the point of view of society, more or less of a new material basis for the next cycle of turnover.[1]

But there is another cause of the rise in the rate of profit at the beginning of a period of prosperity, besides the increased demand previously described. Along with, and as a result of, the increase in demand, the turnover period of capital is shortened. The work period for a given output is reduced because the introduction of technical improvements makes it possible to produce more rapidly. For example, the auxiliary workers in mining are reduced to the minimum required to maintain output, machinery is more intensively utilized by speeding up its running time and especially by extending the working day (through the elimination of idle shifts, overtime, hiring of extra workers). Furthermore, the turnover time is shortened when sales go on uninterruptedly, and it is frequently reduced to zero because work is done to order. Many important branches of industry increase their sales in nearby domestic markets relative to sales in distant foreign markets, and this too shortens the circulation time. All these factors bring about a rise in the annual rate of profit, since the productive capital, including the variable capital which produces surplus value, is turned over more rapidly.

The shortening of turnover time also means that the industrialist has to advance a smaller amount of money capital in relation to his productive capital. In the first place, better use is made of the available productive capital without any greater outlay of money capital, or at least without a correspondingly greater outlay, as a result of shortening the period of work required by accelerating the tempo of machine operations, and in general by using more intensively the available elements of production. Second, the circulation time is reduced, and along with it the amount of capital which the capitalist must keep on hand during the period of circulation, in addition to the capital that is actually functioning in production. In this way the capital used only for purposes of circulation, unproductive capital, is diminished in relation to the profit-producing capital which functions in production. At the same time the contraction of the circulation period and the accelerated turnover reduce the amount of capital which is lying idle in the form of commodity stocks, which represents an unproductive expense. Thus the annual rate of surplus value and profit rises, the latter particularly sharply because of the reduction in the amount of capital devoted to circulation. At the same time the total sum of surplus value increases and along with it the opportunities for accumulation.

Industrial prosperity simply means, therefore, improved conditions for the valorization of capital. But the very conditions which at first make for prosperity contain within themselves potentialities which gradually worsen the conditions for valorization, until finally a point is reached where new capital investment ceases and there is an evident slump in sales.

For example, if the growth of demand in the first phase of the industrial cycle involves a rise in the rate of profit, this rise nevertheless occurs in circumstances which prepare the way for a later fall. During the period of prosperity there is a large amount of new capital investment, reflecting the latest advances in technology. As we know, however, technical improvements are expressed in a higher organic composition of capital, and this involves a decline in the rate of profit, a deterioration of the conditions for the valorization of capital. The rate of profit declines for two reasons: first, because the variable capital diminishes as a proportion of total capital, so that the same rate of surplus value represents a lower rate of profit; and second, because the larger the amount of fixed capital in relation to circulating capital the longer is the turnover period for capital, and this too involves a decline in the rate of profit.

There are other circumstances which extend the turnover time. At the peak of prosperity labour time per unit of output may increase as a result of a shortage of labour, especially skilled labour, to say nothing of wage disputes which are usually more widespread during such periods. There may also be disruptions of the work process, resulting from an overintensive utilization of the constant capital; for instance, through excessive speeding up of machines which may also be damaged by the employment of inexperienced workers, or by the neglect of repairs and maintenance in order to take full advantage of the brief period of industrial boom. As the cycle continues, turnover time increases again. Once domestic demand has been met, more distant foreign markets have to be sought, and the marketing of commodities and their reconversion into money takes a longer time. All these factors bring about a fall in the rate of profit in the second phase of prosperity.

There are also other factors to be considered. During prosperity the demand for labour power increases and its price rises. This involves a reduction in the rate of surplus value and hence in the rate of profit. Furthermore, the rate of interest rises gradually above its normal level for reasons which will be discussed later, and as a result the rate of entrepreneurial profit falls. Of course, the profit of bank capital is thereby increased (a consideration which is usually overlooked). Yet, during a period such as this, the banks are no longer in a position to make their funds available for the expansion of production. In the first place, speculation in both commodities and securities is in full spate and makes increasing demands on the supply of credit. Second, as we shall see presently, the circulation credit which producers extend to each other becomes inadequate to meet the increased demands, and here too the banks must help out. The banks will therefore tend to retain their profit in liquid form, as money, and this impedes its conversion into productive capital, and hence any real accumulation and expansion of the reproduction process. At the same time, this involves a disruption of the process of production, since as a result of the obstacles to the reconversion of the money capital which the banks have attracted by the higher rate of interest and have retained in money form, a part of the productive capital intended for expanded reproduction remains unsaleable. Thus the decline in entrepreneurial profit means increasingly unfavourable conditions for realization, and a lower level of accumulation for the whole capitalist class.

A crisis begins at the moment when the tendencies toward a falling rate of profit, described above, prevail over the tendencies which have brought about increases in prices and profits, as a result of rising demand. Two questions suggest themselves at this point. First, how do these tendencies, which presage the end of prosperity, assert themselves in and through capitalist competition? Second, why does this occur in the form of a crisis, suddenly rather than gradually? The latter question is less important, for it is the alternation of prosperity and depression which is crucial for the wave-like character of the business cycle, and the suddenness of the change is a secondary matter.

This much at least is clear: if price rises during prosperity were general and uniform they would remain purely nominal. If the prices of all commodities were to rise by 10 per cent or 100 per cent, their exchange relationship would remain unchanged.[2] The rise in prices would then have no effect upon production; there would be no redistribution of capital among the various branches of production and no change in the proportional relations. If production is carried on in the proper proportions (as was shown in the schema presented earlier) these relations need not change and no disruption need occur. It is different, however, if the character of price changes is such as to exclude uniformity. The changed price structure may then bring about changes in the proportional relations among the various branches of production; for the changes in prices and profits crucially affect the allocation of capital among these different branches. This possibility becomes a reality once it is evident that the rise in prices must necessarily be accompanied by a shift in the distribution of capital. And indeed, the existence of factors which prevent prices from rising uniformly can easily be shown.

Leaving aside revolutions in technology and considering only the ordinary, constant technical improvements, we may say that the greatest change in the organic composition of capital, which is responsible, in the last analysis, for the fall in the rate of profit, will occur where the use of machinery and of fixed capital in general is greatest. For the larger the amount of machinery, scientific knowledge, etc., that is already employed, the greater will be the opportunity for further rationalization of production, improved techniques, and more scientific methods. Hence the tendencies toward a higher organic composition of capital become even stronger. The higher organic composition of capital, however, is only the economic expression of increased productivity, which means a lower price for the same quantity of commodities. Newly invested capital, therefore, obtains an extra profit, and capital will flow into such spheres of investment. At this point a disruptive factor supervenes. The larger the extra profit to be made from these new investments the more capital flows into these spheres. This movement can only be corrected when the new products of these sectors of industry come on to the market, and oversupply depresses prices.[3] In the meantime, however, the demand of such industries will also have driven up the prices of products in other sectors, which will now attract capital, though on a smaller scale because, owing to their lower level of technological development, the extra profit is smaller. A further consequence is that the price rise is relatively greater in the latter sectors, since they have not increased their capital to the same extent. In the first sector of production the extra profit is considerable, in the second less so, but this situation is gradually equalized by a reduction in the extra profit through the inflow of capital in the first case, and by price increases as a result of a relatively smaller inflow of capital in the second.

With the development of capitalist production the sum of fixed capital grows, and along with it an increasing differentiation among the various industries with respect to the quantity of fixed capital they employ. The larger the amount of fixed capital, however, the longer is the period of time required to install new plant, and hence the greater the difference between various branches of industry in the time required to expand production. The longer it takes to invest in new plant the more difficult it is to adapt to the needs of consumption; and the longer supply lags behind demand the more strongly do prices rise and the more widespread does the pressure to accumulate capital become in such industries.

The larger the mass of fixed capital, the longer does it take for the changes to become effective and productivity to increase. Until that happens, however, supply will continue to lag behind demand. It takes much longer to increase the number of blast furnaces, sink new coal shafts, and complete new railways, than it does to expand textile or paper production. Thus, while a higher organic composition of capital intensifies the causes which must bring about, in the long run, a fall in the rate of profit, these sectors are able, nevertheless, because of the changed conditions of competition resulting from the slower growth of supply in relation to demand, to raise their prices more sharply than other branches of production. Not only do their profits not diminish; on the contrary, the change in organic composition is accompanied by rising prices and profits, and indeed there is a general tendency for prices to rise more steeply where the organic composition of capital is most highly developed. Since capital flows into those sectors which have the highest profit, the new capital which is being accumulated will be largely diverted into them, and this will continue until the new investments have been completed and the stronger competition from new plants makes itself felt. There is thus a tendency toward overinvestment and overaccumulation of capital in the sectors with the highest organic composition in comparison with those which have a lower organic composition. This disproportion becomes apparent when the products of the first sector reach the market. The sale of these new products is impeded because production in those sectors with a lower organic composition has not increased equally, or at the same speed, but more rapidly though less intensively. This explains why crises are most severe in those branches of production which are technologically most advanced; for example, in the textile (cotton) industry at an earlier time, and subsequently in heavy industry. In general, a crisis is most severe where the turnover of capital is most prolonged and technical improvements and innovations are most advanced, and hence, for the most part, where the organic composition is highest.

The crisis itself depresses prices and profits below their normal level, that is, below the price of production and the average rate of profit respectively. Production contracts and the weaker concerns fail, leaving the field to those which can achieve an average profit even at the lower prices. But the average profit is now at a different level. It no longer reflects the organic composition which existed at the start of the industrial cycle, but the changed, higher organic composition of capital.

Conversely, the industries with a smaller amount of fixed capital are able to adapt more quickly to the requirements of consumption, price rises are more limited (leaving aside fluctuations in the prices of raw materials) and there is less pressure to accumulate capital. This is another reason for the emergence of disproportionality, through the concentration of new investment-seeking capital upon those branches of production with the most rapid and extreme price increases, and at the same time a reason for the fact that, in general, the effects of crises are more severe the more extensive the fixed capital, and most severe in those branches of production where the amount of fixed capital is greatest.

It should be added here that the larger the quantity of capital required at any given time by the level of technology in a particular branch of production, the more difficult it becomes to effect a precise quantitative adaptation of increased production to the increased consumption. It is technically irrational and hence uneconomic to increase steel production by making a new investment in a small steel works. The technological imperative here dictates the scale of expansion without any regard for whether such expansion corresponds with the needs of consumption.

Expansion in the heavy industries, once all the available productive forces
are fully utilized (and variations in the possibility of utilization are an
important factor in making adjustments to minor fluctuations in demand)
can only occur on a large scale, in sudden spurts, not on the modest scale
characteristic of the early period of capitalism. The light industries are far
more adaptable in this respect, and hence their price increases in the interim
period are smaller.

In addition to these disproportions in the price structure which result
from the diversity of organic composition there are others which arise from
natural conditions. We have seen that there is a tendency to overaccumulation in those sectors which have a higher organic composition of
capital. These sectors are not only large consumers of raw materials, but
also supply raw materials and semi-manufactured goods (iron, coal) to
other industries. Disruptions of proportionality may also occur here.

We have seen in Volume II that once the commodities have been
converted into money, sold, a certain portion of this money must be
reconverted into the material elements of constant capital, and this
in proportion to the technical nature of any given sphere of production. In this respect, the most important element in all
lines – aside from wages, or variable capital – is the raw material,
including the auxiliary substances, which are particularly important
in all lines of production that do not use any raw materials in the
strict meaning of the term; for instance, in mining and extractive
industries in general. . . . If the price of raw materials rises, it may be
impossible to make it good fully out of the price of the commodities
after deducting the wages. Violent fluctuations of price, therefore,
cause interruptions, great collisions, or even catastrophes in the process of reproduction. It is especially the products of agriculture, raw
materials taken from organic nature, which are subject to such fluctuations of value in consequence of changing yields, etc., leaving
aside altogether the question of the credit system. . . . A second element, which is mentioned at this point only for the sake of completeness, since competition and the credit system are still outside the
scope of our analysis, is this: it is in the nature of things that vegetable and animal substances which are dependent on certain laws of
time for their growth and production, cannot be suddenly augmented
in the same degree as, for instance, machines and other fixed capital
or coal, ore, etc., whose augmentation, assuming the natural requirements to be present, can be accomplished in a very short time in an
industrial country. It is therefore possible, and under a developed
system of capitalist production even inevitable, that the production
and augmentation of that portion of constant capital which consists

of fixed capital, machinery, etc., should run ahead of that portion which consists of organic raw materials, so that the demand for these last materials grows more rapidly than their supply, and their price rises in consequence. The rise in prices carries with it the following results: (1) a shipping of raw materials from great distances, seeing that the rising price covers greater freight rates; (2) an increase in their production which, however, for natural reasons will not be felt until the following year; (3) the use of various hitherto unused substitutes and a better economizing of waste. If this rise in prices begins to exert a marked influence on production and supply, the turning point has generally arrived at which, on account of the protracted rise in the price of the raw material and of all commodities in which it is an element, demand falls so that a reaction in the price of raw material takes place. Aside from convulsions due to the depreciation of capital in various forms, this reaction is also accompanied by other circumstances which will be mentioned shortly.

It is already evident from the foregoing that the greater the development of capitalist production, the greater the means of suddenly and permanently increasing that portion of the constant capital which consists of machinery, etc., and the more rapidly accumulation takes place (as it does particularly in times of prosperity), the greater is the relative overproduction of machinery and other fixed capital, the more frequent the relative underproduction of vegetable and animal raw materials, and the more pronounced the above-mentioned rise in their prices and the subsequent reaction. And the convulsions increase correspondingly in frequency in so far as they are due to the violent price fluctuations of one of the main elements in the process of reproduction.[4]

The closer we approach our own time in the history of production, so much more regularly do we find, especially in the essential branches of industry, the ever recurring alternation between relative appreciation and the resulting subsequent depreciation of raw materials obtained from organic nature.[5]

These disruptions are complemented by others which arise from the manner in which fixed capital is reproduced. We have seen that in simple reproduction, the fixed capital which has been consumed must equal that which is to be newly invested. In fact, this condition is never strictly fulfilled, and to compensate for the discrepancy there must always be available on one side a surplus of elements of fixed capital, a stock of commodities, which represents, on the other side, a reserve of money capital. A certain amount of reserve stock, and a certain amount of hoarding, is a condition of reproduction, which would otherwise always come to a standstill at some point. The elasticity of capital itself also helps to smooth out minor fluctuations and makes possible the satisfaction of particularly urgent needs by speeding up production, overtime working, etc. The feverish harnessing of all the powers of production diminishes the stock of commodities on one side and of money on the other (both relatively and absolutely) and thus eliminates a factor which in normal times helps to compensate any imbalances. This reduction in the money capital reserve becomes absolute on the eve of the crisis, because on one side the industrialist capitalists' demand for money reaches a peak at such a time, and on the other side the demand for money as a means of payment rises rapidly, as the rate at which capital flows back begins to slow down, and along with it the supply of commercial credit. Any further decline in sales cannot now be met by drawing upon reserve money capital and hence leads to bankruptcy.

Proportionality may also be disrupted by a change in the relation between production and consumption. In times of prosperity both prices and profits rise. The rise in commodity prices must necessarily be greater than that in wages, or there would be no increase in profit. Consequently, the share of the entrepreneurial class in the new production increases more rapidly than does that of the workers. In absolute terms there is an increase in consumption, since the entrepreneurs, like the workers, will consume more. But accumulation increases still more rapidly, for this is a period in which the drive to accumulate capital is especially strong, and there is always an interval before luxury consumption begins to grow. The demand for luxury goods is in any case very elastic and easily accommodates itself to the drive toward accumulation. Thus there is a redeployment of profit; a relatively larger part of it is accumulated, a relatively smaller part is devoted to consumption. This means that consumption does not keep pace with the increase in production. It should also be borne in mind that a certain part of consumption remains unchanged since it is based upon fixed salaries, or upon incomes which are not derived directly from production. Such income strata are only affected indirectly by fluctuations in production.

Thus, disproportional relations arise in the course of the business cycle from disturbances in the price structure. All the factors mentioned above involve deviations of market prices from production prices, and hence disruptions in the regulation of production, which depends for its extent and direction upon the structure of prices. It is clear that such disturbances must eventually lead to a slump in sales. They are also accompanied and mediated by various phenomena in the credit system, which we must now analyse.

Credit conditions in the course of the business cycle

At the beginning of a period of prosperity a low rate of interest prevails, which rises only slowly and gradually. Loan capital is plentiful. The expansion of production, and hence of circulation, does indeed increase the demand for loan capital. But the increased demand is easily satisfied, first because the money capital which was lying idle during the depression is available, and second because the onset of a period of prosperity is accompanied by an expansion of circulation credit. Thus, while the commodity capital of industrialists and merchants, which has to be reconverted into money capital, has increased both in volume and in price, the necessary means for circulating it are supplied by the increased amount of credit money. Along with this increase in the amount of credit money its velocity of circulation is also accelerated as a result of the more rapid turnover of commodity capital. The increased supply of loan capital, brought about by the more extensive creation of credit money, is sufficient to meet the increased demand for loan capital without a rise in the interest rate.

In this period the supply of loan capital also grows because the amount of money capital which producers must have available during the turnover period (which depends upon the length of time involved) has diminished as a result of the reduction of turnover time, and the capital thus released comes on to the money market as loan capital.

As prosperity continues, however, these conditions change, and the gradual changes are reflected in the gradual rise in the interest rate. We saw earlier that during a period of prosperity the turnover time of capital is extended, and a disproportion emerges between the various branches of production. The extension of turnover time, that is, the greater sluggishness of sales, also means a slackening of the velocity of circulation of credit money. A bill which falls due in three months cannot be met if the commodity whose money form it represents is only paid for after four months. The bill must either be renewed or settled in cash. Renewal means having recourse to credit, to capital credit provided by the bank, and this involves an increased demand for bank credit. Demand for bank credit will be general because the need to renew bills will not just affect an individual capitalist, but a certain proportion of the whole class of productive capitalists. The increased demand for bank credit, which simply results from the fact that the circulation credit with which the productive capitalists provide each other is no longer adequate, as well as the increased demand for cash, has a direct effect in raising the interest rate.

Increasing disproportionality, which also signifies that sales are slumping, has the same effect. One commodity must be exchanged for another if credit money is to perform its function of replacing cash. If the reciprocal turnover of commodities comes to a halt then cash must take the place of credit money. The bill cannot be met when it falls due because the commodity which it represents has not been sold. If it is, nevertheless, to be redeemed that can only be done by recourse to bank credit which thus takes the place of circulation credit. It is a matter of indifference to the industrialist whether the bill which he has accepted in payment for his commodity is redeemed through circulation credit (which means, in the final analysis, that his commodity is exchanged for another commodity) or through bank credit (in which case his commodity has not as yet been definitively exchanged for another). Of course, he now has to pay a somewhat higher rate of interest, but he does not understand the reason for it, and even if he did understand, this would not change anything and would do him no good. In any case, prices and profits are still high, and he still needs the money capital which he can get for his bill in order to continue production on the same scale. He is quite unaware that the money capital with which he now operates no longer represents the converted form of his own commodity capital, which in reality has not yet been sold at all. Nor is he aware that he is now continuing production with additional money capital made available to him by the banker.

But this is a circumstance of the greatest importance. The incipient disproportionality must show itself in the formation of stocks of commodities. At some point in the circulation process the commodity must come to a halt. This stock of commodities would be bound to affect the market if the commodity had to be sold, in order to continue production with the money realized from its sale. This effect on the market, and the ensuing effect on prices and profits, is avoided by the banks making money capital available to the producers, and in this way credit obscures the incipient disproportionality. Production continues unchanged and is even greatly expanded in some branches where prices are particularly high, because the drawing in of money capital prevents commodities from exerting pressure on the market, thus causing prices to fall. Thus production appears to be in a perfectly healthy condition even though disproportionality between different branches of production has already developed.

The changes in the level of the interest rate, which are primarily

determined by changes in the relations of proportionality in the course of
the cycle, in turn exert a most powerful influence upon the founding of new
enterprises, upon speculation in commodities and securities, and hence
upon the whole state of stock exchange business. In the initial stages of
prosperity the interest rate is low, and other things being equal this raises
the market quotations of fictitious capital. The price of that part of
fictitious capital, such as state bonds and bonds issued by public
corporations, as well as some types of debentures, which has a fixed and
guaranteed return, rises as a direct result of the fall in the rate of interest. In
the case of shares a rise in their price following the decline in the interest
rate is countered by the reduction of dividends and the greater uncertainty
of yields, but prosperity eliminates this counter tendency, and share
quotations rise as the rate of interest remains low, because yields increase
and become more certain. At the same time speculation increases, with the
aim of exploiting the rise in security prices, and the demand for shares
grows, with the result that prices are driven still higher. The expansion of
production leads to greater activity in the promotion of new companies,
while existing ones increase their capital. The banks become very active in
issuing shares, and the high level of share prices, together with the low
interest rate, bring high profits from such issues. The new shares are quickly
taken up on the stock exchange and are easily sold to the public, that is to
capitalists who have loan capital available. It is in this period that
promotional activity is most vigorous, and the profits made by the banks
from their own issues are greatest. Money liquidity favours speculation,
which is dependent upon the availability of credit for its operations.
Thanks to the low rate of interest, speculation can exploit even small
fluctuations in stock exchange prices such as occur during the initial phase
of prosperity. The stock exchange is lively and the turnover considerable,
and even though price fluctuations are modest, they tend overall to
produce a higher level of quotations. This higher level, which results on one
side from the increase in the volume of securities and their higher prices,
and on the other side from the increased turnover, involves greater recourse
to credit for settling balances, which now require larger sums of money.
This is even more the case since during such periods 'bullish' predominates
over 'bearish' speculation, purchases exceed sales, and the balances which
have finally to be settled are inflated. The increased demand for credit
emanating from the stock exchange is not matched by an increased supply,
unlike the increased demand of productive capitalists which is immediately
met by an expansion of circulation credit. Hence the increased demand has
a direct effect in raising the rate of interest, and reinforces those tendencies
emerging in the sphere of production which operate in the same direction.

Similar developments occur in the field of commodity speculation, which
also tries to take advantage of rising prices and to reinforce the upward

trend. On one side, commodities are brought from other markets to a market where the price is particularly high, thus increasing the supply. Since one importer knows nothing about the activities of others, it is all too easy for the supply ultimately to exceed demand, producing a glut on the market. But on the other side speculation in commodities, like speculation on the stock market, strives to maintain, and if possible augment, the rise in prices. Commodities are withheld from the market for as long as possible in order to raise the price; and 'rings' and 'corners' are formed to force up prices by creating artificial shortages. In order to withhold commodities from the market it is again necessary to resort to credit, and this also contributes to the rise in the rate of interest.

Meanwhile, industrial prosperity has become general and has developed into a boom. Prices and profits reach their highest levels. Share prices rise as a result of higher yields. Speculation, which has on the whole shown a profit, has grown enormously. The prospect of speculative gains becomes infectious, and the general public is drawn increasingly into stock exchange dealings, thus providing the professional speculators with opportunity to expand their operations at the expense of the public. Since the interest rate is high the changes in stock exchange prices must be large enough to prevent the higher interest from absorbing speculative gains, if speculation is to be profitable. In fact, these fluctuations now become significant in another way, because the reports from industry are no longer entirely favourable, and although profits continue to rise, there is stagnation here and there, sales are no longer so buoyant, and access to credit begins to be more difficult once the banks begin to consider it hazardous to follow a policy conducive to speculation. This is particularly the case when, with the greater participation of the general public, there is a considerable increase in the number of people who engage in speculation without resources of their own, or with quite inadequate resources. Similar developments occur on the commodity market.

The rising rate of interest tends, however, to depress stock exchange prices, and eventually a point must be reached at which the effort of speculators to force up prices comes to a halt. This point is reached all the more quickly if some of the credit which was previously available is withdrawn from speculation. We have seen that as prosperity advances productive capitalists have to make increasing demands upon the banks, and to the reasons given for that situation we must now add another. The rate of interest is crucial for the level of promoter's profit. The high rate of interest which prevails during a boom reduces promoter's profit and consequently restricts share issues. In addition, at such a time speculation is already satiated and could not absorb further issues at the current high prices. The banks then confront the danger that they will be unable to dispose of the new issue, or will have to do so at relatively low prices.

The needs of industry are now met by the banks themselves. Instead of issuing shares they grant bank credits, on which the productive capitalists must pay the prevailing high rate of interest. But the greater the commitments of the banks to industry the less funds they are able to make available to speculators. Speculation, therefore, has to contract, and this means a decline in the demand for securities and a fall in stock exchange prices. Since the prevailing level of security prices was the basis of the credit made available for speculative purposes, it now becomes necessary to provide additional funds to support the paper which has served as collateral, or in some other way, as a basis of credit; funds which many of the speculators, and particularly their fellow travellers among the public, cannot supply. So there ensue forced sales of pledged shares, a sudden increase in the supply of shares, and a rapid fall in stock exchange prices. This fall in prices is exacerbated by the manoeuvres of the professional speculators who, having recognized the critical state of the market, now rush into 'bearish' operations. The fall in prices leads to a further restriction of credit and new forced sales; the decline becomes a crash, and a stock exchange crisis and financial panic develops. There is a massive devaluation of paper securities, which fall rapidly below the level corresponding to their real yield at the normal rate of interest. This depreciated paper is then bought up by the large capitalists and banks, in order to be sold later at a higher price when the panic is over and share quotations have risen again. This continues until, in the course of the next cycle, the expropriation of some of the speculators, and the concentration of property in the hands of the money capitalists, again takes place, and the stock exchange performs its function of bringing about a concentration of property through the concentration of fictitious capital.

The immediate cause of a stock exchange crisis, therefore, is the changes which occur in the money market and in the credit situation, and since the advent of such a crisis depends directly upon the level of the interest rate, it can well precede the onset of a general commercial and industrial crisis. None the less, it is only a symptom, an omen, of the latter crisis, since the changes in the money market are indeed determined by the changes in production which lead to a crisis.[1]

Developments similar to those in share speculation also occur in commodity speculation, except that here, in the nature of things, there is a closer connection with the conditions of production. Here too the rise in the rate of interest and the restriction of credit make it more difficult to withhold commodities from the market and so to maintain prices. At the same time the high level of prices encourages maximum production, increased imports, and restraint in consumption, until finally the market collapses. If the commodity is one whose price also affects the price of leading securities on the stock exchange, as is the case with copper, for

example, the collapse of commodity speculation may also be the signal for a
collapse of stock exchange speculation.

The change in money market conditions also has a decisive influence
upon the amount and nature of bank profit. At the beginning of a period of
prosperity the interest rate is low and the profits from share issues large. We
have seen that in the course of the cycle they move in opposite directions.
Moreover, during the whole period of the cycle the bank's profit from its
commissions as an intermediary in the provision of circulation credit
increases; the profit on money dealing capital also increases because
productive capitalists are making more payments; and above all, as the rate of
interest rises, bank capital takes an increasing share of the producers' profit
at the expense of entrepreneurial gains, and of speculative profit at the
expense of marginal gains. The higher the rate of interest, the greater is the
share of finance capital in the fruits of prosperity. While prosperity lasts
money capital increases its share of the profit made by productive capital.

We have also seen that in the course of the cycle there is an increasing
demand for bank credit as soon as the volume of circulation credit has
reached its maximum limit. The demand for bank credit develops because
the expansion of production entails an increase in circulation, and that in
turn requires increased means of circulation. Bank reserves are therefore
gradually depleted and this eventually involves resort to the central bank of
issue. Lagging sales retard the circulation of bills of exchange, thus reducing
the volume of circulation credit and making it necessary for bank credit to
fill the gap. But disproportionality, with all its consequences, continues to
grow, and its effect upon bank credit is reinforced by the growing demands
of speculation. Thus bank credit is gradually strained to the point where the
banks are no longer able to expand credit without an excessive reduction in
their reserves. When circulation can no longer be expanded through the use
of credit there is a demand for cash, and as it flows into circulation in
increasing volume reserves are again reduced and the banks are obliged to
place further restrictions on the provision of credit. These restrictions mean
that industry can no longer correct the dislocations arising from disproportionality, because the required money capital is not available. Commodities
must be unloaded on the market in order to obtain means of payment no
longer obtainable through credit. As a result prices begin to fall; but since
the previous price level was the basis of all credit transactions, this means
that bills drawn against these commodities cannot now be met from the
proceeds of their sale. A demand for money in order to make payments
arises at the very moment when the supply of money is contracting. For
circulation credit declines rapidly as the fall in prices devalues bills and
reduces the amount of money that can be obtained for them. At the same
time, bank credit cannot be expanded because falling prices make it
doubtful whether producers will be in a position to repay loans. Thus the

very demand for payment leads to the impossibility of satisfying it, and credit stringency reaches a peak. Not only has the interest rate risen to its maximum, but it is impossible to obtain credit at all, for the convulsions in the credit system have as a consequence that all those who have cash available keep it for their own payments. There is only one way to obtain means of payment; namely, by converting commodities into money. Everyone wants to sell, and for the same reasons nobody wants to buy. Prices fall precipitously, but still commodities remain unsaleable. Sales come to a full stop, and circulation credit is annihilated; for no matter how much circulation is reduced the elimination of credit money reduces still more the means of circulation. Cash must take the place of credit and the demand for means of payment becomes a frantic demand for cash.

The consequences of this demand depend upon the specific circumstances; the collapse of commodity prices has a very detrimental effect on the cash position of industrialists, and makes it doubtful whether they will be able to repay their bank loans. If the bank has placed its funds with insolvent industrialists then the bankruptcy of the latter will also involve the bank, and the credit standing which it enjoyed on the basis of its deposits and the acceptance of the notes which it issued, is suddenly destroyed. There is a run on the bank and the repayment of deposits is demanded in cash, whereas only a minimum amount of such deposits has not been used to make loans. The deposits are wiped out and the panic may spread to the other banks, thus forcing them in turn to close their doors. A bank crisis breaks out. The collapse of the credit system, the reversion to a monetary system as Marx calls it, makes cash the only acceptable means of payment. But the quantity of cash available is inadequate for the needs of circulation, more particularly because there is massive hoarding of it as a result of the panic. In consequence a cash premium emerges, the intrinsic value of money disappears (even under a gold standard, as the recent American crisis once again demonstrated), and the value of money is determined by the socially necessary value required in circulation.

A long period of development separates the use of money as a means of circulation and payment from its function as loan capital. Money in the glittering form of gold is the first passionate love of youthful capitalism. The mercantilist theory is its breviary of love. It is a great and all-consuming passion, radiant with the glow of romanticism. For the sake of winning the beloved capitalism performs innumerable feats of heroism, discovers new worlds, fights ever-renewed wars, creates the modern state, and in its romantic ecstasy even destroys the very basis of all romanticism – the Middle Ages. But with advancing years comes wisdom. Classical theory teaches capitalism to despise the romantic façade and to build a solid family establishment in its own home, the capitalist factory. It looks back in horror upon the costly follies of its youth which led it to neglect domestic bliss. Ricardo instructs it in the damage done by its expensive liaison with gold and joins in lamenting the unproductiveness of the 'high price of bullion'. On commercial paper, bank notes, and bills of exchange, capitalism writes its farewell note to the loved one. But it still seeks to retain certain privileges, and the currency school requires from the more modest paper currency that it should conform to the traditions of its more glamorous predecessor. The tastes of ageing capitalism become ever more refined. Having enjoyed its youth to the full, an extravagant and intense passion no longer satisfies it, mystical longings arise, and salvation is sought in faith. John Law proclaims the new gospel. Capitalism, now satiated, abominates the flesh and seeks refuge in the spirit. Once again it experiences a supreme rapture, but suddenly the old desires, long denied, reawaken, the confidence in satisfaction through faith alone evaporates, and there is a frantic desire to make sure that the old virility remains. Credit collapses, and thus suddenly deserted capitalism returns in despair to its first love, to gold. Shaken by the fever of crisis, no sacrifice is too great in order to attain the loved one. Capitalism thought that it had long since liberated itself from the domination of gold, but now it experiences a bitter disillusionment, and shaken by panic recognizes its continuing dependence. But such crises are cathartic. Gradually capitalism comes to understand the nature of what it fears but cannot forsake. The vain effort to abandon gold is given up, and more jealously than ever capitalism endeavours to hold on to it, and especially to restrain its dangerous propensity to travel abroad. Nevertheless, the more capitalism succeeded in establishing its own domination, the less did it allow itself to be bound by this golden chain. The loved one, once so demanding, learns to be more modest and is eventually satisfied with the role of someone in reserve, to whom the incorrigible philanderer may return as a refuge after each fresh disappointment. Her demands may become excessive, and she may occasionally refuse her favours altogether, but these moods do not last long and things soon return to normal. Gold has lost, once and for all, its absolute domination. . .

A monetary crisis is not an absolutely necessary feature of the crisis, and may not always occur. Even during a crisis the turnover of commodities continues, even though on a much reduced scale. Within these limits circulation can be carried on with credit money, all the more so since the crisis does not affect all branches of production simultaneously or with equal force. Indeed, the slump in sales seems to reach its lowest point only when the situation is complicated by a monetary and banking crisis. If the necessary credit money is made available for circulation the monetary crisis can be averted; and even a single bank whose credit position is unimpaired can do this by advancing credit to industrialists against their collateral. In fact, monetary crises have been avoided whenever such an expansion of the means of circulation was possible, and on the other hand they have always occurred when banks whose credit remained unimpaired were prevented from making credit money available. This was the case in England in 1847 and 1857; an incipient monetary crisis was cut short by suspending the Bank Act which arbitrarily limited the bank note issue (that is, credit money) to the amount of the gold reserve plus £14,000,000. In America, where the law restricts the circulation of credit money in an even more insane way, just when credit is most urgently needed, the monetary crisis of 1907 attained classic proportions.

If one considers the train of events on the national market, then it is evident that the reduction of the cash reserve is due not only to its being drained off into domestic circulation, but also to its flowing out of the country. We have seen that gold functions as world money for the settlement of international payment balances. There is an observable tendency for the balance of payments to deteriorate in a country which has reached the peak of the boom and is close to a crisis. Prices during the boom encourage imports, which rise far above their normal level, whereas exports do not increase to the same extent since the absorptive capacity of the domestic market remains considerable; and in the case of some important export commodities such as ores, coal, etc., there may even be a large absolute decline.

It should also be borne in mind that the principal imports of the advanced capitalist countries are agricultural products, consumer goods, and raw materials, while their exports are mainly manufactured goods. The former, however, are much more subject to speculation, and this alone, aside from other considerations, gives commerce, and market uncertainties, a much more important role here. Hence excessive imports are more likely to occur, and on a larger scale, than excessive exports. The balance of trade, the most important element in the balance of payments, deteriorates and requires a larger quantity of gold for settlement.

Events on the money market take a difference course. In the first place, interest rates are highest in the country where the boom is greatest. Consequently a considerable amount of foreign money is invested there on a long-term or short-term basis. Furthermore, speculation in shares and commodities on the exchanges is in full swing and attracts foreign speculators, with the result that large sums of money flow into the country for the purchase of securities. The particular structure of the balance of payments at any given moment depends upon credit relations in international trade. England, where crises always tend to be preceded by a large outflow of gold, extends relatively large amounts of credit for the payment of its exports, but has little resort to credit to pay for the commodities it imports. This increases the imbalance which, as we have seen, tends to emerge in the balance of trade.

The deterioration of the balance of trade may itself be enough to cause a flight of gold, and any reduction in the gold reserve occurring at a time when credit is already strained generates alarm, drives the interest rate still higher, undermines confidence, and above all restricts speculation. Thus it may give the initial impetus to a stock exchange crisis. The effects of a deteriorating balance of trade may be reinforced by fluctuations in the balance of payments. The boom is an international phenomenon, although it may vary in its intensity and timing from one country to another. Let us assume that the boom began in the United States and has reached its peak there while England is only approaching the peak. The higher interest rates and vigorous speculation have attracted a large amount of English capital to America. Now, however, increasingly insistent demands are being made on the money market in England too and the interest rate as well as the volume of speculation rise to a high level. As a result, money previously invested on the American money market is withdrawn and invested in England just at the time when the American balance of trade has deteriorated. This accelerates the outflow of gold from America, leading to a contraction of credit there, and the outbreak of a stock exchange crisis which itself, as the forerunner of a general business crisis, worsens further the balance of payments situation. Foreign funds which had been invested in speculation are promptly withdrawn. This applies, of course, to funds invested in collateral and contango operations, which can be withdrawn, not to funds tied up in securities. At the beginning of the crisis foreign speculators also try to dispose of their declining securities, and these sales are augmented by the forced sales of those whose 'bullish' speculation now collapses. To the extent that foreign countries are involved the sale of securities has an adverse effect on the balance of payments.

At the same time, however, other factors may come into play which may change the course of events. The stock exchange crisis, and the banking crisis which may be associated with it, produce a violent convulsion in the credit system. The interest rate rises to an extremely high level and encourages the investment of foreign money capital. The depreciation of securities makes them attractive to foreign capitalists, and the substantial export of securities then improves the balance of payments. At the same time the balance of trade improves, the credit upheaval puts an end to speculation in commodities, and it soon becomes apparent that the domestic market is overstocked. Prices fall, a commercial crisis begins, and imports stagnate, while exports – as long as the situation in foreign markets, where the crisis has not yet begun, permits – are pushed in order to obtain means of payment.[2] Bankruptcies begin to occur, but in so far as they affect those who have to pay foreign industrialists for imported goods, the bankruptcies cancel out such payments and to that extent improve the national balance of payments.[3] Thus the export of gold is sooner or later brought to an end, depending upon the specific circumstances, before the onset of the crisis, and is replaced by an influx of gold during and after the crisis. The alternation between exports and imports of gold during a period of crisis represents changes in the areas in which the main incidence of the crisis is experienced.

A more pronounced outflow of gold always affects the interest rate at a time when, as a result of the emerging disproportionalities, circulation credit can no longer be expanded sufficiently to meet the requirements of circulation; but its specific effect is strongly influenced by banking legislation. The essence of mistaken banking legislation is that it severely restricts the expansion of circulation credit and prevents it from reaching those limits which would be reasonable from the standpoint of economic laws. It does so by establishing some arbitrary relation between circulation credit and a sum of values with which in reality it has absolutely no connection in terms of its own economic character. As we know, the bank note is simply another form of the draft, or bill of exchange, and this in turn is only a monetary form of the value of commodities. If the volume of banknotes is not related to the amount of bills and drafts – that is, in the final analysis, to the value of commodities in circulation, as happens in a strictly enforced system of so-called bank coverage for notes issued – but is related instead to a metallic reserve, as in England, or to government bonds, as in the United States, where this kind of insanity has reached a peak and debts are regarded as the best collateral for the amount of credit issued (such insanity being explicable by the insane character of fictitious capital), then an artificial limit is placed upon the supply of loan capital which must obviously have a direct effect upon the rate of interest. In England, where the volume of notes is fixed by law and the needs of circulation can be met only by metallic money (since every note issued in excess of £14,000,000[4] simply represents gold in the coffers of the bank and is actually gold, therefore, in an economic sense) every considerable increase in the outflow of gold must pose a direct threat to circulation. Hence, even if business conditions are perfectly healthy, and credit has not been impaired, the bank cannot convert the same quantity of bills into its own notes to offset an outflow of gold, which may have resulted, for example, from increased imports of wheat following a poor harvest in England. Consequently, whenever there is an outflow of gold, even if one can be sure that it will be temporary, the bank is obliged at once to raise the interest rate in order to protect its gold reserve, thus making credit more expensive; a measure, incidentally, which increases the profit of loan capital, including its own capital, at the expense of entrepreneurial profit. Moreover, the limitation makes it doubtful whether bills can be converted into bank notes, that is into legal tender, or at any rate into generally accepted means of payment. Thus the circulation of credit money required by increased circulation is arbitrarily restricted, although the state of production gives no grounds for this; and it creates artificially, under these circumstances, a total interruption of the circulation of credit money, with its consequences in a monetary and banking crisis, all for the sake of a false theory, the practical application of which, however, brings loan capital advantages which are by no means purely theoretical.

Even more senseless is the situation in America, where the circulation of notes can only be increased if the banks purchase more government bonds. Since the supply of such bonds is limited, the increased demand leads immediately to an exceptional rise in their price, so that despite the high rate of interest the banks find it unprofitable to issue bank notes. If the banks refrain from purchasing bonds and hence from increasing the notes in circulation, there is an exorbitant rise in the interest rate, which not only ensures unusually large profits for the banks and banking capitalists, but makes them masters of the money market and establishes their dictatorship not only over speculation and the stock exchange, but also over production, through their role in share issues and the provision of credit. This is also one of the reasons why the American stock exchanges have acquired such immense importance in the process of concentrating property ownership in the hands of a few money capitalists. If the present banking legislation were to remain in force the redemption of the national debt (in the United States) would play havoc with the note circulation; a kind of madness which has method in it, for it is an excellent way of making money for loan capital and hence successfully resists all attempts at reform.

The restrictions imposed by banking legislation have only been tolerable, up to a point, because – partly as a result of the legislation – in such countries as England and America, where they are most stringent and harmful, the circulation of notes is supplemented by other types of credit money which make the legal regulations considerably less onerous. The development of clearing house arrangements and the use of cheques come under this heading. The clearing house effects a direct settlement of bills, and to the extent that bills cancel out they perform their function as money and do not need to be converted into bank notes. The same is true of cheques. A cheque is drawn upon the drawer's deposit, even though this deposit does not really exist because the bank has loaned it out. When I pay with a cheque drawn upon this non-existing deposit it is the same as if I paid with a bank note, which also has no metallic backing, but is backed, just like the deposits which have been loaned out, only by the bank's own securities. From an economic point of view the substance is the same even if the forms (and fortunately this is all that banking legislators pay attention to) differ. In addition to these various means of economizing on the circulation of notes (and the fact that one type of credit money can be substituted for another demonstrates their essential equivalence) there is also, in England, the further assurance that the splendid Bank Act would be suspended immediately any danger arose that it might be effectively applied.

The effects of bank note legislation may also weaken, or under certain conditions even completely eliminate, the tendencies which are expressed in changes in the balance of payments during a crisis. We saw earlier that changes in the balance of payments always occur as a result of the state of the balance of trade. The latter itself depends in the first place upon the natural conditions of production, and second, upon the level and stage of economic development. A country which has undergone a long period of economic development, is highly developed industrially, has a large export trade in means of production and a low level of raw material production, will have an adverse balance of trade. Thus England, the first country in which advanced capitalist production became established, was only able to promote its exports of means of production so vigorously by supplying them not only as commodities but as capital; that is to say, not by selling means of production abroad but by sending them abroad as capital investments. Thus, for example, when England made a railway loan to South America it was used to buy machines, locomotives, etc., from England. Such exports, which are at the same time exports of capital, cease to depend upon the simultaneous import of commodities. If it were simply a case of commodity exports, South America, for instance, could only import means of production from England over the long term if it could pay for them with commodities of its own, since it has not accumulated enough money to pay for so large a quantity of means of production out of its stock of metal. In fact, a large part of international trade involves this kind of exchange of commodities, which more or less balances out. But if commodities are exported as capital, the volume of exports becomes independent of commodity production in a country which is still undeveloped, and is limited only by its potentialities for capitalist development on one side, and by the accumulation of capital, the existence of a surplus of productive capital, in the advanced country on the other side. This is precisely the reason for the rapidity of capitalist expansion. It enables the most advanced capitalist countries to increase their industrial production and their exports far beyond their imports from the undeveloped countries. Hence the adverse balance of trade is matched by a favourable balance of payments, since the industrial countries receive regular payments in the shape of profits from the exported capital.

The precise influence of the tendencies which determine the import and export of gold depends upon the particular quantitative structure of the balance of trade and the balance of payments. If there is not such a regular outflow of gold from the United States as was the case in England in earlier crises, two distinct factors account for this. The first is the obstacles to the development of circulation credit arising from the legislation governing the issue of bank notes. This raises the interest rate in America above the European level, because the restricted volume of circulation credit is inadequate, and regularly attracts European money capital. It depends upon the pressure on credit in Europe whether it is possible, in a boom period, to draw this money capital back to Europe, thus producing an outflow of gold from America.

The structure of America's balance of trade may also bring about modifications. America is a country which exports predominantly raw materials. Assuming good harvests it is precisely in boom periods that the American balance of trade will improve greatly, since the prices of cotton, copper, and possibly also wheat will rise, and this improvement in the balance of trade may weaken, eliminate, or postpone those tendencies which lead to an outflow of gold, and hence also postpone the onset of a crisis, for which, however, the outflow of gold is by no means a *conditio sine qua non*.

In this connection it should be emphasized that the power of national banks to protect themselves against an outflow of gold varies considerably according to the reasons for which gold is required for export. For example, if the bank discount is 5 per cent in Berlin and only 3 per cent in Paris, French banks will have a motive for transferring funds from France to Germany to take advantage of the higher interest rate. The same thing may happen if there is lively speculative activity in Berlin in which French banks want to participate. Such transfers of gold do not arise from any compelling economic necessity, but are largely arbitrary movements of money capital. For this capital could just as well remain in France if capitalists were content with a lower interest rate or smaller stock market gains. These gold movements can therefore be prevented by appropriate banking policies. The simplest way of keeping these funds at home is to assure them of higher interest by raising the bank discount rate. At the same time this equalizes interest rates in the two countries. But the bank can also prevent such transfers of gold directly, if it is able to refuse to convert bank notes into gold. The Austro-Hungarian bank, which has suspended cash payments, has a legal right to do this; and the Bank of France, which can also make payments in silver, can therefore refuse to pay in gold, ultimately by exercising its right to charge a gold premium,[5] and by thus raising the price, eliminate the advantage to be gained from the difference in interest and so remove the motive for exporting gold. The Bank of England and the German Reichsbank do not have such direct means at their disposal; but the latter attempts at least, by indirect pressure upon gold exporters, to restrict the export of gold when the money market is tight, a policy which, when confined to this particular case, is thoroughly rational from the point of view of the national economy. At the same time, this factual restriction of the mobility of money capital, or in other words, of the export of gold, is one of the factors which obstructs the equalization of national interest rates.

The situation is quite different, however, if there arises, for example, a demand for gold from the German Reichsbank because Germans have to pay for commodities or securities in England. They will initially buy sterling drafts on the Berlin exchange, but if the exchange rate rises above parity they will prefer to pay in gold. If the Reichsbank then refuses to provide gold, the German debtors, who are obliged either to pay or to be declared bankrupt, would once more have to obtain sterling drafts. Their demand would raise the price of bills above parity, involving a depreciation of German currency which it is the primary task of banking policy to prevent.

Hence an outflow of gold which results simply from financial transactions can be prevented by stopping the financial transactions themselves. Conversely, it is impossible to prevent an outflow of gold which is necessary in order to meet obligations already contracted in the course of trade in commodities and securities without devaluing the currency.

Money capital and productive capital during the depression

If we observe the accumulation process after a crisis, it is apparent that initially reproduction takes place on a reduced scale. Social production undergoes a contraction. Because of the 'solidarity of the branches of production' the sector in which overproduction first occurs does not matter. Overproduction in the leading sectors involves general overproduction; hence there is no productive accumulation, no expanded reconversion of profit into capital, no increase in the application of means of production. Productive accumulation has ceased. But what happens to individual accumulation and to particular branches of production? Production continues even if it is on a reduced scale. It is just as certain that a large number of enterprises, especially those which are most technically efficient in their own sector and those which operate in sectors producing the basic necessities of life, the consumption of which cannot be too severely curtailed, still make a profit. A part of this profit can be accumulated. But the rate of profit has fallen, and this decline may also reduce the rate of accumulation. Similarly, the total amount of profit has declined, and this too diminishes the possibility of accumulation. Furthermore, while one part of the capitalist class makes a profit, another part sustains losses which must be defrayed from additional capital if bankruptcy is to be avoided. Real production, however, is not expanded during a depression, and if accumulation takes place, it can only be accumulation in the form of money. Where does the money for the accumulating capitalists come from?

Let us recall the schema of reproduction:

$$\text{I} \quad 4{,}000 \text{ C} + 1{,}000 \text{ V} + 1{,}000 \text{ S} = 6{,}000$$
$$\text{II} \quad 2{,}000 \text{ C} + 500 \text{ V} + 500 \text{ S} = 3{,}000$$

This would represent production which has been reduced by the crisis. Capitalists, however, produce commodities, not money. In order to obtain money, and indeed more money than they already have at their disposal – for otherwise there would be no accumulation of money – they must convert their commodities into money and refrain from reconverting that money into commodities. If department II wants to accumulate say 250 out of its 500 S, it must sell consumer goods (and the producers must sell them to others in the same department because the turnover of II S takes place within department II) without itself buying commodities from other members of the same department. Thus 250 S remain unsaleable in department II. If one producer succeeds in selling then others are left with unsold stocks. Money capital is redistributed, and sellers receive money from the buyers, but the money does not return to the buyers because they cannot sell their 250 of commodities.

We arrive at the same result if we assume that capitalists in department I accumulate half of their surplus value. They would then be able to sell $1,000 V + 500 S$ in the form of means of production to II C, which would pay 1,500 in money for the purchase. Since I S does not buy 2,000 in consumer goods, but keeps 500 in consumer goods, II C therefore has 500 less in money, which remains in I as accumulated money. But if II C does not advance 1,000 in money for the purchase of means of production, and if we assume that I initiates the process, then I will buy 1,500 in consumer goods, II will use the 1,500 to buy means of production, leaving I with 500 unsaleable means of production. Its expectation of accumulation has not been realized. Department II restricts production still further, and begins the process of reproduction with 1,500 C and a correspondingly reduced variable capital. If it possessed 2,000 in money for its turnover with I C, it has now used only 1,500, while the 500 which previously functioned as money capital now lies idle, and to this must be added the reduction in the amount of money advanced as variable capital.

It is evident that the pure accumulation of money at the level of society as a whole is impossible on the assumption of reduced or stationary production. Only individual accumulation can take place, which simply means that accumulation by one capitalist changes the distribution of money capital in the hands of others, and this change is then bound to lead to new disruptions of reproduction. It makes no difference if we look at the class of gold producers themselves. In this case a direct accumulation of money is certainly possible, but this is limited by the size of the accumulated profit in this particular branch of production. The volume of sales by other industries is reduced in proportion to the amount of money thus accumulated, since it is accumulated and retained as a hoard. No matter how this factor is evaluated it is quantitatively too insignificant to play any part in the general process of accumulation.

Nor does the use of credit change matters. The $2,000 (V + S)$ of I must be sold for the 2,000 C of II. An accumulation of money would mean that I sells 2,000 but only buys back 1,500 from II. Whether these turnovers are accomplished by means of credit or not, the fact remains that I can only accumulate 500 in money or credit money – that is, claims upon future production – if II buys 2,000 from I. But II can only do this by paying for it either with its own commodities, which is excluded by our assumption, or out of a reserve fund of money, in which case I simply accumulates what II loses. It is incorrect to say, therefore, that the capital lying idle during a period of depression consists of money capital accumulated in the form of money or credit. It is money capital set free by the contraction of production, which was previously used to effect turnovers but has been rendered superfluous by the decrease in production. Its idleness reflects the idleness of productive capital. The forces of production, as a result of the contraction of production, are only partially employed. The newly produced constant capital is. stored up and finds no application in production. Money capital and the potentialities of the existing system of credit have become too large in relation to the diminished turnover, and so money capital lies idle in the banks awaiting utilization, the precondition for which is an expansion of production.

It is, by the way, an extraordinary notion of the theorists of crises to point precisely to this idle money capital as the most powerful stimulus to an enlargement of reproduction.[1] As if the shutdown of machinery, with its threat of material and moral deterioration, the underutilization of fixed capital in general, which involves not a sacrifice of profit but continuing losses, were not a much stronger incentive to expand production than a lowering of the rate of interest on money capital. The question is not whether the incentive to accumulate after a crisis is reinforced by money liquidity, but whether or not the expansion of reproduction is objectively possible. There is usually great money liquidity immediately after a crisis, and yet it may take years before prosperity is fully restored.[2]

It is very amusing to see how the views of business commentators in the bourgeois press change in accordance with the current state of the business cycle. In the German press, the recent crisis was attributed almost exclusively to dear money or to the scarcity of money capital. Now that the depression persists in spite of the continuing international liquidity they are slowly discovering that prosperity does not depend solely upon the condition of the money market.[3]

The misconceptions about the causes of money liquidity during a depression, and their significance for overcoming the depression, rest ultimately upon the failure to see beyond the determination of economic forms to the material determination of social production which is revealed by Marx's analysis in the second volume of *Capital*. One operates only with such economic concepts as 'capital', 'profit', 'accumulation', etc., and thinks that the problem is solved when one has shown the quantitative relations which make simple or expanded reproduction possible, or conversely, cause disturbances. In this way the fact is overlooked that these quantitative relations reflect qualitative conditions and that not only can value magnitudes, which are directly commensurable, be distinguished, but also specific use values which must possess definite qualities in production and consumption. It is also overlooked, in analysing the reproduction process, that there are not only distinct units of capital in general – so that, for example, a surplus or shortage of industrial capital can be 'compensated' by a corresponding amount of money capital – and not only units of fixed and circulating capital, but that it is a question of machines, raw materials and labour power of a very definite kind (required by the technology) which must be available as use values of this specific kind if disruptions are to be avoided.[4]

In fact, during a crisis, there is idle industrial capital (plant, machines, etc.) on one side, and idle money capital on the other. The same causes which make industrial capital idle also make money capital idle. Money does not circulate, or function as money capital, because industrial capital is not functioning. Money is not employed because industry is not employed. 'Phoenix'* does not cease production because money capital is lacking, nor does it resume production because money capital is abundant; on the contrary money is readily available because production has been reduced. The 'scarcity' of money capital is only a symptom of the stagnation of the circulation process, as a result of overproduction having already begun.

Credit, in the first place, replaces money as a medium of circulation, and second, it facilitates the transfer of money. Theoretically it is possible to ignore credit for the moment by assuming that there is a sufficient quantity of metallic money available for a purely metallic circulation.

It is characteristic of almost all modern crisis theorists that they explain business cycle phenomena in terms of changes in the interest rate, instead of explaining, conversely, the phenomena of the money market in terms of the conditions of production.[5] The reasons for this are not far to seek. The events on the money market are manifest, are discussed daily in the newspapers, and have a decisive influence on the course of the stock exchange and on speculation. In addition, the supply of loan capital at any given moment is a determinate sum, and must appear as a determinate sum, for otherwise it would be impossible to explain how supply and demand could determine the rate of interest. What is generally overlooked is that the supply of loan capital depends upon the state of production; first, upon its volume, and second, upon the proportionality between branches of production, which has a decisive effect on the circulation time of commodities and hence on the velocity of circulation of credit money. What is also generally overlooked is the functional difference between commercial credit and capital (bank) credit, especially since this difference seems to be eliminated by the issue of bank notes, and with the development

---

* The Phoenix Mining and Smelting Co., a well known pre-1914 German enterprise. [Ed.]

of the banking system all forms of credit take on the appearance of bank credit. If this distinction is ignored, however, the course of events on the money market appears in quite a different light, and the relation of dependence now seems to consist simply in the fact that the expansion of production requires more capital. Capital is more or less vaguely identified with money capital. Production expands, the demand for money capital increases, and the rate of interest rises. Finally, a shortage of money capital emerges, the high interest rate wipes out the profits from production, new investment ceases, and the crisis begins. Then during the depression money capital is accumulated instead of being converted into investment capital – a senseless notion since machines, docks, railways, are not produced from gold. The interest rate falls, money capitalists become dissatisfied with the low interest and once again invest their money in production. Prosperity begins afresh.

Leaving aside the barbaric confusion which underlies this conception of the economists, who refer to money, machines, and labour power as capital, and then think that one form of capital, say money, can simply be transmuted into another, such as machinery and labour power (or, as they would put it, circulation capital into investment capital), the contortions of this splendid 'theory', even from the purely statistical aspect, are pure nonsense. In the advanced capitalist countries, the range of variation of the interest rate is at most 5 per cent, judging by the fluctuations of the official discount rates between 2 per cent and 7 per cent; and in my view restrictive banking legislation or inadequate discount policies make these fluctuations larger than rational economic considerations would produce. Now money capital is demanded by producers in order to expand production; which means that the borrowed value, converted into productive capital, realizes value and yields a profit, the size of which depends, *ceteris paribus*, upon prices. The fluctuations in commodity prices during the business cycle, however, are far greater than 5 per cent. A glance at any table of prices would show that fluctuations of 50 per cent, 100 per cent, or even more, are not unusual. Profits may not increase to the same extent because costs of production also increase, but in any event the increase in industrialists' profits during periods of prosperity and at the peak of the cycle is vastly more than 5 per cent. If their profits did not decline for other reasons an interest rate of 7 per cent would certainly not halt the accumulation of capital. For example, if the Rhine-Westphalia Coal Syndicate could sell its entire output at peak prosperity prices, it would not hesitate for a moment to pay interest of even 10 per cent on its borrowed capital, which is only part of its total capital, since even on this part it would make an entrepreneurial profit far higher than the rate of interest.[6]

The extraordinary notion that interest gradually devours entrepreneurial profit is reinforced by the total confusion which reigns concerning categories such as 'profit', 'entrepreneurial profit', 'wages of management', 'Interest', 'dividends', etc.; and with the growth of joint-stock companies this confusion has increased. Dividends are regarded as a kind of interest, though an interest which fluctuates in a remarkable way compared with the permanently fixed interest on loan capital. Loan capital and productive capital no longer seem to be distinguished by the fact that one bears interest and the other produces profit. Instead, both are regarded as interest-bearing capital, and the sole difference between them is that 'liquid' capital always yields a fixed interest which is announced daily on the stock exchange, while 'fixed' capital yields an interest which is only discovered when dividends are declared. The difference in the certainty of the yield is then attributed to the difference between 'liquid', that is, money capital, and 'fixed', that is, industrial capital. When all qualitative distinctions are confused in this way it is no wonder that so many extraordinary notions prevail concerning quantitative differences, and that people then imagine they have found in the fluctuations of the interest rate a sufficient explanation of the mechanism governing the sudden changes in the business cycle.

Changes in the character of crises. Cartels and crises

The development of capitalist production brings about certain changes in the form of crises to which we must now turn our attention. In this account, however, I shall only be concerned to indicate the general lines of development, leaving it to detailed historical studies to depict the variations in the character of crises between particular countries in a comparative perspective.

Here I shall only try to reveal the general in the particular, which is all the more difficult since the development of capitalism has created an ever closer international interdependence of economic processes, such that when a crisis occurs in one country, all the features specific to the stage of technical and organizational development which it has reached have repercussions on the crises in other countries. For example, the events of the most recent European crisis of 1907 can only be understood as repercussions of the American crisis, the distinctive feature of which was an extremely severe monetary and banking crisis such as Europe had not experienced for a long time. This was responsible for some particular developments on the European money markets, and especially the severity of the crisis in some spheres, which might perhaps have been avoided if it had not been for the effects of the American crisis.

On the other hand, it is equally impossible to derive general laws about the changing character of crises from the history of crises in a single country such as England, precisely because the capitalist crisis is a phenomenon of the world market – all the more so if it is a prolonged crisis – and crises in a particular country may undergo various modifications as a result of distinctive features of its capitalist development, so that any generalization based upon this experience could only be misleading.[1]

If we want to establish what changes are taking place in the phenomena of crises, therefore, we must be able to derive them from a theoretical analysis in order to be certain that we are dealing with tendencies inherent in capitalist development, rather than with specific phenomena peculiar to a particular phase of capitalism which may perhaps be purely accidental.

Capitalism develops in a society in which commodity production still occupies a relatively unimportant place. As it expands it generalizes commodity production, and establishes a national market and a constantly expanding world market. With the expansion of the market the conditions also develop in which crises can occur. As long as capitalist production is superimposed upon widespread production for use and non-capitalist, artisanal commodity production intended for a local market, the full impact of crises is felt only by the capitalist superstructure. They affect branches of production where sales may be brought almost to a standstill because the circulation which is absolutely indispensable for the turnover of goods in society is provided by handicraft production or by domestic production. A crisis may cause havoc in the capitalist sector of production, halting sales completely for a time provided the factors producing the crisis are powerful enough to paralyse production, which, as we shall see, is often the case in this period.

As capitalist production develops handicraft and domestic production are largely destroyed. The impact of a crisis is now felt by a system of production, the contraction of which is limited by the necessity of satisfying social needs on a much larger scale, both absolutely and relatively. With the growth of production there is an increase in that part which must be carried on under all circumstances, and whose continued operation prevents the almost complete stagnation of the production and circulation process. This is shown by the fact that the impact of a crisis is less severe in those branches of production which serve the needs of consumption, and all the less severe the more essential the consumer goods they produce and hence the greater the stability of consumption.

Changes in the character of crises are also bound to follow the advance of capitalist concentration. The ability of an enterprise to survive increases with its size. The smaller the firm, the more likely it is that a price collapse will lead to bankruptcy. The small entrepreneur may lose his entire market; the fall in prices and stoppage of work make it impossible for him to convert his commodity capital into money capital. Since he does not have any reserve capital, and particularly in times of crisis cannot obtain credit, he is unable to meet his obligations. The crisis thus leads to a massive collapse of small capitalist enterprises, suspension of credit, wholesale bankruptcies, insolvencies, bank failures, and hence to a panic. The situation is aggravated by the greater technical disparities between firms. Modern plants exist alongside old plants, some of which date from the period of handicraft production or manufacture, and these become completely unviable when prices fall. Their collapse, in large numbers, also drags down enterprises which are in themselves technologically viable.[2]

The large modern firm has quite a different relation to a crisis. Its output is so large that some part of it can continue even during a crisis. The American Steel Trust may perhaps be obliged to reduce its production by half during a crisis, but it need not reduce output below a certain minimum.

Along with the concentration of firms the scale on which production can be maintained also increases.

As capitalist production develops there is therefore an increase, both absolute and relative, in that part of production which can be carried on under all circumstances, and along with it an increase in the volume of commodity circulation which continues undisturbed during the crisis, and of the circulation credit based upon it. Hence the disruption of credit need not be as complete as in crises of the early period of capitalism. Furthermore, the development of a credit crisis into a banking crisis on one side and a monetary crisis on the other is made more difficult, first by the changes in the organization of credit, and second by the shift in the relations between commerce and industry.

A credit crisis develops into a monetary crisis if the collapse of credit produces a sudden scarcity of means of payment.[3] This scarcity emerges less strongly the larger the volume of production which is maintained under all circumstances, for credit money can continue to perform its function to the same extent. The greater the volume of credit transactions the more commercial credit is replaced by bank credit, for the latter is less easily undermined than is the credit of individual industrialists. The decisive factor, however, is that there is no longer any shortage of means of payment because the development of credit has reduced the need for cash money, even during a crisis, since the use of cheques and clearing transactions continues; and the latter means of payment can be supplied by the banks of issue, whose credit remains unimpaired even in a crisis. We have seen that the circulation of bank notes is based upon the circulation of bills, which may contract if its foundation, commodity circulation, contracts. But it contracts more than does the circulation of commodities because commercial credit has been shaken. The bank now substitutes its own credit for commercial credit to the extent that the real circulation of commodities permits, and it can do so on this scale because the continued circulation of commodities provides an assurance that its claims will be honoured. It can therefore make its credit money available for the genuine needs of circulation and satisfy the demand for means of payment. In effect the bank restricts demand for means of payment to the real, essential needs of circulation, and wards off that well-nigh unlimited demand, arising from the fear that it will be impossible to obtain means of payment even against the best collateral, which goes beyond any actual need and leads to large-scale hoarding with a consequent further contraction of the means of payment. If the bank of issue is to act in this way, it is necessary, first, that its credit position should be sound (a condition which a well managed bank of issue should easily be able to fulfil), and second, that the increased note issue should not endanger convertibility. This second condition is met by a policy, dictated by the bank's own self-interest, of issuing bank notes during a crisis only against absolutely reliable collateral, which gives it the assurance that it is really satisfying only the requirements of circulation within the limits imposed by the crisis. Furthermore, convertibility is protected against unforeseen accidents by an adequate cash reserve, especially of gold. This condition is fulfilled, as capitalist production develops, by increased production of gold, by the accumulation of gold in the banks, and by restricting the function of this gold to that of a reserve. With the development of credit the function of gold is increasingly limited to settling the balances on international payments, and although the volume of international payments has increased enormously, the cash required for balancing these payments has not increased to the same extent, nor in proportion to the accumulated gold reserves in the older capitalist countries, as a result of the growing use of credit money in international transactions. This puts the banks of issue in a position to meet the increased demands upon them during a crisis. We are assuming of course that their economic functions are not hampered by legislative controls, as was the case in England with the Peel Act, and in the United States with the nonsensical coverage regulations which have produced typical monetary crises there.

The absence of a monetary crisis protects credit against a complete breakdown and is therefore also a safeguard against the occurrence of a bank crisis. There is no run on the banks and mass withdrawal of deposits, and the banks, if they are otherwise solvent, can meet their obligations. Even where a bank crisis does not result from a credit and monetary crisis, but from the immobilization of bank resources in industry and losses on credit advances, capitalist development tends to mitigate the effects of crises on capital.

The concentration of banking plays an important part here. Through the enormous expansion of the sphere of business activity, and its extension to diverse national economic areas at different stages of capitalist development, it allows a much greater spreading of risk. Furthermore, the increasing concentration of the banks is accompanied by a change in their position *vis à vis* speculation, commerce and industry. In the first place, this concentration involves a redistribution of power in their favour, thanks to their large capital resources. Not only is their capital quantitatively superior to that of their debtors, but they also have a qualitative advantage in disposing over capital which is constantly available, namely money capital. This advantage precludes the possibility that a large, well-managed bank could become so dependent upon the fate of a single enterprise, or a few enterprises, in which it has invested its resources, as to be ruined by their failure during a crisis.

If one examines the causes which militate against a banking crisis the first thing to notice is that speculation, in both commodities and securities, has declined considerably in volume and importance, By speculation in commodities I mean here not only that which takes place on the commodity exchanges, but especially that which is involved in commodity trading, the demand for commodities by merchants who anticipate further price rises, and the accumulation of larger stocks in order to drive up prices by withholding supplies. Such speculation declines, in the first place, because of the elimination of commerce and the growth of direct dealings between producers and consumers, involving the transformation of independent merchants into agents of the syndicates and trusts, working on a fixed commission. To some extent this prevents speculation by merchants from driving prices far above the levels fixed by producers during a boom, and creating the illusion of a lively market when in reality effective demand has already begun to slacken.[4]

But where wholesale trade (and it is only wholesale trade with which we are concerned in this context) has not lost its traditional position, to the benefit of industry or the commodity departments of the large banks, it shows a strong tendency towards concentration itself and sharply reduces the participation of small dealers and outsiders. However, where the commodity exchanges still have an important role, in certain specific conditions, speculative movements are increasingly dominated by the banks, because the development of the credit system gives them a growing control over the whole stock of money capital, and hence the power to confine speculative movements within certain limits.

Finally, commodity speculation is also curbed by the development of means of transport, which has made markets less remote, especially in the case of commodities which are particularly subject to speculation, and of news agencies which give the state of the markets minute by minute. The accumulation of unsaleable products in distant markets while at the point of production output continues on the same, or an increased, scale, becomes more difficult. Furthermore, the decline in the relative share of consumer goods means that speculation in colonial products, which often had a fateful importance in the earlier crises in England, now plays a lesser role; a situation to which the certainty and regularity of imports and the precision and speed of market reports also contribute. In addition, commodity speculation declines in importance with the growth in scale of the capital goods industries, whose products are not subject to speculation because they are increasingly produced to order.

The changes which have occurred in the character of industrial crises, and the growth of the banks' domination of industry, also tend to make the emergence of a banking crisis more difficult. As we have seen, the growing concentration of industrial enterprises gives them greater immunity against the ultimate consequences of a crisis, namely total bankruptcy. Their powers of resistance are further enhanced by the joint stock form of organization which, as I have noted, also greatly increases the influence of the banks upon industry The joint-stock company has this effect because it makes possible the continuation of production without any profit, and even at a loss, since capital can be attracted more readily than is the case with an individually owned firm. Second, it is easier for the joint-stock company to accumulate reserves in good years in preparation for bad years. Third, it is easier to control more rigorously the use of resources and especially the application of borrowed capital. The banks exercise a direct control over the employment of capital in corporations which they support with credit, and this control is applied ever more systematically as the tendency for industry to become increasingly dependent upon the banks progresses. The use of credit for purposes other than those directly related to the conduct of the enterprise is prevented. In earlier crises, an important factor was that individual entrepreneurs engaged heavily in speculation and used their firms' capital for this purpose, while operating their business with borrowed capital. Today a controlling bank would not allow this.

It is, therefore, sheer dogmatism to oppose the banks' penetration of industry, which is a necessary and unavoidable tendency, arising from the laws of capitalist development, as a danger to the banks; and to take the organizationally backward English banking system, with its division of labour between deposit and merchant banks, as an ideal to be attained, if necessary, by legislative compulsion. This doctrinaire view mistakes the appearance of the English banking system for the reality, by overlooking the fact that in England too the banks place their accumulated funds at the disposal of industry, commerce and speculation. There are specific historical causes which explain why this is done through middlemen in England, and directly by the banks in Germany and, with some modifications, in the United States.[5] None the less, the English system is an outmoded one and is everywhere on the decline because it makes control of the loaned-out bank capital more difficult, and hence obstructs the expansion of bank credit itself.

Finally, and here it will suffice to recall what was said in the chapter on the stock exchange, speculation in securities is also declining as a factor making for banking crises. As the power of the banks continues to grow, it is the banks which dominate the movements of speculation, rather than being dominated by them. The general importance of the stock exchange is declining, but more particularly as an aggravating factor in crises.

With the decline of speculation the psychology of the capitalist public has also been undergoing a change. However primitive the mentality of the speculator really is, notwithstanding the efforts of his admirers to discover in him all sorts of prophetic gifts and romantic plans for world improvement, the change in attitude of the speculating public can be explained by the commonplace view of the ordinary capitalist: 'losses make one a wiser man'. The mass psychoses which speculation generated at the beginning of the capitalist era, in those blessed times when every speculator felt like a god who creates a world out of nothing, seem to be gone for ever. The tulip swindle with its idyllic background of a poetic love of flowers, the South Sea Bubble, with its adventure-inspiring fantasies of unheard-of discoveries, Law's projects with their plans for world conquest, all gave way to the naked quest for marginal profit, which came to an end in the crash of 1873. Since then, faith in the magical power of credit and the stock exchange has disappeared, and despite Bontoux,* the beautiful Catholic cult has been destroyed by a sober enlightenment which no longer wants to believe in an immaculate conception by the holy ghost of speculation, but accepts what is natural as natural, and leaves faith to the fools who remain. The stock exchange has lost its faithful and kept only its priests, who make their money from the faith of others. Since faith has become a business, the business of faith has declined. The seductive and lucrative craze has spent itself, the tulips have long since faded, and the coffee bush, though it still yields commercial profit, no longer produces true speculative gains. Prose has vanquished the poetry of gain.

The above-mentioned factors throw light on the causes which have changed the character of crises in so far as the latter result from large-scale bankruptcies, and from stock exchange, bank, credit, and money panics. While these causes do not preclude the occurrence of such crises, they do explain why it is more difficult for them to occur. Whether they do break out or not depends upon the severity of the disturbances and the suddenness of their appearance. Whether these disturbances could become so great as to bring about a failure of one of the large banks in Germany (assuming reasonably competent management) is a *quaesto facti* (a matter of fact) rather than a theoretical question. But all these factors leave unresolved the emergence of an industrial crisis, the cyclical alternation of prosperity and depression. The question arises whether the great change in the form of industrial organization, whether monopolies, through their alleged power to suspend the regulatory action of the capitalist mechanism – free competition – can bring about qualitative changes in the business cycle.

As we know, cartels can effect changes in the level of prices, which produce a different level of profit as between cartelized and non-cartelized branches of production. The phenomena of the business cycle then develop on the basis of these changes, and they are modified, in certain respects, by

---

* Eugène Bontoux was a French engineer and financier who succeeded in enlisting the participation of French clerical and aristocratic circles in his speculative Union Générale for the construction of railways in Eastern Europe. The project collapsed in 1882. [Ed.]

the existence of cartels. But other effects too have been, and are still, attributed to the cartels. They are supposed not only to modify the effects of crises, but to be able to eliminate them altogether, since they regulate production and can always adjust supply to demand. This view ignores completely the inherent nature of crises. Only if the cause of crises is seen simply as the overproduction of commodities resulting from the lack of an overall picture of the market can it be plausibly maintained that cartels are able to eliminate crises by restricting production.

That a crisis is synonymous with the overproduction of commodities, or is caused by overproduction, appears to be certain and undeniable. Is it not a palpable fact, apparent to everyone? Prices are low because supply exceeds demand, that is, because there is a surplus of commodities, and every glance at the market reports shows that warehouses are overstocked, goods unsaleable, that there is indeed overproduction of commodities. But the cartels are in a position to restrict the output of an entire branch of industry. Previously, this was accomplished by the blind operation of the law of price, which brought numerous firms to a standstill, and to bankruptcy, through a fall in prices; but now the same blessed shrinkage of production can be achieved more rapidly and painlessly by the collective wisdom of the cartelized directors of production. Nor is this all. Since the cartel can fix prices and take care of 'the balancing of supply and demand' eliminate speculation, and control and supervise trading (if it does not take it over completely) why should it not be possible, by adapting production precisely to demand, to eliminate crises altogether from this world and to deal with minor disturbances of economic life quickly, without any serious disruption?

This would be too good to be true. Anyone who simply equates crises with the overproduction of commodities misses precisely the essential point: the capitalist character of production. The products are not simply commodities, but products of capital, and overproduction during a crisis is not just overproduction of commodities, but overproduction of capital. This simply means that capital is invested in production in such volume that the conditions of its utilization have come into contradiction with the conditions of its valorization, so that the sale of products no longer yields a profit sufficient to ensure its further expansion and accumulation. The sale of commodities comes to a standstill because production has ceased to expand. That is why anyone who simply equates a capitalist crisis with the overproduction of commodities does not get beyond the first step in the analysis of crises. It is evident that we are not dealing merely with an overproduction of commodities from the fact that soon after a crisis the market shows itself able to absorb a much larger quantity of commodities. Each successive period of prosperity breaks the record set by its predecessor, even though the increase in market capacity cannot be explained either by population growth or by the growth of income available for consumption. There are quite different factors to be taken into account besides the mere capacity to consume.

Cartels do not diminish, but exacerbate, the disturbances in the regulation of prices which lead ultimately to disproportionalities, and so to the contradiction between the conditions of utilization and the conditions of valorization. The effect of cartels is to end competition within a given branch of production, or more precisely, to make it latent, so that it does not exert a downward pressure on prices in that branch of production; and second, to establish competition among the cartelized sectors on the basis of a higher rate of profit than that which prevails in the non-cartelized industries. But cartels are powerless to alter the competition among capitals for spheres of investment, or the effects of accumulation on the price structure, and they cannot, therefore, prevent the emergence of disproportional relations.

We have seen that during a period of prosperity competition in a particular branch of production does not exert a downward pressure on prices, because demand exceeds supply and in such a case competition takes place among buyers, not among sellers. Only when supply outstrips demand does competition among sellers appear, and prices begin to fall. That cartels conform with the price structure, and do not determine it, follows from the mechanism of production. Let us assume that cartels maintain low prices during a period of prosperity; then there will be no increase in profit and no expansion of accumulation. If the prices of the cartelized industries remained low while those of non-cartelized industries rose, capital would flow out of the former, there would soon be overproduction of capital in the non-cartelized branches of production, matched by underproduction in the cartelized ones, hence an extreme disproportionality, leading to a general crisis; for a crisis is also possible when the volume of production remains unchanged, or even when it is reduced. In reality the cartel would probably have been shattered long before, because it would have frustrated instead of satisfying the striving for profit, and so lost its *raison d'être*. Partial regulation, involving the unification of a branch of industry into a single enterprise, has absolutely no influence upon the proportional relations in industry as a whole. The anarchy of production is not abolished by reducing the number of individual units while simultaneously increasing their strength and effectiveness; indeed, it cannot be abolished at all in this gradual and piecemeal fashion. Planned production and anarchic production are not quantitative opposites such that by tacking on more and more 'planning' conscious organization will emerge out of anarchy. Such a transformation can only take place suddenly by subordinating the whole of production to conscious control. Who exercises this control, and is the owner of production, is a

question of power. In itself, a general cartel which carries on the whole of
production, and thus eliminates crises, is economically conceivable, but in
social and political terms such an arrangement is impossible, because it
would inevitably come to grief on the conflict of interests which it would
intensify to an extreme point. But to expect the abolition of crises from
individual cartels simply shows a lack of insight into the causes of crises and
the structure of the capitalist system.

If cartels are not in a position to prevent crises, neither can they escape
their effects. Naturally, if the crisis is identified with an overproduction of
commodities, then the remedy is quite simple. The cartel curtails production and thus achieves more rapidly, and perhaps on a larger scale, what
the crisis would in any case have accomplished by means of bankruptcies
and plant slow-downs. The social consequences, namely unemployment
and wage cuts, would of course be the same. But the cartelized capitalists
would be able to maintain high prices by sharply curtailing supply. Prices
will remain high, but profit will be reduced as a result of lower sales and
higher costs of production. After a certain time the market will have
absorbed the surplus output, and prosperity can return. This line of
argument is as false as it is simple. Two conditions are necessary for
prosperity to return: first, the restoration of proportionality, which is
required in order to bring the depression to an end; and second, an
expansion of production, without which there can be no prosperity. But the
cartel policy which I have outlined above would actually make it more
difficult to establish these two conditions. The curtailment of production
means the cessation of all new capital investment, and the maintenance of
high prices makes the effects of the crisis more severe for all those industries
which are not cartelized, or not fully cartelized. Their profits will fall more
sharply, or their losses will be greater, than is the case in the cartelized
industries, and in consequence they will be obliged to make larger cuts in
production. As a result, disproportionality will increase, the sales of
cartelized industry will suffer still more, and it becomes evident that in spite
of the severe curtailment of production, 'overproduction' persists and has
even increased. Any further limitation of production means that more
capital will be idle, while overheads remain the same, so that the cost per
unit will rise, thus reducing profits still more despite the maintenance of
high prices. The high prices attract outsiders, who can count on lower
capital and labour costs since all other prices have fallen; thus they
establish a strong competitive position and begin to undersell the cartel.
The cartel will not be able to maintain prices any longer, and the price
collapse spreads beyond cartelized industry. Artificial interventions are
corrected, and the price structure follows the laws which the cartels vainly
tried to bypass in their own case.[6] On the basis of the new price structure a
redistribution of capital among the various sectors of production then

takes place, and gradually the relations of proportionality are restored; the depression is overcome. Prosperity can then get under way as soon as technical innovations or new markets generate increased demand, which in turn attracts new investment of productive capital, especially fixed capital.

Cartels, then, do not eliminate the effects of crises. They modify them only to the extent that they can divert the main burden of a crisis to the non-cartelized industries. The difference in the rate of profit between cartelized and non-cartelized industries, which on average is greater the stronger the cartel and the more secure its monopoly, diminishes during times of prosperity and increases during a depression. In the initial period of a crisis and depression the cartel may also be in a position to maintain high profits for longer than the independent industries, thus exacerbating the effects of the crisis for the latter. This circumstance is not without importance, because it is precisely during a crisis and its immediate aftermath that the situation of industrialists is most difficult and their independence most threatened. The fact that just at this time cartel policy denies them any relief in the form of reductions in the price of their raw materials, etc., is an important factor in worsening the situation of the non-cartelized industries and accelerating the process of concentration.

Part V

The economic policy of finance capital

The reorientation of commercial policy

Finance capital signifies the unification of capital. The previously separate spheres of industrial, commercial and bank capital are now brought under the common direction of high finance, in which the masters of industry and of the banks are united in a close personal association. The basis of this association is the elimination of free competition among individual capitalists by the large monopolistic combines. This naturally involves at the same time a change in the relation of the capitalist class to state power.

The bourgeois conception of the state has its origins in the struggle against mercantilist policy and against the centralized and privilege-dispensing state power. It represents the interests of the nascent capitalist manufacturing and factory system in opposition to the privileges and monopolies of the large trading and colonial companies on the one hand, and of the closed handicraft guilds on the other. The struggle against state intervention could only be carried on, however, when it could be shown that economic legislation by the state was unnecessary and harmful. The ascendancy of the laws regulating the economic system itself over state legislation had to be demonstrated.[1]

Thus the policy of the bourgeoisie comes to be based upon political economy and its struggle against mercantilism becomes a battle for economic freedom, which in turn develops into a broader struggle for individual liberty against the tutelage of the state. This is not the place to follow in detail the flowering of these ideas in the *Weltanschauung* of liberalism; but perhaps it should be pointed out that wherever, as in England, the struggle for economic freedom is victorious before the modern scientific outlook has emerged, liberalism does not incorporate this outlook in its view of the world. The revolutionary subversion of all moral and religious ideas, which French liberalism engendered, never took root in the popular consciousness in England, whereas conversely, liberalism became more deeply entrenched there than anywhere on the continent.

Yet even in England the triumph of *laissez-faire* was far from complete; the banking system remained immune, and the theory of banking freedom succumbed to the practical needs of the governors of the Bank of England. The theory of the Manchester School had an even smaller influence on the actual course of foreign policy, which remained the executive arm of English world trade in the nineteenth century just as it had been in the seventeenth and eighteenth centuries. On the continent the movement was limited to achieving freedom of the trades and professions, and remained a rule for domestic policy, while the policy for external trade quite naturally continued on a protectionist basis. England's free trade policy was based, after all, on its lead in capitalist development and on the technical and economic advantage which this gave to English industry. This lead was not due solely to natural causes, although they played an important role; thus until the modern transport system had developed water-borne traffic, and the saving in freight charges resulting from the location of iron ore and coal in close proximity to each other, were bound to have a decisive significance. On the other side, however it should not be forgotten that capitalist development is the accumulation of capital, and the more rapid accumulation in England was due, in large measure, to the outcome of the power struggles with Spain, Holland and France for control of the seas, and hence the control of colonies, as well as to the rapid proletarianization which followed the victory of the large landowners over the peasants.

England's industrial pre-eminence gave her a larger stake in free trade just as, at an earlier time, Holland's lead in capitalist development had committed her to a free trade policy.[2] Internally the development of industry, the growth of population, and its concentration in the cities, very soon made domestic agricultural output inadequate. As a result the price of grain was determined by the particularly high costs of transport which prevailed prior to the revolution in the means of transportation, and by the tariff which was then going into effect. Furthermore, even during the transition period, when good harvests made grain imports unnecessary, while bad ones increased them enormously, the landlords saw to it that through a system of export subsidies famine prices were periodically created, and the inelastic monetary system of England had the effect of bringing about a monetary crisis in the wake of every increase in food prices. This whole system was quite contrary to the interests of industry; manufacturers had no reason to fear the import of foreign industrial products since their own enterprises were technically and economically far superior, and on the other hand, grain prices were the most important element in the 'price of labour', which itself played a part in the industrialists' cost prices that was all the more important because the organic composition of capital was still low and the share of living labour in the value of the total product was therefore relatively high. The openly avowed purpose of the English anti-tariff campaign was to reduce costs by making both raw materials and labour power cheaper.

Similarly, English industrial and commercial capital was greatly interested in encouraging free trade in other countries, but had little interest in the possession of colonies. To the extent that colonies served as markets for industrial products and for the purchase of raw materials, England had to face no competition worth mentioning so long as these areas remained under a regime of free trade. The campaign for an active colonial policy, which was very expensive, raised taxes, and weakened the parliamentary system at home, abated in face of free-trade propaganda. Nevertheless, the idea of abandoning the colonies remained a platonic demand of radical free traders. The most important of these colonies, India, was never regarded as a mere market; dominion over India assured a large and influential class of high incomes as a 'tribute for good government'.[3] Moreover, in this important market 'security' was an essential condition of sales, and it was questionable whether the surrender of England's dominion might not revive old conflicts which would reduce its trading opportunities.[4]

The commercial policy interests on the continent were entirely different. Here the principal champions of free trade were the agrarian suppliers of raw materials and the exporting landowners, because free trade would have enlarged the market for their own produce and lowered the price of imported industrial products. The interest of the industrialists, on the other hand, lay in the opposite direction. There was no question of a tariff on agricultural products, but the overwhelming English competition obstructed or retarded the development of indigenous industry. It was necessary first of all to overcome the difficulties of take-off, to master the obstacles created by the shortage of skilled workers, foreman and engineers, to close the technological gap, to create marketing organizations and promote the development of credit, to accelerate proletarianization by undermining the competitive position of the handicraft producers, and to dissolve the traditional peasant economy – in short to catch up with all the things which gave England her supremacy. In addition, there was a fiscal interest in tariff revenues, which at that time, when the system of indirect taxation was in its infancy, and the existence of a natural economy over large areas of the country posed insuperable obstacles to its extension, were far more important than they are today. The tariff revenues of the continental states, in so far as they came from duties levied on industrial products, were apparently not economically harmful during that period. It is true, of course, that the domestic consumer had to pay more for the product, say, of English industry by the amount of the tariff, but the difference flowed into the state treasury, whereas today the protective tariff not only pours money into the state treasury but also exacts enormous payments from domestic consumers and transfers them to industrialists and landowners. Conversely, the fiscal interest is now coming to the fore in England, because the tax system evolved to date can be perfected only with great difficulty and in the face of fierce resistance, given the present distribution of political power among the various classes. So far as their colonial possessions were concerned, the colonial powers also had to reckon in this case with the overwhelming power of English competition if ever they dismantled the protective tariff barriers and privileges.

Thus the tariff policies of the industrial classes in England and on the continent followed different directions, as a result of the industrial pre-eminence of English capitalism. The continental and American protective tariff systems were given a theoretical justification in the works of List and Carey. List's system is not a refutation of the theory of free trade as it was formulated, for instance, by Ricardo. It propounds an economic policy which would really make the free trade system feasible, by facilitating the development of a national industry for which that system would be appropriate. This was the only purpose which List's 'educational' tariffs were intended to serve, and he therefore proposed low tariffs designed to eliminate the disparity between England's superiority and Germany's backwardness, which would only be imposed for a limited period of time since his policy was intended ultimately to make tariffs unnecessary.

This tariff policy of developing capitalism is transformed into its opposite by the tariff policy of advanced capitalism. List's system was avowedly a system designed for backward capitalist countries. But here again the law of the heterogony of ends asserted itself.* It was not free trade England, but the protectionist countries, Germany and the United States, which became the model states of capitalist development, if one takes as a yardstick the degree of centralization and concentration of capital (that is, the degree of development of cartels and trusts) and of the domination of industry by the banks – in short, the transformation of all capital into finance capital. In Germany the rapid rise of industry after the abolition of internal tariff barriers, and especially after the establishment of the empire, brought about a complete realignment of interests with respect to commercial policy. When the landowners stopped exporting agricultural products they became protectionist. The supporters of a protective tariff in industry made common cause with them, and it was precisely the representatives of heavy industry, particularly the iron industry, who clamoured for protection against the more powerful competition from England. This branch of industry had a high organic composition of capital and could easily bear the rise in food prices, which at that time was moderate, and the effects of which were being offset by nascent agricultural competition from America. On the other hand, industry suffered greatly as a result of the crisis. English competition was all the more difficult to meet

---

* The term 'heterogony of ends' is taken from the psychological theory of Wilhelm Wundt, and refers to the possibility that the consequences of a course of action will lead to a modification of the original end or the emergence of unintended ends. [Ed.]

because the German iron industry lagged far behind the English for natural and technical reasons, especially before the discovery of a method for removing phosphorus from pig-iron. In addition, it was precisely in the industries with a very high organic composition of capital and an exceptionally large component of fixed capital, that it was difficult to overcome the advantages of industries which had developed earlier elsewhere. A part of bank capital, which was intimately associated from an early stage – indeed from the very outset – with the development of heavy industry in Germany, also supported a policy of protective tariffs. The opponents of such a policy were those sectors of industrial capital which had invested in the export industries, and commercial capital. The victory of protectionism in 1879, however, marked the beginning of a change in the function of the tariff from an 'educational' tariff to a protective tariff for cartels.[5]

There is no doubt that the exclusion of foreign competition gives an exceptional impetus to the formation of cartels. It does this directly in so far as a reduction in the number of competitors facilitates agreement among them; and indirectly, because the protective tariff, by its nature and origin – since it is at this stage of development in Europe and the USA the vehicle of the powerful capitalists of the raw materials and semi-finished goods industries – is as a rule more advantageous to these industries than to the export oriented finished goods industries, which had to compete on the world market with similar English products, the cost price of which had not been increased by tariffs. It was this circumstance which necessarily favoured the development of the industries engaged in the production of means of production, placing at their disposal all the capital they needed for their technical equipment, accelerating their advance to a higher organic composition of capital and at the same time their concentration and centralization, thus creating the prerequisites for their cartelization.

There was still another circumstance, stemming originally from the backwardness of German industrial development, which eventually became a cause of the organizational superiority of German industry as compared with that of England. English industry developed so to speak organically and gradually from small beginnings to its later greatness. The factory was an outgrowth of co-operation (simple division of labour) and manufacture, which first developed principally in the textile industry, an industry which required comparatively little capital. Organizationally it remained, for the most part, at the stage of individual ownership; the individual capitalist rather than the joint-stock company predominated, and capitalist wealth remained in the hands of individual industrial capitalists. There emerged gradually, but at an increasing pace, a class of wealthy industrial entrepreneurs, owning large capital resources, whose property consisted of their productive plant. Later on, when joint-stock

companies acquired greater importance, especially with the development
of large transport undertakings, it was mainly these large industrialists who
became shareholders. It was industrial capital, in terms of both its origin
and its ownership, which was invested in these companies. Like industrial
and merchant capital, so too bank capital – and notably the capital used in
share issuing activities – remained exclusively in the hands of individual
capitalists, while the joint-stock banks only provided circulation credit and
so acquired little influence upon industry. The bankers who specialized in
share issues had equally little influence, since as a result of their activities
they had ceased to be bankers and had become, at least to some extent,
industrialists themselves. This predominance of capital accumulation in
the hands of individual capitalists, one of the earlier and, as it were, organic
features of English capitalism, was lacking both on the continent and in the
United States. In addition the large sums flowing in from the colonies,
especially India, and from the exploitation of England's trade monopoly,
were also accumulated in the hands of individual capitalists; and this too
was entirely absent in Germany and America.

Thus when the political obstacles to capitalist expansion were finally
overcome in Germany by the customs union (*Zollverein*) and then by the
establishment of the Empire, so that the way was clear for capitalism, it was
obvious that capitalist development could not simply follow the English
pattern. It was essential, indeed, to put every effort into establishing as the
starting point the technical and economic stage already reached in the more
advanced country. In Germany, however, there was lacking that accumulation of capital in the hands of individuals which was needed if production
in the most highly developed industries were to be brought to the level
already attained in England on the basis of individually owned enterprises.
Hence the joint-stock company had to assume a new function in Germany,
besides those which it had in common with English companies; namely, to
become the instrument for raising the required capital which, as a result of
the smaller scale of accumulation, neither individual capitalists nor the
industrial capitalist class as a whole possessed. Whereas in England the
joint-stock company, particularly in its early days, was essentially an
association of wealthy capitalists, its task in Germany was also to provide
industrialists with the capital they needed and to direct into their
enterprises the money of other classes. This could not be accomplished
through the direct issue of shares on the same scale as was possible through
the services of the banks, in which all the idle money of the capitalists
themselves, but also of other classes, was concentrated and could be made
available to industry. The same cause which favoured the joint stock form
of enterprise in industry was also responsible for the fact that the banks
became joint-stock banks. Thus the German banks, from the very outset,
had the task of providing German industrial companies with the capital

they needed; they were the source of capital credit and not only of circulation credit. In Germany, therefore, and in a somewhat different way in the United States, the relation of banks to industry was necessarily, from the outset, quite different from that in England. Although this difference was due to the backward and belated capitalist development of Germany, the close connection between industrial and bank capital nevertheless became, in both Germany and America, an important factor in their advance toward a higher form of capitalist organization.[6] This conjunction of a protective tariff policy with the financing of industry by the banks necessarily produced, in conditions of rapid industrial growth, those tendencies towards cartelization which themselves then created new groups which had a stake in protective tariffs, because the function of the tariff changed.

The purpose of the old protective tariff, aside from compensating for various natural disadvantages, was to accelerate the emergence of industry within the protected borders. It was intended to guard the developing domestic industry against the danger of being stifled or destroyed by overwhelming competition from a well developed foreign industry. It needed only to be high enough to offset the advantages of foreign industry, and in no circumstances could it be prohibitive because domestic industry could not yet satisfy the entire demand. Above all it was not regarded as permanent. Once it had fulfilled its 'educational' function, and domestic industry had developed to the stage where it could both satisfy domestic demand and begin to think about exports, the protective tariff lost its meaning. It became an obstacle to export promotion, since it induced other nations to adopt similar policies. Under a system of free competition, it would cease to raise prices when the protected domestic industry could satisfy domestic demand and begin to export goods. The price on the protected market would then necessarily be the same as the price on the world market, because the saving of freight charges to more distant foreign markets would make sales on the domestic market more profitable than those abroad and the output of industry would equal or exceed domestic demand. The protective tariff, therefore, was intended to be both moderate and temporary, simply to help an infant industry overcome its initial difficulties.

But matters are different in the age of capitalist monopolies. Today it is just the most powerful industries, with a high export potential, whose competitiveness on the world market is beyond doubt and which, according to the old theory, should have no further interest in protective tariffs, which support high tariffs. If we assume the maintenance of free competition a protective tariff loses its power to raise prices once domestic industry fully satisfies domestic demand. But the protective tariff for industry was one of the most effective means of promoting cartels, first by making foreign competition more difficult,[7] and second, because cartels provided an opportunity to take advantage of the tariff margin even when industry had become capable of exporting. By restricting production quotas for domestic consumption the cartel eliminates competition on the domestic market. The suppression of competition sustains the effect of a protective tariff in raising prices even at a stage when production has long since outstripped domestic demand. Thus it becomes a prime interest of cartelized industry to make the protective tariff a permanent institution, which in the first place assures the continued existence of the cartel, and second, enables the cartel to sell its product on the domestic market at an extra profit. The amount of this extra profit is given by the difference between the domestic price and the price on the world market. This difference, however, depends upon the level of the tariff, and so efforts to raise tariffs have become just as unrestrained as those to increase profits. Cartelized industry has therefore a direct and supreme interest in the level of the protective tariff. The higher the tariff, the more the domestic price can be raised above the price on the world market; and so the 'educational' tariff has evolved into a high protective tariff. The protagonist of friendly agreements and advocate of the gradual reduction of tariffs has become a fanatical high tariff protectionist.

But the cartel does not only benefit from the protective tariff on its own products. As we know, the cartel price, other things being equal, is constrained by the rate of profit in other industries. For example, if the rate of profit of the machine tool industry is increased by a higher duty on imported machinery, the cartels in coal and iron production will be able to raise their prices and so appropriate for themselves part or all of the extra profit of the machine tool industry. Monopolistic combinations thus acquire an interest in tariff protection not only for their own products, but also for those of industries which use their products in a later stage of production.

The protective tariff thus provides the cartel with an extra profit over and above that which results from cartelization itself,[8] and gives it the power to levy an indirect tax on the domestic population. This extra profit no longer originates in the surplus value produced by the workers employed by the cartels; nor is it a deduction from the profit of the other non-cartelized industries. It is a tribute exacted from the entire body of domestic consumers, and its incidence on the various strata of consumers – whether, and to what extent, it is a deduction from ground rent, from profit, or from wages – depends, as with any other indirect taxes imposed on industrial raw materials or consumer goods, upon the real power relations and upon the nature of the article which is made more expensive by the cartel tariff.

An increase in the price of sugar, for example, affects the mass of workers more severely than does an increase in the price of agricultural machinery or of bentwood furniture. But whatever the final outcome of these increases, the fact remains that a part of society's income is seized in this way for the benefit of cartelized industry, protected by tariffs, which is thereby enabled to accelerate enormously its accumulation of capital.

This way of increasing profits was bound to assume greater importance when it became impossible to raise the rate of profit by means of an increase in absolute surplus value, by extending the working day and depressing wages, as a result of the growing strength of labour organizations, which tended to produce a trend in the opposite direction. The fact that the introduction of a protective tariff for industrial goods was accompanied by increases in the duties on agricultural products, had little importance for the heavy industries. Since the organic composition of their capital is high the increased cost of labour power is not an excessive burden, their position in wage disputes is extraordinarily strong, and the modest rise in costs of production as a result of the agricultural tariffs is more than compensated by the extra profit derived from their own protective duties, provided they are high enough.

The increase in prices on the domestic market, however, tends to reduce the sales of cartelized products, and thus conflicts with the trend towards lowering costs by expanding the scale of production. This may well endanger the existence of cartels which have not yet become firmly established. The largest, best equipped concerns, for which the reduction of sales as a result of cartel policy is unacceptable, would renew the competitive struggle in order to destroy the weaker firms and take over their share of the market; and after the battle is over a still stronger cartel may emerge on a new basis. But if a cartel is already well established, it will try to compensate for the decline of the domestic market by increasing its exports, in order to continue production as before and if possible on an even larger scale. On the world market, of course, the cartel has to sell at world prices. If the cartel is efficient and capable of exporting – which is our assumption here – its real price of production $(c + p)$ will correspond with the world market price. But a cartel is also in a position to sell below its production price, because it has obtained an extra profit, determined by the level of the protective tariff, from its sales on the domestic market. It is therefore able to use a part of this extra profit to expand its sales abroad by underselling its competitors. If it is successful it can then increase its output, reduce its costs, and thereby, since domestic prices remain unchanged, gain further extra profit. It can also achieve the same result by paying its domestic customers export subsidies out of the extra profit when they ship its products abroad. The maximum export subsidy in this case, given the size of the economic area and the volume of domestic consumption, is determined by the level of the tariff. When business conditions are good, the cartel will be able to set this subsidy much lower, or even eliminate it altogether, and in this way appropriate a part of the profits of prosperity which would otherwise have gone to its customers. In bad times even the full subsidy may perhaps be inadequate to compensate its customers for the losses resulting from the fall in prices on the world market. The history of cartels shows repeatedly how important it is for their continued existence that they should have the export trade in their hands, since otherwise they are continually threatened by a restriction of exports as a result of the failure to develop an adequate system of subsidies. With the development of export subsidies the function of the protective tariff has undergone a complete change, and indeed has turned into its opposite. From being a means of defence against the conquest of the domestic market by foreign industries it has become a means for the conquest of foreign markets by domestic industry. What was once a defensive weapon of the weak has become an offensive weapon in the hands of the powerful.

English free trade was certainly never regarded by its advocates as an economic policy to be followed by England alone. Indeed, a general extension of free trade was a major interest of English industry, assuring it of its monopoly on the world market. The protective tariff of other states meant a diminution of the marketing possibilities for English goods. There has been a change also in this respect today because capital has found a way of surmounting this obstacle. The introduction or raising of the tariff in another country means indeed, as always, a decline in the marketing opportunities of the country which exports to it, and hence an obstacle to the industrial development of the latter. But the protective tariff also means extra profit in the former country, and this becomes an inducement for other countries to transfer the production of commodities, rather than the commodities themselves, to the foreign country. As long as capitalism was still not fully developed such opportunities were relatively limited, partly because state legislation at that time intervened obstructively, and partly because the economic prerequisites for capitalist production were still inadequate. The lack of public order, the shortage of labour, especially skilled labour, constituted obstacles which could only be overcome slowly and by degrees, and made the transfer of capital extraordinarily difficult. But today these obstacles have, for the most part, been eliminated, and so it has become possible for capital in a developed country to overcome the harmful effects of a protective tariff on the rate of profit by means of the export of capital.

The export of capital and the struggle for economic territory

Whereas on one side the generalization of the protective tariff system tends increasingly to divide the world market into distinct economic territories of nation states, on the other side the development towards finance capital enhances the importance of the size of the economic territory. This has always been extremely important for the development of capitalist production.[1] The larger and more populous the economic territory, the larger the individual plant can be, the lower the costs of production, and the greater the degree of specialization within the plant, which also reduces costs of production. The larger the economic territory, the more easily can industry be located where the natural conditions are most favourable and the productivity of labour is highest. The more extensive the territory, the more diversified is production and the more probable it is that the various branches of production will complement one another and that transport costs on imports from abroad will be saved. Interruptions of production resulting from changes in demand or from natural catastrophes are more easily compensated in a larger territory. There can be no doubt, therefore, that at an advanced stage of capitalist production free trade, which would amalgamate the whole world market into a single economic territory, would ensure the highest possible labour productivity and the most rational international division of labour. But even with free trade industry enjoys certain advantages in its own national market, because of its familiarity with the customs of the country and consumer habits, which makes for an easier relationship with its customers; and above all because of its proximity to the market and the consequent saving in transport costs. All these advantages are, of course, increased by protectionist measures. For a foreign industry, on the other hand, various obstacles arise from the differences of language, law, currency, etc. A protective tariff, however, greatly increases the disadvantages of a smaller economic territory by impeding exports, thus limiting the size of firms, discouraging specialization, and so raising costs of production, which are also raised by the impediments placed in the way of a rational international division of labour. It is above all the size of its economic territory, which permits an extraordinary degree of specialization within plants, that accounts for the rapid industrial development of the United States, even under a regime of protective tariffs. At an advanced stage of capitalist production (that is to say, after the 'educational' tariff has done its work) a state will be more strongly inclined toward free trade the smaller its economic territory. Hence the strong free trade interests of Belgium. Furthermore, the smaller the territory, the more one-sided is the distribution of the natural prerequisites of production, and therefore the smaller the number of branches of industry which it will be able to develop and the greater the interest in importing from abroad those commodities for the production of which its own territory is less suited.

On the other hand, a protective tariff means a constriction of the economic territory, and hence an interference with the development of the productive forces, since it reduces the size of industrial plants, discourages specialization, and impedes, finally, that international division of labour which brings about a flow of capital into those branches of production for which a given country is best suited. This is all the more important in the case of the modern high protective tariff since the tariff rates are frequently fixed less out of regard for the technical conditions of production which prevail in particular branches of production, than as the outcome of a political struggle for power among various industrial groups whose influence upon the state ultimately determines the tariff structure. But although the tariff is a brake upon the development of the productive forces, and hence of industry, it means for the capitalist class a direct increase in its profits. Above all, free trade hampers cartelization, and deprives industries which are capable of being cartelized of their monopoly of the domestic market, if that monopoly is not already assured by protected freight rates (as in the case of coal) or by a natural monopoly (as in the case of German potash production). But then the extra profits which flow from the use of the cartel's protective tariff come to an end.

It is true, of course, that monopolization also progresses even without a protective tariff. But the pace is slowed down, the cartels do not become as firmly established, and there is a danger that international cartels will meet with resistance because they will immediately be regarded as alien forces of exploitation. On the other hand, a protective tariff assures the cartel of the national market and gives it much greater stability, not only by excluding competition, but also because the possibilities for making use of the tariff are a direct incentive to the consolidation of cartelization. International cartelization too, although it would develop eventually on the basis of a much more advanced concentration of capital, even under a free trade system, is accelerated by protective tariffs, which facilitate especially the formation of the type of cartel based upon the allocation of markets, and upon price agreements, since it is not a matter of combining isolated producers on the world market, as would be the case if a free trade regime prevailed, but of combining national cartels which are already well established. The protective tariff establishes the individual cartels as the contracting parties, and thus greatly reduces the number of participants. It also prepares the basis for agreement by reserving the national markets from the outset for the respective national cartels. But the more markets there are which exclude competition by a protective tariff, and are thus reserved for their respective national cartels, the easier it is to reach agreement about free markets, and the more firmly established will be the international arrangements, since if they broke down this would not give outsiders the same prospect of competing successfully as would a free trade regime.

Hence there are two opposed tendencies at work here. On the one hand the protective tariff has become an offensive weapon which the cartels employ in the competitive struggle, thus intensifying the price war, while at the same time they seek to strengthen their competitive position by recourse to the machinery of the state and to diplomatic intervention. On the other hand the protective tariff gives greater stability to the national cartels and so facilitates the conclusion of inter-cartel arrangements. The net result of these two tendencies is that these international agreements represent a kind of truce rather than an enduring community of interest, since every change in the tariff defences, every variation in the market relations between states, alters the basis of the agreement and makes necessary the conclusion of new contracts. More solid structures can only emerge when either free trade more or less eliminates the national barriers, or the basis of the cartel is not the protective tariff but primarily a natural monopoly, as in the case of petroleum.

At the same time cartelization greatly enhances the direct importance of the size of the economic territory for the level of profit. As we have seen, the protective tariff brings the capitalist monopoly an extra profit on its sales in the domestic market. The larger the economic territory, the greater the volume of domestic sales (think, for example, of the proportion of steel output which is exported by Belgium and the United States respectively) and the larger therefore the cartel's profits. The greater this profit, the higher the export subsidies can be, and the stronger therefore is the cartel's competitive position on the world market. Along with the more active intervention in world politics occasioned by the passion for colonies, there has also emerged the desire to extend as much as possible the economic territory, surrounded by a wall of protective tariffs.

In so far as the protective tariff has adverse effects on the rate of profit, the cartel seeks to overcome them by means which the tariff system itself provides. In the first place the development of export subsidies, which have been called into existence by tariff protection, enables the cartel to surmount, at least in part, the tariff barriers of other countries and thus, to some extent, avoid any reduction of output. And this will be all the easier the larger the volume of domestic output, subsidized by its own protective tariffs. This again does not promote an interest in free trade, but rather in the expansion of its own economic territory and in raising tariff rates. Should these means prove ineffective, however, the alternative is to export capital in the form of factories built abroad. A branch of industry which is menaced by the protective tariffs of foreign countries now makes use of these tariffs for its own purposes by transferring part of its production abroad. If this prevents the expansion of the parent concern and excludes the possibility of increasing the rate of profit by reducing costs of production, it is compensated by the increased profit which the same owners of capital receive from the increase in the price of the goods which they now produce abroad. Thus the export of capital, which receives a powerful stimulus from the protective tariff at home in one way, is also promoted by the protective tariff of other countries, and contributes to the penetration of capital into all parts of the world and the internationalization of capital.

In this way the effect of the falling rate of profit, brought about by the restriction of productivity as a result of the modern protective tariff, is cancelled out. From the standpoint of capital free trade thus appears superfluous and harmful; and it seeks to overcome the restriction of productivity resulting from the contraction of the economic territory, not by conversion to free trade, but by expanding its own economic territory and promoting the export of capital.[2]

While modern protective tariff policy intensifies the ever-present drive of capital towards a constant expansion of its territory, the concentration of all idle money capital in the hands of the banks leads to a planned organization of capital exports. The linking of the banks with industry allows them to attach to the provision of money capital the condition that this particular capital will be used in this particular industry. In this way the export of capital in all its forms is enormously accelerated.

By 'export of capital' I mean the export of value which is intended to breed surplus value abroad. It is essential from this point of view that the surplus value should remain at the disposal of the domestic capital. If, for example, a German capitalist were to emigrate to Canada with his capital, become a producer there and never return home, that would constitute a loss for German capital, a denationalization of the capital. It would not be an export of capital but a transfer of capital, constituting a deduction from the domestic capital and an addition to the foreign capital. Only if the capital used abroad remains at the disposal of domestic capital, and the surplus value produced by this capital can be utilized by the domestic capitalists, can we speak of capital export. The capital then figures as an item in the national balance sheet and the surplus value produced each year as an item in the national balance of payments. The export of capital reduces *pro tanto* the domestic stock of capital and increases the national income by the amount of surplus value produced.

The joint-stock company and a highly developed credit system encourage the export of capital and change its character, in so far as they enable capital to migrate out of a country detached from the entrepreneur; ownership then remains for a much longer time, or even permanently, with the capital-exporting country, and the nationalization of capital is made more difficult. Where capital is exported for the purpose of agricultural production nationalization usually occurs more rapidly, as is shown particularly by the example of the United States.

From the standpoint of the exporting country the export of capital can take place in two different forms: it can migrate abroad either as interest-bearing or as profit-yielding capital. In the latter form, it may function as industrial, commercial, or bank capital. From the standpoint of the capital-importing country, a further consideration is what part of the surplus value is used to pay interest. Interest which has to be paid on mortgage bonds held by foreigners involves sending part of the ground rent abroad,[3] whereas interest on the debentures of industrial enterprises represents an outflow of part of the industrial profit.

As European capital has advanced to the stage of finance capital it has frequently begun to migrate abroad in this form. Thus a large German bank establishes a branch abroad, which then negotiates a loan the proceeds of which are used to construct an electrical generating plant, and the construction work is assigned to an electrical company which is connected with the bank at home. Or the process may be simplified further, and the foreign branch of the bank establishes an industrial enterprise abroad, issues the shares at home, and orders raw materials, etc., from enterprises which are connected with the parent bank. Such transactions attain their largest scale when state loans are used for obtaining industrial supplies. It is the intimate connection between bank and industrial capital which is responsible for the rapid development of capital exports.

The precondition for the export of capital is the variation in rates of profit, and the export of capital is the means of equalizing national rates of profit. The level of profit depends upon the organic composition of capital, that is to say, upon the degree of capitalist development. The more advanced it is the lower will be the average rate of profit. Besides this general factor, which is less significant here because we are concerned with commodities on the world market where prices are determined by the most advanced methods of production, we must also consider some more specific factors. So far as the rate of interest is concerned it is much higher in undeveloped capitalist countries, which lack extensive credit and banking facilities, than in advanced capitalist countries. Furthermore, interest in such countries still includes for the most part an element of wages or entrepreneurial profit. The high rate of interest is a direct inducement to the export of loan capital. Entrepreneurial profit is also higher because labour power is exceptionally cheap, and what it lacks in quality is made up by unusually long hours of work. In addition, since ground rent is very low or purely nominal, owing to the large amount of free land resulting either from the bounty of nature or from the forcible expropriation of the native population, costs of production are low. Finally, profits are swelled by special privileges and monopolies. Where products are involved for which the new market itself provides an outlet very high extra profits are also realized, since in this case commodities produced by capitalist methods enter into competition with handicraft production.

But no matter how the export of capital takes place, it always means that the capacity of the foreign market to absorb it is growing. In the past the capacity of foreign markets was an obstacle limiting the volume of European industrial products which could be exported. Their ability to consume was limited to the surpluses which they had available from their natural economy, or in any case undeveloped system of production, which could not increase its output rapidly, and still less be transformed quickly into a system of production for the market. It is understandable, therefore, that English capitalist production, with its enormous versatility and capacity for expansion, very quickly met the needs of the newly-opened markets, and even exceeded them, so that in due course there was overproduction in the textile industry. On the other hand, however, England's capacity to consume the specific products of these newly opened markets was limited, even though it was, of course, very much greater in quantitative terms than that of other foreign markets. But the crucial factor here was the qualitative nature, the use value of the products, which such foreign markets could send back in exchange for the English commodities. In so far as it was a matter of specialized luxury articles, consumption in England was limited, while on the other hand the textile industry was striving to expand as rapidly as possible. The export of textile products, however, increased the import of colonial products intended for luxury consumption, whereas the rapid expansion of textile production required the accumulation of profit at an increasing rate rather than its consumption through spending on luxury products. The result was that every opening of new foreign markets by England ended in a crisis, initiated on the one hand by a fall in the price of textile products abroad, and on the other by a collapse of the price of colonial products in England. Every history of English crises shows the importance of these special causes of such crises. It is worth noting how carefully Tooke follows the prices of colonial products, and how regularly the earlier industrial crises are accompanied by a complete collapse of these branches of commerce. The situation first begins to change with the development of the modern transport system, which shifts the main emphasis to the iron Industry, while simultaneously transactions with the newly opened markets move increasingly towards capital exports rather than mere trade in commodities.

The export of capital in the form of loans itself greatly enlarges the capacity of the newly opened markets to absorb imports. If we assume that a newly opened market is able to export £1,000,000 in commodities, then its capacity to absorb imports – given equal exchange – would also be £1,000,000. But if this sum of value is exported to the country, not in the form of commodities but as loan capital (say in the form of a state loan), then the value of £1,000,000 which the new market can obtain by exporting its surplus will not serve to exchange commodities but to pay interest on capital. It is therefore possible to export to that country a sum of value amounting not to £1,000,000 but say £10,000,000 if it is sent there as capital at 10 per cent interest, or £20,000,000 if the rate of interest is lowered to 5 per cent. This example also shows the great significance of a fall in the rate of interest for the capacity of a market to expand. Keen competition among foreign loan capitals tends to reduce the rate of interest very quickly even in backward countries and thus to increase the opportunities for capital exports. Far more significant, however, than the export of capital in the form of loan capital is the effect produced by the export of industrial capital, and this is why the latter is growing in importance. For the transfer of capitalist production to a foreign market liberates it completely from the limitations of its own domestic capacity to consume. The yield of this new production ensures the valorization of the capital. But the newly-opened market is by no means the only sales outlet; indeed capital in these new territories turns towards branches of production which can be sure of sales on the world market. Capitalist development in South Africa, for example, is quite independent of the capacity of the South African market, since the principal branch of production, the working of the gold mines, has a practically unlimited market for its product, and depends only upon the natural conditions for increasing the exploitation of the gold mines and the availability of an adequate work force. Similarly, the working of copper mines is independent of the capacity of the market in the colony itself, whereas consumer goods industries which must sell most of their output in the new market itself very soon find their growth restricted by the limitations on the capacity to consume.

In this way the export of capital extends the limits arising from the new market's capacity to consume. At the same time the introduction of capitalist methods of transport and production into the foreign country brings about rapid economic development, the emergence of a larger internal market through the dissolution of the natural economy, the expansion of production for the market, and hence an increase in the volume of those products which can be exported and thus serve to pay interest on newly imported capital. While at one time colonies and new markets were established mainly to provide new articles of consumption, new capital investment is now directed principally to branches of production which provide raw materials for industry. As domestic industry, which supplies the requirements of capital export, grows, so the exported capital is applied to the production of raw materials for this industry. In this way the products of the exported capital find a market in the home country, and the narrow sphere in which production moved in England undergoes a great expansion as domestic industry and the products of exported capital nourish each other.

We know, moreover, that the opening of new markets is an important factor in bringing an industrial depression to an end, in prolonging a period of prosperity, and in moderating the effects of crises. The export of capital accelerates the opening up of foreign countries and promotes the maximum development of their productive forces. At the same time it increases domestic production, which has to supply the commodities that are exported abroad as capital. Thus it becomes a very powerful impetus to capitalist production, which enters upon a new period of *Sturm und Drang* (storm and stress)[4] as the export of capital becomes general, during which it seems to be the case that the cycle of prosperity and depression has been shortened and crises have become less severe. The rapid increase in production also brings about an increased demand for labour power which is advantageous to the trade unions, and the tendencies towards pauperization inherent in capitalism appear to be overcome in the advanced capitalist countries. The rapid rise in production inhibits a conscious awareness of the ills of capitalist society and generates an optimistic view of its viability.

The speed with which colonies and new markets are opened up today depends essentially upon their capacity to serve as outlets for capital investment. This capacity is all the greater the richer the colony is in products which can be produced by capitalist methods, have an assured sale on the world market, and are important to industry in the home country. The rapid expansion of capitalism since 1895 has brought about a price increase especially in metals and cotton, and has thereby intensified the drive to open up new sources of these vital raw materials. Hence export capital seeks its sphere of activity principally in regions capable of producing such materials, and is drawn to those sectors, especially mining, which can at once be run on capitalist lines. As a result of this production the surplus which the colony can export is again increased, and this makes possible new capital investments. In this way the tempo of capitalist development in new markets is greatly accelerated. The obstacle to opening up a new country is not the lack of indigenous capital, since this is eliminated by the import of capital, but in most cases quite another disruptive factor, namely, the shortage of 'free', that is to say wage, labour. The labour problem assumes an acute form, and seems to be capable of resolution only by the use of force.

As has always been the case, when capital first encounters conditions which contradict its need for valorization, and could only be overcome much too slowly and gradually by purely economic means, it has recourse to the power of the state and uses it for forcible expropriation in order to create the required free wage proletariat. In the early days of capitalism this was the fate of the European peasants and of the Indians of Mexico and Peru, and today the same is happening to the Negroes of Africa.[5] These violent methods are of the essence of colonial policy, without which it would lose its capitalist rationale. They are just as much an integral part of it as the existence of a propertyless proletariat is a *conditio sine qua non* of capitalism in general. The idea of pursuing a colonial policy without having to resort to its violent methods is an illusion to be taken no more seriously than that of abolishing the proletariat while maintaining capitalism in existence.

There are diverse methods of obtaining forced labour. The principal means is the expropriation of the natives, who are deprived of their land and hence of the very basis of their previous existence. The land is turned over to the conquerors, and there is an increasing tendency to give it not to individual settlers, but to large land companies. This is particularly the case when the exploitation of mineral products is involved. Here, in accordance with the methods of primitive accumulation, there is an instant creation of capitalist wealth in the hands of a few capitalist magnates, while the small settlers are left with nothing. One need only recall the enormous wealth which came to be concentrated in this way in the hands of the groups owning the gold and diamond mines of British South Africa, and on a lesser scale, in the hands of the German colonial companies in South West Africa which are closely linked with the large banks. This expropriation creates at the same time, out of the native population 'liberated' from their land, a proletariat which is bound to become a helpless object of exploitation. Expropriation itself is made possible initially by the resistance which the demands of the conquerors quite naturally provoked among the native population. The violent actions of the settlers themselves generate the conflicts which make necessary the intervention of the state, which then ensures that a thorough job is made of it. The quest of capital for unresisting objects of exploitation becomes the concern of the state, in the form of 'pacification' of the area, for the attainment of which the entire nation, and in the first place the proletarian soldiers and taxpayers of the mother country, has to assume responsibility.

Where expropriation does not succeed immediately in such a radical way, the same end is achieved by the introduction of a system of taxation which requires the natives to make money payments on such a scale that they can only be met by incessant labour in the service of foreign capital. This education for labour has attained perfection in the Belgian Congo, where the methods of capitalist accumulation include not only oppressive taxes, but also chronic violence of the most infamous kind, fraud, and deception. Slavery is reinstated as an economic ideal, and along with it that spirit of brutality which is then transferred back from the colonies to the champions of colonial interests at home and celebrates here its disgusting orgies.[6]

If the native population does not suffice to produce the desired volume of surplus value, either because excessive zeal in expropriating them has deprived them of their lives as well as their land, or because the population is in any case small, or the natives are not sufficiently robust, capital attempts to solve the labour problem by introducing foreign labour. The import of coolie labour is organized, and an ingenious system of contract slavery is devised to ensure that the laws of supply and demand do not exert any undesirable effects on the labour market. Of course, this does not provide capital with a definitive solution of the labour problem. The introduction of coolie labour encounters increasingly strong opposition from white workers in all countries where there is room for white wage labour. At the same time it also appears dangerous to the ruling circles where European colonial policy comes into conflict with the growing expansionist ambitions of Japan, which are bound to be followed in the near future by those of China itself.[7]

If the introduction of yellow-skinned workers is thus restricted, the chances of expanding the area of employment for white labour are still more limited. The process in which the development of capitalism freed workers for industrial employment has largely come to an end in Europe. Indeed, the rapid expansion of capitalism in the most advanced countries has to some extent, during this period of storm and stress, produced a counter tendency.

Thus German capitalism, during the last two periods of prosperity, encountered a labour shortage and had to provide the necessary recruits to the industrial reserve army by encouraging immigration. American capitalism has also had to resort to immigrants, on an even larger scale, whereas the slowing down of development in England is manifested in mounting unemployment. Hence the source of emigration from Europe has become confined to south and south-east Europe and to Russia, while at the same time the demand for wage labour has increased enormously as a result of rapid economic growth.

Those states which exclude Asiatic immigrants for social or political reasons find their development hampered by the limited size of the working population; and this obstacle is most difficult to overcome precisely in those regions where the prospects for capitalist development are best, as for example in Canada and Australia. In these regions, moreover, which have vast tracts of free land, the expansion of agriculture also requires a rapidly growing additional population, and this works strongly against the emergence of a propertyless proletariat. The rate of natural increase of the population in these territories, however, is generally extremely low. But even in the most advanced European countries the rate of population growth is steadily declining, thus diminishing the surplus population available for emigration.[8]

This diminished rate of growth, however, is occurring precisely in those countries which are of great importance for increasing the output of agricultural products, such as Canada, Australia and Argentina; and it results in a tendency towards rising prices for agricultural products, which becomes steadily more pronounced in spite of the inherently great potentialities for increasing agricultural production.

But the limit imposed by population size is never more than relative. It explains why capitalist expansion is not more tempestuous, but it does not in any way halt that expansion. Besides, it carries within itself its own remedy. Leaving aside the introduction of free wage labour or forced labour in the colonial territories proper, and the relative (periodic) unemployment of white workers which emerges continually in the capitalist mother countries as a result of technological progress and may become absolute (permanent) unemployment if the rate of expansion slows down, a more severe restriction of capitalist expansion in the colonial regions where there are white workers would have as a consequence that capitalism would turn increasingly to the still backward agrarian regions of Europe itself, surmounting the political barriers which stand in its way. In this way it would open up new regions where its introduction, by destroying rural domestic industry and setting free a large part of the agrarian population, would provide the material for increased emigration.

Since the new markets are no longer simply outlets for goods, but also spheres for the investment of capital, this has also brought about a change in the political behaviour of the capital-exporting countries. Trade alone, so far as it was not colonial trade which has always been associated with robbery and plunder, but comprised trade with relatively advanced white or yellow peoples who were capable of resistance, for a long time left the social and political relations in these countries basically undisturbed, and confined itself to economic relations. So long as there exists a state power which is capable of maintaining some kind of order, direct rule over these areas is less important. All this changes when the export of capital becomes predominant, for much more substantial interests are then at stake. The risks involved in building railways, acquiring land, constructing harbours, opening and operating mines, in a foreign country, are much greater than in the mere buying and selling of goods.

The backwardness of the legal system thus becomes an obstacle, and finance capital demands ever more insistently that it should be removed, even if that has to be done by force. This leads to increasingly acute conflicts between the advanced capitalist states and the state authorities of the backward areas, and to ever more pressing attempts to impose upon these countries legal systems appropriate to capitalism, regardless of whether the existing rulers are retained or destroyed. At the same time the competition for the newly-opened spheres of investment produces further clashes and conflicts among the advanced capitalist states themselves. In the newly-opened countries themselves, however, the introduction of capitalism intensifies contradictions and arouses growing resistance to the invaders among the people, whose national consciousness has been awakened, which can easily take the form of policies inimical to foreign capital. The old social relations are completely revolutionized, the age-old bondage to the soil of the 'nations without a history' is disrupted and they are swept into the capitalist maelstrom. Capitalism itself gradually provides the subjected people with the ways and means for their own liberation. They adopt as their own the ideal that was once the highest aspiration of the European nations; namely, the formation of a unified national state as an instrument of economic and cultural freedom. This independence movement threatens European capital precisely in its most valuable and promising areas of exploitation, and to an increasing extent it can only maintain its domination by continually expanding its means of coercion.

This explains why all capitalists with interests in foreign countries call for a strong state whose authority will protect their interests even in the most remote corners of the globe, and for showing the national flag everywhere so that the flag of trade can also be planted everywhere. Export capital feels most comfortable, however, when its own state is in complete control of the new territory, for capital exports from other countries are then excluded, it enjoys a privileged position, and its profits are more or less guaranteed by the state. Thus the export of capital also encourages an imperialist policy.

The export of capital, especially since it has assumed the form of industrial and finance capital, has enormously accelerated the overthrow of all the old social relations, and the involvement of the whole world in capitalism. Capitalist development did not take place independently in each individual country, but instead capitalist relations of production and exploitation were imported along with capital from abroad, and indeed imported at the level already attained in the most advanced country. Just as a newly established industry today does not develop from handicraft beginnings and techniques into a modern giant concern, but is established from the outset as an advanced capitalist enterprise, so capitalism is now imported into a new country in its most advanced form and exerts its revolutionary effects far more strongly and in a much shorter time than was the case, for instance, in the capitalist development of Holland and England.

The revolution in transport is a milestone in the history of capital exports. Railways and steamships in themselves are immensely important to capitalism because they reduce the turnover time. This releases circulation capital and then raises the rate of profit. The reduction in the price of raw materials lowers costs and increases consumption. Thus it is the railways and steamships which first create those large economic territories that make possible the giant modern concerns with their mass production. But above all the railways were the most important means of opening up foreign markets. Without them, it would have been impossible to distribute the products of these countries in such vast quantities throughout Europe and to expand the market so rapidly into a world market. Even more important, however, is the fact that the export of capital now became necessary on a vast scale in order to construct these railways, which have been built almost entirely with European, particularly English, capital.

The export of capital was, however, an English monopoly, and it secured for England the domination of the world market. Neither industrially nor financially had England any reason to fear competition from other countries, and so the freedom of the market remained its ideal. Conversely, England's supremacy necessarily made all other states even more determined to maintain and extend their rule over territories which they had already acquired, so that at least within their own borders they would be protected against the overwhelming competition of England.

The situation changed when England's monopoly was broken and English capitalism, which as a result of free trade had never been effectively organized, had to meet the superior competition of America and Germany. The development of finance capital created in these states a powerful drive towards the export of capital. As we have seen, the development of joint-stock companies and cartels generates promoter's profits which flow into the banks as capital seeking application. In addition, the protective tariff system restricts domestic consumption and makes it essential to promote exports. At the same time the export subsidies which are made possible by cartel tariffs provide a means for competing vigorously with England in neutral markets, and this competition is all the more dangerous because the newer large-scale industry of these countries is to some extent technically superior to that of England as a result of its more modern equipment. Export subsidies having become an important weapon in the international competitive struggle, they are all the more effective the larger they are. Their size depends upon the level of tariffs, and raising this level thus becomes a prime interest of the capitalist class in every nation. No one can afford to lag behind in this respect. A protective tariff in one country makes it essential for others to follow suit, and this is all the more certain to happen the more advanced capitalism is in this country and the more powerful and widespread its capitalist monopolies. The level of the protective tariff thus becomes the decisive factor in the international competitive struggle. If it is raised in one country, others must necessarily do the same if they are not to suffer from adverse conditions of competition and to be beaten on the world market. Thus the industrial tariff too becomes what the agrarian tariff is by its very nature, an endless spiral.

But the competitive struggle, which can only be waged by reducing the price of commodities, always threatens to bring losses or at least not to produce an average rate of profit, so that here too the elimination of competition has become the ideal of the large capitalist combines. All the more so because, as we have seen, exports have become an urgent necessity for them under any circumstances, as a result of technological conditions which make imperative the largest possible scale of production. But competition rules on the world market, and there is no alternative but to replace one type of competition by a less dangerous one; to substitute for competition on the commodity market, where the price of the commodity is the only determining factor, competition on the capital market in the provision of loan capital on condition that any loan will subsequently be used for obtaining goods from the country making it. The export of capital has now become a means of ensuring that the capital-exporting country will be the supplier of industrial goods. The customer has no choice; he becomes a debtor and hence a dependent who must accept the conditions imposed by his creditor. Serbia can obtain a loan from Austria, Germany or France only if it undertakes to buy its guns or its rolling-stock from Skoda, Krupp or Schneider. The struggle for markets for goods becomes a conflict among national banking groups over spheres of investment for loan capital, and since rates of interest tend to be equalized on the international market, economic competition is confined here within relatively narrow limits, so that the economic struggle quickly becomes a power struggle in which political weapons are employed.

From an economic standpoint the older capitalist states still retain an advantage in these conflicts. England possesses an old capital-satiated industry which was originally adapted to the needs of the world market in the days of England's monopoly and now develops more slowly than German or American industry, lacking their capacity for rapid expansion. On the other hand, its accumulated capital is extraordinarily large, and vast amounts of profit available for accumulation flow steadily back to England from its overseas investments.[9] The proportion of the accumulated masses of capital to the volume of capital which can be invested internally is at its highest here, which explains why the pressure to invest capital abroad is strongest and the rate of interest lowest in England. The same situation had emerged in France for different reasons. Here also there is a store of old accumulated wealth which is centralized by the banking system (though it is somewhat less concentrated as a result of the property system in France) together with a steady flow of income from foreign investments, and on the other side a stagnation of industrial growth at home; hence a powerful tendency to export capital. The advantage which England and France enjoy can only be made effective politically through strong diplomatic pressure, which is a dangerous, and therefore limited, means, or else economically, by making sacrifices in respect of prices, which would outweigh a possible rise in the rate of interest.

But the intensity of competition arouses a desire to eliminate it altogether. The simplest way of achieving this is to incorporate parts of the world market into the national market, through a colonial policy which involves the annexation of foreign territories. Thus, while free trade was indifferent to colonies, protectionism leads directly to a more active colonial policy, and to conflicts of interest between different states.

Another factor works in the same direction. From a purely quantitative point of view it is more advantageous for a country to export its capital in profit-yielding rather than interest-bearing form, because the profit is greater than the interest. Furthermore, if the exporting capitalists invest their capital as industrial capital, they retain a more direct control over its disposal and use. English capital invested in American railway bonds, that is to say, as interest-bearing capital, has a negligible influence on the American railway barons, whereas its influence is decisive when the industrial enterprise itself is operated with English capital. Today, however, the principal exporters of industrial capital are the cartels and trusts, and this for various reasons. In the first place they are strongest in the heavy industries where, as we have seen, the pressure to export capital is greatest in the search for new markets to absorb their massively increasing output. The major interest of these monopolistic heavy industries is the construction of railways, the exploitation of mines, the growth of the armaments of foreign states, the installation of electricity-generating stations. Behind them stand the large banks which are most closely connected with these branches of industry. Moreover, while the drive to increase production is very strong in the cartelized industries, high cartel prices preclude any growth of the domestic market, so that expansion abroad offers the best chance of meeting the need to increase output. The cartels, thanks to their extra profits, always have at their disposal sums of capital available for accumulation, which they prefer to invest in their own branches of industry where the rate of profit is highest. The link between the banks and industry is also closest here, and the possibility of promoter's profit through the issue of shares in these enterprises becomes a powerful inducement to export capital.

So today we see the strongest drive towards the export of industrial capital in those countries which have the most advanced organization of industry, namely, Germany and the United States. This explains the peculiar circumstance that these countries on the one hand export capital, and on the other hand also import a part of the capital required for their own economies from abroad. They export primarily industrial capital and so expand their own industry, while obtaining their working capital, to some extent, in the form of loan capital from countries with a slower rate of industrial development but greater accumulated capital wealth. In this way they not only gain from the difference between the industrial profit which they make in foreign markets and the much lower rate of interest which they have to pay on the capital borrowed in England or France, but also ensure, through this kind of capital export, the more rapid growth of their own industry. Thus the United States exports industrial capital to South America on a very large scale, while at the same time importing loan capital from England, Holland, France, etc., in the form of bonds and debentures, as working capital for its own industry.[10] In this respect too, therefore, cartelization and trustification, by promoting the export of capital, give an advantage to the capitalists of a country with the most highly monopolized industries over countries whose industries are less well organized, thus arousing in the latter a determination to accelerate the cartelization of their own industries by means of a protective tariff, and at the same time strengthening the resolve of the most advanced countries to maintain the export of capital under all circumstances by excluding any kind of competition from foreign capital.

If capital export in its most advanced form is undertaken by those sectors of capital in which concentration is most advanced, this in turn accelerates the growth of their power and their accumulation of capital. It is the largest banks and the largest branches of industry which succeed in obtaining for themselves the best conditions for the valorization of their capital in foreign markets, and acquire the rich extra profits in which lesser capitals cannot even dream of participating.

The policy of finance capital has three objectives: (1) to establish the largest possible economic territory; (2) to close this territory to foreign competition by a wall of protective tariffs, and consequently (3) to reserve it as an area of exploitation for the national monopolistic combinations. Such aims, however, were bound to come into the sharpest possible conflict with the economic policy which industrial capital carried to a state of classic perfection during its period of absolute rule (in the double sense that commercial and bank capital were subordinated to it, and that it had absolute control of the world market) in England. All the more so since the application of this policy of finance capital in other countries has also increasingly threatened the interests of English industrial capital. Indeed, the country of free trade was the natural target for attack by foreign competition, though of course 'dumping' also has certain advantages for English industry. The processing industry obtained cheaper raw materials as a result of cut-throat competition. But on the other hand this also hurt the raw material industries, and so, as cartelization advanced, as more stages of production were integrated, and as the system of export subsidies was extended, the hour was bound to strike for those English industries which had hitherto profited from 'dumping'. The most important factor, however, is that the tariff opens up the prospect of an era of rapid monopolization with its opportunities for extra profits and promoter's profits, which are a great enticement to English capital.

On the other hand, it would be entirely possible for England to enter into a customs union with her colonies. Most of the self-governing colonies are important primarily as suppliers of raw materials to England[11] and purchasers of industrial products.[12] The protective tariff policy adopted by other states, especially in agriculture, has in any case made England the principal market for the colonies. In so far as English industry could impede the development of their own industries these countries (in the British Empire) are still at the stage of the 'educational' tariff, that is to say at a stage which cannot tolerate a rise in tariffs above a certain level because importation of foreign industrial products is still absolutely essential to supply their own market. It would be quite easy, therefore, to establish a higher cartel tariff for the British Empire as a whole, while retaining the 'educational' tariffs within the empire; and the prospect of establishing such an economic territory, which would be strong enough both politically and economically to counter the expulsion of British industries as a result of other states raising their tariffs, is capable of uniting the whole capitalist class.[13] Furthermore, by far the greater part of the capital used in the colonies is owned by English capitalists, for whom an imperial tariff is much more important than the larger increase that an independent colonial tariff would bring.[14]

The United States is in itself a sufficiently large economic territory even in the age of imperialism, and the direction of its expansion is determined by geography. The Pan-American movement, which found its initial political expression in the Monroe Doctrine, is still in its beginnings and has immense potentialities because of the enormous predominance of the United States.

Things are different in Europe, where the division into independent states has given rise to conflicting economic interests, the elimination of which by means of a Central European customs union encounters very serious obstacles. Here, unlike the British Empire, it is not a matter of mutually complementary parts but of more or less identical, and hence competing, entities confronting each other in hostile fashion.

This hostility, however, is greatly increased by the economic policy of finance capital, as a result of which the antagonisms no longer arise from the efforts to establish unified economic territories in Europe itself, as was the case in the nineteenth century, but from the attempts to annex neutral foreign markets, for which purpose the armed forces of the European nations are now deployed. It is not a matter of annexing highly developed capitalist countries, whose own industry is capable of exporting and would only involve increased competition for the conquering country, and in any case would offer little scope as a sphere of investment for the surplus capital of that country. It is a matter rather of those territories which have not yet been opened up but which can have great importance precisely for the most powerful capitalist groups; that is to say, above all overseas colonial territories. It is here that capital has the opportunity to invest on the grand scale. In particular, the creation of a modern transport system, railways and steamship lines, absorbs enormous quantities of capital.[15]

The state ensures that human labour in the colonies is available on terms which make possible extra profits. In many cases it also guarantees the gross profit. The natural wealth of the colonies likewise becomes a source of extra profits by lowering the price of raw materials and so reducing the cost price of industrial products. In the colonies ground rent is either non-existent or very low. The expulsion or annihilation of the native population, or in the most favourable case their transformation from shepherds or hunters into indentured slaves, or their confinement to small, restricted areas as peasant farmers, creates at one stroke free land which has only a nominal price. If the land is fertile it can supply the home industry with raw materials such as cotton far more cheaply than could the old sources of supply. Even when this is not reflected in prices – for example in the case of cotton where the American price continues to have a determining influence – it means that a part of the ground rent which would otherwise have to be paid to the American farmers now goes into the pockets of the owners of colonial plantations.

The supply of raw materials for the metal working industries is still more important. In spite of all the technological advances the rapid development of these industries tends to raise the price of metals and this tendency is reinforced by capitalist monopolization. That makes it all the more important for a country to have sources of supply for such raw materials within its own economic territory.[16]

The drive for colonial acquisitions thus leads to a steadily growing conflict among the large economic territories and has major repercussions upon the relations between individual states in Europe. The diverse natural conditions which are a source of rapid economic growth in a large unified economic territory such as the United States have the opposite effect in Europe where they are distributed at random, quite fortuitously and hence irrationally from an economic standpoint, among many small economic territories. Here they obstruct economic development and tend to favour the larger economic territories at the expense of the smaller ones, especially since there is no system of free trade to integrate these territories into a higher economic unity. This economic inequality has the same significance for the relations between states as it has for those between social strata within them; namely, the dependence of the economically weak upon the economically powerful. The economic means employed is again in this case the export of capital. The country which is rich in capital exports it as loan capital and becomes the creditor of the borrowing country.

As long as the export of capital served primarily for the construction of a transport system and the development of consumer goods industries in a backward country, it contributed to the economic development, in a capitalist form, of that country. Even so, this method had some disadvantages for the country concerned. The bulk of the profit flowed abroad where it was either spent (without providing employment for the industries of the debtor country) or accumulated. Naturally, this accumulation did not have to take place in the country where the profit originated; but this capitalist 'absentee ownership'[17] slows down enormously the pace of accumulation, and hence the further development of capitalism, in the debtor country. In large economic territories where capitalism would have been bound to develop rapidly because of domestic conditions, a national assimilation of foreign capital soon occurred. Thus Germany quickly assimilated Belgian and French capital, which was particularly important in the mining industry of Westphalia. In the small economic territories, however, this assimilation was more difficult to achieve, because an indigenous capitalist class emerged much more slowly and with greater difficulty.

Such emancipation became quite impossible when the character of capital exports changed, and the capitalist class in the large economic territories became less concerned with establishing consumer goods industries in foreign countries than with acquiring control over raw materials for their ever growing producers' goods industries. Thus the mines and the mining enterprises of the states in the Iberian peninsula came under the control of foreign capital which was no longer exported as loan capital but directly invested in these mines; and the same thing happened – though against stronger opposition – to the mineral wealth of Scandinavia, especially Sweden. Thus at a time when these countries could perhaps have proceeded to establish the most basic of modern industries, an iron industry of their own, they were deprived of their raw materials for the benefit of English, German and French industry. Their capitalist development, and along with it their political and financial development, was stunted at the outset. As economic tributaries of foreign capital,[18] they also became second-class states, dependent upon the protection of the great powers.

On the other hand, the increasing importance of capitalist colonial policy confronted England with the task of defending her colonial empire, which meant retaining her control of the seas and protecting the route to India. For this, however, it was essential to have access to Atlantic ports and so England was obliged to maintain good relations with all the states bordering on the Atlantic. England has been able to achieve this politically because her capital exports enabled her to secure economic control over the smaller of these states. The strength of the British navy necessarily drove France too into an alliance with England when Germany's claim to a share in colonialism brought France into conflict with Germany and made her concerned, like all the other countries which had colonies, about the safety of her possessions. Thus there was a growing tendency not to eliminate the tariff barriers within Europe and so create a large unified economic territory, but rather to group the smaller, and hence economically backward, political units as satellites around the larger ones. These political relationships react in turn upon the economic relationships and make the country which is politically a satellite into a sphere of investment reserved for the capital of its protector. Thus diplomacy serves directly the interests of investment-seeking capital.

As long as the smaller states have not yet been taken 'firmly in hand' they become an arena for competition by foreign capital and in this case too a decision is sought by political means. In order to obtain arms Serbia, for example, has also to make a political decision about whether it should seek French and Russian or German and Austrian aid.[19] Political power thus becomes a decisive factor in economic competition and finance capital acquires a direct profit interest in the power position of the state. The most important function of diplomacy now becomes the representation of finance capital. Purely political weapons are now reinforced by the weapons of commercial policy,[20] and the provisions of a commercial agreement are no longer determined simply by the requirements of commodity exchange, but also by the extent to which a small state is willing to give preferential treatment to the finance capital of a larger state against its competitors. The smaller the economic territory the less power it has to sustain the competitive struggle successfully by means of large export subsidies, and the stronger is the urge to export capital in order to share in the economic development and higher profits of other, greater, powers. The larger the stock of previously accumulated wealth within the country the more readily can this desire be satisfied.

But here also there are opposing tendencies at work. The larger the economic territory and the greater the power of the state, the more favourable is the position of its national capital on the world market. That is why finance capital has come to champion the idea that the power of the state should be strengthened by every available means. But the greater the historically produced disparities between the power of difficult states, the more the conditions on which they engage in competition will vary, and the more bitter – because more rewarding – will be the struggle of the large economic territories to dominate the world market. This struggle is intensified the more developed finance capital is and the more vigorous its efforts to monopolize parts of the world market for its own national capital; and the more advanced this process of monopolization, the more bitter the struggle for the rest of the world market becomes. The English free trade system made this conflict bearable, but the transition to protectionism which is bound to occur very soon will necessarily exacerbate it to an extraordinary degree. The disparity which exists between the development of German capitalism and the relatively small size of its economic territory will then be greatly increased. At the same time as Germany is making rapid progress in its industrial development, its competitive territory will suddenly contract. This will be all the more painful because, for historical reasons which are irrelevant to present-day capitalism (indifferent to the past unless it is accumulated 'past labour') Germany has no colonial possessions worth mentioning,[21] whereas not only its strongest competitors, England and the United States (for which an entire continent serves as a kind of economic colony), but also the smaller powers such as France, Belgium and Holland have considerable colonial possessions, and its future competitor, Russia, also possesses a vastly larger economic territory. This is a situation which is bound to intensify greatly the conflict between Germany and England and their respective satellites, and to lead towards a solution by force.

Indeed this would have happened long ago if there had not been countervailing forces at work. The export of capital itself gives rise to tendencies which militate against such a solution by force. The unevenness of industrial development brings about a certain differentiation in the forms of capital export. Direct participation in opening up industrially backward or slowly developing countries can be undertaken only by those countries in which industrial development has attained its most advanced form, both technically and organizationally. Among them are, first, Germany and the United States, and in the second place England and Belgium. The other countries of long-standing capitalist development take part in the export of capital rather in the form of loan capital than of capital for the construction of factories. This has as a consequence that French, Dutch, and even to a great extent English capital, for example, constitute loan capital for industries which are under German and American management. Various tendencies thus emerge which make for solidarity among international capitalist interests. French capital, in the form of loan capital, acquires an interest in the progress of German industries in South America, etc. Moreover, connections of this kind, which greatly enhance the power of capital, make it possible to open up foreign territories much more rapidly and easily as a result of the increased pressure of the associated states.[22]

Which of these tendencies prevails varies from case to case and depends primarily upon the opportunities for profit which emerge in the course of the struggle. The same considerations which decide whether competition should continue in a given branch of industry, or should be eliminated for a longer or shorter period of time by a cartel or trust, play a similar role here at the international and inter-state level. The greater the disparities of power the more likely it is, as a rule, that a struggle will occur. Every victorious struggle, however, would enhance the power of the victor and so change the power relationships in his favour at the expense of all the others. This accounts for the recent international policy of maintaining the *status quo* which is reminiscent of the balance of power policy of the early stages of capitalism. Moreover, the socialist movement has inspired a fear of the domestic political consequences which might follow from a war. On the other hand the decision as to war or peace does not rest solely with the advanced capitalist states, where the forces opposing militarism are most strongly developed. The capitalist awakening of the nations of Eastern Europe and Asia has been accompanied by a realignment of power relations which, through its effect upon the great powers, may well bring the existing antagonisms to the point where they erupt in war.

Once the political power of the state has become a means of competition for finance capital on the world market, this naturally involves a complete change in the relation of the bourgeoisie to the state. In the struggle against economic mercantilism and political absolutism, the bourgeoisie was the champion of opposition to the state. Liberalism was in reality a destructive force involving the 'overthrow' of state power and the dissolution of old social bonds. The whole painfully constructed system of dependent relationships on the land, and of guild associations with their complex superstructure of privileges and monopolies in the towns, was thrown overboard. The victory of liberalism meant first of all an enormous reduction in the power of the state. Henceforth, at least in principle, economic life was to be excluded entirely from the sphere of state regulation, and politically the state was to confine itself to the maintenance of public order and the establishment of civil equality. Thus liberalism was purely negative, in sharp contrast to the state during the mercantilist period of early capitalism which in principle wanted to regulate everything, and

also to all socialist systems which seek constructively rather than de-
structively to replace anarchy and the freedom of competition by a
conscious regulation of economic life, and a self-organizing society. It is
only natural that the liberal principle should have been realized first in
England where it was championed by a bourgeoisie committed to free trade
which had to appeal to the power of the state only for short periods of time
in its conflict with the proletariat. But even in England its realization
encountered opposition, not only from the old aristocracy which pursued a
protectionist policy and therefore opposed the principle of liberalism, but
also, to some extent, from commercial capital and from bank capital
involved in investment abroad, which demanded above all the maintenance
of England's control of the seas, a demand which was most vigorously
supported by all those groups which had an interest in the colonies. On the
continent, however, the liberal view of the state had to be considerably modified from the very outset before it was able to prevail. While continental
liberalism – and this shows a characteristic contrast between ideology and
reality – as formulated in classical fashion by the French deduced the
theoretical consequences of liberalism in all spheres of political and
intellectual life much more boldly and systematically than did its English
counterpart, since it came upon the scene later with quite a different body of
scientific knowledge, so that it was formulated in a far more comprehensive
way, based upon a rationalist philosophy, English liberalism rested
essentially upon political economy and its practical realization was subject
from the very beginning to definite limitations. Indeed, how could the
liberal demand for the restriction of state power be put into effect by a
bourgeoisie which, in economic terms, needed the state as the most
powerful lever of its development and for which it was a matter not of
abolishing the state, but of transforming it from an obstacle into a vehicle
of its own development? What the continental bourgeoisie needed above
all was to overcome the plethora of petty states and to substitute for the
impotence of these petty states the supreme power of a unified state. The
need to create a national state was bound to make the bourgeoisie from the
very beginning a champion of the state. On the continent, however, it was a
matter of land power, not sea power. The modern army, however, is
entirely different from a navy as a means of establishing the power of the
state *vis à vis* society. It means fundamentally that those who control the
army have the state power in their hands without restraint. On the other
hand, universal military service, which arms the mass of the people, was
bound to persuade the bourgeoisie very quickly that if the army were not to
become a menace to its rule, a strictly hierarchical organization was
required, based upon an exclusive officers' corps which would be a pliable
instrument of the state. If liberalism was thus unable to carry out its
political programme in countries such as Germany, Italy and Austria, its

efforts were also circumscribed in France, where the French bourgeoisie could not dispense with the help of the state in matters of commercial policy. Furthermore, the victory of the French Revolution necessarily involved France in a war on two fronts. She had to defend the revolutionary achievements against continental feudalism; and on the other hand the creation of a new empire of modern capitalism was a threat to the established position which England held on the world market, and so France was obliged at the same time to contest England's domination of the world market. Her defeat enhanced the power of the landed gentry, and of commercial, bank, and colonial capital, in England, and along with it the power of the state over industrial capital, thus delaying the definitive accession of English industrial capital to a position of dominance and the triumph of free trade. On the other hand, England's victory necessarily led industrial capital in continental Europe to support the protective tariff, totally frustrated the advance of economic liberalism, and created the conditions needed for a rapid development of finance capital on the continent.

Thus from the outset, the ideology and the conception of the state of the bourgeoisie in Europe encountered few obstacles in their adaptation to the needs of finance capital. Moreover, the fact that the unification of Germany was accomplished in a counter-revolutionary way was bound to reinforce very strongly the position of the state in the consciousness of the people, whereas in France military defeat led to a concentration of all available forces upon the task of re-establishing state power. Thus the needs of finance capital found various ideological elements to hand which could easily be used for creating a new ideology in harmony with its own interests.

This ideology, however, is completely opposed to that of liberalism. Finance capital does not want freedom, but domination; it has no regard for the independence of the individual capitalist, but demands his allegiance. It detests the anarchy of competition and wants organization, though of course only in order to resume competition on a still higher level. But in order to achieve these ends, and to maintain and enhance its predominant position, it needs the state which can guarantee its domestic market through a protective tariff policy and facilitate the conquest of foreign markets. It needs a politically powerful state which does not have to take account of the conflicting interests of other states in its commercial policy.[23] It needs also a strong state which will ensure respect for the interests of finance capital abroad, and use its political power to extort advantageous supply contracts and trade agreements from smaller states; a state which can intervene in every corner of the globe and transform the whole world into a sphere of investment for its own finance capital. Finally, finance capital needs a state which is strong enough to pursue an expansionist policy and the annexation of new colonies. Liberalism opposed international power politics, and only wanted to secure its own rule against the old forces of aristocracy and bureaucracy by granting them the least possible access to state power, but finance capital demands unlimited power politics, and this would be the case even if military and naval expenditures did not directly assure the most powerful capitalist groups of important markets, which provide in most cases monopolistic profits.

The demand for an expansionist policy revolutionizes the whole world view of the bourgeoisie, which ceases to be peace-loving and humanitarian. The old free traders believed in free trade not only as the best economic policy but also as the beginning of an era of peace. Finance capital abandoned this belief long ago. It has no faith in the harmony of capitalist interests, and knows well that competition is becoming increasingly a political power struggle. The ideal of peace has lost its lustre, and in place of the idea of humanity there emerges a glorification of the greatness and power of the state. The modern state arose as a realization of the aspiration of nations for unity. The national idea, which found a natural limit in the constitution of a state based upon the nation, because it recognized the right of all nations to independent existence as states, and hence regarded the frontiers of the state as being determined by the natural boundaries of the nation, is now transformed into the notion of elevating one's own nation above all others.[24] The ideal now is to secure for one's own nation the domination of the world, an aspiration which is as unbounded as the capitalist lust for profit from which it springs. Capital becomes the conqueror of the world, and with every new country that it conquers there are new frontiers to be crossed. These efforts become an economic necessity, because every failure to advance reduces the profit and the competitiveness of finance capital, and may finally turn the smaller economic territory into a mere tributary of a larger one. They have an economic basis, but are then justified ideologically by an extraordinary perversion of the national idea, which no longer recognizes the right of every nation to political self-determination and independence, and ceases to express, with regard to nations, the democratic creed of the equality of all members of the human race. Instead the economic privileges of monopoly are mirrored in the privileged position claimed for one's own nation, which is represented as a 'chosen nation'. Since the subjection of foreign nations takes place by force – that is, in a perfectly natural way – it appears to the ruling nation that this domination is due to some special natural qualities, in short to its racial characteristics. Thus there emerges in racist ideology, cloaked in the garb of natural science, a justification for finance capital's lust for power, which is thus shown to have the specificity and necessity of a natural phenomenon. An oligarchic ideal of domination has replaced the democratic ideal of equality.

While this ideal appears to embrace the whole nation in the sphere of international politics, it becomes transformed in domestic politics by emphasizing the point of view of the rulers as against the working class. At the same time the increasing power of the workers intensifies the efforts of capital to reinforce the power of the state as a bulwark against proletarian demands.

Thus the ideology of imperialism arises on the ruins of the old liberal ideals, whose naïvety it derides. What an illusion it is, in the world of capitalist struggle where superiority of weapons is the final arbiter, to believe in a harmony of interests. What an illusion to expect the reign of eternal peace and to preach international law in a world where power alone decides the fate of peoples. What stupidity to advocate the extension of the rule of law which prevails within nations beyond their frontiers, and what irresponsible interference with business this humanitarian fantasy which has turned workers into a labour problem, invented social reform at home, and now wants to abolish contract slavery in the colonies, the only possible form of rational exploitation. Eternal justice is a beautiful dream, but morality builds no railways, not even at home. How are we to conquer the world if we have to wait for competition to undergo a spiritual conversion?

But imperialism only dissolves the faded ideals of the bourgeoisie in order to put in their place a new and greater illusion. It is clear-headed and sober in evaluating the real conflicts among capitalist interest groups, and it conceives all politics as a matter of capitalist syndicates either fighting or combining with each other. But it is carried away and becomes intoxicated when it unveils its own ideal. The imperialist wants nothing for himself, but he is also no visionary and dreamer who would dissolve the tangled profusion of races at every level of civilization and of potentiality for further development, into the bloodless concept of 'humanity', instead of seeing them in all their colourful reality. He observes with a cold and steady eye the medley of peoples and sees his own nation standing over all of them. For him this nation is real; it lives in the ever increasing power and greatness of the state, and its enhancement deserves every ounce of his effort. The subordination of individual interests to a higher general interest, which is a prerequisite for every vital social ideology, is thus achieved; and the state alien to its people is bound together with the nation in unity, while the national idea becomes the driving force of politics. Class antagonisms have disappeared and been transcended in the service of the collectivity. The common action of the nation, united by a common goal of national greatness, has taken the place of class struggle, so dangerous and fruitless for the possessing classes.

This ideal, which seems to provide a new bond for the strife-ridden bourgeois society, will doubtless meet with an increasingly enthusiastic reception as the process of disintegration of bourgeois society continues.

Finance capital and classes

We have seen how the process of agglomeration in capitalist monopolies gives capital an interest in strengthening the power of the state. At the same time capital acquires the power to dominate the state, both directly through its own economic power, and indirectly by subordinating the interests of other classes to its own.

The development of finance capital changes fundamentally the economic, and hence the political, structure of society. The individual capitalists of early capitalism confronted each other as opponents in a competitive struggle. This conflict prevented them from undertaking any common action in politics as in other spheres. It should be added that the needs of their class did not as yet call for such common action, since the negative attitude of industrial capital to the state did not allow it to come forward as the representative of general capitalist interests. Instead, individual capitalists defended their own interests as citizens of the state. The great problems which agitated the bourgeoisie were essentially constitutional questions, such as the establishment of a modern constitutional state; problems, that is to say, which affected all citizens alike, uniting them in a common struggle against reaction and the vestiges of feudal and absolutist-bureaucratic rule.

But the situation changed as soon as the triumph of capitalism unleashed the opposing forces within bourgeois society. The petty bourgeoisie and the workers were the first to rebel against the rule of industrial capital. Both groups launched their attack in the economic field. The freedom of enterprise seemed to be threatened by the petty bourgeoisie which demanded combinations reminiscent of the guilds, and by the workers who insisted on legal regulation of the labour contract. It was now no longer a matter of citizens, but of manufacturers and workers, or manufacturers and craftsmen. Political parties now directed their activities openly in terms of economic interests, whereas these were previously concealed behind the slogans of reaction, liberalism, and democracy, through which the three classes of early capitalism – the landowners with their hangers-on at court, in the bureaucracy and in the army; the bourgeoisie; and the combination of petty bourgeoisie and workers – disguised their interests. In the struggle over the industrial system three groups of economic organizations emerged: associations of industrialists, co-operatives and workers' organizations, the first two frequently encouraged by the state, which invested them with legal powers in respect of some of their functions. But while the co-operatives and the trade unions soon became united in the pursuit of common aims, the employers' associations remained divided by conflicts over commercial policy. Furthermore, industrial capital came into conflict politically with commercial and loan capital.

Commercial capital was far more favourably inclined to an increase in the power of the state than was industrial capital, because wholesale trade, especially overseas trade and notably the colonial trade, sought the protection of the state, and yielded readily to a dependence upon privileges. Loan capital, during the period of early capitalism, supported the power of the state with which it had to transact its most important business – state loans – and it was entirely free of that yearning for peace and tranquillity which permeated industrial capital. The greater the financial needs of the state, the greater was its influence, and the more abundant its loans and other financial transactions. These were not only the basis of its direct profits; they were also the backbone of stock exchange transactions, and in addition an important means by which the banks could obtain state privileges. Thus, for example, the privilege of issuing bank notes granted to the Bank of England is closely connected historically with the debt relationship between the state and the bank.

Cartelization, by unifying economic power, increases its political effectiveness. At the same time it coordinates the political interests of capital and enables the whole weight of economic power to be exerted directly on the state. By uniting all capital interests it confronts the state as a far more cohesive body than was the fragmented industrial capital of the era of free competition. Moreover, capital now finds a much greater readiness to support it among other classes in the population.

This must appear strange at first sight, because finance capital seems to be opposed to the interests of all other classes. After all, as we have seen, monopolistic profit is a deduction from the income of all other classes. Cartel profit on industrial products increases the cost of means of production in agriculture and reduces the purchasing power of its income. The rapid development of industry deprives agriculture of labour power and creates a chronic shortage of workers in rural areas along with a technological and scientific revolution in agricultural production. This conflict was bound to make itself increasingly felt so long as the tendency of finance capital to raise the prices of industrial products was not accompanied by a similar tendency in the case of agricultural products.

When capitalist development first got under way it encountered opposition from the agricultural population. Industry destroys peasant domestic production and transforms the essentially self-sufficient peasant economy into an agricultural business geared to the sale of its product on the market. The peasants have to pay a high price for that transformation, and they are therefore hostile to industrial development. But the peasantry is a class in modern society which is incapable of action by itself. Lacking geographical cohesion, isolated from urban culture, and with an outlook confined to narrow parochial interests, it is for the most part only capable of political action when it follows the lead of other classes. At the beginning of capitalist development, however, it stands opposed to the very class which has the greatest power to act in the countryside, the large landowners, who have a direct interest in the expansion of industry. They depend upon the sale of their products, and capitalism creates a large domestic market for them as well as giving them the opportunity to develop agricultural industries such as distilling, brewing, starch and sugar production. This interest of the large landowners is very important because it provides support for capitalism in its early stages, and also ensures the support of the state. Mercantilist policy is also always supported by the landed proprietors, who are the product of the capitalist transformation of landownership.

The further development of capitalism soon destroys this community of interest as a result of the struggle against mercantilism and its executive agent, the absolutist state. This struggle is waged directly against the landed proprietors who largely dominate the state and occupy the highest posts in the army, the bureaucracy and the court, boost their income by economic exploitation of the state, and are the upholders of state power in the rural areas. This conflict becomes more intense after the defeat of absolutism and the creation of the modern state. The development of industry reinforces the political power of the bourgeoisie and threatens the landed proprietors with total political impotence. Political antagonism is then supplemented by an intensification of economic conflict. The development of industry depopulates the countryside, creates a shortage of manpower, and finally turns what was an interest in exports into an interest in imports. In this way there arises the conflict over commercial policy which ends, in England, with the defeat of the landed interests. On the continent, however, the common interest in protective tariffs prevents the conflict from coming to a head. As long as backward industrial development on the continent obliges the large agricultural estates to export, the large landowners maintain a friendly attitude – within certain limits – towards industry and especially towards trade. They support free trade until the emergence of an interest in imports converts them to protectionism and brings them closer to heavy industry in economic policy. But the same industrial development which strengthens them in Germany by raising the prices of agricultural products and increasing ground rents, also plants the seeds of a new conflict. The upsurge of industry, before cartelization, reinforces its commitment to free trade and commercial agreements, and a danger arises that its power will become sufficiently great for its interest in low grain prices to prevail. Industrial development thus becomes a threat to the landed interests; one which is increased when the same development which is transforming Europe into an industrial state lets loose agricultural competition from America which threatens European agriculture with an abrupt fall in grain prices, rents and land values. The development of finance capital, by changing the function of the protective tariff, reconciles these conflicting interests and establishes a new community of interest between large landed property and cartelized heavy industry. Agriculture now has a secure level of prices, and the further progress of industry can only raise this price level. It is no longer the conflict with industry, but the labour question, which is the principal concern of landowners. Resisting the demands of workers is now their most urgent political problem, and hence they also oppose strongly the efforts of industrial workers to improve their conditions because every such improvement would make it more difficult to retain the agricultural labour force. Thus a common hostility to the labour movement brings these two most powerful classes together.

At the same time the power of the large landed proprietors increases as a result of the disappearance, or at least the considerable abatement, of their conflict with the small landowners. The old historic conflict between them has long been settled by the abolition of feudal imposts on land. The period of falling grain prices as well as the difficulties of the labour problem have halted almost completely the expansion of the large estates at the expense of small land-holdings. On the other hand, the common struggle for an agricultural tariff has united the large and small landowners. The fact that the small farmers had a greater interest than the large ones in protection against imports of meat and livestock naturally did not in any way prevent them from co-operating, since a protective tariff could only be achieved by a common struggle. Another factor to be considered is the specific effect of an agricultural tariff on the price of land. The rise in the price of land is of course harmful to agriculture as such, but it is very advantageous to the individual owner of agricultural land. The common struggle with respect to commercial policy thus united all strata of agricultural proprietors in countries which needed to import agricultural products, and so gave finance capital the support of the arable farmers. The medium and small landowners participated all the more fully in these struggles as the rapid development of co-operatives enlarged the commercial market for peasant agriculture and reduced production for the family's own needs. At the same time, the larger proprietors very easily acquired a leading position in these co-operatives since on the one side no stronger interest group opposed them, and on the other they possessed the necessary experience, intelligence, and authority. This, in turn, reinforced the leading role of the large proprietors in the countryside and led to the politics of the arable farming areas being increasingly dominated by them.

The degree of unity among the propertied interests has also tended to increase because their sources of income are becoming more diversified. The tariff policy has rapidly increased income from ground rent, especially during the last decade when overseas agricultural competition became less intense, partly because of the rapid industrial development of the United States.[1] and partly because the agricultural production of the Central and South American states, though rapidly increasing, cannot keep pace with the increase in demand. The increase in demand meant, of course, that the larger proprietors had surplus income at their disposal, but there were difficulties in the way of using it to increase agricultural output, particularly because the distribution of land ownership presented considerable obstacles to the expansion of the cultivable area. These obstacles might be overcome if the upward trend of grain prices were sufficiently vigorous and enduring, thus permitting land prices to rise correspondingly, and (this being a second important factor) if the large landowners were dealing with an impoverished peasantry which had no alternative but to sell its land. But the period from the mid 1870s to the middle of the first decade of the twentieth century was a favourable one for the peasantry. In fact, it was the large wheat producers and cattle breeders who bore the full brunt of overseas competition and who were most adversely affected by the shortage of labour, whereas the great increase in urban demand for the main products of the small farmer – milk, meat, vegetables, fruit, etc. – and the lesser impact of the labour problem, favoured the medium and small farms. The attempt of the large farmers to extend their holdings, which could only be vigorously pursued when the falling trend of grain prices was reversed, thus met with resistance from powerful medium and small farmers whose main products enjoyed constantly rising prices. Hence this surplus income had to be applied primarily to profitable investment in industry. This was also encouraged by the fact that the tumultuous boom which began in 1895 increased the rate of profit in industry, at any rate far above that in agriculture. Such investment was all the easier because the development of the share system created an appropriate form for investments from other spheres of the economy, while the concentration and consolidation of large-scale industry greatly reduced the risk for outsiders. There was also a rapid development of agricultural industries proper which the state, through its tax legislation, helped to become monopolies; an equally rapid development of other industries which were established in the countryside; and finally, in the case of large landowners, the age-old association between agriculture and mining. All these factors transformed the class of large landed proprietors from one which derived its income from ground rent into one which received its income in part, and to an increasing extent, from industrial profit, from participation in the gains of 'mobile capital'.[2]

On the other side, finance capital became increasingly interested in the mortgage business. Other things being equal, it is the level of land prices which is crucial for the expansion of these activities, since the higher the price of land, the larger the amount of mortgage indebtedness can be. A rise in agricultural tariffs thus became a matter of great interest for a not insignificant part of the banking community. At the same time the increased incomes of landowners and tenants tended to attract new capital investment in agriculture and more intensive cultivation; this in turn increased the demand for farm equipment and expanded this particular field of investment for bank capital.

Furthermore, the desire of urban capitalists to enhance their social standing has led them to acquire landed property, or else – and here again we see the principle of personal union – to ally themselves with the large landed proprietors through intermarriage, the most favoured form of social climbing and of defence against the dispersal of property.

Thus the separation of the ownership function from the management of production, brought about by the joint-stock system, makes possible the solidarity of property interests, and this possibility becomes a reality with the increase of ground rent on one side and of extra profits in industry on the other. 'Wealth' is no longer differentiated in terms of the source of income, according to its origin in profit or rent, but now flows from participation in all the sectors of the economy among which the surplus value produced by the working class is distributed.

The connection with the large landowners greatly augments the capacity of finance capital to dominate the state. With them it has won over the elite, and hence on most issues the whole countryside. This support is not unconditional, of course, and it is costly; but the costs, in the form of higher prices for agricultural products, are easily compensated by the extra profit which finance capital obtains through its domination of the state, which is a *conditio sine qua non* for the pursuit of an imperialist policy. The support of the large landed proprietors also assures finance capital of support from the class which occupies most of the highest and most influential offices in the state and controls the bureaucracy and the army. At the same time imperialism involves a strengthening of the state power, an expansion of the armed forces and the bureaucracy in general, and thereby a reinforcement of the community of interests between finance capital and the large landowners.

While finance capital has been supported by the decisive stratum in the countryside in its effort to dominate the state, it was also helped in this attempt, at an earlier stage, by the development of class conflicts among the industrial producers. From the outset finance capital is in conflict with small and medium size capital. As we have seen, cartel profit is a deduction from the profits of non-cartelized industry. It is in the interest of the latter, therefore, to oppose cartelization. But this interest clashes with others. Industries which are not, or not yet, capable of exporting, have a common interest with cartelized industries in the protective tariff, which can be achieved only through combined action since the cartels are the most powerful protagonists of the tariff. But the formation of a cartel undoubtedly accelerates the monopolistic tendencies in other enterprises, and it is just the most powerful and competitive capitalists in the industries which have not yet been cartelized who welcome the formation of cartels, which promote concentration in their own industry and so speed up the process of cartelization. Their way of combating other cartels is to form a cartel of their own, not in the least to fight for free trade. What they want is not free trade, but the opportunity to take advantage of the protective tariff through their own cartel.

It should also be noted that instances of medium and smaller capitalists becoming indirectly dependent on finance capital are increasing. We have seen that this is the case to a very great extent in capitalist commerce. It is true that this produces a conflict while the process is still going on, but once it has been completed it is precisely these groups which come to identify their interests with the cartel. The merchants who today are the agents of the coal syndicate or of the organization of alcohol producers are now only interested in strengthening the syndicate because it fends off the competition from outsiders, and in expanding it in order to increase their sales. The numerous and increasing cases of indirect dependence, in which industrialists are kept going by a department store or a large industrial concern, have the same consequences, for the growth of cartelization in general creates an identity of interest for all owners of capital. The participation of the small and medium capitalists in large-scale industry leads in the same direction. As a result of the possibilities opened up by shareholding, profit accumulated in other branches of industry is partly invested in the heavy industries, first because they are developing more quickly due to the relatively more rapid growth of the production of means of production, and second because cartelization is most advanced here and the rate of profit at its highest.

Finally, the policy of finance capital involves the most vigorous kind of expansion and a constant search for new spheres of investment and markets. But the more rapidly capitalism expands, the longer are the periods of prosperity and the more short-lived the crises. Expansion is the common interest of all capital, and in the era of protectionism it is only possible in the form of imperialist expansion. It should be added that the longer a period of prosperity lasts the less severe is the competition felt by domestic capital in its own country, and the less danger there is of the smaller capitalists succumbing to the competition from the larger ones. This is true for smaller capitalists in all industries, including those which are cartelized. For it is periods of prosperity which are most dangerous for the existence of cartels, while conversely a depression, involving an intensified competitive struggle at home and large quantities of idle capital, is a time when the drive for new markets is most intense.

After being disputed for decades the Marxist theory of concentration has now become a commonplace. The decline of the middle strata in industry cannot be halted. But what interests us here is not so much the decline in their numbers, resulting from the destruction of small businesses, as the structural change which modern capitalist development has brought about in small enterprises both in industry and commerce. A great many of these small businesses are auxiliaries of large enterprises and therefore interested in the latter's expansion. Repair shops in the cities, installers of equipment, etc., depend upon large-scale factory production which has not yet taken over such subsidiary work. The enemy of all repair business of whatever kind is not the factory but the handicrafts which once performed this type of work. These strata are therefore in conflict with the working class, not with big business.

An even larger proportion of small enterprises is indeed only seemingly independent; in reality these businesses have become 'indirectly dependent upon capital' (Sombart) and therefore 'enslaved to capital' (Otto Bauer). They are a declining stratum with little prospect of surviving, lacking organizational ability, and completely dependent on the large capitalist enterprises whose agents they are. In this category, for example, belong the swarm of small innkeepers who are nothing more than sales agents for the breweries, the owners of shoe shops which are fitted out by some shoe factory, etc. It also includes the numerous seemingly independent cabinet makers who work for furniture stores, the tailors who work for clothing manufacturers, etc. It is unnecessary to examine these phenomena more fully here, since Sombart has provided an extensive and striking description of them in *Der moderne Kapitalismus*.

What is important, however, is that in the course of this development these strata have adopted a different political attitude. The conflict of interest between small business and big business, exemplified in the struggle of the handicrafts against the capitalist enterprise in the early stages of capitalism, has been decided in all essential respects. That struggle drove the old middle class to assume an anti-capitalist attitude. The middle class sought to postpone its own defeat by combating freedom of enterprise and by imposing restrictions on the large capitalist enterprises. Legislation was invoked to prolong the existence of the middle class by protecting handicraft workers, reintroducing guild regulations and apprenticeship training, and passing discriminatory tax laws. In this struggle against big capital the middle class received the support of the rural classes, which at that time were equally inclined towards anti-capitalist attitudes. But it encountered the hostility of the working class, which was bound to see these restrictions on productivity as a threat to its vital interests.

The outlook of small business today is fundamentally different. The competitive struggle has been settled in all essential respects so far as competition between the handicrafts and capital is concerned. The struggle over concentration now takes place within the capitalist sphere itself, in the form of a struggle between small and medium business firms and the giant concerns. The small businesses are now essentially only annexes of large enterprises, and even where their independence is not purely fictitious they are only auxiliaries of large firms, as is the case, for example, with firms which install lighting equipment, or the modern urban stores which sell factory products. None of them engage in competition with large-scale industry, but are interested, on the contrary, in seeing it expand as much as possible because they work for it as repair or auxiliary businesses, as dealers or agents. This does not, of course, exclude competition among themselves, nor a movement towards concentration, which also occurs here. But this struggle no longer gives rise to any general anti-capitalist outlook among them; on the contrary, they see their salvation in a still more rapid development of capitalism, which has produced them and broadens their opportunities. On the other hand, in so far as they employ workers they come into increasingly bitter conflict with the working class, because the power of workers' organizations is felt most strongly in small businesses.

But even among those strata where the small business still predominates, as for example in the building industry, the conflict with big capital is becoming less bitter. Not only because these entrepreneurs, who depend upon bank credit, are thoroughly imbued with the capitalist spirit, nor simply because their opposition to the workers is becoming more intense, but also because whenever they present specific demands they meet less resistance, and quite frequently even receive support, from the biggest capitalists. The battle for and against freedom of enterprise was waged with particular intensity between the master craftsmen and the small and medium manufacturers of consumer goods. Tailors, shoemakers, wheel-wrights and building craftsmen on one side, confronted textile and clothing manufacturers, etc. on the other. But today, when this conflict has been settled in essentials, the protection of handicrafts does not affect any of the vital interests of the most advanced branches of capitalist enterprise. The coal syndicate, the steel combine, the electrical or chemical industry, are more or less indifferent to the kind of demands the middle class puts forward today. The interests of the small and medium capitalists, which may suffer as a result, are not their concern, or at least not directly. On the other hand, the people who make these demands are the most vigorous and bitter opponents of workers' demands. In these spheres of small-scale production competition is at its most bitter, and the rate of profit at its lowest. Every new social reform, every trade union success, spells doom for a host of these enterprises. It is here that the workers find their most furious antagonists, and big business and the big landed interests their best mercenaries.[3]

The same interest also assures the middle class of support from the farming class, and so the old conflict of interest between the bourgeoisie and the petty bourgeoisie is disappearing, and the latter becomes a political praetorian guard of big business. The fact that the middle class has not improved its lot even after its demands have been satisfied changes nothing in this situation. Where the state has set up compulsory organizations for small businesses they have always been a complete fiasco. Even where small business is viable, the co-operatives and guilds (for example in the food trade in the big cities) have become quasi-cartels engaged in a common effort to plunder consumers, as has been the case with butchers and bakers. Or else they are employers' associations, whether membership is direct or the guild members as a body join a separate employers' association, which remains closely dependent upon the guild.[4]

However, it is precisely the impossibility for the middle class, unlike the old-time craftsmen, to put forward significant economic demands of its own, which makes it incapable of independent political action and obliges it to act as a political hanger-on. Denied the possibility of pursuing its own class policy, it falls victim to any kind of demagogy which can exploit its hostility to the working class. From being the economic antagonist of the workers it becomes their political opponent, and sees political freedom, which it can no longer utilize itself, as aiding and abetting the strengthening of the political, and hence economic, power of the working class. It becomes politically reactionary, and the smaller its household the greater the value it places upon remaining master of it. Thus it calls for a firm hand in government, and is ready to support any coercive policy as long as it is directed against the workers. Thus it becomes the enthusiastic promoter of strong government, worshipping military and naval might and an authoritarian bureaucracy. In this way it carries out the aims of the imperialist classes and becomes their most valued comrade-in-arms. Imperialism in turn provides it with a new ideology; through the rapid expansion of capital it hopes to see an improvement in its own business, greater opportunities for employment, an increase in the purchasing power of its customers – all of which makes it an enthusiastic fellow-traveller of the imperialist parties. At the same time it is also most susceptible to the means of influencing elections, especially business boycotts, and its weakness makes it a suitable object of political exploitation.

Of course it begins to have doubts when the bill is presented, and the harmony between itself and big business is disturbed for a time. But the taxes are borne mainly by the workers, and even if indirect taxes fall more heavily on the middle class than on big business its power of resistance is nevertheless too weak to dissolve the bond between them. Only a small part of the middle class breaks away from its support of the bourgeoisie and allies itself with the proletariat. Apart from the seemingly independent self-employed, who are actually engaged in domestic industry, most of these belong to the urban strata of small tradesmen who depend on working class customers, and either for business reasons or because they have acquired a working class outlook through constant association with workers, join the workers' party.

An entirely different position is taken by those strata which have come to be described recently by the unfortunate term 'new middle class'. These are the salaried employees in commerce and industry, whose numbers have increased greatly, and who have become the actual managers of production in a hierarchical system, as a result of the development of large-scale production and the corporate form of enterprise. This is a stratum which has grown even more rapidly than the proletariat. The advance towards a higher organic composition of capital involves a relative, and in some cases, or in some branches of industry, an absolute decline in the number of workers. This is not necessarily the case with technical personnel, whose numbers tend rather to increase with the size of the firm, even if not proportionately. For the advance to a higher organic composition of capital means an advance toward the automatic plant, and a change to more complicated machinery. The introduction of new machines makes human labour power superfluous, but it is far from making technical supervision superfluous. The expansion of the mechanized, large-scale capitalist concern is therefore a vital interest of all grades of technical personnel and makes the salaried employees in industry most fervent supporters of large-scale capitalist development.

The development of the joint-stock system has a similar effect. It separates management from ownership and makes management a special function of more highly paid wage earners and salaried employees. At the same time, the higher posts become very influential and well paid positions into which all employees apparently have the opportunity to rise. The interest in a career, the drive for advancement which develops in every hierarchy, is thus kindled in every individual employee and triumphs over his feelings of solidarity. Everyone hopes to rise above the others and to work his way out of his semi-proletarian condition to the heights of capitalist income. The more rapidly corporations have developed, and the larger they have become, the greater also becomes the number of positions, especially the influential and well paid ones. The white collar employees see only this harmony of interests, and since every position seems to be merely a stepping-stone to a higher one they feel less interest in the struggle over their own labour contract than in the struggle of capital to expand its sphere of influence.

This is a stratum which in terms of its ideology and its origins forms part of the bourgeoisie, whose ablest or most ruthless representatives are still rising into the capitalist strata, and who still to some extent have a higher standing than the proletariat because of their income. Members of this stratum come more frequently into contact with capitalist directors, who keep them under close scrutiny and select them very carefully. Any attempt on their part to organize is fought fiercely and implacably. Although development will eventually drive these strata, who are indispensable to production, onto the side of the proletariat, especially when power relations begin to fluctuate, and the power of capitalism, though not yet broken, no longer appears invincible, they are still at present not particularly active in any independent struggle.

Future developments will no doubt gradually change this passive attitude. The decline in opportunities to attain an independent position, which is a consequence of the movement of concentration, obliges the small businessmen and petty capitalists more and more to send their sons into careers as employees. At the same time, as the number of such employees grows, the expenditure on their salaries becomes a more important item in costs, and a tendency arises to depress salary levels. The supply of this kind of labour power is increasing rapidly, but on the other hand there is an increasing division of labour and specialization, even for this highly skilled labour power, in the large firms. Part of the work, which is mechanical in character, is done by less qualified workers; a large modern bank, an electrical corporation, or a department store employs a great many white-collar workers who are little more than trained routine workers, and whose higher education, if they have had one, is more or less a matter of indifference to the employer. They are constantly in danger of being replaced by unskilled, or semi-skilled workers, and women workers offer strong competition, which they have to fight against when the price of their labour power is being determined. Their level of living is declining, and they are only too painfully aware of the fact because they are accustomed to bourgeois pretensions. Furthermore, as the giant concerns expand, it is largely these badly paid positions which increase in number, while there is no corresponding increase in the higher posts. The growth in numbers of giant modern concerns has rapidly increased the demand for all kinds of white-collar workers, but the expansion of existing concerns has by no means involved a similar increase. Moreover, with the consolidation of the joint-stock companies the most remunerative positions are increasingly monopolized by the stratum of big capitalists and the career prospects for white-collar employees deteriorate greatly.[5]

The consolidation of industries and banks into large monopolies brings a further deterioration in the situation of salaried employees. They now confront an overwhelmingly powerful capitalist group; their mobility, and hence the prospect of finding a better job by taking advantage of competition among entrepreneurs for the best employees, becomes uncertain even for the most able and talented among them. The number of salaried employees may also be reduced absolutely as a result of combinations. In the main, this affects the number of highly paid jobs, because management can be streamlined. The rise of combinations, particularly trusts, reduces the number of the highest technical positions, and there is also an absolute reduction in the number of salesmen, commercial travellers, advertising personnel, etc.[6]

But it takes a considerable time for these consequences to make themselves felt in the political attitude of this stratum. Originating in, and recruited from, a bourgeois milieu they continue to adhere for the time being to their old ideology. This is a stratum in which the fear of sinking into the proletariat keeps alive the determination not to be taken for a proletarian, a stratum in which hatred of the proletariat and contempt for proletarian methods of struggle are at their most intense. The commercial clerk regards it as an insult to be called a worker, whereas a privy councillor, and occasionally even the director of a cartel, enthusiastically claims this title for himself, though, of course, what the former fears is the identification with a lower social stratum, whereas the latter puts the emphasis on the ethical value of work. At all events, this ideology keeps the salaried employees at a distance from proletarian views for the time being. On the other hand, the development of corporations, and especially of cartels and trusts, enormously accelerates the pace of capitalist development. The rapid development of the large banks, the expansion of production brought about by the export of capital, the conquest of new markets, all serve to open up new fields of employment for salaried employees of all kinds. Still divorced from the struggle of the proletariat, they see their best prospects in the expansion of capital's sphere of activity. More educated than the middle class which I described earlier, they are more easily seized by the ideology of imperialism, and because of their interest in the expansion of capital, they become prisoners of its ideology. Since socialism is still ideologically alien to them, and too dangerous in practice, they accept the ideology of imperialism as promising a way out, which offers the prospect of advancement in their careers and increases in their salaries. Although its social position is weak, this stratum of salaried employees has considerable influence in forming public opinion, through its connections with petty capitalist circles and its greater facility in public activities. These are the subscribers to specifically imperialist publications, partisans of racialist theory (which they frequently interpret in terms of competition), readers of war novels, admirers of colonial heroes, agitators and electoral fodder for finance capital.

But this is not a definitive position. The more the expansion of capitalism encounters obstacles which slow down its rate of growth, the more complete the process of cartelization and trustification, and hence the growing predominance of those tendencies which produce a deterioration in the position of salaried employees, so the opposition of these strata to capital (for which they perform the most important as well as the most useless functions in production) will increase. At the same time there will be an increase in the numbers of those who even now constitute a majority, the employees who will remain permanently in subordinate positions, badly paid, working excessively long hours, and reduced to the position of routine workers for capital; and they will be driven increasingly to take up the struggle against exploitation alongside the proletariat. The greater the strength of the proletarian movement and the better its prospects of victory the sooner this will happen.

In the end their common interest in halting the advance of the working class increasingly unites all sections of the bourgeoisie. But the leadership of the struggle has long since passed into the hands of big business.

The conflict over the labour contract

The conflict over the labour contract, as is well known, has passed through three stages. In the first stage, the individual manufacturer is opposed by the individual worker. In the second, the individual manufacturer is engaged in conflict with an organization of workers, and in the third, organizations of workers are locked in conflict with employers' organizations.

The function of a trade union is to eliminate competition among workers on the labour market. It tries to achieve a monopoly of the supply of the commodity 'labour power'. Thus it constitutes, in a sense, a quota cartel; or rather, since it is only a matter here, in relation to the capitalists, of buying and selling this commodity, a 'ring'. But every quota cartel or 'ring' suffers from the weakness that it does not control production, and so cannot regulate the extent of the supply. This weakness is inescapable in the case of a trade union. The production of labour power almost always defies regulation. Only when it is a question of skilled labour power can a workers' organization succeed in curtailing production by taking appropriate measures. A strong trade union of skilled workers, by limiting the number of apprentices, extending the period of apprenticeship, and prohibiting the employment of any but skilled workers, as recognized by the union itself, can restrict the production of such labour power and achieve some kind of monopoly position. A good example is provided by the printing unions which have made it a rule, for instance, that only highly qualified 'skilled' compositors can operate type-setting machines, even though less skilled workers with some technical training would be adequate for the job. Under favourable circumstances a strong trade union may even succeed in reversing the relationship and get a certain type of work recognized as 'skilled', and therefore entitled to a high rate of pay, by recognizing as full-fledged workers only those who have spent a considerable time in the trade. That is the practice, for example, in the English textile industry, whose monopoly position on the world market, which it still retains for some products, favoured the formation of a strong trade union and also made it easier for entrepreneurs to grant concessions since their monopoly position allowed them to pass on the cost of higher wages to consumers.

The effort to control the labour market also gives rise to a tendency to prevent competition from foreign workers by increasing the difficulties of immigration, particularly when it is a question of workers who are accustomed to low levels of living and are difficult to organize. Bans on immigration are intended to perform the same service for the trade union as does the protective tariff for the cartel.[1]

But if the trade union, as an organization of living human beings, is to attain its goal, it can do so only through the will of its members. The establishment of a monopoly presupposes that the workers will sell their labour power only through the union and only on the terms set by the union. The price of labour power has to be removed from the play of the forces of supply and demand. This means, however, that the suppliers, that is to say, the unemployed, must not become active on the labour market at prices other than those which have been set. The price is given, fixed by the will of the trade union, and the supply must adjust itself to that price rather than the price to supply and demand. The trade union thus becomes a form of co-operation between the employed and the unemployed. The unemployed must be kept from entering the labour market, in the same way as a cartel protects the market against a glut by storing products whenever production exceeds the volume of supply which suits the purpose of the cartel. The storage costs correspond to the various forms of assistance given by the unions to the unemployed, but the latter are much more important because they are the only means of restricting the supply, whereas a cartel also disposes of the far more effective means of curtailing production. On the other hand, the aim of keeping the unemployed off the labour market can be achieved by various forms of moral pressure, such as outlawing scabs, explaining how class interests are damaged, and in short by an education in trade unionism which welds the working class into a fighting unit.

The problem for the trade union, as for every other monopoly, is to control the market as fully as possible. But here the trade union encounters formidable obstacles. The transient personal interests of the individual worker often clash with the interests of the class as a whole. The organization requires certain sacrifices: dues, expenditure of time, readiness to engage in struggle. Anyone who remains outside the union earns the good will of his employer and avoids conflicts, unemployment, or demotion. The stronger the trade unions become the more the entrepreneur strives to keep his workers out of them. He substitutes his own social security arrangements for those of the trade union, and deliberately exploits the conflict between personal and class interests.

The trade union struggle is a struggle over the labour contract. The worker reproduces the value of c and creates a new value consisting of $(v + s)$, wages and surplus value. The absolute magnitude of $(v + s)$

depends upon the length of the working day. The shorter the working day the smaller is (v + s), and if v remains the same, the smaller is s. If working time remains the same s increases when v declines and vice versa. But this effect is offset by a change in the intensity of labour; with rising wages and a shortening of working time, the intensity of labour grows. The development of piece work and bonus payment systems represents an attempt to increase the intensity of labour to a maximum at a given level of wages and working hours, while the regulation of the speed at which machines are operated provides an objective means of increasing the intensity of labour. The achievements of the working class in reducing hours of work have certainly not reached, and in some cases are very far from reaching, the point at which they would fully compensate for the increased intensity of labour. However important the reduction of working hours has been for the social condition of workers, and however much this achievement and the struggle for it have raised their physical and cultural level, there can be little doubt that this reduction of working time has not altered the ratio of v to s at the expense of s. It has not affected the rate of profit, and from a purely economic standpoint nothing has changed. However, it should be pointed out in passing that in many industries which require high standards of precision and accuracy, longer hours of work would have been impossible, and that in general the reduction of hours of work has improved the quality of work, accelerated technological progress, and increased relative surplus value. So far as the level of wages is concerned, the connection between wage increases and increased intensity of labour is not quite so clear, but it certainly exists, and it remains extremely doubtful whether the relatively small increase in real wages, especially for unskilled workers, has increased v at the expense of s, or whether, as is far more probable, any rise in wages has been fully compensated by an increase in the intensity of labour. But it must obviously be conceded that a certain period must elapse before there is such a compensating effect, during which s is reduced by the increase in v.

Since the value of a commodity – and in this context, since we are dealing with the social relationship, we can use the shortened expression 'value' [instead of 'exchange value'–Ed.] – is equal to constant plus variable capital plus surplus value $(c + v + s)$, a change in v to which corresponds an opposite change in s has no influence on the price of the commodity, and consequently no effect on consumers. Ricardo demonstrated conclusively that a rise in wages and a reduction in working hours can have no effect on the price of commodities. This is indeed quite evident. The annual social product falls into two parts. The first is a replacement for the means of production (machinery, raw materials, etc.) which have been used up, which has to come out of the total product. The second is the new product which has been created by the productive workers during the course of the year. This is at first in the hands of the capitalists and again comprises two parts, one constituting the income of workers, the other accruing to the capitalists as surplus value. The price of the product to consumers equals the sum of both parts [i.e. replacement plus new product – Ed.] and cannot be altered by the proportion in which the second part is divided between workers and capitalists. It is, therefore, completely nonsensical, from a social standpoint, to maintain that a rise in wages or a reduction in working hours increases the price of the product. Nevertheless, this contention is put forward over and over again, and with good reason.

The conclusion we have just reached is directly valid only for the value of commodities, that is to say, only from the standpoint of society. We know, however, that the value of a commodity undergoes a modification as a result of the attempts to equalize the rate of profit. For the individual capitalist, or the capitalist in a particular branch of industry, however, a rise in wages represents an increase in the cost outlay. Suppose that his wage bill has been 100; then using 100 of constant capital, and with a rate of profit of 30 per cent, he sold the product for 260. If the wage bill now rises to 120, as a result of a successful strike, his cost price will be 220, and if he continues to sell at the old price of 260 his profit will fall from 60 to 40 in absolute terms, while his rate of profit will decline from 30 per cent to slightly less than 19 per cent, far below the average rate of profit. An equalization of the rate of profit will have to take place. This means that a rise in wages in a particular branch of production results in a price increase in that branch of production, which takes place on the basis of the formation of a new general rate of profit lower than the one which previously prevailed. But price increases always encounter resistance; they make sales more difficult, and this in turn works against the increase in price. Contracts at the old prices have to be carried out. Above all, it takes some time to make the price increase effective. Strictly speaking, a migration of capital out of this branch of production should follow, because a price increase reduces the volume of sales, and consequently the supply, that is to say production, must be reduced. This danger that sales will fall off varies in the different branches of production and hence also the degree of resistance offered by employers to wage demands. It also depends to a large extent upon business conditions and upon the organization of the industry whether such wage increases can be passed on more or less fully, and how quickly this can be done. Given a general rise in wages, the equalization of the altered rate of profit will result in a fall in the prices of products in those industries with an above average organic composition of capital, and a rise in the prices of products in those with an organic composition of capital below the average. Every increase in wages, however, results in a decline in the average rate of profit, although the decline may be very slight and may take effect very slowly, if it results from a wage increase in a single branch of industry.

Since individual capitalists suffer losses before prices settle at their new level, it is only natural that they should offer resistance, and that the resistance should be all the stronger, the lower the rate of profit. We saw earlier that a lower than average rate of profit prevails in small business and petty capitalist spheres of activity, and for this reason resistance will be most vigorously displayed there, while at the same time the ability to resist is least. The trade union struggle is a struggle over the rate of profit from the employers' point of view; a struggle over the level of wages (including the reduction of working time) from the standpoint of the workers. It can never be a struggle to abolish the capital relationship itself, the exploitation of labour power. For the outcome of such a struggle would always be decided in advance; since the object of capitalist production is the production of profit through the exploitation of the worker, it would appear senseless to the entrepreneur to engage in business if exploitation were eliminated. He would therefore stop production, for whatever his personal situation, it could not possibly be improved by continuing to run the business, and in such a case he would have to rely on starving out his workers. If only his own sphere of activity were threatened he would try to save at least a part of his capital by transferring it to another branch of industry. The struggle for the complete abolition of exploitation thus lies outside the scope of purely trade union activity, and can never be brought to a conclusion simply by trade union methods of struggle, as the syndicalist 'theory' would have us believe. Even where it assumes a trade union form, as in the mass strike, it is not a question of a struggle against the economic position of the entrepreneur, but of a struggle for power waged by the working class as a whole against the organized power of the bourgeoisie, the state. The economic damage inflicted upon the entrepreneur is never more than an auxiliary weapon in the struggle to disrupt the power apparatus of the state. This political task can never be the responsibility of the trade unions as such, but simply brings the trade union form of organization into the service of the political struggles of the proletariat.

But if the trade union struggle is concerned with the rate of profit, it follows that there are definite limits to the objectives that a trade union can pursue. For the employer, it is a matter of calculating whether he is in a position to put the new price level into effect, whether his losses during the transition period will not exceed the losses incurred through a prolonged strike, and finally whether there is not some possibility for him to invest his capital elsewhere, in a branch of production where the rate of profit is not directly affected by the outcome of a strike. It follows from this, however, that certain limits are set in advance to every particular trade union struggle, which it is the difficult task of the trade union leadership to recognize, and which determine their tactics. It also follows that a trade union can as a rule operate more successfully the higher is the rate of profit; whether it is generally higher, as in a boom, or higher in a particular branch of production, in consequence of its monopoly position, the achievement of extra profit through patents, etc. It is beyond the scope of this study to investigate these conditions in detail, but it will be useful to discuss briefly some general aspects of the changes in the power relations between the two classes.

It is obvious that the rise of employers' organizations involves a change in the balance of power between capital and labour. As a rule, the development of employers' organizations has been regarded, quite correctly, as a reaction to the organization of labour. But the pace of their development, as well as their power, depends essentially upon the change in the structure of industry, upon the concentration and monopolization of capital. As long as the isolated employer confronted an organized workforce the trade union had a great many measures available to it which the development of employers' organizations has now rendered ineffective. With the concentration of capital the power of the employer in the struggle over the labour contract increases, but at the same time the possibilities of organization for the more concentrated workforce also increase. Variations in the size of enterprises are responsible for quite different degrees of resistance to trade unions. The more fragmented an industry is, and the smaller the average size of the firms, the greater, in general, is the power of the trade union. Within the same industry, moreover, the power of the trade union is greater in small and medium-size firms than in the large concerns, simply because the small firms, already hard pressed by competition from the large ones, are far less able to sustain the losses involved in a struggle. The struggle of the trade unions generally promotes the trend towards large firms, and hence the growth of productivity, technological progress, a reduction in costs of production, and the emergence of relative surplus value; and in this way it creates the preconditions for obtaining new concessions.

As long as trade unions confront individual employers their position is a favourable one. They can bring their concentrated power to bear upon the isolated employer. The wage struggle is thus decomposed into a series of individual strikes. The workers of the employer concerned are supported by the whole financial strength of the trade union, which does not diminish during the struggle because the members who are still working continue to pay their dues, and perhaps special levies. The employer has to fear that his customers will be taken from him by employers who continue to produce, and that his sales will be considerably reduced even after the strike has ended. He has to make concessions, and from that moment it is in his interest that the terms to which he has agreed should become general throughout the industry, that all the other employers, whether voluntarily or under duress, should concede the same terms of employment. The isolation of the employers enables the trade unions to compel them to come to terms one after the other, through systematically conducted individual strikes, without these strikes putting too great a strain upon the resources of the unions themselves. Their successes increase their power by increasing membership and income from dues, and they emerge from the struggle stronger than before. It is clear that these tactics can be employed all the more successfully, the more tenuous the co-operation between employers, the keener the competition among them, the greater the number of employers involved, and the smaller the power of resistance of each individual employer. All these conditons obtain in those branches of activity in which small and medium-size firms predominate, and it is here that the influence and power of the unions is greatest. Large-scale industry, which can make far more accurate calculations, resists such individual strikes much more strongly, because the large firms are far more insistent on the greatest possible equality of production costs. In this case a strike can only be successful if it is general throughout the industry. An individual strike encounters much greater resistance which is far more difficult to overcome because the power of even a single large employer is far more considerable, and an understanding among a relatively small number of employers can be achieved more rapidly.[2] But the more powerful trade unions become, the stronger too is the resistance they evoke on the part of employers. The combination of workers is now confronted by the combined power of the employers. Since the influence of trade unions is greatest in the small and medium-size enterprises, it is here that resistance will also show itself most strongly. In fact, the organization of employers begins in handicraft production and in the smaller finished goods industries,[3] where the power of the unions is most strongly felt, and where it grows most rapidly in periods of boom.[4] But even though the establishment of employers' associations must unquestionably be regarded as a reaction to the trade unions,[5] and therefore occurs first in the light industries, it is by no means confined to that sphere. Cartelization and trustification merge the interests of the participating capitalists much more strongly and indissolubly, and make them a united body *vis à vis* the working class. The elimination of competition is not confined to the labour market – as it is in the case of the uncartelized light industries – and so the solidarity of employers is enhanced to a much greater extent. It may even go so far as to make any special organization unnecessary in those branches of industry where the position of employers is strongest. The coal syndicate makes an employers' association superfluous, and the Steel Trust makes it impossible. Even if it were true, as is always claimed officially, that German cartels do not concern themselves with labour matters, a united front of employers is taken for granted, and it is just their strength which make the specific functions of an employers' association (such as assistance during strikes) superfluous, since a 'friendly understanding' suffices in each particular case. Even here, however, a trend towards the formation of employers' associations is becoming apparent.

The formation of employers' associations makes it more difficult, if not impossible, for a trade union to achieve success in an isolated struggle, since the individual employer is now backed by his organization, which compensates him for his losses, ensures that the striking workers do not find other jobs, and makes every effort to fill the firm's most pressing orders itself. If necessary it resorts to stronger measures, and takes the offensive by extending the struggle and declaring a lockout in order to weaken the union and force it to capitulate. In such a struggle between the combined employers and the trade unions, the employers' organization is quite often the stronger of the two.[6]

An employers' association creates the possibility, in principle, of deferring a conflict. As long as labour organizations are in conflict with individual employers the choice of timing rests with the workers, and timing is a decisive factor in determining the outcome of a struggle. A work stoppage is most damaging during a boom, when the rate of profit is at its highest and the opportunities for extra profit are greatest, and in order not to lose his whole profit even a major employer would try to avoid a conflict at such a time, for the opportunity to earn that profit will not recur, at least not until the next boom. From the standpoint of the union's chances of success, a strike should be called at a time when production is at its maximum, and it is one of the difficult tasks of trade union educational work to persuade the members of the wisdom of these tactics. For it is precisely at this time that workers' incomes are highest, as a result of regular employment and overtime, and the psychological incentive to go on strike is consequently weakest. This also explains why most strikes occur during a period of prosperity before the peak of the boom is reached.

This choice of timing, however, ceases to be the prerogative of the trade unions once the employers' organization becomes well established, for the latter can now determine the time of the conflict. For them the lockout is a form of preventive war, which can best be waged during a depression when overproduction makes it quite useful to halt production, and the workers' power of resistance is at its lowest because of the excessive supply of labour on the market and the financial weakening of their organizations as a result of the large demand for financial aid and the decline in membership. This ability to postpone the occurrence of a conflict, which results from the development of an employers' organization, in itself represents a massive transfer of power.[7]

The same causes, however, which lead to the formation of employers' organizations also strengthen the trade unions, which now become a refuge for workers everywhere who do not want to be left entirely at the mercy of their employers. The fighting measures adopted by employers are also directed against those who have hitherto remained aloof from unions. Lockouts, and particularly general lockouts, provide very powerful incentives for previously unorganized workers to join the unions, and the rapid growth of membership increases their strength. The employers' associations try to counter this development by a continuing struggle against the trade unions. They attempt, by a process of careful selection, to retain unorganized workers, rather than those who are organized, in employment. The proficiency certificates of the employers' associations systematically give preference to unorganized over organized workers, and the most dangerous among the latter are proscribed by the use of blacklists. By organizing 'yellow' company unions – institutions for breeding class traitors – the employers try to divide the workers with the aid of bribes and the granting of special privileges, and to ensure the availability of a strike-breaking squad.[8] By refusing to negotiate with the union leaders they seek to undermine their moral influence. But they are fighting a vain battle, for in the final analysis the class interests of the workers are identical with their personal interests, and the trade union organization has become a matter of life and death for them. But the battle does retard the progress of the trade union movement and restrict its influence.

Just as in the period before employers' organizations existed the individual employer's power of resistance varied according to the size of the enterprise, so now the power of resistance of employers' organizations varies according to their composition. The associations in large-scale industry are the strongest, and within this group especially those in the large cartelized industries which do not have to fear the desertion or business failure of any of their members. They can rest assured that no competitor will derive any advantage from a stoppage of their plants, and where their monopoly is assured and foreign competition is of little consequence, thanks to the protective tariff, they can ultimately make up the losses sustained in a strike. Orders which have been delayed can be filled later, and the dearth of commodities resulting from the stoppage makes possible price increases, and hence the unloading of losses from the strike onto others.

Here, therefore, resistance is at its strongest, and a struggle against the trade unions easiest to undertake. Hence these industries become the leaders in the struggle of all employers' associations, and the champions of the common interests of employers in their conflict with the working class. The more the small capitalists are forced to make concessions to the trade unions, and the more ominous the power of the workers appears to them, the greater is their sense of solidarity with the big industrialists, the champions of their own cause.

The fact that the weaker associations have to come to terms with trade

unions, though on more favourable conditions than was the case previously for individual employers, makes no difference. For them too, the
association has eliminated the greatest dangers. It has been able to impose a
strike clause for the entire industry, prevent outsiders from taking advantage of the situation by its ability to cut off supplies, thus making suppliers
its allies in the struggle, and finally, assure equality in the conditions of
competition, under all circumstances, by preventing individual
employers from concluding separate agreements. This is best done by the
conclusion of an industry-wide agreement on wage rates and conditions of
employment. Such an agreement is also in the interests of the trade unions
because it immediately extends any gains which have been achieved to the
whole industry. Its disadvantage is that it fixes the date for a renewal of the
contract in advance, and so deprives the union of its ability to decide the
timing of a conflict. But since the very existence of an employers'
association has already deprived the union of an exclusive power to decide
when to renew the conflict, this circumstance affects both organizations in
the same way. Nevertheless, this introduces a fortuitous element into the
coming conflict, and a strong union will therefore try to avoid any wage
agreement the duration of which may make it impossible to take advantage
of a boom period.

The existence of an employers' organization has the further advantage
for the employers that it makes it easier for them to pass on any increase in
costs of production. We know that a successful strike means an immediate
reduction below the average rate of profit of the industry affected. The
equalization which must ensue through an increase in prices is facilitated
and expedited by the common procedure which an employers' association
can easily arrange in such an event, and this can be done even in non-
cartelized industries because the increase in prices corresponds to the
changed cost prices. Hence it is precisely the small capitalists in the non-
cartelized finished goods industries who are disposed to conclude industry-
wide agreements.[9]

Here too arise those trends which lead to the conclusion of trade alliances.
Industries which are not yet capable of forming cartels, because technological factors have kept them fragmented, try to secure a monopoly for
themselves by closing the labour market to outsiders. They leave it to the
trade union to do this for them, and the combined employers then have a
cartel which the trade union protects against the competition of outsiders.
The extra cartel profit is shared between employers and workers, thus
giving the workers a stake in the existence of the cartel.

The relationships which prevail in cartelized industry are different. Here
the rate of profit has already reached the highest possible level under the
existing conditions of production. The price is equal, or roughly equal, to
the world market price plus the protective tariff plus transport costs. In this

case a wage increase cannot be passed on, and the resistance to such increases is therefore exceptionally strong. Furthermore, since the high cartel profit is already taken into account in the price of shares, a reduction in profit depresses share prices and provokes resistance from shareholders to any concessions by the directors. Their resistance is reinforced by the interests of the banks, for whom a smaller profit means smaller promoter's gains when a new share issue is made. On the other side, there is also greater resistance, for psychological reasons, from the non-working, appointed directors of the company, who have lost all contact with the workers and appear to them as representatives of alien interests. Any inclination on the part of an employer who takes personal responsibility to make concessions from time to time seems to these directors a dereliction of duty. The last vestige of personal contact disappears from the relations between workers and capitalists, and the provisions of the labour contract become a question of power, totally divorced from any sentimental considerations.[10]

The features of the industry-wide agreement which the employer finds valuable are those such as the guarantee of equality of costs, which the cartels in any case achieve through the concerted action of employers, or the guarantee of industrial peace over a certain period of time, which the cartels attain through industrial conflict on a scale that precludes frequent disputes. All that remains then is the disadvantage that industry-wide agreements constrain employers in their choice of timing for the next struggle, and have a propaganda value for the unions. Hence the rejection of such agreements in the cartelized sphere. Furthermore, the possibility of forming a cartel without trade union help makes a trade alliance, with its sharing of the extra cartel profit, entirely unnecessary.[11] The position of industries which are primarily engaged in exporting is similar to that of cartelized industry, since their prices are determined on the world market and it is more difficult to pass on wage increases.

The development of employers' and workers' organizations enhances the general social and political significance of wage conflicts. The guerrilla war of the trade unions against individual employers has given way to mass struggles which affect whole branches of industry, and if they grip the most vital sectors of production, which have become interdependent through the division of labour, they threaten to bring all social production to a standstill. The trade union struggle thus expands beyond its own sphere, ceases to be the concern only of the employers and workers directly affected, and becomes a general concern of society as a whole, that is to say, a political phenomenon. At the same time it has become increasingly difficult to bring such conflicts to an end by trade union methods alone. The more powerful the employers' organization and the trade union, the more protracted is the struggle. The question of raising wages and diminishing profits becomes a problem of power. Employers become unshakeably

convinced that every concession they make will weaken their future
position and enhance the moral and actual power of the trade unions; that
a victory today is bound to mean future victories for the trade unions. They
want to decide the conflict once and for all, and are prepared to pay the
costs of warfare if it will ensure them the upper hand for a long time to
come. Their capital is large enough for them to hold out, and to hold out
longer than the trade unions whose resources are rapidly depleted by
payments to strikers. But the conflict does not remain confined to one
particular sphere of industry; it extends to others which supply raw
materials, components, etc., and they too have to shut down plants and
dismiss workers. This is a situation which provokes increasing bitterness
among workers, and more widely in the retail trade which depends upon
working class custom, and it may lead to major social and political
confrontations. There is growing pressure from those who are not directly
involved to end the original wage conflict, and since there is no other means
available for this purpose they call for intervention by the state. The
question of ending the strike is thus transformed from a trade union
question into one of political power, and the more the balance of power has
tilted in favour of the employers as a result of the growth of employers'
organizations the more vital it is for the working class to secure for itself the
strongest possible influence in political bodies, and to have representatives
who will take up boldly and independently the interests of the workers
against those of the employers and help them to be victorious. Such a
victory, however, will not be achieved by political action alone, which
indeed can only be undertaken successfully if the trade unions are strong
enough to wage the purely economic struggle with such intensity and
vigour that the reluctance of the bourgeois state to intervene in labour
questions, against the interests of employers, has already begun to break
down, and the political representatives of labour have only to complete the
process. Far from the working class being able to dispense with the trade
unions and to replace them by a political struggle, the increasing strength of
trade union organizations is indispensable for success. But however strong
the trade unions are, the very scale and intensity of their struggles gives
them a political character and demonstrates to workers organized in the
trade unions how trade union activity is necessarily complemented by
political action. Hence a point is inevitably reached in trade union
development when the formation of an independent political labour party
becomes a requirement of the trade union struggle itself. Once an
independent political party of the workers exists its policy is not confined
for long to those issues which led to its creation, but becomes a policy which
seeks to represent the class interests of workers as a whole, thus moving
beyond the struggle *within* bourgeois society into a struggle *against*
bourgeois society.

On the other hand, the increasing strength of employers' organizations does not by any means make the trade union struggle either unnecessary or hopeless. It would be a very partial view if we were to conclude that because the employers' organization has the ability to hold out patiently until the workers are exhausted, their trade union is financially destitute, and those who are ready to return to work gain the upper hand, trade union struggles must always end in defeat and lockouts must always be successful. For it is not simply a question of power, but of calculating the effect on the rate of profit. A lockout or strike in a period of boom always involves such great losses that it may be more advantageous for employers to accede to wage demands in order to avoid a conflict.[12] Even a trade union previously weakened by a lockout can summon enough strength to wring concessions from employers during a period of boom, although in such a case, of course, since the union also fears the cost of the struggle, these concessions would be more limited in scope than in the days when the trade unions did not yet confront any employers' organizations.

The proletariat and imperialism

The economic policy of the proletariat is fundamentally opposed to that of the capitalists, and the position adopted on every particular issue is marked by this antagonism. The struggle of wage labour against capital is first of all a struggle for that part of the new value in the annual product created by the working class (including the productive salaried employees and the managers of production). The immediate occasion for this struggle is the labour contract, and it then prolongs itself in the conflicts over the economic policy of the state. In commercial policy, the interests of the workers require, first and foremost, an expansion of the domestic market. The higher their wages, the larger is that part of the new value which constitutes a direct demand for commodities, and more particularly for consumer goods. But the expansion of the consumer goods industries, and of the finished goods industries in general, means an enlargement of those spheres which have generally a lower organic composition of capital, or in other words, of industries which are able to employ large numbers of workers. This brings about a rapid increase in the demand for labour and hence a more favourable position for the worker on the labour market, strengthens trade union organizations, and improves their prospects of victory in any new wage struggles. The interests of the employers are just the reverse. An enlargement of the domestic market through wage increases means a fall in their rate of profit, with the prospect of further reductions, and this in turn slows down accumulation. At the same time their capital is forced into the finished goods industries where competition is keenest and the possibilities of cartelization most limited. It is true, of course, that they have an interest in expanding the market, but not at the expense of the rate of profit; and they can attain their end by expanding the external market, while the domestic market remains the same. A part of the new product does not then go into the incomes of workers, and does not increase the demand for domestic products, but is invested as capital employed in production for the foreign market. In that case the rate of profit is higher and accumulation more rapid. The commercial policy of the entrepreneurs is accordingly directed primarily to the foreign market, that of the workers to the domestic market, manifesting itself particularly in the form of a wage policy.

As long as protective tariffs are 'educational' tariffs, mainly for the finished goods industries, they do not conflict with the interests of wage labour. Of course, they hurt the worker as a consumer, but they also promote industrial development and can therefore recompense him as a producer, if the trade unions are sufficiently developed to take advantage of the situation. Those who suffer most in this period are the artisans, those engaged in domestic production, and peasants, rather than factory workers. It is a different matter, however, when the protective tariff becomes a tariff for cartels. We know that cartels emerge principally in those branches of production which have the highest organic composition of capital, and the generation of extra profit in these spheres hinders the development of the finished goods and consumer goods industries. At the same time the increase in food prices which is caused by the unavoidable combination of agricultural tariffs with the industrial tariffs involves a decline in real wages and therefore a contraction of the domestic market in so far as it is determined by the demand of workers for industrial products. Thus the worker suffers both as consumer and as producer through the damage done to those industries which are labour-intensive. Cartelization also strengthens the employers' position on the labour market and weakens that of the trade unions. Furthermore, the cartel tariff provides the strongest incentive to increase capital exports, and it necessarily leads to the expansionist policy of imperialism.

We have seen that the export of capital is a condition for the rapid expansion of capitalism. In social terms, this expansion is an essential condition for the perpetuation of capitalist society as a whole, while economically it is a condition for maintaining, and at times increasing, the rate of profit. The policy of expansion unites all strata of the propertied classes in the service of finance capital. Protective tariffs and expansion thus become the common demand of the ruling class. The abandonment of the free trade policy by the capitalist classes makes it a lost cause. For free trade is not a positive demand of the proletariat, only a means of defence against a protectionist policy which involves more rapid and thorough cartelization, accompanied by an increase in the strength of employers' organizations, intensification of national antagonisms, increasing armaments, a growing burden of taxes, a rise in the cost of living, a growth in the power of the state, the weakening of democracy, and the emergence of an ideology which glorifies force and is hostile to labour. Once the bourgeoisie has abandoned free trade the struggle for it becomes quite futile, for the proletariat alone is certainly too weak to impose its policy upon the rulers.

But this does not mean at all that the proletariat must now become converted to the modern protectionist policy which is indissolubly bound up with imperialism. The fact that it has recognized the necessity of this policy for the capitalist class, and therefore its ascendancy so long as the capitalist class wields power, is no reason for the proletariat to forego a policy of its own and capitulate to the policy of its enemies, or to succumb to any illusions about the alleged benefits which the generalization and intensification of exploitation would mean for its situation as a class. But this does not prevent the proletariat from perceiving that imperialist policy spreads the revolution which capitalism entails, and along with it the conditions for the victory of socialism. Nevertheless, however strong its conviction that the policy of finance capital is bound to lead towards war, and hence to the unleashing of revolutionary storms, it cannot abandon its implacable hostility to militarism and the war policy, nor can it in any way support capital's policy of expansion on the ground that this policy may prove to be, in the end, the most powerful factor in its own eventual triumph. On the contrary, victory can come only from an unremitting struggle against that policy, for only then will the proletariat be the beneficiary of the collapse to which it must lead, a collapse which will be political and social, not economic; for the idea of a purely economic collapse makes no sense.

Protective tariffs and cartels mean a rise in the cost of living. Employers' organizations increase capital's power to resist the onslaught of the trade unions. Armaments and colonial policy lead to a rapid growth in the burden of taxes imposed on the proletariat. The inevitable outcome of this policy, a violent collision between capitalist states, will bring an unparalleled increase in misery. All these forces which revolutionize the mass of the people can only be made to serve a reconstruction of the economy if the class which is destined to become the creator of a new society anticipates in thought the policy as a whole and its necessary outcome. This can only happen if the inevitable consequences of such a policy, inimical to the interests of the mass of the people, are explained to the people again and again; and this, in turn, can only be achieved through a steadfast, relentless struggle against the policy of imperialism.

While capital can pursue no other policy than that of imperialism, the proletariat cannot oppose to it a policy derived from the period when industrial capital was sovereign; it is no use for the proletariat to oppose the policy of advanced capitalism with an antiquated policy from the era of free trade and of hostility to the state. The response of the proletariat to the economic policy of finance capital – imperialism – cannot be free trade, but only socialism. The objective of proletarian policy cannot possibly be the now reactionary ideal of reinstating free competition by the overthrow of capitalism. The proletariat avoids the bourgeois dilemma – protectionism or free trade – with a solution of its own; neither protectionism nor free trade, but socialism, the organization of production, the conscious control of the economy not by and for the benefit of capitalist magnates but by and for society as a whole, which will then at last subordinate the economy to itself as it has been able to subordinate nature ever since it discovered the laws of motion of the natural world. Socialism ceases to be a remote ideal, an 'ultimate aim' which serves only as a guiding principle for 'immediate demands',* and becomes an essential component of the immediate practical policy of the proletariat. It is precisely in those countries where the policy of the bourgeoisie has been put into effect most fully, and where the most important social aspects of the democratic political demands of the working class have been realized, that socialism must be given the most prominent place in propaganda, as the only alternative to imperialism, in order to ensure the independence of working class politics and to demonstrate its superiority in the defence of proletarian interests.

Finance capital puts control over social production increasingly into the hands of a small number of large capitalist associations, separates the management of production from ownership, and socializes production to the extent that this is possible under capitalism. The limits of capitalist socialization are constituted, in the first place, by the division of the world market into national economic territories of individual states, a division which can only be overcome partially and with great difficulty through international cartelization, and which also prolongs the duration of the competitive struggle which the cartels and trusts wage against one another with the aid of state power. Socialization is also limited by another factor which should be mentioned here for the sake of completeness; namely, the formation of ground rent, which is an obstacle to concentration in agriculture; and finally, by measures of economic policy intended to prolong the life of medium and small enterprises.

The tendency of finance capital is to establish social control of production, but it is an antagonistic form of socialization, since the control of social production remains vested in an oligarchy. The struggle to dispossess this oligarchy constitutes the ultimate phase of the class struggle between bourgeoisie and proletariat.

The socializing function of finance capital facilitates enormously the task of overcoming capitalism. Once finance capital has brought the most importance branches of production under its control, it is enough for society, through its conscious executive organ – the state conquered by the working class – to seize finance capital in order to gain immediate control of these branches of production. Since all other branches of production depend upon these, control of large-scale industry already provides the most effective form of social control even without any further socialization. A society which has control over coal mining, the iron and steel industry, the machine tool, electricity, and chemical industries, and runs the

---

* The allusion is to Bernstein's argument in *Evolutionary Socialism*. [Ed.]

transport system, is able, by virtue of its control of these most important spheres of production, to determine the distribution of raw materials to other industries and the transport of their products. Even today, taking possession of six large Berlin banks would mean taking possession of the most important spheres of large-scale industry, and would greatly facilitate the initial phases of socialist policy during the transition period, when capitalist accounting might still prove useful. There is no need at all to extend the process of expropriation to the great bulk of peasant farms and small businesses, because as a result of the seizure of large-scale industry, upon which they have long been dependent, they would be indirectly socialized just as industry is directly socialized. It is therefore possible to allow the process of expropriation to mature slowly, precisely in those spheres of decentralized production where it would be a long drawn out and politically dangerous process. In other words, since finance capital has already achieved expropriation to the extent required by socialism, it is possible to dispense with a sudden act of expropriation by the state, and to substitute a gradual process of socialization through the economic benefits which society will confer.

While thus creating the final organizational prerequisites for socialism, finance capital also makes the transition easier in a political sense. The action of the capitalist class itself, as revealed in the policy of imperialism, necessarily directs the proletariat into the path of independent class politics, which can only end in the final overthrow of capitalism. As long as the principles of *laissez-faire* were dominant, and state intervention in economic affairs, as well as the character of the state as an organization of class domination, were concealed, it required a comparatively mature level of understanding to appreciate the necessity for political struggle, and above all the necessity for the ultimate political goal, the conquest of state power. It is no accident, then, that in England, the classical country of non-intervention, the emergence of independent working class political action was so difficult. But this is now changing. The capitalist class seizes possession of the state apparatus in a direct, undisguised and palpable way, and makes it the instrument of its exploitative interests in a manner which is apparent to every worker, who must now recognize that the conquest of political power by the proletariat is his own most immediate personal interest. The blatant seizure of the state by the capitalist class directly compels every proletarian to strive for the conquest of political power as the only means of putting an end to his own exploitation.[1]

The struggle against imperialism intensifies all the class contradictions within bourgeois society. The proletariat, as the most decisive enemy of imperialism, gains support from other classes. Imperialism, which was initially supported by all other classes, eventually repels its followers. The more monopolization progresses the greater is the burden which extra profit imposes upon all other classes. The rise in the cost of living brought about by the trusts reduces living standards, and all the more so because the upward trend in food prices increases the cost of the most essential necessities of life. At the same time the tax burden increases, and this also hits the middle classes, who are increasingly in revolt. The white collar employees see their career prospects fade, and begin to regard themselves more and more as exploited proletarians. Even the middle strata in commerce and industry become aware of their dependence upon the cartels, which transform them into mere agents working on commission. All these contradictions are bound to become unbearably acute at the moment when the expansion of capital enters a period of slower development. This is the case when the development of corporations and cartels no longer proceeds so rapidly, and when the emergence of new promoter's profits, together with the drive to export capital, slows down. And it is bound to slow down when the rapid opening up of foreign countries by the introduction of capitalism tapers off. The opening up of the Far East, and the rapid development of Canada, South Africa and South America, have made a major contribution to the dizzy pace of capitalist development, interrupted only by brief depressions, since 1895. Once this development begins to slow down, however, the domestic market is bound to feel the pressure of the cartels all the more acutely, for it is during periods of depression that concentration proceeds most rapidly. At the same time, as the expansion of the world market slows down, the conflicts between capitalist nations over their share in it will become more acute, and all the more so when large markets which were previously open to competition, such as England, for example, are closed to other countries by the spread of protective tariffs. The danger of war increases armaments and the tax burden, and finally drives the middle strata, whose living standards are increasingly threatened, into the ranks of the proletariat, which thus reaps the harvest of the decline in the power of the state, and of the collisions of war.[2]

It is a historical law that in all forms of society based upon class antagonisms the great social upheavals only occur when the ruling class has already attained the highest possible level of concentration of its power. The economic power of the ruling class always involves at the same time power over people, disposal over human labour power. But that itself makes the economic ruler dependent upon the power of the ruled, and in augmenting his own power he simultaneously increases the power of those who stand opposed to him as class enemies. As subjects, however, the latter appear to be powerless. Their power is only potential, and can only materialize in the struggle to overthrow the power of the ruling class, while the power of the ruler is self-evident. Only in a collision between the two powers, in revolutionary periods, does the power of the subjects prove to be a reality.

Economic power also means political power. Domination of the economy gives control of the instruments of state power. The greater the degree of concentration in the economic sphere, the more unbounded is the control of the state. The rigorous concentration of all the instruments of state power takes the form of an extreme deployment of the power of the state, which becomes the invincible instrument for maintaining economic domination; and at the same time the conquest of political power becomes a precondition of economic liberation. The bourgeois revolution only began when the absolutist state, having overcome the autonomous regional power of the large landowners, had concentrated in its own hands all the means of power; and the concentration of political power in the hands of a few of the largest landowners was itself a precondition for the victory of the absolute monarchy. In the same way the victory of the proletariat is bound up with the concentration of economic power in the hands of a few capitalist magnates, or associations of magnates, and with their domination of the state.

Finance capital, in its maturity, is the highest stage of the concentration of economic and political power in the hands of the capitalist oligarchy. It is the climax of the dictatorship of the magnates of capital. At the same time it makes the dictatorship of the capitalist lords of one country increasingly incompatible with the capitalist interests of other countries, and the internal domination of capital increasingly irreconcilable with the interests of the mass of the people, exploited by finance capital but also summoned into battle against it. In the violent clash of these hostile interests the dictatorship of the magnates of capital will finally be transformed into the dictatorship of the proletariat.

Notes

Notes to Introduction by Tom Bottomore

1 Otto Bauer, 'Das Finanzkapital', *Der Kampf,* III (1909–1910), pp. 391–7.
2 Karl Kautsky, 'Finanzkapital und Krisen', *Die Neue Zeit*, XXIX (1911), pp. 764–72, 797–803, 838–46, 874–83.
3 V. I. Lenin, *Imperialism, the Highest Stage of Capitalism* (1916).
4 He had come into contact with the Austro-Marxist school during his stay in Vienna between 1912 and 1914, and it was during this time that he wrote his first book, an attack on the Austrian marginalist economic theory, *The Economic Theory of the Leisure Class*. Stephen Cohen, in his biographical study, *Bukharin and the Bolshevik Revolution,* observes that 'Austro-Marxism, particularly Hilferding's *Finance Capital* . . . . was to have a lasting influence on Bukharin', and that even after 1917, when the Austro-Marxists were dismissed as 'reformists', 'Bukharin retained a grudging admiration for their theoretical achievements' (p. 21).
5 Cohen, op. cit., p. 25.
6 See J. A. Schumpeter, 'Zur Soziologie der Imperialismen' (1919), and *Capitalism, Socialism and Democracy* (1942).
7 Eugen von Böhm-Bawerk (1851–1914) was a leading representative of the Austrian marginalist school of economics, and a vigorous opponent of socialism, who published his critical study of Marxian economics under the title *Zum Abschluss des Marxschen Systems* in 1896. Hilferding's reply, *Böhm-Bawerks Marx-Kritik,* appeared in the first volume of *Marx-Studien* (Vienna, 1904). Böhm-Bawerk's study and Hilferding's rejoinder have been published together in English translation in a volume edited and introduced by Paul Sweezy.
8 Unabhängige Sozialdemokratische Partei Deutschlands. This new party was created in April 1917 at a conference in Gotha attended by all the Social Democratic opposition groups, and numbered among its leading members, besides Hilferding, Hugo Hasse, Karl Kautsky, Rosa Luxemburg, Karl Liebknecht, Eduard Bernstein, Franz Mahring, and Kurt Eisner. For a brief account of the foundation, and subsequent dissolution, of the party, see Julius Braunthal, *History of the International,* vol. II, pp. 59–61, 123–4, 224. A full account is given in Eugen Prager, *Geschichte der Unabhängigen Sozialdemokratischen Partei Deutschlands.*
9 See Braunthal, op. cit., pp. 233–6.
10 Notably to the *Zeitschrift für Sozialismus, Der Kampf,* and the new *Vorwärts* (under the pseudonym 'Richard Kern').
11 The exact date and manner of Hilferding's death remain uncertain, and so

far as I can discover, no organization in Germany (or elsewhere) has ever
made any serious attempt to investigate it, or to identify and bring to justice
those who were responsible.

12 See note 7.

13 For a brief account of the school, see Tom Bottomore and Patrick Goode
(eds) *Austro-Marxism*, Introduction.

14 Otto Bauer, 'What is Austro-Marxism?', in Bottomore and Goode, *Austro-
Marxism,* pp. 45–8. Bauer notes particularly that the Austro-Marxists 'had
to come to terms with the so-called Austrian school of political economy';
that is, with the marginalist school, whose leading thinkers, besides Böhm-
Bawerk, were Carl Menger (1840–1921) and Friedrich von Wieser
(1851–1926). The first substantial Austro-Marxist criticism of the marginalist theory had been made by Gustav Eckstein, 'Der vierfache Wurzel des
Satzes vom unzureichenden Grunde der Grenznutztheorie', *Die Neue Zeit,*
XX (1901–2), pp. 810–16.

15 Peter Gay, *The Dilemma of Democratic Socialism*, notes that the marginalist analysis of value (which was also formulated independently by an
English economist, William Stanley Jevons) acquired great influence among
the Fabian socialists, to whom Eduard Bernstein was indebted for many of
his ideas. Bernstein himself came to believe that both the Marxist and the
marginalist concepts of value contained part of the truth, and hinted
vaguely at a synthesis of the two, but in the main he favoured the second,
saying that 'We search for the laws of price formation more directly today,
and avoid the detour of the convolutions of that metaphysical thing,
"value" ' (cited by Gay, p. 174).

16 The publication of *Capital*, vol. III, in 1894 provided the occasion for
Böhm-Bawerk's study.

17 Paul M. Sweezy, *The Theory of Capitalist Development*, p. 26n.

18 See the comments of reviewers mentioned above, p. 1

19 J. A. Schumpeter, *History of Economic Analysis*, p. 881. Undoubtedly some
parts of Hilferding's analysis would need to be reconsidered today; for
example, his rejection of the possibility of a 'pure paper currency', his insistence upon the need for gold in international transactions (pp. 57-8
below), and his underestimation of the role of consumer credit.
But these later developments in the functioning of money do not
necessarily invalidate the underlying principles of his theory. Schumpeter's
comment seems less than just, for in his own review of the theories of money (in Chapter 8) he suggests that there was little progress in theoretical
understanding during the period under consideration (up to Keynes); and
some of the theories he singles out for criticism had already been criticized
by Hilferding (that of Knapp, for instance). Moreover, even today the
theory of money remains one of the least satisfactory parts of economic
theory, as may easily be seen from the confusion and controversy which
prevail in discussions of inflation. It is arguable, I think, that what is nec-
ded in order to form an adequate conception of money is a *social*, rather
than a narrowly economic, theory. One such theory, which provides the
starting-point for Hilferding's analysis, is of course Marxism; another, not
wholly unrelated, is that to be found in Georg Simmel's *The Philosophy of
Money*.

20 See p. 67 below. For a more recent Marxist discussion of this question see Ernest Mandel, *Marxist Economic Theory*, pp. 664–8.

21 As he writes at the beginning of Chapter 4: 'Only the hope that by this

means we can discover the secret of how the processes of circulation themselves endow capitalist credit with the power eventually to dominate the whole social process, can give the reader courage to traverse patiently the "stations of the cross" in the present chapter' (p. 67 below).

22 I have used the terms 'joint stock company' and 'corporation' interchangeably, preferring one or the other according to the context.

23 p.107 below.

24 pp. 111 – 14 below.

25 Hilferding also makes clear, however, that the concentration and centralization of capital is strongly affected by technological progress, which makes necessary much larger capital investments. See Chapter 11 below.

26 pp. 118 – 20 below.

27 p. 368 below.

28 See Jacob Riesser, *Die deutschen Grossbanken und ihre Konzentration.*

29 Eduard Heimann, *History of Economic Doctrines*, p. 165.

30 Paul Sweezy, *The Theory of Capitalist Development*, pp. 267–9. Sweezy argues that 'Hilferding mistakes a transitional phase of capitalist development for a lasting trend', and suggests that once the large monopolistic corporations are well established they can rely upon their own internally generated funds for further growth, and thus become less dependent upon the banks. He therefore proposes as a more appropriate term to describe this latest stage of capitalism, 'monopoly capital' rather than 'finance capital'.

31 See Hilferding, 'Gesellschaftsmacht oder Privatmacht über die Wirtschaft' (1931).

32 Even in this case a number of critics, among them Riesser (op. cit.), pointed out that in several leading German industries bank capital had never had a dominant role.

33 In Austria, particularly, the connection between the banks and industry were extremely close, as is shown in the recent work by Bernard Michel, *Banques et banquiers en Autriche au début du XXe siècle.* See also the comments of Eduard März in his introduction to the new German edition of *Finance Capital* (1968), p. 14. It is also worth noting here that Hilferding himself (in Chapter 21 particularly) explicitly draws attention to the substantial differences between Germany and Britain with regard to the role of the banks. Furthermore, in the course of his discussion he comments on some related aspects of the development of British capitalism which still seem highly relevant to Britain's continuing industrial decline in the late twentieth century.

34 März, op. cit., pp. 13–15.

35 Michael Barratt Brown, *After Imperialism*, Preface to 2nd edn, p. xxx.

36 März, op. cit., p. 15.

37 Barratt Brown, op. cit., p. xxxi.

38 See chapters 16 and 17 below.

39 p. 241 below.

40 From a quite different theoretical standpoint Tugan-Baranowsky, in his *Studien zur Theorie und Geschichte der Handelskrisen in England* (in Russian, 1894; German version, 1901), also outlined a 'disproportionality' theory. He and Hilferding were both vigorously criticized, in due course, by the 'orthodox' (Bolshevik) Marxists, as 'revisionists' and 'reformists' (see, for example, Sweezy, *The Theory of Capitalist Development*, pp. 156–62), but this kind of criticism is of little interest today, after the disintegration

of 'orthodox' Marxism itself. In any case, Hilferding made very clear his own disagreements with Tugan-Baranowsky; see pp. 421 – 2 below.

41 See chapter 20 below.

42 See chapters 21–25 below.

43 J. A. Schumpeter, 'Zur Soziologie der Imperialismen' (1919).

44 Otto Bauer made an important contribution, upon which Hilferding draws, in his book *Die Nationalitätenfrage und die Sozialdemokratie* (1907).

45 It may be claimed that the First World War showed that Hilferding had entertained illusions in this respect; but still it should be noted that while he did not accept the idea of the *inevitability* of war, he did emphasize very strongly the inherent drive toward war and the particular danger of an armed conflict between Britain and Germany (p. 331 below).

46 See Cohen, *Bukharin and the Bolshevik Revolution*, p. 27, where this difference is brought out clearly.

47 This became the general standpoint of the Austro-Marxists. Karl Renner, for example, who noted in his essays on 'Probleme des Marxismus' (1916) how the war economy had strengthened these tendencies, wrote that 'our opponents . . . are bewildered by the idea that the sovereign state now has the function of selling potatoes and trading in livestock' and that 'we demand, and our opponents contest, the new tasks'. For an English translation of excerpts from these essays, see Tom Bottomore and Patrick Goode (eds), *Austro-Marxism*, pp. 91–101.

48 It should be noted, however, that Hilferding does *not* equate this action with the achievement of socialism, but makes clear that it is only a preliminary step.

49 This term was used by Otto Bauer in his essay on Fascism (1938); and it came to be very widely employed after 1945.

50 It may be claimed indeed that Hilferding set the stage for all subsequent discussion up to the present time of the political significance of the 'new middle class' (although he disliked this particular term) in relation to the labour movement.

51 p. 347 below.

52 As we shall see later, this idea was further developed by Hilferding in his last work.

53 No comprehensive major study of Hilferding's life and work has yet been published. In the following brief account I have drawn upon the work by Wilfried Gottschalch, *Strukturveränderungen der Gesellschaft und politisches Handeln in der Lehre von Rudolf Hilferding*, which provides much information about Hilferding's political career, but I have also consulted numerous other sources, which are cited at relevant points below and are also listed in the Bibliography. In addition, through the kindness of the late Professor David Spitz, and of his widow, Professor Elaine Spitz, I have been able to look at the extensive manuscript material which Morris Watnick had prepared with a view to writing an introduction to *Finance Capital*, and this has helped me considerably both in tracing sources and in interpreting Hilferding's political views. Finally, I have benefited greatly from Dr Peter Milford's detailed comments on the first draft of my introduction. I should emphasize, however, that none of the people I have mentioned bear any responsibility for the eventual judgments on Hilferding's politics which I express here.

54 See his letters to Kautsky, from 1902 to 1937, deposited in the International Institute of Social History, Amsterdam.

55 See his articles in *Die Neue Zeit*, XXII, 1 (1903–4) 'Zur Frage des Generalstreiks', and XXIII, 2 (1904–5) 'Parlamentarismus und Massenstreik'. See also the discussion in Gottschalch, op. cit., pp. 70–81.
56 See his article, 'Ausbau des Rätesystems', in *Freiheit*, 5 February 1919.
57 On 'socialization' see Patrick Goode, *Karl Korsch: A Study in Western Marxism*, chapter 2; and F. L. Carsten, *Revolution in Central Europe, 1918–1919*, chapters 5–7.
58 The report on the coal mining industry seems to have been the only important work which the general Commission accomplished.
59 See especially his speech against Zinoviev at the USPD conference in Halle (1920), published under the title 'Revolutionäre Politik oder Machtillusionen?'
60 The importance of unity in the labour movement was strongly emphasized by Otto Bauer at a later date in his essay 'What is Austro-Marxism?' See Bottomore and Goode, op. cit., pp. 45–8.
61 The recent publication of the minutes of Hermann Müller's cabinet makes available a useful source for an eventual study of Hilferding's second term of office. There are short accounts of his work as finance minister in Gottschalch, op. cit., pp. 20–26, and in E. Eyck, *Geschichte der Weimarer Republik*, vol. II, Chapter 18, on which I have drawn here.
62 Gottschalch, op. cit., p. 21.
63 J. A. Schumpeter, 'Erbschaftsteuer' (1928), quoted in Gottschalch, op. cit., p. 24.
64 Julius Braunthal, *History of the International, Vol. II, 1914–1943*, p. 354.
65 See the discussion in Braunthal, op. cit., pp. 356 60. This policy was strongly opposed by the left wing in the party, grouped around the journal *Der Klassenkampf*. Max Adler, who was one of the editors of this journal, belonged to the left-wing group in the Austrian party; see his comments on the German situation in his essay 'Metamorphosis of the Working Class' (1933), translated in Bottomore and Goode, op. cit.
66 Otto Bauer, in his report to the Fourth Congress of the Labour and Socialist International in July 1931, reiterated, in the context of the rise of fascism in Germany and Austria, his doctrine of 'defensive violence', saying

> We do not want Socialism to come out of a bloody civil war; we do not want it to come as the result of another war among nations and countries; we do not want Socialism to emerge out of a sea of blood upon the ruins of civilization. We want the road of democracy to Socialism and to use the methods of democracy to achieve Socialism.

Quoted in Braunthal, op. cit., p. 364. I have discussed this aspect of Austro-Marxist doctrine in my Introduction to Bottomore and Goode, op. cit., pp. 40–43.
67 See Braunthal, op. cit., pp. 372–5, 380–6, and E. Matthias, 'Social Democracy in the Weimar Republic', in A. Nicholls and E. Matthias (eds), *German Democracy and the Triumph of Hitler*.
68 See, for example, Lewis J. Edinger, 'German Social Democracy and Hitler's "National Revolution" of 1933: A study in Democratic Leadership' (1953). Edinger points out that while the average age of the twelve most important SPD leaders (among them Hilferding) was 58, that of the twelve Nationalist Socialist Reichsführer was 37. By 1931 only 19 per cent of SPD members were under 30, compared with 38 per cent of Nazi party members (p. 335, n. 2). See also the discussion of the problems of 'legal opposition' by

Bracher, in Karl Dietrich Bracher, Wolfgang Sauer and Gerhard Schulz, *Die nationalsozialistische Machtergreifung,* pp. 62 – 6.

69 Bracher *et al.,* op. cit. See also p. 15 below.
70 Quoted in Braunthal, op. cit., p. 369.
71 Hilferding, 'Zwischen den Entscheidungen' (1933).
72 op. cit., pp. 224–5.
73 Hilferding first used the term in his essay 'Arbeitsgemeinschaft der Klassen?' (1915), and expounded his conception more fully in 'Probleme der Zeit' (1924).
74 Hilferding, 'Realistischer Pazifismus' (1924).
75 Hilferding, 'Die Aufgaben der Sozialdemokratie in der Republik' (1927).
76 'Arbeitsgemeinschaft der Klassen?' (1915).
77 In 'Die Sozialisierung und die Machtverhältnisse der Klassen' (1920) and 'Probleme der Zeit' (1924).
78 Gottschalch, op. cit., chapter 6. He quotes here Siegfried Marck's description of Hilferding as 'the theorist of coalition politics in the period of capitalist stabilization' (p. 207). However, Gottschalch does also acknowledge in his concluding discussion that Hilferding succeeded in identifying some important long-term trends in capitalist development (p. 265).
79 The limits of German liberal and democratic thought are well illustrated in the political writings of Max Weber, which are, more than anything else, intensely nationalistic. See, for an excellent brief account of Weber's views, Wolfgang Mommsen, *The Age of Bureaucracy.*
80 These aspects of the rise of National Socialism are given considerable weight by Bracher, op. cit., Introduction.
81 See his article 'Revolutionärer Sozialismus' (1934) and later articles (under the pseudonym Richard Kern) in *Neuer Vorwarts,* and the comments by Lewis J. Edinger, *German Exile Politics,* pp. 183 – 4, 197. By the late 1930s, as Edinger and others have noted, Hilferding's outlook had become increasingly pessimistic, in face of the concentrated power – military and other – of the totalitarian states, and this is reflected in his writings of that period. It may also account for the fact that he seems not to have made very strenuous efforts to escape into a more remote exile after the fall of France.
82 The manuscript was first published, with an introduction by Benedikt Kautsky, in *Zeitschrift für Politik* (1954), and my references in the text are to the page numbers in that journal. I hope to publish, in due course, a complete English translation of the work.
83 Notably Karl Renner, in his articles on 'Probleme des Marxismus', referred to in note 47 above, but also in many later writings, including his posthumously published work, *Wandlungen der modernen Gesellschaft* (1953).
84 In the concluding paragraphs Hilferding observes that Marxists had expected the state to wither away in a socialist society: 'But history, that "best of all Marxists", has taught us another lesson. It has taught us that, in spite of Engels's expectations, the "administration of things" may become an unlimited "domination over men", and thus lead not only to the emancipation of the state from the economy but even to the subjection of the economy by the holders of state power.'
85 *Das historische Problem,* p. 296.
86 op. cit., p. 297. This is very similar to the analysis made later by a Polish sociologist, who had experienced the totalitarian state in two forms, first under the Nazi occupation, afterwards under the Stalinist regime, and who wrote in a study of class structure:

In situations where changes of social structure are to a greater or lesser degree governed by the decision of the political authorities . . . we are a long way from classes conceived of as groups arising out of the spontaneous activities of individuals or at the most of spontaneously created class organizations . . . where the political authorities can overtly and effectively change the class structure; where the privileges that are most essential for social status, including that of a higher share in the national income, are conferred by a decision of the political authorities; where a large part or even the majority of the population is included in a stratification of the type to be found in a bureaucratic hierarchy – the nineteenth century concept of class becomes more or less an anachronism, and class conflicts give way to other forms of social antagonism (Stanislaw Ossowski, *Class Structure in the Social Consciousness*, p. 184).

87 *Das historische Problem*, p. 315. Hilferding then argues that this interpretation is valid only for some, not for all, historical periods.
88 op. cit., p. 320.
89 op. cit., p. 324.

Chapter 1 The necessity of money

1 The great diversity of acts of exchange makes it absurd to look for a uniform law governing all such acts in completely different social formations.
2 J. Karner (Karl Renner), *Die soziale Funktion der Rechtsinstitute [The Institutions of Private Law and their Social Functions]* (1904). There are, therefore, laws of a specific type, appearing only in a given social system, which disappear with that system, and have causal force only as long as that system lasts. The task of economic theory is to understand these laws.
3 'Their (the commodity producers') social relations appear simply as private exchange arrangements. After all, exchange as such is essentially a personal transaction. All that is necessary for an act of exchange is that the parties have things to exchange and the desire to exchange them. In that sense, exchange is a phenomenon known to all social systems because they are all familiar with property.

   In fact, the exchange of a pen for a piece of chalk in school, or the exchange of a horse for an automobile between two members of a socialist society, is a private affair, of no interest to theoretical economics. It is the basic error of the marginal utility theory that it seeks to discover the laws of capitalist society by an analysis of exchange as a purely private transaction'. R. Hilferding, 'Zur Problemstellung der theoretischen Nationalökonomie bei Karl Max', *Die Neue Zeit, XXIII*, 1 (1904–5), p. 106.
4 In a commodity producing society, things must enter universally into a relation with each other, and they do this as the expression of socially necessary labour time. Only as such an expression are they commensurable. The essence of the theory of value is that commodities are products of socially necessary labour time, that is, products of society; but it is not an essential feature of the theory that labour time must in all cases be the same on both sides of the exchange relationship. This is a secondary factor, which determines exchange ratios only under the most simple forms of commodity production.

5 The extent to which this proposition needs to be modified in the light of modern forms of paper currency will be examined later.

6 Every commodity has value in so far as it incorporates socially necessary labour time, and is the outcome of a social process of production. It enters the process of exchange as a bearer of value. This is the sense of Marx's remark that, 'the act of exchange gives to the commodity converted into money, not its value, but its specific value form'. *Capital*, vol. I, p. 103.

7 Karl Marx, *A Contribution to the Critique of Political Economy*.

8 At least for the time being, pending the consummation of the trend toward an exclusive gold standard.

9 An example of this practice is the currency of the Hamburg Bank since 1770. Sales were cleared by transfer operations at the Hamburg Giro Bank. A bill of credit was honoured only against payment in silver at the full weight. The money medium was silver, the unit being the Cologne mark (in fine silver) rated at 27.25 marks in the accounts of the bank. In other words, the book money which served the trade of Hamburg until 1872 was secured by the uncoined silver within the city. It made no difference, in this instance, that the silver itself was kept in the vaults of the bank and only certificates of ownership (quite different from bank notes) circulated. Fully backed 'paper money', which is merely a certificate showing that the owner has deposited bullion that is actually in the possession of the bank, is a purely technical expedient and a protection against the wear and tear of the metal. It does not modify any of the laws of the circulation of money, any more than would the circulation of pieces of silver wrapped in leather or paper.

The only part the state can play in the matter is the one outlined in the text. This serves to dispel Knapp's illusion that money originates by state fiat. Moreover, it enables us to see that, historically, money originated in circulation and is therefore primarily a medium of circulation. Only after it has become a general standard of value and the general equivalent of commodities, does it become a general means of payment, notwithstanding Knapp's view to the contrary (see Knapp, op. cit., p. 2).

Chapter 2 Money in the circulation process

1 *Capital*, vol. I, p. 134.

2 ibid., p. 139.

3 When Wilson declares that idle money entails a loss to the community he judges matters from the standpoint of bourgeois society. It is possible to go further and say that the whole mechanism of circulation, to the extent that it involves an outlay of value, is a *faux frais*. A mature bourgeois attitude regards gold, used as a circulating medium, as an unproductive outlay, as an expenditure which does not produce a profit, and therefore looks for ways to avoid it. This idea was an obsession with the champions of the mercantilist system. See James Wilson, *Capital, Currency and Banking*, p. 10.

4 *Capital*, vol. I, p. 125.

5 The law holds good that 'the issue of paper money must not exceed in amount the gold (or silver, as the case may be) which would actually circulate, if not replaced by symbols'. *Capital*, vol. I, p. 143.

6 Having begun with the mistaken notion that money was originally only a piece of metal of specific weight, Knapp is subsequently surprised to find

that it can be replaced by a mere token acceptable to society. Had he recognized (and failure to do so still prevents economists from formulating a
fruitful theory of money) that money is a social arrangement in material
form, he would not have found it the least bit puzzling that in certain circumstances this economic relationship takes the form of socially acceptable
tokens, chosen by deliberate agreement, namely, government legal tender
paper money. Of course it is true that a real problem results from any such
arrangement, namely, the limits of this conscious social regulation by the
state. But precisely this economic problem is excluded by Knapp from his
inquiry.

7 As is well known, free coinage means the right of an individual to take
whatever quantity of the money substance he pleases to the government
mint of a country and have it coined according to the fixed standard of the
mint. Coinage is suspended when the government refuses to accept bullion
for coinage.

8 Strictly speaking, monetary appreciation was no problem at all to these
authors. Writing under the influence of the English restrictions on the issue
of bank notes, they showed boundless naiveté in applying the laws of paper
money to metallic currency. See William Blake, *Observations on the
Principles which Regulate the Course of Exchange, etc.*, (pp. 68 9): 'It is
obvious, that as the nominal price of commodities will be increased by the
over issue of currency, so, for the same reasons, the contraction of it below
the natural wants of circulation will diminish the *nominal* prices in the same
proportion . . . . Bullion will then be of less value in the market than in the
form of coin, and the merchant will carry it to the mint to obtain the profit
attending its conversion into specie.'

9 K. Helfferich, *Money*, vol. I, p. 73.

10 ibid., p. 76.

11 D. Spitzmüller, 'Die österreichische-ungarische Währungsreform',
Zeitschrift für Volkswirtschaft, Sozialpolitik und Verwaltung, XI, 1902,
p. 339.

12 The gold guilder, worth 1/8th of an 8-guilder piece, which was coined only
for foreign trade and not for domestic circulation, was equal to 20 francs in
gold content.

13 Spitzmüller, op. cit., p. 311.

14 ibid., p. 341.

15 ibid., p. 311.

16 K. Helfferich, op. cit., vol. I, p. 77.

17 Helfferich, vol. II, p. 393.

18 A. Arnold, *Das indische Geldwesen unter besonderer Berücksichtigung seiner
Reformen seit 1893*, p. 227.

A friend who returned from a visit to India once told me the following
story. He had observed some Europeans buying silver ornaments at an
Indian bazaar. The Indian merchant, in an effort to prove that he was not
defrauding them, offered to weigh the silver objects and suggested payment
in silver rupees according to the weight of these objects. The Europeans
agreed with the greatest pleasure, delighted at the prospect of paying for
the metal only and obtaining the benefits of the workmanship gratis.
Obviously, they were unaware that, thanks to the currency legislation, they
were paying a price 100 per cent in excess of the value of the metal. It was
a fit punishment for economic ignoramuses and the pity is that it cannot be
inflicted more generally.

19 'It may indeed be doubted whether, since the new system of the Bank of England payments has been fully established [meaning the suspension of bullion payments and the beginning of legal tender for notes of the Bank of England – R.H.], gold has in truth continued to be our measure of value; and whether we have any other standard of prices than that circulating medium, issued primarily by the Bank of England, and in a secondary manner by the country banks, the variations of which in relative value may be as indefinite as the possible excess of that circulating medium'. Report of the Select Committee of the House of Commons on the High Price of Gold Bullion, June, 1810. [Reprinted in J. R. McCulloch, *Scarce and Valuable Tracts on Paper Currency and Banking*, p. 418. Ed.]
The Report leaves its own question unanswered.

20 Lindsay quite correctly stated before the Committee on Indian Currency in 1898: 'Under the present currency system the rupee is nothing but a special type of non-negotiable metal with legal tender, subject to all the laws of non-negotiable paper money.' Lindsay credits Ricardo with the original formulation of these laws. (Cited by M. Bothe, *Die indische Währungsreform*, p. 48.)

21 M. Bothe, op. cit., pp. 44 ff. The way Bothe poses the question is quite characteristic: 'What was the standard of value in India after June 26, 1893? Clearly ... silver ceased to be the standard of value once the gold value of the rupee exceeded the gold value of the pure silver content of the rupee. Or perhaps, the rupee has become the standard of value in India in the sense implied by Professor Lexis in his article "Paper Money" in the *Handwörterbuch der Staatswissenschaften*; that is to say, in the sense that non-negotiable legal tender bank notes become money in their own right, and consequently, a standard of value? Being legal tender, they must always be accepted as a valid means of payment, and thus acquire a value in terms of commodities. Or again, perhaps, gold became the standard of value in India when coinage was discontinued? To credit the rupee with the characteristics of a standard of value is tantamount to saying that an abstraction can be a standard of value; for after June 26, 1893, the value of the rupee ceased to depend on the use value [!] of the material from which it was coined. The material only supplied the minimum limit to the ceaseless fluctuations which depended on the accepted notions of the usefulness of the rupee and had nothing to do with the material as such.
In the same vein, John Lubbock is of the opinion that, since the closing of the mints "exchange" had become a standard of value, which is but another way of saying, not without some hesitation [!], that an abstraction can be a "standard of value".' Voila tout! It is evident that only a high regard for the authority of Professor Lexis prevents the author from criticizing the lack of a capacity for theoretical 'abstraction' which Lexis exhibits in his famous abstraction! But the word 'confidence' always manages to crop up at the right moment when a concept of value is lacking! See Arnold's cogent polemic against Lexis, op. cit., pp. 241 *et seq.*

22 Karl Marx, *A Contribution to the Critique of Political Economy*, p. 234.

23 David Ricardo, 'The High Price of Bullion', in *The Works of David Ricardo*, ed. J. R. McCulloch, p. 264.

24 ibid., p. 264.

25 Karl Marx, *A Contribution to the Critique of Political Economy*, pp. 156–7.

26 David Ricardo, *Principles of Political Economy and Taxation*, chapter XXVII, pp. 238–9.

27 J. Fullarton, *On the Regulation of Currencies*, pp. 60–61.
20 ibid., pp. 61–2.
29 In a report presented to Congress in mid January 1908, the American
    Secretary of the Treasury, Cortilyon, estimated the total sum of cash money
    hoarded by the public from the time the Knickerbocker Trust Company
    suspended payments until confidence was restored, at about $296,000,000.
    This sum represents about 10 per cent of the money in circulation in the
    United States.
30 In accordance with the old law that bad money drives good money out of
    circulation. As Macaulay noted: 'The first writer who noticed the fact that
    when good money and bad money are thrown into circulation, the bad
    money drives out the good money, was Aristophanes. He seems to have
    thought that the preference which his fellow citizens gave to the light coins
    was to be attributed to a depraved taste such as led them to entrust men
    like Cleon and Hyperbolus with the conduct of general affairs. But if his
    political economy will not bear examination, his verses are excellent:

> Πολλάκις δ'ημῖν ἔδοξεν ἡ πόλις πεπονθέναι
> ταὐτὸν ἔς τε τῶν πολιτῶν τοὺς καλους τε κἀγαδούς
> ἔς τε τἀρχαῖον νόμισμα καὶ το καινον χρυσιον.
> οὔτε γὰρ τούτοισιν οἴσιν οὐ κεκιβδηλευμένοις
> ἀλλὰ καλλίστοῖς ἁπάντων, ὡς δοκεῖ, νομισμάτων,
> καὶ μόνοις ὀρθῶς κοπεῖσι, καὶ κεκωδωνισμένοις
> ἔν τετοῖς "Ελλεσι καὶ τοῖς βαρβάροισι πανταχοῦ,
> χρώμεθ' οὐδέν, ἀλλὰ τούτοις τοῖς πονηροῖς χαλκιοις,
> χθές τε καὶ πρωῆν κοπεῖσι τῷ καχίστῳ κόμματι.
> Τῶν πολιτῶν θ'οὓς μὲν ἴσμεν εὐγενεῖς καὶ σώφρνονας
> ἄνδρας ὄντας, καὶ δικαίονς, καὶ καλούς τε κἀγάθούς,
> καὶ τραφέντας ἐν παλαιστραις καὶ χοροῖς καὶ μουσικῆ,
> προυσελοῦμεν. τοῖς δὲ βαλχοῖς, καὶ ξένοις, καὶ πυῤῥίαις,'
> καὶ πονηροῖς, κἀχ πονηρῶν, εἰς ἄπαντα χρώμεθα."

Lord Macaulay, *History of England*, vol. V, p. 2563 in the edition by C.
Firth, London, Macmillan, 1913–15.
[From Aristophanes, *The Frogs*. English translation by David Barrett,
Penguin, 1964, pp. 182–3.

> I'll tell you what I think about the way
> This city treats her soundest men today:
> By a coincidence more sad than funny,
> It's very like the way we treat our money.
> The noble silver drachma, that of old
> We were so proud of, and the recent gold,
> Coins that rang true, clean-stamped and worth their weight
> Throughout the world, have ceased to circulate.
> Instead, the purses of Athenian shoppers
> Are full of shoddy silver-plated coppers.
> Just so, when men are needed by the nation,
> The best have been withdrawn from circulation.
> Men of good birth and breeding, men of parts,
> Well schooled in wrestling and in gentler arts,
> These we abuse, and trust instead to knaves,

Newcomers, aliens, copper-pated slaves,
All rascals – honestly, what men to choose!]"

31 Its explanation by modern economists is still awaited with great impatience.
The idea of suspending free coinage was under discussion in England in the
middle of the 1890s when gold production rose rapidly, the supply of money increased, and interest rates were low (the market discount in London
was less than 1 per cent).

The same problem occupied Tooke. The occasion was the controversy
about the desirability and effects of the introduction of a charge for coinage (seignorage). Ricardo had already expressed himself in favour of a fee
of 5 per cent. 'A debased coin, or one subject to seignorage, if not accompanied by a principle of limitation as to the total amount of money in
circulation, will, naturally, not be of the same value in exchange as if the
coin were perfect or if a principle of limitation were strictly enforced or
maintained.' As an illustration, Tooke then assumed the following case:
'Suppose the circulation of the whole country be confined to gold, and to
consist of twenty millions of sovereigns of the present weight and standard;
if, by some sudden process, each piece were reduced by 1/20 or 5 per cent,
but the whole number of pieces strictly confined to the same amount of
twenty millions; then, other circumstances being the same, the relation of
commodities, etc., to the numerical amount of coin being undisturbed, there
would not, it is evident, be any disturbance of prices; and if gold bullion in
the market were previously at £3 17s 10½d per ounce, it would, other things
remaining the same, continue at that price; or, in other words, £46 14s 6d
in gold coin, weighing 19/20 of a pound, would purchase in the market a
whole pound of uncoined gold of the same standard. But if the quantity of
gold taken out of each individual coin is coined into an additional quantity
of coins and thrown into circulation, the 21 millions would then exchange
for no more than the original 20 million. All commodities will rise 5
per cent in price, and with them, the gold bullion, which would then cost
£4 1s 9¼d. Or, in other words, £46 14s 6d minted will exchange for 19/20 of
a pound of uncoined gold.

'This is the keystone to all reasoning on the subject of currency, and the
application of it is clear enough as to the power of the state, by the monopoly of issue to raise the nominal, as compared with the intrinsic value
of the coin, in a currency wholly metallic.' T. Tooke, *A History of Prices*,
vol. I, pp 120–21.

32 *Capital*, vol. III, p. 607. Incidentally, when one reads Marx, certain pas-
sages dealing with monetary problems leave the impression that the conclusions which follow from his theory of money clashed in his thinking with
ideas suggested by the empirical facts of his day, a conflict which could not
be reconciled satisfactorily in purely logical terms. The most recent experiences do in fact confirm the ultimate conclusions which are deducible
from Marx's theory of value and money.

Marx emphasizes that there can be only as much paper in circulation as
the amount of gold required; but it is important to remember, in order to
understand modern currency, that since the value of gold is given, its quantity is determined by the social value of circulation. If the latter falls, gold
flows out of circulation, and vice versa. In a system of paper currency or
suspended coinage, however, this flow in and out of circulation cannot take

place because the non-circulating paper certificates would depreciate in value. Here one must revert to circulating value as the determining factor, and it does not suffice to regard a money certificate simply as a symbol of gold, as Marx does in *A Contribution to the Critique of Political Economy*.

It seems to me that Marx formulates the law of paper currency (or any currency with suspended coinage) most correctly when he says: 'The worthless tokens are signs of value only in so far as they represent gold within the sphere of circulation, and they represent it only to the extent to which it would itself be absorbed as coin by the process of circulation; this quantity is determined by its own value, the exchange value of the commodities and the rapidity of their metamorphosis being given' (*A Contribution to the Critique of Political Economy*, p. 155). The detour by which Marx proceeds – first determining the value of the quantity of coins and then, from that, the value of the paper money – seems superfluous. The purely social character of that determination is far more clearly expressed when the value of paper money is derived directly from the social value in circulation. The fact that, historically, paper currency had its origin in metal currency is not a reason for regarding it in this way theoretically. The value of paper money must be deducible without reference to metallic money.

33 Hence, Helfferich is wrong when he says: 'Theoretically, it would be possible completely to adapt the issue of a pure and simple paper currency to the fluctuations of the country's economic demand for money and to obviate thereby certain disturbances which may occur in the case of a metallic standard currency through displacements in the equilibrium between money supply and demand.' K. Helfferich *Money*, vol. II, p. 491.

34 Paper money as such, therefore, is not 'defective' or 'bad' or 'debased' money. When present in circulation in the correct amount it does not do violence to any economic law. Only lack of clarity on this point leads most 'metallists' to blame all paper currencies for abuses which are committed deliberately or out of ignorance of theory. Hence, they are left in a state of superstitious panic by an inconvertible government paper certificate, and even by the most harmless small convertible bank note. Goliaths, though not in theory, they fear David; and the smaller the bank note, the greater is their panic.

35 *A Contribution to the Critique of Political Economy*, pp. 150–51.

Chapter 3 Money as a means of payment. Credit money

1 I refer to the intrinsic economic guarantee. The formal, legal guarantee that contracts shall be honoured is, of course, always taken for granted.

2 In the clearing business of the German Reichsbank, 1 pfennig of cash supported, in 1894, a turnover of 4 marks 35 pfennigs; and in 1900 a turnover of 8 marks 30 pfennigs.

3 *Capital*, vol. I, pp. 154–5.

4 Germany requires from nine to fifteen times as much cash as England to transact all its business. Cheque transactions save about £140,000,000 in sterling notes. Given present legal regulations the current money reserve of about £35,000,000 would have to be increased fourfold in order to provide coverage for that sum. See E. Jaffé, *Das englische Bankwesen*, p. 121.

Chapter 4 Money in the circulation of industrial capital

1 In a letter to Rudolf Meyer, Rodbertus says: 'Metallic money is not merely a measure of value and a means of payment. These are characteristics associated with the general idea of money. They do not require that the receipt or claim for commodity value has to be written upon such a valuable material as a precious metal. Money today is also a regulator of production, thanks to the high value of its content. If you want to introduce commodity notes, you must also be able to tell every entrepreneur how much he shall produce. The idea of the commodity note touches the most interesting point in political economy, but as a permanent medium of circulation (and not merely a temporary loan certificate) it is feasible only if the value of commodities is constituted by labour, and the commodity note is inscribed with the value of a commodity measured in terms of labour. I do not doubt the possibility of such money, but if it were made the only medium of circulation, property in land and capital would have to be abolished.' Rudolf Meyer (ed.), *Briefe und sozialpolitische Aufsätze von Dr Rodbertus-Jagetzow,* vol. II, p. 441.

    This and other passages show that Engels did Rodbertus an injustice when he put him together with the petty bourgeois labour-money Utopians such as Gray, Bray, *et al.,* who believed that labour money is possible without the social control of production.

2 The difficulty in understanding the concept of 'capital', and economic concepts generally, is due to the appearance they give of inhering in things themselves, whereas they are only definite social relationships in which the same thing may assume quite diverse roles. Thus gold as money, in one sense, only reflects the state of affairs during a certain period in the development of commodity exchange; it is a medium of circulation. In a different context, it becomes capital. To ask whether gold, or money, is capital is a misleading question. In many circumstances, it is money, in others, also capital. But as capital, it can only perform the functions of money; it is the money form of capital as distinct from the commodity form. Thus, to endow particular things with the attributes of capital is just as incorrect as to regard space as adhering to things. It is only our perception which gives objects their spatial form, just as it is only certain stages of social development which endow things with the form of money or capital.

3 *Capital,* vol. II, pp. 42–3.

4 *Capital,* vol. II, p. 138.

5 ibid., p. 176.

6 ibid., p. 297.

7 ibid., p. 303.

8 ibid., p. 317.

9 ibid., p. 303. Marx's numerical examples differ from those given in the text. I have interposed my own numbers in Marx's statement for the sake of simplicity.

10 I can only indicate the most important factors here. In the second volume of *Capital,* Marx examined the problem in detail, and its further elaboration may be left to pedants. Yet the fundamental significance of these investigations for understanding the credit system has previously been overlooked.

11 ibid., pp. 87–8.

12 ibid., p. 524.
13 'The transactions disposing of the annual product in commodities can no more be dissolved into a mere direct exchange of its individual elements than the simple circulation of commodities can be regarded as identical with a simple exchange of commodities. Money plays a specific role in this circulation, which is particularly marked by the manner in which the value of the fixed capital is reproduced' (ibid., p. 525).
14 ibid., p. 330.
15 ibid., p. 363.
16 ibid., pp. 363–4.
17 ibid., p. 364.
18 ibid., p. 334.
19 ibid., pp. 361–2.
20 The activities of those banks which transfer to industrial districts the money capital which is released by agricultural districts with their sharp seasonal variations in the demand for money are based on this fact. On the other hand, the following illustration taken from modern shoe manufacturing shows the extent of the influence of traditions. The fact that the circulating capital does not turn over more than twice a year, although the manufacture of a shoe only takes, on the average, three to four weeks, can be explained by the circumstance that the main orders during the year require delivery before Easter or Whitsuntide. The product is finished in the interim but it remains in stock because it cannot be sold to the shoe merchant before that time, or at least his obligation to pay begins only with the delivery date.

At the same time, these circumstances have a definite effect on the use of credit. 'The peculiarity of the seasonal business in the shoe industry also obliges the shoe factories to co-operate with the banks. The large sums flowing in after the season is over are transferred to the banks, which in turn make available to factories the sums they require for wages and other production costs and also take responsibility for the payments for raw materials through endorsements or cheques.' (See Karl Rehe, *Die deutsche Schuhgrossindustrie*, pp. 55, 57.)
21 *Capital*, vol. II, p. 122. Here we have a prevision of the dominance of the banks over industry, the most important phenomenon of recent times, written when even the germ of this development was scarcely visible.

Chapter 5 The banks and industrial credit

1 Anyone who sees only that bills are based on the exchange of commodities, and overlooks the fact that the exchange does not have the sanction of society until the bills have been cancelled against each other, the balances settled in cash, and the unredeemed bills replaced by money, is simply dreaming of a utopia of commodity-notes, labour money, etc.; in other words, of credit certificates divorced from bullion which are supposed to represent the value of commodities directly and independently.
2 The volume of bills put into circulation annually has been (in thousands of marks) as follows: 1885, 12,060; 1895, 15,241; 1905, 25,506. Of these, bank acceptances amounted to 1,965 or 16 per cent, 3,530 or 23 per cent and 8,000 or 31 per cent respectively, although these figures also include bills

which do not circulate, such as bills deposited as security, warehouse receipts, etc. See W. Prion, *Das deutsche Wechseldiskontgeschäft,* p. 51.

3 If, however, the normal circulation of commodities is interrupted by unusual non-economic, accidental events, such as revolutions or wars, etc., it is reasonable not to count the period of interruption as part of the normal circulation time, and to wait until such events have passed. This happens when the law decrees a moratorium on bills.

4 By productive capitalists, I mean those capitalists who realize an average profit, that is, industrialists and merchants, in contrast to loan capitalists who receive interest, and property owners who receive rent.

5 J. Wilson, *Capital, Currency and Banking,* p. 44.

6 Naturally, the banks will continue to do a discount business with these notes, and in so far as they are issued against bills of exchange and other forms of collateral they will fulfil the function of credit money as before. But that does not alter their status as state paper money. The proof that they constitute paper money is that they begin to depreciate when they are issued in excess of the requirements of the social minimum of circulation. Where there is no excessive issue, there will not be any depreciation. Since the advances made to the state in England, which increased the quantity of paper in circulation in excess of the needs of trade and industry, even during the period of bank restrictions, remained small, there was only a slight depreciation. Diehl is mistaken, however, when he writes: 'But we cannot even go so far as to call non-negotiable bank notes which are actually legal tender "paper money"; for however disquieting the absence of a redemption requirement may be [a disquiet which Diehl, ignoring the experience of the Austrian currency, exaggerates–R.H.] even under this system bank notes are not issued in order to put money into circulation, but as loans to the state or to merchants on the basis of claims which the bank secures. It depends therefore on the way the bank is managed, not on the quantity of notes, whether and to what extent, under these conditions, the issue of bank notes serves only the legitimate credit needs of the state and business, or whether it leads beyond this to a paper money economy which endangers the whole credit system.' Karl Diehl, *Sozialwissenschaftliche Erläuterungen zu Ricardos Grundgesetezen der Volkswirtschaft* part II, p. 235. Diehl overlooks the essential difference between the issue of notes, based on the discounting of bills of exchange, as credit to facilitate the circulation of commodities, and the issue of notes as loans to the state. In the former case, the bank note replaces the bill of exchange; one form of credit money takes the place of another, and the bill represents real commodity value. But in the latter case, the notes are issued in return for the state's promise to pay, and they make it possible for the state to buy commodities for which it cannot pay cash. If the state contracts a debt on the money market, it receives money already in circulation, and when this money is spent it simply returns to the money market. There is no reason in this case why there should be any change in the quantity of money in circulation. But the state has recourse to the bank precisely because it has no other source of credit, and it makes the notes legal tender to protect the bank from bankruptcy. The notes thus issued as a loan to the state are an addition to circulation and can depreciate. It is exactly as if the state itself were to issue directly the paper money it required to make its payments, rather than doing so indirectly through the bank. The only difference is, of course, that the indirect procedure is profitable to the bank, since it receives

interest on the 'loan' for which it has incurred only printing costs. This is precisely what aroused Ricardo's ire against the Bank of England and prompted him to demand that the issue of paper money be made a monopoly of the state, though he confused state paper with bank notes. It is also interesting to observe that Ricardo's well known suggestions in his *Proposals for an Economical and Secure Currency*, were actually realized, in many respects, in Austria's 'pure paper currency', and it was this very experience in Austria which clearly revealed the errors in Ricardo's theoretical argument.

7 In currency legislation capitalist society faces a purely social problem. But this society is not aware of its own essential characteristics. Its own laws of motion remain hidden from it and must be laboriously discovered by theory. The self-interest of its leading strata, moreover, prevents acceptance of the theoretical conclusions. Ignoring, for the moment, the narrow and selfish interests of money capitalists, who are commonly regarded as the outstanding experts in matters of banking legislation, the insuperable obstacle to a knowledge of the laws of money and note circulation has been the hostility to the labour theory of value. This accounts for the triumph of the Currency School in English banking legislation, notwithstanding its reduction to historical and theoretical absurdity in the works of Tooke, Fullarton and Wilson. It is a fine irony of history that this theory could, with some justification, find support in Ricardo; that same Ricardo who otherwise spared no effort to apply the labour theory of value in a consistent way, but in this case, influenced by the practical experience of English paper money, abandoned his own theory.

It is the anarchic character of capitalist society which makes it so difficult to establish any conscious and rational way of dealing with a social problem. Capitalism may learn more adequate principles, slowly and laboriously, from the bitter and costly experiences of diverse countries and periods, but it cannot find the power within itself to generalize them; as the maintenance of American, English, and to a lesser extent, German legislation and policies with regard to banks of issue demonstrates. Still less is capitalism capable of evolving a consistent theory which would provide an understanding of recent monetary history. In fact, the capitalist world is shocked even by the boldness of a Knapp, who neither evaluates nor explains away the recent data, but at least creates a systematic terminology for them.

Since the management of money and credit circulation is a purely social task there arises a demand to assign this task to the state. But as the capitalist state is riven by class interests, such a proposal at once arouses suspicions among those who have reason to fear an increase in the power of the strata dominating the state. The struggle usually ends in a compromise, with the state exercising extensive supervision over a privileged private corporation. The private interest of the capitalist, which is supposed to be indispensable, must nevertheless be eliminated or at least curtailed. The significance of the power wielded by the directors of the national banks is unrelated to their private interests; and indeed, if the free reign of the profit motive led them to use the national credit for their private ends untold harm would result. The social character of the task makes absolutely indispensable the elimination or rigorous curtailment of the profit motive.

8 'I have no hesitation in professing my own adhesion to the decried doctrine of the old Bank Directors of 1810, "that so long as a bank issues its notes

in the discount of *good* bills, at not more than sixty days' date, it can never
go far wrong". In that maxim, simple as it is, I very strongly believe, there
is a nearer approach to the truth, and a more profound view of the principles which govern circulation, than in any rule on the subject, which since
that time has been promulgated.' J. Fullarton. *On the Regulation of
Currencies,* p. 198.

9 'The bill of exchange is the most important means of settling accounts in
international commerce. In the past, settlements between different states
were made by commercial bills, but the bank draft has come increasingly to
the fore in the past century. Behind the bank note stands the commercial
bill as well as obligations arising from other sources, for example, from
stock exchange transactions. The commercial bill of exchange deprives the
act of purchase of its unique character. And, in harmony with the trend of
the times, the bank draft has carried the process of abstraction still further,
so that it is no longer possible to say today that it is based upon the exchange of commodities. The most that can be said is that it is required to
meet money claims arising from some sort of economic transaction.
International credit can now readily make use of this method of payment.'
A. Sartorius von Waltershausen, *Das volkwirtschaftliche System der
Kapitalanlage im Ausland,* pp. 258 *et seq.*

10 Money loaned out always earns interest and therefore represents a capital
to its lender; and conversely it is always regarded as capital after it has
been loaned out, regardless of what use is made of it, whether as a starting
point for new productive capital or as a means of circulation for capital
already in existence. Hence the demand for money as a means of payment
is confused with the demand for money capital.

11 *Capital,* vol. III, p. 553.

12 When economists undertake an analysis of commodities, they always confine themselves to the content of the exchange act and overlook its specific
form. When dealing with the more developed forms of credit and with
stock exchange operations, however, they follow the opposite procedure of
ignoring their content, and instead, spend untold hours brooding upon their
various forms. In my opinion, even Jeidels, in his otherwise excellent study,
Die Verhältnisse der deutschen Grossbanken zur Industrie, attaches exaggerated importance to the various forms of credit operations.

13 E. Jaffé, *Das englische Bankwesen,* p. 200.

14 'In almost all branches of business the same trend can be observed which
had already become characteristic of transactions in raw materials and
semi-finished goods; namely, the increased substitution of cash payment [in
which, however, Prion also included bank payments – R.H.] for commercial
bills. With the aid of bank credit, especially in the form of acceptances, the
merchant pays in cash by making a giro transfer or by writing a cheque,
with the result that the use of pure commodity bills is increasingly restricted. This was bound to affect the largest and best commodity bills most,
since capital wealth has already grown considerably by absorption in the
upper levels of commerce. Even in large scale overseas commerce, which
has given rise to the best bills to date (for example, in the wheat trade) it is
customary to pay by sight drafts, if bank acceptances are not used, rather
than by 2 or 3 month notes. This new trend arises from the fact that, by
paying in cash, a buyer can always buy on better terms, which remain more
favourable even if the buyer is obliged to have greater recourse to bank
credit. Since some commodity bills still actually enter circulation, there is

great competition for them between the Reichsbank and the credit banks, as well as among the different groups of credit banks. The enormous amounts of capital accumulated in the large banks seek suitable investment in bills, and the competition for these commodity bills depresses the price of the good ones far below the discount rates of the Reichsbank to the discount level of the private banks.' Prion, op. cit., p. 120.

15 A specific example of the size of such credits can be seen from a notice which appeared in 1902 in the *Aktionär*, according to which it has become usual in many instances for industrialists to have to pay bank interest on 20 per cent to 40 per cent of their capital. At a shareholders' meeting of the Neusser Eisenwerke (previously Rudolf Daelen), a shareholder estimated that the debts of this firm in the years 1900 to 1903 amounted to 26, 85, 105 and 115 per cent of its liquid assets. Out of a debt of 718,000 marks in 1903, 500,000 marks were bank debts as compared with a share capital of 1,000,000 marks. See Jeidels, op. cit., p. 42.

16 Jeidels, op. cit., p. 32.

17 E. Jaffé, *Das englische Bankwesen*, p. 60.

18 'The essential feature of credit on current account is that it permits the debtor to make use of the credit agreed upon, either wholly or in part, or to pay back the credited sum at all times in the same way. This feature of credit granted on current account is of great advantage to the debtor because he can use the funds in such a way as to adjust them to the needs of his business and thus economize on their costs. On the other hand, by extending funds through credit on current account, the banks are investing their funds with sufficient security because, although the time of payment is not limited, the debtor is nevertheless enabled to repay the loan at all times.' Prion, op. cit., p. 102.

Concerning the level of interest charges on such credit in Germany, we are told that 'the rate of interest on current account credit is usually adjusted to the lending rate of the Reichsbank, although when the bank rate falls, it does not fall below a certain minimum which usually amounts to 5 per cent. Besides, although interest rates are generally calculated uniformly, in actual practice they depend, in the case of this particular form of credit, on the character and quality of the collateral and the type of bank. They also include a commission based on the quality of the business connections, and in most cases, the commission depends on the amount of credit used and on the speed of turnover. In any case, this commission changes the level of the true interest to the disadvantage of the credit-receiver to such an extent that, in practice, it is sometimes necessary, depending on the terms of the agreement, to pay 2 per cent or 3 per cent more than the normal current rate of interest' (ibid.).

19 Jeidels, op. cit., p. 32.

Chapter 6 The rate of interest

1 *Capital*, vol. III, pp. 398–9.

2 In order to explain prices by the relationship between supply and demand the latter must be assumed to be fixed and given quantities. That is why the marginal utility theory always endeavours to make the assumption that supply is constant, and to take a given stockpile for granted. Schumpeter, in *Das Wesen und der Hauptinhalt der theoretischen Nationalökonomie*, is per-

fectly consistent, therefore, in his attempt to uphold the marginal utility
theory by reducing political economy to a static system; whereas it should be
dynamic, providing a theory which formulates the laws of motion of capitalist society. The contrast with Marxism is very aptly and precisely expressed here, as is the complete sterility of the marginal theory, 'the final
futility of final utility' as Hyndman jokingly described it. The problem is that
an economic explanation of the scale of supply would involve explaining the
scale of production by formulating the laws which govern production.
Demand itself is detemined by production and distribution, by the laws
which govern the distribution of the social product. Similarly, in any attempt
to explain the rate of interest, the difficulty lies in showing what factors
determine the extent of the supply.

3 *Capital*, vol. III, pp. 586–7.

4 Such comparative empirical data as are available do not in any way support
the dogma of a declining rate of interest. Smith tells us that in his day, the
government of Holland paid 2 per cent, and private borrowers with good
credit 3 per cent interest. For a time after the war (1763) not only private
borrowers of the best credit standing but also some of the largest London
trading houses usually paid 5 per cent as compared with the previous rate of
from 4 to $4\frac{1}{2}$ per cent. Tooke, citing the latter facts, remarks on this point:
'In 1764, 4 per cent stock certificates fell below par; navy bills were discounted at $9\frac{5}{8}$ per cent; consols which stood at 96 in March, 1763, fell to 80 in
October. But in 1765, the 3 per cent stock certificates, of which a new issue
followed, stood generally at par, and at times above par; and 3 per cent
consols rose to 92.' Thomas Tooke, *A History of Prices and of the State of
the Circulation*, vol. I, pp. 240–41. Schmoller, in *Grundriss der allgemeinen
Volkswirtschaftslehre*, vol. II, p. 207, tells us further that in 1737 the 3 per
cent consols stood at 107. The price of state paper, which is also influenced
by other factors, is certainly not an absolutely reliable criterion of the level
of the interest rate, although it merits some attention.

　　Nor does an examination of the discount rate of banks of issue reveal any
uniform decline in the rate of interest. Table 1 is taken from an interesting
article by Dr Alfred Schwoner, 'Zinsfuss und Krisen im Lichte der Statistik',
in the *Berliner Tageblatt* of 26 and 27 November 1907. [The symbol C indicates a crisis year, although in 1895 and 1882 (the Bontoux crash) it was a
matter of purely speculative crises – R.H.]

Table 1　Average discount rates of the four leading
European banks during the past 55 years

	Bank of England	Bank of France	German Reichsbank (1874–5 Prussian Bank)	Austro-Hungarian Bank (formerly the National Bank)
1907 (first 10 months)	4.54	3.3	5.72	4.72
1906	4.27	3.0	5.12	4.4
1905	3.08	3	3.82	3.68
1904	3.3	3	4.2	3.5

	1903	3.76	3	3.77	3.5
	1902	3.33	3	3.32	3.55
C	1901	3.9	3	4.1	4.08
C	1900	3.94	3.2	5.33	4.58
	1899	3.75	3.06	5.04	5.04
	1898	3.19	2.2	4.27	4.16
	1897	2.64	2	3.81	4
	1896	2.48	2	3.66	4.09
C	1895	2	2.1	3.14	4.3
	1894	2.11	2.5	3.12	4.08
	1893	3.06	2.5	4.07	4.24
C	1892	2.52	2.7	3.2	4.02
C	1891	3.35	3	3.78	4.4
	1890	4.69	3	4.52	4.48
	1889	3.65	3.16	3.68	4.19
	1888	3.3	3.1	3.32	4.17
	1887	3.34	3	3.41	4.12
	1886	3.05	3	3.28	4
	1885	2.92	3	4.12	4
	1884	2.96	3	4	4
	1883	3.58	3.08	4.4	4.11
C	1882	4.14	3.8	4.54	4.02
	1881	3.48	3.84	4.42	4
	1880	2.76	2.81	4.24	4
	1879	2.38	2.58	3.07	4.33
	1878	3.75	2.2	4.34	5
	1877	2.85	2.26	4.42	5
	1876	2.62	3.4	4.16	5
	1875	3.25	4	4.71	4.6
	1874	3.75	4.3	4.38	4.87
C	1873	4.75	5.15	4.95	5.22
	1872	4.12	5.15	4.29	5.55
	1871	2.85	5.35	4.16	5.5
	1870	3.12	3.9	4.40	5.44
	1869	3.25	2.5	4.24	4.34
	1868	2.25	2.5	4	4
	1867	2.5	2.7	4	4
C	1866	7	3.67	6.21	4.94
	1865	4.75	3.66	4.96	5
	1864	7.5	6.51	5.31	5
	1863	4.5	3.66	4.96	5
	1862	2.5	3.73	4.2	5.06
	1861	5.25	5.86	4.2	5.5
	1860	4.25	3.56	4.2	5.12
	1859	2.75	3.47	4.2	5
	1858	3	3.68	4.2	5
	1857	6.7	6	5.76	5
	1856	5.8	5.5	4.94	4.27
	1855	4.8	5	4.08	4
	1854	5.1	4.37	4.36	4
	1853	3.4	3.23	4.25	4
	1852	2.5	3.18	4	4

Schwoner comments on the table as follows:

'If we try to draw some general conclusions about the movement of the rate of interest from these statistics of the bank discount rate in the nineteenth century, it becomes apparent that no definite tendency, upward or downward, is demonstrable. True, official discount rates below 4 per cent appeared in the course of time, sooner or later according to the economic development of the country. In this respect English was far in advance of other countries. As far back as 1845, the discount rate went down to 2 per cent for the first time. In the case of the Bank of France, the discount rate stood at 3 per cent for the first time in 1852, at $2\frac{1}{2}$ per cent in 1867, and at 2 per cent in 1877. The Berlin Bank had a minimum discount rate of 3 per cent as far back as the twenties of last century, but during the period of the Prussian Bank and the German Reichsbank the interest rate fell below 4 per cent for the first time in 1880 [sic]. In the Austro-Hungarian Bank, a $3\frac{1}{2}$ per cent interest rate first appeared in 1903 during the first depression experienced by the Dual Monarchy after the reform of the currency system. Some progress may be discerned in so far as the rate of interest has declined with the technical perfecting of banking organization and the currency system.'

Schwoner also provides the following figures (Table 2).

Table 2   Average discount rates over the past five decades

Decade	Bank of England	Bank of France	German Reichsbank	Austro-Hungarian Bank	Overall Average
1897–1906	3.52	2.85	4.28	4.05	3.67
1887–1896	3.04	2.71	3.59	4.21	3.38
1877–1886	3.19	2.96	4.11	4.26	3.63
1867–1876	3.25	3.89	4.34	4.85	4.09
1857–1866	4.28	4.48	4.83	5.06	4.79

'The overall average was at its highest by far in the decade 1857–1866, when it amounted to 4.79 per cent, and remained very high in 1867–1876 at 4.09 per cent. In 1877–1886, it fell to 3.63 per cent and reached its lowest point in 1887–1896, at 3.38 per cent. In the last decade, the average was 3.67 per cent, higher, therefore, than in the preceding two decades, but far below the average during the first twenty years of the financial and industrial upswing, 1857–1876.'

The conclusion to be drawn from all this is that the rate of interest is not determined by the rate of profit, but by the stronger or weaker demand for money capital resulting from variations in the rate of development, and the tempo, intensity and duration of periods of prosperity.

A study of excessively high rates of interest will show that their causes are always to be found in the regulation of the monetary system. Thus, for example, the discount rate in Hamburg rose to 15 per cent in 1799, and even at this rate, only the best bills, in limited amounts, were accepted (Tooke, op. cit., vol. I, p. 241). The cause lies in the absence of a flexible monetary system, as is shown at present by the exceedingly high interest rates and their violent fluctuations in the United States. They have nothing to do with any changes in the rate of profit.

5 Adam Smith's principle that 'wherever a great deal can be made by it [money] a great deal will commonly be given for the use of it; and wherever little can be made by it, less will commonly be given for it' (*Wealth of Nations*, bk I, ch. IX), although illuminating, is not demonstrated and not correct.

Chapter 7 The joint-stock company

1 This sentiment seems also to have guided Erwin Steinitzer when he entitled his work on the corporation *Ökonomische Theorie der Aktiengesellschaft*. Nevertheless, he too fails to recognize the distinctive economic characteristics of the joint-stock company, although his work is otherwise rich in cogent and perceptive observations.
2 'The value of money or of commodities employed in the capacity of capital is not determined by their value as money or commodities but by the quantity of surplus value which they produce for their owner.' *Capital*, vol. III, p. 418.
3 The only relation between the price of a share and the value of the productive capital is that the share price cannot fall below that part of the value of the capital which, if the enterprise became bankrupt, and after its other creditors had been satisfied, would fall due to it as an aliquot part.
4 *Briefe und sozialpolitische Aufsätze von Dr Rodbertus-Jagetzow*, R. Meyer (ed.), vol. I, p. 259.
5 This is not correct. A corporation is not a technical form of production, but a form of business enterprise.
6 ibid., p. 262.
7 ibid., p. 285.
8 Nevertheless, this conservative socialist had an accurate premonition of the revolutionary significance of the corporation: 'This form of business which can merge tributaries from a thousand small sources of capital into a single stream, has a mission to perform. It will have to complete God's handiwork by penetrating land barriers and countries which the Almighty had forgotten or regarded as unready for penetration. It will have to connect countries separated by oceans, through submarine or surface links. It will have to pierce mountain barriers and so forth. The pyramids and the squared blocks of the Phoenicians were as child's play compared with what share capital will create.' In this vein, Rodbertus abandons himself to romantic fantasies reminiscent of Saccard in Zola's *L'Argent*. He continues: 'Moreover I have a very special personal enthusiasm for them. And why? Because they do such a thorough job of sweeping away all obstacles. And what sweepers they are! Traditional free trade, without the benefit of the corporate form, is a miserably inadequate handbroom. Combined with corporations, it becomes a steam-driven sweeper which will sweep away in 10 years what it would take the Sabbath broom 100 years to do. The hand of the corporation is indeed powerful! The solution of the social problem requires this scavenger. After all, even without the corporation, we would need a thoroughgoing cleaning' (ibid., p. 291). Equally apposite is the following remark: 'The corporate enterprise will eliminate both the individual entrepreneur and the loan capitalist' (ibid., p. 286).
   Van Borght therefore was incredibly naive when he wrote in the chapter on corporations in the *Handwörterbuch der Staatswissenschaften*: 'The task and objective of corporate enterprises can be just as much the enlargement

and improvement of personal labour power, and of the knowledge and experience of the entrepreneur, as the strengthening of the power of capital.' This is just about as brilliant as would be the statement in a scientific cookery book that the task and objective of a plum pudding is to stimulate the appetite and to provide a livelihood for the cook!

9 *Capital*, vol. III, pp. 516 *et seq.*

10 The following report in the evening edition of the *Berliner Tageblatt* (16 May 1908) will illustrate the schematic presentation in the text: 'Recently the shares of the Kopenick nitrate plant were introduced on the stock exchange at a premium of more than 80 per cent. From 1901 to 1906, this enterprise operated as a limited company with a modest capital of 300,000 marks. After operating at a loss for several years, the company made a gross profit of 100,000 marks one year, followed by another of 300,000 marks, and paid dividends of 15,000 marks and 75,000 marks. The founders of the enterprise accordingly decided that it was time to transform it into a joint-stock company with a capital of 1,000,000 marks, in which the original capital of 300,000 marks was included. In order to balance the assets and liabilities of the new corporation, the corporation had to take over the land, with a book value of 60,000 marks, for 210,000 marks; the buildings, valued at 45,000 marks, for 140,000 marks; and the machinery, equipment and materials, valued at 246,000 marks, for 400,000 marks. The new corporation has now been operating for two years, during which period it has distributed dividends of 15 per cent and 16 per cent respectively, although the account for the land (exclusive of improvements) still carries a deficit of 200,000 marks, that for the building a claim of 150,000 marks. Only the equity on the machines and equipment (the overvaluation of which seemed most questionable) was written down to 250,000 marks. The output of the corporation is based on two patents, one of which will expire in a year, the other having been purchased from the inventor for 50,000 marks. On the basis of these facts, the issue houses felt themselves entitled to stipulate a price of 180 per cent; in other words they allowed themselves to be paid 1,800,000 marks for the original capital of 300,000 marks, including 100,000 marks in cash, which were the basis of the corporation!' In this instance, the promoter's profit is increased because the enterprise makes an extra profit from its exploitation of the patents, which is, of course, also capitalized.

11 The following table, taken from the *Berliner Tageblatt* of 1 June 1907, shows that the capital invested in shares for the first or new investment yields its owner a dividend which is not very much above the average rate of interest. The discount rate of the Reichsbank was $5\frac{1}{2}$ per cent at the time.

	Share price index per cent (May 30)	Dividend per cent	Yield per cent
Berliner Handelsgesellschaft	150.75	9	5.97
Darmstädter Bank	129.30	8	6.18
Deutsche Bank	223.60	12	5.36
Diskontogesellschaft	169	9	5.32
Dresdner Bank	141	8.5	6.02
Nationalbank	121.50	7.5	6.17
Bochumer Gussstahl	224.25	15	6.68

Laurahütte	223.30	12	5.32
Harpener Bergbau	207.60	11	5.29
Gelsenkirchener Bergwerk	195.50	11	5.62
Phönix Bergbau	205.30	15	7.30
Rombacher Hüttenwerke	204.50	14	6.84
Donnersmarckhütte	264.50	14	5.29
Eisenwerk Kraft	166	11	6.62
Eisenhütte Thale (preferred)	123	9	7.31
Allgemeine Elektrizitäts-gesellschaft	198.50	11	5.54
Lahmeyer Elektrizität	122	8	6.55
Hoffmann Waggonfabrik	335	22	6.56
Gaggenauer Eisenwerk	105	8	7.61
Schering Chemische Fabriken	263	17	6.46
Chemische Fabrik Oranienburg	184.50	10	5.42
Schulteiss Brauerei	288.50	18	6.23
Vereinsbrauerei, Aktien	210.50	12	5.70

12 The same thing has occurred in the formation of English joint-stock com
panies. In describing the community of interests between a mixed pig-iron
enterprise and a steel company, Macrosty says: 'It is to be observed that
while the aid of the public was called in to assist in the extension of the
business [through the issue of debentures, preferred shares – R.H.] control
lay solely with the vendors (the firm of Bill Bros and Dorman Long & Co.)
so long as debenture interest and preference dividends were maintained.
This is quite a common feature of British flotations, and it demands from
the cautious investor a careful scrutiny of the purchase conditions.' Henry
W. Macrosty, *The Trust Movement in British Industry,* p. 27. 'In many
cases, the ordinary stock is held largely or solely by the original vendors in
order that they may retain control, in which case the amount of the ordinary dividend is of less consequence to the public' (ibid., p. 54).
    Similar in purpose to ordinary shares – the monopolization of the be-
nefits resulting from the development of the corporation by the
promoters – were the so-called 'promoters' rights' in the former German
(and Austrian) company law. The promoters stipulated certain privileges
for themselves; for example, that new share issues had to be offered to
them at par. However, such privileges conflicted with the process of mobilizing capital and were therefore eliminated. The *Berliner Tageblatt* of 24
September 1907, had this to say on the subject: 'Like a memorial of an age
long past, the institution of promoters' rights survives today, still observed
by many corporations. These rights derive from a period when company
law was not as developed as it is today. In the past, it was considered per-
missible to grant the founders of a corporate enterprise permanent special
privileges, a condition which in view of the mobility inherent in shares, was
bound to prove onerous and unjustified. The 1884 amendment of company
law already made a breach in the system of promoters' privileges, but it
was first completely abolished as regards the founding of new corporations
by the Commercial Code which came into force on 1 January 1900. It is
true that this new commercial law was not retroactive, so that the promoters' privileges of former times remain unchanged, and in so far as they
have not been eliminated by voluntary agreement they are still unpleasant

reminders to shareholders in corporations "blessed" with promoters' rights
. . . . In the case of Berliner Elektrizitätswerken – to mention one typical example of the effects of these promoters' rights – the Allgemeine
Elektrizitätsgesellschaft has the privilege of taking for itself half of any
newly issued shares at par. The profit which this privilege brought to the
Allgemeine Elektrizitätsgesellschaft as a result of the issue of shares by the
Berliner Elektrizitätswerken in the years 1889, 1890, 1899 and 1904 alone is
estimated at about 15,000,000 marks. Neither the founders nor their heirs
can be blamed for profiting from their duly acquired privileges.
Nevertheless, it has become obvious that the modern view of the stock
market rightly demands the abolition of perpetual promoters' privileges.'

13 The most notable example is provided by the history of the American Steel
Trust (See *Report of the Industrial Commission*, 1901, vol. XIII, pp. xiv–xv).
It combined companies which were already overcapitalized. The report
calculates the 'real worth' by adding together only the preferred shares of
the constituent companies, which would give a real share capital standing at
par, and comes to the conclusion that $398,918,111 are counted for 'good-
will' alone. The following account in the *Frankfurter Zeitung* of 29 March
1909 gives an even better idea of the 'overcapitalization', or more precisely
of the difference between the capital which was actually at work and the
share capital: 'The Gary works will cost about $100,000,000 and produce
over 2,000,000 tons of steel. The other plants of the trust are capitalized at
almost $1,500,000,000 and have a capacity of 10,000,000 tons. The disparity
is glaring.' It remains glaring even if we take into account that valuable ore
property and other items are also included in the capitalization.

This has not prevented the Steel Trust from regularly paying a dividend
of 7 per cent on its preferred shares, nor has it hindered the ordinary shares
from yielding dividends on an increasing scale. The trust was organized in
the spring of 1901. The period 1901 to 1903 was one of prosperity and the
ordinary shares received dividends of 4 per cent. In 1903 the dividends
dropped to 3 per cent, and in 1904 and 1905 no dividends were paid, but
by 1905 there was an improvement in business conditions and the Steel
Trust would have had about $43,000,000 available to distribute as di-
vidends, equivalent to a dividend of 8.5 per cent. But the trust used the
amount for write-offs, new investments, and the building of reserves. Then,
in 1906, it again paid 2 per cent.

But this dividend is quite disproportionate to the profits of the Steel
Trust, for 1906 was a very good year and the trust had almost $100,000,000
available for dividends. Of this sum some $25,000,000 were used for pay-
ments on preferred shares. The balance on the books amounted to 14.4 per
cent on the ordinary shares. But the shareholders only received $10,166,000,
while $50,000,000 were invested in new construction (including the second
instalment on the Gary Steel works at $21,500,000), and $13,000,000 were
put into the reserves. The directors followed the same policy in 1907, when
earnings were even greater than in 1906. The amount available for distribution to ordinary shareholders would have provided a dividend of 15.6
per cent. But again the shareholders only received 2 per cent for the year,
or 0.5 per cent a quarter, while $54,000,000 were spent on new construc-
tion, of which $18,500,000 went into the Gary works, and $25,000,000 were
added to reserves. 1908 was not as good as the previous years, but still the
Steel Trust earned enough to pay a little over 4 per cent on its ordinary
shares. In fact, the ordinary shareholders received only 2 per cent. Nothing

was spent on new construction, but $10,000,000 were added to reserves, so that by the end of the year 1908 these amounted to $1,330,500,000. The first quarter of 1909 was better than the same period of the previous year, but a good deal worse than the last two quarters of 1908, mainly as a result of the collapse of prices on the American market for iron. As was the usual practice since 1900, a quarterly dividend of 0.5 per cent was paid on the ordinary shares and more than $3,000,000 were added to reserves (see *Berliner Tageblatt*, 28 July 1909). For the second quarter of 1909 the steel trust declared a dividend of 0.75 per cent, equivalent to 3 per cent per annum. For the third quarter, the dividend was 1 per cent, or 4 per cent per annum, on ordinary shares. Most of these shares had remained in the hands of the founders, or had become favourite targets for speculators, and were bought up again during and after the panic of 1907 by financial groups at very low prices. Hence this dividend policy of withholding earnings for many years at the expense of the shareholders, only to pour them out at the most appropriate time, was the source of an enormous accession of wealth to the financial groups which dominated the Steel Trust.

14 A detailed description of the technique of financing is beyond the scope of the present work. Nevertheless, the following typical example, describing the financing of the Rock Island railway system, will serve to illustrate what has been said in the text (see the *Frankfurter Zeitung*, 6 October 1909). At the head of the system is a holding company, the Rock Island Company, without any secured debentures, and with an authorized capital of $54,000,000 in preferred shares and $96,000,000 in ordinary shares, of which $42,129,000 and $89,730,000 respectively have been issued. Only the preferred shares carry voting rights. The company owns the entire share capital of $145,000,000 in the Chicago, Rock Island and Pacific Railroad Company, which in addition has secured debentures of $70,199,000 4 per cent Collateral Trust Bonds and $17,361,000 5 per cent Collateral Trust Bonds. These are bonds which are backed by securities in the hands of the trustees (on Collateral Trust Bonds, see Thomas L. Greene, *Corporation Finance*). This Railroad Company in turn owns two railways: (1) The Chicago, Rock Island and Pacific Railroad Company with a funded debt of $197,850,000, with shares amounting to $74,859,000 of which $70,199,000 are in the hands of trustees as collateral for the abovementioned 4 per cent Collateral Trust Bonds; and (2) The St Louis and San Francisco Railroad Company with a funded debt of about $227,000,000 and a share capital of $5,000,000 class A preferred shares, $16,000,000 class B preferred shares, and $29,000,000 ordinary shares of which the Rock Island Company has acquired $28,940,000. The latter gave $60 of 5 per cent Collateral Trust Bonds belonging to Chicago, Rock Island and Pacific Railroad Company and $60 of its own shares for every $100 of shares of the former. Both large companies now have, in turn, their own subsidiary companies.

The purpose of this ingenious financing is evident. The control of the whole immense railway system rests with the owners of the preferred shares of the Rock Island Company which alone carry voting rights. At the time of its formation in 1902 the shares stood at between 40 and 70. The founders needed at most $15,000,000 to obtain the $27,000,000 of preferred shares which were necessary to control the entire railway system.

15 E. Loeb, 'Das Institut des Aufsichtsrates, etc.' in *Jahrbuch für Nationalökonomie und Statistik,* Third series, vol. 23, 1902 estimates the income from directorships for the year 1900 at about 60 million marks. In a

very thorough investigation of boards of directors of German corporations in the same periodical (Third series, vol. 32, 1906, pp. 92 *et seq.*) Franz Eulenberg estimates the sum at 70 million marks for 1906. Every corporation distributes on average 6/10 per cent of its nominal capital as bonuses, and each director receives on average 1/10 per cent. In the large corporations the absolute amount is naturally greater – about 6,000 to 8,000 marks, or more. Thus the Dresdner Bank distributed 21,000 marks; Felton und Guillaume 34,000 marks; Dürkopp 10,000 marks; Deutsche Bank 32,000 marks; Hörder Bergwerke, 15,000 marks; Gelsenkirchen 87,000 marks; Bayerische Hypothekenbank, 13,000 marks, in bonuses.

16 A personal union is the starting point or culmination of combinations among companies which, for external reasons, must remain organizationally and institutionally separate, but can attain their full effectiveness only by combining their forces in a single top management. The personal union between Austria and Hungary is all that remains of their former ties, and is perhaps only significant today in so far as it may serve as the point of departure for another kind of union. The combination of the political and economic organizations of the working class through a unified leadership at the top reinforces the strength of both types of organization. The same kind of fusion of economic with political organization is to be found among German landowners in the Bund der Landwirte, and is particularly developed in the organizations of Prussian Poland.

17 This is why large bank loans to an individually owned enterprise often presage its conversion into a joint-stock company.

18 The large banks seek 'to develop a network of connections with industrial enterprises in different areas and fields of industry, and to remove such inequalities in geographical and industrial representation as arise from peculiarities in the development of particular institutions. Along with this, they also try to base their relations with industry on sustained and permanent business dealings, to make them effective, and to extend and deepen them, through a systematic policy of placing their representatives on boards of directors.' O. Jeidels, *Die Verhältnisse der deutschen Grossbanken zur Industrie*, p. 180. According to the table given by Jeidels the banks had the following representation in corporations in 1903:

	Deutsche Bank	Diskontogesellschaft	Darmstädter Bank	Dresdner Bank	Schaaffhausenscher Bankverein	Berliner Handelsgesellschaft	Total
Managing directors	101	31	51	53	68	40	344
Board members	120	61	50	80	62	34	407
	221	92	101	133	130	74	751

Thus the six large Berlin banks alone controlled a total of 751 positions on boards of directors.

According to the latest directory of managing directors and board members (1909) there are 12,000 such positions in Germany, but 2,918 of them are held by only 170 persons. The record is held by Mr Karl Fürstenberg of the Berliner Handelsgesellschaft who has 44 positions, while Mr Eugen Gutmann of the Dresdner Bank has 35. Of the various occupations represented on these boards of directors, the banking profession has the leading place, and it is among bankers, therefore, that there is the greatest accumulation of positions by individuals. (For details, see Eulenberg, op. cit.)

Naturally, the same situation exists in the United States. In 1906 the firm of J. P. Morgan & Company was represented on the boards of directors of five banks, fifty railways, three shipping lines, eight trust companies, eight insurance companies, and forty industrial enterprises. (See Steinitzer, op. cit., p. 158.)

19 Conversely, the board of directors does not play in any way the role which is prescribed for it by a legal fiction. Thus, the chairman told the general meeting of the Elektrische Licht- und Kraftanlagen Aktiengesellschaft in Berlin frankly: 'The notion that any board of directors, or any member of a board can do what the law prescribes is mistaken. The legislators did not know what they were doing when they passed such a law. Imagine a member or an entire board of directors trying to follow in detail, even for a single day, the activities of all the branches of one of our big corporations. While the man is inquiring into the affairs of one branch, ten big mistakes can be made elsewhere. A board of directors can only issue general directives for running a corporation. It can ensure that the management does not violate any laws or regulations, but the details of auditing are matters with which only auditors are competent to deal' (*Berliner Tageblatt*, 28 November 1908).

20 In speaking of 'social capital', in this context, I mean that the private entrepreneur is limited by the size of the individual capital, whereas the corporation is limited only by the size of the whole stock of free money capital seeking new investment which is available in capitalist society.

21 'The stock company is the keenest and surest and hence the favourite weapon which the capitalist system can use in its struggle for concentration. In itself, the stock company represents a form of concentration, viz, the union of small and scattered units of property, in most cases too small to be fitted for productive uses, into a single mass of capital suited and intended for industrial or productive purposes under a single management. The facility with which the shares can be marketed or transmitted by inheritance, the probability of a longer term of existence for the corporation, owing to the far greater degree to which it is independent of the personality of the entrepreneur as compared with other forms of business organization, and finally the absence (at least in theory) of any limitations on the amount of dividends that may be expected on the combined capital – all these elements give the corporation a great power to attract available capital. More than any other form of business organization, the stock company has the means of satisfying its need for credit and for expansion by capital increases. The ease with which additional capital can be secured naturally stimulates the tendency toward capital increases. This tendency grows at a constantly increasing rate by reason of what may be regarded as an economic law in the realm of industry, trade and banking alike, according to which a twofold increase of capital means more than a twofold increase of production and sales. [But this does not necessarily mean the doubling of profits – R.H.] For this reason the tendency towards capital increases is enhanced by this very growth of capital, and thereby is far more important

under larger capitals than under the smaller.' Jacob Riesser, *Zur Entwicklungsgeschichte der deutschen Grossbanken*, pp. 151–2.

[This passage was incorporated by Riesser in his later book on German banking, *Die deutschen Grossbanken und ihre Konzentration*, and was translated by M. Jacobson for the National Monetary Commission under the title, *The German Great Banks and Their Concentration* (Senate Document 593, 61st Congress, 2nd Session, Washington, 1911). Following the indications given by Watnick, I have used this translation, on pp. 605–6 of the Senate Document, in the above note. Ed.]

22 'The Commission of 1886 heard a very large number of complaints against the competition of corporations. Many witnesses argued that the main reason for low commodity prices was that corporations had grown enormously in many lines of industry and that they continued in business even when they failed to earn a profit. The motive of the people who ran these enterprises was to continue production regardless of whether or not a profit was being earned.' M. Tugan-Baranowsky, *Studien zur Theorie und Geschichte der Handelsksisen in England* p. 162

23 *Capital*, vol. I, pp. 685–6.

24 On the distinction between these two concepts see *Capital*, vol. I, pp. 681 *et seq.*

25 The tendency for bank capital to increase may be accentuated by legislative intervention. Thus, the provision of the German Companies Law requiring that when a privately owned enterprise is converted into a corporation, the shares cannot be released on the stock exchange until one year later, makes it impossible to mobilize bank capital during one whole year, so that it remains in the form of industrial capital for that year and cannot revert to the form of money. Consequently, promotional activities, especially the promotion of large enterprises, were monopolized by the very large banks which had a large capital of their own, and this, in turn, also intensified the tendency to concentration in the banking system. The promoter's profit also accrued, of course, to the same large banks.

26 E. S. Mead, *Trust Finance*, p. 243.

Chapter 8 The stock exchange

1 See the informative work by W. Prion, *Das deutsche Wechseldiskontgeschäft*.

2 *Nota bene*: I am not referring here to so-called 'bucket shop' transactions, where no securities are actually delivered, and speculation is concluded by payment of the difference in share quotations. In the economic sense, every speculative gain is a marginal profit. In this respect the technique of stock exchange transactions is just as immaterial as is the circumstance that capitalists – and also some economists – regard all capitalist profit as marginal, regardless of whether it is a matter of industrial or commercial profit, rent, interest, or speculative gains.

3 This is not all. They must also make the valuations at the same time and in the same degree. A speculative profit is still possible, for instance, if one speculator purchases a security at a higher price at a later time than another has been selling at, or if one speculator pays a higher price than another, who is already selling at this price, has paid.

4 To cite one striking example of this: 'A report circulated recently that Phoenix had received a very large order for steel tubes from America; a

value of several million marks was mentioned. The stock exchange, without any misgivings, gave full credence to the report and drove up the price of our domestic steel securities, especially those of Phoenix. Yet it was known, of course, that conditions in America had not improved significantly over the last few months . . . . But in the country, in the industrial districts, and especially among the directors of Phoenix, there must have been a good deal of secret laughter at the sensational report which evoked so much optimism on the Berlin stock exchange. It subsequently turned out that the order, for several millions, and for an American account, was attributed to an enterprise which does not even produce steel tubes, and does not have a quota for tubes as a member of the German Steel Combine. In short, it was a bare-faced swindle.' *Berliner Tageblatt,* 15 July 1909.

When, therefore Mr Arnold (*Deutsche Börsenenquete,* Part I, p. 444) talks of speculative intelligence, he is really speculating on the lack of intelligence of his audience. In any case, he has to concede the accidental and irrational character of speculation for the bulk of small investors and the general public.

5 On the concept of 'productive labour' in the narrower sense, see Karl Marx, *Theories of Surplus Value,* vol. I, chapter IV.

6 In the terminology of J. Karner (Karl Renner) there is a change in the function of a legal institution without a simultaneous change in the legal norm. See *Marx-Studien,* vol. I, p. 81. [See Karl Renner, *The Institutions of Private Law and their Social Functions,* pp. 74–7 – Ed.]

7 Perhaps the most important recent example is the take-over of the Tennessee Steel & Coal Company by the Steel Trust during the panic in the autumn of 1907. The Tennessee Steel & Coal Company was an important competitor of the Steel Trust. An indignant correspondent writes in the *Berliner Tageblatt* (17 November 1907): 'Well informed sources have now confirmed that the two representatives of J. Pierpont Morgan who have been in Washington for several days, E. H. Gary (of the Steel Trust) and H. C. Frick, presented the following ultimatum to President Roosevelt: either quietly countenance the absorption of the Tennessee Steel & Coal Company by the Morgan Trust, and promise that the government will take no preventive action on the basis of the existing anti-trust legislation, or be prepared for the worst panic in the history of the country and the suspension of all bank payments.

This threat to the president at the most turbulent and dangerous point of the economic crisis naturally bore fruit. Bowing to necessity, the president had to abdicate his power to the stock exchange. He was brutally compelled to foreswear temporarily his highest duty as the first officer of the government, and to disregard the existing laws. The executive power was rendered powerless, and the worthy Morgan, in return for "saving" the Trust Company of America and the Lincoln Trust Company, secured a monopoly of the country's iron and steel for his Steel Trust. A few days later, in the course of his rescue activities, he succeeded in another *coup*, by taking over the C. W. Morse Coastwise Steamship Co.

This indicates the present state of affairs in the republic of the United States of America, founded by selfless patriots like George Washington, Benjamin, Jefferson, and other outstanding men.'

8 *Capital,* vol. III, p. 496.

9 *Stenographischer Bericht der deutschen Börsenenquete* (Verbatim Report of the German Stock Exchange Inquiry) 1893, vol. I., p. 190.

10 Thus, for example, London 'has had a Stock Exchange Clearing since 1874, through which all transactions involving the leading securities are, so far as possible, settled; so that cheques need only be drawn for the balance. The result has been that only about 10 per cent of the transactions on the capital market are paid by cheque while 90 per cent of the reciprocal claims are settled by simple balancing.' E. Jaffé, *Das englische Bankwesen*, p. 95. Similar institutions also exist in other stock exchange centres.

11 'The various forms of stock exchange procedure are not only important for ascertaining prices. The conditions for taking part in and concluding stock exchange operations are more than legal and technical aids in such transactions; they are themselves factors in price-formation whose importance should not be underestimated, even though, in the final analysis, supply and demand are the deciding factors. Whether it is securities or commodities that are dealt in, whether the transactions take place in cash or in futures, whether in long-term or short-term futures, whatever units the deals are concluded in, whatever the commodity traded, whatever the stock exchange group involved (kerb trader or member); all these as well as other formal considerations are important factors, not only in ascertaining prices correctly, but also in forming them. Every change in these conditions has an influence on the course which prices will take over time in an organized market.' M. Landesberger, 'Die Reform der landwirtschaftlichen Börsen in Deutschland', *Zeitschrift für Volkswohlfahrt, Sozialpolitik und Verwaltung*, vol. XI, 1902, p. 36.

12 *Deutsche Börsenenquete*, vol. I, report of the Commission, pp. 75 *et seq.*

13 This can also occur for other reasons. 'On the continent, it is not unusual for the banks to pursue a contango policy of their own. It happens, for example, that banks preparing a large issue of shares, reduce the contango rate in order to provoke a "bullish" mood; they can make good the losses sustained in this way by their profit on the shares issued.' E. von Philippovich, *Grundriss der politischen Ökonomie*, vol. II, part II, p. 181.

14 See the *Deutsche Börsenenquete*, vol. III, p. 1930, where one expert witness, König, maintains that futures operations are undesirable for industry, and justifies his opinion as follows: 'All these securities involved in the futures trade float about on the stock exchange, for the most part in the hands of people who have no permanent interest in them. They are only interested in the shares, not in the businesses as such, and their sole interest lies in driving the share prices up or down. Given the procedures which exist in the futures trade, it is extraordinarily easy for almost anyone to acquire influence in an enterprise through contango operations which enable him to obtain a large number of shares at the end of a month when there is a general meeting of stockholders. He suddenly appears as the owner of a few million shares, which do not really belong to him, in front of the regular shareholders, who suspect nothing, but are taken by surprise and sold all sorts of beautiful schemes which they never imagined.'

15 See the testimony of Meier (*Börsenenquete*, vol. III, p. 1608) who attributes the powerful development of the futures business in England to the fact that there has always been a considerable volume of floating capital available for contango operations.

16 *Börsenenquete*, vol. I, p. 347. Testimony of Arnhold.

17 See, for example, the following statement of a 'prominent member of the Berlin banking community', as reported by the *Berliner Tageblatt* of 25 February 1908. 'Do not forget that only a comparatively small proportion

of all turnovers are actually concluded at the official cash prices. The concentration in German banking is responsible for the fact that a large part
of purchase and sale orders are cancelled out in the offices of the large
banks. Only dealings in the top securities are settled on the Berlin
exchange.'

In Austria there is a similar development. At the general meeting of the
Vienna Giro- und Kassenverein, one shareholder complained: 'Owing to
the fact that the commercial life of the Monarchy is being increasingly
concentrated in the hands of the banks, with the result that all the weaker
private houses are bound to disappear, dealings on the stock exchange do
not even require, in a great many cases, the services of brokerage offices.
Every bank is a clearing house without any expenses or officials. The securities business prospers in the banks, while there is an associated reduction
in the brokerage services of the Giro- und Kassenverein' *Neue Freie
Presse*, 1 February 1905).

18 *Berliner Jahrbuch für Handel und Industrie*, 1905.
19 *Frankfurter Zeitung*, 21 June 1907.
20 Thus the *Frankfurter Zeitung* of 28 January, 1906, writes: 'There is hardly
any such thing as a monthly settlement today. True, renewal rates are published, but most of the postponements are arranged in the big banks which
also have the right to set their own rates. It is quite impossible to form any
idea of the volume of floating commitments because, as was said, only a
very small proportion of the dealings are finally settled on the stock
exchange.'

To some extent stock exchanges abroad are in a different position. In
particular, the New York stock exchange plays a much more important role
than do European exchanges in the transfer of property, that is expropriation. The unique system of fiscal regulation complements the techniques
of the stock exchange. The New York stock exchange only allows cash
business in which differences must be settled daily. When there are strong
market movements, and especially when they are all in the same direction,
a strong demand for money arises. If the money market is tight, the
American bank note legislation, with its lack of flexibility, is calculated to
produce exorbitant interest rates which small speculators cannot pay. This
is the moment for the large suppliers of money to 'throw them out of
speculation' and to acquire their securities cheaply on the occasion of
forced liquidations.

Chapter 9 The commodity exchange

1 Mr Russel of the Diskontogesellschaft offers the following definition: 'The
essence of mercantile speculation consists in anticipating changes in business conditions in order to take advantage of them when they occur,
through futures trading' (*Börsenenquete*, vol. I, p. 417).
2 *Börsenenquete*, vol. II, p. 2072.
3 The use of such artificial methods has been the source of many abuses and
difficulties, which disappear when there exists a real and easily verifiable
interchangeability, as for example in the case of spirits (alcoholic content)
or, to some extent, sugar (degree of polarization).
4 'This special form of the futures trade is not only designed to facilitate
actual trading but also serves, in the final analysis, to give the capitalist or

speculator who possesses capital which is available for the time being, the opportunity to invest it temporarily or for a longer term, in a given branch of trade, even if he is completely ignorant of the commodity concerned or of the procedures, of that trade. This capitalist . . . differs from the grain merchant mainly in the motive for his activity.' The latter wants to deal in grain, the former to make a profit out of price fluctuations. The capitalist here assumes the risk. (See Fuchs, 'Der Warenterminhandel', in *Schmollers Jahrbuch für Gesetzgebung*, 1, 1891, p. 71.) It should be added that the profit motive is common to all capitalist activities; only the means by which profit is acquired differs.

5 Thus Offermann reports that in 1892, 2,000 bales of wool were actually sold on the Le Havre Wool Exchange, whereas 16,300 bales were sold on the futures markets. Similarly, futures trading in cotton was ten times greater than the actual trade. The harvest yielded 8 to 9 million bales, but some 100,000,000 bales were turned over on the futures market (*Deutsche Börsenquete*, vol. III, p. 3368).

6 Nevertheless, the power of insiders in commodity futures trading should not be exaggerated: 'If it were possible to foresee the future state of the market, or the appropriate prices, by reading market reports, that would be a splendid thing. From long experience I can only say; intuition is everything. It is admirable to be well-informed, but that is just a catchword, it doesn't lead anywhere, and merchants frequently make mistakes . . . . The merchant is as ignorant of these things as the farmer, and if he studies all the reports, he becomes more confused than ever, and things usually turn out differently', the dealer Domme frankly admits (*Deutsche Börsenenquete*, vol. II, p. 2858).

7 The protective tariff does not equalize the price, but simply raises the German price above the world price by an amount which brings the grain producer a profit even when the price on the world market is low.

8 Mr Kampf, chairman of the Berlin Chamber of Commerce, has this to say about participation in the futures trade generally: 'When the waves are high everyone takes part, but when they are not very high, it is only the wealthier people who do business of this kind' (*Dentsche Börsenenquete*, vol. III, p. 2459).

9 There is a delightful dialogue between Mr von Gamp and Mr Horwitz concerning the pain that a businessman is morally obliged to feel at the thought of the losses suffered by small speculators. But that is not in the nature of the businessman. Either do away with him altogether, or let him retain his proper nature (*Deutsche Börsenenquete*, vol. III, p. 2459). For the ethical school of political economy the exchange has above all the function of a moral public lavatory. Its other functions remain concealed from them.

10 See *Deutsche Börsenenquete*, Report of the Commission, p. 90.

11 'The small non-professional dealers have withdrawn from the coffee trade, which is now dominated by large syndicates' (*Deutsche Börsenenquete*, p. 2065). The expert, van Gülpen, explains this as follows: 'Much can be achieved with large capital resources if they are directed to trade in single articles.'

   The big London grain firms oppose the introduction of futures trading because it would democratize the trade and they would lose their dominant position (ibid., p. 3542).

12 H. Ruesch, 'Der Berliner Getreidehandel unter dem deutschen

Börsengesetz', in *Conrads Jahrbuch für Nationalökonomie und Statistik*,
Third Series, XXXIII, 1, 1907, p. 53.

13 ibid., p. 87. Cf. also Landesberger's prediction of this development:
'Significantly, the very largest grain merchants do not participate in futures
trading, but arrange their own insurance. The abolition of futures trading is
thus bound to result in a concentration of the grain trade in the hands of
the firms with the largest capital resources, with the same necessity as the
prohibition of futures trading in certain types of securities delivered this
branch of securities trading into the hands of the large German banks.' op.
cit., p. 45.

14 *Deutsche Börsenenquete*, vol. III, pp. 3373 *et seq.* Testimony of Offermann.

15 *Berliner Tageblatt*, 19 October 1907.

16 *Kontradiktorische Verhandlungen der deutschen Kartellenquete über die
Verbände in der deutschen Spiritusindustrie.* Testimony of the managing
director of the central office for regulating the sale of alcohol,
Bourzutschky.

17 Landesberger is quite right when he says: 'Some important economic facts
explain the farmers' opposition to the futures trade. Agriculture, more than
any other branch of production, depends upon seasonal and geographical
conditions of production. Hence its costs of production are less variable
than in other sectors of the economy. This is also connected with the fact
that capital is immobilized in agriculture, with the considerable mortgage
burden on land, and with the difficulty, arising from natural conditions, of
employing so extensively or successfully such important defensive measures
as are used by other branches of production (specialization of production,
temporary expansion or contraction of output) in order to counter the
effects of a depression. In no other branch of production does the impersonal movement of the business cycle override to the same extent personal
factors, namely, costs of production. For many decades now Central
European agriculture has encountered extremely adverse business conditions . . . . The business cycle, however, is expressed in the futures trade.
Commerce, which cannot avoid business fluctuations at both poles of its
economic activity, in procurement and in distribution, is obliged to respond
by developing a specific new function. The organ which performs this function is the futures trade, and its task is to depict as clearly as possible
world market conditions, rendering them intelligible from an economic
point of view. Purged of all errors and abuses, it would be a perfect mirror
of business conditions. But in that kind of mirror agricultural producers
would see mainly unfavourable market conditions; which explains the natural desire to smash the mirror.' Landesberger, op. cit., pp. 44 *et seq.*
It is well known that when any country prohibits trading in futures, the
ban is circumvented by the merchants with large capital resources, and by
speculators, who resort to futures trading in another country. Thus the
cotton manufacturer, Dr Kuffler, tells us: 'In Bremen, where almost all the
cotton importing business for central Europe is done, there is no trading in
futures, yet each and every deal is based upon futures, that is, in Liverpool
or New York.' (See the conference report of the Association of Austrian
Economists, in *Zeitschrift für Volkswirtschaft, Sozialpolitik und Verwaltung*,
vol. XI, p. 83.) Similarly, the ban on futures trading in grain in Austria has
only led to the transfer of speculation to Budapest.

18 The expert, Mr Simon, is therefore quite right in saying: 'The desire for

marginal gain is the real basis of every business enterprise.' On the other hand, when the president of the Reichsbank, Koch, retorts that mercantile transactions differ from marginal transactions in that their object is to transfer a commodity from one hand to another, the rejoinder is altogether beside the point, and even Simon does not understand it. The only difference between these two types of transaction is that, in the one case, the profit is constituted by the average profit, while in the other, it is a marginal gain in the absolute sense of the term (*Deutsche Börsenenquete*, vol. II, p. 1584).

Bourgeois economics always confuses the social functions of economic actions with the motives of the actors, and ascribes the performance of these functions to the actors' motives even though they are, naturally, unconscious of them. Hence it fails to see the specific problem of economics: namely, to reveal the functional interdependence of economic actions which makes social life possible as the outcome of quite different motives, and then to understand the motivation of the capitalist agents of production in terms of these necessary functions themselves.

19 *Deutsche Börsenenquete*, vol. II, p. 2079.

20 *Deutsche Börsenenquete*, vol. II, p. 2135. In the following pages, similar examples are given for grain and alcohol; in the latter case rectified alcohol cannot be supplied in place of crude alcohol.

21 'Like primitive production and manufacturing industry, commerce and speculation are particular kinds of production. Commerce is that kind of production which has the task of overcoming local scarcity of any of nature's economic goods. Speculation, on the other hand, has the same task with regard to the scarcity of goods in time. From the economic standpoint of private industry, commerce makes use of geographical price differences, speculation of temporal price differences.

'Stock exchange opinion influences prices on the basis of all kinds of reports which stream into the exchange, some true, others false, some regarding what has already happened, others concerned with what will happen. The latter are discounted by stock exchange opinion in advance, according to their importance. If it takes advantage of low prices to build up stocks for the future, and high prices to make possible disposal over present and future stocks, it is operating productively, otherwise not.' R. Ehrenberg, 'Börsenwesen', in *Handwörterbuch der Staatswissenschaften*, 2nd edn.

22 *Deutsche Börsenenquete*, vol. II, pp. 3523 *et seq.*

Chapter 10 Bank capital and bank profit

1 For further details, see *Capital*, vol. III, part IV: 'Conversion of commodity capital and money capital into commercial and financial capital'.

2 *Capital*, vol. III, pp. 371–2.

3 ibid., pp. 379 – 80.

4 The following schematic calculation will serve as an illustration. Let us assume that the production capital is 1,000 and produces a profit of 200. The commercial capital amounts to 400 (a somewhat exaggerated proportion) and the money-handling capital to 100. The profit must be distributed over a total capital of 1,500, so that the average rate of profit is $13\frac{1}{3}$ per cent. The industrialists will therefore receive $133\frac{1}{3}$ from the total of 200, the merchants

$53\frac{1}{3}$, and the money dealers $13\frac{1}{3}$. [Following the indications given by Watnick I have corrected an arithmetical error contained in the original text – Ed.]

5 It is therefore a childish fantasy to expect that an increase in the capital belonging to a bank of issue, for example, the Deutsche Reichsbank, will necessarily result in a reduction of the interest rate.

6 The banking system is 'indeed the form of a universal book-keeping and of a distribution of products on a social scale, but only the form . . . . It places at the disposal of industrial and commercial capitalists all the available or even potential capital of society, so far as it has not been actively invested, so that neither the lender nor the user of such capital is its real owner or producer. This does away with the private character of capital, and implies in itself, to that extent, the abolition of capital . . .

'Finally, there can be no doubt that the credit system will serve as a powerful lever during the transition from the capitalist mode of production to production by means of associated labour; but only as one element in connection with other organic revolutions of the mode of production itself. On the other hand, the illusions concerning the miraculous power of the credit and banking system, as nursed by some socialists, arise from a complete lack of familiarity with the capitalist mode of production, and the credit system as one of its forms. As soon as the means of production have ceased to be converted into capital (which includes also the abolition of private property in land) credit as such has no longer any meaning . . . . But so long as the capitalist mode of production lasts, interest-bearing capital, as one of its forms, also continues and constitutes actually the basis of the credit system.' *Capital*, vol. III, pp. 712–3.

Chapter 11 Surmounting the obstacles to the equalization of rates of profit

1 Hobbes conceives this striving in universal terms: 'The general inclination of all mankind is a perpetual and restless desire of power after power, that ceaseth only in death. And the cause of this is not always that a man hopes for a more intensive delight than he has already attained to; or that he cannot be content with a moderate power; but because he cannot assure the power and the means to live well which he hath at present without the acquisition of more.' *Leviathan*, ch. XI, para 2.

That great portrayer of personified social types, Zola, has shown us, in Gunderman, the quintessence of the capitalist principle: profit for the sake of profit. Gunderman's entire consumption needs have been reduced to milk, but he continues to profiteer unremittingly. Hence his triumph – the triumph of the capitalist principle – over Saccard, whose passion for profit is clouded by elements alien to capital, such as the lust for power, cultural preoccupations, and the desire for luxury. In Gunderman the most senseless type of capitalist, the moneylender and stock exchange speculator, is admirably portrayed; much better than in Ibsen's *John Gabriel Borkman*, where social need is violated by capitalism. For Borkman bases his activities on social needs, rather than on an interest in profit; that is, on a motive alien to the capitalist. The tragic theme of capitalist drama is always this conflict between social interests and profit, which may account for their lack of realism. The personal suffering of the miser may, in some circumstances, convey a tragic impression, but the real capitalist is not a dramatic figure, only an episodic type in a novel.

2 From the motives of active economic subjects, which themselves are determined by the nature of economic relationships, nothing more can be
   inferred than the tendency to equalize economic conditions: equal prices for
   equivalent commodities, equal profit for equal capital, equal wages and an
   equal rate of exploitation for equal work. But one can never get to the
   quantitative relationships themselves in this manner, by starting out from
   subjective motives. In order to discover the quantitative characteristics of the
   individual parts one must first know the size of the aggregate social product,
   in the distribution of which these equalizing tendencies take effect. Determinate quantitative conclusions can never be derived from psychological factors.

3 The extent to which the participation of living labour has been reduced in
   modern rolling mills is illustrated by the following example: 'Lifting gear
   alone reduced the size of crews employed in rail rolling from 15–17 to 4–5
   men. In America, the wage per ton (in cents) fell as follows:

   For rail rollers, from 15 in 1880 to less than 1 in 1901;
   For wire rollers, from 212 in 1880 to less than 12 in 1901;
   For wire billet smelters, from 80 in 1880 to less than 5 in 1901,'

   Hans Gideon Heymann, *Die gemischten Werke im deutschen
   Grosseisengewerbe*, p. 23.

4 Heymann, op. cit., pp. 13 *et seq.*
5 K. Rehe, *Die deutsche Schuhgrossindustrie*, p. 54.
6 Heymann, op. cit., p. 26.
7 The tendency towards the equalization of the rate of profit is important for
   understanding the movement of capitalist production and the mode of
   operation of the law of value as a law of movement. The law of value does
   not control directly each individual act of exchange but only the totality of
   exchanges, of which the individual exchange act is simply a part conditioned by the whole. From another aspect individual inequality of profits
   is important for the distribution of the total profit, for accumulation and
   concentration, and finally for the development of combinations, mergers,
   cartels and trusts.
8 There can be no doubt that the different course of development taken by
   the banking system in England, which gives the banks far less influence over
   industry, is one cause of the greater difficulty of cartelization in England,
   and of the fact that when cartels have been formed, they have in most cases
   involved loose price agreements which achieve extraordinarily high prices
   during periods of prosperity and then collapse in a depression. (For
   numerous examples of such collapse see Henry W. Macrosty, *The Trust
   Movement in British Industry*, pp. 63 *et seq.*) Improvements in the organization of English industry, particularly the growth of combinations in
   recent years, are due to American and German competition. English
   industry has been retarded by its monopoly on the world market; the best
   proof that competition is necessary in the capitalist system.
      The development of English banking also shows another characteristic.
   In Germany and the United States the common interests of industry are
   mainly represented by bank directors, through personal connections,
   whereas in England this is less important, because there the personal
   relations are established among directors of industrial corporations.
9 Thus in mid June 1907 the entire output of the German and English spinning mills for the first quarter of 1908 had already been sold many times
   over. German coal consumers had placed firm orders with the coal syn-

dicate in January 1907 for deliveries until March 1908, that is, 15 months ahead (*Frankfurter Zeitung*, 16 July 1907).

10 *Capital*, vol. III, pp. 228–9. The following passage cited by Marx is also quite *à propos*: 'If each man of a class could never have more than a given share or aliquot part of the gains or possessions of the whole, he would readily combine to raise the gains (he does it as soon as the proportion of demand to supply permits it); this is monopoly. But where each man thinks he may in any way increase the absolute amount of his own share, though by a process which lessens the whole amount, he will often do it; this is competition.' (*An Inquiry into those Principles respecting the Nature of Demand, etc.*, London, 1811, p. 105, Anonymous.) In times of prosperity the 'given share' is fixed, and equals the entire product which a single entrepreneur can produce, but during a depression he must fight for his market.

11 'Experience has shown that even if cartels can be described as "children of necessity", and although in most cases the efforts to unite members of a trade find the most fertile soil in times of declining economic activity or crisis, nevertheless it is easiest to form cartels when business is good, and in a period of prosperity, for the prospect of maintaining favourable prices, linked with strong demand, provides the most powerful incentive to the unification of common interests. On the other hand, the attempt to obtain orders at all costs, even at the lowest price, and to take them away from competitors impedes any concerted action.' (Dr Völcker, in his paper on the Association of German Newsprint Producers, in *Kontradiktorische Verhandlungen über deutsche Kartelle*.) On the history of cartels, see also Heinrich Cunow, 'Die Kartelle in Theorie und Praxis,' *Die Neue Zeit*, XXII, 2, p. 210.

12 Thus Levy observes, after citing the fact that despite the fluctuations of the world market price and the prices of raw materials, the price of steel rails in the United States remained unchanged at \$28 from May 1901 to the summer of 1905: 'It appears that this organization, the pool, has always lost its power during bad times only to regain it during good times.'

'Thus, as soon as prices fell in 1892, the rails pool broke up, as a result of conflicts between its principal constituents, the Carnegie Steel Co. and the Illinois Steel Co. Similarly, the second pool broke up in 1897 after the brief upswing of 1896. A general demoralization of the market followed, which induced producers to take concerted action once again at the end of 1898, and to reconstitute the rails cartel.' Hermann Levy, *Die Stahlindustrie der Vereinigten Staaten*, p. 201.

13 In the Ruhr, opening a new mine takes from 5 to 7 years. In the USA installing a steel works and rolling mill requires 2 years; longer, if it is combined with a blast furnace (Heymann, op. cit. p. 221).

The process described in the text is a phenomenon of competition, which explains why an analysis of it did not come within the scope of the investigation undertaken in *Capital*. Yet Marx did allude in passing to a similar phenomenon in another context: 'It is in the nature of things that vegetable and animal substances which are dependent on certain laws of time for their growth and production cannot be suddenly augmented in the same degree as, for instance, machines and other fixed capital, or coal ore, etc., whose augmentation, assuming the natural requirements to be present, can be accomplished in a very short time in an industrial country. It is therefore possible, and under a developed system of capitalist production even inevitable, that the production and augmentation of that portion of the constant capital which consists of fixed capital, machinery, etc., should run ahead of that portion which consists of organic raw materials, so that the demand for the latter grows more rapidly than their supply, and their price rises in consequence' (*Capital*, vol. III, p. 140). The discrepancy described in this passage is due to the difference in turnover times. In the case of organic raw materials, the causes lie in nature; in the case of inorganic materials, the cause is the size of the capital, particularly the fixed capital.

14 Levy, op. cit., p. 31.
15 ibid., p. 98.
16 ibid., p. 121.
17 ibid., p. 136.
18 Heymann, op. cit., p. 223. In America, it was the demand of the railroads, which itself depended upon the size of harvests, which was the crucial factor in the fortunes of the iron industry during the initial stages of its development. Hence the violent fluctuations and large price variations in the course of the business cycle, and the early drive to form combinations in the United States. Cf. Levy, op. cit., p. 77.
19 *Capital*, vol. I, pp. 381–2.
20 It should be noted here that an association is already monopolistic if it has a decisive influence in determining market prices. The continued existence of some independent firms, which always follow the lead of the combination in fixing their prices, does not alter the fact that free competition in the theoretical economic sense no longer exists in this branch of production. But in order not to offend any pedantic scruples, I refer to such combinations as 'monopolistic' rather than as fully-fledged consortia or mergers. Cf. R. Liefmann, *Kartelle und Truste*, p. 12.
21 ibid., p. 13.
22 Levy, op. cit., pp. 156 *et seq.* Levy then illustrates what he has said with the following figures of pig-iron production. These include, to be sure, the production of poured and puddled iron in which the corporation had an insignificant stake, but as data illustrating the points made above they are striking. Production of pig-iron was as follows:

Year	By the corporation (gross tons)	By independents (gross tons)	%share of the corporation in total production
1902	7,802,812	9,805,514	44.3%
1903	7,123,053	10,693,538	39.9%
1904	7,201,248	9,286,785	43.9%

The corporation's output therefore declined in 1903 compared with the previous year, while that of outsiders increased, so that its share in the total output fell from 44.3 per cent to 39.9 per cent. But in the depression year 1904 the corporation's production still increased somewhat, while the output of the outsiders fell by the enormous amount of 1,400,000 tons; that is, below the 1902 level.

In passing it should be remarked how superficial are the views of those who regard everyone outside a cartel as some kind of moral freak and economic criminal. This is ridiculous even from the standpoint of the profit interests of the cartel, let alone from that of society, because it is just the competition of outsiders which can be extremely valuable for the technical and organizational development of the monopolistic combination, leaving aside the interests of consumers.

23 *Kontradiktorische Verhandlungen über deutsche Kartelle, I, 1903.* Testimony of Kirdorf, p. 80.

24 On the other hand, the possession of patents may make unification more difficult under certain circumstances, if the extra profit achieved thereby is large enough to make the continuance of competition advantageous. 'Each branch of the textile machinery trade contains but a few names. Eight large firms in Lancashire manufacture cotton machinery, and, in addition to monopolizing the home trade, export to the value of about £4,500,000 annually. Repeated suggestions have been made for an amalgamation of their interests but they have always broken down. Mechanical industries lend themselves to inventions which, when patented, produce a monopoly for a term of years and while it lasts a patent is an argument against combination. Unwillingness to sink a world-famous name, especially when it has been gained by the exercise of individual enterprise and ingenuity, in an impersonal amalgamation must be reckoned as a powerful deterrent'. H. Macrosty, op. cit., p. 48.

In this case the small monopoly is the foe of the large one. Yet it is just the desire to pool patents which may provide the incentive to form a consortium. The agreements in the German chemical industry and between the Deutsche Allgemeine Elektrizitätsgesellschaft and the American Westinghouse Co. fall into this category.

Chapter 12 Cartels and trusts

1 It is the type of cartel which Engels had in mind when he wrote: 'The fact that the rapidly and enormously growing productive forces grow beyond the control of the laws of the capitalist mode of exchanging commodities, inside of which they are supposed to move, this fact impresses itself nowadays more and more even on the minds of the capitalists. This is shown especially by two symptoms. First, by the new and general mania for a protective tariff, which differs from the old protectionism, especially by the fact that now the articles which are capable of being exported are the best protected. In the second place, it is shown by the trusts of manufacturers of whole spheres of production for the regulation of production and thus of prices and profits. It goes without saying that these experiments are practicable only so long as the economic weather is relatively favourable. The first storm must upset them, and prove that, although production assuredly needs regulation, it is certainly not the capitalist class which is fitted for that task. Meanwhile the trusts have no other mission but to see to it that the little fish are swallowed by the big fish still more rapidly than before.' *Capital*, vol. III, pp. 142–3, footnote by Engels.

2 'The cartel wants a mass product which no longer shows any appreciable differences of quality, form, material, etc. This can, of course, be promoted by artificial means, as happens on the commodity exchanges, which also presuppose a certain interchangeability of commodities and therefore establish by special prescription what standard a commodity must meet in order to be traded on the exchange. Cartels attain the same end either by selecting certain standard articles upon which the flow of business in a branch of

industry mainly depends, or by setting out specifications to which all manufacturers must conform in producing their goods, so that differences of quality are eliminated. The international plate glass cartel, for example, prescribed for its members plate glass between 10 and 15 millimetres in
thickness.

'The Austro-Hungarian twine cartel; on the other hand, imposed standards
for all types of twine to be produced, and obliged all its members to produce
their goods in conformity with these standards. In the same way, the Austro-
Hungarian jute cartel prescribed specific types of jute bags to be produced.'
J. Grunzel, *Über Kartelle,* pp. 32 *et seq.*

3 That cartels also exert a certain measure of influence on the production and
technology of firms is shown, for example, by the following statement of
Schalterbrand, Chairman of the Board of Directors of the Deutscher
Stahlwerkverband (Association of German Steel Works): 'We must examine
further how we can manage our sales in the future business of the combine
so as to derive the maximum advantage; how to introduce a division of
labour which will enable us to produce more cheaply by relieving each separate enterprise of the necessity of producing all types of output'
(*Kontradiktorische Verhandlungen über deutsche Kartelle,* 10, p. 236). The
Austrian machine tools cartel has also introduced a far-reaching division of
labour among its different enterprises. The profits flow into a common treasury and are then distributed according to a quota system.

4 When, therefore, J. Grunzel (op. cit., p. 14) expresses the view that 'cartels
differ from trusts in kind rather than degree, and I know of no single instance in the course of three decades of vigorous cartel formation in Europe
in which one form of organization developed into the other', he simply
mistakes the legal form of the organization for its essence. The fact that
a transition from cartel to trust is not frequent simply shows that the two
forms have the same content. Nevertheless, we should not overlook the fact
that the increasing limitation of the independence of the cartelized enterprises
brings them steadily closer to the status of the trust. The difference in form
is attributable to wholly different circumstances, above all to the development of the banks and their connections with industry, and in part also, to
various forms of legislative intervention. It is well known, for instance, that
American legislation against cartels has encouraged the trust as a form of
combination.

Chapter 13 The capitalist monopolies and commerce

1 The following information appeared in various newspapers at the beginning
of July 1908: It has recently become known that the Swiss department store
chain of Braun in Zürich has been turned into a limited liability company
with the participation of a German consortium. It is not longer unusual for
department stores to be 'promoted' as public companies today, but there
are special reasons why the promotion of this Swiss firm merits general
attention. The management of the German consortium is in the hands of
the firm of Hecht, Pfeiffer & Co. in Berlin which is considered to be one of
the most important German export firms. It has developed into a purchasing agent for many department stores in various countries. The agreement
with the Braun department store of Switzerland provides that the firm of
Hecht, Pfeiffer & Co. will in future take care of all its purchases and will

also pay for these purchases. The firm maintains a far-flung purchasing organization, and early last year it formed a consortium with M. I. Emden & Sons of Hamburg which is so close knit that Hecht, Pfeiffer & Co. now also makes all the domestic purchases for 200 businesses which are members of the M. I. Emden group. Furthermore, the firm also maintains contacts with a New York department store for which, according to a statement in the *Konfektionär,* it makes purchases in Germany of some 60 million marks annually. The economic advantages of the large department store, not the least important of which is that they can purchase in bulk, has led to the establishment of central purchasing agencies which have made most of the business houses they serve financially dependent on them.

2 See the interesting summary account provided by Algernon Lee, 'Die Vertrustung des Kleinhandels in den Vereinigten Staaten', *Die Neue Zeit,* 27 (2), pp. 654 *et seq.* To safeguard their independence, cigar merchants had organized a trade association called the Independent Cigar Stores Co. As a counter move, the Tobacco Trust founded the United Cigar Stores Co. with a capital of $2,000,000. 'This company bought up many of the existing retail establishments and, in addition, opened many new ones which offered better goods, a wider choice and more attractive store displays, than their competitors. Prices were reduced and finally a system of rebates was introduced which assured the corporation a permanent body of customers. The struggle did not last long. Within a year the Independent Cigar Stores Co. was obliged to sell out to the United Cigar Stores Co., on terms dictated by the latter. By resisting, the small merchants had only hastened their doom . . . . There is not the slightest doubt that the trust will continue in this way, probably even more rapidly, until it has conquered everything worth conquering in the retail trade of this branch of industry.'

Lee then goes on to describe the concentration in the retail trade in coffee, tea, milk, ice, fuel, groceries, etc., and incisively sums up the trend toward concentration as follows: 'Concentration proceeds, and the class of small independent traders loses ground, in the following diverse ways, which all lead to the same result:

1 Some of the industrial trusts, after having attained supremacy in production, extend their operations to retail trade, entirely eliminating the small tradesmen, and selling their products directly to consumers.

2 Some large industrial corporations do indeed still sell their commodities to the consumer through the small trader, but treat him as their agent rather than an independent tradesman.

3 In large cities, department stores have already taken a considerable part of the retail trade away from the small tradesman, and this process is accelerating. Many of these stores have a capital of hundreds of thousands, or even millions, of dollars, in many cases several of them belong to a single company, and a beginning has already been made in applying the principle of concentration on a still larger scale in this field. In this way the department stores are brought into still closer contact with groups involved in high finance, with the wholesale trade, and with the industrial trusts.

4 Those large business houses which concentrate almost exclusively on the mail order business injure the small tradesmen in rural areas just as the chain stores do in the cities. The rapid development of the telephone and tramways in the cities, and the expansion of free postal delivery in the rural districts, have greatly increased the scope of this kind of busi-

ness, and in many cases these mail order concerns belong to the same
company as operates chain stores in the city.
5 Competition among the small tradesmen themselves only strengthens
the trend toward concentration, just as it did in the industrial field at the
beginning of the capitalist era. Many a tradesman finds a way of getting
some advantage over his competitors, and is then able to expand his
business, thus gaining new advantages and restricting still further the
scope of his competitors' business.'
   See also Werner Sombart, *Der moderne Kapitalismus,* vol. II, chapter 22.
3 It is a characteristic of the organization of the Bohemian lignite trade that
the sales agent is both a mine owner and a shareholder in the companies he
represents. Both coal commission firms, J. Petschek and E. J. Weinmann,
have established organizations in Aussig 'which take care of the sale of
lignite for the large Bohemian companies . . . both coal companies were
originally only middlemen. Early in the 1890s a change came about in this
situation, starting with the strong development of the Brüx Mining
Company. The Weinmann firm had for a long time engaged in selling for
this company. The Brüx concern acquired very cheaply the flooded Osseg
seams, and by that means rose to be the leading enterprise in the Bohemian
lignite industry. Meanwhile there was a change in the ownership of the
Brüx shares; a majority of the shares were transferred to a syndicate led by
the Petschek concern, and as an expression of the changed power relations
the coal retailing was transferred to this firm. A new relationship was thus
established; the coal commissioner was also a large shareholder in the enterprise, who concluded sales agreements with himself, as it were, and had
the controlling voice in the conduct of the business and in production. The
competing firm had to follow suit, and it too was able to acquire, through
the ownership of shares, a dominant influence and a permanent interest in
the enterprises which it represented.' *Neue Freie Presse,* 25 February 1906.
4 The *Neue Freie Presse* of 18 June 1905 describes the take-over of one of the
large sugar firms of Prague by the Kreditanstalt as symptomatic, and continues: 'The sugar trade has fallen victim almost completely to these tendencies. As far back as the early 1890s, the marketing of most of the
Bohemian sugar refineries was already in the hands of the wealthy sugar
merchants of Prague, who drew a substantial profit from the sale of sugar
for the producers, carrying on the business to suit themselves. Their large-
scale transactions and their connections with foreign markets constituted a
distinct phenomenon in Prague. The sugar operations of the banks were
limited to commission sales for their own refineries, and to the provision of
credit in the normal course of banking activity. During the last decade
many of these private sugar refineries went out of business entirely, or were
taken over by the banks, while others were forced to curtail their business,
and of all the sugar magnates of Prague, only one large trading house has
survived, which even now represents thirteen sugar refineries and still sells
many hundred thousand metric hundredweights of sugar annually. The very
largest private sugar refineries, which supply both halves of the Empire,
dispense entirely with the services of middlemen in their marketing and take
care of their own wholesaling. The medium size and smaller firms have
entered into a more or less close relationship with the banks, which supply
them with the credit they need, and sell their goods both for export as well
as for the retail trade at home, but also frequently assume the full risk
involved in the sale of sugar. Thus the once large and prosperous

middlemen's trade in sugar has been completely dislodged from its position, and two-thirds of the sales of the Bohemian sugar refineries pass through the sugar departments of the Prague banks (most of which are in any case branches of Viennese banks).

'The starting point for this reorganization of the sugar trade was the provision of credit and the establishment of new sugar refineries. In the 1880s and 1890s numerous new refineries were established in Bohemia and Moravia, sponsored by the large export houses of the Elbe region. Most of them were built with foreign capital, and the banks which supplied the necessary funds stipulated that they retain the commission sales of the output of the new refineries. The small and medium unrefined sugar factories which sprang up like mushrooms after the formation of the cartel were frequently established with insufficient capital and were therefore entirely dependent on their sources of credit. Even the existing establishments required considerable funds to modernize and expand their plants, and entered into a closer relationship with those who could supply the funds, so that ultimately all sales were transferred to the creditors. Thus the Prague branches of the Viennese banks, as well as some of the local banks, gained a firm foothold in the sugar business and transferred the bulk of their activities to that field. The Länderbank represents fifteen refineries . . . . The Anglo-Bank takes cares of the commission sales of eleven unrefined sugar factories. Five large enterprises have their business affairs concentrated in the Kreditanstalt. The Zivnostenska Bank is the selling agent for numerous rural sugar refineries. The banks buy the output of the unrefined sugar producers and transfer it to the refineries, after which they take the white sugar from the refineries and place it on sale in domestic and foreign markets. When in the course of time exports assumed an even greater importance for Austrian factories, the nature of the activities of the banks also changed. Exports required a continuous operation in the various foreign markets, and the modest fees from the commissions become less important as compared with the large profits earned from arbitrage and speculative transactions . . . . But trade on one's own account was closely connected with international business, and very few domestic producers were in a position to undertake such operations, which are often necessarily extended over a long period of time. Thus the last link in the chain of the sugar trade was forged when the banks gained complete control. The factories sold their output to the banks with which they were connected, and they in turn tried to make the maximum profit from it by exploiting any advantage on domestic and foreign markets. Trade on their own account is certainly not yet the general rule, and a few cautious banks refrain from it as a matter of principle, but compared with the commission business it already enjoys considerable importance and it cannot be denied that business development is moving in this direction.

'An even larger commodity business is done by those banks which have close connections with cartels and handle the marketing for the industries which they control. Thus, for instance, the Länderbank controls the sales of the cartels in matches, syrup, enamelware, wrapping paper, and starch, and the output of some chemical industries. The Bankverein is similarly placed with regard to pasteboard mills, and the Kreditanstalt controls sales of the combined brass enterprises. All these are only commission operations, which do not involve any trade in the strict sense of the word, but the middlemen after all, have been ousted from these positions by cartelization and the concentration of sales in central selling agencies. Thanks to competition among the banks, the benefits of the commission business in commodities have decreased and now amount to only a modest proportion of the former substantial commission fees. The decline in the gains from ordinary banking business has given some banks which have commodity branches the idea of developing trading operations on their own account, and there are many indications of new attempts to expand business in this direction.'

5 In specific cases, as a result of the different relations between industrial and commercial capital in particular branches of industry, price changes may occur. Let us assume that in one branch, for example the machine tool industry, productive capital equals 1000 and commercial capital 200. Given an average rate of profit of 20 per cent the commercial profit will be 40. The total price to consumers would be $1,000 + 200$ (the price at which the industrialists supply their product to the merchant) plus 240 (which reproduces the merchant's capital plus profit), that is, a total of 1,440. But suppose that in the textile industry commercial capital of 400 must be added to the productive capital of 1,000. The price of the product would then be 1,680. Now assume that a cartel succeeded in a eliminating commercial capital and reducing commercial expenses by half in both cases. The machine tool manufacturers would then obtain a profit of 340 on a capital of 1,100, while the textile manufacturers would make a profit of 480 on their capital of 1,200. The inequality of rates of profit could lead to equalization processes which would then be reflected in price changes. But what textile consumers gained the buyers of machine tools would lose. In fact, such equalization would be a very difficult and incomplete process because cartelization would interfere with it.

The case is different if independent merchants are replaced by consumer co-operatives, wholesale purchasing societies, agricultural co-operatives, etc.; for this means that organized consumers take over the activities of the merchant capitalists and also receive the commercial profit. Equally, the increased concentration would mean a saving of circulation costs.

6 The wholesale merchant, Engel, says quite correctly: 'The efforts of the syndicate are intended to create a monopoly for itself and to eliminate the wholesale trade entirely. Naturally prices will not be any lower for the retailer. If the motives were not to obtain for the factory and the syndicate the same benefits which accrue to the wholesale merchant, the whole movement would be without purpose.' *Kontradiktorische Verhandlungen über den Verband deutscher Druckpapierfabriken*, part IV, p. 114.

The same is true of the coal syndicate. It 'uses its monopoly of the haulage and wholesaling business to levy a tribute on the small consumers, without any overt increase in coal prices, by raising transportation rates, while ensuring that the higher prices which consumers are obliged to pay benefit the producers rather than as hitherto the merchants', R. Liefmann, *Kartelle und Truste*, p. 98.

7 *Kontradiktorische Verhandlungen*, vol. I, p. 236.

8 ibid., p. 235.

9 ibid., pp. 228 *et seq.*

10 ibid., p. 230.

11 ibid., p. 229.

12 ibid., p. 230.

13 ibid., part II, p. 455.

14 ibid., part II, p. 380.
15 The hypocritical language of the worthy syndicate agent is truly delightful: 'As commercial firms we considered this legitimate, because our main concern is to promote and protect domestic business.' Plundering the domestic market, interfering with the finishing industries by the creation of artificial shortages of coal, coke and iron, maintaining high domestic prices by dumping abroad – this is the patriotism of the profit motive!
16 *Kontradiktorische Verhandlungen,* 6th session, p. 444.
17 ibid., p. 445.
18 ibid., p. 447. On the other hand, the same Gerstein also shows (ibid., p. 556) how strictly the large firms deal with their smaller suppliers: 'A large steel plant which owns mines has printed conditions for the procurement of material for tools, in which it requires tenders from suppliers, and continues: "Quantity: Our requirements for the calendar year 1904 without obligation on our part to take any specific quantity. Delivery at our request."'
19 *Kontradiktorische Verhandlungen über den Verband deutscher Druckpapierfabriken,* IV. Testimony of Reuther, pp. 110 *et seq.*
20 'The syndicate therefore undertook to eliminate the existing wholesale trade in newsprint. After it had succeeded in eliminating a great many agents, who sold other types of paper besides newsprint, there still remained a large number of dealers who handled only newsprint, and the syndicate then decided to refuse to sell its paper to firms which engaged in speculation, and also to prevent the entry of new dealers into the field. It therefore refused in many cases to sell newsprint, even to paper merchants who were already planning to extend their trade to newsprint at the time when the syndicate was being organized' (ibid., p. 111).
21 *Kontradiktorische Verhandlungen,* vol. I, pp. 94 *et seq.* In the autumn of 1899 the German Coke Syndicate obliged its customers to place their orders for the two years 1900–1901; and it should be noted that the syndicate used its power to raise the price, which had been fixed at 14 marks in February 1899, to 17 marks for these two years. The steel mills had to accept these terms, under the threat that otherwise they would not receive their supplies of coke.
    This case is also interesting because it shows how little influence syndicates have upon crises. The agreements were concluded in 1899, about 27 months before the crisis. Business began to decline about mid 1900, and 1901 was a depression year, but the high prices for coke were maintained. As a result the crisis was exceptionally severe for the processing industries. *Kontradiktorische Verhandlungen,* 3rd Session, pp. 638, 655, 664.
22 Industrial Commission, *Preliminary Report on Trusts and Industrial Combinations,* 56th Congress, Senate Document 476, part I, 1901, p. 223.
23 ibid., p. 63. 'I do not care 2 cents' worth for your ethics'. He adds that it is a proper business principle to reduce prices to the point where they destroy competition. For as he puts it later, 'trusts are not in business for their health' (p. 223).
24 Consider the penalties threatened by the *Deutsche Agrarkorrespondenz* (No. 8, 1899) which is close to the Bund der Landwirte (the Farmers' Union): 'The German distiller who refuses to join the association foregoes any claim to professional recognition. These people should be shunned, and if such a fine gentleman were later to be hit in his pocketbook, no better or more merited punishment could be imagined.'

25 *Kontradiktorische Verhandlungen.* Testimony of General Secretary Köpke.
26 *Deutsche Börsenenquete,* vol. I, p. 464. The statement was made by Russel, the lawyer of the Diskontogesellschaft.
27 *Handwörterbuch der Staatswissenschaften,* pp. 181 *et seq.*
28 *Deutsche Börsenenquete,* vol. II, p. 2151. Testimony of von Gülpen. But not only in this case: Mr V. Guaita assures us that 'If they make life miserable for him (the provincial banker) he is obliged to deal in fraudulent paper more than he did previously' (ibid., p. 959).
29 *Deutsche Börsenenquete,* vol. II, p. 2169.

Chapter 14 The capitalist monopolies and the banks. The transformation of capital into finance capital

1 The American Sugar Trust was formed in 1887 by Havemeyer through the amalgamation of fifteen small companies which reported their total capital as being 6.5 million dollars. The share capital of the Trust was fixed at 50 million dollars. The Trust immediately raised the price of refined sugar and reduced the price of unrefined sugar. An investigation conducted in 1888 revealed that the Trust earned about $14 on a ton of refined sugar, which allowed it to pay a dividend of 10 per cent on the share capital, equivalent to approximately 70 per cent on the actual capital paid in when the company was formed. In addition, the Trust was able to pay extra dividends from time to time, and to accumulate enormous reserves. Today the Trust has 90 million dollars of share capital, of which one half comprises preference shares entitled to a 7 per cent cumulative dividend, the other half being ordinary shares which at present also bring in 7 per cent (*Berliner Tageblatt,* 1 July 1909). There are numerous other examples in the Reports of the Industrial Commission on Trusts and Industrial Combinations.
2 We are concerned here with the 'price of capital', which is equivalent to the capitalized profit.
3 In fact 'the usurer was the principal agent for the accumulation of capital since he took a share of the rents of landowners. But industrial and commercial capital more or less joined forces with landowners against this outmoded form of capital.' Marx, *Theories of Surplus Value,* vol. I, p. 19.

Chapter 15 Price determination by the capitalist monopolies and the historical tendency of finance capital

1 At the same time there is a change in the nature of cartel profit. It still consists of unpaid labour, surplus value, but in part of the surplus value which workers employed by other capitalists have produced.
2 I refer here, of course, only to the average organic composition of capital in non-cartelized industries, not to the composition of the total social capital.
3 An interesting form of extra profit for a cartel can be seen in the following instance. Until the 1890s, America was almost the sole supplier of shoe machinery to German industry. The American factories which supplied these machines to Germany organized a combination, the 'Deutsche Vereinigte Schuhmaschinen-Gesellschaft' (DVSG). The machines are not sold, but are leased out at a fixed royalty. A Factory which wants to procure a machine has

to sign a contract for a term of 5 to 20 years. 'The contract requires the supplying firm to install the machine, to repair it without charge, to introduce all the latest improvements and to supply spare parts at reasonable prices. In return, the shoe manufacturer pays a flat rate rent which more or less covers the cost of producing the machine, and in addition a periodic sum for every 1,000 revolutions of the machine . . . . These payments amount to 15–25 pfennigs per pair of shoes, which the manufacturer has to pay to the DVSG, a tribute on a scale which we can only conceive when we learn that in 1907 "three shoe factories in Erfurt employing 885 workers and working mostly with these machines, paid 61,300 marks for their use over a period of one year".' K. Rehe, *Die deutsche Schuhgrossindustrie*, p. 32. The interesting aspect is that the use of these machines gave German manufacturers an extra profit because it gave them an advantage over their competitors. The American trust obliges them to give up a part of this extra profit, but not all of it, since there would then be no reason to use the machinery. The stipulation of an annual rental makes it easier for them to acquire the machines, and increases the manufacturer's dependence upon the trust because he is now tied to this machine. All new imporvements in the machinery are immediately applied, increasing the extra profit and along with it the manufacturer's turnover as well as the payments to the trust which thus acquires a part of someone else's extra profit. The main beneficiary of the improved techniques was the trust. The users of the machines benefited to a much lesser extent, and the consumers least of all.

Chapter 16 The general conditions of crises

1 Aside from its survival in the peasant economy, domestic production still has a role in capitalist society wherever the product of an enterprise itself becomes an element in reproduction (for instance, grain for sowing, coal which is consumed in coal mines, etc.). This type of production for use increases with the growth of combination. It is domestic production because the commodity is not intended for the market, but for use as an element of constant capital in the same enterprise which produced it. Nevertheless, it differs *toto cælo* [as heaven from earth] from the domestic production of previous social formations, directed to the satisfaction of needs, because it serves commodity production, not consumption.

2 'It is a pure tautology to say that crises are caused by the lack of effective consumption or effective consumers. The capitalist system does not know any other modes of consumption but paying ones, except that of the pauper or the thief. If any commodities are unsaleable, it means that no solvent purchasers have been found for them; in other words, consumers (whether commodities are bought in the last instance for productive or individual consumption). But if one were to attempt to clothe this tautology with a semblance of profounder justification by saying that the working class receive too small a portion of their own product, and the evil would be remedied by giving them a larger share of it, or raising their wages, we should reply that crises are precisely always preceded by a period in which wages rise generally and the working class actually get a larger share of the annual product intended for consumption. From the point of view of the advocates of healthy, "simple" (!) common sense, such a period should rather remove a crisis. It seems, then, that capitalist production comprises

certain conditions which are independent of good or bad will and permit
the working class to enjoy that relative prosperity only momentarily, and at
that always as a harbinger of a coming crisis.' *Capital,* vol. II, pp. 475–6.
To which Engels adds this comment: 'Advocates of the theory of
Rodbertus are requested to take note of this.'

3 *Capital,* vol. III, pp. 286–7.
4 'But the problem is to follow the further development of the potential
   crisis – and a real crisis can only be explained by the actual movement of
   capitalist production, competition and credit in so far as it can be derived
   from the functional characteristics of capital, peculiar to capital as such,
   rather than to the forms it takes in commodities and money.' Marx,
   Theories of Surplus Value, chapter xvii, Section 10.
5 M. Tugan-Baranowsky deserves credit for calling attention to the significance of these investigations for the problem of crises in his *Studien zur
   Theorie und Geschichte der Handelskrisen in England.* The curious thing is
   that this needed to be pointed out at all.
6 *Capital,* vol. II, p. 546.
7 For further examples see *Capital,* vol. II, pp. 596 *et seq.*
8 *Capital,* vol. II, pp. 576–7.
9 ibid., pp. 577 – 8.
10 ibid., p. 581.
11 ibid., pp. 581 – 2.
12 ibid., pp. 582 – 3.

Chapter 17 The causes of crises

1 *Capital,* vol. II, p. 211.
2 At first sight a period of prosperity seems to be characterized by general and
   uniform price rises and a period of depression by a similar fall in prices. This
   is the reason why the cause of crises has been sought so long and so per-
   sistently in changes in the value of money. The superstitious faith in the
   quantity theory of money draws its strongest support from this view.
3 'Undoubtedly, the economic development of mining and the iron industry
   has been much too rapid in the Lorraine-Luxembourg area. The effects of
   this were particularly noticeable because the new concerns came into operation at a late stage, and for a long time, during the period of peak prosperity, helped to increase demand. But the new plants went into production
   at the end of 1899 and in the spring of 1900, when the high point of development had already passed, so that they merely increased the supply . . . .
   When they ceased to be consumers, and now appeared on the market with
   their own output, productive capacity increased enormously and overproduction became inevitable.' 'Die Störungen im deutschen Wirtschaftsleben
   während der Jahre 1900 ff.' in *Montan- und Eisenindustrie,* vol. 2, p. 48.
4 *Capital,* vol. III, pp. 139–41.
5 ibid., p. 143.

Chapter 18 Credit conditions in the course of the business cycle

1 I am considering the stock exchange crisis here, of course, only as a factor in
   the general commercial crisis. Stock exchange and speculative crises can also

occur as isolated phenomena, and a stock exchange crisis often emerges during the initial phase of industrial prosperity if speculators exploit the nascent upswing prematurely. This was the case in Vienna in 1895.

2 Thus, during the last American monetary crisis cotton and wheat exports to Europe were vigorously promoted in order to obtain gold in return.

3 This is, of course, an old experience. An anonymous 'Continental Merchant' said as much to the members of the famous Bullion Committee in 1810. 'In fact, I only know of two means to liquidate an unfavourable balance of trade. It is either by bullion or bankruptcy.' Report of Committee on the High Price of Bullion, reprinted in J. R. McCulloch, *Scarce and Valuable Tracts on Paper Currency and Banking*, p. 422.

4 This refers to the time of Peel; today, the volume of notes not backed by gold can amount to some £18,500,000.

5 'The Bank of France often charges a premium when money is withdrawn, and if there is a strong demand from abroad this may amount to 8 per cent or even 10 per cent. Since foreign buyers only want gold, the discounter is obliged to add this premium to the domestic discount rate. In general, one can be sure that the gold premium will be used whenever discount rates abroad are high, and those in Paris significantly lower. It increases the interest on a three-month 5 per cent bill by about 2 per cent a year.' Sartorius, *Das volkswirtschaftliche System . . .*, p. 263.

Chapter 19 Money capital and productive capital during the depression

1 Not only Tugan-Baranowsky, but also Otto Bauer in his otherwise penetrating and suggestive exposition of the Marxist theory of crises (*Die Neue Zeit*, XXIII, pp. 133 *et seq.*) succumbed to this temptation arising out of certain economic phenomena.

2 This was the case, for instance, in the depression period after 1890. The entire year 1893 was marked by an unusually plentiful supply of money and low interest rates. The London bank rate was 2 per cent at the end of February 1894, while the private discount rate stood at 1 per cent in mid March. In mid January 1895 the private discount rate in London was between $\frac{1}{2}$ and $\frac{7}{8}$ per cent. Yet in spite of the prolonged and extreme liquidity, the recovery began only in the second half of 1895.

3 Recently, as theoretical analysis has fallen into neglect, a bad habit has spread which consists in drawing general conclusions from a small number of observations over a period of a few years, and elevating the experience of a partial phase of the industrial cycle, or at best the experience of a particular, unique cycle, to the level of general 'laws'. For that reason, others abjure all generalizations and console themselves with the folk wisdom of *qui vivra verra*. They deliberately reduce political economy to the level of a cheap joke.

4 An extreme instance of this confusion is to be found in Tugan-Baranowsky's theory of crises. By taking account only of the formal economic categories of capitalist production, it overlooks the natural conditions of production which are common to all systems of production, whatever their historical form, and thus arrives at the curious conception of a system of production which exists only for the sake of production, while consumption is simply a tedious irrelevance. If this is 'madness' there is method in it, and a Marxist one at that, for it is just this analysis of the specific historical structure of

capitalist production which is distinctively Marxist. It is Marxism gone mad, but still Marxism, and this is what makes the theory so peculiar and yet so suggestive. Without being quite aware of it, Tugan seems to sense this. Hence his vigorous polemic against the 'sound common sense' of his critics.

5 And not only in recent times. 'The superficiality of political economy is shown among other things by the fact that it regards the expansion and contraction of credit, which is a mere symptom of the periodic changes in the industrial cycle, as their cause.' *Capital,* vol. I, p. 695.

6 The following example shows that high interest rates do not produce a crisis. England had an adverse balance of payments in 1864. Cotton imports from America had fallen off in consequence of the Civil War, and imports of cotton from the East Indies and Egypt increased, thus raising total imports from these countries; for the East Indies from £15,000,000 in 1860 to £52,000,000 in 1864, and for Egypt from £10,000,000 to nearly £20,000,000. The bank raised its discount rate to check the outflow of bullion. During 1864 it fluctuated between 6 per cent and 9 per cent. Yet the crisis was confined entirely to the money market. 'The increases in commodity prices were insignificant and in spite of the high discount rates, which were to be met with only during periods of money shortage in the past, commerce and industry did not experience any marked disturbances . . . . Notwithstanding a continuous cotton shortage, English trade was certainly not depressed.' Tugan-Baranowsky, op. cit., p. 139.

Chapter 20 Changes in the character of crises. Cartels and crises

1 Incidentally, this is an error which Tugan-Baranowsky does not seem always to have avoided in the conclusions which he draws from his excellent and reliable account of the history of crises in England.

2 'The crisis of 1857, and still more that of 1873, involved an unusually large number of enterprises (in the iron industry) which did not differ greatly in their productivity. The general collapse therefore included many firms which, from a technological point of view, were quite viable and deserved to survive. In the crisis of 1900 the giant enterprises of basic industry were operating alongside many firms which would be considered antiquated today, the non-integrated firms which had risen to the top on the wave of prosperity. The fall in prices and the shrinkage of demand were calamitous for these non-integrated firms, whereas the giant combines were either not affected at all, or only for a short time. That is why the recent crisis resulted in a greater degree of concentration than previous crises, for example the crisis of 1873 which, although it eliminated some firms, did not give the survivors a monopoly in the prevailing state of technology. Today, however, thanks to a complex technology, elaborate organization and large capital resources, a very high degree of monopoly is enjoyed by the giant concerns in the modern iron and electrical industries, and to a lesser extent in the machine tool industry, as well as in some engineering, transport and other firms. If this does not apply to some "light" industries, and the effects of crises have not essentially changed for them, it is all the more easy to see how the recent development of the banking system affects the first category of industry.' O. Jeidels, *Die Verhältnisse der deutschen Grossbanken zur Industrie,* p. 108.

3 This condition alone is sufficient, regardless of any other fundamental causes that might bring about the crisis. In an account of the Amsterdam stock

exchange crash of 1773, the following description of the results of one big failure occurs: 'No one knew what the loss would amount to, nor how many other firms it would ruin. The general uncertainty drove away credit, and suddenly it was impossible to obtain cash. Some feared that their bills would not be accepted; others were concerned that they would be unable to recover the sums which their debtors owed them; still others tried to take advantage of the general distress. Everyone was on the lookout for a chance to buy at the lowest prices, but feared to pay out any cash, and circulation almost came to a standstill.' *Der Reichtum von Holland,* pp. 444 *et seq.,* cited by Sartorius von Waltershausen in *Das volkswirtschaftliche System der Kapitalanlage im Ausland,* p. 377.

Compare with this the following description of the condition of the German stock exchanges on the outbreak of war in 1870: 'On 4 July 1870 the mood of the Berlin stock exchange was excellent. It began to waver in the next few days, became very uneasy on 8 July, and on 11 July lost its head. The panic lasted 8 to 10 days and then, with the return of confidence, the downward trend came to an end . . . . Money had vanished from the stock exchange as if by a magic wand. The discount of the Bank of Prussia rose to 9 per cent and the rate for collateral loans rose to 10 per cent in Leipzig, 9 per cent in Lubeck and 8 per cent in Bremen. What had happened to the money which could easily be had a few days previously for 3 per cent and 3.5 per cent? The government could not possibly have absorbed the money for mobilization purposes, because at that time the note issuing banks in Germany were decentralized and much of the money was in the hands of banks which did not issue notes, or of private bankers. Most of the money stayed where it was, but was hoarded, and anyone who succeeded in getting any money added it to his hoard. Thus, for example, it was reported from Munich: "For a time, it was impossible to obtain 500 florins for the best paper and collateral. On the other hand, even private individuals felt obliged to create a cash reserve for themselves, whatever the sacrifice, in order to be prepared for the worst." In Frankfurt "the bankers had only one thought, to get back their loans, in view of the public clamour for the return of deposits. The rapid increase of clearing credits in the banks shows that both bankers and the public tried to assure themselves of a large supply of cash in preparation for any eventuality."

'The following is reported from Hanover concerning the premium on cash: "Every banker, and above all the Hanover Bank, thought only of himself . . . treasury certificates and the notes of the private banks in Prussia were proscribed, and the solid citizen who had done any business with money bills or Prussian bonds had to accept a loss of 5 per cent, while the peasant whose fear made him ready to sell at any price was forced to accept a loss of 10 per cent or even more."'

And just as this situation shows in embryo all the typical features of the recent American monetary crisis, so also were the remedies the same. 'During the money shortage in the second half of July, various measures were taken to secure relief. In Bremen, the Senate and the City Council decided to recognize certain foreign gold coins as legal tender, but this was of little help because this money, like the city's own currency, was retained in private hoards. In Stuttgart, a clearing company was founded which issued six-month 3 per cent notes in denominations of 50 to 500 florins. Similar bonds were issued by the Hypotheken- und Wechselbank in Munich, and in Frankfurt leading banking houses offered the local bank of issue a collective guarantee. Precious metals were imported from abroad as quickly as possible. By the end of July, the banking and import houses of Bremen had acquired considerable sums in sovereigns. Frankfurt obtained gold from England and silver from Vienna. These measures proved to be reasonably effective in countering the shortage of money as a means of payment, but could not bring enough capital on to the loan market to satisfy government requirements.' Sartorius von Waltershausen, op. cit., pp. 323 *et seq.*

4 To that extent, the following comment by Marx needs to be qualified in respect of present-day conditions: 'Under the modern credit system, it [merchant capital] disposes of a large portion of the total capital of society, so that it can repeat its purchases even before it has definitely sold its previous purchases . . . aside from the separation of C–M from M–C, which follows from the nature of the commodities, a fictitious demand is here created . . . . Hence, we note the phenomenon that crises do not show themselves nor break out first in the retail business, which deals with direct consumption, but in the spheres of wholesale business and banking by which the money capital of society is placed at the disposal of the wholesale business.' *Capital,* vol. III, pp. 358–9.

5 It makes no difference in this respect if a trust company is interposed between the bank and the enterprise, since it remains directly dependent upon the bank.

6 This is illustrated by the behaviour of the Steel Trust. It reduced its production to a minimum in 1907–1908 in order to maintain prices. A year later the iron market collapsed, dragging with it all the other metal markets.

Chapter 21 The reorientation of commercial policy

1 Since the essence of political economy is the discovery of economic laws, the struggle against mercantilist economic policy became one of the most powerful driving forces in the development of economic theory. The other stimulus, antedating it, and of greater fundamental importance, was the attempt to solve the key problem of economic legislation at the beginning of modern capitalism, that of establishing a sound monetary system. By raising the problem of money Petty became the founder of classical political economy, because this question leads directly to the problem of value, and hence to the basic law of political economy.

2 'Dutch supremacy in trade and seafaring reached its peak during the period from the founding of the East India Company to the wars against Cromwell and Charles II (1600–75). At the end of this period, Colbert estimated the entire merchant marine of the European states at 20,000 seagoing vessels, of which 16,000 belonged to Holland alone, thus earning for the Dutch the title of the freight carriers of Europe. They created an enormous colonial empire in Asia, in South and North America, and in Africa; a large insurance business grew up; the leading stock exchange was that in Amsterdam, which was virtually the world market for money, and its low interest rates always stood industry and commerce in good stead. No other nation could rival the Dutch in herring fishing and whaling. Holland's commercial policy was the most liberal of that period. There were no competitors whom the Dutch had any reason to fear.' Sartorius, *Das volkswirtschaftliche System,* p. 369.

3 The amount of the pensions alone which stream into England each year from India is currently estimated at 320,000,000 marks. These are supplem-

ented by the enormous contributions for the salaries of English officials, for
the maintenance of the army, and for the conduct of some of England's
colonial wars in Asia.

4 'Despite Cobden, England did not give up her colonies. The leading liberal
statesman of the day, Lord John Russell, probably expressed the sentiment
of his party when he declared that the time had not yet come to give them
up. In the meantime, England would have to do everything in its power to
educate the colonies for self-government. In fact, under the influence of the
Manchester School, England had rejected its previous point of view that
colonies were useful possessions. Sir Robert Peel had declared that "in every
one of our colonies, we have a second Ireland". England now began to build
up a voluntary relationship with its colonies, endowing them with parliamentary institutions. The adherents of the Manchester School thus
became – quite unwittingly – the founders of a new British Empire which
could not have been held together by redcoats.' Schultze-Gävernitz, *Der
Britischer Imperialismus*, p. 75.

5 See Rudolf Hilferding, 'Der Funktionswandel des Schutzzolles', in *Die Neue
Zeit*, XXI, 2 (1902/3); and Robert Liefmann, *Schutzzölle und Kartelle*. A
wealth of illustrative material is to be found in Hermann Levy, 'Einfluss der
Zollpolitik auf die wirtschaftliche Entwicklung der Vereinigten Staaten',
Conrads Jahrbücher, XXXII (1909) and 'Entwicklungsgeschichte einer amer-
ikanischen Industrie', *Conrads Jahrbücher*, XXIX (1905).

6 That a similar development, for which the founding of the Crédit Mobilier
paved the way, proved abortive in France can be explained by the same
causes which frustrated the industrial expansion of France in general. These
included a distribution of land unfavourable to capitalist development, its
consequences in the two-child family, and hence the absence of a sufficiently
large industrial reserve army, an excessively protective tariff policy, and the
excessive export of capital itself, caused by the existence of a rentier class
based upon the petty bourgeoisie, the small peasants, and the luxury
industries.

The testimony given by Alexander at the Stock Exchange inquiry,
(*Deutsche Börsenenquete*, Part I, p. 449) throws light on the relation between
the nationalization of capital and the reinforcement of the banks' influence
on industry as a result of the fact that German industrialists lack capital
resources of their own. According to him a large number of coal mines such
as Herne, Bochum, etc., were owned until recently (1892) by French and
Belgian shareholders. At the same time a process of concentration was taking place. The banking institutions acted as middlemen in purchasing the
shares because the companies themselves did not have the necessary liquid
resources. The banks could only undertake these transactions because they
were certain that they would soon be able to dispose of these securities, in
which they had tied up their funds, through futures operations.

It may be assumed, moreover, that the weakening of the stock exchanges
through legal restrictions, especially those which limit trading in futures,
tends to increase the influence of the banks over industry, because industry
then becomes more dependent upon the services of the banks than would be
the case if there were a vigorous stock exchange. And in fact the consequences of German stock exchange legislation were very advantageous to
the banks.

7 Naturally, manufacturers are well aware that free trade tends to impede the
formation of cartels. An English manufacturer, writing in *The Times* of 10

October 1906 proposed the formation of a cartel of English electrical manufacturers. The writer admitted that 'in a free trade country, high prices or underproduction would merely throw the trade into the hands of foreign rivals'. Another manufacturer answered, 'If we had protection in this country, it is possible that we might do something in the way suggested in this letter, but we have found from experience that it is absolutely impossible to attempt any combination, as things are, to keep prices up on the lines suggested by your correspondent. We are all suffering at present from overproduction, and until this is rectified, either by manufacturers restricting their output or going out of trade altogether, we shall continue to suffer.' H. J. Macrosty, *The Trust Movement in British Industry*, p. 319. Macrosty himself writes: 'The weakness of every form of combination in the United Kingdom is due to the free admission of foreign competition. If that can be removed their strength is enormously increased and all the conditions of the problem are altered' (op. cit., p. 342).

8 The extent to which this has served as an incentive to cartelization is shown by the great shock which the German and Austrian sugar cartels sustained when the sugar duty was reduced to 6 francs, as required by the Brussels Convention. The Austrian duty of 22 kroner, for example, gave the refineries united in the cartel an extra profit which was so high that it far outweighed any advantages which the largest and most technically advanced firms might have gained from competing with and eliminating the smaller firms and it was the main inducement to forming a cartel. At the same time it was much easier to accept the allocation of production quotas, even though they imposed heavier burdens on the largest and technically most advanced firms, because the level of the tariff and the resulting increase in domestic prices more than compensated for the disadvantages. This example shows that it is not just the tariff itself, but its level, which is significant for cartelization.

Chapter 22 The export of capital and the struggle for economic territory

1 See Otto Bauer, *Die Nationalitätenfrage und die Sozialdemokratie*, pp. 178 *et seq.*

2 The following example is characteristic and gives a picture both of an international cartel and of the effect of the export of capital. 'A very important branch of industry, long established in Great Britain, and especially in Scotland, is the sewing thread industry. The four largest firms dominating the industry – Coats & Co., Clark & Co., Brook Bros, and Chadwick Bros – combined into one enterprise in 1906 under the well known name of J. & P. Coats Ltd, which also includes many smaller English factories and some fifteen American companies. This so-called 'Thread Combine', with a capital of £5,500,000, constitutes one of the largest industrial combines in the world. Even before the combine was formed the protectionist policy of the United States prompted the firms of Coats and Clark to establish their own factories in the United States in order to bypass the high tariff rates directed against their products. The new combine continued this practice, and also acquired a large number of shares in other companies in this industry in North America and other countries (involving a considerable emigration of capital) which gave it control of these firms. Thus English industrialists produce abroad, and the cost, in the form of loss of employment, is borne by English workers and in the last resort by the whole na-

tion. The Thread Trust has every reason to continue this policy, for it can be said without fear of contradiction that its profit of £2,580,000 in the year 1903 – 4 came largely from the factories established abroad. However, it is only a matter of time before foreign industry will be strong enough to throw off the yoke of "English control" and reduce its tribute of interest.' M. Schwab, *Chamberlains Handelspolitik*, p. 42.

3 Thus, for example, a part of Hungarian ground rent flows into Austria as interest payments on the mortgage bonds of Hungarian mortgage companies circulating in Austria.

4 The very apt expression used by Parvus, *Die Handelskrisen und die Gewerkschaften.*

5 See the examples given in Parvus, *Die Kolonialpolitik und der Zusammenbruch*, pp. 63 *et seq.*

6 Consider, for example, the shameful enthusiasm shown by the land of poets and thinkers for a person such as Carl Peters. [1856–1918. An explorer who helped to establish the German East African protectorate of Tanganyika and was deprived of office in 1897 for his ill-treatment of Africans. Ed.] This relationship was already evident to the British free traders who emphasized it to good effect as a means of agitation against colonialism. Thus Cobden declared: 'Is it possible that we can play the part of despot and butcher there (in India) without finding our character deteriorate at home?' Cited by Schultze-Gävernitz, *Britischer Imperialismus*, n. 104.

7 On this subject, see the discussion of the immigration problem in *Die Neue Zeit* (1907–8), XXVI, 1, especially Otto Bauer, 'Proletarische Wanderungen', and Max Schippel, 'Die fremden Arbeitskräfte und die Gesetzgebung der verschiedenen Länder'.

8 On this subject see, for example, the data provided in Paul Mombert, *Studien zur Bevölkerungsbewegung in Deutschland.* Thus in Europe the average annual number of live births per 1,000 inhabitants was:

1841–50	37.8	1881–85	38.4
1851–60	37.8	1886–90	37.8
1861–70	38.6	1891–95	37.2
1871–75	39.1	1896–1900	36.9
1876–80	38.7	1901–	36.5

The decline in the birthrate is also very noticeable in the United States, and in Australia it is remarkable. In New South Wales, for example, the number of children born per 1,000 married women between the ages of 15 to 45 was 340.8 in 1861 and 235.3 in 1901. See also the data in Schultze-Gävernitz, op. cit., p. 195. He quotes the following cry of distress by the government statistician Coghlen: 'The problem of the falling birth rate is of paramount importance, and more so for Australia than for any other country. It depends upon the satisfactory solution of this problem whether our country will ever have a place among the great nations of the world.'

Population growth in the above-mentioned regions can be attributed entirely to the substantial decline in the mortality rate, which has fallen more sharply than the birthrate. This has also been the case in Germany. 'If the decline in the latter (the birthrate) continues a point must be reached, in the nature of things, when the decline in the morality rate will be slower, so that the relationship between the two will be reversed. The surplus of births would then necessarily tend to decline.' Mombert, op. cit., p. 263. This is already happening, for instance, in England and Wales, in Scotland, and in Sweden.

Mombert's conclusion is very relevant to the present stage of capitalist expansion: 'Perhaps in the not too distant future the crux of the population problem in other nations as well as France will be seen as consisting in an excessively low, rather than excessively high, rate of population growth' (op. cit., p. 280).

9 British capital investments abroad were estimated in 1900 at £2,500 million, growing annually at the rate of £50 million of which £30 million is in securities. Apparently its capital investments abroad increase more rapidly than those at home; at all events, the total income of Britain between 1865 and 1898 only doubled, while its income from abroad increased ninefold in the same period according to Giffen. Detailed figures are given in a lecture by George Paish published in the *Journal of the Royal Statistical Society*, September 1909, which shows that the income from Indian government loans in 1906–7 amounted to £8,768,237; from the rest of the colonies, £13,952,722; and from all other countries, £8,338,124, making a total of £31,059,083 as compared with £25,374,192 in 1897–8. Income from other securities (railways!) is estimated at £48,521,000. The amount of capital invested abroad is estimated at £2,700 million of which £1,700 million are invested in railways. The income from this capital is put at £140 million, which is equivalent to interest at 5.2 per cent. These estimates are probably lower than the actual figures.

French capital invested abroad was estimated by P. Leroy-Beaulieu at 34,000 million francs. By 1905 it had apparently increased to 40,000 million francs. New annual investment is estimated at 1,500 million francs.

German holdings abroad were estimated by Schmoller in his well-known report to the *Börsenenquete-Kommission* at 10,000 million marks, and by W. Christians at 13,000 million marks, yielding an annual return of between 500 and 600 million marks. Sartorius estimates that in 1906 the amount was 16,000 million marks in securities and 10,000 million marks in other foreign holdings, yielding an annual return of about 1,240 million marks. For further details see Sartorius, op. cit., pp. 88 *et seq.*

10 Even where European capital is invested in the form of American shares, it often obtains no more than interest, because the entrepreneurial profit is included beforehand in the promoter's profit going to American banks.

11 'In the last twenty years imports of wheat and other grains from foreign countries rose by £4,000,000 or 9 per cent; those from British possessions on the other hand by £9,250,000 or 84 per cent. Meat imports from foreign countries showed an increase of £16,500,000, or 79 per cent and from British possessions, £8,000,000, or 230 per cent. The increase in butter and cheese imports from foreign countries was £9,500,000, or 60 per cent, while the same imports from British possessions rose by 630 per cent.

'Imports of all types of cereals from British possessions rose from £7,722,000 in 1895 to £20,345,000 in 1905, an increase of £12,623,000 or 163 per cent. During the same period, imports from foreign countries rose only from £45,359,000 to £49,684,000, an increase of £4,325,000, or 9.5 per cent. In 1895, foreign countries provided 85.4 per cent of the cereal requirements of the United Kingdom, the colonies 14.6 per cent. In 1905 foreign countries supplied 71 per cent, the British colonies 29 per cent.' W. A. S.

Hewins, 'Das britische Reich', in *Die Weltwirtschaft*, edited by Ernst von
Halle, vol. I., 1906, part II, p. 7.
12 According to the figures of the Chamberlain Tariff Commission (cited by
Schultze-Gävernitz, op. cit., p. 216) the *per capita* value of imports from
Great Britain by the following countries was:

Germany, Holland and Belgium	£0.	11.	8
France	0.	9.	0
United States	0.	6.	3
Natal	8.	6.	0
Cape Colony	6.	19.	6
Australia	5.	5.	6
New Zealand	7.	5.	7
Canada	1.	18.	4

In 1901, the British colonies imported:

From the mother country	£123,500,000
other British colonies	68,000,000
foreign countries	90,000,000

Exports of the United Kingdom (in £ millions) were:

	1866	1872	1882	1902
To British possessions	53.7	60.6	84.3	109.0
Europe	63.8	108.0	85.3	96.5
non-British Asia, Africa and South America	42.9	47.0	40.3	54.1
United States	28.5	40.7	31.0	23.8

13 That is why this point of view is always emphasized in Chamberlain's agitation. 'It seems to me that the tendency of the time is to throw all power
into the hands of the great empires. The smaller nations – those which do
not progress – seem destined to fall into a subordinate place. But if Greater
Britain remains united no empire in the world can ever surpass it in area, in
population, in wealth, and in the diversity of its resources.' Speech by
Chamberlain, 31 March 1897, cited in Marie Schwab, *Chamberlains
Handelspolitik*, p. 6.
14 Professor Hewins summarizes the general capitalist interest in tariff reform
and imperialism, including that of the finishing industries (set skilfully in
the foreground) which were until recently, or still are, in favour of free
trade. 'The United Kingdom today imports its means of sustenance from
certain countries with which it has not concluded any reciprocity treaties.
Hence it must rely on the complicated mechanism of international trade to
pay for its means of sustenance and is forced constantly to search for new
markets all over the world for its manufactured goods and to liquidate its
debts through multilateral arrangements among the various countries.
Apparently this commercial policy cannot go on indefinitely for the following reasons:
  1 The number of countries thus importing from Britain is constantly
declining. In the markets of the Far East, for example, we will doubtless
encounter the irresistible competition of Japan in the very near future.
  2 The necessity of constantly searching for markets for our products

outside countries like Germany and the United States, omitting for a moment the role of the colonies, has a harmful effect on the course of economic development in England. The natural course has been for English industries to advance steadily, employing more skilled labour and increasing their technical efficiency. Actually, however, the course of development may depart considerably from this pattern. The civilized and advancing markets are closing. Forced to trade with the backward parts of the world, English industry is therefore compelled to produce such goods as will meet their needs.

   3   Two divergent tendencies are thus brought into direct conflict. It is in the field of these great staples that the more recent industrial countries are also making considerable progress. Germany, Belgium, the United States, and even Japan can compete with us in these lines and establish themselves in these countries. But on the other hand, there is also a tendency in English industry to turn increasingly to specialties rather than to staples and hence to produce the more expensive articles. And thus it happens that Great Britain is fighting a rearguard action in those very areas on which it has always been depending most for paying for its means of sustenance. These, however, are the considerations which give the movement throughout the empire to organize British industrial life on a wider basis its significance.' Hewins [in Halle], op. cit., p. 37

15 The importance to England of colonial railway construction, for example, is indicated by the following details:

   'In 1880 the British Empire had 40,000 miles of railway, of which three-eighths were in the United Kingdom and five-eighths in overseas possessions and colonies. By 1904 the rail network had increased to 95,000 miles, of which only two-ninths were within the United Kingdom. In other words, the increase in mileage amounted to 26 per cent at home and 223 per cent overseas. Naturally, the rapid development of colonies is based upon the rapid penetration of areas which previously had no railways or at best very primitive ones. Since 1880 railway mileage has trebled in India and Canada, quadrupled in Australia and quintupled in South Africa.

   'Outside the United Kingdom, the greatest density of railways in relation to population is to be found in the Australian Commonwealth where there are 3.86 miles of railway per 1,000 inhabitants, as against 3.76 in Canada and 0.19 in India.

   'It is worth nothing that the UK railway network, though large in itself, is small compared with that of the USA where, according to Poor's Railroad Manual 1904, 212,349 miles were in operation, or more than double the mileage in the whole British Empire, despite the fact that the population of the latter is five times as large. The railways of the empire may therefore be expected to develop and increase in mileage almost without limit.

   'Almost all the capital for the construction of these railways was raised in the United Kingdom. The sums invested in British railways outside the UK are estimated at about £850 million, the annual income at £75 million gross and about £30 million net. Bearing in mind the figures for the UK itself, I estimate the total capital invested in the railways of the British Empire at £2,100 million, appreciably closer to the corresponding figure for the US (£2,800 million) than the mileage length. The net income of the railways amounts to about £70/75 million a year, or a return of 3 per cent on invested capital.' Hewins, op. cit., p. 34.

16 Herr Dernberg therefore understood very well the mentality of the capi-

talists when he emphasized time and again in his propaganda speeches the possibility that German colonies would free German capitalists from their dependence upon America for cotton and copper. [Dernberg was the governor of German South West Africa in the decade before the First World War. Ed.]

17 See the penetrating analysis of the consequences of this phenomenon for Russia in Kautsky, 'Der amerikanische Arbeiter', *Die Neue Zeit* (1905–6), XXIV, pp. 676 *et seq.*

18 The same is true of Russia, except that the size of her territory makes it easier to assimilate this capital, and the process is already under way to some extent. The most radical means for attaining this end is the bankruptcy of the state.

19 Conversely, when negotiating about loans, small states find it difficult to impose any conditions concerning the delivery of industrial products, partly because their own industries are less efficient. 'The Dutch banks have rightly been accused of providing foreign countries with capital without imposing any conditions at all . . . . The stock exchange provided foreign countries, most recently South America (in 1905) with large amounts of capital, without exacting any terms favourable to Dutch industries, as frequently happens in Belgium, Germany and England.' G. Hesselink, 'Holland', in Halle's *Weltwirtschaft*, part III, p. 118.

20 On the advantages enjoyed by a larger economic territory in this respect, see Richard Schüller, *Schutzzoll und Freihandel*, p. 247. 'The foreign trade of a relatively small territory is large in relation to its total production and hence important to it, whereas for the large foreign nations from which it imports goods and to which it wishes to export, this trade is of minor importance in relation to their total output. A small state, therefore, seldom succeeds in protecting its interests in trade agreements, or in persuading the other states to adapt their trade policies to its needs.'

21 See Karl Emil, 'Der deutsche Imperialismus und die innere Politik', in *Die Neue Zeit*, XXVI, 1 (1907/8). [As noted in the introduction, 'Karl Emil' was one of the pseudonyms Hilferding used in his earlier writings. Ed.]

22 An example of such a development is afforded by the preliminary outcome of the conflict over Morocco in which the combine formed by Krupp and Schneider-Creuzot for the joint exploitation of Moroccan and Algerian ores resulted in an agreement between the two states (France and Germany). Morocco will not find it as easy to resist their pressure as it did when it could play one country off against the other.

23 Consider, for example, how important it was for Germany, in concluding recent international trade agreements, that Russia's political power was so weakened as a result of entanglements in the Far East that she could not exert any political pressure.

24 See Otto Bauer, *Die Nationalitätenfrage und die Sozialdemokratie* pp. 491 *et seq.* 'Imperialism and the Principle of Nationality'.

Chapter 23 Finance capital and classes

1 Wheat exports from the United States constituted 33 per cent of total wheat production in 1901, 29 per cent in 1902, 19.5 per cent in 1903, and 10.5 per cent in 1904. See I. M. Rubinow, *Russia's Wheat Trade*.

   A report of the Department of Commerce and Labor in Washington (cited

by M. Schwab, *Chamberlains Handelspolitik*, p. 73) states: 'The fall in
exports of bread grains, foodstuffs and cotton which has taken place in recent years, and especially in the last year, 1903–4, cannot be ascribed either
to poor harvests at home or to low prices abroad. Last year the output of
corn, wheat and cotton was not below average, and in fact, in most instances, exceptionally high. The main reason for the steady decline in the
proportion of farm products in total exports is obviously the increasing
demand in the United States. The quantity of wheat retained in the country
for internal consumption up to 1880 never reached 275 million bushels, but
in 1883 it exceeded the 300 million mark and continued to increase steadily
with the growth of population. It was more than 400 million bushels in 1889,
500 million bushels in 1902, and in the fiscal year ending 30 June 1904 it
reached 517 million bushels. This is the largest figure to date.'

'Between 1880 and 1900, the population of the United States increased
from 50 million to 76 million, or 52 per cent, whereas the wheat acreage of
the republic only increased from 34 million to 42 million, or 23.5 per cent.
The entire cereal growing area increased only from 136 to 158 million acres,
or 16.5 per cent' (ibid., p. 72).

2 For Prussia, see K. Kühnert, 'Das Kapitalvermögen der selbständigen
Landwirte in Preussen', in *Zeitschrift des königlich-preussischen statistischen
Landesamtes,* vol. 48, 1908. This is based on Prussian statistics showing the
assessment of income tax and supplementary taxes for 1902 in respect of
landowners paying a minimum of 60 marks in land tax, thus covering the
really independent farmers. 'Actual capital wealth' does not refer here to
landed property, working capital for agriculture and forestry, or fixed and
circulating capital in plants and mines, but to capital claims of every kind,
such as shares, savings deposits, mining stocks, etc. Thus what is meant is
capital wealth exclusive of fixed and circulating capital used in manufacture
or agriculture. It appears that the owners of land paying at least 60 marks in
land tax, who numbered 720,067, had an aggregate capital wealth of
7,920,781,703 marks, of which 3,997.549,251 marks (50.5 per cent) belonged
to the 628,876 owners who derived most of their income from agriculture or
forestry – that is, those whose main occupation is independent
farming – while 3,923,232,452 marks (49.5 per cent) belonged to the 91,191
owners for whom agriculture and forestry provide only a supplementary
income, and constitute a secondary occupation.

Of the total gross wealth of the 720,067 independent Prussian farmers,
amounting to 39,955,313,135 marks, 74.1 per cent consisted of landed property, 19.8 per cent of capital wealth, 5.9 per cent of fixed and circulating
capital, and 0.2 per cent of exclusive rights and privileges; more specifically,
in the case of the 28,541,502,216 marks owned by the 628,876 farmers whose
main source of income was agriculture the percentages were: 84.9, 14.0, 1.0,
0.1, while for the 91,191 for whom agriculture is a secondary calling, with a
total wealth of 11,413,811,919 marks, the figures were: 47.1, 34.4, 18.3 and
0.3.

3 Just how well aware the large industrialists are of this fact is shown by the
position taken by Freiherr von Reiswitz, the general secretary of the
Hamburg-Altona Employers' Association and the chief advocate of the principle of mixed employers' associations. He cites as advantages of mixed
associations that, in the first place, 'they are extremely educational' for employers because there is almost always a strike in one of the participating
branches so that the association, 'finds itself, so to speak, in a constant state

of war', while on the other hand – and this is the main thing – they make
possible a united approach by big business, small firms, and craftsmen.
Freiherr von Reiswitz sets great store by this collaboration among all sections of industry, for political reasons. The craftsman is the best fighter in
the guerrilla war against Social Democracy, and hence big business has a
major interest in keeping him going economically. See Reiswitz, *Gründet
Arbeitgeberverbände*, pp. 22 *et seq.*, cited by Gerhard Kessler, 'Die deutschen
Arbeitgeberverbände', in *Schriften des Vereins für Sozialpolitik*, vol. 124
(1907), pp. 106 *et seq.*

4 Kessler, op. cit., p. 15.
5 According to a report in the *Berliner Tageblatt*, 14 June 1909, on the conference of the German Bank Employees Association, Fürstenberg (Berlin)
the chairman of the executive committee declared: 'The movement of concentration in banking has fortunately come to an end. Even so, at present 90
per cent of all bank employees in Germany have no prospect of ever becoming independent.'
6 The formation of the Whiskey Trust made 300, the Steel Trust 200 commercial travellers redundant. See J. W. Jenks, *The Trust Problem*, p. 24.

Chapter 24 The conflict over the labour contract

1 This is not the place for a more detailed examination of the immigration
problem, and it is in any case unnecessary in view of the thorough treatment in the issue of *Die Neue Zeit* referred to earlier. [See ch. 22, note 7.
Ed.]
2 Consequently, in countries where the development of trade unions comes
relatively late and faces highly developed large-scale industry from the
outset, they are as a rule weaker than in a country such as England, for
example, where they developed in step with the growth of industry.
3 See Gerhard Kessler, 'Die deutschen Arbeitgeberverbände', in *Schriften des
Vereins für Sozialpolitik*, vol. 124 (1907), p. 40.
4 ibid., p. 37.
5 ibid., p. 20. 'As long as the workers in a firm remain an unorganized mass,
even an individual employer has the upper hand. He does not need an
employers' association . . . . As long, therefore, as the German trade union
movement was fighting desperately to survive, roughly up to the 1880s . . .
there was no need for employers' associations in Germany. But since the
end of the 1880s, and especially since the repeal of the anti-socialist laws,
when a great upsurge of the trade union movement began, accompanied by
wave after wave of wage demands and strikes, employers began to combine
in employers' associations in their own branches of industry – a natural
reaction to the activities of the trade unions. The trade union always appears first, followed by the employers' association. By its very nature, the
trade union is always the aggressor and the employers' association the
defender (and the fact that occasionally the roles are reversed does not
affect the general truth of this proposition). In its youth, the trade union is
mainly a strike organization and the employers' association an anti-strike
organization. The sooner a strong trade union appears in an industry, the
sooner too will a full-blown employers' association be formed. In short, an
employers' association is an organization of the employers of an industry
for the purpose of regulating their relations with organized labour.'

6 See the following comments on the situation in the United States:
'Employers' associations in the United States are probably stronger and
more militant than those in other countries. Almost every industry has its
central, state and local associations, not to mention the combinations of
these associations. The two most important are the National Association of
Manufacturers and the Citizens' Industrial Association of America. The
former consists almost exclusively of manufacturers and was formed in
1895 primarily in order to expand foreign markets for American products.
In the last five years it has taken an active part in the fight against labour
organizations and has sought to influence public opinion and federal
legislation in favour of employers. In 1905 it prevented the passage of two important bills introduced in Congress at the request of labour
federations. One sought to introduce an 8-hour day for all work carried out
by or for the federal government, while the other sought to restrict the
power of the courts to grant injunctions in labour disputes.

The Citizens' Industrial Association has a different character in that it is
a federation of all local, state and national employers' and civic associations in the United States. It was organized in 1903 on the initiative of
the National Association of Manufacturers for the purpose of uniting all
individuals and associations into a fighting organization to combat the
demands of trade unions, especially the demand for the 'closed shop' (that
is, the employment of union members only in an enterprise). It has grown
rapidly, and has several hundred thousand members in its national, regional
and local associations. It combats all intervention in business affairs whether by the government or by the trade unions. At its third annual conference in St Louis in November 1905 it adopted resolutions on the establishment of vocational schools and certificates of proficiency (under the
jurisdiction of associations) so as to provide employers with workers without regard to union membership.

Aside from the National Association of Manufacturers, two of the most
important organizations connected with this Citizens' Industrial Association
are the National Metal Trades Association and the National Foundries
Association. When they were first organized five years ago they concluded
agreements with the machine and foundry workers' unions. But these have
since been cancelled, and in 1905 the Foundries Association began a struggle with the powerful foundry workers' union which has since spread to all
the plants in the United States. [Halle], *Weltwirtschaft*, vol. III, p. 62.

7 This is not altered by the fact that, for a time, when the development of an
employers' organization and of its mode of operation is still in its early
stages, the shift in timing is not fully apparent. The statistics of lockouts, as
given by Kessler (op. cit., p. 259) show, first, that the number of lockouts is
growing rapidly, and second, that their number is greater during a boom
than during a depression. This can be explained simply by the fact that
those lockouts which serve as counter-measures against strikes would naturally increase most rapidly during periods of boom, when strikes also
occur most frequently. But this does not in any way refute the view that, as
employers' associations grow, conflicts are more frequently postponed by
employers to periods of depression and aggressive lockouts increase in
number. Kessler remarks on this point (p. 243): 'Aside from sympathetic
lockouts, programmatic lockouts have become frequent, particularly in
recent times. The author uses this term to denote all layoffs of workers

which take place without a preceding strike, in order to impose upon
workers a programme specifying wage rates, hours of work, job assignments,
and any other general or specific conditions of employment . . .

'It is quite likely that programmatic lockouts will become more important in the near future, since after the failure of negotiations for the renewal
of a wage agreement, the employers' association is often more interested in
the conclusion of a new wage agreement as quickly as possible than is the
union, even if it has to be imposed through a conflict. Programmatic lockouts sometimes resemble aggressive strikes, and at other times defensive
strikes, but more frequently the latter, which is more in accord with the
character of employers' associations. Very seldom does an employers' association attempt directly to worsen the conditions for employment by means
of a lockout, and this will continue to be so in the future. What happens
more frequently is that workers are locked out in order to obtain a renewal
of the wage agreement for some years ahead, without any improvements,
and to ward off wage increases' (p. 243).

After evaluating the available statistics, Kessler reaches the conclusion
that 'almost all the larger lockouts ended in complete or partial success for
the employers . . . . Generally speaking, the lockout is a weapon against
which workers have no defence. This is reason enough for trade union
leaders to restrain any strike fever among the rank and file as much as
possible, and to deal quickly with unofficial walkouts. It is also a reason
for employers not to be unreasonably alarmed by the growth of labour
organizations. In any case, the high costs and losses entitled by every lockout, even when the employers win, will certainly prevent this extreme
weapon from being used too frequently or in clearly unjustified cases.
Neither group will lose its head and go to extremes' (p. 263).

8 'While in America it has become a specialized business to hire out gangs of
professional strike-breakers, resembling the *condottieri,* who can be put at
the disposal of this or that employer when he needs them, for a fee, in our
own giant factories permanent squads of strike-breakers are maintained
under the guise of welfare institutions. Thus these institutions are not a way
of promoting social peace, but a weapon which makes for social conflict
and strengthens the hand of one of the parties to that conflict.' Lujo Bren-
tano in *Verhandlungen des Vereins für Sozialpolitik,* vol. 115 (1905), p. 142.

9 On the other hand, the conclusion of industry-wide agreements strengthens
the unions, and many workers who previously remained aloof now flock to
them. This increases the resistance of the employers. Thus the most powerful German manufacturers' organization, the Zentralverband Deutscher
Industrieller, passed the following resolution in May 1905: 'The Central
Association of German Industrialists considers the conclusion of industry-
wide agreements between employers' organizations and labour organizations extremely dangerous for German industry and its future progress.
Such agreements deprive the individual employer of that freedom to control
his own workers which is essential to the proper conduct of his enterprise,
just as they inevitably subject the individual worker to the rule of the labour organization. In the view of the Central Association, which is fully
confirmed by the experience of England and America, industry-wide agreements are a serious obstacle to the technological and organizational progress of German industry.' Cited by Adolf Braun, *Die Tarifverträge und die
deutschen Gewerkschaften,* pp. 47–8.

10 See also the speech by State Councillor Leidig, in *Verhandlungen des Vereins für Sozialpolitik,* 1905, vol. 115 p. 156, and that by Dr Harms, p. 201.

11 Adolf Braun has shown that trade alliances should also be rejected from the general standpoint of the working class: '[It] should be pointed out that employers are beginning to expect far-reaching results from industry-wide agreements, including the elimination of all forms of inconvenient competition, the guarantee of higher prices, and the exploitation of the consuming public. The same employers who not so long ago, and still to some extent today, were outraged by work stoppages, the restriction of immigrant labour, and the general influence exerted by trade unions on the labour market, are now considering whether it might not be a good idea, when negotiating a wage agreement, to ask trade unions to agree to clauses guaranteeing the maintenance of fixed minimum prices for the commodities produced. Besides the wage scales governing the payment of workers, there would be a schedule of prices to be charged to consumers. Trade unions bound by such a wage agreement would then be required to stop all work, as well as the supply of labour, in all cases where an employer sold his commodities at lower prices than those established by the general price schedules of the employers' associations. The trade unions would thus be forced not only to promote the rise in price of the necessities of life, and to give public support to it, but they would also become the conscious agents of the employers' interests and would be held responsible by public opinion for the rise in the cost of living. There are of course exceptional cases in which the objectives of a trade union cannot be attained in any other way, where the concessions in questions do not affect mass consumption, and where they might therefore appear justifiable. But as a rule, making such concessions in order to obtain an industry-wide agreement seems to be incompatible with the principles of the labour movement and with the objectives of trade unions.' Adolf Braun, op. cit., p. 5.

12 It is throwing the baby out with the bath water when Naumann says: 'The sphere in which strikes can be brought to an end in the normal way (through a wage agreement) is practically coterminous with medium-size enterprise. Of course, some attempts have been made to extend wage agreements beyond that point. Nevertheless, this is a distinctive sphere in which workers can be recommended to strike, in accordance with the old liberal recipe, in order to get a wage agreement, whereas beyond this sphere there is another where a wage agreement cannot be achieved by a strike alone, for the simple reason that the elementary question "Which of us can hold out longest?" can be answered from the outset by any thinking person. If we should ever experience another miners' strike . . . both participants and outsiders know in advance that the workers could not win the kind of victory they used to achieve in the old peace negotiations, and that such strikes belong to a new species of demonstrative strikes. For even if we were to assume that one of these strikes were actually won – an entirely hypothetical assumption – the large industrial combinations have ample resources to arm themselves against the recurrence of such an event. Not long ago one of our younger bankers made the following simple calculation for me: "How much interest shall we lose if we keep a constant reserve for x or y months which will protect us completely against a possible defeat in a strike (meaning a strike in the old sense) during that period?" What follows from this? Simply that if the worker wants to improve his con-

dition he will have to regard the strike simply as a means of appealing to the rest of the population.' F. Naumann, in *Verhandlungen des Vereins für Sozialpolitik*, vol. 115 (1905), p. 187.

Chapter 25 The proletariat and imperialism

1 'The modern system of protective tariffs – and this is its historical significance – ushers in the final phase of capitalism. In order to check the fall in the rate of profit which is the law of motion of capitalism, capital eliminates free competition, organizes itself, and, thanks to this organization, is able to seize state power in order to use it directly in promoting its exploitative interests. It is no longer the workers alone, but the entire population, who are subordinated to the desire for profit of the capitalist class. All the instruments of power available to society are consciously mobilized and converted into means by which capital can exploit society. It is the immediate precursor of socialist society because it is the complete negation of that society; a conscious socialization of all the economic potentialities of modern society, in a form which does not benefit society as a whole, but is intended to increase the rate of exploitation of the entire society to an unprecedented degree. But it is just the clarity and self-evidence of this situation which makes its continuance impossible. It arouses the proletariat to action against the activities of the capitalist class, which has concentrated its thought and action along with the concentration of the means of production, a proletariat which need only become conscious of its power to make it irresistible.' Rudolf Hilferding, 'Der Funktionswechsel des Schutzzolles', *Die Neue Zeit*, XXI, 2 (1902–3).
2 See Karl Kautsky, *The Road to Power*, especially the concluding chapter, 'A New Age of Revolutions'.

Bibliography

I The principal writings of Rudolf Hilferding

1 Books and monographs

Böhm-Bawerks Marx-Kritik, Vienna, Wiener Volksbuchhandlung, 1904
(*Marx-Studien,* vol. I). An English translation by Eden and Cedar
Paul was first published about 1920 and is reprinted in the volume
edited and introduced by Paul Sweezy, which includes both Böhm-
Bawerk's monograph and Hilferding's criticism: New York,
Augustus M. Kelley, 1949.

*Das Finanzkapital. Eine Studie über die jüngste Entwicklung des
Kapitalismus,* Vienna, Wiener Volksbuchhandlung, 1910 (*Marx-
Studien,* vol. III). The most recent German edition is that of 1968,
with an introduction by Eduard März. Frankfurt: Europäische
Verlagsanstalt. The book has been translated into several languages,
including French, Italian and Russian.

Das historische Problem. This unfinished study, on which Hilferding
was working in the last few years of his life, was first published,
edited and introduced by Benedikt Kautsky, in *Zeitschrift für Politik*
(New Series), vol. I, 1954.

2 Articles

'Der Funktionswechsel des Schutzzolles. Tendenz der modernen
Handelspolitik', *Die Neue Zeit,* XXI, 2, 1902–3.
'Zur Frage des Generalstreiks', *Die Neue Zeit,* XXII, 1, 1903–4.
'Parlamentarismus and Massenstreik', *Die Neue Zeit,* XXIII, 2,
1904–5.
'Historische Notwendigkeit und notwendige Politik', *Der Kampf,* VIII,
1915.
'Arbeitsgemeinschaft der Klassen?', *Der Kampf* VIII, 1915.
'Probleme der Zeit', *Die Gesellschaft,* I, 1, 1924.
'Realistischer Pazifismus', *Die Gesellschaft,* I, 2, 1924.
'Zwischen den Entscheidungen', *Die Gesellschaft,* X, 1933.

'Revolutionärer Sozialismus', *Zeitschrift für Sozialismus*, I, 1933–4.
'Macht ohne Diplomatie – Diplomatie ohne Macht', *Zeitschrift für Sozialismus*, II, 1934–5.
'State Capitalism or Totalitarian State Economy', *Socialist Courier*, New York, 1940. Reprinted in *Modern Review*, I, 1947.

3   Published speeches

'Zur Sozialisierungsfrage', 10th Congress of the German trade unions, Nuremberg, 30 June – 5 July 1919. Berlin, 1919.
'Revolutionäre Politik oder Machtillusionen?', speech against Zinoviev at the annual conference of the USPD in Halle, 1920. Berlin, 1920.
'Die Sozialisierung und die Machtverhältnisse der Klassen', 1st Congress of Works Councils, 5 October 1920. Berlin, 1920.
'Die Aufgaben der Sozialdemokratie in der Republik', Annual conference of the SPD in Kiel, 1927. Berlin, 1927.
'Gesellschaftsmacht oder Privatmacht über die Wirtschaft'. 4th AfA (Allgemeiner freier Angestelltenbund) trade union congress in Leipzig, 1931. Berlin, 1931.

II   Works on Hilferding

Gottschalch, Wilfried, *Strukturveränderungen der Gesellschaft und politisches Handeln in der Lehre von Rudolf Hilferding*, Berlin, Duncker & Humblot, 1962.
Kersten, Kurt, 'Das Ende Breitscheids und Hilferdings', *Deutsche Rundschau*, 84, September 1958, pp. 843–54.
Kurata, Minoru, 'Rudolf Hilferding: Wiener Zeit. Eine Biographie (I)', *The Economic Review*, XXVI, 2, October 1975, Hokkaido, Japan.
Stein, Alexander, *Rudolf Hilferding und die deutsche Arbeiterbewegung. Gedenkblätter*, Hamburg, Hamburger Buchdruckerei and Verlagsanstalt, 1946.
In addition, the following works contain important references to aspects of Hilferding's life and thought:
Braunthal, Julius, *In Search of the Millennium*. London: Victor Gollancz, 1945. On pp. 241–5 Braunthal reports a conversation with Hilferding on the failure of the German revolution in 1918–19.
Edinger, Lewis J., *German Exile Politics: The Social Democratic Executive Committee in the Nazi Era*, Berkeley and Los Angeles, University of California Press, 1956. Chapter 6 gives an account of the increasing pessimism of Hilferding and other SPD leaders in exile, and of the reasons for it.
Eyck, Erich, *Geschichte der Weimarer Republick*. 2 vols. Erlenbach-Zürich und Stuttgart: Eugen Rentsch Verlag, 1956. In the second volume, pp. 255 *et seq.* and pp. 287 *et seq.* the author examines

Hilferding's projects and problems during his two terms of office as finance minister.

Wheeler, Robert F. *USPD und Internationale: Sozialistischer Internationalismus in der Zeit der Revolution.* Frankfurt/Main: Ullstein Verlag, 1975. This is based upon an unpublished Ph.D. thesis, 'The Independent Social Democratic Party and the Internationals: an examination of socialist internationalism in Germany, 1915 to 1923', University of Pittsburgh, 1970 (on microfilm, University Microfilms, Ann Arbor, Michigan, 1972). Contains numerous references to Hilferding, and discusses particularly his role in opposing the affiliation of the USPD to the Third International.

III   Other works mentioned in the introduction and in the text

Adler, Max, *Kausalität und Teleologie im Streite um die Wissenschaft.* Vienna: Wiener Volksbuchhandlung, 1904 (*Marx-Studien,* vol. I).

Aristophanes, *The Frogs,* English trans. by David Barrett, Harmondsworth, Penguin, 1964.

Arnold, A., *Das indische Geldwesen unter besonderer Berücksichtigung seiner Reformen seit 1893,* Jena, G. Fischer, 1906.

Baran, Paul A., and Sweezy, Paul M., *Monopoly Capital,* New York, Monthly Review Press, 1966.

Barratt Brown, Michael, *After Imperialism,* 2nd edn, London: Merlin Press, 1970.

Bauer, Otto, *Die Nationalitätenfrage und die Sozialdemokratie,* Vienna, Wiener Volksbuchhandlung, 1907 (*Marx-Studien,* vol. II). Second enlarged edition with a new preface, 1924.

Bauer, Otto, 'Der Faschismus', in *Der Sozialistische Kampf* (Paris), 16 July 1938, pp. 75–83. Reprinted in *Die Zukunft* (Vienna), February 1948, pp. 33–41. English trans. of the major part in Bottomore and Goode, *Austro-Marxism,* pp. 167–86.

Bernstein, Eduard, *Die Voraussetzungen des Sozialismus und die Aufgaben der Sozialdemokratie,* 1899, English trans. under the title *Evolutionary Socialism,* New York, Huebsch, 1909.

Blake, William, *Observations on the Principles which regulate the course of Exchange and on the present depreciated State of the currency,* London, Edmund Lloyd, 1810.

Böhm-Bawerk, Eugen von, *Zum Abschluss des Marxschen Systems.* 1896. English trans. in Paul Sweezy (ed.), see section I.

Bothe, M., *Die indische Währungsreform,* Stuttgart, J. G. Cotta, 1904.

Bottomore, Tom, and Goode, Patrick (eds), *Austro-Marxism,* Oxford University Press, 1978.

Bracher, Karl Dietrich, Sauer, Wolfgang, and Schulz, Gerhard *Die nationalsozialistische Machtergreifung,* Köln und Opladen, Westdeutscher Verlag, 1960.

Braun, Adolf, *Die Tarifverträge und die deutschen Gewerkschaften*, Stuttgart, J. H. W. Dietz, 1908.

Braunthal, Julius, *History of the International*, vol. II, 1914 – 1943. London, Thomas Nelson & Sons, 1967.

Bukharin, Nikolai, *Imperialism and World Economy* (1918), London, Merlin Press, 1972.

Bukharin, Nikolai, *The Economic Theory of the Leisure Class* (1919), London, Martin Lawrence, 1927.

Bukharin, Nikolai, *The Economics of the Transformation Period* (1920), New York, Bergman, 1971.

Carsten, F. L., *Revolution in Central Europe, 1918–1919*, London, Temple Smith, 1972.

Cohen, Stephen, *Bukharin and the Bolshevik Revolution: A Political Biography, 1888–1938*, London, Wildwood House, 1974.

Diehl, Karl, *Sozialwissenschaftliche Erläuterungen zu Ricardos Grundgesetzen der Volkswirtschaft*, 2nd edn, vol. II, Leipzig, W. Engelmann, 1905.

Edinger, Lewis J., 'German Social Democracy and Hitler's "National Revolution" of 1933: A Study in Democratic Leadership', *World Politics*, April 1953, pp. 330–67.

Fullarton, J., *On the Regulation of Currencies*, 2nd edn, London, John Murray, 1845,

Gay, Peter, *The Dilemma of Democratic Socialism: Eduard Bernstein's Challenge to Marx*, New York, Columbia University Press, 1952.

Goode, Patrick, *Karl Korsch: A Study in Western Marxism*, London, Macmillan, 1979.

Greene, Thomas L., *Corporation Finance*, New York, G. P. Putnam's Sons, 1897, 3rd edn, 1901.

Grunzel, Joseph, *Über Kartelle*, Leipzig, Duncker & Humblot, 1902.

Halle, Ernst von (ed.), *Die Weltwirtschaft*, Yearbook published from 1906. Leipzig und Berlin, B. G. Teubner.

Heimann, Eduard, *History of Economic Doctrines*, New York, Oxford University Press, 1945.

Helfferich, K., *Money* (1903), English trans. by L. Infield, 2 vols, London, Ernest Benn, 1927.

Heymann, Hans Gideon, *Die gemischten Werke im deutschen Grosseisengewerbe*, Stuttgart und Berlin, J. G. Cotta, 1904.

Hobbes, Thomas, *Leviathan*, London, Andrew Crooke, 1651.

Jaffé, E., *Das englische Bankwesen*, Leipzig, Duncker & Humblot, 1905.

Jeidels, Otto, *Die Verhältnisse der deutschen Grossbanken zur Industrie*, Leipzig, Duncker & Humblot, 1905.

Jenks, J. W., *The Trust Problem*, New York, McClure, Phillips, 1901.

Kautsky, Karl, *Der Weg zur Macht* (1909), English trans. by A. M. Simons, *The Road to Power*, Chicago, S. A. Block, 1909.

Knapp, G. F., *Staatliche Theorie des Geldes* (1905), abridged English trans. by H. M. Lucas and J. Bonar, *The State Theory of Money*, London, Macmillan, 1924.

Kontradiktorische Verhandlungen über deutsche Kartelle, Berlin,
   Franz Siemenroth, 1903.
Lenin, V. I., *Imperialism, the Highest Stage of Capitalism* (1916),
   English trans. Moscow, Foreign Languages Publishing House, 1947.
Levy, Hermann, *Die Stahlindustrie der Vereinigten Staaten von Amerika
   in ihren heutigen Produktions- und Absatz-Verhältnissen,* Berlin, J.
   Springer, 1905.
Levy, Hermann, 'Entwicklungsgeschichte einer amerikanischen
   Industrie', *Conrads Jahrbücher für Nationalökonomie und Statistik,*
   XXIX, 1905, pp. 145–81.
Levy, Hermann, 'Einfluss der Zollpolitik auf die wirtschaftliche
   Entwicklung der Vereinigten Staaten', *Conrads Jahrbücher für
   Nationalökonomie und Statistik,* XXXII, 1909, pp. 607–56.
Liefmann, Robert, *Schutzzoll und Kartelle,* Jena, G. Fischer, 1903.
Liefmann, Robert, *Kartelle und Truste,* Stuttgart, E. H. Moritz, 1905.
Loeb, E., 'Das Institut des Aufsichtsrates', *Jahrbuch für
   Nationalökonomie und Statistik,* XXIII, 1902.
Luxemburg, Rosa, *The Accumulation of Capital,* trans. Agnes
   Schwartzschild, London, Routledge & Kegan Paul, 1951.
Lürmann, Fritz W., *Die Fortschritte im Hochofenbetrieb seit 50 Jahren,*
   Düsseldorf, Gedruckt bei August Bagel, 1902.
Macaulay, Lord, *History of England,* London, Longman, 1849–61.
McCulloch, J. R., *A Select Collection of Scarce and Valuable Tracts and
   other publications on Paper Currency and Banking,* London, privately
   printed, 1857.
Macrosty, Henry W., *The Trust Movement in British Industry: A Study
   of Business Organization,* London, Longmans, 1907.
Mandel, Ernest, *Marxist Economic Theory,* 2 vols, London, Merlin
   Press, 1968.
Marx, Karl, *A Contribution to the Critique of Political Economy* (1859).
   Various English translations.
Marx, Karl, *Capital,* vol. I (1867), II (1885), III (1894). Various
   English translations. References in the text are to the English trans-
   lation of *Capital,* 3 vols, Chicago, Charles H. Kerr, 1915.
Marx, Karl, *Theories of Surplus Value,* 3 vols (1905–10). Various
   English translations.
März, Eduard, See under I, *Das Finanzkapital.*
Mead, Edward S., *Trust Finance,* New York, D. Appleton, 1903.
Meyer, Rudolf H. (ed.), *Briefe und sozialpolitische Aufsätze von
   Dr Rodbertus-Jagetzow,* 2 vols, Berlin, A. Klein, 1882.
Michel, Bernard, *Banques et banquiers en Autriche au début du XXe
   siècle,* Paris, Presses de la Fondation nationale des sciences poli-
   tiques, 1976.
Mombert, Paul, *Studien zur Bevölkerungsbewegung in Deutschland in
   den letzten Jahrzehnten,* Karlsruhe, G. Braun, 1907.
Mommsen, Wolfgang, *The Age of Bureaucracy: Perspectives on the
   Political Sociology of Max Weber,* Oxford, Basil Blackwell, 1974.

Nicholls, Anthony and Matthias, Erich (eds), *German Democracy and the Triumph of Hitler*, London, Allen & Unwin, 1971.

Ossowski, Stanislaw, *Class Structure in the Social Consciousness*, London, Routledge & Kegan Paul, 1963.

Parvus (Alexander Helphand), *Die Handelskrisen und die Gewerkschaften*, Munich, Druck von M. Ernst, 1901.

Parvus (Alexander Helphand), *Die Kolonialpolitik und der Zusammenbruch*, Leipzig, Leipziger Buchdruckerei, 1907.

Philippovich, E. von, *Grundriss der politischen Ökonomie*, Tübingen, J. C. B. Mohr, 1909.

Prager, Eugen, *Geschichte der Unabhängigen Sozialdemokratischen Partei Deutschlands*, Berlin, Verlagsgenossenschaft 'Freiheit', 1922.

Prion, Willi, *Das deutsche Wechseldiskontgeschäft*, Leipzig, Duncker & Humblot, 1907.

Rehe, Karl, *Die deutsche Schuhgrossindustrie*, Jena, G. Fischer, 1908.

Renner, Karl, *The Institutions of Private Law and their Social Functions* (1904, revised edn 1929), London, Routledge & Kegan Paul, 1949.

Renner, Karl, *Wandlungen der modernen Gesellschaft. Zwei Abhandlungen über die Probleme der Nachkriegszeit*, Vienna, Wiener Volksbuchhandlung, 1953.

Renner, Karl, 'Probleme des Marxismus', *Der Kampt*, IX, 1916. Excerpts trans. in Bottomore and Goode, *Austro-Marxism*.

Ricardo, David, *Principles of Political Economy and Taxation*, London, J. Murray, 1817.

Ricardo, David, *The High Price of Bullion*, London, J. Murray, 1810.

Ricardo, David, *Proposals for an Economical and Secure Currency*, London, J. Murray, 1816.

(The preceding two pamphlets were reprinted in *The Works of David Ricardo*, edited by J. R. McCulloch, London: J. Murray, 1846; to which Hilferding refers.)

Riesser, Jacob, *Zur Entwicklungsgeschichte der deutschen Grossbanken*, Jena, G. Fischer, 1905.

Riesser, Jacob, *Die deutschen Grossbanken und ihre Konzentration*, 4th revised and enlarged edn, Jena, G. Fischer, 1912.

Rubinow, I. M., *Russia's Wheat Trade*, Washington, DC, Government Printing Office, 1908.

Sartorius von Waltershausen, A., *Das volkswirtschaftliche System der Kapitalanlage im Ausland*, Berlin, G. Reimer, 1907.

Schmoller, G., *Grundriss der allgemeinen Volkswirtschaftslehre*, Leipzig, Duncker & Humblot, 1904.

Schüller, Richard, *Schutzzoll und Freihandel*, Vienna, F. Tempsky, 1905.

Schultze-Gävernitz, G. von, *Britischer Imperialismus und englischer Freihandel zu Beginn des zwanzigsten Jahrhunderts*, Leipzig, Duncker & Humblot, 1906.

Schumpeter, J. A., *Das Wesen und der Hauptinhalt der theoretischen Nationalökonomie*, Leipzig, Duncker & Humblot, 1908.

Schumpeter, J.A., *Capitalism, Socialism and Democracy* (1942), 5th enlarged edn with a new Introduction, London, Allen & Unwin, 1976.

Schumpeter, J. A., *History of Economic Analysis* (1954), London, Allen & Unwin, 1972.

Schumpeter, J. A., 'Zur Soziologie der Imperialismen' (1919), English trans. in *Imperialism and Social Classes*, edited with an introduction by Paul M. Sweezy, New York. Augustus M. Kelley, 1951.

Schwab, Marie, *Chamberlains Handelspolitik*, Jena, G. Fischer, 1905.

Simmel, Georg, *The Philosophy of Money* (1900), London, Routledge & Kegan Paul, 1978.

Smith, Adam, *An Inquiry into the Nature and Causes of the Wealth of Nations*, London, 1776.

Sombart, Werner, *Der moderne Kapitalismus*, Leipzig, Duncker & Humblot, 1902.

Steinitzer, Erwin, *Ökonomische Theorie der Aktiengesellschaft*, Leipzig, Duncker & Humblot, 1908.

Sweezy, Paul M., *The Theory of Capitalist Development*, New York, Oxford University Press, 1942.

Tooke, Thomas, *A History of Prices and of the State of the Circulation*, 6 vols, London, Longman, 1857.

Tugan-Baranowsky, M. I., *Studien zur Theorie und Geschichte der Handelskrisen in England* (1894), Jena, G. Fischer, 1901.

Wilson, J., *Capital, Currency and Banking*, London, The Office of the Economist, 1847.

Zola, Émile, *L'Argent*, Paris, 1871.

Index

absolutist state, 339, 370
accumulation, 364; capital wealth,
  326, 330; process, 282–4
Adler, Max, member Austrian Social
  Democratic Party (SPÖ), 375n65;
  ed. *Der Klassenkampf*, 375n65;
  and *Marx-Studien*, 2; study of
  causality in social sciences, 23 and fn
advertising, 190, 213
Africa, forcible expropriation of
  Negroes, 319
agricultural products, advantages of
  cartelization, 164; exchange
  trading, 152; foreign imports,
  428n4; nationalization, 315; prices,
  164, 321; supply and demand, 153;
  techno/scientific revolution, 338
agriculture: capital investment, 342;
  cartel profit and 338; competition
  from America, 340; co-operatives,
  164, 417n24; English, maintenance
  of famine prices, 302; population
  shortages, 321; tariffs, 309, 340,
  342, 365; variation in output, 166
America (US); agriculture, 432nl;
  balance of trade, 280; banking
  system, 277, 278, 291, 293, 307,
  408n8; capitalism, 6, 92, 304, 320,
  399n18; cartels, 412n4; colonial
  possessions, 331; in competition
  with England, 323; economic
  growth, 328–9; employers'
  associations, 434n6;
  and export of capital, 326, 331;
  geographically determined
  expansion, 327; immigration, 320;
  industrial organization, 312, 324,
  326, 341; iron and steel industry,
  194, 288, 289, 423n; labour

organizations, 434n6; monetary
  and currency systems, 46, 49,
  53–4, 85; monetary crises, 275,
  288, 423n; Monroe Doctrine, 327;
  population, 427n8, 432nl;
  protectionism, 304, 426n2;
  railroads, 119, 397n14, 410n8,
  430n15; Steel Trust, 396–7n13,
  400–1n4; Stock Exchange, 117,
  403n20; Sugar Trust, 418n1; tariff
  policies, 304; Tobacco Trust, 209,
  413n2
arbitrage transactions, 96, 146, 162
Argentina, agricultural prices, 321
Aristophanes; bad money drives out
  good, 381n30
armaments, 325, 330, 365, 366
armed forces, annexation of neutral
  foreign markets, 328; and state
  power, 333, 342
Arnold, A., and fluctuating return on
  shares, 143
Asia, 332
Association of Socialist Students, 2
associations, business, 196, 197,
  198; divisions among industrialists,
  338; monopolistic character,
  410n20; of similar industries, 197
Australia, population, 321, 427n8;
  railway network, 430n15
Austria: banking system, 213,
  373n33, 403n17, 414–15n4; cartels,
  412n3, 428n8; currency system and
  policy, 57, paper, 40, 46, 387n6,
  silver, 40–2, 46, 47, 48; fascism,
  15; industry/bank relationship,
  373n33; monetary system, 22,
  40–2, 45; reorganization of sugar
  trade, 414n4, 415

Index